Created Equal

Books by Benjamin DeMott:

The Body's Cage
Hells & Benefits
You Don't Say
A Married Man
Supergrow
Surviving the Seventies
America in Literature
Scholarship for Society
Close Imagining
The Imperial Middle
Created Equal
The Trouble with Friendship

Created Equal

Reading and Writing About Class in America

Benjamin DeMott
Amherst College

HarperCollins*CollegePublishers*

Senior Editor: Patricia A. Rossi
Project Coordination, Text and Cover Design: York Production Services
Cover Photo: Keith Tishken
Electronic Production Manager: Mike Kemper
Manufacturing Manager: Helene G. Landers
Electronic Page Makeup: York Production Services
Printer and Binder: R.R. Donnelley & Sons Company
Cover Printer: Phoenix Color, Corp.

For permission to use copyrighted material, grateful acknowledgment is made to the copyright holders on pp. 520-521, which are hereby made part of this copyright page.

Created Equal: Reading and Writing About Class in America

Copyright © 1996 by Benjamin DeMott

HarperCollins® and ® are registered trademarks of HarperCollins Publishers Inc.

All rights reserved. Printed in the United States of America. No part of this book may be used or reproduced in any manner whatsoever without written permission, except in the case of brief quotations embodied in critical articles and reviews. For information address HarperCollins College Publishers, 10 East 53rd Street, New York, NY 10022.

Library of Congress Cataloging-in-Publication Data

DeMott, Benjamin, 1924–
  Created equal: reading and writing about class in America / Benjamin DeMott.
    p. cm.
  Includes index.
  ISBN 0-06-501316-6 (Student Edition)
  ISBN 0-06-501317-4 (Instructor's Edition)
  1. Readers—Social sciences. 2. Social classes—United States—Problems, exercises, etc. 3. English language—Rhetoric. 4. College readers. I. Title.
PE1127.S6D46   1995
808'.0427—dc20
                                         95-8951
                                            CIP

To Richard Hoggart, friend and mentor

Contents

Introduction for Instructors   xi
Introduction for Students   xv

1. Superiors and Inferiors (I): Coping with Higher-Ups   1

John Langston Gwaltney
    CLEANING UP AFTER THE MASTERS   3

Robert Coles and Jane Hallowell Coles
    THE MAID AND THE MISSUS   7

Studs Terkel
    A PECKING ORDER   13

Anna Quindlen
    THE SKIRT STANDARD   22

David Mamet
    MY HOUSE   25

Brent Staples
    A BROTHER'S MURDER   28

Lorene Cary
    TURNING OUT THE PRIVILEGED   32

2. Toward a Definition of Class   37

Paul Fussell
    A TOUCHY SUBJECT   39

Mortimer Levitt
    TOWARD A DEFINITION OF CLASS   46

Donna Gaines
    DIRTBAGS, BURNOUTS, METALHEADS, AND THRASHERS   54

3. Discoveries: Working Class, Underclass, Plutocrats   67

Barbara Ehrenreich
    THE DISCOVERY OF THE WORKING CLASS   69

Michael Katz
    THE EMERGENCE OF THE UNDERCLASS AS A PUBLIC ISSUE   82

Kevin Phillips
    A BIRD'S EYE VIEW OF AMERICAN PLUTOGRAPHICS   93

4. Making It Big: American Visions of Riches — 113

Richard Huber
   THE AMERICAN IDEA OF SUCCESS   115
Russell Conwell
   WHERE TO GET RICH   125
Tony Parker
   HAROLD ALBERT, THE RICHEST MAN IN THE WORLD, AND LOUIE, HIS WIFE   133

5. Equality and Mobility: The Sacred Ground — 145

Alexis de Tocqueville
   MORE EQUAL THAN IN ANY OTHER COUNTRY   147
The Editors of Life
   A SOCIOLOGIST LOOKS AT AN AMERICAN COMMUNITY   150
Howard M. Bahr
   UPS AND DOWNS: THREE MIDDLETOWN FAMILIES   156
Benjamin DeMott
   CLASS STRUGGLE IN HOLLYWOOD   164
Mark Crispin Miller
   TV AND ALL THE RIGHT COMMODITIES   170

6. Lives of the Elites — 179

C. Wright Mills
   THE POWER ELITE   181
Lewis Lapham
   MONEY AND CLASS IN AMERICA   192
Nelson Aldrich
   OLD MONEY, THE MYTHOLOGY OF AMERICA'S UPPER CLASS   212

7. The Great Equalizer: School — 225

Benjamin DeMott
   I SHOULD NEVER HAVE QUIT SCHOOL   227
Mike Rose
   THE STRUGGLE AND ACHIEVEMENTS OF AMERICA'S UNDERPREPARED   239
Jonathan Kozol
   SAVAGE INEQUALITIES OF PUBLIC EDUCATION   254

8. Superiors and Inferiors (II): The Problem of Guilt — 273

Garrison Keillor
   PROTESTANT   275
Thomas Geoghegan
   FREE TRADE   283
Richard Sennett and Jonathan Cobb
   THE HIDDEN INJURIES OF CLASS   299
Marianna De Marco Torgovnick
   ON BEING WHITE, FEMALE, AND BORN IN BENSONHURST   307

Richard Rodriguez
    The Achievement of Desire   318
Anthony Appiah, Henry Louis Gates Jr., bell hooks, Glenn Loury, Eugene Rivers, and Cornel West
    Forum on the Responsibility of Intellectuals   330

9. Class Consequences: Five Public Issues   343

William G. Smith
    The Affluent Draft Resister   345
Elliott Currie
    The Futile War on Drugs   351
Christopher Lasch
    The Ethics of Limits and the Abortion Debate   368
Ellen Goodman
    Censoring Studs   377
Charles Krauthammer
    Death of a Princess   380

10. Tomorrow's Class Politics   387

Mickey Kaus
    The Case for Class-Mixing   389
Derrick Bell
    Racism's Secret Bonding   400
James MacGregor Burns and Stewart Burns
    The Nurturing of Rights   406

11. Class Textures (I): Adventure, Superstition, Enigma   421

Bobbie Ann Mason
    Sorghum   423
Charles Dickinson
    The Jinx   436
Gish Jen
    The Water-Faucet Vision   444
John Cheever
    The Superintendent   452

12. Class Textures (II): Varieties of Human Love   465

Tillie Olsen
    I Stand Here Ironing   467
Stuart Dybek
    Chopin in Winter   475
Sandra Cisneros
    Woman Hollering Creek   491
Russell Banks
    Sarah Cole: A Type of Love Story   501

Acknowledgments   520
Index   522

Introduction for Instructors

This book is intended to help college students engage in acts of writing rooted in personally significant acts of discovery. Good undergraduate writing—papers that students enjoy producing and teachers like to read—demands mastery of many skills, including those of prewriting and revision. But it demands something more as well. This book's basic assumption is that the chance that good writing will occur is much improved when students are awakening to their worlds with newly curious eyes—and when they believe, correctly, that the discoveries they're making will mean something to others as well as to themselves.

Writing teachers have long been aware of the need for subjects that arouse student interest. The distinctiveness of *Created Equal* lies not in its philosophy of composition but in the practical ways it implements the philosophy. The widely variegated readings assembled here—interviews, personal testimony, autobiographical narratives, a forum, stories, essays, political, historical, and sociological studies—center on issues of social class in America. And what is notable about these issues is that they're at once engrossing and fresh. They have the capacity to rivet attention, and to repay—in the coin of discovery—young writers' efforts at understanding them. Equally important, the discoveries in question can take place at many different levels of sophistication, which means satisfaction for the inexperienced as well as the experienced.

Why do readings on class have such power? For two reasons. First, because social class is a pervasive force in American life; second, because the workings of social class are regularly neglected or even misrepresented. It's true, to be sure, that commentators of varying political stripes often seek to alert Americans to the significance of class. "America is supposed to be a classless society when obviously we're not," says George Will (on the ABC news show "This Week with David Brinkley"). The fundamental issue in this country is "class, not race," Senator Daniel Patrick Moynihan tells the *Wall Street Journal*, adding that it's essential "to at least start thinking about it, start talking about it. Let's be honest. We're not doing that." American historians speak out about "the evasions and self-deceptions that make it so difficult for Americans to confront the truth about their society" (Christopher Lasch), and about the "cant and myth" concerning class that needs to be "cleaned out of the American mind" (Arthur Schlesinger Jr.).

But over the years these and numberless other attempts to heighten awareness of social stratification and its consequences have had little impact. And as a result the facts about class, mobility, and related matters remain obscure—for college students as for many of their elders.

What flows from this, pedagogically, is that readings that address social differences offer opportunities to teachers and students alike: chances to deal at close quarters with ideas in action, situations in which analysis of media and other texts by students functions not as a stale exercise but as a means of advancing toward better comprehension of major contemporary political and cultural debates, and toward self-recognition. In my own decades as a writing teacher I have tried many approaches and worked with many themes. None has produced papers as alive or discussions as absorbing as those arising from concentration on social class and social mobility.

Organization of the Book

The link between quality of composition and quality of thought is obvious to all writing teachers. No less clear is that quality of thought usually improves as students achieve a stronger grasp of the need for—and the uses of—perspectives that reach beyond off-the-cuff statements of personal opinion. It's not a matter of students needing to learn to discount their gut responses; it's a matter of students learning how to train a beam of critical light on shoot-from-the-hip opinions—how to use intellectual resources (including techniques of prewriting and revision) to deepen understanding of the origins, the strengths, and the limits of personal views.

The structure of *Created Equal* is shaped by a recurring movement from easily accessible personal narrative and anecdotal materials to more generalized, impersonal, and speculative versions of experience. Divided into twelve chapters, the book begins with autobiographical pieces, opens out into broader-scaled argument and essays, returns at intervals to personal materials, and ends with short fiction in which imaginative writers work with class themes. The assumption, to repeat, is that students' ability to handle complex concepts grows fastest when the links between those concepts and the immediate daily experience of people like themselves are vividly and continuously realized.

Chapter 1 (Superiors and Inferiors [I]) focuses discussion and writing on the behavior and feelings of individual Americans in situations involving class differences. The readings draw students directly into the lived emotional realities of daily experience. The "Questions for Writing" seek out students' opinions and judgments of these realities; they also provide means by which students can inquire into their own social backgrounds without bogging down in theory and abstraction.

Chapters 2 and 3 (Toward a Definition of Class and Discoveries) introduce the subjects of social classification and social ascent. We are taking a first step toward theoretical perspectives on experience of the sort described in Chapter 1. The selections remain for the most part entertaining and readily accessible. One or two that present higher levels of difficulty for the student reader are preceded by headnotes offering hands-on help in navigating; the headnotes explain how and why the effort to grapple with the difficulties will pay off.

Chapters 4 and 5 (Making It Big and Equality and Mobility) look into the matter of influences on American class realities: in particular, the power of history in molding the ideal of classlessness, and the power of the media to persuade Americans that they live in a classless society. The section balances accounts of movies and TV sitcoms familiar to students with overviews of the American past and excerpts from inquiries into family mobility. Again the movement in the readings, "Questions for Writing," and the end-of-part excercises is from objects of immediate student experience to perspectives that are more theoretical, detached, academic.

Chapter 6 (Lives of the Elites) provides examples of writing by authors whose descriptions of immediate class situations not only are less personal than those with which the book begins but have a sustained critical edge, moral or political. The writers share no politics but have in common a sharp consciousness of class as a determining influence on the actualities they're describing. In "Questions for Writing" the student is asked to focus on differences in ways of writing—different methods of articulating personal responses while probing and reporting events, or developing theoretical positions.

Chapter 7 (The Great Equalizer: School) turns to education, each selection contrasting myths and ideals about schooling with classrooms as they are. Writing assignments encourage students to draw on their own experiences of school as a shaper of social distinctions. Chapter 8 (Superiors and Inferiors [II]) contains analyses, based on personal experience, of problems of social identity and allegiance arising partly from upward mobility. Chapter 9 (Class Consequences) consists of selections that relate class realities to highly specific sociopolitical and cultural issues, from drugs to the military draft. "Questions for Writing" concentrates on both the substance of the arguments on the issues and on rhetorical or antirhetorical strategies that figure in their expression.

In Chapter 10 (Tomorrow's Class Politics), three writers address the future of class issues in America. Two propose methods of diminishing the impact of class differences; the third writer lays out reasons for doubting that any solution is possible in the near-term. In "Questions for Writing" students are asked to express and justify their own sense of the immediate prospect.

Chapters 11 and 12 (Class Textures I and II) conclude the book with short fiction in which class themes are prominent. The "Questions for Writing" elicit personal opinion and judgment, but they encourage, in addition, student use, in interpretation and assessment, of the nonfictional materials engaged in earlier sections. The aims are to bring home the meanings of the concept of "contexts of criticism," and to establish the feasibility of connecting abstract ideas with the experience of reading imaginative literature.

As this summary should indicate, the subject of class and mobility in America is rich and various, and actually gains in interest as its bearings on the whole of public and private life grow clearer. The structure of *Created Equal* allows students to stay in touch with their own base yet, simultaneously, to get a feel for the kind of papers they will be asked to write during college study. And it shows students practical ways of coping with the writing problems that need to be overcome to ensure academic success. Among the latter are the problem of how to marshall new knowledge, linking it persuasively with personal experience and belief; the problem of setting up relations between abstract ideas and a body of factual matter; the problem of winnowing substance both from understated, "objective" writing and from rhetorically charged arguments.

Lively and interesting in themselves, the readings introduce several major humanities and social science disciplines. The pattern of the book's organization, the guiding headnotes on the subject matter, and the "Questions for Writing" following each reading launch a sustained engagement with moral and political issues central to college courses in several different fields. An Instructor's Manual built on solid classroom experience with the texts provides straightforward opinions both about strategies for discussion and about grading papers written in response to the specific questions.

Acknowledgments

I'm extremely grateful to my daughter Megan DeMott Quigley for imaginative suggestions and editorial help. The reader-consultants for *Created Equal* were: Libby Bey (Rockland Community College), Nick Coles (University of Pittsburgh), Kim Flachmann, (California State University, Bakersfield), Sandra Jamieson (Drew University), Michael Meyer (University of Connecticut), Mike Rose (University of California, Los Angeles), Irwin Weiser (Purdue University), and Dexter Westrum (Ottawa University). Each made highly individual, finely animated contributions, and I enjoyed responding to their critiques. My friend Eric McKitrick helped valuably with a design problem. Because of Tracey Topper and Susan Free, production was a pleasure. Warmest thanks to Patricia Rossi, my editor; her shrewdness, patience, and grace made the work matter and made it fun.

B.D.

Introduction for Students

Purposes of This Book

Created Equal has two purposes. The first is to help you, the student, to improve your writing. The second is to help you sharpen your understanding of the immediate world in which you study, work, entertain yourself, interact with others, and arrive at your basic convictions.

These two goals are closely related—because good writing depends on sharp thinking. Grammar, spelling, and punctuation are important. So, too, are the skills of prewriting and revision to which your teacher may introduce you. But there is no substitute for fresh, clearheaded, penetrating thought and observation. Your teachers want you to steer clear not just of mechanical errors. They want you never to settle for stale, sloppy arguments, or unsupported conclusions. To make your standards match theirs, you need to ask more of yourself when you sit down to write than you do when you're relaxing in casual conversation.

What exactly is involved in "asking more of yourself"? That is what this book is about, and no capsule answer to the question can be fully satisfactory. At one level, asking more of yourself as a writer means digging below the surface to the sometimes blurry, unconsciously held assumptions on which basic beliefs often rest, and setting those assumptions under critical scrutiny. At another level, asking more of yourself means probing for the historical factors that play a role in shaping everybody's assumptions, including your own. At still another level, asking more of yourself means finding out what application academic learning has on your opinions—how your views stand up when considered in light of reasoned, research-based knowledge developed in the academic disciplines.

This makes it sound as though writing well is a demanding assignment—and that, in fact, is the truth. But as a college student you have solid ground for confidence that you can master this skill. The reason is that personal experience—personal knowledge—is a highly important element in every first-rate piece of writing. Good writing draws on many resources besides the gut responses of the writer, but it seldom treats those gut responses dismissively. Your best work as a writer is likely to express much more than your off-the-cuff personal opinion. It will seek out and evaluate points of view and contexts of knowledge whose pertinence may well not have been in your mind when you first began thinking out the paper. But the direction of what you write will usually reflect your life-experience and observation—and your personal decisions about which perspectives on your subject are most valuable.

You come to class, in other words, with significant resources of your own. Your writing at its best will combine private, personal awareness and understanding with disciplined knowledge of both the broader world and of techniques of composition—knowledge that's available to everyone willing to pursue it. From the blend of individual and public perspectives comes writing that you yourself will enjoy producing and that teachers like to read.

The Need for a Subject

You need a subject, of course, and this book is designed to meet that need. The readings in *Created Equal* are widely variegated—reporting, autobiographical narrative, stories, essays, historical studies, sociological surveys. All are focused on *social class* and *social mobility*.

The prefatory headnotes before the selections offer guidance about each author's individual slant or direction. The "Questions for Writing" and other exercises that follow the selections offer guidance about where to jump off in your own thinking and writing about each selection. One especially helpful aid to you as a writer will be the relations and connections among the selections. The selections in each chapter shed light on each other *and* on the selections in the chapters ahead; together they build up a body of knowledge on which you'll be able to draw more deeply from week to week.

The subject of class is rich in dimensions. It's germane to race relations and to relations between the sexes, and it figures centrally in politics, education, the pattern of careers, the "messages" in popular entertainment. What makes the subject particularly useful to you as an undergraduate writer is that it's fresh. As a young writer you can contribute significantly to clarifying its intricacies.

In the 1990s class differences are becoming increasingly prominent in political discussion. Conservatives and liberals alike are insisting that these differences deserve closer attention. Leaders like the columnist George Will and Senator Daniel Patrick Moynihan are asserting that there's much to be learned about major national problems and controversies by looking at them from the perspective taken up by the writers represented in this book. Personal and career situations become more comprehensible when looked at in terms of social class relationships. The same holds for the myth-like versions of American life served up every day in the media. The subject on which you are now launching an investigation may well yield fascinating discoveries.

But the primary concern remains improving your writing. You're working on the problem of connecting personal experience and belief with general ideas...the problem of linking a body of factual matter with abstract ideas...the problem of weighing the risks and benefits of interpreting imaginative writing from a single intellectual point of view. By producing carefully thought-out, connected sentences and paragraphs responding to the exercises in this book, you should be able to raise by several notches the level of your writing performance. At the same time you'll be introducing yourself to a number of the major disciplines of the humanities and, in the bargain, coming to terms with fascinating realities of our country's present and past. Just ahead, in short, lies a genuine learning adventure.

Benjamin DeMott
Worthington, MA

1

Superiors and Inferiors (I)
Coping with Higher-Ups

Finding out where you stand on the social ladder isn't easy. No official placement office helps with the work of self-location. People often disagree about where they themselves and others should be placed. Many individual Americans have the sense that they occupy two or even more spots in the pecking order during the course of their normal workday.

But despite these and other uncertainties and puzzles, one thing is clear: situations involving social standing have the power to arouse strong feelings. They can cause hurt, stir rage or powerfully competitive ambition—even compel people to conclude that human life is unjust, meaningless or worse. Or, at the opposite extreme, they can create intense self-satisfaction and pride, or a truly obnoxious smugness.

The readings in Chapter 1 provide examples of this range of feelings. They also provide opportunities for you to test your ability to describe and analyze the reactions of other human beings caught up in complicated social situations—and to compare those reactions with your own. The questions that follow each reading are meant as starting points; as you address them, your own experience, thoughts, and feelings may well take you in surprising new directions.

CLEANING UP AFTER THE MASTERS
John Langston Gwaltney

Levels of awareness of social differences differ from person to person, partly for reasons having to do with occupation. People who deal every day both with blue-collar workers *and* with managers are likely to be more conscious of those differences than people who deal exclusively with workers—or with managers. Al Davidoff, who speaks in "Cleaning Up After the Masters" below, makes it plain that his awareness of class is constant and acute.

The interview with Davidoff is by John Langston Gwaltney, professor of anthropology at Syracuse University. Gwaltney's first collection of interviews, *Drylongso: A Self-Portrait of Black America,* won a Robert F. Kennedy Book Award honorable mention in 1981.

1 My whole name is Alan Harry Davidoff, but everyone calls me Al Davidoff and that's what I go by. I went to the New York State School of Industrial Labor Relations at Cornell University. By the end of my junior year I'd been involved in a number of labor-oriented projects and programs and was very involved in student politics. I was the president of the student government at my college. At that point there was an employee association beginning to form. It was avowedly not a union drive, it was openly saying this is not going to be a union, we want to work within the channels of the University. And I thought that it wouldn't work and that ultimately people would be interested in turning toward something more serious as an alternative. I saw that association as the best thing happening at Cornell and immediately got involved with the people who were the leaders. Just in a very, you know, helping-hand kind of way, not trying to give them direction or anything so presumptuous, but just trying to offer what I knew and leg work. Then I left that summer to do some organizing and research in Albany, sort of assigned through an organization called Frontlash, which is a youth labor organization, and when I came back I committed myself to getting active in building the organization at Cornell.

2 I took a full-time job at the University while I was still a full-time student, which was a very bizarre arrangement to be in. And I began working in a girls' dorm. Cleaning it. So the sudden transformation from how I was perceived in one part of my day from the other part was absolutely personally devastating for a while. For instance, I'll tell you. The first way I realized it was kind of funny. I had a fairly good personal social life. I'd

---

From John Langston Gwaltney, *Drylongso* (1981).

gone out with a number of different girls and had a nice time and basically positive experiences and was fairly active in a social kind of a way. This was when I was a senior, when you're a little bit better off status wise, and here I was, going into a freshman dorm cleaning it all day as a janitor. A lot of them never knew me as anything other than the janitor and the thing that really struck me was the girls, the young women, the freshmen—I'm there very early so I'm there when they're waking up—they'd run out with like their panties on and a little towel or a T-shirt or something like that, half-naked, totally oblivious to me, 'cause I'm a custodian. I'm like a broom or a mop or a pail and I'm not a person who could conceivably be a sexual being. That's the way they viewed me, I really do think so. On the other hand, these were the same girls who I might be, eight hours later coming back around trying to meet in a social way and they would never have done that, acted so, treated me as an inanimate object, if I had been there eight hours later. They would have made sure they had something on before they ran by me.

3   I think it's a class problem, or maybe not a problem, I don't know how you'd put it. I've talked to some of the other male custodians about this. It's a depersonalizing and a castrating kind of experience to be with all these young co-eds and to have them being so oblivious to you as anything other than a sort of a deadened person. And you know, for me, being roughly close to them in age and, again, functioning in the other part of my life as a peer, it was a shocking kind of experience for me.

4   Another kind of depersonalizing experience is being treated as a sort of a servant. There's a specific series of things you're supposed to clean and it doesn't include going into the student's rooms to do any of their cleaning, and occasionally one particularly presumptuous, obnoxious person would sort of give me an order, you know, about doing something a little extra or something like that. For instance, I had a very firm code of what I would clean and what I wouldn't clean. There was a kitchen and if they made an absolute mess, spilled stuff all over, that's a little excessive, and I would try to find out who did it and ask them if they would get it to a reasonable state before I cleaned it. But many of them argued. They'd say, "Hey, it's your job, I pay all this money to come here to go to school and you're paid to do this, what can you do, sucker?" And there were grosser problems along those lines. Students getting drunk and throwing up all over the place and missing the toilet.

5   I guess there just comes a point where it's a shame thing. It's a personal indignation that cuts too deep and is a personal affront. Everybody draws the line somewhere. Maybe if I did it for the next twenty years, I don't know if I'd still have that code. There's a line I'd say two-thirds of the people I work with won't cross. There's some point that they personally establish that their pride won't stomach. The question of politeness is very important. There's all the world of difference with the people I work with if the student *asks* as opposed to *orders*. If you knew the average Cornell student, they are the masters of our society. Twenty years from now

they're the people that are gonna be runnin' the show and that's the way they view themselves. And the truth is, economically, many of 'em are from a fairly well-to-do background. They have servants at home. But working at Cornell there are people whose lives have been downtrodden. There are a lot of people who have very little education, have no sense of self-worth, who feel lucky to have a job making minimum wage at Cornell and will do anything to avoid jeopardizing it. These are the people that are, of course, very hard to get oriented toward standing up and fighting. And I'd say we've taken a lot of those people and, through the organizing, transformed them. Some of the most miraculous changes have occurred.

6   The girls in the dorm I cleaned were unaware of who I was. I mean, I wouldn't come back and try and date them per se. I was tempted, when feeling down and downtrodden and, you know, trying during that eight hours of work to find some self-definition that gave me dignity. Oh yeah, I felt down, very much so. It was very depressing. One of the temptations that I am, in a sense, ashamed of is that I would be tempted to let them know who I was. That's something obviously that I could do that none of the people that I was working with could do. Let them know that I was really a student still. It transforms the way they look at you—it's very tempting.

7   But to get back to the union, during the bargaining—logistically it's really interesting. It's what you'd imagine. You sit face to face. It's you on one side of the table with six or seven of your fellow workers and the fellow from the international union helping us, and four or five or six people from management on the other side. All the differences are so clear—the dress, the style of speech, the general attitude. I've been in meetings on different issues with the leadership of Cornell University and I would have thought I'd be somewhat self-controlled in a situation like this, less easily enraged, but the truth of it was that I ended up being the one who got pissed off all the time. I just started getting into nasty back-and-forths with management. Why? Part of it has to do with getting back to my mother, the gut-level sense of right and wrong. Management themselves are such an affront to what I believe in. I mean, these are people who are full-time out to keep the people that I'm working with in a lousy position. I mean, that's all they *do!* They're not just doing this part-time, occasionally. This is their life! And the people that were on our bargaining committee were a group of high-minded, wonderful individuals who were, for the first time, standing up as workers. The bargaining process is supposed to be one of equals bargaining with each other and yet management consistently adopted a tone of superiority that infuriated me. Part of it was because I was probably less frightened of them and was more willing to get them mad at me than some of the other people, although they were very brave in standing up. They also are probably a little more up-tight with becoming the bitter enemy personally of management. But I swear, the main reason I did it was I was enraged. I think largely because of two reasons.

Because of some of my basic background, but I think also because of being so close to the other people on our side of the table. They're just some very precious people to me. People who have lived very hard lives who have finally, in their forties or fifties, blossomed as human beings because of the union drive and the chance to really have a say in their own lives. Seeing the people on the other side of the table, management, so interested in stopping that flowering, I think that's where the rage came from.

Points for Review and Discussion

1. Davidoff is critical both of coeds in the dorms and of management at the bargaining table. What are the grounds of his criticism?
2. What quality does Davidoff appear to admire most in other people? What quality does he most detest?
3. How does Davidoff explain his belief in the extreme importance of politeness?

❧ Questions for Writing

1. Al Davidoff sees himself as having lost social standing in at least three different ways. Describe each of those losses in your own words and, giving reasons for your choices, tell which strikes you as the most painful.
2. "I had a very firm code of what I would clean and what I wouldn't clean," says Davidoff (¶ 4). He claims, in addition, that most people he's worked with over the years also have a code—"a line [they] won't cross" (¶ 5). Davidoff thinks people draw that line out of pride. But does this tell us enough? What other factor or factors can you see driving workers to develop their own rules about what they will and will not do on the job?
3. Davidoff gets infuriated at the "people from management" because they "consistently adopted a tone of superiority" (¶ 7). What makes people adopt such a tone? Is it simply that they think they're better than the rest of us, or are there other explanations? Explain.
4. Imagine this situation: Some of the people Al Davidoff refers to as "masters of our society" hear him talking harshly about them and decide to talk back to him. They tell him to his face to grow up. The only reason he's resentful of them, they insist, is that he's just plain envious of them—and envy is a bad thing. What do you think of this as a critique of Al Davidoff's attitudes? Does it make good sense to you? Again, explain your reasoning.
5. Using your reflections on the issues raised above as a means of opening up your own experience, write a short personal essay (500 words) focused on a situation in which social difference became, for you yourself, a matter of serious emotional and/or intellectual concern.

The Maid and the Missus
Robert Coles and Jane Hallowell Coles

In some situations superiors, or bosses, try to behave as though there's really no difference between them and the bossed or inferior. That happens in the upper-middle-class family in Cambridge, Massachusetts, whose lives and attitudes are described, in the following selection, by "Helen," the family's cook/cleaning woman. The interview with Helen was conducted by Robert Coles and his wife Jane Hallowell Coles for their study *Women of Crisis: Lives of Struggle and Hope* (1978). A Harvard Medical School faculty member, Robert Coles is also the author of *Children of Crisis* (1978), a multivolume account of the lives of young Southerners in the period of the civil rights struggle.

1   A white woman from Somerville, a so-called streetcar suburb outside of Boston, has for a long time worked in the home of a prominent, quite well-off Cambridge family. Helen has cleaned for them, cooked for them. She has taken care of their two children. She knows them well—and herself, too; and knows the difference. "I come over there every day. When they go away, I stay. They've given me a room. They say I can live with them. They mean to be nice, but I get upset. They don't stop and think that I have a family, too.

2   "You get used to the way the rich live, and you go home at night, and suddenly you're poor again. I tell my husband he's lucky he works on a truck. He doesn't see what I do, so he doesn't miss what I do.

3   "I'll be working, and I'll hear them talk. The missus is a big talker. She goes gab, gab all the time when she's home. She has a lot of money but she works, too. She's in public relations, she tells me. She helps the museums. She writes articles. She calls a lot of people up and goes see them. She has an office in Boston. She used to do volunteer work, a lot of it; but she said she should *work*, like men do. My husband thinks she's crazy, and so do I. If I had money, I'd quit this job and go home and stay home for a thousand years. I'd be with my own kids and not someone else's. Does it make sense? The missus says that she has to get out and work or else she'll 'stagnate'—her favorite word. She's always worrying about 'stagnating.' She says women are in danger of 'stagnating.' Maybe in her dictionary I'm not a woman!

4   "It's different being a woman like the missus and being a woman in the neighborhood where my family lives. We were brought up to wait on our men, hand and foot. Here in this house, the missus is the equal of the mister. She speaks and he listens as much as he speaks and she lis-

---

From Robert Coles and Jane Hallowell Coles, *Women of Crisis* (1978).

tens. I think she runs the money, and she doesn't *ask* him for anything. She *tells* him: 'I'll do this, and I want to do that!' In my family, my mother always let my father run things; and that's the way I am with my husband. He wouldn't have it any other way. He says women are getting out of line these days. Maybe he's right; I don't know. I don't envy the rich women I see over in that Cambridge house! A lot of them have husbands who are doctors or lawyers or professors, and they have more money than I'd know what to do with; but I'll look at one of them, a pretty lucky woman, I'll think for a second or two, and she's not at peace with herself—that's how I'd put it. The missus I work for—she weighs herself twice a day. If she gains a pound—*one* pound!—she tells her husband she's 'depressed,' another of her words. He asks why. She says she doesn't know. But I know. I've seen her face when she's been on the scale. I can tell what she'll say afterwards. Her husband never uses the scale. He's not fat. He looks thin and healthy to me. He doesn't worry about himself the way his wife does. She's always buying clothes and putting them on and taking them off and looking in one mirror and then another mirror. I can't figure her out. I guess she's a rich, spoiled woman."

No Respect

5   "She tells her children that they should feel sorry for the poor, and if they ever see a colored person, they should put themselves in that person's shoes. The way those kids order me around, I know they're not fighting over who gets to try out my shoes!

6   "I come there, and the house is full of talk, even early in the morning. He's read something that's bothered him, and she's read something that's bothered her. They're both ready to phone their friends. The kids hear all that and they start complaining about what's bothering *them*—about school, usually. They're all so *critical.* I tell my kids to obey the teacher and listen to the priest; and their father gives them a whack if they cross him. But it's different when I come to fancy Cambridge. In that house, the kids speak back to their parents, act as fresh and snotty as can be. I want to scream sometimes when I hear those brats talking as if they know everything. They have no respect for anyone, older or younger. They're taught to be in love with themselves—but they keep saying how much they love other people. They can dance like they do in Africa and they can sing all those songs from foreign countries, and they love the one or two colored kids handpicked for their classrooms. But they can be so rude to me and the cleaning woman and anyone else who doesn't just run to them when they snap their fingers. And they have no God. They worship themselves—and their 'causes.'

7   "She asked me whether I'd work if I didn't need the money. I told her no, I wouldn't. She said I'd change my mind once I was at home all day, sitting and waiting for people to come back from school and work so that

I could wait on them. I didn't know how to answer her. I guess I got flushed, and she could see I was upset. I didn't say a word. I just looked into my cup of Sanka. I swallowed all there was left of it and got up. I started cleaning up.

8   "All I hear the missus talk about is how 'free' she thinks women ought to be. Her friends will come over—women who live nearby—and they say they're glad to have their careers, and they're glad they're not just 'housewives.' I guess I'm not just a 'housewife' either. It's crazy: they say they're glad to get out of the house, and all my friends, who work in supermarkets or factories, keep on wishing the day will come that they don't have to go to work. And they envy me for at least having the kind of work I do: housework!

9   "They ask me when they see me how they live here in this neighborhood of Cambridge, and I'll tell my girl friends that it's not only a picnic. The woman I work for *thinks* she's so 'free' and 'independent' and 'equal' with her husband, but I know different. I've heard her husband tell her off. I've heard her manipulate him. She's a clever one. She talks in a soft voice, but she's tough underneath. She pretends to be a little dumb—when she wants to get him to change his ideas. She's no different from any other woman; she uses her wiles when she needs to.

10 "The missus talks one way with her women friends and another way with her husband. In fact, she talks with all the men who come for dinner differently from all the women. She's either very tough when she talks with men or she becomes silly and sarcastic and makes them laugh. With her women friends she relaxes; with men, she's always watching herself. I don't see how that's any different from what I saw go on between my mother and my father. When the missus has an argument with her husband, she speaks and he speaks. Neither gives in. Then she changes. She starts crying. Then he collapses and says yes to her. I heard her tell one of her women friends that she has her 'final weapon,' if nothing else works. I think she stays away from him until he surrenders! What's so smart about that! Is she really 'liberated'? I'd never do that! I'd rather scream and shout and throw dishes than hold out on my husband that way. It's being sneaky and dishonest.

11 "The trouble with those two is that they think they're so honest with each other, and she thinks she's equal with her husband. But she acts like a woman and he acts like a man, and that's how they get through their troubles."

"Stop Kidding Yourself"

12 "I get annoyed at the girl and her mother—all their pretense that men and women are equal. They're not equal. My husband is stronger than I'll ever be. My father was stronger than my mother. I couldn't do the work my husband does. The trouble with these people is that they're *all* soft and weak, because none of them does much physical work. They sit

and use their voices. They move around in their chairs. He says he's going to go jogging. Big deal: an hour every other morning! She does her Canadian exercises; I hear her going thump, thump, upstairs. Her biggest exercise is keeping her hands away from those butterscotch candies she says she buys for her husband; but he doesn't know the half of it—how many she's taken before he gets home. Then she says out loud, as if the cleaning woman and I are supposed to pay attention, that she doesn't know *where* all those candies go! I feel like coming into that study of hers and saying, 'Come on, lady, stop kidding yourself!' I don't like those candies!

13   "A lot of things stick to my teeth! When I go home I need an hour to adjust to my own home. I'll hear my son talking with his friend about airplanes and spaceships. Both boys want to be pilots. They'll talk about 'reentry' problems—I guess spaceships coming back to earth. I think to myself: I have one of those problems every night. I'll hear something at work, and even when I'm really back in the swing of my own family, I can't get the words out of my mind. The other day I heard the missus talking to her daughter. The girl was throwing a fit over something, and I was glad I didn't have her as my child. Then I heard the mother trying to be nice, and the girl only got nastier. I wanted to go and give her a whack—but God forbid! In that house they don't believe in using 'physical force' on children. The missus once asked me if I used 'physical force' on my children. I said no, but I sure hit them when they get fresh or rude, especially when they act like spoiled brats. She looked at me for a while, and I thought I'd said the wrong thing. She seemed interested, though. She asked me where I hit the kids, and how many times. I told her any place, and the number depended on what they did and my mood. Then she gave me one of her smiles—as if to say that *she* was *above* that kind of behavior! I thought of her daughter and got snobby myself: I would never have a girl who acted like that one does!

14   "The girl came home the other day and was upset. She spoke up in class, and the teacher didn't agree with her. It's a fancy school she goes to—a private school. The mother gets angry with the teachers in front of her daughter and tells the girl she's going to get the woman fired. I don't understand how a woman who is always talking about the way women are unfairly treated can speak of a schoolteacher, a woman, as if she's dirt to be brushed aside.

15   "She gets nervous because of me, I know. She has all these good wishes for the whole world, and she wants to 'liberate' everyone, so it's embarrassing when she has to stop and think about *me!* I'm not her slave, but I do a lot of her dirty work, and she knows it. But if I were in her shoes, I'd be doing what she does—I'd be hiring myself a maid or two and doing other things with my time. If I were rich, I'd swim in a swimming pool outside my house, and travel a lot, and I'd have a lot of flowers around my

house—and I'd hire the gardener she hires. That man could turn a desert into a jungle; he's got two green thumbs and eight green fingers. I'd keep him working all spring and all summer!"

Sour Milk

16 "I don't hold it against her that she has money. Some have it, most don't. That's the way it is. What can you do? If it were the other way around, I hope I'd be as considerate of her as she (mostly) tries to be of me. She slips up every once in a while. She shows the bad side of herself. She forgets herself. She turns as sour as month-old milk. She starts shouting at all of us working for her, especially the cleaning lady and me. The gardener is a man! She forgets all that 'women's liberation' talk I hear her speaking on the phone or during those 'dinner parties' of hers. She sounds like my neighbor, with her tongue that needs to be washed with soap once a week. She sounds like a 'male chauvinist pig.' I've learned that expression from her—and the morning talk shows.

17 "My boss is a woman who worries a lot that women aren't getting all they should be. You can't help doing a lot of thinking, after you've heard her talk. You can't help asking yourself things. She goes to see a psychiatrist, and then I'll hear her telling her husband that she's the way she is now because of the way she was treated by her parents when she was a little girl. I don't know why anyone like her should go see a psychiatrist. She's got everything in the world, you'd think. She should be happy. I wish I had her life! But all I hear her talk about on the days she goes to that doctor is the bad trouble she went through a long time ago. I guess her father wanted her to marry a certain boy she'd known since she was a little girl, and she didn't like the boy when she was little, and she didn't like him when she grew up either. So the father didn't like *her*—I think that's what happened.

18 "I wonder whether she'd really like it better if I sat and read a fancy book from her husband's library. He doesn't read those books, and she doesn't either. They skim some new books, and then they tell people they've read them, and then they laugh and confess to each other how they 'fake it' when they talk about those books. Meanwhile, I'm 'wasting my time' watching those 'stupid' television programs. I hear her speak like that to her children. 'Don't watch the "stupid" TV.' I'm one of her children, I guess! I'll tell you what she doesn't know about the world—that because of who she is and who I am, we're not just two women, the way she pretends we are sometimes when she tries to be nice to me; we're something else—the boss and the one who's being bossed. Sure, I'm 'wasting my time' watching her television set; but I wonder if she knows how I feel when I get up before the sun does and start getting myself over to her house. I'll be drinking my coffee, and I'll say to myself: Another day down

the drain, and all for *the almighty buck*—my dad's words. I remember him saying over and over: *the almighty buck*. He said *the almighty buck* is the lord and master of everyone—except those who have lots and lots of bucks.

19   "When I sit and watch those quiz shows, I figure I'm gaining a few minutes—and I can see someone win a few dollars without being made to get up at five or five-thirty, and without getting a dirty look for taking a break after working pretty damn hard, I'll tell you. Who wants to read a lot of heavy stuff—and then go back to the washing machine and the vacuum cleaner and the stove and the refrigerator, and none of them mine! I'd like her to come and work in my house every day, and see what she'll want to do with her coffee break and her lunch hour! After doing that, she might end up glad to go home—*and stay home.*"

Points for Review and Discussion

1.   What are the chief differences between Helen's life situation and that of her "Missus"?
2.   How does Helen explain her readiness to let her husband "run things"?
3.   Why does Helen take satisfaction in quiz shows? What do they do for her that reading doesn't do?

◆ *Questions for Writing*

1.   Helen has many reservations about her employers. Name two or three points in her complaint that strike you as persuasive and explain what inclines you to believe them.
2.   Helen says at one point: "I'll tell you what she doesn't know about the world—that because of who she is and who I am, we're not just two women, the way she pretends we are sometimes when she tries to be nice to me; we're something else—the boss and the one who's being bossed" (¶ 19). Helen's voice as she speaks sounds angry. What causes this anger? Why do people sometimes get mad when their "superiors" attempt to treat them as equals?
3.   Write a carefully detailed account of a real-life or imagined situation in which you occupy either Helen's situation (one in which a "superior" treats you as an equal), or the situation of Helen's employer (one in which you yourself treat an "inferior" as an equal).

A Pecking Order
Studs Terkel

Where a person stands in the social pecking order depends, of course, on who's looking. The same worker who sees himself or herself as badly placed in a hierarchy may be seen by others—even perhaps by some whose opinions matter deeply—as a success. In the following interview, an airline stewardess speaks bitterly more than once about where she ranks in relation to others. But she knows that some of her own loved ones are far from sharing her estimate of her position.

The stewardess's interviewer is Studs Terkel, famous for the radio show he conducted for decades, beginning in 1952, on Chicago's WFMT. Terkel was born in New York City in 1912, graduated from the University of Chicago Law School, and for a time acted in radio soap operas. His best-selling works include *Working, Division Street: America,* and *Hard Times*.

1 *Terry Mason has been an airline stewardess for six years. She is twenty-six-years old, recently married. "The majority of airline stewardesses are from small towns. I myself am from Nebraska. It's supposed to be one of the nicest professions for a woman—if she can't be a model or in the movies. All the great benefits: flying around the world, meeting all those people. It is a nice status symbol.*

2 *"I have five older sisters and they were all married before they were twenty. The minute they got out of high school, they would end up getting married. That was the thing everybody did, was get married. When I told my parents I was going to the airlines, they got excited. They were so happy that one of the girls could go out and see the world and spend some time being single. I didn't get married until I was almost twenty-five. My mother especially thought it would be great that I could have the ambition, the nerve to go to the big city on my own and try to accomplish being a stewardess."*

3 When people ask you what you're doing and you say stewardess, you're really proud, you think it's great. It's like a stepping stone. The first two months I started flying I had already been to London, Paris, and Rome. And me from Broken Bow, Nebraska. But after you start working, it's not as glamorous as you thought it was going to be.

4 They like girls that have a nice personality and that are pleasant to look at. If a woman has a problem with blemishes, they take her off. Until the appearance counselor thinks she's ready to go back on. One day this

---
From Studs Terkel, *Working* (1972).

girl showed up, she had a very slight black eye. They took her right off. Little things like that.

5   We had to go to stew school for five weeks. We'd go through a whole week of make-up and poise. I didn't like this. They make you feel like you've never been out in public. They showed you how to smoke a cigarette, when to smoke a cigarette, how to look at a man's eyes. Our teacher, she had this idea we had to be sexy. One day in class she was showing us how to accept a light for a cigarette from a man and never blow it out. When he lights it, just look in his eyes. It was really funny, all the girls laughed.

6   It's never proper for a woman to light her own cigarette. You hold it up and of course you're out with a guy who knows the right way to light the cigarette. You look into their eyes as they're lighting your cigarette and you're cupping his hand, but holding it just very light, so that he can feel your touch and your warmth. (Laughs.) You do not blow the match out. It used to be really great for a woman to blow the match out when she looked in his eyes, but she said now the man blows the match out.

7   The idea is not to be too obvious about it. They don't want you to look too forward. That's the whole thing, being a lady but still giving out that womanly appeal, like the body movement and the lips and the eyes. The guy's supposed to look in your eyes. You could be a real mean woman. You're a lady and doing all these evil things with your eyes.

8   She did try to promote people smoking. She said smoking can be part of your conversation. If you don't know what to say, you can always pull out a cigarette. She says it makes you more comfortable. I started smoking when I was on the airlines.

9   Our airline picks the girl-next-door type. At one time they wouldn't let us wear false eyelashes and false fingernails. Now it's required that you wear false eyelashes, and if you do not have the right length nails, you wear false nails. Everything is supposed to be becoming to the passenger.

10   That's the whole thing: meeting all these great men that either have great business backgrounds or good looking or different. You do meet a lot of movie stars and a lot of political people, but you don't get to really visit with them that much. You never really get to go out with these men. Stewardesses are impressed only by name people. But a normal millionaire that you don't know you're not impressed about. The only thing that really thrills a stewardess is a passenger like Kennedy or movie stars or somebody political. Celebrities.

11   I think our average age is twenty-six. But our supervisors tell us what kind of make-up to wear, what kind of lipstick to wear, if our hair is not the right style for us, if we're not smiling enough. They even tell us how to act when you're on a pass. Like last night I met my husband. I was in plain clothes. I wanted to kiss him. But I'm not supposed to kiss anybody at the terminal. You're not supposed to walk off with a passenger, hand in hand. After you get out of the terminal, that's all yours.

12   The majority of passengers do make passes. The ones that do make passes are married and are business people. When I tell them I'm married,

they say, "I'm married and you're married and you're away from home and so am I and nobody's gonna find out." The majority of those who make passes at you, you wouldn't accept a date if they were friends of yours at home.

13   After I was a stewardess for a year, and I was single, I came down to the near North Side of Chicago, which is the swinging place for singles. Stewardess, that was a dirty name. In a big city, it's an easy woman. I didn't like this at all. All these books—*Coffee, Tea and Me.*

14   I lived in an apartment complex where the majority there were stewardesses.* The other women were secretaries and teachers. They would go to our parties and they would end up being among the worst. They never had stories about these secretaries and nurses, but they sure had good ones about stewardesses.

15   I meet a lot of other wives or single women. The first minute they start talking to me, they're really cold. They think the majority of stewardesses are snobs or they may be jealous. These women think we have a great time, that we are playgirls, that we have the advantage to go out with every type of man we want. So when they first meet us, they really turn off on us.

16   When you first start flying, the majority of girls do live in apartment complexes by the airport. The men they meet are airport employees: ramp rats, cleaning airplanes and things like that, mechanics, and young pilots, not married, ones just coming in fresh.

17   After a year we get tired of that, so we move into the city to get involved with men that are usually young executives, like at Xerox or something. Young businessmen in their early thirties and late twenties, they really think stewardesses are the gals to go out with if they want to get so far. They wear their hats and their suits and in the winter their black gloves. The women are getting older, they're getting twenty-four, twenty-five. They get involved with bartenders too. Stewardesses and bartenders are a pair. (Laughs.)

18   One time I went down into the area of swinging bars with two other girls. We just didn't want anybody to know that we were stewardesses, so we had this story made up that we were going to a women's college in Colorado. That went over. We had people that were talking to us, being nice to us, being polite. Down there, they wouldn't even be polite. They'd buy you drinks but then they'd steal your stool if you got up to go to the restroom. But when they knew you weren't stewardesses, just young ladies that were going to a women's college, they were really nice to us.

19   They say you can spot a stewardess by the way she wears her make-up. At that time we all had short hair and everybody had it cut in stew school exactly alike. If there's two blondes that have their hair cut very

---

* "In New York, stewardesses live five or six girls to one apartment. They think they can get by because they're in and out so much. But there's gonna be a few nights they're all gonna be home at once and a couple of 'em will have to sleep on the floor."

short, wearing the same shade of make-up, and they get into uniform, people say. "Oh, you look like sisters." Wonder why? (Laughs.)

20   The majority of us were against it because they wouldn't let you say how *you'd* like your hair cut, they wouldn't let you have your own personality, *your* makeup, *your* clothes. They'd tell you what length skirts to wear. At one time they told us we couldn't wear anything one inch above the knees. And no pants at that time. It's different now.

21   Wigs used to be forbidden. Now it's the style. Now it's permissible for nice women to wear wigs, eyelashes, and false fingernails. Before it was the harder looking women that wore them. Women showing up in pants, it wasn't ladylike. Hot pants are in now. Most airlines change style every year.

22   *She describes stewardess schools in the past as being like college dorms: it was forbidden to go out during the week; signing in and out on Friday and Saturday nights.* "They've cut down stewardess school quite a bit. Cut down on how to serve meal classes and paperwork. A lot of girls get on aircraft these days and don't know where a magazine is, where the tray tables are for passengers... Every day we used to have an examination. If you missed over two questions, that was a failure. They'd ask us ten questions. If you failed two tests out of the whole five weeks, you would have to leave. Now they don't have any exams at all. Usually we get a raise every year. We haven't been getting that lately."

23   We have long duty hours. We can be on duty for thirteen hours. But we're not supposed to fly over eight hours. This is in a twenty-four-hour period. During the eight hours, you could be flying from Chicago to Flint, to Moline, short runs. You stop twenty minutes. So you get to New York finally, after five stops, let's say. You have an hour on your own. But you have to be on the plane thirty minutes before departure time. How many restaurants can serve you food in thirty minutes? So you've gone thirteen hours, off and on duty, having half-hours and no time to eat. This is the normal thing. If we have only thirty minutes and we don't have time to eat, it's our hard luck.

24   Pilots have the same thing too. They end up grabbing a sandwich and eating in the cockpit. When I first started flying we were not supposed to eat at all on the aircraft, even though there was an extra meal left over. Now we can eat in the buffet. We have to stand there with all those dirty dishes and eat our meals—if there's one left over. We cannot eat in the public eye. We cannot bring it out if there's an extra seat. You can smoke in the cockpit, in the restrooms, but not in the public's eye.

25   "We have a union. It's a division of the pilots union. It helps us out on duty time and working privileges. It makes sure that if we're in Cleveland and stuck because of weather and thirteen hours have gone by, we can go to bed. Before we had a union the stew office would call and say,

'You're working another seven,' I worked one time thirty-six hours straight."

26   The other day I had fifty-five minutes to serve 101 coach passengers, a cocktail and full-meal service. You do it fast and terrible. You're very rude. You don't mean to be rude, you just don't have time to answer questions. You smile and you just ignore it. You get three drink orders in a hurry. There's been many times when you miss the glass, pouring, and you pour it in the man's lap. You just don't say I'm sorry. You give him a cloth and you keep going. That's the bad part of the job.

27   Sometimes I get tired of working first class. These people think they're great, paying for more, and want more. Also I get tired of coach passengers asking for something that he thinks he's a first-class passenger. We get this attitude of difference from our airlines. They're just dividing the class of people. If we're on a first-class pass, the women are to wear a dress or a nice pants suit that has a matching jacket, and the men are to dress with suit jacket and tie and white shirt. And yet so many types of first-class passengers: some have grubby clothes, jeans and moccasins and everything. They can afford to dress the way they feel . . .

28   If I want to fly first class, I pay the five dollars difference. I like the idea of getting free drinks, free champagne, free wine: In a coach, you don't. A coach passenger might say, "Could I have a pillow?" So you give him a pillow. Then he'll say, "Could you bring me a glass of water?" A step behind him there's the water fountain. In first class, if the guy says, "I want a glass of water," even if the water fountain is right by his arm, you'd bring it for him. We give him all this extra because he's first class. Which isn't fair . . .

29   When you're in a coach, you feel like there's just head and head and head of people. That's all you can see. In first class, being less people, you're more relaxed, you have more time. When you get on a 727, we have one coatroom. Our airline tells us you hang up first-class coats only. When a coach passenger says, "Could you hang up my coat?" most of the time I'll hang it up. Why should I hang up first class and not coach?

30   One girl is for first class only and there's two girls for coach. The senior girl will be first class. That first-class girl gets used to working first class. If she happens to walk through the coach, if someone asks her for something, she'll make the other girls do it. The first stew always stays at the door and welcomes everybody aboard and says good-by to everybody when they leave. That's why a lot of girls don't like to be first class.

31   There's an old story on the airline. The stewardess asks if he'd like something to drink, him and his wife. He says, "I'd like a martini." The stewardess asks the wife, "Would you like a drink?" She doesn't say anything, and the husband says, "I'm sorry, she's not used to talking to the help." (Laughs.) When I started flying, that was the first story I heard.

32   I've never had the nerve to speak up to anybody that's pinched me or said something dirty. Because I've always been afraid of these onion

letters. These are bad letters. If you get a certain amount of bad letters, you're fired. When you get a bad letter you have to go in and talk to the supervisor. Other girls now, there are many of 'em that are coming around and telling them what they feel. The passenger reacts: She's telling me off! He doesn't believe it. Sometimes the passenger needs it.

33   One guy got this steak and he said, "This is too medium, I want mine rarer." The girl said, "I'm sorry, I don't cook the food, it's precooked." He picked up the meal and threw it on the floor. She says, "If you don't pick the meal up right now, I'll make sure the crew members come back here and make you pick it up." (With awe) She's talking right back at him and loud, right in front of everybody. He really didn't think she would yell at him. Man, he picked up the meal ... The younger girls don't take that guff any more, like we used to. When the passenger is giving you a bad time, you talk back to him.

34   It's always: the passenger is right. When a passenger says something mean, we're supposed to smile and say, "I understand." We're supposed to *really* smile because stewardesses' supervisors have been getting reports that the girls have been back-talking passengers. Even when they pinch us or say dirty things, we're supposed to smile at them. That's one thing they taught us at stew school. Like he's rubbing your body somewhere, you're supposed to just put his hand down and not say anything and smile at him. That's the main thing, smile.

35   When I first went to class, they told me I had a crooked smile. She showed me how to smile. She said, "Kinda press a little smile on"—which I did. "Oh, that's great," she said, "that's a *good* smile." But I couldn't do it. I didn't feel like I was doing it on my own. Even if we're sad, we're supposed to have a smile on our face.

36   I came in after a flight one day, my grandfather had died. Usually they call you up or meet you at the flight and say, "We have some bad news for you." I picked up this piece of paper in my mailbox and it says, "Mother called in. Your grandfather died today." It was written like, say, two cups of sugar. Was I mad! They wouldn't give me time off for the funeral. You can only have time off for your parents or somebody you have lived with. I had never lived with my grandparents. I went anyway.

37   A lot of our girls are teachers, nurses, everything. They do this part-time, 'cause you have enough time off for another kind of job. I personally work for conventions. I work electronic and auto shows. Companies hire me to stay in their booth and talk about products. I have this speech to tell. At others, all I do is pass out matches or candy. Nowadays every booth has a young girl in it.

38   People just love to drink on airplanes. They feel adventurous. So you're serving drinks and meals and there's very few times that you can sit down. If she does sit down, she's forgotten how to sit down and talk to passengers. I used to play bridge with passengers. But that doesn't happen any more. We're not supposed to be sitting down, or have a magazine or read a newspaper. If it's a flight from Boston to Los Angeles, you're supposed to have a half an hour talking to passengers. But the only time we

can sit down is when we go to the cockpit. You're not supposed to spend any more than five minutes up there for a cigarette.

39   We could be sitting down on our jump seat and if you had a supervisor on board, she would write you up—for not mixing with the crowd. We're supposed to be told when she walks on board. Many times you don't know. They do have personnel that ride the flights that don't give their names—checking, and they don't tell you about it. Sometimes a girl gets caught smoking in the cabin. Say it's a long flight, maybe a night flight. You're playing cards with a passenger and you say, "Would it bother you if I smoke?" And he says no. She would write you up and get you fired for smoking in the airplane.

40   They have a limit on how far you can mix. They want you to be sociable, but if he offers you a cigarette, not to take it. When you're outside, they encourage you to take cigarettes.

41   You give your time to everybody, you share it, not too much with one passenger. Everybody else may be snoring away and there's three guys, maybe military, and they're awake 'cause they're going home and excited. So you're playing cards with 'em. If you have a supervisor on, that would be a no-no. They call a lot of things no-no's.

42   They call us professional people but they talk to us as very young, childishly. They check us all the time on appearance. They check our weight every month. Even though you've been flying twenty years, they check you and say that's a no-no. If you're not spreading yourself around passengers enough, that's a no-no. Not hanging up first-class passengers' coats, that's a no-no, even though there's no room in the coatroom. You're supposed to somehow make room. If you're a pound over, they can take you off flight until you get under.

43   Accidents? I've never yet been so scared that I didn't want to get in the airplane. But there've been times at take-offs, there's been something funny. Here I am thinking, What if I die today? I've got too much to do. I can't die today. I use it as a joke.

44   I've had emergencies where I've had to evacuate the aircraft. I was coming back from Las Vegas and being a lively stewardess I stayed up all night, gambled. We had a load full of passengers. The captain tells me we're going to have an emergency landing in Chicago because we lost a pin out of the nose gear. When we land, the nose gear is gonna collapse. He wants me to prepare the whole cabin for the landing, but not for two more hours. And not to tell the other stewardesses, because they were new girls and would get all excited. So I had to keep this in me for two hours, wondering, Am I gonna die today? And this is Easter Sunday. And I was serving the passengers drinks and food and this guy got mad at me because his omelet was too cold. And I was gonna say, "You just wait, buddy, you're not gonna worry about that omelet." But I was nice about it, because I didn't want to have trouble with a passenger, especially when I have to prepare him for an emergency.

45   I told the passengers over the intercom: "The captain says it's just a precaution, there's nothing to worry about." I'm just gonna explain how to

get out of the airplane fast, how to be in a braced position. They can't wear glasses or high heels, purses, things out of aisles, under the seats. And make sure everybody's pretty quiet. We had a blind woman on with a dog. We had to get people to help her off and all this stuff.

They were fantastic. Nobody screamed, cried, or hollered. When we got on the ground, everything was fine. The captain landed perfect. But there was a little jolt, and the passengers started screaming and hollering. They held it all back and all of a sudden we got on the ground, blah.

I was great. (Laughs.) That's what was funny. I thought, I have a husband now. I don't know how he would take it, me dying on an airplane. So I thought, I can't die. When I got on the intercom, I was so calm. Also we're supposed to keep a smile on our face. Even during an emergency, you're supposed to walk through the cabin and make everybody feel comfortable with a smile. When you're on the jump seat everybody's looking at you. You're supposed to sit there, holding your ankles, in a position to get out of that airplane fast with a big fat smile on your face.

Doctors tell stewardesses two bad things about them. They're gonna get wrinkles all over their face because they smile with their mouth and their eyes. And also with the pressurization on the airplane, we're not supposed to get up while we're climbing because it causes varicose veins in our legs. So they say being a stewardess ruins your looks.

A lot of stewardesses wanted to be models. The Tanya girl used to be a stewardess on our airline. A stewardess is what they could get and a model is what they couldn't get. They weren't the type of person, they weren't that beautiful, they weren't that thin. So their second choice would be stewardess.

What did you want to be?

I wanted to get out of Broken Bow, Nebraska. (Laughs.)

POSTSCRIPT: *"Every time I go home, they all meet me at the airplane. Not one of my sisters has been on an airplane. All their children think that Terry is just fantastic, because their mom and dad—my sisters and their husbands—feel so stupid, 'Look at us. I wish I could have done that.' I know they feel bad, that they never had the chance. But they're happy I can come home and tell them about things. I send them things from Europe. They get to tell all their friends that their sister's a stewardess. They get real excited about that. The first thing they come out and say, 'One of my sisters is a stewardess.'*

"My father got a promotion with his company and they wrote in their business news that he had a family of seven, six girls and a boy, and one girl is a stewardess in Chicago. And went on to say what I did, and didn't say a word about anything else."

Points for Review and Discussion

1. Terry Mason's attitude toward her work appears to have changed over the years. What factors account for this change?
2. Terry's parents remain impressed by the fact that she's a stewardess. How does she explain this?
3. What kinds of pleasure does Terry Mason take in her job?

⋆◊ Questions for Writing

1. Terry Mason's teacher at stewardess school tries to make her change her smile, but she "couldn't do it. I didn't feel like I was doing it on my own." Point to other places in this interview where the stewardess chafes at instruction about her appearance and behavior. How does this kind of on-the-job instruction affect people's sense of their social standing? What do they do to fight back?
2. One night Terry Mason and two other stewardesses pretended they were "young ladies that were going to a women's college" (¶ 18). Recalling that when the bar patrons "knew you weren't stewardesses ... they were really nice to us," Terry speaks as though she learned something from this experience. In your own words tell what you think that lesson was. Name another moment in the interview in which Terry's learning experience resembled that which she had in the bar.
3. Terry Mason and Al Davidoff among others believe that college students enjoy relatively high social standing in the eyes of the general public. Are they correct in this belief? Support your answer with evidence drawn from personal experience.
4. Give an example either from your own experience or that of somebody you know in which matters of social standing figured significantly. Compare and contrast the lessons of that experience with those taught to Terry Mason.
5. Write a short character profile of Terry Mason, basing your interpretation of her personality and values—your account of the kind of person she is—on specific details found in the text.
6. Write a short personal essay (500 words) focused on a work or school experience in which either you yourself or someone you know coped, successfully or unsuccessfully, with a problem of regimentation and control comparable to the problems described by Terry Mason.

The Skirt Standard
Anna Quindlen

Questions of social standing are often tightly connected with gender issues. In the following selection Anna Quindlen, a columnist for the *New York Times*, finds herself confronting this connection head-on. Quindlen, author of two novels, worked as a reporter and editor for the *Times* between 1977 and 1985 before becoming a columnist. Her fame grew as the result of a series of intensely personal newspaper articles about the trials and rewards of her life as a working woman, wife, and mother. She began a career as a bestselling novelist in 1991, with *Object Lessons*, and retired from the *Times* in 1994 to devote herself primarily to the writing of fiction. Quindlen was born in New York and has lived her entire life in that city.

1   This time around, we were the ones who didn't get it.

2   Senator Bob Packwood had always been someone feminists could count on, to support abortion rights and family leave, to vote against confirming Clarence Thomas for the Supreme Court. And then one morning we discovered that, like a Capitol Hill Dorian Gray, the Senator was suspected of keeping an ugly portrait in the attic of his character. Ten women told the *Washington Post* that he had sexually harassed them over what had been a long and, until now, illustrious career. Kissing, fondling, sexual suggestions—there was nothing subtle about the behavior they alleged.

3   But there was something emblematic about it.

4   For while it is important that the Senate investigate these charges fully, it's also important not to compartmentalize this as the Packwood problem. It's not even useful to think of it only as a power problem, the arrogance of the man at the top who believes he can do what he pleases.

5   The problem of sexual harassment is emblematic of what hasn't changed during the equal opportunity revolution of the last 20 years. Doors opened; opportunities evolved. Laws, institutions, corporations moved forward. But many minds did not.

6   At the time of Anita Hill's testimony, a waitress told me of complaining to the manager of the coffee shop in which she worked about his smutty comments and intimate pats. He replied, "You're a skirt." Then he told her that if she didn't like it, there were plenty of other skirts out there who would take the job—and the abuse.

7   She needed the money and she got the message—there is one standard for people, and there is another standard for skirts. This is the way the world works for many women: the boyfriend pops you in the eye, the boss

---

From Anna Quindlen, "The Skirt Standard" (*New York Times*, Op-Ed page, December 6, 1992).

feels you up. It all seems very distant from Sandra Day O'Connor, Sally Ride, the admission of women to medical school, or the rest of what we characterize as progress for women.

8   Several weeks ago a Federal judge in New Jersey named Maryanne Trump Barry gave a speech about sexual harassment in which she complained about women overreacting to small remarks and incidents. "I like a little chivalry, I like to receive flowers, I like taking care of a son and a husband," the judge said, "and in my judgment those who recoil from these things don't know what they're missing."

9   I'm disappointed that Judge Barry perpetuated the nutty antifeminist myth that the world is full of overbearing women who go berserk if you send them roses. And I would hope a woman in such a visible position would use it to say publicly over and over again that the number of women who take excessive umbrage at an off-color joke is very small compared with those who have been humiliated by something considerably more.

10   The International Labor Organization, a United Nations agency, recently released a report on sexual harassment in 23 countries, including the United States. The report said between 15 and 30 percent of working women questioned in surveys the group studied said they had been subjected to frequent harassment, including "unwelcome requests for sexual intercourse."

11   The report concludes: "The likelihood of being harassed is most closely associated with the perceived vulnerability and financial dependency of the victim." In other words, female Federal judges are rarely sexually harassed.

12   Judge Barry recommended the deft riposte in the face of boorish behavior. But the deft riposte is the purview of the professional woman with the showy résumé. The bitter shrug is more like it for the waitress who puts up with the filthy comments about her physique so she can afford to buy shoes for the kids.

13   Just as we fooled ourselves that the end of discriminatory laws would soon lead to racial harmony, so we thought that increased access to education, advancement and male-only arenas would erase the attitudes that have led some men to treat women like children, fools and punching bags. The allegations against Senator Packwood—the alleged chasm between public acts and private attitudes—illustrate the changes that still need to come. After equal opportunity and role models and life choices comes the hard part, the hearts and minds of the men we live and work with. Fairness. Civility. The end of the skirt standard.

Points for Review and Discussion

1.   Explain the contrast Anna Quindlen draws between the "standard for people" and the "standard for skirts."
2.   Judge Barry's assertion that she herself "likes a little chivalry" disappointed Quindlen. Why so?

3. On what grounds does Quindlen justify her assertion that contemporary women have "fooled [them]selves?"

❧ Questions for Writing

1. Explain in your own words why Quindlen thinks it's wrong to "compartmentalize" Senator Bob Packwood's behavior as "the Packwood problem" (¶ 4).
2. Put yourself in the place of the coffee shop manager who's guilty of "smutty comments and intimate pats" (¶ 6). What does he mean when he replies to the waitress's complaint by saying, "You're a skirt" (¶ 6)? Is he simply dismissing her because she's a woman?
3. In her concluding paragraph Quindlen argues that the change that's now necessary to achieve fairness must take place in "the hearts and minds of the men we live with and work with" (¶ 13). And it's clear that the change she has in mind concerns men's fundamental attitudes toward women. Do you agree or disagree that changing those attitudes can end the harassment described in the International Labor Organization report? Explain your answer.

My House
David Mamet

The link between social standing and occupation is obvious; less obvious is the link between social standing and choices of clothes, furnishings, general decor, pets and so on. In "My House" the Pulitzer Prize–winning playwright and screenwriter David Mamet explores the changes in his choices that have occurred over the years. Mamet grew up on Chicago's South Side; his best-known work is *Glengarry Glen Ross*, the film version of which starred Al Pacino, Jack Lemmon, and Alec Baldwin.

1 In my younger days in New York everyone I knew lived in a walk-up apartment building, and I didn't know anyone who lived below the fifth floor.

2 At least that is the way my memory has colored it.

3 I remember the industrial wire spools that served as coffee tables, and the stolen bricks and boards out of which everyone constructed bookcases. There were red-and-yellow Indian bedspreads on the wall, and everyone had Milton Glaser's poster of a Medusa-haired Bob Dylan displayed.

4 That was how the counterculture looked in Greenwich Village in the sixties. We considered ourselves evolved beyond the need for material comfort, and looked back on a previous generation's candle-in-the-Chianti bottle as laughable affectation.

5 We children of the middle class were playing proletariat, and, in the process, teaching ourselves the rules of that most bourgeois of games: the Decoration of Houses.

6 The game, as we learned it, was scored on cost, provenance, integrity of the scheme, and class loyalty.

7 Now, in those days, status was awarded to the least costly article, and, as for provenance, those articles that were stolen ranked highest, followed immediately by those that had been discarded, with those that had been merely borrowed ranking a weak third.

8 Objects were capable of being included in the *ensemble* if they were the result of or made reference to the Struggle for a Better World; and points were given to the more geographically or politically esoteric items.

9 I look around my living room today and see that, of course, none of the rules have changed. They stand just as Thorstein Veblen described them a hundred years ago. The wish for comfort and the display of status contend with and inform each other in the decoration of the living place, and I'm still pretending.

From David Mamet, *The Cabin* (1993).

10 Now, however, I am faking a long-term membership in a different class.
11 I live in an old row house in Boston.
12 The house is in an area called the South End, specifically in that section called the Eight Streets. These streets are lined with near-identical bow-front brick row houses, built in the 1870s as part of a housing development and intended as single-family residence. The panic of 1873 wounded the real estate market, and the row houses were, in the main, partitioned and rented out by the room.
13 My house, the local historical association tells me, is one of the few that were not partitioned. Consequently, it retains most of the architectural detail with which it was adorned a hundred and some years ago. It has beautiful mahogany banisters and intricate newel posts, the stairwell and the rooms on the parlor floor have ornate plaster molding, there are pocket doors with etched glass—the house was built with new mass-construction techniques that enabled the newly bourgeois to suggest to themselves that they were living like the rich.
14 I bought the house and thought to enjoy the benefits of restoring it to a Victorian grandeur that it most probably never enjoyed. I recalled the lessons of the sixties, and obtained the services of a decorator, who, in this case, was not a security-lax construction company, but a very talented Englishwoman named Susan Reddick.
15 Now, if fashion is an attempt by the middle class to co-opt tragedy, home decor is a claim to history.
16 I grew up on the South Side of Chicago, surrounded by sofas wrapped in thick clear plastic. My parents and the parents of all my friends were the children of immigrants, and they started their American dream homes with no artifacts and without a clue, so, naturally, that history to which I laid claim was late-Victorian Arts and Crafts.
17 That is the era which I am pretending bore and endorsed me—a time which was genteel yet earthy, Victorian in its respect for the proprieties, yet linked through its respect for craft to the eternal household requirement for utility and the expression of that truth in pottery and textiles. What a crock, eh?
18 But that is whom I am pretending to be, a latter-day William Morris, who suggested that a man should be able to compose an epic poem and weave a tapestry at the same time.
19 And that is the fantasy which my house probably expresses.
20 There are a lot of fabrics woven on a hand loom by a neighbor in Vermont, some nice examples of American art pottery, and rooms painted various unusual colors, and applied with several arcane techniques of stippling, striation, and what may, or at least should, be called dappling.
21 My wife and I are very comfortable here. We spend a lot of time lounging on overstuffed furniture and reading or writing or talking in our own two-person Bloomsbury salon.
22 It is, as we would have said in Chicago, a real nice house.

Points for Review and Discussion

1. Mamet describes "the Decoration of Houses" as the most bourgeois of games. What reasons does he give for calling decorating a game?
2. Mamet also describes decorating as "a claim to history." What are his reasons for calling it that?
3. What distinctions does Mamet draw between himself and his parents in regard to home decorating?

◆ Questions for Writing

1. Mamet details three separate efforts to achieve social standing through dwelling places, furnishings, and the like. Describe each of these efforts briefly in your own words, and, giving reasons for your choice, tell which of them seems to you most deserving of respect.
2. Under some circumstances, according to Mamet, an apartment furnished with cheap stuff can confer higher social standing on its tenants than they could achieve with expensive furnishings. What's behind this seeming reversal of values? Why might a person gain social status by having, say, stolen property on the premises?
3. Mamet seems to make fun of social pretensions—his own and those of others—at many places in this piece. Point to one or two passages where you detect ridicule, and, again giving reasons, explain why the writer's attitude seems to you appropriate or inappropriate.
4. In a personal essay describe a choice of possessions that you yourself made which, in your opinion, has helped you gain higher social standing. Describe the background of the choice, the reasons it mattered to you, and the reasons that acting on the choice lifted your status.
5. Compare the attitudes toward social standing taken by Al Davidoff, Terry Mason, and David Mamet. Which of these attitudes seems to you most admirable and least admirable? Why? To which of these individuals is the matter of social standing most important? Why does he or she take it so seriously?

A Brother's Murder
Brent Staples

Opinions about race in America continue to be influenced by prejudices and stereotypes (all blacks are the same). Individual and social differences are commonly ignored. "A Brother's Murder"—a poignant account of division within one black family—reveals the absurdity of stereotypes. It also reminds us of social factors that are powerful enough to open a vast gulf between human beings who belong to the same race, family, and generation. Brent Staples, born in 1951, serves on the editorial board of the *New York Times*. His articles appear frequently in the "Notebook" column on that paper's editorial page, and his autobiography, *Parallel Time*, appeared in 1994.

1   It has been more than two years since my telephone rang with the news that my younger brother Blake—just 22 years old—had been murdered. The young man who killed him was only 24. Wearing a ski mask, he emerged from a car, fired six times at close range with a massive .44 Magnum, then fled. The two had once been inseparable friends. A senseless rivalry—beginning, I think, with an argument over a girlfriend—escalated from posturing, to threats, to violence, to murder. The way the two were living, death could have come to either of them from anywhere. In fact, the assailant had already survived multiple gunshot wounds from an incident much like the one in which my brother lost his life.

2   As I wept for Blake I felt wrenched backward into events and circumstances that had seemed light-years gone. Though a decade apart, we both were raised in Chester, Pa., an angry, heavily black, heavily poor, industrial city southwest of Philadelphia. There, in the 1960's, I was introduced to mortality, not by the old and failing, but by beautiful young men who lay wrecked after sudden explosions of violence. The first, I remember from my 14th year—Johnny, brash lover of fast cars, stabbed to death two doors from my house in a fight over a pool game. The next year, my teenage cousin, Wesley, whom I loved very much, was shot dead. The summers blur. Milton, an angry young neighbor, shot a crosstown rival, wounding him badly. William, another teen-age neighbor, took a shotgun blast to the shoulder in some urban drama and displayed his bandages proudly. His brother, Leonard, severely beaten, lost an eye and donned a black patch. It went on.

From Brent Staples, "A Brother's Murder" *New York Times Magazine* (March 30, 1986).

3   I recall not long before I left for college, two local Vietnam veterans—one from the Marines, one from the Army—arguing fiercely, nearly at blows about which outfit had done the most in the war. The most killing, they meant. Not much later, I read a magazine article that set that dispute in a context. In the story, a noncommissioned officer—a sergeant, I believe—said he would pass up any number of affluent, suburban-born recruits to get hard-core soldiers from the inner city. They jumped into the rice paddies with "their manhood on their sleeves," I believe he said. These two items—the veterans arguing and the sergeant's words—still characterize for me the circumstances under which black men in their teens and 20's kill one another with such frequency. With a touchy paranoia born of living battered lives, they are desperate to be *real* men. Killing is only *machismo* taken to the extreme. Incursions to be punished by death were many and minor, and they remain so: they include stepping on the wrong toe, literally; cheating in a drug deal; simply saying "I dare you" to someone holding a gun; crossing territorial lines in a gang dispute. My brother grew up to wear his manhood on his sleeve. And when he died, he was in that group—black, male and in its teens and early 20's—that is far and away the most likely to murder or be murdered.

4   I left the East Coast after college, spent the mid- and late-1970's in Chicago as a graduate student, taught for a time, then became a journalist. Within 10 years of leaving my hometown, I was overeducated and "upwardly mobile," ensconced on a quiet, tree-lined street where voices raised in anger were scarcely ever heard. The telephone, like some grim umbilical, kept me connected to the old world with news of deaths, imprisonings and misfortune. I felt emotionally beaten up. Perhaps to protect myself, I added a psychological dimension to the physical distance I had already achieved. I rarely visited my hometown. I shut it out.

5   As I fled the past, so Blake embraced it. On Christmas of 1983, I traveled from Chicago to a black section of Roanoke, Va., where he then lived. The desolate public housing projects, the hopeless, idle young men crashing against one another—these reminded me of the embittered town we'd grown up in. It was a place where once I would have been comfortable, or at least sure of myself. Now, hearing of my brother's forays into crime, his scrapes with police and street thugs, I was scared, unsteady on foreign terrain.

6   I saw that Blake's romance with the street life and the hustler image had flowered dangerously. One evening that late December, standing in some Roanoke dive among drug dealers and grim, hair-trigger losers, I told him I feared for his life. He had affected the image of the tough he wanted to be. But behind the dark glasses and the swagger, I glimpsed the baby-faced toddler I'd once watched over. I nearly wept. I wanted desperately for him to live. The young think themselves immortal, and a dangerous light shone in his eyes as he spoke laughingly of making fools of the policemen who had raided his apartment looking for drugs. He cried out as I took his right hand. A line of stitches lay between the thumb and index finger.

Kickback from a shotgun, he explained, nothing serious. Gunplay had become part of his life.

7   I lacked the language simply to say: Thousands have lived this for you and died. I fought the urge to lift him bodily and shake him. This place and the way you are living smells of death to me, I said. Take some time away, I said. Let's go downtown tomorrow and buy a plane ticket anywhere, take a bus trip, anything to get away and cool things off. He took my alarm casually. We arranged to meet the following night—an appointment he would not keep. We embraced as though through glass. I drove away.

8   As I stood in my apartment in Chicago holding the receiver that evening in February 1984, I felt as though part of my soul had been cut away. I questioned myself then, and I still do. Did I not reach back soon or earnestly enough for him? For weeks I awoke crying from a recurrent dream in which I chased him, urgently trying to get him to read a document I had, as though reading it would protect him from what had happened in waking life. His eyes shining like black diamonds, he smiled and danced just beyond my grasp. When I reached for him, I caught only the space where he had been.

Points for Review and Discussion

1.   Summarize the chief differences between the life stories of Brent and Blake Staples.
2.   How does Brent Staples account for the differences between his life and his brother's?
3.   What link does Brent Staples make between the experience of Vietnam veterans and that of his brother, who never served in the military?

•◦ Question for Writing

1.   Staples explains that his brother and others like him "kill one another with such frequency" because they suffer "a touchy paranoia born of living battered lives" and are "desperate to be *real* men" (¶ 3). Explain in your own words the connection between the experience of living a battered life and the desire to be "a *real* man." What exactly do these two things have to do with each other?
2.   Staples speaks of himself as having become "overeducated and 'upwardly mobile'" about ten years after leaving home for college (¶ 4). By what means did he improve his social standing? Could it be said, truthfully, that Staples' murdered brother was engaged in an effort to improve *his* social standing? How so?
3.   Al Davidoff speaks of the "rage" he feels at the management people with whom he deals at the bargaining table. Do you see any connection between that rage and the feelings that lie behind the violence described in "A Brother's Murder"?

4. Lives and attitudes in the sections of Roanoke where gunplay is routine differ vastly from lives and attitudes on Brent Staples's "quiet, tree-lined street" (¶ 4). And clearly race isn't pivotal in shaping the differences. In your view what factors *are* pivotal?

5. In a short (500 words) paper explain as clearly as you can how social standing figures in the contemporary problem of urban violence that's treated in "A Brother's Murder."

Turning Out the Privileged
Lorene Cary

First or early encounters with social difference sometimes trigger explosions of pride and combativeness. People—young people especially—are determined not to be put down. In "Turning Out the Privileged" Lorene Cary writes about the feelings she and a friend experienced when they were thrust—as the result of a special recruiting drive—from ordinary life in black middle-class Philadelphia into the deluxe and self-satisfied world of an exclusive New Hampshire boarding school. After succeeding in this school, the author went on to the University of Pennsylvania and became a writer for *Time* and an editor at *TV Guide*. Her autobiography, *Black Ice* (1991), tells the full story of what it was like to take on the elite white Establishment with no help other than that provided by a barely average junior high education.

The passage below shows us Lorene Cary on her first night at boarding school. Earlier in the day she caught glimpses of the somewhat imposing families of her fellow students—parents bringing their offspring for the start of school. "There were fancy white people in big foreign sedans, the women emitting, as I passed near them, a complex cosmetic aroma; there were plain, sturdy people whose hair and nails alike were cut in blunt, straight lines and whose feet were shod in brown leather sandals. Less exotic families emerged from chrome-and-wood station wagons; they wore baggy beige shorts. Almost no one was fat." Lorene's own parents are on their way home in their car; Lorene has just said goodbye to them.

1   Still barefoot, I ran into my house to cry. Even when I closed the door to my room, however, I could hear girls. They were talking and laughing. Who could cry? I washed my face . . . and took the long route back to my room by making a circle down past the common room and peeked in. Two black students, a boy and a girl, smiled back at me.

2   Jimmy Hill, one of the skinniest boys I had ever seen, had arrived that morning from Brooklyn. He had extravagant brown eyes. His black satin jacket, emblazoned on the back with a red-and-yellow dragon, hung open to reveal a fishnet T-shirt that cast tiny shadows on his chest.

3   Annette Frazier was a ninth grader (or "Third Former," as I was learning to say) whose theatrical mannerisms made her seem older than she was. She had an appealing face, rounded, with regular features that she used to great effect. When we met, she pantomimed our wariness with a quick movement of her eyes. She caught precisely our exposure and our collusion.

From Lorene Cary, *Black Ice* (1991).

4   We shouted with laughter and touched hands. Had anyone told me two hours before that I would be engaging in such high-decibel, bare-naked black bonding, I would have rolled my eyes with scorn. We sat in our small circle until Annette decided that it was time for her to get back to unpacking her things. I wondered if she was as organized and as self-assured as she looked. Neither Jimmy nor I could face our rooms, so we left together in search of a place to smoke.

5   We found one next to the squash courts. It was marked by a sand-filled stone urn and a few butts. We liked the place, because we could smoke there, and because we had a solid wall to lean on and buildings with which to swaddle ourselves against the open sky.

6   I was not afraid to go to St. Paul's School, although it was becoming clear to me from the solicitous white faces that people thought I was—or ought to be. I had no idea that wealth and privilege could confer real advantages beyond the obvious ones sprawled before us. Instead, I believed that rich white people were like poodles: overbred, inbred, degenerate. All the coddling and permissiveness would have a bad effect, I figured, now that they were up against those of us who'd lived a real life in the real world.

7   I knew that from a black perspective Yeadon [Lorene Cary's hometown] had been plenty cushy, but after all, I had been a transplant. West Philly had spawned me, and I was loyal to it. Jimmy felt just as unafraid, just as certain as Darwin that we would overcome. Jimmy had grown up in the projects, the son of a steadfast father and a mother who was a doer, a mover who led tenant-action and community groups. Together, his parents had raised a boy who had a job to do.

8   "Listen to me, darling," he said. "We are going to turn this motherfucker out!"

9   And why not? I, too, had been raised for it. My mother and her mother, who had worked in a factory, and her mother, who had cleaned apartments in Manhattan, had been studying these people all their lives in preparation for this moment. And I had studied them. I had studied my mother as she turned out elementary schools and department stores.

10 I always saw it coming. Some white department-store manager would look at my mother and see no more than a modestly dressed young black woman making a tiresome complaint. He'd use that tone of voice they used when they had *important* work elsewhere. Uh-oh. Then he'd dismiss her with his eyes. I'd feel her body stiffen next to me, and I'd know that he'd set her off.

11 "Excuse me," she'd say. "I don't think you understand what I'm trying to say to you . . ."

12 And then it began in earnest, the turning out. She never moved back. It didn't matter how many people were in line. It didn't matter how many telephones were ringing. She never moved back, only forward, her body

leaning over counters and desk tops, her fingers wrapped around the offending item or document, her face getting closer and closer. Sometimes she'd talk through her teeth, her lips moving double time to bite out the consonants. Then she'd get personal. "How dare you," would figure in. "How dare you sit there and tell me . . . " Finally, when she'd made the offense clear, clearer even than the original billing error or the shoddy seam, she'd screw up her eyes: "Do you hear me? Do you hear what I'm saying to you?"

13   They'd eventually, inevitably, take back the faulty item or credit her charge or offer her some higher-priced substitute ("like they should've done in the first place," she'd say, and say to them). They would do it because she had made up her mind that they would. Turning out, I learned, was not a matter of style; cold indignation worked as well as hot fury. Turning out had to do with will. I came to regard my mother's will as a force of nature, an example of and a metaphor for black power and black duty. *My* duty was to compete in St. Paul's classrooms. I had no option but to succeed and no doubt that I could will my success.

14   Jimmy understood. He knew the desperate mandate, the uncompromising demands, and the wild, perfect, greedy hope of it. If we could succeed here—earn high marks, respect, awards; learn these people, study them, be in their world but not of it—we would fulfill the prayers of our ancestors. Jimmy knew as I did that we could give no rational answer to white schoolmates and parents who asked how we had managed to get to St. Paul's School. How we got there, how we found our way to their secret hideout, was not the point. The point was that we had been bred for it just as surely as they. The point was that we were there to turn it out.

Points for Review and Discussion

1. How does Lorene Cary react when she finds two black students in the common room?
2. For what reason does Lorene's mother stiffen when she hears the store manager's voice?
3. Why do Lorene and Jimmy "feel unafraid" to go to St. Paul's School?

•◆ Questions for Writing

1. Explain in your own words the meaning of the phrase "turning out" as the phrase is used by Lorene Cary and Jimmy Hill.
2. Lorene believes that "rich white people were like poodles: overbred, inbred, degenerate. All the coddling and permissiveness would have a bad effect, I figured, now that they were up against those of us who'd lived a real life in the real world" (¶ 6). This way of thinking suggests that there's at least one important aspect of privilege that Lorene Cary doesn't yet understand. What is this aspect?

3. Part of Lorene's confidence in herself derives from the feeling that success is her *duty*—she has no other options. In what sense is this feeling a strength and in what sense is it a weakness?

4. Write a short personal essay (about 500 words) assessing your own level of competitive spirit, your own confidence (or lack of it) that you can hold your own against those who think they're your betters. In the course of the essay, name the influences that you consider to have been crucial in shaping your level of confidence.

5. Compare the state of mind and feeling in which Lorene Cary approaches a situation involving her so-called superiors with the state of mind and feeling in which Al Davidoff, Terry Mason, or Brent Staples's brother approached similar situations.

Connecting the Parts in Chapter 1: Assignment for Extended Essay

Several selections in Part 1 are written from the point of view of people who see themselves as, in one sense or another, underdogs in a social struggle. We hear their complaints and are told how they see themselves, and we're given their versions of the top dogs. But we don't hear how the top dogs see them, or what the top dogs have to say for themselves.

Write a 1000-word essay in which you look at one or more of the social situations described by these authors from a viewpoint more inclusive—and therefore, perhaps, fairer—than theirs. One way to begin this essay might be to consider the following questions about Al Davidoff's situation.
1. Davidoff speaks of the management representatives as people whose only purpose is to keep wage workers "in a lousy position." How else might the management representatives' behavior be explained?
2. Assume that both the behavior of the coeds and that of the management representatives is as reprehensible as Davidoff finds it. What steps might help change such behavior?

Leads for Research

1. Explore the subject of how individual workers see their bosses by reading extensively in the interviews conducted by Studs Terkel in *Working* (1972) and *Division Street: America* (1967) and by consulting contemporary databases and indexes such as *Social Science Index*, *Sociological Abstracts*, and *Social SciSearch*. Write a paper classifying the dominant patterns of thought and feeling, and describing their main features.
2. Research the subject of current managerial attitudes to workers by examining pertinent articles in the current issues of each of the following journals: *Harvard Business Review*; *Management*; *Management Quarterly*; *Human Relations*; *Personnel*. Make notes as you read on recurring attitudes, and develop your paper as an evaluation of current management thinking about how to get the most from employees.
3. The subject of sexual harassment in relation to social position that Anna Quindlen takes up in "The Skirt Standard" figured in a 1993 date-rape controversy that centered partly on Katie Roiphe's *The Morning After* and Naomi Wolf's *Fire With Fire*. Read the two books and the reviews that greeted them (see *Book Review Digest* and *Book Review Index* for references). Then write a paper comparing and contrasting Roiphe's, Wolfe's, and Quindlen's perspectives on the subject.

2

Toward a Definition of Class

For each of us social identity is particular and personal. We become conscious of it mainly in concrete situations and seldom think of stepping back and taking a detached look at the whole social scene of which we're a part.

Still, a "whole social scene" does in fact exist, and people interested in analyzing social distinctions often strive for a detached view. Attitudes among those who share this interest range from morally intense to amused, and there's a good deal of disagreement about what class actually means. The essays ahead, in Chapter 2, sample the disagreements.

Paul Fussell sees class as a more or less impersonal system of "hierarchical status orderings." Mortimer Levitt and celebrity friends connect class with personal character. Donna Gaines treats class as a powerful force whose malevolent, hidden operations can induce destructive self-hatred in the young. These commentators have nothing in common but this: they write about class in a language that seeks to rise above the limits of merely personal feelings and background.

A Touchy Subject
Paul Fussell

In the following essay Paul Fussell explains why the subject of class is touchy for his fellow Americans. The essay is drawn from a book—*Class* (1983)—in which Fussell offers an anatomy of class differences in America. Studying everything from favorite pets to the styles of driveways to features of speech, clothing, and preferred recreation, the author arrives at the conclusion that the United States has nine separate social classes: (1) top out-of-sight; (2) upper; (3) upper middle; (4) middle; (5) high proletarian; (6) mid-proletarian; (7) low proletarian; (8) destitute; (9) bottom out-of-sight.

Paul Fussell is Professor of English at the University of Pennsylvania. His book *The Great War and Modern Memory* won a National Book Award in 1976.

1   Although most Americans sense that they live within an extremely complicated system of social classes and suspect that much of what is thought and done here is prompted by considerations of status, the subject has remained murky. And always touchy. You can outrage people today simply by mentioning social class, very much the way, sipping tea among the aspidistras a century ago, you could silence a party by adverting too openly to sex. . . .

2   Especially in America . . . the idea of class is notably embarrassing. In his book *Inequality in an Age of Decline* (1980), the sociologist Paul Blumberg goes so far as to call it "America's forbidden thought." Indeed, people often blow their tops if the subject is even broached. One woman, asked by a couple of interviewers if she thought there were social classes in this country, answered: "It's the dirtiest thing I've ever heard of!" And a man, asked the same question, got so angry that he blurted out, "Social class should be exterminated!"

3   Actually, you reveal a great deal about your social class by the amount of annoyance or fury you feel when the subject is brought up. A tendency to get very anxious suggests that you are middle-class and nervous about slipping down a rung or two. On the other hand, upper-class people love the topic to come up: the more attention paid to the matter the better off they seem to be. Proletarians generally don't mind discussions of the subject because they know they can do little to alter their class identity. Thus the whole class matter is likely to seem like a joke to them—the upper classes fatuous in their empty aristocratic pretentiousness, the middles loathsome in their anxious gentility. It is the middle class that is highly

---

From Paul Fussell, *Class* (1983).

class-sensitive, and sometimes class-scared to death. A representative of that class left his mark on a library copy of Russell Lynes's *The Tastemakers* (1954). Next to a passage patronizing the insecure decorating taste of the middle class and satirically contrasting its artistic behavior to that of some more sophisticated classes, this offended reader scrawled, in large capitals, "BULL SHIT!" A hopelessly middle-class man (not a woman, surely?) if I ever saw one.

4   If you reveal your class by your outrage at the very topic, you reveal it also by the way you define the thing that's outraging you. At the bottom, people tend to believe that class is defined by the amount of money you have. In the middle, people grant that money has something to do with it, but think education and the kind of work you do almost equally important. Nearer the top, people perceive that taste, values, ideas, style, and behavior are indispensable criteria of class, regardless of money or occupation or education. One woman interviewed by Studs Terkel for *Division Street: America* (1967) clearly revealed her class as middle both by her uneasiness about the subject's being introduced and by her instinctive recourse to occupation as the essential class criterion. "We have right on this street almost every class," she said. "But I shouldn't say class," she went on, "because we don't live in a nation of classes." Then, the occupational criterion: "But we have janitors living on the street, we have doctors, we have businessmen, CPAs."

5   Being told that there are no social classes in the place where the interviewee lives is an old experience for sociologists. "'We don't have classes in our town' almost invariably is the first remark recorded by the investigator," reports Leonard Reissman, author of *Class in American Life* (1959). "Once that has been uttered and is out of the way, the class divisions in the town can be recorded with what seems to be an amazing degree of agreement among the good citizens of the community." The novelist John O'Hara made a whole career out of probing into this touchy subject, to which he was astonishingly sensitive. While still a boy, he was noticing that in the Pennsylvania town where he grew up, "older people do not treat others as equals."

6   Class distinctions in America are so complicated and subtle that foreign visitors often miss the nuances and sometimes even the existence of a class structure. So powerful is "the fable of equality," as Frances Trollope called it when she toured America in 1832, so embarrassed is the government to confront the subject—in the thousands of measurements pouring from its bureaus, social class is not officially recognized—that it's easy for visitors not to notice the way the class system works. A case in point is the experience of Walter Allen, the British novelist and literary critic. Before he came over here to teach at a college in the 1950s, he imagined that "class scarcely existed in America, except, perhaps, as divisions between ethnic groups or successive waves of immigrants." But living awhile in Grand Rapids opened his eyes: there he learned of the snob

power of New England and the pliability of the locals to the long-wielded moral and cultural authority of old families.

7   Some Americans viewed with satisfaction the failure of the 1970s TV series *Beacon Hill*, a drama of high society modeled on the British *Upstairs, Downstairs*, comforting themselves with the belief that this venture came to grief because there is no class system here to sustain interest in it. But they were mistaken. *Beacon Hill* failed to engage American viewers because it focused on perhaps the least interesting place in the indigenous class structure, the quasi-aristocratic upper class. Such a dramatization might have done better if it had dealt with places where everyone recognizes interesting class collisions occur—the place where the upper-middle class meets the middle and resists its attempted incursions upward, or where the middle class does the same to the classes just below it.

8   If foreigners often fall for the official propaganda of social equality, the locals tend to know what's what, even if they feel some uneasiness talking about it. When the acute black from the South asserts of an ambitious friend that "Joe can't class with the big folks," we feel in the presence of someone who's attended to actuality. Like the carpenter who says: "I hate to say there are classes, but it's just that people are more comfortable with people of like backgrounds." His grouping of people by "like backgrounds," scientifically uncertain as it may be, is nearly as good a way as any to specify what it is that distinguishes one class from another. If you feel no need to explicate your allusions or in any way explain what you mean, you are probably talking with someone in your class. And that's true whether you're discussing the Rams and the Forty-Niners, RVs, the House (i.e., Christ Church, Oxford), Mama Leone's, the Big Board, "the Vineyard," "Baja," or the Porcellian. . . .

9   Class should be a serious subject in America especially, because here we lack a convenient system of inherited titles, ranks, and honors, and each generation has to define the hierarchies all over again. The society changes faster than any other on earth, and the American, almost uniquely, can be puzzled about where, in the society, he stands. The things that conferred class in the 1930s—white linen golf knickers, chrome cocktail shakers, vests with white piping—are, to put it mildly, unlikely to do so today. Belonging to a rapidly changing rather than a traditional society, Americans find Knowing Where You Stand harder than do most Europeans. And a yet more pressing matter, Making It, assumes crucial importance here. "How'm I doin'?" Mayor Koch of New York used to bellow, and most of his audience sensed that he was, appropriately, asking the representative American question.

10   It seems no accident that, as the British philosopher Anthony Quinton says, "The book of etiquette in its modern form . . . is largely an American product, the great names being Emily Post . . . and Amy Vanderbilt." The reason is that the United States is preeminently the venue of new-

comers, with a special need to place themselves advantageously and to get on briskly. "Some newcomers," says Quinton, "are geographical, that is, immigrants; others are economic, the newly rich; others again chronological, the young." All are faced with the problem inseparable from the operations of a mass society, earning respect. The comic Rodney Dangerfield, complaining that he don't get none, belongs to the same national species as that studied by John Adams, who says, as early as 1805: "The rewards . . . in this life are *esteem* and *admiration* of others—the punishments are *neglect* and *contempt*. . . . The desire of the esteem of others is as real a want of nature as hunger—and the neglect and contempt of the world as severe a pain as the gout or stone. . . . " About the same time the Irish poet Thomas Moore, sensing the special predicament Americans were inviting with their egalitarian Constitution, described the citizens of Washington, D.C., as creatures

> Born to be slaves, and struggling to be lords.

Thirty years later, in *Democracy in America,* Alexis de Tocqueville put his finger precisely on the special problem of class aspiration here. "Nowhere," he wrote, "do citizens appear so insignificant as in a democratic nation." Nowhere, consequently, is there more strenuous effort to achieve—*earn* would probably not be the right word—significance. And still later in the nineteenth century, Walt Whitman, in *Democratic Vistas* (1871), perceived that in the United States, where the form of government promotes a condition (or at least an illusion) of uniformity among the citizens, one of the unique anxieties is going to be the constant struggle for individual self-respect based upon social approval. That is, where everybody is somebody, nobody is anybody. In a recent Louis Harris poll, "respect from others" is what 76 percent of respondents said they wanted most. Addressing prospective purchasers of a coffee table, an ad writer recently spread before them this most enticing American vision: "Create a rich, warm, sensual allusion to your own good taste that will demand respect and consideration in every setting you care to imagine."

11 The special hazards attending the class situation in America, where movement appears so fluid and where the prizes seem available to anyone who's lucky, are disappointment, and, following close on that, envy. Because the myth conveys the impression that you can readily earn your way upward, disillusion and bitterness are particularly strong when you find yourself trapped in a class system you've been half persuaded isn't important. When in early middle life some people discover that certain limits have been placed on their capacity to ascend socially by such apparent irrelevancies as heredity, early environment, and the social class of their immediate forebears, they go into something like despair, which, if generally secret, is no less destructive.

12 De Tocqueville perceived the psychic dangers. "In democratic times," he granted, "enjoyments are more intense than in the ages of aristocracy,

and the number of those who partake in them is vastly larger." But, he added, in egalitarian atmospheres "man's hopes and desires are oftener blasted, the soul is more stricken and perturbed, and care itself more keen."

13   And after blasted hopes, envy. The force of sheer class envy behind vile and even criminal behavior in this country, the result in part of disillusion over the official myth of classlessness, should never be underestimated. The person who, parking his attractive car in a large city, has returned to find his windows smashed and his radio aerial snapped off will understand what I mean. Speaking in West Virginia in 1950, Senator Joseph R. McCarthy used language that leaves little doubt about what he was really getting at—not so much "Communism" as the envied upper-middle and upper classes. "It has not been the less fortunate or members of minority groups who have been selling this nation out," he said, "but rather those who have had all the benefits . . . , the finest homes, the finest college education. . . . " Pushed far enough, class envy issues in revenge egalitarianism, which the humorist Roger Price, in *The Great Roob Revolution* (1970), distinguishes from "democracy" thus: "Democracy demands that all of its citizens begin the race even. Egalitarianism insists that they all *finish* even." Then we get the situation satirized in L. P. Hartley's novel *Facial Justice* (1960), about "the prejudice against good looks" in a future society somewhat like ours. There, inequalities of appearance are redressed by government plastic surgeons, but the scalpel isn't used to make everyone beautiful—it's used to make everyone plain.

14   Despite our public embrace of political and judicial equality, in individual perception and understanding—much of which we refrain from publicizing—we arrange things vertically and insist on crucial differences in value. Regardless of what we say about equality, I think everyone at some point comes to feel like the Oscar Wilde who said, "The brotherhood of man is not a mere poet's dream: it is a most depressing and humiliating reality." It's as if in our heart of hearts we don't want agglomerations but distinctions. Analysis and separation we find interesting, synthesis boring.

15   Although it is disinclined to designate a hierarchy of social classes, the federal government seems to admit that if in law we are all equal, in virtually all other ways we are not. Thus the eighteen grades into which it divides its civil-service employees, from grade 1 at the bottom (messenger, etc.) up through 2 (mail clerk), 5 (secretary), 9 (chemist), to 14 (legal administrator), and finally 16, 17, and 18 (high-level administrators). In the construction business there's a social hierarchy of jobs, with "dirt work," or mere excavation, at the bottom; the making of sewers, roads, and tunnels in the middle; and work on buildings (the taller, the higher) at the top. Those who sell "executive desks" and related office furniture know that they and their clients agree on a rigid "class" hierarchy. Desks made of oak are at the bottom, and those of walnut are next. Then, moving up, ma-

hogany is, if you like, "upper-middle class," until we arrive, finally, at the apex: teak. In the army, at ladies' social functions, pouring the coffee is the prerogative of the senior officer's wife because, as the ladies all know, coffee outranks tea.

16   There seems no place where hierarchical status-orderings aren't discoverable. Take musical instruments. In a symphony orchestra the customary ranking of sections recognizes the difficulty and degree of subtlety of various kinds of instruments: strings are on top, woodwinds just below, then brass, and, at the bottom, percussion. On the difficulty scale, the accordion is near the bottom, violin near the top. Another way of assigning something like "social class" to instruments is to consider the prestige of the group in which the instrument is customarily played. As the composer Edward T. Cone says, "If you play a violin, you can play in a string quartet or symphony orchestra, but not in a jazz band and certainly not in a marching band. Among woodwinds, therefore, flute, and oboe, which are primarily symphonic instruments, are 'better' than the clarinet, which can be symphonic, jazz, or band. Among brasses, the French horn ranks highest because it hasn't customarily been used in jazz. Among percussionists, tympani is high for the same reason." And (except for the bassoon) the lower the notes an instrument is designed to produce, in general the lower its class, bass instruments being generally easier to play. Thus a sousaphone is lower than a trumpet, a bass viol lower than a viola, etc. If you hear "My boy's taking lessons on the trombone," your smile will be a little harder to control than if you hear "My boy's taking lessons on the flute." On the other hand, to hear "My boy's taking lessons on the viola da gamba" is to receive a powerful signal of class, the kind attaching to antiquarianism and museum, gallery, or "educational" work. Guitars (except when played in "classical"—that is, archaic—style) are low by nature, and that is why they were so often employed as tools of intentional class degradation by young people in the 1960s and '70s. The guitar was the perfect instrument for the purpose of signaling these young people's flight from the upper-middle and middle classes, associated as it is with Gypsies, cowhands, and other personnel without inherited or often even earned money and without fixed residence.

17   The former Socialist and editor of the *Partisan Review* William Barrett, looking back thirty years, concludes that "the Classless Society looks more and more like a Utopian illusion. The socialist countries develop a class structure of their own," although there, he points out, the classes are very largely based on bureaucratic toadying. "Since we are bound . . . to have classes in any case, why not have them in the more organic, heterogeneous and variegated fashion" indigenous to the West? And since we have them, why not know as much as we can about them? The subject may be touchy, but it need not be murky forever.

Points for Review and Discussion

1. Fussell says that in America the idea of class is "notably embarrassing" (¶ 2). How does he account for this embarrassment?
2. What reasons does Fussell give in support of his assertion that class "should be a serious subject in America" (¶ 9)?
3. Fussell observes that foreigners frequently make mistakes about class in America. What mistakes? How do foreigners correct them?

•◆ Questions for Writing

1. Fussell refers to "the official myth of classlessness" (¶ 13), as though everyone knew the content of this myth. What *is* the content and where have you encountered the myth?
2. Commenting on the reader who wrote BULL SHIT in the margins of a library book, Fussell says: "A hopelessly middle-class man (not a woman, surely?) if I ever saw one" (¶ 3). Both the tone and substance of this remark are meant to define the author's social place. What is that place? What relation do you see between Fussell's assumed social position and his way of writing—his style?
3. Where do you yourself stand on the question of whether Americans, in their heart of hearts, "don't want agglomeration but distinctions" (¶ 14)? Explain your answer.

Toward a Definition of Class
Mortimer Levitt

A self-made millionaire, Mortimer Levitt founded a chain of custom shirt shops that now has branches in dozens of American cities. For years he was an active theatrical and television producer, while serving on the boards of several major cultural organizations in New York City. In 1984 Levitt produced a book called *Class*, offering guidance to people intent on becoming classy. There are chapters on "What You Say and How You Say What You Say," "How You Look," and "What You Do: A. How You Live Your Life, B. How You Entertain." The book begins with the following essay defining class.

1 In practical terms, then, what might class consist of? As I see it, there are four basic components:

1. What you say
2. How you say what you say
3. How you look
4. What you do

I prepared a preliminary list of items in each of the four categories, and it is interesting that the list on "what you do" is twice as long as the other three categories put together. And why not—what you do is the substance of class; how you do it is the style.

2 That, then, presents the question Can class be achieved? My good friend, Dorothy Cullman, a much-traveled woman, and sometime producer for Broadway and television, says emphatically, No.

> For me, class cannot be bought or acquired. It is an inner quality found without regard to financial status or family background. I think its essential quality is integrity, intelligence, and lack of pretension. Education can expand the horizon of a person with so-called class, but it will not give class to someone born without it. It is a state of grace that few people have.

I think Dorothy's general position is sound, but I disagree with her on the point that one must somehow have class from the beginning or not at all.

3 I happen to be a high-school dropout, born on the wrong side of the tracks and certainly without the appurtenances of class as it is usually understood. One of the many that I lacked was a middle name, having been born simply Mortimer Levitt. Being quick on the draw, I adopted the middle name of Harold. I was fourteen, and moved in one gigantic step from

---

From Mortimer Levitt, *Class* (1984).

Mortimer Levitt to Mortimer H. Levitt. It happened that Mrs. Wrightman, a close friend of my mother, gave her the top part of a bathing suit her son had outgrown. (In those days men were never topless at the beach.) The top was emblazoned with a crimson H. I didn't know the H stood for Harvard. I assumed it stood for Harold, the name of Mrs. Wrightman's son, and claimed it as my middle initial, a claim no one bothered to challenge. Many, many years later, having acquired other and more important appurtenances, I felt sufficiently secure to drop Harold and become, once again, Mortimer Levitt.

4   Although I lacked the appurtenances, I did have something that was my very own—a sense of self. I knew that I was not like the people my family grew up with. I knew that I was not born to live and die in Brooklyn. I had a hunger for something else without being sure what that something else was. I too undoubtedly confused class with its appurtenances, not realizing that my own sense of self was indeed a beginning. . . .

5   [My] premise [is] that class can be achieved, at least to a degree, and I will offer practical suggestions toward that end. But at this point the operative question may well be, can class be *defined*? To that question I received a wide range of responses from the friends I consulted. As they are all individuals of considerable achievement and experience, I think you may agree that their comments, as diverse and, often, divergent from one another as they appear, will help us shape a reasonably precise working definition of the term. Let us see. . . .

6 *William Bernbach, Chairman and Founder, Doyle Dane Bernbach:*
Class is unostentatious quality. It is restraint. It is modesty, an elegance of behavior, a willingness to let time measure your performance rather than a strident, meretricious "selling" of your personal wares. Class is a quiet pursuit of excellence that abhors all pretension.

7 *Robert Ludlum, Author:*
"Class" is not something I dwell on, but trust it is something I recognize. In behavior and appearance, I think "class" is the impact that comes with the simplicity of understatement. That impact is almost always accompanied by a directness in conversation and a willingness to listen. I guess it boils down to a genuine regard for other people because you have the same regard for yourself.

8 *Herbert Salzman, Former Ambassador to the Organization for Economic Cooperation and Development in Paris:*
"He has class" is the ultimate compliment. It indicates a person with instinctive generosity; it is a spontaneous expression of a person's character. Such a person is totally unconcerned

with making an impression upon others. It derives from utter personal security and usually stems from an upbringing that can afford clear standards of "what is done," but may also develop regardless of station in life (leaving aside the Sicilian Brotherhood of the Black Hand). A person may be said to have "class" who is never in doubt as to the "right" thing to do and does it instinctively. Such a person is "inner-directed" in the sense that he takes his own behavior for granted and the approval of the group is immaterial—he knows that whatever he is doing is "right" because it meets his own standards.

9   "Style" is frequently used as a synonym for "class" because the American culture likes to think of our society as democratic, and "style" doesn't imply the historical meaning of "class." Those who voluntarily remained aboard the S.S. *Titanic* and sang "Rock of Ages" as the ship went down can truly be said to have made their exit in style, to have shown "class." Although it was the ship's orchestra who played while the passengers sang, it is, oddly enough, only the singers who are remembered, all of whom were first-class passengers.

10 *Roger Starr, Editorial Board, the* New York Times:
"Class" used as an adjective in the sentence, "Joe DiMaggio has class," for example, means that the person so described embodies the virtues of the social class to which he belongs, or would like to belong. In any case, it's the nobility to which everyone assumes everyone else would like to belong, and so class is simply a rough version of the word *noble;* it's really the lingering remnant of what was called chivalry, meaning the code of conduct of people able to own horses in the medieval economy. Class, or chivalry, involves a *style of dress*, a set of manners, and a code of conduct that is a highly refined version of the art of war: generosity in victory, calm in defeat, deportment that calls attention not so much to individual behavior but rather to conformity with socially acceptable ideals. We assume that noble people are immune to self-doubt, qualms, vanity, envy. Maybe they are. I never knew any well enough to be absolutely certain.

11 *Elise MacLay, Author:*
Class is like happiness. It is acquired with casual grace in the attainment of something else. But the something else must be noble and the pursuit of it must be true. So it is that Mother Theresa has class and the Duchess of Windsor does not. Class is caring about what is eternal and not caring about what is not.

12 *Manya Starr, Screenwriter:*
Class is what you ain't got if everybody knows it except you.

13 *Gay Talese, Author:*
I always thought of class as a convincing manifestation of poise under pressure—something many of us aspire to, but rarely does the effort achieve the ideal.

14 *William Honan, Cultural News Editor, the* New York Times:
Although class has many strongly positive connotations, it also brings to mind some dark thoughts. That's because originally the notion of "class" was an admiring reference to the conduct of the aristocracy. Now, of course, there never really was and there never really will be anything to admire about the way rich and privileged people behave. Generally, throughout history, they have behaved badly. And, thus, it is an unfortunate comment on our short memories and our present shallowness that "class" has come to mean something quite positive, something we all crave to possess.

15   Nevertheless, we are so far removed from the worst evils of a rigidly structured class system that we forget that a century or more ago "class" was an approving term for the license, irresponsibility and spoiled-brat behavior of those who found themselves, by birth or by good luck, on top of the heap. We forget that today. We think of class as the noble bearing of Jacqueline Kennedy at her husband's funeral and we don't recognize that class was also a mark of the conduct of Edward Kennedy at Chappaquiddick. That, too, was class. Nobody but a spoiled aristocrat would have behaved as Teddy behaved then, and certainly no one else would have gotten away with only losing his driver's license; excepting perhaps a U.S. Senator with the very best legal services. So, you see, I have a good deal of trouble thinking that "class" is simply a wonderful thing to have or possess, because I remember the origin of the terms.

16 *Jack Garfein, Producer and Director:*
Class is when you're not concerned about it.

17 *Ruth Spears, Author:*
Because "class" is not a classy word, there is nothing I can say about it.

18 *Judy Price, President and Publisher,* Avenue Magazine:
   Few of the people I meet have it. Many are stylish; many, successful; some, even unique. But few have that special combination of qualities: a sense of self without egotism; a sense of worth without wealth; and a sense of style achieved with ease rather than by artifice.

19 *William F. May, Dean, Graduate School of Business, New York University:*
   A person with class possesses assurance but not arrogance; pride but not conceit; sympathy but not sycophancy—one that has a deep unpretentious nobility.

20 *Skitch Henderson, Composer/Conductor/Pianist:*
   Class to me means the assimilation of culture, whether it be the best bricklayer, carpenter, composer, or conductor. With many professions there is an organized dress code, and, speaking as a working musician, well-tailored but comfortable clothes give me an inward class and warmth which helps my professional life.

21 *Brendan Gill, Author and Critic,* The New Yorker:
   The adjective "classy" is an old-fashioned slang term, which nobody likely to be so described would ever employ. The highest degree of class is the least visible; the odds are very much against its being achieved in a single lifetime and certainly not through effort or a sedulous aping of one's betters. F.D.R. has class, but Eleanor Roosevelt had far more class than her husband did. She was at ease with all kinds of people, while he was at ease only with his peers; he talked down to the so-called lower orders, though they never seemed to notice. Few presidents and still fewer business executives have class, and no wonder: scrambling for place is ruthless as well as untidy, and nice guys do tend to finish last. Scott Fitzgerald said, "I speak with the authority of failure." No self-pity, no plea for sympathy—in a word, "class."

22 *Vada Stanley, Marketing Executive:*
   Class is the art of being true to oneself under all circumstances and with all people. A person with class treats a charwoman the same as a duchess, or, in the manner of Henry Higgins, a duchess the same as he treats a charwoman. He doesn't toady and he doesn't bully: he doesn't condescend, nor does he fawn. No one can intimidate him. I think being gracefully unintimidate-able is the height of class.

23 *Harold Proshansky, President, the Graduate School and University Center of the City University of New York*
    I have often referred to people as either having or lacking class and while I have often meant this in terms of how they look and dress, more often I have meant how they deal with a problem or a conflict. For example, people who "continually wash their dirty linen in public" lack class, and, for me, people who lie either to avoid problems or create false solutions also lack class. Even among some of the most distinguished corporate leaders of the nation—what little experience I have had with them—I am able to tell you those who have class and those who have not.
24   While education and money help in establishing class, I can assure you I have found it in people who lack both.

25 *Edward Koch, Mayor, New York City:*
    Class or classy is a state of mind, both in the person who is perceived as classy and the observer who makes that determination. It is a matter of distinctive style, a manner, and an outlook which demonstrate independence and solid substance, something that is worth emulation.

26 *Molly Haskell, Author:*
    Class has an ethical as well as an aesthetic side. That is, it implies virtue, selflessness, as well as style. It's a modish way of paying tribute to morality by people who wouldn't be caught dead using *that* old word—even before Jerry Falwell appropriated it. To attribute class to somebody is to express admiration without envy. That's rare enough these days, and as beauty is in the eye of the beholder, we hope to rise a bit in our own esteem by acknowledging "'class" in others.

27 *Jonathan Reynolds, Author and Playwright:*
    First and foremost, I think class is morality—because it demands of the individual the most rigorous precept of all; that he be truly himself, and therefore unique. Although aware of fashion (political or sartorial), the person with class must be flexible enough to follow fashion when it complements that uniqueness and to shun it when it doesn't. However, the particular uniqueness must be admirable: several folks who live on the Bowery are decidedly unique but couldn't be considered to have class.
28   Second, I think class has very little to do with birth and almost everything to do with upbringing: class is usually

learned, seldom inherited. There are far too many classless aristocrats, from Princess Margaret of England to Huntington Hartford of America, and there are far too many people without genetically privileged backgrounds who do have class, from Diana Ross to Cary Grant. I think one may learn from a privileged background, but it is still learning.

29   And, finally, just to negate the above, class, like its opposite, kitsch, is always in the eye of the beholder: one man's Fred Astaire is another man's Sammy Davis, Jr.

30 *Mrs. William Woodside, Special Consultant, Drug and Alcohol Rehabilitation:*
To get class, choose your parents wisely.

31 *John Mack Carter, Editor-in-Chief,* Good Housekeeping:
Class is the act of living without compromise, hewing unfailingly to an individual and self-imposed standard of performance. Prime examples in fiction are Sidney Carton and Gunga Din, in real life Robert Moses and Jacqueline Onassis.

32 *Sally French, Banker:*
Class is a human condition that occurs when one has used inherent skills to their full potential without hurting anyone else in the process. It is achieved when one has gone through adversity without becoming bitter or cynical. It is thinking of others before thinking of one's self. And, of course, class means having a collar that fits your neck.

33 *A. E. Hotchner, Author:*
Class is a unique self-quality possessed by certain people that sets them apart and incites admiration in their fellow man. It is compounded of:

- A sense of knowing who they are, where they are headed and being extremely good at what they do.
- A total lack of hostility, jealousy or envy.
- A polite consideration for the rights and talents of others.
- A controlled ambition.
- Wisdom nurtured from experience.
- A disdain of complaining, especially about fate.
- A tendency toward having good luck.

34 *Bill Blass, Designer:*
Class means the Yale Class of '22.

35   Based upon this diversity of quotations, you may agree that it is almost impossible to say precisely what class is—in fact, it is almost easier to say what class is *not* . . .

36   ... One cannot say "up to this line, no class; step over this line, pouf, class." *Therefore, we should be flexible and perhaps rate ourselves on a class scale of one to ten.*

Points for Review and Discussion

1.   Summarize Mortimer Levitt's own class background on the basis of what he himself says about it.
2.   What point is most stressed by Levitt's "authorities" in their definitions of class?
3.   To what class do the quoted authorities appear to belong?

•● Questions for Writing

1.   Levitt says that, since he was "born on the wrong side of the tracks," he was "without the appurtenances of class as it is usually understood" (¶ 3). Fussell, on the other hand, appears to believe that nobody, regardless of place of birth, can be without the appurtenances of class. Account for this conflict by explaining the difference between Fussell's and Levitt's definitions of class.
2.   Reread William Honan's comments (¶ 14). The tone of these remarks is unlike that of many of the other responses to Levitt's question. How would you describe this tone? What strengths or weaknesses (or both) do you see in the attitude toward class that Honan expresses?
3.   From among the other responses in this essay to Levitt's question, choose one that you strongly approve or disapprove of, and explain your reaction to it.

Dirtbags, Burnouts, Metalheads, and Thrashers
Donna Gaines

One way to decide what class means is to sort people out into different classes according to their behavior and tastes. Another way is to ask people what they think it means. Still another way is to choose a sector of society and spend time familiarizing yourself with it—learning how people think and feel who belong to that sector, discovering how they explain their social situation to themselves, assessing the degree to which the factor of their social class affects the course of their lives.

Donna Gaines, a teacher and journalist with advanced degrees in sociology, chose this third path, centering her inquiries on high school dropouts in suburban Bergenfield, New Jersey, and in several Long Island towns. Seeking to understand working-class, often self-destructive teenagers, Gaines lived in their alienated world and studied its customs and agonies. She published her findings in *Teenage Wasteland* (1991) and is now a features writer for the *Village Voice*.

The selection below offers Gaines' account of what social class means and how it works in the case of young men and women tracked into vocational education.

1   Dirtbags, burnouts, metalheads, and thrashers alike could find pride and purpose in Bergen County's trade schools. Here, as in other suburban towns, the local vocational and technical school is usually called "heavy metal high school" because of all the metalheads who attend.

2   Vocational high school may be viewed by academically oriented educators as a convenient dump site for troublemakers with low test scores. But for the kids who end up there, it's often a pretty cool scene. Especially here in Bergen County, where every dirtbag shuttled over to a vocational school has the additional prestige of knowing S.O.D.'s lead singer went to one. Wherever I went in Bergen County, if music was seriously discussed, people made sure to tell me that S.O.D.'s powerful front man, Billy Milano, was from Bergen County. So what if the jocks were winning state competitions—the dirts had Billy and S.O.D. for their regional pride.

3   Meanwhile, there were guys like Roy. I had met him on the Ave one night, talking to Jeanne and Nicole. Roy rarely hung out anymore, now

---

From Donna Gaines, *Teenage Wasteland* (1991).

that he was learning to labor on the cars of America. It was a great career choice, and it seems to have happened quite by chance. It's a familiar story, though.

4   This is how it goes: The teacher calls you down to talk about your record. Or maybe it's the guidance counselor. "So, Roy, what do you see yourself doing five years from now?" And Roy is thinking what did I do wrong, what does she want me to say, what is going to come down on me now? And then the guidance counselor will say something about Roy's lack of spectacular grades—"not on any teams or in any clubs, are you, Roy?" And Roy starts feeling stupid and maybe he fiddles with himself nervously, and says the first thing that comes to his head, like how much he enjoys working on his car. Like she shouldn't think he's a total loser. And that's that! He's never really given much thought before now, but today, the future is laid out before him and now Roy's going to vocational high school and he's going to learn about cars.

5   He's so relieved that he's not in trouble, and that this adult hasn't figured out that he really hasn't got a clue about what he's going to do with his life because nobody ever asked him about it. Or impressed upon him that what he wants might be important. Until today, most of what Roy has been concerned with has been keeping out of trouble, keeping out of his teachers' way. So Roy is satisfied because now he has a future, and with it, an identity and plans. Maybe he'll do well at it. His foster mother is proud of him. He's almost grown, and now he's got a direction.

6   In the suburban high schools of America the greasers have always been found hanging around outside "shop." There are many "hoody"-looking types who have good academic grades, who are book-smart, but that's not the stereotype. Working-class males smoking cigarettes and bonding around labor. Girls gathered around small office machines and hair-setting apparatus. This territory is now the domain of America's metalheads. Dirtbags, metalheads, thrashers, burnouts. Black and Hispanic kids are part of this too.

7   Bergen County's Vocational Technical School, where Roy was now enrolled, was in Hackensack. When I mentioned this to some guy I met at Hav-A-Pizza in the Foster Village Shopping Center, he said. "Oh yeah, that's a real burnout school." The school has a great street rep. So I drove out to Roy's school that afternoon, to find out what this school was doing right.

8   The campus is situated near Roy Rogers, which is right away a good spot for a school. In the parking lot an unidentifiable thrash band's snarecore drumroll propels two long-haired dudes deep into the engine of an old light-green Chevy Nova. Many of the grand bombs of the Ave will have been resurrected here. Engines and bodies and hoods and fenders and hair. Here, the celebration of car culture becomes a legitimate practice, and it's okay to be yourself. You learn what you like to learn. That's why you're here.

9   There are greenhouses, and clusters of girls in smocks. Before I introduce myself to the authorities I meander through the halls. The school is clean and cheerful, although clearly "not for kids." Serious business is conducted here. On display are the successful liaisons of youth and industry, career ladders in various trades, union wage schedules. I am stopped by a man who is a teacher. We chat comfortably. This is far from Bergenfield and he is delighted that I am interested in the school.

10   For more information he suggests the guidance counselor's offices, and directs me there. I am told that someone can see me in about twenty minutes, as a door shuts behind a middle-aged woman with dark hair and a young girl. Meantime, would I mind waiting in the library?

11   I walk by a room filled with computers. A few moments later I am seated near some kids doing library time, working on a report, relaxing and quietly talking. I pick from a table of magazines: *Psychology Today, BYTE, Horticulture, The Conservationist, Parents, New Jersey Outdoors, Family Computing, Gourmet.* Something for everyone.

12   A glamorous teenage girl shows off an earring someone made for her in shop. It's delicate metal sculpture, something nice enough to wear to a show. A boy in a concert polo shirt teases her, all the while viewing the librarian for sanctions. The librarian glares once or twice, but goes on to other business. The students seem more physically relaxed than their counterparts in regular schools. They're more stylish too, from a street point of view. That makes sense; these are specialized programs for kids interested in food preparation, cosmetology, carpentry, commercial art, and the interest in grooming and styling is strong. Also, they will be working with the public in some of these fields, so personal appearance is important.

13   The time passes quickly in this sunlit airy room. I am greeted by the dark-haired guidance counselor, Dolores Bentivegna. We sit down in her office and I ask her, simply, why kids seem to like this school so much. By now I understand the basic breakdown: Kids with behavior problems are sent to special services—emotionally disturbed kids, school phobics, and disabled kids. And kids with low grades are often encouraged to come here, dumped into vocational education. That way teachers can spread scarce resources efficiently, focus on the more intellectually responsive kids, the college material. Keep the school looking good, the test scores robust, all so their "brighter" kids have a better chance.

14   I also understand from the kids that getting farmed out to the vocational high school involves some degree of coercion. But once they get here, they like it, they are happy. So I ask this guidance counselor what is the secret of this school's success.

15   Mrs. B. explains that this school has the longest school day in the district, no study hall, a short lunch break. Half the day is academic, half is for work in one's chosen field. The program is highly structured. Not all the kids can handle it. That makes sense, I say, since a number of kids who have been encouraged to come here say they have no real interest in vocational training. . . .

16   Following a good hour of her time, Mrs. B. gives me her card, and I thank her.

17   That night it occurs to me that most of the guys I knew from Metal 24, guys in my neighborhood, were "B.O.C.E.S." graduates—New York State's version of Bergen Vo-Tech. The Board of Cooperative Educational Services of Nassau County was famous for many things. Some kids were sent there for vocational training or for programs in the arts, and they spoke lovingly of their high school experiences. Some programs were directly related to Long Island's aerospace and technology industries.

18   Other kids were "special," like Nicky and Joe and Randy, too "emotionally disturbed" for the mainstream classroom. These guys were sent to the school in Baldwin Harbor because they were even too rowdy for the "rubber rooms" in their own districts. They just took it in stride: the label, the Ritalin, the warehousing.

19   Then there was "B.O.C.E.S. for chicks"—that's what the guys call the traditionally feminine fields of cosmetology, flower arranging, data processing, food preparation, and dental assisting. I live near Nassau Tech, a major B.O.C.E.S. site that is known for its low-cost, high-quality lunch cafeteria. The kids do the cooking and the public gets a great deal on a meal.

20   My "research consultants" at the convenience store, Eddie and Cliff, also agreed that life in vocational courses had a lot more dignity than life in regular high school. Eddie says he was coming to his school drunk every day, so they steered him over to B.O.C.E.S. When asked what he wanted to study, Eddie figured food preparation, because this was where all the pretty girls hung out and he wanted to meet them. So he embarked upon a career in "food prep." This eventually landed him a job baking donuts, then making sandwiches at a deli.

21   Of course Eddie couldn't support himself on five dollars an hour, so, like many local entrepreneurs, he began moonlighting in the underground youth economy. This illicit activity got him sent up for two years. In prison, he had the opportunity to take some college courses. Eddie says he would like to complete his B.S. degree some day, but he's got no money for tuition. Besides, he says, he's not in any rush for school right now. So he's just working at the convenience store and playing in a local band.

22   Cliff studied graphic arts and printing, but had also worked in a deli. He hoped to buy one of his own but needed a chunk of cash to do it. His parents died before he was twenty-one; there really wasn't anyone to help him out. At one point he was going to go in on a limo partnership, hoping to drive and work for himself. But he needed to put up heavy cash for it. So for now he's working at Metal 24. Late at night it's arts-and-crafts time at Metal 24. Eddie will be writing lyrics, Cliff setting up designs for future tattoos. Sid and a few of the other guys will be playing video games and Cliff's girlfriend, Ann, and I are probably discussing horoscopes.

23   Sid is another B.O.C.E.S. alum who studied auto body. He offers to do a light compounding on my car. He did an impressive piece of work on his

Boxcar; he won't take any money from me because we're friends. He works at the parts counter at Auto Barn.

24   The "disposable" heroes in my neighborhood are all working in fields related to the training they got at B.O.C.E.S. Ann works in hair, and she sweeps the floors of a local beauty parlor. The other girls have babies now, so they don't hang out anymore. A few hold jobs as cashiers or hostesses and you rarely see them. One girl goes to Nassau Community College at night and works in a video store during the day.

25   Meanwhile Cliff dreams of being a bass player, Eddie is writing lyrics. Sid plays drums, Ann wants to have a family. Friends from the neighborhood who are my age hung out at Metal 24 when it was a drive-in hamburger stand. Many people here live the same lives, ten years after, with some of the same dreams.

26   In the scheme of things average American kids who don't have rich or well-connected parents have had these choices: Play the game and try to get ahead. Do what your parents did—work yourself to death at a menial job and find solace in beer, God, or family. Or take risks, cut deals, or break the law. The Reagan years made it hard for kids to "put their noses to the grindstone" as their parents had. Like everyone, these people hoped for better lives. But they lived in an age of inflated expectations and diminishing returns. Big and fast money was everywhere, and ever out of reach. America now had an economy that worked sort of like a cocaine high—propped up by hot air and big debt. The substance was absent. People's lives were like that too, and at times they were crashing hard.

27   In the meantime, wherever you were, you could still dream of becoming spectacular. A special talent could be your ticket out. Long Island kids had role models in bands like the Crumbsuckers, Ludichrist, Twisted Sister, and Pat Benatar. North Jersey was full of sports celebrities and rock millionaires—you grew up hoping you'd end up like Mike Tyson or Jon Bon Jovi. Or like Keith Richards, whose father worked in a factory; or Ozzy, who also came from a grim English factory town, a hero who escaped the drudge because he was spectacular. This was the hip version of the American dream.

28   Kids who go for the prize now understand there are only two choices—rise to the top or crash to the bottom. Many openly admit that they would rather end it all now than end up losers. The nine-to-five world, corporate grunt life, working at the same job for thirty years, that's not for them. They'd prefer to hold out until the last possibility and then just piss on it all. The big easy or the bottomless pit, but never the everyday drone. And as long as there are local heroes and stories, you can still believe you have a chance to emerge from the mass as something larger than life. You can still play the great lottery and dream.

29   Schools urge kids to make these choices as early as possible, in a variety of ways. In the terse words of the San Francisco hardcore band MDC, "There's no such thing as cheating in a loser's game." Many kids who start out as nobody from nowhere with nothing will end up that way.

Nevertheless, everyone pretends that everything is possible if you give it your best shot. We actually believe it. While educators hope to be as efficient as possible in figuring out where unspectacular students can plug into the work force, kids try to play at being one in a million, some way of shining, even if it's just for a while.

30   A few years playing ball, or in a band, and then you get a job. My boyfriend K. had a father employed as a mechanic at Grumman Aerospace. His father offered to get him a job in management there, since K. was "quick with the words." But K. had other plans. He got a part-time job in shipping at the age of seventeen. He kept it after high school, and held on to it for ten years while he played in the Grinders and other bands. The music was always his first priority. Over the years, he's picked up some more hours, and he's glad to have good Teamsters benefits.

31   But during those years he also got to play at CBGB's and Max's Kansas City, and he cut a few albums. Periodically there was champagne and limousines, and so once in a while K. got to be spectacular.

32   Girls get slightly different choices. They may hope to become spectacular by virtue of their talents and their beauty. Being the girlfriend of a guy in a band means you might get to live in his mansion someday if you stick it out with him during the lean years. You might just end up like Jon Bon Jovi's high school sweetheart, or married to someone like Cinderella's lead singer—he married his hometown girlfriend and helped set her up in her own business. These are suburban fairy tales.

33   Around here, some girls who are beautiful and talented hope to become stars too, like Long Island's local products Debbie Gibson and Taylor Dayne. Some hope to be like actress Heather Locklear and marry someone really hot like Motley Crue's drummer, Tommy Lee. If you could just get to the right place at the right time.

34   But most people from New Jersey and Long Island or anywhere else in America don't end up rich and famous. They have some fun trying, though, and for a while life isn't bad at all.

35   Yet, if you are unspectacular—not too book-smart, of average looks and moderate creative ability—there have always been places for you. Much of your teacher's efforts will be devoted to your more promising peers, and so will your nation's resources. But your parents will explain to you that this is the way it is, and early on, you will know to expect very little from school.

36   There are still a few enclaves, reservations. The shop and crafting culture of your parents' class of origin is one pocket of refuge. In the vocational high school, your interests are rewarded, once you have allowed yourself to be dumped there. And if the skills you gather there don't really lead to anything much, there's always the military.

37   Even though half the kids in America today will never go to college, the country still acts as if they will. At least, most schools seem to be set up to prepare you for college. And if it's not what you can or want to do, their attitude is tough shit, it's your problem.

38   And your most devoted teachers at vocational high school will never tell you that the training you will get from them is barely enough to get your foot in the door. You picture yourself getting into something with a future only to find that your skills are obsolete, superficial, and the boss prefers people with more training, more experience, more promise. So you are stuck in dead-end "youth employment jobs," and now what?

39   According to the William T. Grant Commission on Work, Family and Citizenship, twenty million people between the ages of sixteen and twenty-four are not likely to go to college. The "forgotten half," as youth advocates call them, will find jobs in service and retail. But the money is bad, only half that of typical manufacturing jobs. The good, stable jobs that don't require advanced training have been disappearing rapidly. From 1979 to 1985 the U.S.A. suffered a net loss of 1.7 million manufacturing jobs. What's left?

40   In my neighborhood, the shipping and warehousing jobs that guys like the Grinders took, hedging their bets against rock stardom, are now seen as "good jobs" by the younger guys at Metal 24. I am regularly asked to petition K. to "find out if they're hiring" down at his shipping company. Dead-end kids around here who aren't working with family are working "shit jobs."

41   The skills used in a typical "shit job" like the ones Cliff and Eddie have involve slapping rancid butter on stale hard rolls, mopping the floor, selling Lotto tickets, making sure shelves and refrigerators are clean, sorting and stacking magazines, taking delivery on newspapers, and signing out videos. They are also advised to look out for shoplifters, to protect the register, and to be sure that the surveillance camera is running. Like most kids in shit jobs, they are most skilled at getting over on the boss and in developing strategies to ward off boredom. It is not unusual to see kids at the supermarket cash register or the mall clothing shop standing around with a glazed look in their eyes. And you will often hear them complain of boredom, tiredness, or whine, "I can't wait to get out of here." Usually, in shit jobs this is where it begins and ends. There aren't many alternatives.

42   Everywhere, such kids find getting into a union or having access to supervisory or managerial tracts hard to come by. Some forms of disinvestment are more obvious than others. In a company town, you will be somewhat clear about what is going on. At the end of the 1980s, the defense industry of Long Island seemed threatened; people feared that their lives would soon be devastated.

43   But the effect of a changing economic order on most kids only translates into scrambling for a new safety zone. It is mostly expressed as resentment against entrepreneurial foreigners (non-whites) and as anomie— a vague sense of loss, then confusion about where they might fit in.

44   Through the 1980s, people articulated their sense of loss in songs. Springsteen's Jersey was a suicide rap, a death trap. The Pretenders' Chrissie Hynde found that her industrial city, her Ohio, was gone, turned into shopping malls. Billy Joel's "Allentown" mourned for the steelwork-

ers of Pennsylvania who had lost their America. To those of us who relate to music nonlyrically, the middle 1980s "industrial noise" bands, the postpunks, and the death-metal merchants were saying the same thing: when old ways die out, before new ones are firmly established, all that remains is a vacuum, a black hole. . . .

45 So where are we going? Some people fear we are polarizing into a two-class nation, rich and poor. More precisely, a privileged knowledge-producing class and a low-paid, low-status service class. It is in the public high school that this division of labor for an emergent postindustrial local economy is first articulated. At the top are the kids who will hold jobs in a highly competitive technological economic order, who will advance and be respected if they cooperate and excel.

46 At the bottom are kids with poor basic skills, short attention spans, limited emotional investment in the future. Also poor housing, poor nutrition, bad schooling, bad lives. And in their bad jobs they will face careers of unsatisfying part-time work, low pay, no benefits, and no opportunity for advancement.

47 There are the few possibilities offered by a relative—a coveted place in a union, a chance to join a small family business in a service trade, a spot in a small shop. In my neighborhood, kids dream of making a good score on the cop tests, working up from hostess to waitress. Most hang out in limbo hoping to get called for a job in the sheriff's department, or the parks, or sanitation. They're on all the lists, although they know the odds for getting called are slim. The lists are frozen, the screening process is endless.

48 Meantime they hold jobs for a few months here and there, or they work off the books, or at two bad jobs at once. They live at home, in a finished basement. If they get pregnant, they still remain with their parents. Nobody has health insurance. Unless they are sucked in by car salesmen who urge them to buy on credit and are paying off heavy car loans, they drive old cars.

49 And they don't marry. Some think it's hopeless because of the inevitability of divorce. But many girls have told me marriage is their dream, since it is their one shot at a home of their own. In 1985, only 43 percent of high school dropouts had incomes high enough to support a three-person family above the poverty level. That's a decline of 60 percent since 1973. In 1985, 3.1 million family households headed by youth under twenty-five had incomes below the poverty level, nearly double the rate of the early 1970s. If we disengage the romanticism normally ascribed to "adolescence," these are simply poor people with few options and no understanding of the social relations that permit adults to keep young Americans poor, disenfranchised, and without skills. Young people are poor people without rights, poor and powerless even without any added burdens of region, class, race, and sex. In the absence of a "youth" movement of magnitude or any memory of intergeneration politics, many kids are simply stuck.

50   In *Learning to Labor*, a study of British working-class kids, Paul Willis argued that by messing up at school, kids tricked themselves into reproducing their parents' bad lives. Willis was writing in the middle 1970s. By now, his "lads" and my "kids" don't even have those same bad options, since so many working-class jobs are disappearing. Today, dropping out of school in a society that is curtailing production and moving toward technical knowledge is the kiss of death.

51   Working-class kids have learned patterns of coping with an educational system originally designed by middle-class reformers to elevate the masses. It is generally agreed that the values and "cultural capital" needed to survive and thrive in this environment have given middle-class kids a bigger advantage. Traditionally, working-class kids had a number of strategies mentioned earlier, shop strategies adapted from the parent culture (sabotage, workplace solidarity, after-hours fraternizing). But if the parent culture itself is dying out, the strategies learned from it have no value. They won't lead to reproducing one's parents' lives in industrial labor. They'll lead you nowhere.

52   Kids who bomb out at school, who express their outrage and defy the regime by ignoring it, will now pay a worse price than ever before. They have higher expectations because of the inflated rhetoric of the Reagan years, and lower life chances because of global transformations in the economy that most people cannot even comprehend. Older guys I know who are struggling to keep their jobs in American companies say we should be more organized, be like the Japanese. Labor blames management and management blames labor. The public buys American out of loyalty and then curses the shitty product. Beyond that, nobody has a clue.

53   Responsibility for containing young people, for prolonging their entry into the work force, is now shared among families, school, the military, and juvenile jails. Meanwhile, life outside, in the real world, has changed drastically.

54   So if kids fuck off in school, they have nothing to fall back on. They are tracked, early on, for life. According to the Grant Commission, kids with math and reading scores in the bottom fifth as compared with their peers in the top half were almost nine times more likely to leave without a diploma, have a child out of wedlock, almost five times more likely to have incomes below the poverty line, and twice as likely to have been arrested the previous year.

55   In 1986, high school dropouts between the ages of twenty and twenty-four earned 42 percent less than similar kids did in 1973. In 1984, 12 percent of them had no earnings at all. So kids who make up the forgotten half and are unspectacular are now learning to labor at the bottom of the economy. These undereducated and underemployed kids will be tracked into low-paid, futureless jobs. The drop-out rates, all the invisible kids bombing out to nowhere, foreshadows the career possibilities available to whole classes of Americans.

56   Unspectacular children of the baby bust—*Los Olvidados*. And these will become America's invisible classes. They will remain as unseen and unheard as the legions of young people who now serve the baby boom and others, in fancy eateries, video stores, and supermarkets. Adult employers regularly complain that such kids have "poor work habits," are unreliable, "tardy," and perform badly at whatever they're told to do. The kids today lack "basic skills." Half the time they don't even show up for work. The impression is that for most kids, work is a low priority. They lack the discipline. They just don't seem to care about anything except having a good time.

57   Before I knew better, I asked Nicky what he was planning to do after he graduated. Was he going to college? He had decent grades. He could study music. Nicky was annoyed that I would even suggest something so idiotic. He laughed right in my face. "Yeah, right. I'll go to college for four years, be bored to death, and come out owing all this money and then I can get a job that pays less than what some guy pumping gas is making." For him, school is a joke. He wants the diploma but beyond that, education serves no purpose.

58   For Nicky, there also doesn't seem to be any desire to try to live differently from his parents. Nicky has dreams; he'd like to make it someday as a drummer. This is his shot at becoming spectacular. He was practicing, he said. Maybe he'd get in a band. Meanwhile Nicky was planning to put in some applications. Maybe get a job as a stock boy at Rickel's, a huge home-improvement chain.

59   After school he'd go right to work. If he didn't leave north Jersey he would probably look for a place around here. Or stay home and save money. I asked him if he wanted to get out of here, leave the area for good. Maybe; he might like to move to California someday. Maybe he'd move there with his old girlfriend. But Nicky also told me he didn't want to leave his friends or his family. He was always saying, "This place sucks." He was always complaining about how boring it was. But when it came down to making a move, he doubted there was any place else he'd rather live. It would be hard to get started where you didn't have people you knew. His friends agreed.

60   But even for kids who finish school, have good records, and obey the rules, there is no guarantee they'll make it into productive careers. The American dream won't work for them, and nobody has bothered to explain why. So they find their concentrated effort and motivation only lead to an extra dollar an hour. At best, they'll earn a promotion to another boring job.

61   Stuck without hope, dreaming of jobs that no longer exist, with the myths of better days further convincing them of their individual fate as "losers," kids today are earning almost one-third less, in constant dollars, than comparable groups in 1973. For white kids, the drop in income is almost 25 percent; for black kids, it's 44 percent. The

scars of race discrimination run deep, and minority youth feel hopeless because they get the message that this nation does not value its nonwhite citizens.

62 White kids have scars too, but with no attending socioeconomic explanation, they personalize their plights. They are "losers" because they are shit as people. They are failures because they are worthless. Either way, it hurts.

63 The understanding of how class works in "classless America" eludes everyone. Parents can teach kids what to expect, help shape attitudes toward their "lot in life." If your parents are losers, it's because their parents were. It's just that way.

64 In nonaffluent white suburbia, all this is hidden. The big picture isn't there. You're middle class, you think. You believe that this country works for you. You do what you are told. It doesn't work, even though you're sure you made all the right moves. So who's fault is it? Yours. You have shit for brains and you'll never be anybody. This feeling becomes part of you.

Points for Review and Discussion

1. Summarize the dominant student attitudes toward school and work that Donna Gaines describes in here.
2. Kids who "bomb out" (¶ 52) in school pay a worse price today, Gaines believes, than ever before. What reasons does she give for this belief?
3. Cite two examples of "suburban fairy tales" (¶ 32) that, in Gaines's opinion, influence her interviewees.

•• Questions for Writing

1. Gaines says that "the understanding of how class works in 'classless America' eludes everyone . . . . The big picture isn't there" (¶ 63). What is the content of the "understanding" to which she refers? Look back over the essay, making notes on what seem to you the most important elements in the big picture of "how class works" in this setting. Then write a paragraph summarizing how class works for teenagers on the voc ed track in suburban New Jersey.
2. The author argues that it's because knowledge of class eludes everyone that the kids she studies "personalize their plights" (¶ 62). Where and how does this "personalizing" take place? What exactly do the kids in question tell themselves about the causes of their situation? Do you agree with Gaines that their analysis of the causes is mistaken? Explain your answer.

3. The language and tone of "Dirtbags" differs vastly from those of the essays by Mortimer Levitt and Paul Fussell. Select representative passages from their essays and compare and contrast them with a related passage of "Dirtbags."
4. Obviously Fussell, Levitt, and Gaines have different conceptions of class. Adopting the perspective of one of these authors, explain to either of the other two what his or her conception of class omits.

Connecting the Parts in Chapter 2: Assignments for Extended Essays

1. Imitating Fussell, develop your own "hierarchy of social classes" on the basis of your personal observations of life in the dorms, in classes, in the dining hall, and at sports and social events. Then write an essay in which you name and define your class categories, explain their relations to money and family and educational background, and assess the extent to which the people you have observed are aware of the particular hierarchy you are explicating.
2. Conduct your own survey of opinion regarding class by asking acquaintances and strangers for their definitions of the word. Then write an essay that draws out the meanings of the responses to your survey. Among the questions worth considering are these: What definitions of class appear to have widest acceptance? How are the differences between your sources and Levitt's sources reflected in the differences between the definitions you and he elicited? What do these latter differences tell you about the relation between social class and ideas about social class?

Leads for Research

1. Explore the intellectual backgrounds of the concept of class. Start by reading *The Communist Manifesto* (1848), part 2 ("Bourgeois and Proletarian"), by Karl Marx, and Jean L. Cohen's *Class and Civil Society: The Limits of Marxian Critical Theory* (1982). What differences do you see between the Marxian concepts of class and those evident in Fussell, Levitt, and Gaines? To what degree are these differences attributable to social change?
2. Social scientists' understandings of class take into account Marxian concepts but a variety of other thinking as well. Acquaint yourself with some of these understandings by reading and taking notes on the entries in the *Encyclopedia of Social Sciences* (1930) on "Class" (by Morris Ginsberg), "Middle Class" (by Alfred Meusel), "Bourgeoisie" (by Carl Brinkman), and "Status" (by Max Radin). Look also at the article on "Social Status" by Morris Zelditch Jr. in the *International Encyclopedia of the Social Sciences* (1968).
3. The phrase "class consciousness" is much used but poorly understood. Begin your research on its meaning by looking into E. P. Thompson, *The Making of the English Working Class* (1963). Read with particular care the preface and Chapter 16 on "Class Consciousness."

3

Discoveries
Working Class, Underclass, Plutocrats

In a society in which the classes are increasingly isolated from each other, ideas about class characteristics tend to be based on stereotypes. Writers and researchers on social and economic topics often find they have no choice except to work at breaking down those stereotypes—cutting through false images.

The first step toward that end is turning a beam of light on the stereotypes themselves—focusing on specific details, one by one, of currently accepted images of the classes. An equally important step is that of explaining how the stereotypes came into existence in the first place—what historical events, for instance, helped to mold them. (One writer argues, below, that the national image of the working class is still much influenced, even now, by the attack launched, on May 8, 1970, in Manhattan's Wall Street district, by hundreds of hardhat construction workers, on a peaceful student demonstration against the Vietnam War.) Finally, breaking down stereotypes requires some hard probing of statistical realities, in order to test opinions about socioeconomic circumstances against solid, relatively objective evidence.

The next three essays contend, in separate ways, against American class stereotypes: false images of the working class, the so-called underclass, and the rich.

The Discovery of the Working Class
Barbara Ehrenreich

Barbara Ehrenreich's *Fear of Falling: The Inner Life of the Middle Class* (1989) is among the best-known, recent, popular studies of American attitudes concerning social difference. The author, who graduated from Reed College in 1963 and holds a Ph.D. in biology from Rockefeller University, writes a monthly column on political and other subjects for *Time* and is also a novelist; she has a son and daughter in their twenties. The following essay probes the origins of blue-collar, hard hat stereotypes.

1   The student rebellion [of the late Sixties] awakened middle-class adults to the uneasy awareness that they were, in some sense, an elite. But an elite relative to whom? Except for the extremes of wealth and poverty, everyone was still part of a monolithic "middle class." Commentators and professors still spoke sonorously of a *we* that included themselves and the majority of Americans, from auto workers to ad men. Radical students at Columbia or Harvard still fancied themselves representatives of "youth." No one felt disqualified—by virtue of wealth, education, or occupation—from speaking for "the common man."

2   Then came what Nora Sayre has described as the "huge, crude astonishment" at the discovery of the "working/forgotten/average man." Here was the missing part of the picture: a vast segment of the population that was not middle class, and relative to whom the professional middle class was indeed an elite: paid better, and privileged to sit while others stood or moved about, to speak while others listened.

3   The commentators, professors, and Ivy League radicals awoke with a rude jolt to the idea that they were no longer the authentic voice of the American people but something more like a special-interest group, a minority, or, as some were eventually to decide, a "new class" unto themselves. "Most of us in what is called the communications field are not rooted in the great mass of ordinary Americans," confessed columnist Joseph Kraft at the very dawn of the discovery, in the summer of 1968, but represent only "the outlook of upper-income whites."

4   Working-class whites, unlike the amorphous category of the poor in the early sixties, *had* done something to signal their existence. They showed scattered signs of discontent that became, in the media, a full-scale backlash: against the civil rights movement, the antiwar movement,

---

From Barbara Ehrenreich, *Fear of Falling: The Inner Life of the Middle Class* (1989).

and apparently against middle-class liberalism in general. More specifically, *some* members of the traditionally Democratic, white working class, in some parts of the country, were suddenly rallying to public figures who appealed to racist sentiments: Louise Day Hicks, the leading opponent of school integration in Boston; Charles Stenvig, policeman-turned-politician in Minneapolis; Anthony Imperiale, organizer of neighborhood vigilante squads in Newark; Mario Proccacino, the law-and-order challenger to New York's upper-class, liberal mayor, John Lindsay; and above all, George Wallace, the Alabama segregationist who, having been beaten in the 1958 gubernatorial primary by a Ku Klux Klan member, had vowed never to be "out-niggered" again.

5   According to British journalist Godfrey Hodgson, the moment of awakening to the existence of this irascible new social class occurred in the summer of '68, in the aftermath of the violence that surrounded, and virtually swallowed up, the Democratic convention. Tens of thousands of youthful radicals had converged in Chicago to protest the war and the front-running Democratic candidate, liberal but pro-war Hubert Humphrey. Mayor Richard Daley's police attacked, mercilessly and indiscriminately. Not only did the yippies, pacifists, radicals, and sundry countercultural types fall under the billy clubs; so did stray convention delegates, bystanders, and, most importantly, reporters and camera crews. Even the maverick publisher Hugh Hefner had his moment of confrontation. Stepping out in a rare excursion from the Playboy Mansion (then located in Chicago), he was struck by a policeman's club and instantly retreated back inside, an angrier and, one must imagine, wiser man. In a rare moment of collective courage, the editors of all the nation's major newspapers telegrammed a strong protest to Mayor Daley. Chet Huntley told the nation on the evening news that "the news profession in this city is now under assault by the Chicago police."

6   Then came a sobering message from the viewing public. Polls taken immediately after the convention showed that the majority of Americans—56 percent—sympathized with the police, not with the bloodied demonstrators or the press. Indeed, what one could see of the action on television did not resemble dignified protest but the anarchic breakdown of a great city (if only because, once the police began to rampage, dignity was out of the question). Overnight the press abandoned its protest. The collapse was abrupt and craven. As bumper stickers began to appear saying "We support Mayor Daley and his Chicago police," the national media awoke to the disturbing possibility that they had grown estranged from a sizable segment of the public. "I was stunned by the public reaction to Chicago," said NBC's documentary producer Shad Northshield. "We all were. I was stunned, astonished, *hurt*. It's the key thing that opened my eyes to the cleavage between newsmen and the majority."

7   Media leaders moved quickly to correct what they now came to see as their "bias." They now felt they had been too sympathetic to militant minorities (a judgment the minorities might well have contested). Hence-

forth they would focus on the enigmatic—and in Richard Nixon's famous phrase—silent, majority. The switch was announced in the trade journal *Editor and Publisher* and, on the same day, September 27, 1969, in *TV Guide*, in an article that quoted one penitent network official after another: "We didn't know it [the white, adult majority] was *there!*" one admitted. "The world doesn't end at the Hudson," another claimed to have discovered. To NBC's Fred Freed the fault lay in the peculiar parochialism of the men who dominated the media:

> The blue- and white-collar people who are in revolt now do have cause for complaint against us. We've ignored their point of view. . . . It's bad to pretend they don't exist. We did this because we tend to be upper-middle-class liberals.

8   Sooner or later the producers of ideas and images would inevitably have discovered the "forgotten" or "troubled" majority, if just for a change of pace. Former Housing and Urban Development undersecretary Robert Wood, who had been one of the first to point out the existence of the (largely white) working class as early as 1966, suggested that the discovery might just be a matter of "the liberal academic and interpreter getting tired of the minority kick and looking for a new folk hero, who happens to be white."

9   But it was not only the search for novelty that sent media people and intellectuals in search of "a new folk hero." Godfrey Hodgson suggests that the media's discovery of the "middle Americans" was prompted by something darker: the "fear [that] haunts all elites . . . the fear of being out of touch with the majority." Indeed, they had been out of touch. In a nation where one-quarter of the citizenry were poor by any reasonable definition, America's intellectuals and media people had not known poverty existed until Michael Harrington pointed it out to them. And in a nation where the great majority of people are not newsmen or media executives or professors, they had been too caught up in their own world—blinded, perhaps, by their success and affluence—to notice that the majority was, somehow, different from themselves.

10   There were reasons, then, for the wave of contrition that swept through the professional middle class at the end of the sixties. They had presumed to speak for everyone, and now "everyone" turned out to be social group almost as baffling and exotic as the poor had been at the time of their discovery. For the next few years media people, intellectuals, and others of their class would work overtime to make up for their embarrassing neglect of this new social "other." They would examine, fearfully and almost reverently, that curious segment of America: the majority. And within it, they would find that supposedly extinct—or at least thoroughly assimilated—category, the working class.

11   Like the poor before it, the working class *as discovered* was the imaginative product of middle-class anxiety and prejudice. This discovery occurred at what was for many middle-class intellectuals a time of waning

confidence and emerging conservatism. Professional authority was under attack; permissiveness seemed already to have ruined at least one generation of middle-class youth. And so, in turning to the working class, middle-class observers tended to seek legitimation for their own more conservative impulses. They did not discover the working class that was—in the late sixties and early seventies—caught up in the greatest wave of labor militancy since World War II. They discovered a working class more suited to their mood: dumb, reactionary, and bigoted.

"Middle Americans" in the Media

12 Beginning in the fall of 1969, the networks geared up to show "what's right with America," offering soothing new dramas such as *Country Preacher* and *Small Town Judge*. Then, in 1970, came the ambiguous caricature represented by Archie Bunker in *All in the Family*. Almost simultaneously, academia, foundations, and policy-makers discovered the "forgotten majority." The Nixon administration commissioned a task force on "The Problem of the Blue-Collar Worker." The Lindsay administration in New York (for which I worked as "program-planning analyst" for several months in 1968–69) almost overnight began to search for white neighborhoods to reward with new municipal services, even though none of them were anywhere near as needy as the city's black and Puerto Rican communities. The Ford Foundation, which had been generously funding black community activism, suddenly switched its attention to white ethnic groups and devoted a January 1970 staff conference to "the blue-collar problem." Writers and academics moved quickly to fill in the general ignorance with books and studies, some of them—such as *The White Majority*, *Middle Class Rage*, *The Radical Center*, and *The Troubled American*—quite thoughtful and sensitive. And in the fall and winter of 1969, every major newsmagazine ran a cover story on the "middle Americans," the "troubled Americans," or the "forgotten Americans."

13   The newsmagazines were strangely unembarrassed to announce their discovery. It was one thing to discover the poor, most of whom cannot afford to subscribe to newsmagazines anyway. But it was quite another thing, one might have thought, for a magazine to "discover" a majority that overlapped with its readership. "Now the pendulum of public attention is in the midst of one of those great swings that profoundly change the way the nation thinks about itself," *Newsweek* announced, not bothering to explain that it, and the media generally, were the ones pushing the pendulum. *Time* was more honest, explaining that the "Middle Americans" were "'discovered' first by politicians and the press," and attributing this belated discovery to a "pervasive discontent" and, mysteriously, to "the character and achievements of the astronauts." *U.S. News and World Report* merely observed that "the common man is beginning to look like a Very Important Person in-

deed," leaving the reader to wonder about the elite perspective from which the "common man" must have looked, until just now, so insignificant.

14 The Middle Americans that the media discovered were, of course, a far larger category than the blue-collar working class. In fact, in their haste to get away from the no-longer-newsworthy blacks, hippies, radicals, and poor people, most media analysts were content to define Middle Americans as almost anybody but the members of those disturbing groups. In a Gallup poll commissioned by *Newsweek*, for example, Middle Americans were defined more or less as white people. Although the poll claimed to be presenting a sketch of "the little guy," 28 percent of the people polled were in families dependent on wage-earners in business and professional occupations. For its definition of Middle America, *Time* felt it could exclude only "the nation's intellectuals, its liberals, its professors, its surgeons," and, naturally, its blacks. This left quite a large chunk of the population, which the magazine struggled to shape into a meaningful social category:

> The Middle Americans tend to be grouped in the nation's heartland more than on its coasts. But they live in Queens, N.Y., and Van Nuys, Calif., as well as in Skokie or Chillicothe. . . . They are defined as much by what they are not as by what they are. As a rule, they are not the poor or the rich. Still, many wealthy business executives are Middle Americans. . . . They are both Republicans and Democrats.

"Above all," *Time* concluded, apparently exhausted by this effort at definition, "Middle America is a state of mind."

15 Defining that state of mind, though, was almost as difficult as defining the social group that shared it. The "pervasive discontent" *Time* and *Newsweek* discovered ranged through almost every possible issue. Predictably, Middle Americans complained about drugs and crime and what they saw as the violent tactics of black and student activists. They complained about antiwar demonstrators and about the war itself; about high taxes and welfare expenditures and also about government inaction in the face of pressing social problems, such as poverty. "They spend $50 million to send a f——— monkey around the moon and there are people starving at home," a Milwaukee garage man "growl[ed]" to *Newsweek*. They complained about being poor themselves: "Why, I can't even afford a color-TV set!" a Los Angeles plumber "explod[ed]" in the same cover story. They complained about environmental pollution and the breakdown of community. In fact, if a Middle American complained about anything at all, the media were now eager to record it, as in this case from *Time's* cover story:

> Mrs. Dorothy King, 47, a mother of three and wife of an Atlanta manufacturer's representative, reads a book a week—a somewhat un-Middle American habit in a television age—but finds fewer and fewer books to her taste:

"I read one book about a brother and sister living together. 'This is sick,' I told myself."

16   If there was any kind of journalistic core to the otherwise empty notion of Middle America, it was the blue-collar working class. "The essence of the 'silent majority,'" *U.S. News and World Report* asserted, "turns up most strongly among the blue-collar workers of America." *Newsweek* told its readers:

> The disgruntlement of Middle America finds its cutting edge in the nation's traditional working class—families whose breadwinners have at most a high-school education, hold blue-collar jobs and bring home incomes of $5,000 to $10,000 a year.... It is in this group that troubled discontent shades closest to angry violence.

17   On most of the key "backlash" issues, as defined by the media, it was hard to distinguish the blue-collar people singled out by the newsmagazines from the rest of the Middle Americans. In the Gallup poll commissioned by *Newsweek*, blue-collar respondents stood out in two respects: They were more likely to be pessimistic about the future than white-collarites and less likely to be sympathetic to black economic demands.* However, some of the most viciously racist statements collected by the pollsters came not from blue-collar workers but from brokers, finance managers, businessmen, and even one unnamed MIT professor, who opined that successful Negroes are "almost all light-colored." And it was an "investment advisor" who, when asked how he would define "law and order," responded, "Get the niggers. Nothing else." But, as the news media presented it, a blue-collar vanguard was leading Middle America in its shift to the right.

18   There were, on the sidelines, a few dissenters. The *Nation* observed that the Middle American category was "ambiguous ... assembled for the most part by intellectuals whose knowledge of the people alleged to constitute the group is no more than marginal." These "intellectuals" (a per-

---

* Seventy-nine percent of blue-collar respondents felt blacks "could have done something" about living conditions in the slums (compared to 69 percent of the white-collar respondents), and 49 percent felt that blacks actually had a better chance of getting a job than they did. But as Richard Lemon explained in his book *The Troubled American*, based on the *Newsweek*/Gallup poll, even the racist blue-collar respondents were by no means consistently hostile to government action on behalf of black Americans:

> Of the blue-collar workers who said the Negro could have improved his own slums, the largest number, 48 percent, also would use a [federal budget] surplus to improve conditions, and 34 percent favored spending more on housing for the poor, while only 16 percent were opposed. Of those who said that the Negro already had a better chance at a good job than they themselves did, 54 percent also favored job training for the unemployed. Nor did their answers suggest that they wanted such programs for themselves. Sixty-one percent of them said that the country had changed for the better in providing opportunities for themselves.

haps overly flattering description of the media people in question) were guilty of reporting "loosely and inaccurately" on social groups they saw only remotely as "anthropological subjects." Other critics from the left, such as the authors of *The American Melodrama*, objected to the media's singling out of working-class Americans as the vanguard of reaction:

> By repeating the rather comforting doctrine that racial hostility was to be found among the working class and particularly among . . . "the ethnics," rather than among "people of substantial place and means," the media were spreading an unproven simplification and one that was in danger of being self-verifying.

19 But the mainstream media's very distance from blue-collar America made it an attractive place to locate the "essence" and "cutting edge" of Middle American reaction. From the vantage point, for example, of the contrite network executives quoted in *TV Guide*, blue-collar Americans were genuinely exotic folk. People like Mrs. King, the anomalous book-reader, and the male white-collar representatives of Middle America had the kind of faces you might see on any page of a national magazine in any week. Average people, selected for their averageness, do not add much to a magazine page, especially because they look so deceptively like actual newsmakers—statesmen, business leaders, authors. Blue-collar people add much more visual interest precisely because neither they nor anyone who looks like them are usually seen as newsmakers. *Newsweek*'s most arresting photographs were of hard-faced, beer-bellied men standing in bleachers and pudgy women in beehives and miniskirts. If indeed some affinity for the novel and striking had once led the media to overemphasize hippies, black militants, and white radicals, that same affinity now drove them to select blue-collar people—out of all the possible Middle Americans—as the vanguard of the backlash.

20 Besides, the blue-collar people expressed themselves in ways not usually found in the national media, providing titillating opportunities to print such well-known one-letter words as *f*——— and *s*———. The most ominous, and colorful, backlash sentiments *Newsweek* reported came from two middle-aged men, an auto mechanic and a house repairer:

> "Paint your face black and you can get a new Cadillac and the county will come in and feed your family . . . " says [Frank] Reis. . . . "There's only one way to solve this, and that's gonna be with a revolution. I'm for fighting it out between us," [David] Pedroza says angrily. . . . "What do you call dragging the American flag on the ground and burning draft cards and all that s———?" asks Reis. . . . "We should have a Hitler here to get rid of the troublemakers the way they did with the Jews in Germany."

21 In addition to their vivid language, there was another way that the blue-collar (or "lower-middle-class") people featured in the magazines differed from the mass of Middle Americans. If they were relatively unsympathetic to blacks, they were actively hostile to the professional middle

class. *Newsweek* saw this hostility as a spillover from working-class racism, warning, "The hunt for scapegoats goes beyond the blacks to their allies: the liberal white elite." And the press, which after Chicago believed it epitomized that elite, had to admit that the hostility went both ways. *U.S. News and World Report*, which could at least not be accused of liberalism, was perhaps the most direct:

> Affluent "liberals" are inclined to deplore such [conservative, "silent majority"] views. Intellectuals look down their noses. Young radicals say it figures: "*Squares! Racists! Pigs!*"

22 An ugly incident underscored the tensions between the working class and the professional middle class, and seemed to confirm the image of the blue-collar male as a violent reactionary. On May 8, 1970, hundreds of helmeted construction workers attacked a peaceful student antiwar demonstration in Manhattan's Wall Street district, leaving seventy students and bystanders injured. It was a terrifying event—not only to the student protesters but to the normal denizens of Wall Street. One of the injured was a young Wall Street lawyer, who, one may safely assume, was unprovocatively attired in short hair and a business suit.

23 But the attack, which quickly became emblematic of blue-collar sentiments, was neither spontaneous nor representative of blue-collar union men. At the time of the incident, some of the nation's largest unions, including the thoroughly blue-collar Teamsters, United Auto Workers, and Oil, Chemical, and Atomic Workers, had taken official stands against the war in Vietnam. Peter Brennan, president of New York City's Building Trades Council, had not; he was a hawk and a Nixon supporter. A few members of Brennan's union disclosed to the press that the workers' attack had been planned and announced through the union in advance. Bystanders reported that the attack had been directed by teams of gray-suited men. Nevertheless, the rampaging construction workers were widely taken to be representative of their class and race. In no time at all, the term *hardhat* replaced *redneck* as the epithet for a lower-class bigot.

The Blue-Collar Stereotype

24 In *An Introduction to Sociology*, a textbook published in 1976, well after the discovery of the working class, there is a photograph captioned "Stereotypical Image of the Blue-Collar Worker." In it, an overweight, middle-aged man wearing overalls, T-shirt, and a workman's cap stares dully into the middle distance, apparently at some point just above the Rheingold beer can set in front of him on the table. Next to him, a thin, bright-eyed woman, who has no Rheingold can to consider, stares inquisitively at him, this "worker" who is perhaps her husband. She may be wondering the same thing the reader is: Is this an accurate stereotype,

in which case the caption should have read "Typical Blue-Collar Worker"? Or are the distancing words *stereotypical* and *image* meant to warn us that he is a representative of a widely held prejudice, rather than of blue-collar men in general? Despite the heading on the same page, "Life Styles and Class Values," the text offers no enlightenment. The message to the student seems to be: "This is what we, the authors, think blue-collar men are like, though we do not have any way of supporting our view. But at least this picture may help you to identify them, should you encounter any."

25 One more point, before we set aside this intriguing illustration: It is clear from the focus of the woman's attention that it is the man who is both the "worker" and the "image." Her questioning gaze locates her on the side of the sociologists, examining, as it were, a sociological specimen. In other words, *she* is not the problem. And, in general, middle-class fascination with the working class in the years immediately following its discovery was fascination with the working-class male—in particular, the white working-class male. Poverty, as discovered, had a feminine cast: its victims were portrayed as passive, aimless, beaten down. In the mid-sixties, poor black women even became objects of special concern and study in their own right—thanks to their supposedly prodigious fecundity and matriarchal power over men.

26 But the working class, from the moment of its discovery, was conceived in masculine terms. In part, this was because work, and especially manual labor, was still considered a masculine activity. Also, sociologists and other commentators believed that working-class women were more middle-class in their values and attitudes, partly because they were more enmeshed than their husbands in the consumer culture. Certainly, as we observed in the first chapter, the daily lives of homemakers—shopping, cleaning, caring for children—still did not vary as radically from class to class as the daily lives of men. Furthermore, the major outside occupations of working-class women—clerical and sales work—demanded at least the appearance of middle-class gentility. The working-class woman might be unstylishly overweight, unfashionably dressed, and, by middle-class standards, tastelessly made-up, but she was not a social alien, not a *threat*.

27 The working class, as discovered, was also white. In reality, the American working class—defined broadly and crudely as people who work for hourly wages, rather than salaries—was becoming increasingly female, black, and Hispanic. Middle-class expectations also dictated that workers were white, just as poor people who were not Appalachians were commonly envisioned as black. All the working-class stereotypes we will consider are images of white males—a group that is sometimes imagined to be exempt from the burden of prejudice.

28 At the time of the discovery, there were few available images of the working-class male (or female) to draw on. As we have seen, sociologists tended either to toss the working class in with the poor as one vast lower

class, or, more optimistically, to absorb it into the catchall middle class. Popular culture was not much help. Fifties movies provided only two outstanding working-class characters, Marty, and Terry Malloy in *On the Waterfront*. Both were dumb, likable, and mistakenly loyal to their working-class comrades—a fault overcome by marriage in Marty's case, and by the betrayal of his comrades in Terry's case. And unless one counts cowboys and the occasional anachronistic juvenile delinquent, the working class had been banished from the screen in the sixties.

29   Recent social science offered one major reflection on the character of the working class, Seymour Martin Lipset's 1959 essay "Working-Class Authoritarianism." Fascism had put authoritarianism, understood as a personality trait, on the sociological agenda. Anticommunism kept it alive as an issue in the fifties, especially for scholars like Lipset who saw fascism and communism as two manifestations of the same slavish predilection on the part of the masses. In his analysis, the working class was responsible for totalitarianism of all varieties, at all times, because working-class people were inherently narrow-minded, intolerant, and most of all, "authoritarian." The paradoxical—and, one might say, self-serving—implication was that the only people with any talent for democracy were the members of privileged elites. In Lipset's words, "Acceptance of the norms of democracy requires a high level of sophistication," an indefinable quality possessed only by the professional middle class and well-read members of the aristocracy of wealth.

30   Lipset's description of the working-class personality, which, even at the time, at least some sociologists rejected as fanciful, has since been painstakingly refuted. Thanks to the work of historian Richard F. Hamilton, we know now, for example, that Nazism was not a movement of the "masses"—the lower middle class or working class—but received its strongest backing from wealthy urbanites and the rural gentry. Similarly, Hamilton has shown that other notorious outbreaks of "authoritarianism" and intolerance, such as lynchings in the American South or McCarthyism in the 1950s, tended to be initiated by the wealthy and only later embraced by the lower classes. In an exhaustive analysis of American survey and voting data from the late forties through the sixties, he found *no* significant or consistent evidence for any inherent working-class authoritarianism, intolerance, or hostility to democratic norms.

31   Lipset's study is still valuable, however, as a summary of middle-class prejudices. The "lower-class individual," Lipset wrote—using *lower-class* and *working-class* interchangeably, as was the custom in the fifties—is a bundle of "deep-rooted hostilities expressed by ethnic prejudice, political authoritarianism, and chiliastic transvaluational religion." The blame for these exotic-sounding personality defects lay less with the individual himself than with the company he kept—namely, other working-class individuals. His parents had exposed him to "punishment, lack of love, and a general atmosphere of tension and aggression." In school, his associations with "others of similar background" canceled the efforts of his teachers. At work, the bad influences continued: "He is surrounded on the

32   The working class, in short, is bad company. Lipset quoted the 1926 book *Social Differentiation* to establish that the working-class social environment operates to "limit the source of information, to retard the development of efficiency in judgment and reasoning abilities, and to confine the attention to more trivial interests in life." For Lipset, the limited intellect of the working-class individual—especially "trivial interests," "an impatience with talk," and "a desire for immediate action"—accounted for the class's historic predilection for left-wing (or otherwise "extremist") political movements. There was a catch, however, which Lipset readily acknowledged: Left-wing working-class movements, both in Europe and America, have historically fought not only for "trivial" bread-and-butter goals but for political freedoms, such as suffrage and freedom of speech and association, which were often bitterly resisted by the more "sophisticated" elites. For this apparent anomaly, Lipset offered two explanations. First, that the *leaders* of working-class movements were usually better educated and more middle class in their values than their followers. Second, that the witless rank and file did not understand what they were fighting for anyway: "The fact that the movement's ideology is democratic does not mean that its supporters actually understand the implications."

33   Alas, the members of this benighted class could do nothing right! If they supported "extremist" movements, it was because they were more or less impelled to by their "authoritarian personalities." If they supported liberal, civil-libertarian causes, it was because they didn't know what they were doing. And when they had the right attitude, according to the middle-class fashion of the day, it was for the wrong reason. Thus in the 1981 edition of *Political Man*, Lipset had to confront a recent study showing that the American working class had been more opposed to the Korean and Vietnamese wars than the middle class. The explanation? Working-class opposition reflected not pacifist feelings but archaic and conservative "isolationist sentiments." Presumably, the relatively pro-war stance of the middle class was an expression of a healthy, concerned interventionism, or something to that effect.

34   Lipset's explanation of why the working class was historically too left-wing lent itself readily to the sociological concern in the late sixties and early seventies that the working class had now become too right-wing. Introductory sociology text books published in the seventies solemnly repeated the prejudices Lipset had dignified as political science: Blue-collar people are "more ethnocentric, more authoritarian, and more isolationist than people at higher levels," instructed *Sociology*. In another introductory text we find that the "lower-blue-collar" person is "reluctant to meet new people and new situations, to form new social relationships, and above all, to initiate contact with strangers. On the contrary, he values and seeks out, more than anybody else, the routine, the familiar, the predictable."

35 By the seventies, the Middle American blue-collar backlash began to introduce an uneasy element of self-consciousness into the sociological generalizations. It was clear that, though the blue-collar person might be authoritarian, one kind of authority he did *not* respect was that of the middle-class expert, including perhaps even the sociologist. Thus we find, in a 1976 introductory text, the somewhat bad-tempered observation that the working-class person (here still labeled *lower-class*)

> appears reluctant to accept new ideas and practices and is suspicious of the innovators. . . . Their limited education, reading habits, and associations isolate the lower class from a knowledge of the reasons for these changes, and this ignorance together with their class position makes them suspicious of the middle- and upper-class "experts" and "do-gooders" who promote the changes.

The next step would have been to acknowledge that some sort of Heisenberg-like Uncertainty Principle applied to the sociology of social classes: that observations made by the middle-class experts were no doubt routinely distorted by the hostility of the lower classes for these experts—not to mention the hostility of the experts for the lower-class objects of their study.

36 One text, published in 1972, went so far as to suggest that the official stereotypes might have their own real existence in the eye of the sociological observer. First, the student is given the familiar summary of lower- or working-class traits: "He usually has little ability to take another person's point of view" (as opposed, of course, to the middle-class author). "His perspective is limited, and so is his ability to understand the world around him." He is "traditionalistic, 'old-fashioned' . . . patriarchal." In fact, "not many of these people are given to 'listening to reason.'" In the copy of this text that I read, these passages had been copiously underlined by some anxious undergraduate. Unmarked, and possibly unread, was the thoughtful footnote on the same page:

> AUTHOR'S NOTE: Some sociologists and psychologists have been guilty of distorting evidence in this general area to serve their own moral purposes. . . . In the literature, terms applied to this "class" are often pejorative: why is "authoritarian" consistently used instead of, for example, "respectful of authority"?

37 As Richard F. Hamilton observed in *Class and Politics in the United States,* also published in 1972, the myth of working-class intolerance and authoritarianism is one of the most cherished beliefs of American sociologists. Even when confronted with directly contradictory evidence, they will simply assert their class-based prejudices. For example, a 1966 study on occupational mobility and racial tolerance cited evidence that "the higher one's class of origin or class of destination the more likely that one prefers to exclude Negroes from one's neighborhood." But the authors refused "to contemplate seriously" that such an unflattering finding could

be true. Hamilton comments that "years of training" in effect brainwash sociologists into a kind of "perceptual distortion," whereby they see only such data as seem to support their preconceived notions: "It seems likely that such perceptual distortion goes on continuously, social scientists either 'not seeing' contrary evidence . . . or, if seeing it, not remembering it."

Points for Review and Discussion

1. Summarize each of the various definitions of "middle Americans"(¶ 12) that Ehrenreich evaluates in this essay.
2. Ehrenreich distinguishes sharply between "the working class *as discovered*" and the "working class that was"(¶ 11). What is the distinction and what are her reasons for finding it significant?
3. How does Seymour Lipset characterize "the working class personality" (¶ 30)? How has this characterization been refuted?

◆ Questions for Writing

1. Reread paragraph 13. How would you describe Ehrenreich's attitude toward the newsmagazines? Cite words and phrases that provide clues and explain your choices.
2. The author believes that the hostility of "experts" and "lower classes" to each other hastens the rush to stereotypes that distort the human realities. Explain how this might work, using as your example the relationship between high school guidance counselors ("experts") and teenagers ("lower classes") of the kind studied by Donna Gaines in Bergenfield, New Jersey (pages 54–64).
3. Assume that Ehrenreich is correct: working-class people *are* stereotyped by those socially above them, and the stereotypes are hostile. Write an essay on what you see as the worst damage done by this stereotyping. In your conclusion spell out the steps society should take to counteract the effects of stereotyping.

The Emergence of the Underclass as a Public Issue
Michael Katz

The most persistent social stereotypes are those that combine class feelings with attitudes toward race. Throughout his career, Michael Katz has centered his research on this subject. (Katz is professor of history at the University of Pennsylvania and the author of *The Undeserving Poor* [1989], a study of American attitudes toward the indigent from the late nineteenth century to the present.) In the selection below Katz takes up the historical development of the concept of "the underclass"—a concept that has gained great respectability since it was introduced in the late 1970s.

This essay is not easy reading and needs to be approached with an open mind. The point of view it espouses is unfamiliar; the point of view it opposes is one that has received so much public acclaim in recent years as to render it, at first glance, almost impregnable. But the doubts Katz raises about standard views of the "underclass" can't be ignored by anyone determined to think straight about American social issues. Keep in mind as you read that this essay is first of all an attack on a stereotype—a critique of a false image of millions of living Americans. To master its argument you need only to concentrate on the reasons it sets forth in support of the charge that the image in question is false.

1 In 1987, the *New York Times* pointed to the recent discovery of an underclass by American social science:

> Social scientists have focused new energies on an "underclass" of Americans who live in near total isolation from mainstream society, and scholars are trying to learn more about the deteriorating inner-city areas where not working is the norm, crime is a commonplace and welfare is a way of life [italics in original].

2 Two groups—black teenage mothers and black jobless youths—dominated the images of the underclass. The former received the most attention, and antipoverty policy, redefined as welfare reform, came to mean intervening in the alleged cycle of dependency in which young, unmarried black women and their children had become trapped. Black males became less a problem for social welfare and more of one for the police. Instead of training and employment, public policy responded by putting more of them in jail. Rates of incarceration in the United States soared above those in every other Western industrial democracy. Recidivism and prison over-

---

From Michael Katz, *The Undeserving Poor* (1989).

crowding became the equivalent of welfare dependency and escalating AFDC rolls, and the privatization of prisons worked no better as a policy response than Ronald Reagan's early expectation of turning much of public welfare over to private charity.

3   Not only did poverty discourse pay less attention to the joblessness of black males, it virtually ignored both the majority of the poor, who were not black and did not live in female-headed families, and the explosive growth of poverty among white adult males. Most writing about the underclass reinforced these tendencies. From the work of Ken Auletta and Nicholas Lemann, for instance, as well as from the mass media, the concept emerged as imprecise, with its sources specified either inadequately or inaccurately. The underclass seemed little more than the most modern euphemism for the undeserving poor. By contrast, in his 1987 book, William J. Wilson refocused the debate on what he viewed as the major cause of black family instability: black male joblessness.

4   For all its menace, the underclass was a comforting discovery. However defined, it remained a minority among the poor and a tiny share of the American population. It was small and concentrated enough to be the object of effective help, and if assistance failed, to contain. Its prominence not only refocused attention on culture and behavior; it deflected it away from the more intractable, growing, and potentially subversive problems of the working poor: increasing income inequality and the bifurcation of America's social structure.

5   Consider, as a prime example, the first major announcement of the underclass in the mass media, *Time* magazine's cover story, "The American Underclass," in its issue of August 19, 1977. "Behind [the ghetto's] crumbling walls lives a large group of people who are more intractable, more socially alien and more hostile than almost anyone had imagined. They are the unreachables: the American underclass." *Time* defined the underclass primarily by its values and behavior, which differed sharply from those of other Americans. "Their bleak environment nurtures values that are often at odds with those of the majority—even the majority of the poor. Thus the underclass produces a highly disproportionate number of the nation's juvenile delinquents, school dropouts, drug addicts and welfare mothers, and much of the adult crime, family disruption, urban decay and demand for social expenditures." As the description continued, the image became even more menacing. "Rampaging members of the underclass carried out much of the orgy of looting and burning that swept New York's ghettos during the July blackout.... They are responsible for most of the youth crime that has spread like an epidemic through the nation." Most persons in the underclass were "not looters or arsonists or violent criminals," admitted *Time*, but they remained "so totally disaffected from the system that many who would not themselves steal or burn only stand by while others do so, sometimes cheering them on."

6   Like other commentators, the authors of the *Time* article failed to define the underclass clearly and consistently. For they described it not only

by its behavioral pathology and deviant values, but by its relation to the process of social mobility as well. "Underclass" referred to people "stuck at the bottom, removed from the American dream," and therefore left unclear just who composed the underclass, whether its members represented a population disadvantaged by lack of mobility, in which case their numbers would include many poor people untainted by drugs, promiscuity, or criminality, or whether the term should be reserved as a label for behavior. *Time* stressed that the underclass differed from the rest of America. They were aliens, alarming strangers in our midst. Indeed, for *Time* the American underclass consisted of international outcasts: A confluence of factors—"the weakness of family structure, the presence of competing street values, and the lack of hope amidst affluence"—had created in America an "underclass unique among the world's poor people."

7   During the next decade, mass media interpretations of the underclass changed very little. In 1986, *U.S. News and World Report's* cover story, "A Nation Apart," reinforced the image of poor people of color in America's inner cities as strangers, aliens in their own country, defined primarily by their deviant values. A "second nation" had emerged within black America, "a nation outside the economic mainstream—a separate culture of have-nots drifting further apart from the basic values of the haves. Its growth is now the central issue in the country's urban centers." Little more than a year later, an article in *Fortune* reinforced the same interpretation. It defined "underclass communities" as "urban knots that threaten to become enclaves of permanent poverty and vice" and impose severe social and economic costs on the rest of American society, leaving business without a work force sufficiently skilled for jobs in the twenty-first century. Not so much their poverty or race as their "behavior—their chronic lawlessness, drug use, out-of-wedlock births, non-work, welfare dependency, and school failure," asserted the author, defined the underclass: "Underclass describes a state of mind and a way of life. It is at least as much a cultural as an economic condition."

8   Social scientists did relatively little to modify the popular image of a menacing underclass defined by behavior rather than poverty. Indeed, when American social science discovered the underclass, it paid more attention to its behavior than to its origins in the transformations that intensified poverty within postindustrial cities. As early as 1969, Lee Rainwater criticized this constricted vision. Social scientists, he wrote, had neglected to analyze "the central fact about the American underclass—that it is created by, and its existence is maintained by, the operation of what is in other ways the most successful economic system known to man."

9   Douglas Glasgow's *Black Underclass* (1980) tried to direct debate along the path urged by Rainwater and later taken by Wilson. Glasgow used the concept to frame his research on the young men who had participated in the great Watts riot of 1965. The emergence of an underclass as a "permanent fixture of our nation's social structure," he wrote, repre-

sented "one of the most significant class developments in the past two decades." By underclass, he meant "a permanently entrapped population of poor persons, unused and unwanted, accumulated in various parts of the country." Blacks, disproportionately represented among the poor, remained particularly vulnerable to the magnetic force of the underclass. "Structural factors found in market dynamics and institutional practices, as well as the legacy of racism, produce and then reinforce the cycle of poverty and, in turn, work as a pressure exerting a downward pull toward underclass status." Serious misconceptions, argued Glasgow, detracted attention from the obstacles confronting blacks. For example, references to statistics that pointed to improvements in blacks' economic status between 1959 and 1974 failed to note that white unemployment fell about twice as far as black, widening the unemployment gap between races, and that the proportion of blacks among the poor actually had increased. In both 1959 and 1974, blacks' poverty rate exceeded that of whites by about three times. The argument that significant numbers of blacks had moved into the middle class also misdirected interpretations of black experience. First, figures that showed increasing incomes for black families reflected the joint wages of employed husbands and wives. In fact, as individuals black men and women continued to earn less than their white counterparts, and the increasing number of single-headed black families offset the gains by those with two wage earners.

10   Most serious were the unemployment problems of black youth. Their lack of work opportunity in the primary labor market locked many young blacks permanently into the underclass. Nor did all blacks who worked escape, because their low wages and occupational immobility trapped them in poverty despite their commitment to the work ethic. (Glasgow stressed that research has demonstrated the eagerness for work among black youths. He dismissed as a cruel myth the idea that they were unwilling to enter the labor market.) Blacks' detachment from the "standardized institutions" feeding the primary labor market reinforced their entrapment in the underclass. Indeed, this inability to escape poverty was, for Glasgow, the component that differentiated the underclass from a lower class, whose members realistically could expect mobility if not for themselves, then for their children.

11   Therefore, "underclass" did not "connote moral or ethical unworthiness" or "any other pejorative meaning." Rather, it described a new population, "not necessarily culturally deprived, lacking in aspirations, or unmotivated to achieve," but the static poor, trapped in their situation by a variety of forces, primarily constricted opportunities and "limited alternatives provided by socialization patterns." Rejection by mainstream institutions, especially schools, fed the rage and desperation of ghetto youth. Rejection often maimed and broke them by denying their individuality and integrity. As a result, behavior considered destructive by many remained their "one great protection" against a system that assured them failure. Economic trends also trapped black youths in the underclass by

eliminating entry-level jobs and reducing the need for unskilled labor. Of all the forces sustaining the underclass, however, racism remained the strongest. Despite the virtual disappearance of legal discrimination, computers now excluded people ostensibly "on the basis not of 'race' but of 'social profile.'" What, then, was the answer? What would help break up the underclass and move blacks out of poverty? The key was jobs, whose provision should be the prime goal of policies to alleviate the underclass crisis in America's cities.

12 Glasgow's interpretation of the underclass excluded two themes that would dominate most subsequent discussion. First, he wrote only about men. Second, he scarcely mentioned black family structure.... Within a few years, however, writers on poverty associated with the conservative political revival had reestablished culture and family structure on the agenda of social science and public policy. This new legitimacy for old concerns—feminist attention to women's poverty—and demographic trends in the 1970s served to focus even moderate and liberal poverty discourse on family and culture. In the process, "underclass" assumed a connotation quite different than Glasgow had intended. One major example is Ken Auletta's book *The Underclass* (1982), which popularized the concept and pointed to its emerging meaning....

13 Auletta defined the underclass as a relatively permanent minority of the poor with "four distinct categories": "(a) the *passive poor*, usually long-term welfare recipients; (b) the *hostile* street criminals who terrorize most cities, and who are often school dropouts and drug addicts; (c) the *hustlers*, who, like street criminals, may not be poor and who earn their livelihood in an underground economy, but rarely commit violent crimes; (d) the *traumatized* drunks, drifters, homeless shopping-bag ladies and released mental patients who frequently roam or collapse on city streets." For Auletta as well as Glasgow, lack of mobility defined the underclass. However, Auletta remained more concerned with the behavior of the underclass than its origins and focused on strategies that taught its members how to enter the mainstream working world.

14 Although he intended his book to be nonideological, Auletta's account fit within the historic tradition of American poverty discourse. (This, certainly, is one explanation for the book's popularity and influence. Another is its resonance with a new consensus about the source of social problems.) Like those who wrote on poverty two centuries before him, Auletta began by separating poor people into two categories and identifying one of them primarily by its deviant behavior. Economic and occupational criteria did not determine class membership. In his definition, the source of stratification lay elsewhere. The underclass was a moral, not a sociological, category. Its members were the new undeserving poor. In the tradition of nineteenth-century social critics who fused crime, poverty, and ignorance into interchangeable eruptions of moral pathology,

Auletta linked disparate groups into one class. His definition subsumed women on welfare, street criminals, hustlers, and homeless drunks, drifters, and bag ladies into one interchangeable unit identified not by income or dependence, but by behavior.

15 Auletta's discussion of poverty subordinated employment. It redirected discussion to family and behavior.... When Auletta presented thirteen "facts about poverty and the underclass" which were "undebatable and unavoidable," women and family headed the list. His first fact was, "Poverty has become feminized," and his second, "Whether family dissolution is a cause or an effect of poverty, it unquestionably cannot be overlooked." None of his facts specified joblessness as a source of poverty....

16 Most subsequent commentaries on the underclass also used imprecise definitions that stressed family and behavior and rested on implicitly moral conceptions of class structure. Consider the two long and widely read articles in *The Atlantic* (1986) by Nicholas Lemann.

17 In "The Origins of the Underclass," Lemann describes life in the ghettoes as "utterly different" from the American mainstream. Using (without acknowledgement) a thesis first argued by William J. Wilson, Lemann laments "the bifurcation of black America, in which blacks are splitting into a middle class and an underclass that seems likely never to make it. The clearest line between the two groups is family structure." The result is the total isolation of the underclass. "As apart as all of black life is, ghetto life is a thousand times more so, with a different language, economy, educational system, and social ethic." The statistic that most accurately captures the distinction is the rise in out-of-wedlock births, which are "by far the greatest contributor to the perpetuation of the misery of ghetto life." Lemann revives the culture of poverty thesis to explain underclass behavior because he sees its "distinctive culture," rather than unemployment or welfare, as "the greatest barrier to progress by the black underclass." His argument, he stresses, "is anthropological, not economic; it emphasizes the power over people's behavior that culture, as opposed to economic incentives, can have."

18 Lemann's idea of *underclass* remains even less precisely defined than Auletta's, but he shares Auletta's moral conception of class structure. Membership in Chicago's underclass, for instance, which contains between 200,000 and 420,000 of the city's 1.2 million blacks, is not simply a function of poverty or blocked mobility. Rather, it results from behavior that should not be sanctioned by the well-meaning relativism of white liberals or the misplaced racial pride of black militants. Underclass behavior has crystallized into a pathological and self-perpetuating culture, on which public policy should launch a major assault.

19 Lemann explains the origins of the underclass as the product of southern blacks' migration into northern cities and of northern middle-class movement to the suburbs. "Every aspect of the underclass culture in the

ghettos," asserts Lemann, "is directly traceable to roots in the South—and not the South of slavery but the South of a generation ago. In fact, there seems to be a strong correlation between underclass status in the North and a family background in the nascent underclass of the sharecropper South." Unfortunately for Lemann's thesis, all the available data contradict it. Southern black migrants to northern cities have enjoyed higher employment rates, better wages, and less dependency on welfare than northern-born blacks. In the 1960s, northern-born blacks, in fact, accounted for the increased welfare rates. Women, according to Gerald Jaynes, headed fewer than 10 percent of households in the rural south because sharecropping *presupposed* a family labor system. Southern-born blacks did not import an underclass culture to northern cities. The harsh experiences they encountered there—of which the most serious was the lack of employment—broke down their culture. Indeed, Jaynes argues, developments within black communities in the 1960s represented a sustained acceleration of trends rather than a new departure. (In contrast to the South, the ability of black women in northern cities to support themselves has fueled the increase in female household heads among them, just as improving employment opportunities have had a similar effect among white women.)

20 Along with Auletta, Lemann reinforced the identification of a menacing underclass with unmarried black women. The coincidence of their views with popular stereotypes distracted casual readers from their imprecision, contradictions, and weak evidence, and "underclass" swiftly became the most fashionable term in poverty discourse. Marian Wright Edelman highlights the dangers of an imprecise definition of underclass:

> References to the underclass will add nothing to our understanding of poverty, but will erode public confidence in our ability to do something about it. If applied too loosely to all who have remained persistently poor, the term underclass may reinforce the misguided belief that poverty is the product solely or primarily of individual pathology, ignoring the institutional forces in our society which help perpetuate deprivation. By implying that there are major differences in the character of the poor vis-à-vis the nonpoor, the term undermines our confidence and desire to try to help.

21 The underclass emerged no more clearly from social science than from journalism. As they summarized their review of the social science literature on the urban underclass, Martha Gephart and Robert Pearson, Social Science Research Council staff associates to the council's urban underclass committee, concluded that definitional and conceptual problems would "undoubtedly continue to confront scholars because there are unlikely to be easily agreed-upon definitions of the underclass available to those who seek to understand it."

22 Drastically different estimates of the size of the underclass reflected its imprecise definition. Erol R. Ricketts and Isabel V. Sawhill, using 1980 census data, estimated the underclass as about 500,000. Peter Gottschalk and Sheldon Danziger, two economists who specialize in poverty re-

search, using different types of measures, reached an estimate of less than 1 million in 1984. By contrast, the estimate offered by two other researchers Patricia Ruggles and William P. Marton, was 8 million for 1985. Two estimates by other experts for 1979 varied between 1.8 million and 4.1 million people.

23 In 1987, the publication of William Julius Wilson's *The Truly Disadvantaged* focused even more national attention on persistent and concentrated urban poverty. It also brought more sophistication to the debate. Although he accepted its usefulness as a term, Chicago sociologist Wilson rejected explanations that traced the origins of an underclass to female-headed families and a culture of poverty. He tried to redirect debate to where he believed its origins lay: black male joblessness.

24 In *The Declining Significance of Race* (1978), William Julius Wilson stressed the emergence of class stratification among blacks. No longer constrained by discrimination, a black middle class had moved into both better jobs and neighborhoods, its upward mobility no longer hampered by race. The situation of blacks left behind in inner cities, however, had worsened. Wilson's thesis provoked a major controversy that centered on his description of improvements in the circumstances of the black middle class and neglected his argument about the "deteriorating conditions of the black underclass."

25 Incorrectly labeled a conservative, Wilson, who thought of himself as a social democrat, decided to focus on the ghetto underclass and spell out the policy implications of this thesis. The result was *The Truly Disadvantaged*. Wilson argues that neutral terms, such as lower class or working class, fail to address the recent transformations within American cities that resulted in dramatic increases in the concentration of poverty. The exodus of the black middle and working class left neighborhoods to the most disadvantaged, a "heterogeneous grouping of families and individuals who are outside the mainstream of the American occupational system." These include "individuals who lack training and skills and either experience long-term unemployment or are not members of the labor force, individuals who are engaged in street crime and other forms of aberrant behavior, and families that experience long-term spells of poverty and/or welfare dependency." This, for Wilson, is the underclass. As he uses it, underclass refers to "the groups that have been left behind" and are as a consequence "collectively different from those that lived in these neighborhoods in earlier years."

26 Wilson's definition of the underclass incorporates geography, occupation, behavior, and history. It is geographical because it assigns a key role to social concentration with a distinct territory. It identifies members of the underclass by their existence outside the mainstream of the "American occupational system." It stresses the development of behaviors at variance with "mainstream patterns and norms," and it rests on a version of recent history that views the underclass as unprecedented.

27 To Wilson, the sources of the underclass are both demographic and economic. He argues that vast migrations of blacks to cities aroused latent

racial consciousness and spurred the creation of barriers in housing and employment. This growing black central city population was "relatively young," and "youth is not only a factor in crime; it is also associated with out-of-wedlock births, female-headed homes, and welfare dependency." Thus, the increase in the number of young people by itself explains much of what is "awry in the inner city." However, changes in urban economic structure that reduced demand for unskilled labor contributed more than demography to the creation of the underclass. Earlier immigrants entered cities when manufacturing was expanding and the demand for unskilled and semiskilled labor growing. Blacks now confront the shift away from a manufacturing to a service economy. As blue-collar jobs dwindle, the service jobs that replace them demand high educational qualifications or, at the other extreme, pay little and offer minimal career opportunity. On almost every measure of the labor market, Wilson points out, the economic position of blacks has deteriorated. So serious has joblessness among black youths become that "Only a minority of noninstitutionalized black youth are employed."

28   Population concentration further exacerbated the impact of age structure and joblessness. From 1970 to 1980, the population rose by 12 percent in the nation's fifty largest cities and the number of persons living in poverty areas increased by more than 20 percent. The total black population in "extreme-poverty" areas soared by 148 percent during these years, compared to a 24 percent rise among whites. This "growth of the high- and extreme-poverty areas," observes Wilson, "epitomizes the social transformation of the inner city."

29   The migration of middle- and working-class families out of many ghetto neighborhoods removed a key "social buffer" that might have deflected the full impact of prolonged and increasing joblessness on behavior. When inner city neighborhoods were more socially diverse, their basic institutions (churches, schools, stores, recreational facilities) remained viable, and by their presence, mainstream role models nurtured "the perception that education is meaningful, that steady employment is a viable alternative to welfare, that family stability is the norm, not the exception." Without them, social isolation—that is, "the lack of contact or sustained interaction with individuals and institutions that represent mainstream society"—has increased, with serious consequences. Because it leaves people outside job networks and fails to develop behavior essential for successful work experience, it exacerbates the difficulty of finding jobs. Because of its relation to attitudes and behavior, social isolation leads Wilson to an emphasis on culture. But unlike earlier writers on the culture of poverty, he defines culture as "a response to social structural constraints and opportunities."

30   As Wilson realizes, *The Truly Disadvantaged* should be read as a hypothesis about inner-city poverty based on the incomplete evidence available for its analysis. Indeed, he has mounted an unprecedented research project in Chicago, which will gather data with which to test many of his ideas. Social scientists have already begun to probe Wilson's hypotheses.

Does neighborhood, they are asking, exert an independent influence on behavior? Has racial segregation ceased to be as important an influence on black residential patterns as Wilson implies? Would higher employment rates for black males reduce adolescent pregnancy by encouraging or permitting family formation? Whatever the answers to these questions turn out to be, no one has contradicted Wilson's emphasis on the importance of black male joblessness and its relative neglect by social science and public policy.

31   Wilson points out that American poverty discourse, both liberal and conservative, has neglected jobs, which are the key to unlocking opportunities and freeing the underclass from their ghetto neighborhoods. Debate has focused on ameliorating the condition of disadvantaged people with income supports and social services and on eradicating the cultural traits that retard their economic progress. As a result, female-headed families remain more central to the poverty debate than good jobs. Indeed, very little current poverty discourse focuses on the working poor or on the rate of poverty among white adult males, which has increased dramatically in contrast to the rate among female household heads, which has remained almost static.

32   How should we explain the neglect of so transparently critical a factor? Although contemporary conservatives have misread and made selective use of economic data, liberals have been equally negligent. Part of the reason is historic: the three major preoccupations of American poverty discourse (classifying poor people, debating the effects of welfare on their behavior, and worrying about the limits of social obligations) and lack of attention to the forces that generate poverty. In this sense, contemporary debate follows well-worn grooves, which had a certain logic before the era when technology and government gained the capacity to transform scarcity into abundance. By slighting the unavailability of work, poverty discourse reinforces the hostility to working-age men almost always reflected in relief policy. The assumption that any able-bodied man could find work underlay the reluctance of welfare administrators and reformers to grant men outdoor relief, the consignment of men to poorhouses, and the vicious war against tramps late in the nineteenth century. Except for the Great Depression of the 1930s, even abundant evidence that jobs were scarce failed to shake the belief that men were unemployed because they were lazy. Poverty discourse that focuses on behavior echoes and reinforces these old stereotypes and nourishes popular preconceptions about poor people that influence the policy directions chosen by politicians. But it is not only because they fit popular images that policies reflecting behavioral and cultural explanations of poverty are politically easiest to enact. They also conflict with the fewest vested interests because they do not require income redistribution or the sharing of power and other resources. At the same time, they suit intellectuals. For poor people who lack the capacity to mobilize in their own self-interest need advocates, organizers, and therapists. All these factors connect to focus attention on the behavior of the poor rather than on their lack of jobs.

Points for Review and Discussion

1. Summarize the chief media interpretations of the underclass that Katz surveys in this essay.
2. Describe in detail the substance of current stereotypes of the average member of the urban underclass.
3. What reasons does Katz give for the neglect, by both conservatives and liberals who address underclass problems, of the critical factor of jobs?

•◆ Questions for Writing

1. The underclass is, says Katz, "a comforting discovery"(¶ 4). Explain in your own words what is comforting about the concept of an underclass. Whom does its existence comfort, and why?
2. In the opening pages Katz and the scholars he quotes speak frequently of "misconceptions" and "misdirected interpretations" of black experience (¶ 9). Choose one of these misconceptions and spell out what you yourself believe it omits or obscures.
3. "Except for the Great Depression of the 1930s," Katz writes, "even abundant evidence that jobs were scarce failed to shake the belief that men were unemployed because they were lazy" (¶ 32). Why is this belief so hard to shake? Why do you think people persist so stubbornly in the view that joblessness is the fault of the jobless? Is there anything to be said for this stubbornness? Write a short essay in which you shape your answers to these three questions into a connected argument.

A Bird's Eye View of American Plutographics
Kevin Phillips

No book published in the last decade has had more impact on American political debate and economic policy than Kevin Phillips's *The Politics of Rich and Poor* (1990). The author first came to power as chief political analyst for the Nixon presidential campaign in 1968, and from that time on has played major roles in national politics as a columnist, TV commentator, and advisor and strategist for conservative political candidates.

The message sent by *The Politics of Rich and Poor* was that the period of the 1980s was not one of advance for this country's "middle class," and that the vaunted go-go years actually saw a worsening of the financial situation and prospects of most Americans.

But the book developed other themes as well. Directly and indirectly it raised questions about the extent to which the popular vision of the rich as self-made go-getters matched the facts. The chapters were studded with charts and statistics that made for difficult reading; that difficulty is evident in the selection below. But one can extract the gist of Phillips's meaning without bogging down in numbers and trying to master each statistical distinction. It's necessary only to bear in mind that, once again, this essay's main importance is as a critique of a stereotype. Implicit throughout is an argument against the popular view that the key reason for the huge recent successes of the rich and the decline of the less well-off lies in the superior daring, braininess, and industriousness of the one and the ignorance and laziness of the other.

1. It is not enough to describe the United States as the world's richest nation between 1945 and 1989. The distribution of its wealth conveys a more provocative message. By several measurements, the United States in the late twentieth century led all other major industrial countries in the gap dividing the upper fifth of the population from the lower—in the disparity between top and bottom. Chart I displays one 1984 attempt at global comparison. Five years later economic polarization had intensified, conceivably even moving the United States ahead of France, the generally acknowledged citadel of concentrated wealth among Western nations. Calculations like these lack precision, of course, but the *generalization*, at least, seems fair: among major Western nations, the United States has displayed one of the sharpest cleavages between rich and poor. Opportunity has counted for more than equality, and in the 1980s, opportunity took on a new boldness and dimension.

From Kevin Phillips, *The Politics of Rich and Poor* (1990).

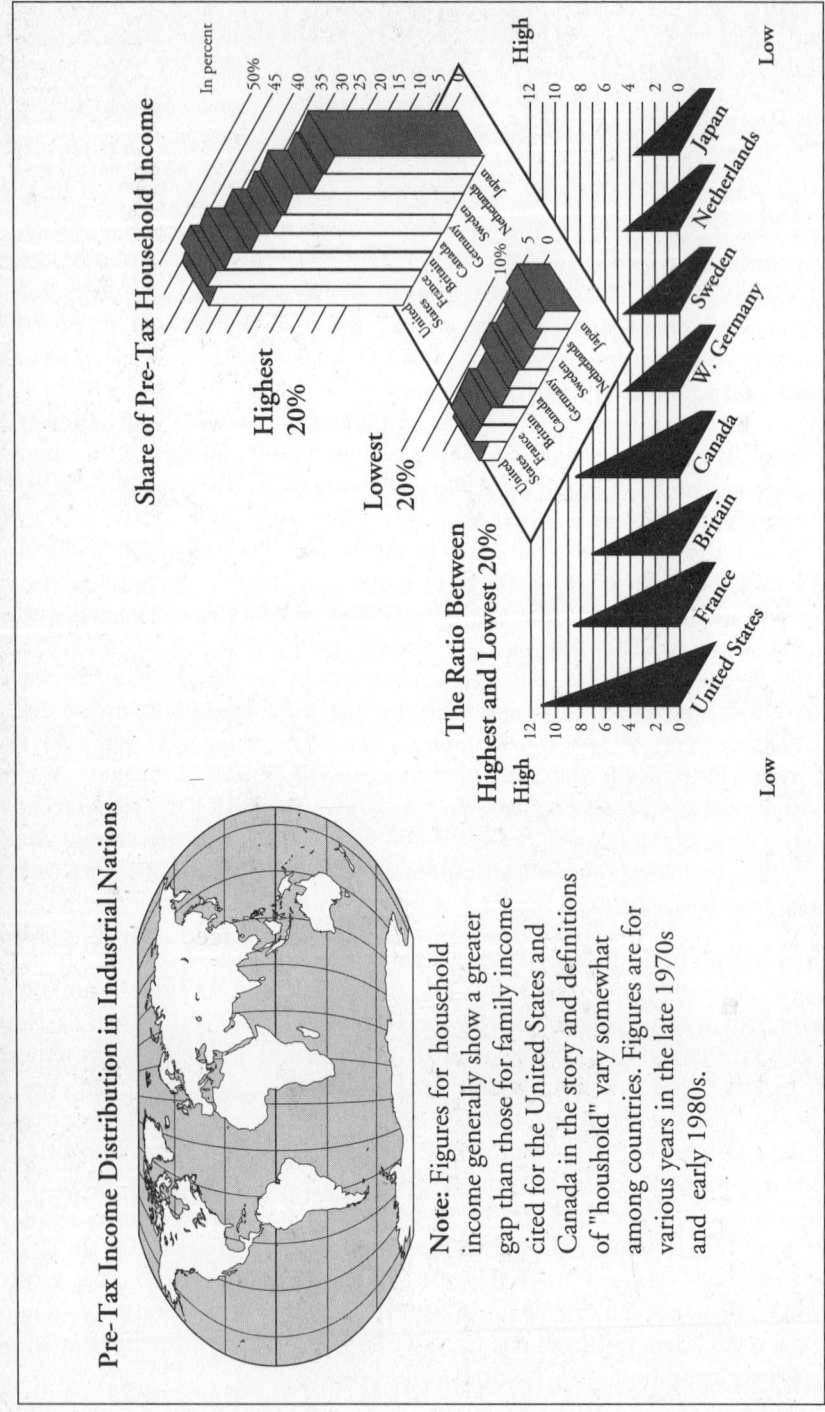

Comparative Concentration of Income in the Major Western Nations (Circa 1980)

Share of Pre-Tax Household Income

Highest 20% (In percent, 0–50%)
- United States
- France
- Britain
- Canada
- Germany
- Sweden
- Netherlands
- Japan

Lowest 20% (0–10%)
- United States
- France
- Britain
- Canada
- Germany
- Sweden
- Netherlands
- Japan

The Ratio Between Highest and Lowest 20% (High to Low, 0–12)
- United States
- France
- Britain
- Canada
- W. Germany
- Sweden
- Netherlands
- Japan

Pre-Tax Income Distribution in Industrial Nations

Note: Figures for household income generally show a greater gap than those for family income cited for the United States and Canada in the story and definitions of "household" vary somewhat among countries. Figures are for various years in the late 1970s and early 1980s.

Sources are individual governments and the World Bank.
Source: *Los Angeles Times*, October 21, 1984.
Note: The ratios for Japan changed significantly in the late 1980s.

94

2   By the middle of Reagan's second term, official data had begun to show that America's broadly defined "rich"—the top half of 1 percent of the U.S. population—had never been richer. Federal policy favored the accumulation of wealth and rewarded financial assets, and the concentration of income that began in the mid-1970s was accelerating. In 1988, approximately 1.3 million individual Americans were millionaires by assets, up from 574,000 in 1980, 180,000 in 1972, 90,000 in 1964, and just 27,000 in 1953. Even adjusted for inflation, the number of millionaires had doubled between the late seventies and the late eighties. Meanwhile, the number of billionaires, according to *Forbes* magazine, went from a handful in 1981 to 26 in 1986 and 49 in 1987. As of late 1988, *Forbes* put that year's number of billionaires at 52, and *Fortune*'s September assessment hung the billion-dollar label on 51 American families. Who these new millionaires and billionaires were and where their money came from we will shortly examine in more detail. *No parallel upsurge of riches had been seen since the late nineteenth century, the era of the Vanderbilts, Morgans and Rockefellers.*

3   And it was equally conspicuous. Rising luxury consumption and social ambition prompted *New York* magazine to observe that for the third time in one hundred twenty-five years "a confluence of economic conditions has created arrivistes in such great numbers and with such immense wealth that they formed a critical mass and created a whole new social order with its own new rules of acceptable behavior." The 1980s were of a magnitude comparable with that of the post–Civil War period and the 1920s, and "each of these watershed eras for New York came at a time when the need to raise capital thrust finance to the front of the national agenda and Wall Street to the center of public attention. And each era created a new class of wealthy who had so much money, so much power and so much momentum that they more or less displaced the older Establishment...."

4   Incomes and wealth were concentrating for several reasons. Global and national economic restructuring—the late twentieth century's worldwide revolution in trade, technology and finance—provided the underlying context. Commercial chaos is brutally Darwinian; it favors skills, enterprise and imagination. A second circumstance was that wages—the principal source of middle- and lower-class dollars—had stagnated through 1986 even while disinflation, deregulation and commercial opportunity were escalating the return on capital. Most of the Reagan decade, to put it mildly, was a heyday for unearned income as rents, dividends, capital gains and interest gained relative to wages and salaries as a source of wealth and increasing economic inequality. By 1983, as the bull market that had begun in August 1982 kept soaring, *Fortune* magazine profiled its biggest winners: Each of fifty-three stockholders had already made profits of over $100 million! One, David Packard, cofounder of

Hewlett-Packard Inc., found himself richer on paper by $1.2 billion. Nine others gained over $300 million. More and bigger gains would follow in the mid-1980s, augmented by reduced tax rates on these swollen unearned incomes. In the wake of the 1978 capital gains tax reductions and the sweeping 1981 rate cuts, the effective overall, combined federal tax rate paid by the top 1 percent of Americans dropped from 30.9 percent in 1977 to 23.1 percent in 1984. No other group gained nearly so much.

5   Wealth data, of course, always display more concentration than income statistics. Upper-income taxpayers do a lopsided share of the accumulating. In 1986 the Joint Economic Committee released Federal Reserve Board findings, overstated at first and later modified, that the share of wealth held by the naïvely labeled "super-rich"—the top one half of 1 percent of U.S. households—had risen significantly in the 1980s after falling during the prior four decades.... By the JEC's revised measurement, America's top 420,000 households alone accounted for 26.9 percent of U.S. family net worth—in essence, 26.9 percent of the nation's wealth. The top 10 percent of households, meanwhile, controlled approximately 68 percent. Accumulation and concentration would be simultaneous hallmarks of the 1980s.

6   On the income side of the ledger, the results, while less skewed, were striking enough. Here, too, the decade's biggest advances were scored by those already doing well—the business owners, investors, financiers and service-industry professionals. "The economy," said Stanford University professor Robert Hall, "has shifted in the direction of a meritocracy," and there was no mistaking how the smart, the well-educated and the highly motivated commanded a large share of the gain. The chart on p. 97 and the accompanying table show the percentage of family money income received by each quintile of the population from 1969 to 1988. One computation grabbed most of the publicity: between 1980 and 1988, the income share taken by the upper 20 percent of Americans rose from 41.6 percent to 44.0 percent, the highest ratio since the Census Bureau began its official measurements in 1949. Parenthetically, the share of the top 1 percent climbed from 9 percent to over 11 percent during the same period, suggesting that this particularly affluent subgroup—and not those with a more middle-class position in the eightieth to ninety-ninth percentiles—took the overwhelming share of the top quintile's advance. Concentration like this is rare.

7   If anything, some experts argued, the Census Bureau understated the realignment of the 1980s. They contended that the Federal Reserve Board's distribution of income series offered a better profile because it included capital gains not included in standard Census Bureau income definitions. By this calculus, the income share of the top 10 percent climbed from 29 percent to 33 percent from 1969 to 1982. Liberal economist Lester Thurow observed, "That's a real earthquake if the top 10 percent of the population can add four percentage points to their total share of income. The four percentage points are a big fraction of somebody's income lower down the spectrum." By the late 1980s data series including capital in-

Rising U.S. Income Inequality
Mean Incomes of Population Quintiles, 1954–86
Thousands of 1986 Dollars

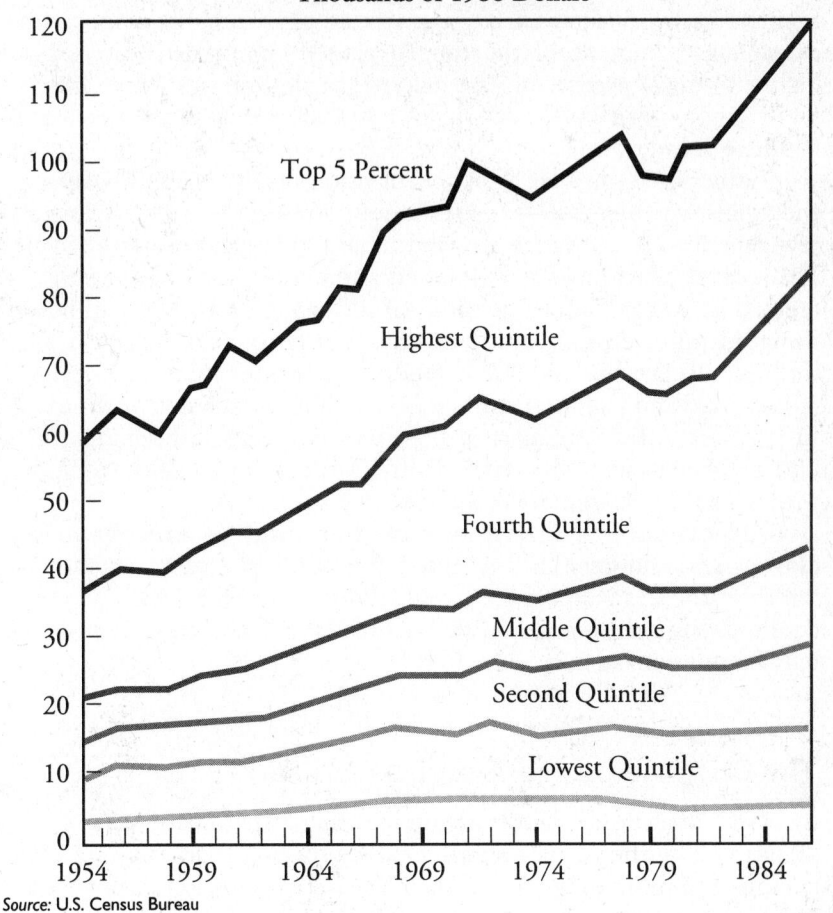

Source: U.S. Census Bureau

come were even more revealing: Experimental census income tabulations for 1986, published just before Christmas 1988, saw the top quintile's share of aggregate household income thereby expand to over 50 percent of the total. Capital gains were so concentrated at the top that their inclusion boosted the top quintile's share from 46.1 percent under the standard computation to a huge 52.5 percent. Federal and state taxes brought it down to 50 percent. Another computation that included capital gains in income, this time a 1989 analysis by Brookings Institution economist Joseph Pechman, found that the top 1 percent of taxpayers in 1981 had 8.1 percent of total reported income. By 1986, with the help of soaring stock markets, that share had risen to an unprecedented 14.7 percent.

Different data series and (necessary) adjustments for inflation can make trend analysis seem like Greek. But Ohioans Ross LaRoe and John Charles Pool put one set of comparative 1977–87 income trends in simple language for Middle America. Using data from the nonpartisan Congressional Budget Office, they wrote that "since 1977, the average after-tax family income of the lowest 10 percent, in current dollars, fell from $3,528 to $3,157. That's a 10.5 percent drop. During the same period, average family income of the top 10 percent increased from $70,459 to $89,783—up 24.4 percent. The incomes of the top 1 percent, which were 'only' $174,498 in 1977, are up to $303,900—a whopping 74.2 increase over the decade."

9   Suffice it to say that the concentration of income and wealth during the 1980s was unusual—the kind of buildup that occurs only once every few generations. Although distributional ratios had not quite returned to 1920s levels, favorable economic circumstances and federal policies had created an extraordinary pyramid of affluence—a record number of billionaires, three thousand to four thousand families each worth over $50 million, almost one hundred thousand with assets over $10 million, and at least one and a quarter million households with a net worth exceeding $1 million. Affluent Americans weren't thronging the Hamptons, Gold Coast Florida and California's Palm Desert area by accident. Unprecedented disposable income brought them there.

10 The caveat was that if two to three million Americans were in clover—and another thirty to thirty-five million were justifiably pleased with their circumstances in the late 1980s—a larger number were facing deteriorating personal or family incomes or a vague but troubling sense of harder times ahead.

The Downside of the American Dream

11 By 1988 anecdotal proof abounded that the imperiled "American dream" had become an emerging battleground of national politics. The average manufacturing wage seemed to buy less. Low-income households were in trouble, especially female-headed ones. Here and there, off the main roads, large patches of small-town America were dying. Big-city poverty was on the rise. Young married couples, needing two incomes to meet bills, postponed having children and gave up buying their own homes. And in blue-collar factory towns, where a job on the production line at Ford or Bethlehem Steel had helped two generations of workers climb into the middle class, the next generation saw no such opportunity.

12 But if hearsay evidence was everywhere, a precise statistical portrait was a lot harder to come by—in part because there was such a confusion of numbers. Different data series gave different—and often contradictory—pictures. Take national per capita income. As figured in constant 1987 dollars, it had expanded almost automatically during the decade as a growing percentage of Americans (women especially) went to work, rising from $10,740 in 1980 to $11,301 in 1984 and $12,287 in 1987. But critics called

this a deceptive measurement and pointed instead to inflation-adjusted weekly *per worker* income, which went down during the same period, dropping from $366 in 1972 to $318 in 1980 and $312 in 1987. Others preferred to cite the weakness in inflation-adjusted U.S. family median incomes.

13   Defenders of 1980s prosperity found family income data a problem. The average millionaire's income might be soaring, but the average family's was stagnating. In constant 1987 dollars, the median had reached $30,820 in 1973, declined slightly to $30,668 in 1979, then plummeted in the early 1980s under both Carter and Reagan. Only by 1987 did it reach $30,853, essentially recovering 1973 levels. *After-tax* 1987 median family incomes were still well below those of the late 1970s. This, critics said, was the better measure of households in pain.

14   There were partial rebuttals. Families in 1988, having shrunk over the prior decades, were no longer comparable to earlier groupings. Families averaging 3.19 people in 1987 *did* require less consumption than those of 1970 averaging 3.58 people, which did distort comparisons of family income. Even so, the weakness in inflation-adjusted family median incomes commanded symbolic attention, as did the similar slump in real disposable (after-tax) family income. For many Middle Americans stagnant purchasing power *was* a day-to-day reality—and a stark offset to the glitter of exploding wealth in Manhattan or Beverly Hills.

15   There were other data, too: reams of them on both sides. And perhaps that was the most telling barometer of all. During the thirty years after World War II, when the American dream was indisputably working, no statistical profiles had really been necessary. People knew they were better off. No one could quibble.

16   By 1988 quibbling and ambiguity were everywhere. Too much could be made of any single broad yardstick of family, per capita or household income. As each index measured something slightly different, virtually every pundit or politician might find some statistics to document a particular case. And critics overplayed their thesis of a whole economy in decline. The Congressional Budget Office, looking for a moderate middle ground, calculated in 1987 that family income went up 11 percent from 1973 to 1986, with a meaningful percentage increase between 1981 and 1986. In many ways, though, the larger story—and the worrisome symptom—was not the slight *overall* growth in median family income. It was the comparative advances or regressions of families in different brackets. "If you look at subgroups you can see that inequality is rising more than it seems to be if you just look at the aggregate numbers," said Sheldon Danziger, a sociologist at the University of Michigan. "There's a lot more going on in the pieces than in the larger picture."

17   Politically the economic viability of U.S. families had started to become an important issue. Academicians and politicians might be able to play ping-pong with statistics seeking to define *overall* family trends, but there was no way to argue with the official government portrait of a shift of income between 1980 and 1988 away from the bottom 80 percent of the

Income Gains and Losses 1977–88

Changes in Average Family Income (1987 Dollars)

Income Decile	Average Family Income 1977	Average Family Income 1988*	Percentage Change 1977–88	Change in Average Family Income 1977–88
First	$ 4,113	$ 3,504	−14.8%	$ −609
Second	8,334	7,669	−8.0	−665
Third	13,140	12,327	−6.2	−813
Fourth	18,436	17,220	−6.6	−1,216
Fifth	23,896	22,389	−6.3	−1,507
Sixth	29,824	28,205	−5.4	−1,619
Seventh	36,405	34,828	−4.3	−1,577
Eighth	44,305	43,507	−1.8	−798
Ninth	55,487	56,064	1.0	577
Tenth	102,722	119,635	16.5	16,913
Top 5%	134,543	166,016	23.4	31,473
Top 1%	270,053	404,566	49.8	134,513
All Families	33,527	34,274	2.2	747

*CBO projection of 1988 incomes

Source: *Challenge to Leadership,* Urban Institute

U.S. population toward the most affluent fifth. The Income Gains table on this page shows how less affluent segments of the population were slipping downward even as the top strata were enjoying a major surge of income and wealth.

18   Previous Republican and laissez-faire eras, periods of competitive, capitalist resurgence, have *always* produced broad ranks of losers as well as winners. And by Reagan's last year in office, evidence of a wide range of occupational declines—for manufacturing employees, farmers, people in the oil industry, young householders and the working poor—was more or less irrefutable. *Money* magazine's midyear polls, those in which 60 percent of Americans described the U.S. economy as "not so good" or "poor," reflected popular disillusionments that extended far beyond much publicized Farm Belt foreclosures or shut-down factory towns.

19   Previous economic dislocations in the United States during the twentieth century could be tied to events; those of the 1980s could not. In 1987 Frank Levy, professor of public policy at the University of Maryland, wrote that during the Carter and Reagan years:

> ... there was little mass unemployment [in the 1980s] and few people were forced to take money wage cuts. To the contrary, *money wages* were rising briskly, but prices were rising, too, and few people gained ground.
>
>   We knew that something was wrong, but we lacked the language to describe it. Conflict among regions, industrial sectors, and generations was

clearly on the rise, and we spoke of growing inequality as if census statistics would show the income distribution splitting apart. But official income inequality increased only modestly, and the real change in inequality has been harder to measure. It involved a mixture of family arrangements, when people bought their homes, and how established they were in their careers. It involved their current income but also their outlook for the future and the likelihood of attaining their aspirations. It was an inequality of prospects in which many people who had attained the middle-class dream could ride out the period while people who aspired to the dream—people who were banking on rising living standards—saw the future shrink.

20 White males serving as their family's only breadwinner were, as a category, particularly conspicuous. By one calculation, their median inflation-adjusted income fell 22 percent between 1976 and 1984. After the 1983 recovery, many squeezed or depressed households discovered that their economic problems weren't simply recession hangovers. As domestic and global economic restructuring continued, well-paid manufacturing jobs and the purchasing power of manufacturing paychecks shrank. For *all* workers, white-collar as well as blue-collar, their real average weekly wage—calculated in constant 1977 dollars—fell from $191.41 a week in 1972 to $171.07 in 1986.

21 But even that decline disguised the larger negative impact on men partly offset by a slight overall rise for women. Well-paid male blue-collar union members suffered the greatest loss, especially younger men and those with no more than a high school diploma. According to Marvin Kosters, a conservative economist at the Washington-based American Enterprise Institute, the median real earnings of men between the ages of twenty-five to thirty-four, measured in constant 1985 dollars, were $10.17 an hour in 1973, $9.70 an hour in 1980 and $8.85 in 1987. For men of all ages with nothing more than high school diplomas the figures were $9.90 in 1973, $9.37 in 1980 and $8.62 in 1987. Frank Levy observed that "back in the early 1970s, the average guy with a high school diploma was making $24,000 in today's dollars. Today a similar guy is making about $18,000."

22 The high-paying jobs lost in Hibbing or River Rouge had been more than just employment; they had been cultural and economic ladders to middle-class status for millions of families all across industrial America. Newspaper writers from Appalachia to the Iron Range wrote more or less the same story: "Once blue-collar sons could follow their fathers into the plants and make $13, $14 an hour. That meant the middle class, a car, maybe a little cabin on a lake, a chance for kids to go to college. Once, but not anymore." Caste and class restraints that had eased after World War II began to reemerge.

23 Public frustration had distinct regional accents, too. Despite a partial rebound in 1987–88 in agriculture and manufacturing, the Reagan decade favored what Democratic politicians in 1986 started calling the "bicoastal economy." Even in 1988, national income data would show the Rocky Mountains, Farm Belt and Oil Patch lagging.

...times in the Great Lakes factory towns were less persistent. ...alf of the decade had been weak, and in 1986 wages fell in 47 ... Illinois's manufacturing jobs, where the average reduction was 8 percent. Then in 1987–88, Great Lakes manufacturing began to rebound as the falling dollar stimulated exports. What was surprising, though, was how little the rebound carried over to wages. On average, the manufacturing jobs being created in 1987–88 were not as well paid as the ones lost earlier—and the pressures of global competitiveness kept wage increases behind modestly resurgent inflation. The General Accounting Office reported the resurgence of sweatshops—businesses that regularly violate wage, child labor, safety and health laws—not just in New York, Chicago and Los Angeles but in virtually all sections of the country.

25 On the eve of the Democratic National Convention, Lester Thurow, dean of the Sloan School of Management at MIT, urged Dukakis to make the lack of "good jobs at good wages" the central issue of the campaign: "The real hourly wages of production or non-supervisory workers—after correcting for inflation—were no higher in the first quarter of 1988 than they had been in 1980. And in recent years, wages have been falling. In 1987, real hourly wages fell 1.1 percent. The fall continued in the first quarter of 1988. Weekly wages, a measure that takes into account both hourly pay and hours of work, were even more of a disaster. In the first quarter of 1988, they were 2.4 percent *below* where they had been in 1980 and falling at a rate in excess of 1 percent per year." The political issue, Thurow contended, was that real GNP was rising despite the falling real wages, which meant that *someone's* income was going up—"and that someone has been the top 20 percent of the population."

26 Major 1988 contract negotiations showed that labor was still defensive. General Electric's 198,000 domestic workers settled for a 2.5 percent wage increase in the first year and 1.5 percent in each of the next two years, far below projected inflation.[†] But there was also another side to the story. "We concentrate on what our memberships want, and a lot of unions have decided to give up wages for guaranteed jobs and for retraining programs," said an AFL-CIO economist in Washington.

27 Moreover, many people were not in the work force at all: members of the underclass, for example, or those no longer looking for a job. The 5.3 percent unemployment rate was misleading because definitions of the work force excluded a growing number of Americans. By the summer of 1988, 45.3 percent of New York City residents over the age of sixteen could not be counted as labor force participants because of poverty,

---

[†] Martin Neil Bailey, a fellow at the Brookings Institution in Washington, found it "surprising—with the current economy—that we have not seen a rise in real wages yet. What we are seeing so far is higher profits rather than higher wages." ("Pay Isn't Keeping Pace with the Economy," *Philadelphia Inquirer*, July 27, 1988).

lack of skills, drug use, apathy or other problems. Similar circumstances were reported in Detroit and Baltimore, while the ratio of uncountables for the nation as a whole was 34.5 percent. Thus the paradox: *millions of jobs might be going begging, but huge numbers of Americans remained either unemployed or unemployable.* Circumstances like this resulted in the destitution and homelessness that perturbed cities and suburbs everywhere as economic polarization intensified.

28   Many women had also been losers. Families were not just shrinking; they were breaking down. Households headed by females ranked well down the income scale—especially those with children. In the spring and summer of 1988 polls showed that half of all men characterized the U.S. economy as "excellent" or "good," but only one third of the women did so. Women preferred the Democrats largely for economic reasons, not only because of broken homes, but, as we have seen, because of the pressure on family life when wives and mothers take marginal jobs. Families were sacrificing psychic income for dollar income, a trade-off that the Census Bureau chose not to quantify, but which was probably considerable. One survey found that Americans' leisure time declined by 37 percent between 1973 and 1987—from 26.2 hours a week to 16.6 hours.

29   By the mid-1980s a new two-tier wage system had arisen in troubled industries as senior employees kept their previous pay scales but *new* hires—from airline pilots to supermarket checkout clerks—came in at lower rates. At the same time, more people could find only part-time jobs as employers spread work and costs more carefully. This "contingent work force"—part-timers and temporaries—had doubled between 1980 and 1987, expanding to include roughly one quarter of the total work force, while the percentage of the working poor with short periods of unemployment rose. Not surprisingly, given these pressures, the uncertainty and unreliability of employment also grew as an issue; a 1988 poll found "job security" reemerging as employees' number one concern. Emphasis on the low official unemployment rate was deceptive to the extent that it ignored these offsets.

30   Corporate chairmen and presidents as a class feasted in the 1980s, but the number of mid-level management jobs lost during those years was estimated to be as high as 1.5 million. In 1987 one survey found 41 percent of respondents acknowledging job-loss fears premised on corporate restructuring or foreign competition. Blue-collar America had paid a larger price, but suburbia, where fathers rushed to catch the 8:10 train to the city, was quietly counting its casualties, too. In September 1988, Peter Drucker observed that "the cynicism out there is frightening. Middle managers have become insecure, and they feel unbelievably hurt. They feel like slaves on an auction block."

31   Thus "downward mobility" emerged as a real fear within the U.S. work force, white-collar and blue-collar alike. The *Los Angeles Times* reported in 1988 that "not in half a century has the United States seen so many 'givebacks' affecting so many people. But from musicians with the

Honolulu Symphony Orchestra to lumbermen in the Pacific Northwest, from steelworkers in West Virginia to Greyhound bus drivers in Montana, thousands of Americans with years of experience are experiencing the vicissitudes of MAAD—middle-aged and downward."

32   In 1986, 59 percent of the baby boomers paying Social Security taxes said they didn't ever expect to collect their benefits. At the same time, amid job switches and family breakups, *private pension* coverage also began to shrink. Between 1950 and 1980 the percentage of American workers included under retirement plans had risen from 22 percent to 45 percent. By 1986 coverage had shrunk to 42.6 percent.

33   Many families found themselves emptying savings accounts and going in debt, often to meet the soaring price of homeownership or to put a child through college. For a family with 1985 earnings equal to the median national income, keeping a child in a four-year private college or university would have taken 40 percent of that income, up from 30 percent in 1970. Buying a house was even tougher. Homeownership had reached a record 65 percent of U.S. households in 1980, after climbing steadily from 1940, when 43.6 percent of households owned their own residences. After 1980, however, the homeownership rate would drop year by year, falling to 63.8 percent in 1986 and leveling off. Young people, in particular, found that home buying was next to impossible.

34   In 1980, 21.3 percent of people under twenty-five owned their own homes. By 1987 that rate was down to 16.1 percent. Among those between twenty-five and twenty-nine the rate fell from 43.3 percent to 35.9 percent. For persons between thirty and thirty-four the decline was from 61.1 percent to 53.2 percent. And among those thirty-five to thirty-nine the drop was seven points—from 70.8 percent to 63.8 percent. In 1988 presidential campaign rhetoric touched on the problem, but not convincingly. To more and more citizens, the American dream of homeownership was becoming just that—*a dream.*

35   For much of Middle America, then, the Reagan years were troubling and ambiguous as the contrast intensified between proliferating billionaires and the tens of millions of others who were gradually sinking. Under the superficial economic glitter of *Lifestyles of the Rich and Famous* and *Architectural Digest,* powerful polarizing forces were at work.[‡] Through much of the late spring and summer of 1988 Republican strategists couldn't understand the dissonance between strong economic statistics and the voters' doubts about George Bush, but one explanation was per-

---

[‡] In the late 1920s economist Stuart Chase had proved a kindred polarization in a cautionary book entitled *Prosperity: Fact or Myth* (New York: Charles Boni Paperback Books, 1929). Beneath the patina of the soaring stock market, new millionaires, two-lane highways crowded with new automobiles, and the excitement of radios, the first talking movies and Charles Lindbergh's unprecedented solo flight across the Atlantic, lots of Americans had gained little during the decade, Chase contended. Many had actually *lost* ground. By the late 1980s Reagan's critics had begun pointing to similar contradictions.

Rising Average Total Corporate CEO Compensation (in thousands of dollars)

	1983	1984	1985	1986	1987	1988
Business Week	900	1,100	1,200	1,250	1,800	2,025

Source: Published *Business Week* data and information furnished by *Business Week* regarding yearly percentage increases

vasive national uncertainty about the shape of the American dream—and suspicion that the Republicans were administering it on behalf of the few, not of the many.

36   In April 1988 *Business Week* released a startling statistic: during 1987, a year with just 4 percent inflation, the average CEO compensation at 339 of the nation's largest publicly held corporations rose by 48 percent to $1.8 million. It rose 14 percent more in 1988–to $2.02 million. At *Forbes*, that magazine's survey of the chief executive officers of the "Forbes 800" top companies turned up an average total compensation of $1.28 million in 1987, a 28 percent jump from the year before. And *Electronic Business* magazine reported that the one hundred highest-paid executives in high-tech companies earned an average of $785,000 in 1987, and seventeen received more than $1 million. Table 2 shows the 1983–88 rise in CEO salaries using the data from the annual *Business Week* survey.

37   Where stock options were involved, vice presidents and others below the CEO level occasionally outgained their chairmen. However, surveys based only on salary and bonus confirmed a widening gap between CEOs and other executives during the 1980s. According to one sampling of 1987 pay levels in thirty major companies, the median total *cash* compensation for chief executives was $1,087,500. For the company's second-ranking executive it dropped to $645,000; for the third, fourth and fifth in the hierarchy, to $520,500, $460,500 and $433,800, respectively. The results added up to "a widening of the differential" between the man at the top and the next-ranking executives. Not surprisingly, there was also a sharp contrast between top-officer salary increases—up 56.8 percent from 1983 to 1987–and the lesser 32.6 percent increment going to the average merit-recipient white-collar employee. Meanwhile the disparity between CEOs and workers was accelerating even more. In 1979 CEOs made twenty nine times the income of the average manufacturing worker. By 1985 the multiple was forty. By 1988, *Business Week* said the total compensation of the average CEO in its annual survey had risen to ninety-three times the earnings of the average factory worker, prompting the magazine to editorialize that "executive pay is growing out of all proportion to increases in what many other people make—from the worker on the plant floor to the teacher in the classroom." The chart on p. 106 profiles the extraordinary, unprecedented divergence that occurred during the Reagan years.

38   Furthermore, there was a negligible correlation between increases in CEO compensation and shareholder gains. One professor dismissed pay-for-performance relationships as "almost non-existent in a lot of companies." The same was true of golden parachutes. For the top one tenth of 1

The Divergence Between the Pay of Workers and Corporate Chief Executives During the 1980s

American Pay, 1965 = 100

Average annual pay	Hourly-paid production workers	Chief executives' total compensation
1968	$6,370	$157,000
1978	$12,962	$373,000
1988	$21,735	$773,000

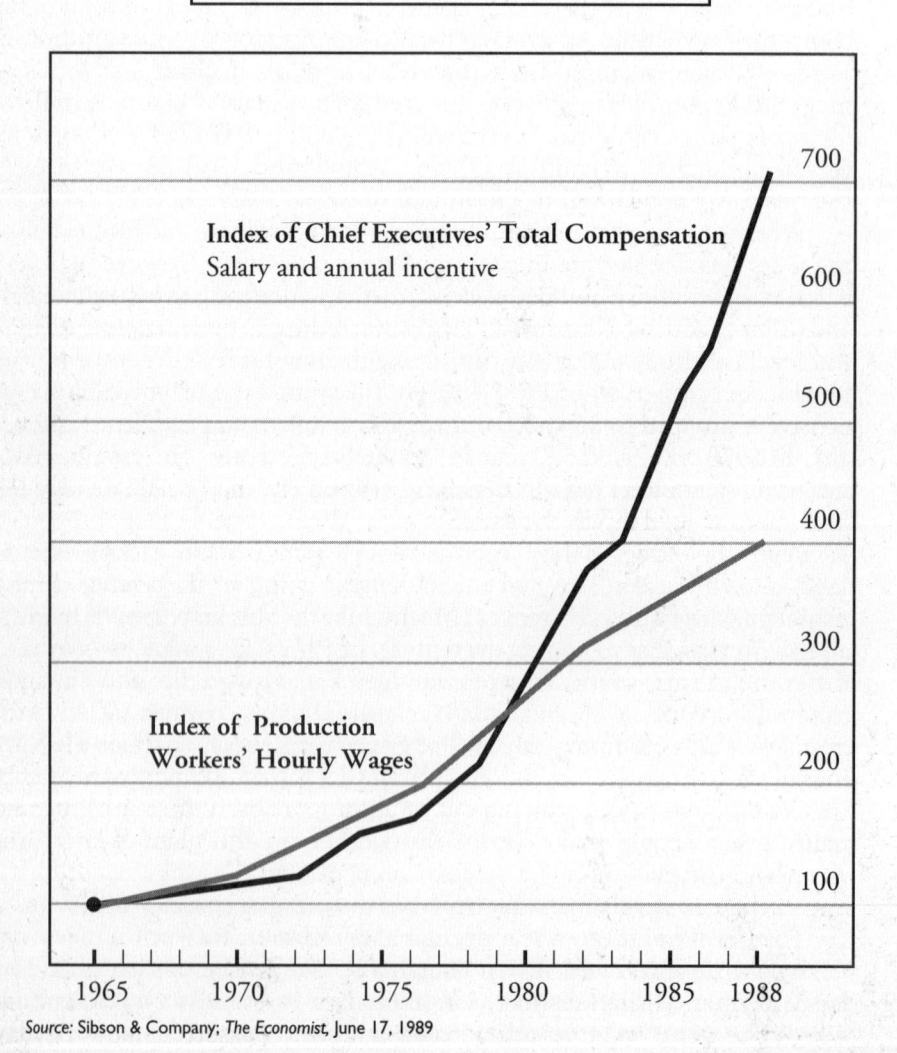

Index of Chief Executives' Total Compensation
Salary and annual incentive

Index of Production Workers' Hourly Wages

Source: Sibson & Company; *The Economist*, June 17, 1989

The Ten Largest Corporate Golden Parachutes, 1988

	Company	Reason for Payment	Total package* ($ thousands)
F. Ross Johnson, CEO	RJR Nabisco	Leveraged buyout	$53,800
E. A. Horrigan, Vice-Chmn.	RJR Nabisco	Leveraged buyout	45,700
Gerald Tsai Jr., Chmn.	Primerica	Commercial Credit takeover	46,800
Edward P. Evans, Chmn.	Macmillan	Maxwell takeover	31,900
Kenneth A. Yarnell, Pres.	Primerica	Commercial Credit takeover	18,400
John D. Martin, Exec. VP	RJR Nabisco	Leveraged buyout	18,200
Sanford C. Sigoloff, Chmn.	Wickes	Leveraged buyout	15,900
Whitney Stevens, Chmn.	J. P. Stevens	West Point-Pepperell takeover	15,700
Philip I. Smith, Chmn.	Pillsbury	Grand Metropolitan takeover	11,000
Wilhelm A. Mallory, Sr. VP	Wickes	Leveraged buyout	7,500

*Includes final salary, bonus, long-term compensation, certain retirement benefits and estimated future annuity payments as well as parachute.

Source: *Business Week*, May 1, 1989.

percent of Americans, national economic restructuring involved negligible risk and enormous gains. Participation in paper entrepreneurialism—even as a loser—was beginning to be its own reward.

39   These raw compensation numbers understated the full benefit to top-executive bank accounts, for the top tax rates had fallen, as mentioned before, from 70 percent to 28 percent, a boon to the corporate elite, but useless to most workers whose combined income tax and Social Security tax burdens remained much the same.

40   Highly rewarded participants in one particularly burgeoning American business, entertainment—movies, records and the like became second only to aircraft as a U.S. export in the late 1980s—included not only executives but performers and promoters. Tabulations for the 1986–88 period showed that their compensation was on a par with that of the financial community. Twenty entertainment moguls made the Forbes 100 in 1988, and tabulations of entertainment's top forty earners for the years 1988–89 started with singer Michael Jackson ($125 million) and producer Steven Spielberg ($105 million), took note of actor Bill Cosby ($95 million) and finished with actor Mel Gibson ($20 million). Performers earning less than that over those two years didn't make the list.

41   As the decade closed, the distortion of American wealth raised questions not just about polarization but also about trivialization. Less and less of the nation's wealth was going to people who produced manufactures or commodities. Services were ascendant—from fast food to legal advice, investment vehicles, data bases and videocassettes. New heyday

wealth has always been scorned for representing unfamiliar or unfashionable vocations or sectors—the "beer barons" of Victorian England are an example. Similar disdain applied to late-1980s fortunes made in everything from candy bars to pet food, cosmetics, cable television and electronic games. The mounting concentration of wealth in the service industries, however, raised a larger problem. It was one thing for new technologies to reduce demand for farmers, steelworkers and typists, enabling society to concentrate more resources on health, money management and leisure. But the distortion lay in the disproportionate rewards to society's economic, legal and cultural manipulators—from lawyers and investment advisers to advertising executives, merchandisers, consumer finance specialists, fashion designers, communicators, media magnates and entertainment promoters. Unfortunately, heyday biases in these directions are as American as apple pie. As disposable income concentrates even more strongly than usual in the hands of the upper 10 to 20 percent of Americans, vocations dealing in short-term objectives and satisfactions profit. Humdrum activities and long-term objectives suffer.

[42] A related boom occurred in nonfinancial assets—art and homes, in particular—linked to the taste and demand of investors, entrepreneurs, corporate managers, lawyers, doctors and other service-sector elites. Inasmuch as the value of housing in the United States represented most Americans' principal asset and added up to several times the value of all the stocks on the New York Stock Exchange, the effect of the 1980s on residential housing values significantly amplified regional and sectoral wealth trends.§ Paralleling circumstances in Britain and Japan, the biggest gains came in areas in or near the nation's financial centers. Between 1981 and 1989 home values soared 50 to 125 percent on a metropolitan area-wide or statewide basis in Boston, Connecticut, New York City, Washington, D.C., Philadelphia, Los Angeles, San Francisco, San Diego and Hawaii, with the largest increases in the better residential neighborhoods. In sharp contrast, inflation-adjusted housing prices actually fell for the 1981–89 period in many places, from Tulsa and Baton Rouge to Denver and Omaha, where local economic troubles mirrored agriculture, energy or declining manufacturing sectors. Although home prices started sagging in 1989 in parts of the Northeast and California, the decade's revaluations in the U.S. housing market had quietly redistributed hundreds of billions of dollars (at least on paper)—and done so with even more bias than income shifts.

[43] In the process, some Americans lost not just housing value or opportunity but also the roof over their heads. By 1989 tent cities and shantytowns were taking shape, from New York City to San Francisco, and

---

§ According to the Census Bureau, in 1984 home ownership was reported by two thirds of all households and accounted for 41 percent of net worth. For the nearly 80 percent of the population with a net worth below one hundred thousand dollars, a lopsided 77 percent of that net worth was represented by equity in homes and cars.

homeless people were organizing temporary tent cities in front of the Illinois and California state capitols. Across the nation, requests for emergency shelter were rising steadily, in small regional centers and big cities alike. In May 1989 Congressman Henry Gonzalez, chairman of the House Committee on Banking, Finance and Urban Affairs charged that by the Reagan administration's reduction of low- and moderate-income housing programs in the face of rising prices "we have made Americans nomads in their own land. Talk about refugees—we have families roaming this land, some of them living in cars and under bridges.* We're headed for the way of . . . Brussels, West Berlin, London and Paris, where 12 to 15 years ago they were having rent squatters, they were having forcible evictions and violence."

44   For America's richest two or three hundred thousand families, by contrast, art and antiques roughly tripled during the Reagan era, witness the increase in value from 1981 to 1989 in a cross section of art categories from the Sotheby's Index. . . . While homelessness mounted at the lower end of the economic spectrum, the art and furnishings of a representative eleven-room cooperative apartment on New York's Park Avenue could well have risen from a $675,000 value in 1981 to $1.5 million in 1989 simply by the workings of supply and demand. Similar, if lesser, explosions in art prices had taken place in the 1920s and Gilded Age booms. When the top one half of 1 percent of Americans are rolling in money, the residential luxuries they crave—from Picassos and eighteenth-century English furniture to Manhattan town houses and Malibu beach homes—soar in markets virtually auxiliary to those in finance.

45   By 1989 the realignment of American wealth was beginning to evoke criticism, albeit less than in Britain and Japan. Following the revelation of Michael Milken's $550 million earnings for 1987, a conservative Southern survey, the Long Marketing North Carolina Poll, found a 53 percent local majority favoring a cap on the incomes of professional athletes, corporate executives, movie stars, stockbrokers and the like. Survey taker W. H. Long observed that "clearly, in America today and certainly in North Carolina today, a slowly growing majority detest excess in the earnings market." Yet by any reasonable yardstick, American populist resentment was still far less than in the early 1890s or the early 1930s. Lester Thurow was not alone when he said in 1989 that "it looks like America (again) has an oligarchy," but the implications he raised awaited further events. Americans do not react against wealth per se. As we have seen, however, some upper-bracket wealth accumulation was a result of favoritism in Washing-

---

* Nomadism and homelessness have been recurrent characteristics of U.S. financial heydays and their aftermath. The circumstances of the late 1920s and (especially) 1930–36 are well known. But similar trends were unmistakable in the 1880s and 1890s, especially in the wake of the 1893 depression: in December of that year Governor Lorenzo Lewelling of Kansas issued by executive proclamation the so-called Tramp Circular drawing parallels to Elizabethan England and prerevolutionary France.

ton policies ranging from tax cuts to tight money, permissive financial deregulation and abnormally high real interest rates. Only if that favoritism could later be said to have hurt other Americans and jeopardized the *larger* economy—important charges during prior heydays—would the scene be set for a classic populist reaction against an abusive, self-serving economic elite.

Points for Review and Discussion

1. Summarize the main changes in the objective economic situation of the rich and the poor that Phillips discusses in this selection.
2. Summarize the chief causes Phillips cites as responsible for the development of a "pervasive national uncertainty about the shape of the American dream" (¶ 35).
3. Phillips describes as "startling" a *Business Week* statistic about average CEO compensation (¶ 36). Why in his opinion is this figure so significant?

◆ Questions for Writing

1. The point raised throughout this selection is that economic policy in recent years has been unfair. Cite some examples of unfairness that you found most telling, and explain who or what you believe to have been responsible for them.
2. After quoting a Stanford professor who says that "the economy has shifted in the direction of a meritocracy," Phillips adds that "there was no mistaking how the smart, the well-educated and the highly motivated commanded a larger share of the gain" (¶ 6). Later he notes that the ratio of management income to worker income was more than three times higher in 1988 than in 1979 (¶ 37). Presumably this change in income ratios didn't occur because management became three times smarter than workers over a period of a decade. How does the essay explain the change?
3. Phillips speaks of a "pervasive national uncertainty about the shape of the American dream—and suspicion that the Republicans were administering it on behalf of the few, not of many" (¶ 35). The idea of the American dream as something "administered" by a party in power—either to benefit the few or the many—conflicts with the idea of success as the result of individual striving. Write a short paper exploring this conflict as you understand it.
4. Express in your own words what happens to the stereotype of the rich man or woman as self-made when huge personal success appears to result from particular government decisions and policies.

Connecting the Parts in Chapter 3: Assignments for Extended Essays

1. Compensation packages for chief executive officers are often put together by committees of corporation trustees appointed by the corporation board chair. In the past, at Superbig, Inc., the compensation committee has usually worked harmoniously, bringing in a unanimous recommendation without hassle. But not this year. Superbig is coming off its most profitable year in history, and one comp committee member moves to reward the CEO with a flat $1 million raise. A second committee member has been reading Kevin Phillips and violently opposes the motion, arguing that Superbig should either hold the line or actually decrease the executive's pay. Write a paper in which you imagine this committee battle and report it fully, quoting not only the arguments on both sides but what is said by the third committee member who undertakes to find some middle ground. Your paper can be set up as a transcript, or as secretarial minutes, or as a report brought back to the full board by the compensation committee chair.

2. A presidential advisor—brilliant but sometimes seen as excessively individualistic if not eccentric—meets in the White House with speechwriters to plan a presidential commencement address to be delivered this spring at Famous U. The advisor has been trying to sell the president on the idea that it's time to begin educating the public out of its simpleminded if not racist views of so-called "minority problems." He outlines to the speechwriters an address that would try to shape a new public attitude both toward the "underclass" and toward federal policy designed to meet the problem. (The advisor has obviously been reading Michael Katz.) One speechwriter reacts violently against the idea, on political, moral, and other grounds. She and the advisor go at each other fiercely for a quarter of an hour. Write a paper reporting dramatically and incisively on the content and tone of this dispute.

Leads for Research

1. Explore the ramifications of the jobs issues that figure in Katz and Phillips by looking into the relation between those issues and corporate restructuring and trends in manufacturing. Start your research by consulting two books by Barry Bluestone and Bennett Harrison, *The Deindustrialization of America: Plant Closings, Community Abandonment and the Dismantling of Basic Industry* (1982) and *The Great U-Turn: Corporate Restructuring and the Polarization of America* (1988), and Gerald Burtless, ed., *A Future of Lousy Jobs? The Changing Structure of U.S. Wages* (1990). If your reading suggests to you a ground for criticism either of Katz or of Phillips, work up the critique into an essay.

2. Look into the content and shaping of attitudes toward blue-collar work by examining Peter M. Blau and Otis Dudley Duncan, *The American Occupational Structure* (1977). Conduct your own survey of student attitudes toward occupations and use it, together with Blau and Dudley, as a basis for a paper about changes in work status in recent decades.

3. Debate about federal initatives to help the underclass has been much influenced by the standard view holding that Great Society programs instituted under President Lyndon Johnson were a failure. Begin your reexamination of this view by reading John Ervin Schwarz's *America's Hidden Success* (1983, rev. 1987) on the impact of U.S. economic and social policy on poverty between 1960 and 1980. (Also look up reviews of Schwarz's book that appeared in the *New York Times, Washington Post, Atlantic,* and *Commentary.*) Write a paper suggesting ways in which clearer public understanding of yesterday's federal programs could contribute to better policymaking now.

4

Making It Big
American Visions of Riches

Visions of riches have haunted some American minds from the time of the first settlers. But the idea of success has seldom been one-dimensional. Puritan doctrines held that profit-making by producing and marketing goods was virtuous in a religious as well as practical sense, and that ascent from humble beginnings to high place was equally virtuous. Historians have had much to say about the links between Protestantism and the rise of capitalism. The popularity of twentieth-century works by ministers preaching on the goodness of success testifies to the continuing belief in the religious significance of making it big. (At midcentury the most famous of these works was the Reverend Norman Vincent Peale's *The Power of Positive Thinking*.)

The readings in this section inquire into the backgrounds of our positive images of moneymaking and social ascent; they focus also on American fascination with *quick* riches.

The American Idea of Success
Richard Huber

> Richard Huber's *The American Idea of Success* (1971, 1987) traces the remarkable history of this country's popular thought about riches. That history includes John D. Rockefeller Sr.'s pronouncement that "I believe the power to make money is a gift of God...." It includes the Gospel of Wealth promulgated by Andrew Carnegie, immigrant boy from Scotland who, as Hubert says, "became an industrialist and financier, made hundreds of millions of dollars, and then gave most of it away." It includes the fictional heroes invented by Horatio Alger—Ragged Dick, Phil the Fiddler, many more—all of whom "started poor and finished rich."
>
> Richard Huber holds a doctorate in American Studies from Yale. His story of our ways of thinking about material advancement begins with the Puritan heritage and Ben Franklin.

The Heritage

1 The idea of success was a force which drove men on to build America. At the center was the individual. Self-confident in his God-given rights, he entered a free world of expanding opportunities. How he seized upon three thousand miles of virgin land and bounteous natural resources to develop those opportunities into the most productive nation the world has ever known has for many always been the thrill of the American achievement.

2 In America, making money had dignity. Here was no mere plundering operation, as in feudal cultures, no apologetic back-sliding of an aristocracy, as in eighteenth-century England. The American sought money as he loved his wife or worshipped his God, sure that every extra dollar permitted him a higher tilt of his head.

3 In the beginning the words were freedom and opportunity. The bold ones who crossed an ocean to a new land in Colonial times were eager to make the most of it. Those who pulled up roots for the new land were generally more ambitious and adventurous than the stay-at-homes. Decade after decade shiploads of middle- and working-class Europeans spilled onto the east coast of America, dissatisfied in one way or another with things at home and anxious for a fresh start to get ahead in the new world.

4 Under American conditions, swiftly and clearly, there developed a hunger for wealth. It was not the sensuous hunger of an oriental potentate, but a moral hunger fed on the awareness that one's self-esteem de-

---

From Richard Huber, *The American Idea of Success* (1971).

pended on results. Free of the ascribed inequalities of Europe, the American soon relied on wealth as a criterion of recognition. The means to success were equally functional. If the pioneer was to land feet first on the frontier and not go under, he had to keep at it, work hard, and save his money. The farmer's day was a long day, and America was a nation bound to the soil. The Revolution was fought by a country in which nineteen out of twenty people were farmers. For those who were urban rather than agrarian capitalists, the same qualities were mandatory for anything more than mere survival. It was a scarcity economy demanding frugality and hard hours of toil.

5 The early Colonists were children of the Renaissance and Reformation. Theirs was a self-assertive age which had rebelled against the disapproval in the Middle Ages of getting ahead by competition in business. Indeed, what had been considered a vice in the Middle Ages—the making of a profit through the exchange of goods—had in the Colonists' economic system become a virtue. That it was a virtue was assured by the doctrines of Puritanism. The economic system which encouraged the accumulation of wealth was capitalism. Religion worked in harness with economics toward the goal of individual success. Religious values encouraged and justified economic behavior.

6 In the later seventeenth and early eighteenth centuries no one spoke with greater authority for the religious interpretation of what we have termed the character ethic than Cotton Mather. A New England divine of great influence and power, Mather spoke for God while saturating the idea of success in Calvinism and the Old Testament. He introduces us to the Puritan concept that every Christian has two callings. In the general calling, Mather instructed his flock, a good Christian should "serve the Lord Jesus Christ and save his own soul in the services of religion. . . ." In his personal calling, a Christian should have a "particular employment by which his usefulness in his neighborhood is distinguished." In his personal calling, or what we would call a job, a Christian should spend most of his time in "some settled business . . . so he may glorify God by doing of good for others and getting of good for himself." Unless disabled by infirmities, a man without a job is "unrighteous" towards his family, community, and country, as well as being open to temptations from the Devil. "Every man ordinarily should be able to say, 'I have something wherein I am occupied for the good of other men.'"

7 Many of the pressures of our own day to get ahead lay heavy upon those early immigrants and their children—except the hand of God increased the pressure. In Proverbs, Mather pressed on, it is written: "'He becomes poor who dealeth with a slack hand, but the hand of the diligent maketh rich.' Such lessons are so frequent in the Book of God that I wonder how any man given up to slothfulness dare look into his Bible. . . . Come, come, for shame, away to your business. Lay out your strength in

it, put forth your skill for it. . . . 'Solomon, seeing that the young man was industrious, he made him a ruler.' I tell you with diligence a man may do marvelous things. Young man, work hard while you are young; you'll reap the effects of it when you are old. Yea, how can you ordinarily enjoy any rest at night if you have not been well at work in the day? Let your business engross the most of your time."

8   Mather saw a dangerous paradox. Laziness is a sin, but hard work, greedily motivated, and the fruits of hard work, unplucked for pious uses, may lead to a greater sin. "The business of your personal calling" must not "swallow up" your general calling. With a vivid image Mather caught the nature of a properly balanced life. The Christian in his two callings is like a man in a boat rowing toward heaven. If he pulls only one oar (either the spiritual or the worldly one), he "will make but a poor dispatch to the Shoar of Eternal Blessedness." You should pull hard on the oar of worldly achievement, but do not neglect the oar of your soul and its salvation through union with Jesus Christ. Row always in the fear of God and strive to be holy and diligent in both your callings. (Mercifully, however, it is true that "the poorest labourer among you all, tho' of a low degree on earth, may be of an high account in heaven.") Say your prayers, be faithful to God, and remember that "at no time of the day may we expect that our business will succeed without God's blessing. . . . All will fall out as God shall order it."

9   In essays of power and persuasion, Mather forged the links between success and God. He asks us to consider "what we are told in Deut. 8:18, 'Thou shalt remember the Lord thy God, for 'tis he that gives the power to get wealth.'" Mather observes that the reverse is also true. It is God who denies us the power to become rich. But, we ask, if this be so, what control have we over our own destiny? Is God's control over our fortunes subject to divine whim, or can we influence God to act favorably towards us? Mather replies that if we serve God faithfully in both our callings, say our prayers twice a day, obey the Sabbath, stay honest, and liberally disburse our income to pious uses as a steward of the Lord, then God will smile favorably upon us. "By these things you will obtain the blessing of God upon your business." If we fail, probably we have displeased God by being dishonest, gluttonous, unthankful, or full of pride. It is God, then, who controls our fortune, but by thought, word, and deed we can influence God to exercise his control in our favor. At the same time, however, we should never forget that material things are not only ephemeral but can corrupt the soul. The highest success is measured by our treasures in heaven.

10   Wherever Calvinism, or the Biblical ideas which it expressed, stamped their mark, the message was similar. Puritanism in America was a modified expression of the Calvinist branch of Protestantism. Though some religious leaders denounced Calvin, Puritanism was especially strong among the Presbyterians, Congregationalists (Reformed), and Methodists. The Quakers were no friends to Puritan theology, but they endorsed Cal-

vin's implicit support of capitalism. In Philadelphia, William Penn tried to teach his children that "Diligence is [a] Virtue useful and laudable among Men: It is a discreet and understanding Application of one's Self to Business; and it avoids the Extreams of Idleness and Drudgery. It gives great Advantages to Men. . . . It is the Way to Wealth." Cultivate the virtues of frugality, industry, prudence, order, and honesty, the ideology counselled, worship God and live in his image, and he will bless you with material prosperity which you can regard as a visible sign that you are living "in the Light."

11 If the Philadelphia Quakers emphasized order and a benevolent compassion for the poor more strongly than did the Boston Congregationalists, they were no less insistent on the intimate relation between religion and worldly affairs. While the getting of wealth was exalted, the ancient dilemma that the fruits of one's labors could rot on the tree of virtue was recognized. An extravagant passion for accumulation should be checked lest it destroy individual rectitude and tempt some to forget that their purpose was to erect temples of holiness and righteousness in the new land.

12 There was nothing uniquely American in all this. The idea of success was not produced by the frontier or by any other indigenous environmental force. America has always been a part of Western Civilization, with a particular indebtedness to English culture. Similar forces and ideas which shaped the means and goal of success in England operated in the new land. The colonies often lagged twenty or so years behind the mother country in painting, architecture, and furniture design. No such obedient imitation enslaved the idea of success. When the intellectual baggage of the colonists was unpacked in the new land, the idea of success took on its own independent existence. It paralleled, but did not imitate, developments in the mother country.

13 Cotton Mather and William Penn were drawing upon a two-hundred-year tradition of popular writing on the subject. The middle classes were on the move in England and they did not find themselves wanting in either advice or justification. In the eighty years after Elizabeth's accession to the throne in 1558, more than twenty works were printed which were devoted to success. Their message was the same—"put money in thy purse" by hard work, frugality, and the like. The tradesman who thrilled to Shakespearean adventures of warriors and kings could read in books of lesser art about the righteousness of material gain and count himself no less noble. From Hugh Latimer through William Perkins to Richard Baxter of the later seventeenth century—clergymen all—came the moral assurance, at once comforting but filled with possibilities of guilt, that one served God by laboring ceaselessly in an earthly calling.

14 When the theology-dominated seventeenth century gave way to the Enlightenment of the eighteenth, the presentation of success literature in England shifted with the times. Western Civilization was breaking out of its intellectual strait jacket and pouring its released energy into exciting discoveries based on reason and science. There was a neo-classic concern

for clarity, balance, and a delight in epigrams and aphorisms. The style of British success books swung into line with the prevailing literary fashion. Any tradesman with touches of elegance in his pen and a few fresh comments on life could satisfy his longing to be a writer. In a confusion of extended titles, gross plagiarism, and pirated editions, a sort of inter-library loan of ideas operated. They thieved from one another after the fashion of the time, plundered the rich storehouse of life about them, invoked a nimble classical allusion whenever possible—and often ignored the Bible as a source of authority.

15 In America, it was the eighteenth century which produced the most influential success apostle in the history of the American experience. In his writings on success, which were to be handed down by Americans from generation to generation, Benjamin Franklin took the position that wealth was the result of virtue. In his own life, and in other writings less influential, Franklin reflected the eighteenth-century patrician view that virtue was the result of wealth. A man of many parts, it is Franklin the success writer who is important for establishing the American heritage of the success idea.

16 Benjamin Franklin made a fortune in his own lifetime—then expanded it by telling others how he did it. He started on the road to success by writing about it. There was little that was original in his contribution. He did not link into new connections ideas which were swirling about in the air. As we have indicated, his bourgeois ideology had been sold wholesale in England long before his time and diffused to America where it already had a grip on the mind of the colonists. It was Franklin's significance, as the ideal eighteenth-century bourgeois, that he swept together into a number of writings the thinking of a nation. This was altogether fitting and proper, for unlike England, with its diversity of classes, America *was* a rising middle class to which this doctrine offered a wider appeal. The colonists were eager to get ahead in a nation on the make. When the time came, they broke away from the mother country to prove it.

17 "The supreme symbol of the American spirit is Benjamin Franklin," Harold Laski has maintained, "for he made a success of all that he attempted.... In his shrewdness, his sagacity, his devotion to making this world the thing that a kindly and benevolent soul would wish it to be, Franklin seems to summarize in a remarkable way the American idea of a good citizen." He was a hard-driving businessman, sage philosopher, pioneer scientist, inventor of a stove and an arm for retrieving books from high shelves, founder of a college, sire of three children (one illegitimate), representative of his country to France, a steady hand at the Constitutional Convention—the list seems endless. His accomplishments were fantastic even for an age which could boast a considerable number of great men. The emperor by popular acclaim of the character ethic, so crafty a manipulator and so shrewd a self-promoter was Franklin that success writers have served him up as a model in our own age of persuasion. A

man of action as well as ideas, it was typical of his versatility that toward the end of his life, when the gout and stone had him down, he longed for "a balloon sufficiently large to raise me from the ground . . . being led by a string held by a man walking on the ground."

18 One episode in his life, which he tells on himself, is particularly significant for American popular thought. The scene pictures a seedy youth strolling up Market Street in Philadelphia munching a great puffy roll of bread and convulsing his future wife by his ludicrous appearance. Described by Franklin with relish and pride, it remains to this day the most vivid and popular pictorial symbol of the social origins of the self-made man in America.

19 Franklin was both a mirror of his own age and a tutor to succeeding generations. That part of his writings which has exerted the most influence on popular thought and stimulated the widest appeal was devoted to success. The first was *The Way to Wealth*, a compilation of Poor Richard's maxims setting down the proper procedures for making money. Most of the sayings were freely borrowed, for Franklin was heir to a long tradition of writing on this subject. The second was his *Autobiography*, a case study of the first, which describes how an earnest young man employs these maxims to emerge "from the poverty and obscurity in which I was born and bred, to a state of affluence and some degree of reputation in the world. . . ."

20 What qualities should an ambitious youth cultivate in order to get ahead? Franklin exalts two. The first is *industry:* ("Early to bed, and early to rise, makes a man healthy, wealthy, and wise." "Then plough deep, while sluggards sleep, and you shall have corn to sell and to keep.") The second is *frugality:* ("A fat kitchen makes a lean will." "Rather go to bed supperless than rise in debt.") Conversely, idleness and extravagance produce their own results: ("Laziness travels so slowly, that poverty soon overtakes him.") The means and the goal were crisply stated in *Advice to Young Tradesmen:* "In short, the way to wealth, if you desire it, is as plain as the way to market. It depends chiefly on two words, *industry* and *frugality*; that is, waste neither *time* nor *money*, but make the best use of both."

21 To these cardinal virtues, eleven more were added in the *Autobiography:* temperance, silence, order, resolution, sincerity, justice, moderation, cleanliness, tranquillity, chastity, and humility (the latter being added to the original list after a Quaker friend "kindly informed" Franklin that he was generally thought proud, overbearing, and insolent in conversation). Always a practical man, Franklin went on to explain more specifically how these virtues might be achieved. He drew up a lined chart with the days of the week at the top and the virtues on the left-hand side. Each week he concentrated on one virtue and would ruthlessly fail himself by a black mark on the days that he did not measure up to the self-examination. In this manner, he reported, one could go through a complete course in thirteen weeks, and four courses in a year.

22   There is compulsion in Franklin's efforts to purge himself of any vices which might hinder his ascent in the world. There is a sense of overwhelming duty in his intense dedication. It is not simply expediency or naked self-interest which propels him forward. He is burning with a moral conviction that a good person *should* and *must* drive himself without mercy until the little chart stands clean of black marks. And his chart was there for everyone. He ignored the importance of luck, contacts, family influence, and native intelligence. The start was equal for all.

23   To tie Benjamin Franklin too closely to Puritanism, as some have done, is to slip over a significant point of distinction. Both Mather and Franklin were in the same boat, but one was rowing for the "Shoar of Eternal Blessedness" while the other was making for a different port. Both agreed that cultivating certain ascetic virtues led to wealth, but Mather justified it primarily as a way of worshipping God. Franklin also justified it as a means to a final end, but an end less concerned with religious implications. These ends were the leisure which money provided to enable him to do what he wanted in life, such as an opportunity for humanitarianism or enough leisure to study.

24   The distinction is revealed in the concept of the stewardship of wealth. Mather charged that every man should give at least a tenth part of his income to the service of God and the relief of the miserable. Franklin's benevolence was primarily secular. For Franklin it was all quite simple. "Poverty often deprives a man of all spirit and virtue: 'Tis hard for an empty bag to stand upright...." Since being poor is undesirable, train yourself in the qualities that make money. The justification for accumulating wealth is utilitarian and instrumental. It is a way to moral perfection, but not necessarily a way to worship God. One can use wealth to become healthy and wise, or to do good to others. But the final ends are up to every individual. In other words, what Franklin did was to preserve the means and immediate goal of wealth of Puritanism, but then went on to diminish its theological sanction by emphasizing a utilitarian justification. The consequence may have been unintended, but the result was that any man lacking in religious convictions could make money and still consider himself virtuous.

25   Franklin did, of course, believe in the existence of God and the power of Providence to intervene in the affairs of mankind. He immediately confessed in the opening pages of his autobiography that "now I speak of thanking God, I desire with all humility to acknowledge that I owe the mention'd happiness of my past life to his kind providence, which led me to the means I us'd and gave them success." It is true, "*God helps them that help themselves,*" but "do not depend too much upon your own *Industry,* and *Frugality,* and *Prudence,* though excellent Things, for they may all be blasted without the Blessing of Heaven...."

26   Franklin was in accord with the Puritan belief that God was a means to success, but broke with the tradition at that point. Success was a vis-

ible sign of God's favor, but the wealth that success brought was not primarily justified as a way of worshipping God. It was justified, in the ideology of the Enlightenment's emphasis on the environment, because it benefited mankind and because it gave the individual the opportunity to become virtuous in whatever way he wished to define that term. Franklin catches this feeling in an anecdote. A friend of his who was a preacher was coming to Philadelphia and had no lodgings. When Franklin offered accommodations at his house, he reported that the minister replied that "If I [Franklin] made that kind offer for Christ's sake, I should not miss of a reward. And I returned, 'Don't let me be mistaken; it was not for Christ's sake, but for your sake.'" Benevolence, then, was to be done in the name of a secular humanitarianism with man as the final purpose, not a ritual faith in God. Making money was justified because it made this possible and simply because it was easier to be virtuous with a full pocketbook than an empty one.

27   From a philosophical viewpoint, Franklin's contribution to the American heritage of the success idea was to invigorate what we have termed the secular interpretation of the character ethic. The tradition he represented cut the cables holding the idea of success to its religious anchor and sent it drifting into a sea of pragmatism.

28   One difficulty in understanding this great man is that for generations Americans quite naturally assumed that Franklin and Poor Richard were the same person. This impression was encouraged by the *Autobiography*, a lopsided account of his life. But the way Franklin actually lived his life and the way he said he lived it were not at all the same. In living his life, money for Franklin was obviously a means to an end. Money meant freedom, and freedom meant, among other things, leisure. Without money and the free time of leisure, how could one play the eighteenth-century gentleman of intellectual pretensions? The sage of Philadelphia longed to play the Enlightenment's model of the cultivated patrician, which is to say he followed the classic Greeks in their conception of the *summum bonum* in life. Franklin would have nodded approval to Aristotle's definition of happiness in *The Nicomachean Ethics*: "The active exercise of the mind in conformity with perfect goodness or virtue."

29   But it was Franklin the tough-minded bourgeois, not the cultivated patrician, who spoke directly to the needs of the American people. Franklin's success advice for popular consumption was composed in the spirit of a frontier pragmatist more interested in means than ends. In the *Autobiography* and *The Way to Wealth*, he does not reflect on what the final goals in life should be. In certain obscure places in his writings he did state that success has ruined many a man and that avarice could never lead to happiness. But compared to many writers of the nineteenth century who publicly instructed ambitious young men on how to get ahead, he appears to be a shallow materialist disinterested in the dangers of materialism and what the final goals in life should be.

30 From a symbolic viewpoint, Benjamin Franklin's influence was immense. The *Autobiography* kindled the fires of ambition in countless numbers of young men. He was not only America's first famous self-made man, but has remained, since the eighteenth century, the supreme symbol of the poor boy who made good. He represented the hope of rising in the world, the thrill of identification with the saga of rags to riches, the pride in a country where getting ahead was based on individual effort. Through the image of Benjamin Franklin, all America, by reason of hard work and diligence, not only stood before kings, but dined with one of them. Franklin's father would have liked that. He frequently recited to young Ben a proverb of Solomon's which reechoed down the corridors of the next century as a loud favorite of success writers: "Seest thou a man diligent in his business? He shall stand before kings; he shall not stand before mean men."

31 Because Franklin was a business success as well as a founding father of the Republic, he became that rare kind of hero suitable for occupational emulation as well as emotional devotion. And there always seemed to be more of the American in him than Washington or Jefferson. While Washington was remote and formidable and Jefferson a kind of well-bred intellectual of political theory and national expansion, Franklin was common, intimate, cozy, and practical.

32 Unlike most heroes in America, Benjamin Franklin was his own best public relations agent. The first in the tradition of successful men who told their own story, Franklin was the Johnny Appleseed of the idea of success. The author of a best-selling almanac and the most popular autobiography in American literature, he cast his seeds across the meadows of the American mind. He became, as Hawthorne noted, "the counselor and household friend of almost every family in America." Perhaps there is some validity in the claim, made towards the end of the nineteenth century, that *The Way to Wealth* had been printed and translated more often up to that time than any other work from an American pen. For Franklin was not only a tutor to those who actively aspired to success; he was a mentor to whom other writers on the subject went to school.

33 As America moved into the nineteenth century, two basic themes were already running through the character ethic. Both themes expressed agreement about the means to money-making, but disagreed on the justification. Cotton Mather, and the more religious writers, justified the accumulation of wealth primarily as a way of glorifying God. Benjamin Franklin, and those of a more secular persuasion, justified success by a philosophy which owed little or nothing to divine sanction. The great German scholar, Max Weber, had assumed that by Franklin's time the "religious basis" of "Puritan worldly asceticism ... had died away." But, in fact, throughout the history of the nineteenth century a religious as well as a secular basis for the character ethic was vigorously supported. The overwhelming majority of success writers made their choice between one or the other of these philosophical positions.

Points for Review and Discussion

1. Summarize the main tenets of Cotton Mather's thinking on the subject of work and success.
2. Summarize the main tenets of Ben Franklin's thinking on the subject of work and success.
3. Huber argues that it's a mistake "to tie Benjamin Franklin too closely to Puritanism" (¶ 23). What reasons does he give in support of this view?

⁌ Questions for Writing

1. Huber writes that Franklin's tradition "cut the cables holding the idea of success to its religious anchor and sent it drifting into a sea of pragmatism." (¶ 27). The metaphor of drifting suggests lack of focus and general aimlessness. Do you believe contemporary ideas of success lack focus? Give reasons for your answer.
2. "[Franklin] ignored the importance of luck, contacts, family influence, and native intelligence. The start was equal for all." (¶ 22). This time-honored faith that in America the starting line is the same for everybody supports the stereotypes discussed in Chapter 2 of this book. Choose one of those stereotypes—for example, the stereotype of the jobless person as lazy and undeserving—and explain why "the start was equal for all" tends to support it.
3. For many generations Ben Franklin "remained . . . the supreme symbol of the poor boy who made good" (¶ 30). But lately other symbols have commenced to replace him. Who in your opinion functions now as "the supreme symbol" of the possibility of starting at the bottom and rising to the top? What "virtues" might this hero or heroine list as all-important when setting down success maxims of the kind Franklin listed in his autobiography?

WHERE TO GET RICH
Russell Conwell

A great popular entertainment in the late nineteenth and early twentieth centuries was listening to lectures—out of doors in tents or in large public auditoriums. A favorite theme of the lecturers was moneymaking and the American dream. And arguably the most famous speaker on this subject was Russell Conwell.

Born in 1843 on a humble farm in western Massachusetts, Conwell worked his way through Yale, became a lawyer and world traveler, served as a colonel in the Civil War and joined the ministry in the late 1870s. With the fortune he amassed from lecturing, he founded Temple University and three charitable hospitals in Philadelphia, and, in addition, provided college scholarships for more than 10,000 indigent but ambitious young men.

Conwell's best-known lecture, "Acres of Diamonds," was published in various forms during and after his lifetime. (He died in 1925.) He gave the lecture no less than 6000 times in his career, earning millions in fees and inspiring countless listeners with visions of backyard riches. Most versions of the talk began—like the one below—with a story about "an ancient Persian" that Conwell claimed to have heard from a tour guide. They went on to answer the question, "Where can I get rich?"

1   Many hundred years ago there lived near the shore of the river Indus an ancient Persian by the name of Ali Hafed. He dwelt in a beautiful cottage, from which he could look down the mountain side upon the magnificent river, and even away to the great sea. He had a lovely wife and intelligent children. He had an extensive farm, with fields of grain, orchards of fruit, gardens of flowers, and miles of forest. He owed no one, and had money at interest. He was a wealthy and contented man. Wealthy because he was contented, and contented because he was wealthy. One day this old Persian was visited by one of the wise priests of Budda. He was sincerely welcomed, and given the best which the house and farm produced. One evening the old priest sat by Ali Hafed's fireside, and told the farmer how this world was made. He said that this great solid globe was once a mere bank of fog, and that the great overruling Spirit thrust his finger into the bank of fog. Then he began slowly to turn his finger about in a circle within the fog, and gradually increased the speed of his finger until in its swiftness it whirled that bank of fog into a solid ball of fire. Then he sent it shooting through the universe, burning its way through other

---

From Russell Conwell, *Acres of Diamonds* (1887).

cosmic banks of fog, condensing them into floods of rain, which cooled the outward crust of this great ball of fire. Then its internal flames burst the cooling crust and threw up the hills and the mountain ranges and made the beautiful valleys. How the world became flat afterwards could not be discovered. But, when the internal fires burst out, if in the flood of rain the melted substance cooled very quickly, it became granite; that which cooled more slowly became copper; that which cooled less quickly formed silver, and the last to congeal became gold. Then the first beams of sunlight condensed on the world's surface into diamonds. Diamonds were but congealed or condensed beams of sunshine. The old priest told Ali Hafed that a drop of sunlight the size of his thumb was worth more than large mines of copper, silver, or gold; that with one he could buy many farms like his; that with a handful he could buy a province, and with a mine of diamonds he could purchase a whole kingdom.

2 Ali Hafed went to his bed that night a poor man. He had not lost anything. But he was poor because he was discontented, and discontented because he thought he was poor. Poverty is only discontent. Early the next morning the Persian farmer awoke the priest, and anxiously inquired where he could find a mine of diamonds. "What do you want of diamonds?" inquired the astonished priest.

3 "I wish to be rich and place my children on thrones through the influence of their wealth."

4 "All you have to do," replied the priest of Budda, "is to go and search until you find them."

5 "But where shall I go?" asked the eager farmer.

6 "Go anywhere—North, South, East, or West—anywhere."

7 "How shall I know when I have found the place?"

8 "When you find a river running over white sands between high mountain ranges, in those white sands you will find diamonds," answered the priest.

9 "But is there any such river?" asked Ali Hafed the Persian.

10 "Oh, yes, plenty of them. Many mines of diamonds are yet undiscovered. All you have to do is to start out and go somewhere—away, away."

11 "I'll go," said the farmer, and turned hastily to make his preparations. He sold his farm at a forced price, collected his money which had been at interest; he left his fine family in charge of a neighbor, and away he went in search of diamonds. He began his real search at the Mountains of the Moon away beyond Arabia. He came down into Egypt. He wandered around through Palestine. Years went by. At last, his money gone, himself in starvation and rags, he stood on the great bay on the coast of Spain—no diamonds, no friends, no property, no hope. On that sad day an immense tidal wave swept up the shore. Poor Ali Hafed could not resist the awful temptation to throw himself into the incoming tide. So he sank beneath that foaming crest, never to rise in this life again.

12   The guide's story seemed to be completed, and he stopped my camel to arrange the baggage in the train, which had become displaced. The story did not seem to have much point to it, and I decided to ask him why he told all that to me. But that was the first story I ever read or ever heard told in which the hero was killed in the first chapter. He had told me only the first chapter. He soon came back to lead my camel, and went on with the tale.

13   Ali Hafed's successor on the old Indian farm was an observant man and contented. He had no ambition to wander away for diamonds. One day he led his camel into the garden to drink. As the animal put its nose into the clear water of the brook Ali Hafed's successor noticed a flash of light from the white sands of the shallow stream. The gleam came from a very black stone. He reached down and picked up the stone. A clear eye of crystal strangely varying in its brilliant hues shone in one side of the pebble. The old farmer took it to the house and left it on a shelf near the earthen hearth where in cool weather they made the fire. Then he went to his rice-field and forgot all about it.

14   A few days later the same old priest who had instructed Ali Hafed how the world was made and where diamonds were to be found called to visit the new owner of the farm. The moment he entered the room he noticed that flash of light from the mantel or shelf. He rushed to it in great excitement: He shouted: "Here is a diamond! here is a diamond! Has Ali Hafed returned?"

15   "Oh, no; Ali Hafed has not returned," said the host, "and that is not a diamond, either. That is nothing but a stone I found out in my garden."

16   "I tell you," said the priest, "I know a diamond when I see it: I tell you that is a genuine diamond!"

17   Together they rushed out into the garden. They stirred up the white sands with their fingers, and lo! other gems more valuable, more beautiful than the first came to the surface. Thus, said the guide, were discovered the ancient diamond mines of Golconda.

18   The story was finished. But the guide had the moral yet to add. He took off his Turkish red cap and swung it in the air, struck an oratorical attitude, while the thin sash which had bound his head as a turban came unrolling to the ground, and exclaimed: "Had Ali Hafed remained at home—had he dug in his own garden, or in his own fields—instead of poverty, starvation, death in a strange land he would have had *Acres of Diamonds*. For every shovelful of that old farm, as acre after acre was sifted over, revealed gems with which to decorate the crowns of emperors and moguls."

19   Surely "Acres of Diamonds" might have been his own had Ali Hafed stayed at home and used his ordinary powers of observation. Acres of diamonds ... can be had for the taking; but, alas! so many wander away, away, and fail of finding anything of value. Can I show you where your diamonds are? I sincerely believe I can.

20   Where can [you] get rich? Right where you are. At home. Not somewhere else. Not a man has secured great wealth by going away who might

not have secured as much by some other means if he had stayed at home. To secure wealth is an honorable ambition, and is one great test of a person's usefulness to others. Money is power. Every good man and woman ought to strive for power, to do good with it when obtained. Tens of thousands of men and women get rich honestly. But they are often accused by an envious, lazy crowd of unsuccessful persons of being dishonest and oppressive. I say, Get rich, get rich! But get money honestly, or it will be a withering curse. Money being power, it ought to be entirely in the hands of good men and women. It is now more largely so than many are willing to admit. We hear of the speculator, and the mine operator, and the gambler, who, like a burning meteor, crosses our vision with his cursed ill-gotten gains, which burn him as he flies; but not much is said of the thousands on thousands of solid men and women whose millions in the aggregate completely hide the gambler's fortune. One hundred men at least get rich honestly where one succeeds in filling his pockets with stolen, blood-stained gold. The very laws of nature and social life all set against dishonorable methods, and give a double momentum to rightful means.

21 The person who has a great deal to sell will get much money. He who can confer great benefit is entitled to great profit. He who offers pure diamonds in the market will get wealth in return naturally and honorably. Nearly every man and nearly every woman has some talent, some possession, some valuable gift, which the world needs. God has given each many acres of diamonds for which the world anxiously waits.

22 Men should and do receive an honest equivalent for the good they confer. The exceptions are talked about a great deal, and hence thoughtless ones dream only of obtaining wealth without giving anything for it. But the great rule is ever the same. He that gives the most is entitled to the most. He who can do the most good, or give the most happiness, should be and is the richest man. A little thought and a little exercise of common sense will soon convince any reader that such is the case. He who works along the smooth lines of God's laws and keeps in the open highway of conscientious duty is not often mentioned. He may accumulate millions, and yet make no sensation. Because he is right. It is impossible for the newspapers to tell of men's good deeds. They do not think of doing that. The pure love, the sweet self-sacrifice, the truthfulness, the honorable dealings and the flood of honestly settled accounts are too common things to be told in a newspaper. So we always read of the exceptions. The more startling strange the exception the more we hear about it. If you are going to get rich, as I mean you shall, let not your heart be moved from the sure lines of success by such sensational rare exceptions.

23 The way to get rich is to have something to sell which people want. The way to obtain the good things you desire is to have something equally valuable to exchange for them. Those things you possess, and could quickly gain the others if you only knew your own wealth. A man in Genoa lived on a pittance for years, groaned in his poor attic and made

common fellowship with the rats; in his unlocked trunk, given him by a sailor uncle, was a fortune in gold. He had never examined the trunk underneath the sailor clothes.

24   A lady in Baltimore lost a valuable diamond bracelet at a ball, and thought it was stolen from the pocket of her cloak. Years afterwards she washed the steps of the Peabody Institute to get money to purchase food. One day she cut up an old worn and ragged cloak in order to get material to make a hood for her head. Lo, there in the lining of the cloak was the flashing diamond bracelet. She was worth thirty-five hundred dollars. So long as she did not know she had it she was as poor as though no diamonds were in her cloak. But yet she owned them all those years. That we all own diamonds, or own the means to purchase wealth and happiness, there is no question. It would be a waste of time in discussing self-evident propositions to talk of that.

25   We all have riches. The all-important question is, Where are they? We can at once get one step nearer the solution of the difficult problem, and say, At home! Not away off at the Moon Mountains; not on Palestine's shores; not on Spain's inhospitable promontories; but at home. Your wealth is close to the spot where you sit to read these pages; perhaps within your fingers' reach. It may be at the shop, or in the store, in your attic, cellar, or back-yard. But not far from you now is all the wealth your heart should desire, and more than you will ever need. Do you mean money and property? Yes. That is just what I mean. It requires but little knowledge of the experience of successful men to see that thousands of others had just the same opportunity to acquire wealth that they had.

26   The demands of mankind are always in advance of the supply. Yet the supply is always close to the touch of many fingers and under the eyesight of many unobservant possessors. One man found a fortune in his coal-bin as he examined a piece of coke accidentally made. Another found it in his potato cellar while examining the difference in the number of sprouts on different kinds of potatoes. Another became rich out of the fish culture which followed his discovery of trout in a streamlet which passed through his back-yard. One became a railroad magnate on the profits of the soap he found could be extracted from a waste heap of ashes over the garden wall. One acquired a fortune by watching his baby boy manipulate a cradle. Another found paint in the mineral deposit at the bottom of his well. Another found a mine of emery while sweeping off his cellar wall. One became a millionaire by watching the effect of certain medical appliances on his aged horse.

27   Among the millionaires who in 1886 held their heads above the usual current of society in New York, Philadelphia and Boston, I find that at least ninety-four out of every hundred found their first fortune in some humble place at home. Look at the list of things which have made men millionaires in those three cities, and the proportion of rich men is just as great in the other districts of our nation. Here are the foundations of wealth: rats, dogs, fence-posts, birds' eggs, blacking, cheese, whey, apple

grafts, limestone, boiling spring, cooking, old bones, binding old files of papers, extract of lilacs and roses, plaster of hemlock tar, ice house, cement, reapers, soup ladle, hairpins, watchcase, dried apples, fancy stock, hens' eggs, plows, shoe nails, delivery of groceries, oil lamps, bricks, weaving, ventilation, locks, carpet yarn, advertising, gossamers, faucets, window glass, books, grist mill, ferry boats, cog-wheels, jack-knife, eye-glass, buttons, teeth-filling, traps, music, tinware, wall paper, silkworms, street cars, spices, clothes-pins and fly-traps. In all these cases the fortune was found at home. The instances could be multiplied from the history of other cities and countries, and prove beyond any question that every person's fortune is in the shop where he works, in the store where he waits, in the house where he sits, or on the farm where he cultivates the soil. Acres of diamonds flash all about, inviting the owner, and for which the world eagerly waits. One of the richest men in Massachusetts told me in 1879 that he made his fortune watching his wife try on her ill-fitting bonnet. It led him to the manufacture of bonnet-frames. A young lady in Hartford, Conn., improvised a button fastening for her dress which, when applied to the manufacture of sleeve-buttons at Attleboro, Mass., led to the wealth of herself and husband a few years later. Your riches are within your present reach. Yet every one thinks he could do better somewhere else. All look away—away to some imagined Eldorado or Isles of the Blessed, while the gems they seek are at their feet. The shepherds of Brazil organized a party of emigrants to go to California to dig gold, and took along a handful of clear pebbles to play checkers with on the voyage. After arriving in Sacramento, the emigrants discovered, after they had given or thrown nearly all the pebbles away, that they were all diamonds. They hastened home to find that the mines were taken up by others and sold to the local government.

28   Professor Agassiz, it is said, was greatly amused by an anecdote of a Pennsylvania farmer, and the professor told it to his summer class in mineralogy the year before his death. He laughed long and heartily whenever he referred to it. The farmer owned many hundred acres of unprofitable rocks and woods, and concluded to get into a more profitable position. His cousin was collecting coal oil, and agreed to employ the farmer if he would study up the whole process. So the agriculturalist devoted himself to the study of mineralogy, coal measures and coal oil deposits. He studied long and hard. He experimented and consulted wise men. Then when sufficiently skilled, he sold his farm for a few hundred dollars, and went into the coal oil business two hundred miles away. He had been gone but a few weeks from his old farm before his successor discovered at a place where the cattle drank a wonderful flood of coal oil which the previous owner had ignorantly and unsuccessfully tried to drain off. The oil wells on that farm have since made many men and women wealthy. The former owner is still poor.

29   A professor of mineralogy in Massachusetts inherited the homestead, and sold it to obtain funds to go prospecting for copper in Wisconsin. The

farm he sold held a valuable silver mine, which was discovered in plain sight in a rock at the end of the door-yard wall. The richest Nevada gold and silver mine was owned and claimed by a man who sold out for forty-two dollars to get money to pay his passage to the Dutch Flat mines. One of the salt mines of Western New York was owned by a grocer who, hearing of a successful salt well in the next county, ignorantly sold out his store and farm to move to the salt region. A very successful manufacturer of steel pens in Philadelphia sold out one unprofitable part of his business and thought it a wonderful trade. The portion he sold has made the purchaser rich. The former owner is abjectly poor. A bedridden cripple, of Worthington, Mass., was obliged to employ his weary hours on a sewing machine and little embroidery figures. He invented the improved machine needle and a button-hook, which, however, appeared later patented by another, but he received his share of the profits. He earned and received more than any other healthy man in the town. He was compelled to look for any gain close to his chair.

30   Men are continually becoming rich out of the trifles which others threw away. All the waste ashes and slag of the iron furnaces are now being worked over at immense profit; and the scraps of the shoe-shop, the iron filings of the machine-shop, the cotton waste of the mill, and the waste seed are all sources of present wealth. The sewers of Paris were richer than mines of gold to the early contractors, who began to use their chemical wealth.

31   Not a tree in your grounds, not a stone in your well, not a plant in your window, not an animal about your farm, not a waste piece of metal or clothing in your lumber-room, but could make you rich if you understood its suggestions and possibilities. There is not a piece of household furniture, nor a kitchen utensil, but will soon be improved by some one. There is not an article of food on your table but is demanded in some different form. There is not a vegetable in your garden, a kind of grain in your field, or a specimen of fruit in your orchard, but which is capable of many unknown uses to civilized man, in the discovery of which, wealth must flow to that public benefactor. There is a great need of the compositions and improvements you can make, and the world will enrich you if you do your duty.

32   A man sat in a chair in Boston, and said, according to the address at his funeral: "What can I do to help mankind?" The chair he occupied was expensive, but uncomfortable. He complained about it. A friend said, "I should think it would be a good thing to begin by getting up an easier and cheaper chair." His hand was on the arm of the chair. "I'll do it!" he exclaimed, leaping up and examining the chair in close detail.

33   "Rattan would be better," he said, and, on inquiry, he found plenty of it thrown away by the East India merchant ships, whose cargoes were wrapped in it. He began the manufacture of rattan goods, and now the variety coming from the prosperous factories is a continual astonishment to the world. When he was sighing for work and for great possessions his

hand was on the chair. How many thousands like him place their hands directly on a pile of diamonds and weep because there is no wealth in sight for them! The only reason why he became so rich and they remain so poor is simply because he looked for his riches close at hand, while they are still seeking for them beyond the horizon of their vision.

Points for Review and Discussion

1. The main theme of "Where to Get Rich" is that riches are near at hand. What reasons does Conwell give for this belief?
2. In Conwell's view, what happens to people who forget the truth that the riches they seek "are at their feet" (¶ 27)? How does he account for this fate?
3. "There is a great need of the compositions and improvements you can make, and the world will enrich you if you do your duty" (¶ 31). Explain what Conwell means here by "doing your duty."

•◦ Questions for Writing

1. Conwell tells his audience that "the very laws of nature" (¶ 20) prohibit people from getting rich dishonestly, and he asserts confidently that money is "now more largely in the hands of good men and women . . . than many are willing to admit" (¶ 20). Where does this confidence of his come from? Do you see any relation between it and the Puritan heritage or the maxims of Ben Franklin or both? Explain your answer.
2. "He who can confer great benefit is entitled to great profit" (¶ 21). Imagine that Russell Conwell returned to life and witnessed the making of the great fortunes of the 1980s (see Kevin Phillips, pages 93–110). Would he regard these chief executive officers as people who confer great benefit or would he view them more negatively? Base your answer on the definition of "great benefit" implicit in Conwell's talk.
3. A lecture like "Where to Get Rich" doubtless could not hold 6000 audiences today, even if it didn't have to compete with visual media, rock concerts, and the like. Why so? Is it that we are smarter or less naive than Conwell's audiences? Or are there other reasons why we would reject his themes? Write a page exploring this topic.

Harold Albert, the Richest Man in the World, and Louie, His Wife

Tony Parker

Generalizations about *the* American attitude toward riches are risky, of course. The country is big enough to embrace a multitude of contradictions, and the national uniformity implied by such a phrase doesn't exist. Tony Parker, widely considered to be England's best interviewer, came to this country in 1987 in search of a truly representative American place—an "ordinary" American town filled with "ordinary" Americans. He settled on Bird, Kansas (population under 2000) as a place that filled the bill.

But the interviews he published in *Bird, Kansas* (1989) revealed many attitudes that didn't jibe with foreigners' conceptions of "American character." In the interview below with Harold and Louie Albert, the richest people in this part of the world, Tony Parker encounters attitudes toward personal wealth that obviously cause him some surprise.

<blockquote>HAROLD ALBERT, the richest man in the world,
and LOUIE, his wife</blockquote>

Their house was one of the smallest and plainest in Bird, Kansas, halfway down South Adams Street. Outside it stood an ordinary Buick pickup truck: last year's model or the year before's.

He was tall, long-legged and wiry: he wore a check shirt and blue twill overalls, the legs tucked into the tops of cowboy-style calf-length boots. She was short, in a plain brown blouse and a shapeless navy skirt. Her gray hair was cut in a schoolgirl fringe. She had bare legs, and white canvas tennis shoes on her feet. A big table in the sitting room was piled with newspapers and magazines, and there were three chairs and an old settee. Several cardboard boxes were scattered around on the floor, full of files and papers. Under a side window a large extractor fan in the wall was motionless, not working: instead a rattling fan swung noisily from side to side at the far end of the room.

> HAROLD: This here's Louie my wife. She ain't feeling too good today, she's got trouble with some bad teeth. She'll just set there and listen to us, but she doesn't feel up to talking much.
> LOUIE: I'll say something if I want.
> HAROLD: You bet.
> LOUIE: If you say something wrong or I don't agree with.

From Tony Parker, *Bird, Kansas* (1989).

HAROLD: Shouldn't be all that long before you start speaking then. I didn't know after when I met you in the library that day whether you'd come around visiting with us or not. I've not had an education and I don't talk all that good but I'll tell you anything you think's interesting you want to know. About our early life and everything, you said?
LOUIE: How'd you know that?
HAROLD: He told me it one time last week when I saw him on Main.
LOUIE: You didn't tell me you saw him on Main.
HAROLD: Oh, him and me we've met a time or two. Once when him and the Sheriff were drinking coffee with Lester, and one time when you came into Dorothy's with that woman right?
LOUIE: That's something to say, that's no way to speak about his wife.
HAROLD: It wasn't his wife, it was a lady he maybe doesn't want folk to know about.
LOUIE: It's no place to take her to isn't Dorothy's, if he doesn't want folk to know about her. Who was it?
HAROLD: I don't know who it was.
LOUIE: Oh sure.
HAROLD: Listen, that's all I'm saying about her. You just set there and give your teeth a chance, else they'll never get better. You should have had them fixed sooner like I said.
LOUIE: They weren't so bad sooner.
HAROLD: OK well you tell him about your teeth later, only right now I'm going to tell him about my early life OK? Well now: the first thing is I'm 74 years of age and she's a little bit older.
LOUIE: Only a little bit older.
HAROLD: Only a little bit right. And I wasn't born here in Bird.
LOUIE: I was.
HAROLD: I was born on a farm out near Milton Reservoir six miles east of here, and she—
LOUIE: I was born right here in Bird: number 238 South Third only it ain't there no more.
HAROLD: It used to be South Third but now it's South Jefferson.
LOUIE: And the house ain't there no more, there was a fire.
HAROLD: She was a local girl but I wasn't. My Mom and Pa, they was simple folk: I was their eldest son, but they had a girl older than me. They ran what was a grocer's store on the corner of Main and Lincoln, which was then Sixth Street. It's gone long since, it's now Joe Hagan's garage. First of all I had to get me some education, but I wasn't much of a one for schooling: when I got up to eighth grade which was when I was 14, I decided that was enough for me. So I asked my Ma and Pa if I could go work with my sister in the store instead, and they said yes, so that's what I did. I just worked ordinary in the store, I took care of the eggs and the potatoes and the sugar, and I packed things in and out as well. I got paid 35 cents an hour plus four dollars a week pocket money, and out of that I had to give a half back to my folks to pay for my keep. In those days at the store we used to sell 100 cases eggs a week, 100 cases cream, and maybe 75 or 80 those big bags of flour.
LOUIE: There wasn't all the fancy things you can buy in packets those days, you just did your home cooking with the ordinary things you could get.
HAROLD: And that's how we met, one day when she came by the store for some eggs.

LOUIE: Sugar. It was sugar I came by for, not eggs.

HAROLD: OK sugar, eggs, it's not important.

LOUIE: I was still at school, and my Mom sent me into the store to get some sugar for to bring home after school. And I took to going into the store to meet him when I was on my way home from school other days too.

HAROLD: She didn't talk much those days either, she just used to stand there while I talked to her. I was supposed to be working, carrying things around, and she used to stand there while I talked to her. She got me into trouble for talking and not getting on with my work.

LOUIE: I never got no chance to talk because of how much he talked all the time. He used to tease me and make up tales to tell me about things he'd done and things he'd seen, see if I believed him. If I did he used to laugh and tell me I must be pretty dumb if I'd believed him. To tell you the honest truth, I didn't really care for him at all.

HAROLD: If you didn't really care for me, how come you used to stop by so often then?

LOUIE: Only 'cause I'd got nothing else to do.

HAROLD: Well, you had nothing else to do for six years. That's how long it took me talking to her, to persuade her to marry me.

LOUIE: I never knew if he really meant it or not, what's why. I never knew if he really meant anything he said to me at all. Lordy, fifty-two years ago that was.

HAROLD: Fifty-two years ago that we was married, that's not bad for these days. I must have meant what I said then, when I said I wanted to be married with you.

LOUIE: You said lots of things you didn't mean though. Do you know one thing he said to me? I can remember it to this day, he said if I married him I'd never want for a new dress. And one day after we was married, I said to him I needed a new dress and I wanted a new dress, and he'd told me I'd never want for one. You know what he said? He said he couldn't afford to buy no new dress for me, so I'd better stop wanting it, then I wouldn't be wanting for a dress.

HAROLD: Well that's how it was then. You could have a new dress now if you wanted one, but in those days things was hard. When we got married, my folks said we could have the running of the store with my sister. It wasn't enough to keep all of us, but they could go back and manage for themselves on the farm if we took the store. So that's exactly what we did: we got married in the church in the morning, then after we'd had something to eat everyone together, then her and me and my sister, we went back to the store and we opened it up and it was business as usual for the rest of the day. And that's how it was, from that day onwards all we did was work.

LOUIE: We bought this little house here, and we ran the store a few years: then his sister, she didn't want to go on doing that any more so she sold out her share to us. Then it was even harder work, we had to go careful a long long time didn't we?

HAROLD: We sure did, we had some pretty hard times too.

LOUIE: We had some hard times, but there was one thing we always did, we always paid our bills. Whether it was for the store or for ourselves, we always paid our bills on the day. We're still that way, if there's one thing I don't like to see in the mail box it's a bill. I just feel it shouldn't ever be there: it ought to have been we paid it on the nail when we bought something.

HAROLD: The other thing we did those days was no matter how little money there was, we'd always kept some of it aside for savings. She's always been pretty good at figuring so she looked after the money, and she looked after it real good. We kept our prices low in the store: we didn't go after making big profits out of folk, so we had a small business but a regular business. And even in the hardest times, she could figure how much of a quantity of something we should buy, how much we should get when we sold it and how much we'd have left afterwards to live on.

LOUIE: And how much we could put by. The hardest times were after the Depression in what they called the Dust Bowl Years: those were the hardest time, I reckon.

HAROLD: Those were terrible times, the 1930s and through up to the beginning of the 1940s. It was like the whole of the state of Kansas was blowing right away. I can tell you, life was as tough as a boot. I've seen Main Street three o'clock of an afternoon, the air was so dark with dust you couldn't see your hand this close in front of your face. Automobiles was all stalled up with dust in the engines and wouldn't run: you had to have a kerchief over your mouth just so's you could breathe. Real tough. But in those days you took things like that in your stride, you thought nothing of them.

LOUIE: You might have thought nothing of them, but I didn't. They blew for days, you had to put wet sheets and blankets up at all the windows there to try and block up the cracks and stop it coming in. You never could though, it got into everywhere: on and on it went blowing, one day after the next.

HAROLD: You know, that dust used to get so thick on the backs of the cows, when it rained it made it solid. And seeds were in it, I've seen cattle had thistles growing on their backs.

LOUIE: That's an old farmers' tale, I've heard him tell that story a hundred times or more. It ain't true.

HAROLD: It is too, I've seen it, I've seen it myself.

LOUIE: It used to be just you knew a man who'd seen it.

HAROLD: Well still, those dust storms they were really something all right.

LOUIE: They really were. But we survived.

HAROLD: By hard work. And this isn't no farmers' tale, this is true: the only time we shut the store the whole year round was two hours at noon on Christmas Day, so we could eat our Christmas dinner. And people used to come by Christmas afternoon, they'd say "Where were you? I thought something was wrong, I was by an hour ago for some butter and the store was closed."

LOUIE: Hard work but we enjoyed it.

HAROLD: Every minute.

LOUIE: No not every minute: I didn't enjoy it when you went away with the truck and left me on my own to mind the store.

HAROLD: I bought me this truck, and I figured if I made the trip to Colorado for good fresh vegetable produce myself, it'd soon come out a mighty bit cheaper than paying someone else to haul it for me. Chiefly tomatoes, peaches and green string beans, and some fruits too. It was something over 600 miles the round trip, but most times you could do it in the day, if you started in the morning early enough.

LOUIE: And sometimes to Texas you used to go, for grapefruit. That used to take him all day and a night to get there, and the same to come back. I used to think he often went only because he enjoyed driving his truck.

HAROLD: Oh, it was a real classy vehicle that one was: a huge big thing, the biggest around here for miles. It was called a Diamond T. In all the years I had it, I can't once remember it ever broke down.

LOUIE: That was because you looked after it so good.

HAROLD: I did all the servicing of it myself. I like mechanical things, I always have. I learned it from watching other people right from when I was a kid: if I saw an automobile mechanic in a repair shop, I'd ask him could I watch what he was doing. That way I picked up how to do it myself. Same with everything in the house: the plumbing, the electrics, the sewering, everything that needed doing, I always did it myself. I still do. Out in the garage there I've got all the tools necessary to do everything could ever want doing. Whatever it is, I can fix it. It makes me happy that I'm like that.

LOUIE: And obstinate.

HAROLD: What's obstinate got to do with it?

LOUIE: Obstinate's got everything to do with it. Tell him about that air-conditioning plant we've got in the wall there.

HAROLD: What's there to tell about it? It only needs taking down and putting together again.

LOUIE: That air-conditioning there, it's getting on for fifty years old now: it was one of the first ones like that that they ever invented. When he put it in, it was just about as modern as you could get. Now it's broken down, and there ain't a single person left living can fix it.

HAROLD: Except me.

LOUIE: OK except you: so why don't you fix it?

HAROLD: I'm going to, I keep telling you: or if I can't fix it, I'm going to put a whole new system in.

LOUIE: You're too old to put a whole new system in. Why not just call someone up and ask them to come along and put a new system in?

HAROLD: Pay some young feller 30 dollars an hour to do something I can do myself?

LOUIE: You see what I mean by obstinate? We could have a whole new house now if we wanted to, with a brand-new system in it.

HAROLD: OK go ahead let's have a whole new house: only any time we talk about that, it's always you says you don't want to move, you want to stay here.

LOUIE: I don't want to move, why should I want to move, we're happy right here.

HAROLD: So then OK you'll have to wait until I get around to fixing the air-conditioning.

LOUIE: And how long's it going to be?

HAROLD: I don't know how long it's going to be. Let's talk now about when the oil came into our lives huh?

LOUIE: When the oil came into our lives, that was when all the headaches came too. I sometimes think that.

TP: *What happened?*

HAROLD: Well it was a strange strange time at the beginning I can tell you, it sure was. There'd been talk for years, you know, that there was oil under some of the land around these parts. Off and on over the years one or other of the oil companies had come and done a little test drilling, but nobody ever found no oil so they went away and forgot about it again. Then when one of them came six or seven years back once more, and said they were going to start looking again, no one paid much attention to them. They drilled a bit here and they drilled a bit there, and then one day they found they had a hole that had some oil. So they said they were going to make a proper run with it, and if they found one that made ten barrels of oil a day, then it'd just about be worth their while and they'd pump it. We had some little piece of land we owned ourselves out that way, and they said they'd do a test drill there too. And that one, the one on our land, before we knew what was happening, it was making not ten barrels a day but fifty barrels a day: every day, bang, bang, bang, just like that. So they sank another one on our land and then another one. Every single one of them produced oil, some of them a lot and some of them a big lot. Came the time we had a total of 24 wells on our land, and one of them alone was producing 400 barrels of oil a day. That's going on towards nine ten thousand barrels almost a day. For each oil well they pump on your land, they give you a royalty of one-eighth of what it produces, day by day according to the price of oil.

So that was it, there we were, we had a very big strike on our land. There's very few times anyone ever strikes as lucky as that. One of the oil company men, he told me they reckon on average it's once in maybe 500 times they drill that they find a well that produces anything at all. So that's how it was, we had all them wells and they was all producing, day after day after day. It got to be called Little Saudi Arabia out there. The type of oil, its gravity, its quality and that it was so near the surface and easy to pump out: all these things were what made it such a big find. They said even after 5 years it was still only 200 feet down from the surface. Well, it's starting to go down a little now, and it won't go on forever, nothing ever does. Oil prices is going down too, so I don't reckon it can go on that much longer now.

LOUIE: We didn't reckon ever that it was going to go on much longer. No one else had that much oil found, but some had some: and some of those who did, they lived like it *was* going to go on forever. But we lived just like we'd always lived, that was all. And then one day the local newspaper printed a story about it. It was nothing much, no big splash about it: and then one of the Kansas City daily newspapers got on to it, and they printed a story about it. And then one of the New York papers, and Washington, and Los Angeles, and Houston Texas, and Alberta Canada: and somebody even told us some newspapers in Europe. Which ones and where, we never did know: but what we did know was that letters started to come, cables, long-distance telephone calls, it was like suddenly everybody in the world knew about it and was begging us for our help. Some of the letters, they were ten pages long: people sent us letters from their doctors telling us their whole medical histories. Or they'd get their kids to write: "My Daddy just died, and my Mommy said you'd got a big lot of money and you sounded to be good kind people, please will you send her some money to help her."

HAROLD: One guy wrote us he needed a half a million dollars that's all, to build this church he had in mind some place in South America. Or another time we had a cable, all it said was "Desperate for money, please send all you can spare" and nothing else but that and a name and address. I mean how do folk think someone's going to respond to something like that?

LOUIE: Sad thing was you know, we reckoned some of the stories people told us about how much they needed money was true. But it was just like one of them avalanches, they kept on and on coming, and how could you tell? You'd need your whole life to sort out which was which, true or false: and we're not that kind of folk, we're just simple people and always have been. It got so bad, we just used to set us down here and look at all the letters we'd divided up into piles: those we thought were really sad and had big troubles, and which a little bit less, and those who sounded like folk who just thought they'd like money for some scheme or other they'd got. And every one of the piles, they all got bigger and bigger and we felt we were getting sick, it was making us feel like that, worrying about how to decide. So then one day someone said to us we couldn't go on like that, there was no way we could ever decide who to help and who to not to: what we should do was think of something else instead to do with our money, throw all the letters in the boiler, and not even read no more that came. So that's just what we did.

HAROLD: We set ourselves down, and we talked about this and that, and in the end we decided what we'd do. We don't have no children, so there was nothing to think of there. All we have is a few what you might call immediate members of the family, so we first of all made sure they would be all right for the rest of their days. Then we got to thinking what we could do which would be to the benefit of everyone around here, not just a few folks, but everyone. It was our feeling that the stroke of luck we'd had, we'd got it out of the ground of Auburn County and the town of Bird in particular, so what we ought to do was somehow give some of it back because this is where we'd lived our lives. To put it to you shortly, when you've got to both our ages and you've had a good life you've been happy with, there's nothing you really need or want more than what you've already got. I'll let Louie tell it you how it was we finally decided what to do.

LOUIE: I'd been to that old library of ours like I did most weeks to get me a couple of books to read, 'cause I like to read. And as I was walking home one day, down along South Adams here, I got to thinking. So when I came in that door I says to him "Harold," I said, "I've thought of an idea for something to do with our money. I've just been in the town to that old library, to get me a couple of books to read. You know what? I'm getting real tired of climbing up those library steps every time I go there: it bothers my knees, my arthritis is getting real bad now. So why don't we give the town a proper decent library where folk can walk right on in and choose a book for themselves without having to climb all them steps?"

HAROLD: I thought that was a real neat idea. The more I thought about it the more I seemed to like it. So I says to her "I think that's a real neat idea. They've got a good-looking library over in Conway City, why don't we go over there and have another look at it, and ask them whose idea it was to build it like that." So that's what we did, we went over there and got the names of the architects, then we asked a couple of other folk if they'd do us some plans and drawings of an idea for it too. We had a talk with Mrs. Oberlin and asked her what she thought about it too, and she said she liked the idea. And we all thought it'd be kind of nice in years to come, if folks went by and they wondered how it was a small place like Bird had got such a nice good library like that setting there.

LOUIE: You'll have folks tell you here and there how it was their idea for to have a library. But it wasn't their idea, not in the first place: it was mine, because of my knees.

HAROLD: So there she sets: and we like looking at it, and folks all say they like to look at it and they like going there, and that's the way we hope it stays for as long as Mr. Carnegie's building's been there.

LOUIE: You going to tell him about the letter?

HAROLD: You mean the letter this week from those people out East?

LOUIE: We had a letter this week from some people in New York, what was it, the American Libraries Association or something is it called?

HAROLD: Something like that.

LOUIE: They want to make us a presentation.

HAROLD: It's no big deal.

LOUIE: They want to make us a presentation because we built the library. He won't go.

HAROLD: Sure I won't go. New York, do you know how far that is? I looked it up in my atlas, and New York, that's somewhere close on to 1,500 miles away, that's just as the crow flies. How many days would that take on a train to get to New York?

LOUIE: Like I said, we don't have to go on a train, we could go on an airplane.

HAROLD: You can go on an airplane if you like, but I'm not going to. It's OK for some folk, they say they're fine and dandy. But I'm never going to get me inside of one of them things, no sir that's for sure. If they want to make a presentation to us they can come here and do it here, or they can mail it to us, I don't mind which.

LOUIE: Obstinate see, like I told you. Well I guess we'll never get to New York for no presentation, that's for sure.

HAROLD: We could go on the train.

LOUIE: How could we go on the train?

HAROLD: We could go to Kansas City, Missoura, and we could go on the train from there.

LOUIE: And how long would that take?

HAROLD: It wouldn't matter.

LOUIE: Look just a minute ago you were saying it was too far and it'd take too long. And anyway you don't like the trains they've got nowadays.

HAROLD: They might have some of the old sort. We could inquire. If they had one of the old sort, it'd be real good to go on a train like that all the way from Kansas City, Missoura, to New York.

LOUIE: They wouldn't let you drive it.
HAROLD: They might too.
LOUIE: They wouldn't let you drive it. And anyway they don't have that sort. Do you know what he's talking about? He's talking about them old steam trains they used to have, the ones with a big chimney on the front shaped like that, and a cowcatching gate, and an old steam whistle that you pulled the chain and it went "woo woo."
HAROLD: "Woo woo woo," that's how they went: they went "woo woo woo." You know, when I was a boy they used to go across the plains, I could see them in the distance from the farm that we had, you'd see them going across the skyline. That was the Union Pacific Line, the Atchison, Topeka & the Santa Fe.
LOUIE: It wasn't nothing of the kind, you're getting it all mixed up with the words of that song. And anyhow, you couldn't see that railroad from there, it was a hundred miles away.
HAROLD: I could too. Anyhow, I could see a railroad and I could hear those whistles. And you know, those men who drove those trains, they could play a tune almost on those whistles of theirs. They'd go along all day long like that, and they were, they were playing a song. And the smoke from their chimney going up in the sky, it was a beautiful sight, they sure don't have trains as beautiful as that these days, all they've got are those real ugly diesel things with their horns and big engines all full of black smoke. Sometimes I reckon you know if I'd been a young man when we had all this money come to us, maybe only half the age I am now, thirty-five or forty or somewhere around there, you know what I reckon I might have done? That was the one thing I always wanted: and I might have gone off and bought me one of them trains, and driven it all day to my heart's content. I'd have said to Louie here, I'd have said "Louie I'm going off for a while, I'm going to get me a train and drive it across the prairie some."
LOUIE: I shouldn't believe all that if I were you. He just makes things up as they come into his head.
HAROLD: I didn't make that up about that train and its whistle, I've always wanted one of those.
LOUIE: I know you have. But all that about going off and driving it around the prairie, that's just talk. On your own: you'd have wanted me to go along with you and sit in the carriage behind the engine and cook your dinner for you, that's what you'd have wanted. One day of going off and driving the engine and pulling the whistle, that'd have been enough for you: as soon as you got hungry or had a hole in your sock, you'd have come hollering for me.
HAROLD: Well. Well maybe I would and maybe I wouldn't. You never can tell. Say all this talking we've been doing: I'll go see if we've some beer or something.

When he'd gone to the kitchen, I asked her any way she could see having money had changed him. She thought for quite a while before she replied.

LOUIE: Not one bit do I see it's changed him, not how in any way at all. He's just exactly what he always was, ever since I've first knowed him: a sweet, nice, gentle man.

Points for Review and Discussion

1. Summarize Harold and Louie's attitudes toward work and savings at the start of their marriage. How do they themselves explain these attitudes?
2. Where and for what reasons does Louie praise Harold? Where and for what reasons does Harold praise Louie? How do you account for this difference?
3. Choose a passage of the interview that amuses you, and explain why.

◆ Questions for Writing

1. Tony Parker doesn't ask Harold and Louie to say how they felt when oil worth nearly an acre of diamonds was discovered in their backyard. But it's possible to speculate about their feelings on the basis of what this interview reveals about the Alberts' character. Make a list of their traits as you understand them, and then go on to write a paragraph in which you imagine what Harold and Louie felt once they realized that "we had a very big strike on our land." How does this response differ from those depicted in TV ads showing the reactions of winners in Publishers Clearing House lotteries?
2. Harold and Louie are upset to the point of actually feeling sick as they read the avalanche of mail from people needing help. What in your opinion causes this disturbance? Why does their own good fortune make the Alberts feel so miserable?
3. Reread the section of the interview about the new air conditioning system and buying "a whole new house." Are these people cheap? Do they lack imagination? Are they worried about what the neighbors will think? How do you yourself explain the couple's reluctance to buy themselves the comforts they can clearly afford?

Connecting the Parts in Chapter 4: Assignment for an Extended Essay

Write an autobiographical essay recounting your own education from childhood to the present concerning the values of work, success, and luck.

One part of the essay should focus on your mentors: parents, teachers, friends, others from whom you learned the lessons that shape your current thinking. Tell who these teachers were, and when, where, how, and what they taught you.

Another part of the essay should focus on experience: events that drove lessons home that weren't verbalized by others but that nevertheless had clear meaning for you.

Still another part of the essay should look into the relations between what you now believe and themes articulated by Cotton Mather, Ben Franklin, and Russell Conwell.

Finally, consider the matter of whether your attitudes are or are not in tune with those prevailing in the general society? For instance: how do you view state-run gambling? (What would Franklin or Conwell make of state-sponsored lotteries or riverboat gambling?) Is it in or out of step with your views?

Your overall purpose is to write an account that situates your own beliefs in relation to the particulars both of your life and of important currents of American thought.

Leads for Research

1. The American idea of success is richly entangled with American concepts of individualism and has undergone complex evolution since Ben Franklin. Research some twentieth-century versions of the success theme by reading Kenneth S. Lynn, *Dream of Success: The Modern American Imagination* (1955), John G. Cawelti, *Apostles of the Self-Made Man* (1965), and Moses Rischin, ed., *The American Gospel of Success: Individualism* (1965). Write a paper explaining distinctions between Franklinian "self-madeness" and later models.

2. Research the recent history of ambivalence about "making it big" by examining newspaper and magazine treatments of the careers of Michael Milken or Ivan Boesky or Donald Trump. (For listings of articles and editorials, consult *Readers' Guide to Periodical Literature*, *The New York Times Index*, *The Wall Street Journal Index*, and *Business Periodicals Index*.) Write a paper discussing contemporary criticism of success and power compulsions.

3. In recent decades ideas about getting to the top and staying there have been codified in an academic field called "Leadership Studies." Research the development of this field and write a paper on the subject of

whether Franklinian gospel has or has not been discarded by the new theorists of success. Begin your project by consulting the standard history of twentieth-century leadership studies—Bernard M. Bass, *Bass & Stogdill's Handbook of Leadership* (1990)—as well as Warren Bennis and Burt Nanus, *Leaders. The Strategies for Taking Charge* (1985), and Tom Peters and Nancy Austin, *A Passion for Excellence: The Leadership Difference* (1985). For a quite different perspective on leadership and success, read the opening Chapter of Ronald A. Heifetz, *Leadership Without Easy Answers* (1994).

5

Equality and Mobility
The Sacred Ground

Dreams of wealth and success haunt many American minds—but they are less potent in ordinary life than our national beliefs in equality and social mobility. Belief in equality holds that no system of social stratification—no official bestowal of inherited privilege—awards one person higher status than the next on the day of their birth.

Belief in social mobility holds that any American who is determined to rise, willing to work, eager to develop native skills and talents, cannot be held back. There's no claim that wealth and heroic success are within everybody's range; there is a claim that the combination of will, ambition, and hard labor can usually be counted on to bring about significant improvement in a person's life conditions.

The writers in Chapter 5 treat major aspects of these two American beliefs: their origins, the ways in which the beliefs have been kept alive in the past and nourished down to the present, the interaction of the beliefs with values of the emerging consumer society.

More Equal Than in Any Other Country
Alexis de Tocqueville

In 1831 a Frenchman named Alexis de Tocqueville traveled to America and wrote a commentary on the new nation's people and institutions—*Democracy in America*. Just 26 at the time, Tocqueville had been commissioned by his government to investigate the penal system in the United States. During his stay, he became an extraordinary enthusiast of the American people as a whole, and he paused often in the course of his work to salute them: "I have lived a great deal with the people in the United States, and I cannot express how much I admire their experience and their good sense."

As Tocqueville traveled the length and breadth of the country, nothing struck him more than the general equality of condition of the inhabitants. At one point he remarked with amazement that "the Americans never use the word 'peasant,' because they have no idea of the peculiar class which that term denotes."

The great truth disclosed in *Democracy in America* is that, a century and half ago, the universal American belief in equality was in no respect mysterious. Everywhere one looked one saw people who simply *were* each other's equals.

1. In the United States ... the English laws concerning the transmission of property were abolished ... at the time of the Revolution. The law of entail was so modified as not to interrupt the free circulation of property. The first generation having passed away, estates began to be parcelled out, and the change became more and more rapid with the progress of time. At this moment, after a lapse of a little more than sixty years, the aspect of society is totally altered; the families of the great landed proprietors are almost all commingled with the general mass. In the State of New York, which formerly contained many of these, there are but two who still keep their heads above the stream, and they must shortly disappear. The sons of these opulent citizens become merchants, lawyers, or physicians. Most of them have lapsed into obscurity. The last trace of hereditary ranks and distinctions is destroyed—the law of partition has reduced all to one level.

2. I do not mean that there is any deficiency of wealthy individuals in the United States; I know of no country, indeed, where the love of money has taken stronger hold on the affections of men, and where the profounder contempt is expressed for the theory of the permanent equality of property. But wealth circulates with inconceivable rapidity, and experience shows that it is rare to find two succeeding generations in the full enjoyment of it. ...

From Alexis de Tocqueville, *Democracy in America* (1835).

3   It is not only the fortunes of men which are equal in America; even their requirements partake in some degree of the same uniformity. I do not believe that there is a country in the world where, in proportion to the population, there are so few uninstructed and at the same time so few learned individuals. Primary instruction is within the reach of everybody; superior instruction is scarcely to be obtained by any. This is not surprising; it is in fact the necessary consequence of what we have advanced above. Almost all the Americans are in easy circumstances, and can therefore obtain the first elements of human knowledge.

4   In America there are comparatively few who are rich enough to live without a profession. Every profession requires an apprenticeship, which limits the time of instruction to the early years of life. At fifteen they enter upon their calling, and thus their education ends at the age when ours begins. Whatever is done afterwards is with a view to some special and lucrative object; a science is taken up as a matter of business, and the only branch of it which is attended to is such as admits of an immediate practical application. In America most of the rich men were formerly poor; most of those who now enjoy leisure were absorbed in business during their youth; the consequence of which is, that when they might have had a taste for study they had no time for it, and when time is at their disposal they have no longer the inclination.

5   There is no class, then, in America, in which the taste for intellectual pleasures is transmitted with hereditary fortune and leisure, and by which the labors of the intellect are held in honor. Accordingly there is an equal want of the desire and the power of application to these objects.

6   A middle standard is fixed in America for human knowledge. All approach as near to it as they can; some as they rise, others as they descend. Of course, an immense multitude of persons are to be found who entertain the same number of ideas of religion, history, science, political economy, legislation, and government. The gifts of intellect proceed directly from God, and man cannot prevent their unequal distribution. But in consequence of the state of things which we have here represented, it happens that, although the capacities of men are widely different, as the Creator has doubtless intended they should be, they are submitted to the same method of treatment.

7   In America the aristocratic element has always been feeble from its birth; and if at the present day it is not actually destroyed, it is at any rate so completely disabled that we can scarcely assign to it any degree of influence in the course of affairs. The democratic principle, on the contrary, has gained so much strength by time, by events, and by legislation, as to have become not only predominant but all-powerful. There is no family or corporate authority, and it is rare to find even the influence of individual character enjoy any durability.

8   America, then, exhibits in her social state a most extraordinary phenomenon. Men are there seen on a greater equality in point of fortune

and intellect, or, in other words, more equal in their strength, than in any other country of the world, or in any age of which history has preserved the remembrance.

Points for Review and Discussion

1. Describe the two kinds of equality among Americans that Tocqueville finds most impressive.
2. Tocqueville claims that "wealth circulates with inconceivable rapidity" (¶ 2) in the United States. How does he account for this and why does he regard it as so significant?

•◦ Questions for Writing

1. Tocqueville writes that America exhibits "greater equality ... than in any other country of the world" (¶ 8). If this Frenchman were to observe America in the 1990s, would he come to the same conclusion? Explain your answer.
2. "In America most of the rich men were formerly poor; most of those who now enjoy leisure were absorbed in business during their youth; the consequence of which is, that when they might have had a taste for study they had no time for it, and when time is at their disposal they have no longer the inclination" (¶ 4). If Tocqueville were to observe American education in the 1990s, would he come to the same conclusion? Again, explain your answer.
3. "There is no family or corporate authority, and it is rare to find even the influence of individual character to enjoy any durability" (¶ 7). If Tocqueville were to observe "authority" in America in the 1990s, would he come to the same conclusion? Yet once more, explain your answer.

A Sociologist Looks at an American Community
The Editors of Life

Well before the middle of the twentieth century, American sociologists had begun studying the country's class structure—and inevitably those studies raised doubts about the claim that people in this society were more equal than in any other society on earth. Published in small academic journals or in books, the research reached mass audiences only slowly, and often in forms that tended to blunt the force of its sometimes pessimistic conclusions.

The article below, which appeared in *Life* magazine in 1953, is an example of the manner in which popular media introduced large audiences to the "un-American" notion of class divisions. At midcentury *Life* had been a potent cultural force in middle-class America for nearly two decades. Its article on class was accompanied by a "photo-essay" on the town of Rockford, Illinois; it contained shots of the town's wealthy and of people "on the way up," and it illustrated the local range of dwellings and workplaces. In addition, there were tables showing how sociologists assessed a person's social prestige through a point system that evaluated the person's house, occupation, and sources of income.

1 Rockford, ILL.—so named because it was founded at the site of a ford across the Rock River—is a pleasant, tree-smothered city 90 miles northwest of Chicago. It is as nearly typical of the U.S. as any city can be. Parking meters line the streets of the shopping district. A fleet of cabs lines up at the station to meet the seven daily passenger trains. On Saturdays farmers pour in from the surrounding country to shop while their children go to the movies or roller-skate at a rink across the street from C.I.O. headquarters.

2 There are many different ways of looking at a town like Rockford. Industrialists searching for new factory sites are interested chiefly in finding adequate electric power and dependable workers. Pollsters ring doorbells to find what people's attitudes are on politics. Specialists like Dr. Kinsey look for information of another kind. Of all these roving, note-taking experts the hardest-working are the sociologists, whose systematic studies of the U.S. people, their problems and their habits are filling in a detailed picture of the American society. Their work is beginning to attract popular attention and John P. Marquand's best-selling novel, *Point of No Return*, is based partly on a contemporary sociological study named *Yankee City*.

From The Editors of *Life*, "A Sociologist Looks at an American Community" *Life* (Vol. 27, 1949).

3   The author of *Yankee City* and one of the best known U.S. sociologists is W. Lloyd Warner, professor of sociology at the University of Chicago. In a recent book, titled *Social Class in America,* Warner describes in detail the social structure of a typical American community which he calls Jonesville. Though most of its citizens do not know it, one of the three communities which make up Warner's hypothetical Jonesville is Rockford.

4   Like the other U.S. communities which Warner and his researchers have visited, Rockford is a gregarious town. It supports 63 churches and 375 lodges and clubs. But it also has its social schisms. Each of the clubs has its own clique of members. And Rockford's people talk about each other just as people do everywhere. They talk about their "country-club set" or "400," and about their local "riffraff."

5   The six people who represent a cross section of Rockford's 104,000 ... include a transient worker, a grocer, a civic booster and the matriarch of an old Rockford family. Each of them lives in a different section of town, has a different circle of friends, a different way of life and a different position in Rockford's community life. And each is a representative of one of the six social classes which Warner has found to be the basis of U.S. society.

6   Each of the three generally recognized American classes (lower, middle and upper) is divided by Warner into subclasses which he calls "lower-lower," "upper-lower," "lower-middle," "upper-middle," "lower-upper" and "upper-upper." Warner's reason for this subdivision is that the social structure of the U.S. is too complex to be explained in terms of three groups. Within the middle class, for example, there are people who have just moved up from the lower class and others who are ready to move on into the upper class. This phenomenon of social "mobility"—the opportunity to move rapidly upward through the levels of society—is the distinguishing characteristic of U.S. democracy and the thing for which it is famous and envied throughout the world.

7   Warner's study reflects what Warner and his assistants have heard people throughout the U.S. say about themselves. When asked to talk about their social life and contacts with other people some of Warner's subjects said, for example, that they were anxious to move to a better part of town. Sometimes they mentioned that they had failed to make friends and felt out of place in a certain neighborhood. After Warner had gathered volumes of this kind of information he sorted it out and converted what he had learned about neighborhoods, homes and jobs and the values people put on them into [a "system"].

8   Warner's system is based on four major factors ... of social prestige: (1) the house a person lives in, (2) the neighborhood in which he lives, (3) the type of job he holds, and (4) the sources of his income. Warner rates each factor mathematically. ...

9   [The rating for house] depends upon the size and condition of the house and the extent of landscaping around it. For example a trailer

ranks low and an elegantly kept old house often ranks over a spanking new one. A person with an extensive, well-kept house in a rundown area would be averaged down in his social status because of his neighborhood. Occupation is rated according to the prestige generally accorded different jobs by people whom Warner has interviewed. Professional men like doctors and lawyers rate high, farm owners have higher status than tenant farmers, skilled workers rate over unskilled workers, insurance salesmen over auto salesmen.

10   Source of income, and not the amount of it, affects social standing. Inherited wealth ranks highest, with earned wealth next. Then come profits, salary, wages and relief in that order. A grocer getting $3,000 in profit from his own business ranks higher socially than a store manager who receives a $5,000 salary. [*Editor's note:* The figures reflect living costs and dollar values a half-century ago.]

11   Warner's study merely organizes into a sociological system, and therefore helps to clarify, what every American knows but frequently forgets: his democracy is like a ladder. Anyone can climb it, but there are already some who have reached the rungs above and there are others who are coming up from below.

12   A stranger to Rockford who asks to meet its most representative people will undoubtedly be told, by almost anyone he talks to, that he should by all means meet Mrs. Walter Forbes: "She is every bit as sweet as she looks." "That's what all the elite ought to be like." "She is really Rockford." In this way Rockford's citizens have themselves placed Mrs. Forbes at the top of their social structure.

13   Her husband's grandfather, a Scotch molder, founded the Gunite Foundries Corporation in Rockford in 1854. Today, with her two sons and nephews, matriarchal Mrs. Forbes owns and runs (4 points) the business which they inherited (3 points). The foundry employs 550, many of them old workers like Alex Armato who are loyal to the company and respect the integrity of the Forbes family. Mrs. Forbes is also a founder of the local Community Fund, a member of the board of Rockford College, president of the Boys' Farm School, a member of the Rockford Woman's Club and of the Monday Club, which is reserved for the daughters of Rockford's oldest families. She is a nominal Republican and her son Seely was elected alderman and probate judge with Republican aid. The town's Old Guard respects her for her philanthropic and social work, and the younger crowd finds her a sympathetic and trusted adviser. Last year the Junior League had a minor crisis. It had passed a resolution favoring more state aid for needy children. Conservative members, anxious to avoid a political controversy, asked Mrs. Forbes to attend and help retract the resolution. Mrs. Forbes attended but warmly supported the welfare measure. Said one of her old friends with utter seriousness, "Marie, you're a traitor to your class." Mrs. Forbes thinks this story is very amusing.

A Sociologist Looks at an American Community   **153**

14   Professor Warner began his study of social classes 20 years ago. His *Yankee City*, a five-volume description of the mores of New England, is a 10-year-old classic. In it he outlined the boundaries of the six social classes which make up the U.S. society. With his rating system he has been able to determine not only the social status of individuals but the average social rating of whole groups of people who tend to join the same clubs and make most of their contacts with people of the same social class.

15   Americans have always thought of their society as being without class distinctions. They are right insofar as rigid economic barriers are concerned. But, as Warner has discovered, they are also becoming increasingly aware of the social differences in the U.S. today.

16   The daughter of an upper-middle-class merchant had this to say about her community when she was interviewed by one of Warner's assistants: "There's not supposed to be classes in this town, but actually there are. There's a higher class and then there's a middle class and there's a lower class. Then there are those in between. Families like us are in between the higher class and the middle class. Income, I guess, is the main thing in class, but—well, it's more than that, too. Part of it is the way you use your money, and the way that you act and what you do in town. The things that you are in and stuff like that."

17   This girl's first sentence ("There's not supposed to be classes in this town, but...") is a typical example of an American attitude which disturbs Warner a great deal and which has caused him to spend so much time on his study. "We Americans have a dream of a perfect democracy, with real equality for all," he says. "And we are often reluctant to face the fact that we have not been able to achieve this ideal. We should not be surprised and we should not be hurt. The saving grace of the American social system is that our social positions are not fixed artificially, as they are in the so-called 'classless' society of Russia. The citizens of Rockford ... are remarkable proof of the vitality of our system. Each, in his own way, is making the most of the mobility which our democracy affords."

18   Though Warner is convinced that social classes are the natural outgrowth of a healthy free-enterprise system, he is not so sure that this will always be so. The channels through which an ambitious American can move are changing and may be drying up. For one thing labor unions tend to freeze the chances of individuals. Warner puts it this way: "Where previously many laborers were interested only in their own mobility, they are working now for the advancement of the total labor group. In this process mobility is slowed down." At the same time many businesses which once rewarded enterprising foremen with positions of formal prestige now reserve these niches for the sons of management and college-trained technicians. "More and more top jobs in industry," Dr. Warner warns, "are being filled by men coming up from technical and engineering schools or from universities. The route up for them is

no longer through a hierarchy of increasing skill as it was two generations ago. The prudent mobile man today must prepare himself by education if he wishes to fill an important job." In this age of technical wizardry and large-scale industry, the most prudent man will master a field like engineering or business administration to gain a maximum chance at promotion to the inner circles of management and planning.

19   Education, then, is the route by which a man can best get from rung to rung. But it is not always sure-fire either. "Despite our free schools, the educational conveyor belt," says Warner, "drops many lower-class children at the bottom of the route and carries those from the higher classes a longer distance." The U.S., he thinks, must look around and see if its channels are being kept open. This country was built from scratch because the way was left open for a man to move from the bottom toward the top as far as his ambition and ability could carry him. He had the freedom to find whatever level he thought it was worth trying for. [Many individuals in Rockford] are showing ... that the process of mobility has been working fine. But if the people of Rockford and other communities are to keep moving, Warner warns, they ought first to understand the realities of their system. "The lives of many are destroyed because they do not understand the workings of social class. The two fundamental propositions of the American Dream are that all of us are equal and that each of us has the right to climb for the top. But no society with a large population can exist without a division of labor to perform the tasks necessary for its survival. And no society like ours can exist without a system of rank to channel this energy. Though all are not equal in ability, the Dream is still true. For given the tools, the education, the will to do and a little luck, we can start at the bottom and climb to the top."

Points for Review and Discussion

1. Summarize the basics of Warner's sociological system for analyzing class as that system is spelled out by the editors of *Life*.
2. What reasons does Warner give for his belief that we should not be surprised or hurt that our "dream of a perfect democracy, with real equality for all" (¶ 16) hasn't been achieved?

•◊ *Questions for Writing*

1. One obvious difference between Warner's system and Paul Fussell's (pages 39–44) is that Warner thinks there are six classes, whereas Fussell argues for nine. Look back at page 44 of Fussell's essay—the section in which his analysis of class focuses on musical instruments. In your opinion are these social differences more or less trivial than those on which Warner concentrates? Explain your answer.

2. The editors of *Life* tell their readers that Warner's study contains nothing new—merely "helps to clarify ... what every American knows but frequently forgets: his democracy is like a ladder" (¶ 11). What is the point, in your opinion, of telling several million readers that they are already fully familiar with the idea that America has social classes?

3. The final paragraph quotes Warner's "two fundamental propositions." Restate these propositions in your own words and explain why you do or do not find them contradictory.

Ups and Downs: Three Middletown Families
Howard M. Bahr

The strongest bulwark of belief in social mobility is, of course, personal experience of social ascent or descent. People who can trace a rise in their family's social position over a period of a generation or two are unlikely to doubt claims that America remains an open society in which equality and mobility are key values.

But statistical and other records show that, although social ascent is by no means uncommon, it's seldom as dramatic as rags to riches stories imply. The following report looks into the life-patterns of three American families in a much-studied community—Muncie, Indiana. It provides details about both social advance and social regression. The author, Howard Bahr, is a professor of sociology at Brigham Young University and is well known for his intergenerational studies of Muncie families.

1   *Middletown*, published in 1929 by Robert and Helen Lynd, was the nation's first sociological bestseller. Together with a sequel, *Middletown in Transition* (1937), written during the Great Depression, it secured a reputation for Muncie, Indiana, as the archetypal middle American city. Muncie, rhapsodized the editors of *Life* in 1937, was "every small U.S. city from Maine to California," a place where pollsters and market researchers could flock to take the pulse of America.

2   *Life* claimed more for Muncie than the Lynds did. They said only that Muncie was not demonstrably *atypical*. Their cautious proposition still holds: When compared to the national population, Middletown's people still turn out to be fairly average.

3   *Middletown* was about work and the way it defines one's life. Middletown, said the Lynds, had two relatively static classes. About two-thirds of its people were working-class, laboring with their hands and backs, while members of what the Lynds called the "business class" earned their livings as clerks, salesmen, managers, and teachers.

4   "The mere fact of being born upon one or the other side of the watershed roughly formed by these two groups," the Lynds wrote in 1929, "is the most significant single cultural factor tending to influence what one does all day long throughout one's life; whom one marries; when one gets up in the morning; whether one belongs to the Holy Roller or Presbyterian church; or drives a Ford or a Buick; . . . whether one belongs to the Odd Fellows or the Masonic Shrine; whether one sits about evenings with one's necktie off; and so on indefinitely throughout the

---

From Howard Bahr, "Ups and Downs: Three Middletown Families," *The Wilson Quarterly* (Winter, 1987).

daily comings and goings of a Middletown man, woman or child." When the Lynds revisited Middletown in 1937, they found that the Great Depression had nudged the classes even further apart.

5   Fifty years have wrought enormous changes in Middletown, and in the United States. The city's population has nearly doubled, to 74,000. Blue-collar work is cleaner, safer, and better paid; many married women have joined the labor force; and the economy has created whole new varieties of white-collar jobs, many of them highly paid.

6   Today, Middletown's traditionally black neighborhoods are still black, and the old South Side remains a working-class haven. But even Middletown's "better" neighborhoods now have at least a sprinkling of black residents, and a few homes there are owned by plumbers rather than doctors. We do not know whether, overall, upward *mobility* in Middletown has increased since 1929. But, partly because of the increasing affluence of wage earners, there are fewer social barriers between the classes and more social contacts across class lines than there were during the Lynds' time.

7   Consider, for example, the families of Henry Franklin and Robert Michaels,* two men whom the Lynds might have met 50 years ago. Henry Franklin was a crack salesman who sold paper during most of a long career. Robert Michaels worked as a farm-implement mechanic. His son, Tom, and Henry Franklin's daughter, Margery, both attended Central High. They dated, and in 1948, they married.

8   The marriage of Tom and Marge Michaels, now both in their late fifties, is a "mixed" marriage in several senses. She grew up in the business class, he in the working class; her family was Catholic, his Protestant; she has been a white-collar professional since 1975, while he has been a blue-collar worker during much of his working life.

9   Tom Michaels' career shows how misleading a simple answer to a social scientist's query—"Occupation?"—can be. He has often held two, sometimes three, jobs at a time, a burden imposed in part by the need to support the eight children the couple raised together. He has hopped back and forth across the class divide several times. He drove a truck for a stock rendering plant, worked as a mechanic, owned his own service station, built and sold houses in a business with his father, ran a fleet of school buses, and, after 1960, served in the city police department. He now teaches at the state law enforcement academy.

10   Tom Michaels exemplifies the optimistic "Middletown spirit" described by the Lynds, the belief that "hard work is the key to success." The rewards for the Michaels are a big, rambling, white frame house in one of Middletown's respectable old neighborhoods, a late model Buick and a new Ford light truck, occasional dinners out, the prospect of retirement and travel, and the satisfaction of a close family, although the children now have families of their own.

*All names in this essay are pseudonyms.

Fathers and Sons

11 Like many American couples, the Michaels won their piece of the American Dream partly by means once considered unorthodox. During the 1920s, almost half of Middletown's working-class women had jobs, but other married women generally stayed home to look after their children and husbands. Today, in Middletown, as throughout the United States, women of all classes work—by 1980, almost half of the employed people were women. Like many women of her generation, Marge Michaels spent more than 20 years as a homemaker before returning to work part-time, later full-time, as a university librarian. She also returned to school, earning an undergraduate and a master's degree.

12 The Michaels' children and their spouses exemplify the progressive erosion of class divisions in Middletown. This single generation includes professionals and laborers, blue-, pink-, and white-collar workers. Overall, the story of the Michaels' family is one of upward mobility: salesman and mechanic in the first generation; police officer and university librarian in the second; and in the third, police officer, accountant, attorney, bank trust officer, technician, and warehouse worker.

13 There is also downward mobility in Middletown, but it is less common. Some movement upward has been built into the U.S. economic system: As the number of higher status jobs as clerks or service workers has grown, the fraction of the city's population employed as menial laborers and domestic help has shrunk.

14 It is still fairly common for sons to grow up to do the same work their fathers did. But sometimes a closer look reveals that the nature of the job has changed, even when the title remains the same, or that a father and son who do the same job differ sharply in educational achievement or general outlook.

15 Take, for example, the Winslows. Great-grandfather Winslow worked in Middletown's factories, rising to foreman in an auto parts company. Grandfather Winslow followed him, eventually becoming a supervisor in a plant that made tire recapping equipment. His three sons are all blue-collar workers. Two are skilled tool and die makers, and one, Duane, is a welder at Middletown's Westinghouse plant.

16 Duane Winslow, now 53, grew up on Middletown's South Side, at a time when working-class families were separated from those of the business class by the great gulf the Lynds described. He attended the prestigious Burris High School, but as one of only three boys from blue-collar families in his class, he chafed at his inferior status. "It was a stigma in my life when I was young, up until I graduated," he says, and his account of a recent 30-year class reunion demonstrates that his sense of injury lingers. Most of his classmates, he says, are now college-educated, professional, even prominent men. And yet, "I'm as good as any of 'em," he says. "I'm as wealthy as any of 'em ... I live *here*."

17   "Here" is a fashionable West End area. When he was growing up, it was among the most affluent neighborhoods of the city. By 1935, the Lynds said, subdivisions like his had supplanted the "aristocratic old East End" in prestige, and the "ambitious matrons of the city" were moving their families there. When Duane was in high school, many of the boys who snubbed him lived there. If the neighborhood is less distinguished today, it retains enough of its eminence to give him a sense of personal progress. The Winslows live in a brick ranch-style home, unassuming on the outside, well furnished within.

No "Working Stiff"

18 "Back when I was a kid," Duane says. "I used to think, 'I'll never live here. I could never attain that.' But I live in a country, and work for a corporation that thought enough of me that I could do it."

19   After graduating from high school, Duane followed his father to the firm that made recapping equipment, and, in 1960, moved to Warner Gear, a plum of a job in Middletown's manufacturing economy. It did not last long. After the company laid him off during a business downturn, he sold insurance for a year. He liked the work but not the travel, so, in 1962, he jumped at the chance to join Westinghouse. He has worked there ever since, in a variety of shopfloor and management positions, and will retire in five years, at 58, as a supervisor of welders.

20   "As a working man," Duane says, "I am proud of what I have attained. I'm not a poor man. My wife [who also works at Westinghouse] and I live here, and my home is paid for. I have money in the bank."

21   Duane calls himself a "working man," like his father, but when asked if that means he identifies with blue-collar workers or labor unions, he is adamant: "I'm middle-class." Trim and energetic, he jogs, plays racquetball, and reads three newspapers a day, including the *Wall Street Journal*. He is not a stereotypical "working stiff."

22   Like many fathers of his generation, Duane worries that his children have had it too easy. Duane's daughter, 24, is married to a house painter and works as a receptionist; his bachelor son Don, at 27, recently landed a job as a tool and die maker at Warner Gear but still lives at home. "Don looks at what I've attained, and thinks, 'Why in the hell can't I do that?' Well, I didn't have that when I was 27 either. That's what I try to get through to him [but] it's never sunk in."

Where the Grass Is Greener

23 Don meanwhile, is trying to "get his time in" (i.e. six months without a layoff) so that he can gain a measure of job security under the union contract. He first applied for a job at Warner Gear nine years ago, and was hired at last, he thinks, because he "knew someone." The money is good

(about $23,000 annually) and "the job's not all that hard." He hopes to stay at Warner Gear until he retires.

24   Duane admits that his son faced a far more difficult job market than he did. During the recession of the early 1980s, many local plants closed or cut back, and unemployment rates soared to half again as high as the national average, peaking at 14 percent in 1982. By 1985, Middletown's jobless rate was still nine percent.

25   Reflecting a growing skepticism among Middletowners, Duane does not have much faith that a college education would have been the answer for his son. "Many people I work with have college educations. They have master's degrees, they have B.A. degrees . . . and they cannot find a job in their field."

26   In contrast to Tom Michaels, Duane is gloomy about the future. He hopes above all that his son will secure a safe berth at Westinghouse or Warner Gear: In the end, security and stability mean more to Duane than upward mobility.

27   For one group of Middletown workers, opportunities clearly have blossomed since the Lynds' time. "The cleft between the white and the Negro populations of Middletown," they wrote in 1937, "is the deepest and most blindly followed line of division in the community."

28   Before 1950, blacks were almost entirely excluded from Middletown's business class; racial discrimination was overt. By 1980, however, one-sixth of Middletown's employed black men and half the working black women held sales, clerical, managerial, or professional positions. Still, the black-white split is closing much more slowly than the class divide. In Middletown, it appears that bridging the gap will be a matter of six generations, or perhaps nine, rather than three.

29   "Across the tracks," in southeast Middletown, is one of the city's two black districts. Ada Jackson and many of the other black domestic servants who served what the Lynds called the "ambitious matrons" of the West End used to live there. Now their children and grandchildren do. Ada cleaned house for white people for over 40 years. Her husband, Lucas, had a good job as a wire drawer at Indiana Steel and Wire, but even during the best of times the family needed both incomes to make ends meet.

30   Ada and Lucas were high school graduates, and their daughter Lila, now in her sixties, remembers that they valued education. "There was always books, there was always newspapers," she says. But Lila only got as far as the 10th grade before, in 1937, she dropped out, married, and began working as a part-time domestic. Her husband was an auto body mechanic, and also a high school dropout. In 1945, he left Lila and their four children, and she began working full-time as a maid. Lila had two more children under circumstances she does not discuss.

31   During the mid-1960s, both of Lila's parents and one of her grown daughters died within two years. It was a turning point. "I went back to school and went back to church," Lila says. In 1967, three decades after dropping out, she graduated from high school.

32 Lyndon B. Johnson's War on Poverty was in full swing, and Lila was hired under the auspices of her Methodist church, as a federally funded outreach "volunteer with a stipend" while she continued to work part-time as a maid. Finally, in 1971, she was able to quit cleaning houses for good. Ever since, she has been a full-time counselor to adult university students and to young blacks seeking schooling. She has also found time to help herself by working toward a bachelors degree in political science and social work at Ball State University, a thriving (enrollment: 17,513) branch of the state system in Middletown. She will graduate this year.

33 Despite her own success, Lila does not believe that Middletown's blacks have made much progress during her lifetime, and her negative view is widely shared among the city's blacks. "Most black people who are educated have to leave," Lila says. "The opportunities just aren't here for black people."

34 Lila will admit to slight local gains. But she is sure that the prospects for Middletown's blacks are worse now than they were during the late 1970s, when there seemed to be many more local blacks attending Ball State. (Partly as a result of federal budget cutbacks, black enrollment fell from 808 in 1977 to 621 last year.)

Backing Into the Future

35 Lila is a great-grandmother now, and she speaks from the experience of kin as well as clients. The jobs of her children and in-laws, now in their thirties and forties, support her dim view of the pace of black progress in Middletown: two males unemployed, the rest blue-collar workers, with the exception of a daughter-in-law who is an accountant.*

36 In part, the fate of Lila's family, especially her sons, is a reminder of a larger social problem—the rise of female-headed families, especially among blacks. Hence, in Middletown, as in other American cities, black women bear heavier family burdens than white women, and the children suffer. In 1980, 34 percent of Middletown's black families were headed by women without husbands, compared to 14 percent of its white families. Middletown's black women are almost as likely to be employed as are the men. (In 1980, 44 percent of black women and 51 percent of black men were employed, compared to 44 and 62 percent, respectively, among whites.) The women tend to have higher status jobs.

37 While Lila's family may not appear to be an example of great occupational upward mobility, there are signs of progress. Lila's eldest

---

* The occupations of Lila's children and their spouses: (1) May, a homemaker, married to a factory worker; (2) Dolores, a utility company teller, married to a factory worker; (3) Sandra (now deceased), was a hospital x-ray technician; (4) William, a former bartender, now unemployed; (5) Samuel, a factory worker; (6) Edward, a former hotel clerk, now unemployed, married to an accountant.

daughter, May, 47, represents the third generation of Jackson women in domestic work, but she served as a maid for only two years. Over the years, she supplemented her husband's factory paychecks with various other part-time jobs. The couple stayed together. In 1980, she passed the high school equivalency exam, and enrolled as a social work major at her mother's alma mater, Ball State. She will graduate this year.

38   Three of May's six children are grown. One daughter manages a public housing project in Middletown. Her first and second sons, both in their mid-twenties, have degrees from Ball State in telecommunications. They are, in part, victims of their own high expectations. "Neither one ... wanted to work in the factory," May says. "They said the work was too hard. They had seen my husband drag in after work. . . . The children do have more alternatives than I had." One son is now an enlisted man in the Air Force; the other works in a fast food restaurant while he looks for another job.

39   Because of discrimination, May is not sure that education will be a key to the local job market for her family. But she has worked hard to get her own university degree, and has pushed her children to finish high school and go on to college. Unlike many of Middletown's whites, she remains convinced that education ultimately will make things better.

40   The Michaels, Winslows, and Jacksons have all "moved up" since the Lynds studied Middletown, but they have advanced unequally, and in different ways.

41   Only the Michaels followed the stereotypical path of fairly steady generation-to-generation improvement in income and status. But the Winslows seem equally satisfied, even though their gains have come chiefly through a rising standard of living. Crumbling class barriers have allowed Duane Winslow and his family to feel that they have moved up to become a part of the vast American "middle class," even though they remain, after three generations, a blue-collar family. By contrast, the Jacksons have, in a sense, come further than the Winslows, but they are still cut off from the larger community. And, despite their gains, they remain near the bottom of the economic ladder. Yet, as their commitment to education suggests, they are also aiming somewhat higher than some of their white counterparts.

42   To the Lynds, all of this might seem quite astonishing. By 1937, when they published *Middletown Revisited*, they had moved sharply to the political left, partly in reaction to the Great Depression. By then, they were impatient with Middletown's working class, unable to understand why widening inequality did not foster greater class consciousness and activism. They concluded their book with a quotation from R. H. Tawney, which seemed to apply to Middletowners: "They walked reluctantly backwards into the future, lest a worse thing should befall them." Viewed in retrospect, that walk has moved Middletown's people a considerable distance up the incline to "success."

Points for Review and Discussion

1. Robert and Helen Lynd published two sociological studies of Muncie, Indiana, in 1929 and 1937. Summarize the chief findings of these books concerning social class, as Bahr reports them.
2. Bahr believes that blacks in Muncie have made much progress since 1937. What reasons does he give for this belief?
3. In his closing paragraph Bahr appears doubtful that the Lynds were right to be impatient with the relative passivity of Muncie's working class. What are the grounds of his doubt?

◆ Questions for Writing

1. Drawing on the relatively positive examples Howard Bahr cites, explain what the belief in social mobility is likely to mean in the case of average Americans in average American communities.
2. Drawing on the relatively negative example Bahr cities, explain what disbelief in social mobility is likely to mean—again in the case of average Americans in average American communities.
3. Write an account of the upward or downward social mobility of an American family known to you at firsthand. Who or what do you see as responsible for this social movement? Give reasons for your answer.

Class Struggle in Hollywood
Benjamin DeMott

Not the least reason that belief in the United States as a citadel of equality remains vigorous is that the country is regularly presented as such a citadel in popular culture. The following article deals with the treatment of class differences in movies in the early 1990s; it argues that that treatment "strengthens the national delusion that class power and position are insignificant." DeMott is Mellon Professor of Humanities at Amherst College and the author or editor of many works on American culture, including this book.

1 Increasingly in recent years movies have been dealing with power issues and class relationships—interactions between masters and servants, executives and underlings, yuppies and waitresses, millionaires and hookers, rich aristocrats and social-nobody lawyers. Think of "Reversal of Fortune" and "The Bonfire of the Vanities." Think of "White Palace" and "Pretty Woman." Think of Michael Corleone's struggle for social acceptance in "The Godfather Part III." Think of "Working Girl," or "Driving Miss Daisy" or "Dirty Dancing." Script after script links up clout and cloutlessness, often to stunning box-office effect.

2 Not every movie version of the power theme speaks specifically about class relationships, and some versions are only loosely linked to social reality. The two worlds of "Edward Scissorhands," for example—hilltop mansion and tract house; solitary helpless artist versus artist-baiting mob—are derived less from everyday experience than from fairy tales, allegory and satire.

3 Usually, though, conventional realism is the chosen mode, and class skirmishes are sketched. The camera in "White Palace" studies St. Louis's fancier suburbs and its rundown Dog Town; class conflict erupts at the movie's crisis point. Nora, the waitress-heroine (Susan Sarandon), listens smolderingly to her yuppie lover's upper-middle friends and relations uttering their hypocritical socio-political pieties, and explodes. Storming her way out, she cries: *"I'm* working class!"

4 At first glance the angry explicitness of her outcry and the movie's declaration of difference look promising. They could signify that Hollywood is reaching toward maturity, trying to teach itself and the nation how to think straight about social hierarchy—the realities of class and class power. The need for such instruction is patent. This country has an ignoble tradition of evading social facts—pretending that individual episodes of upward mobility obviate grappling with the hardening so-

---

From Benjamin DeMott "Class Struggle in Hollywood," *New York Times* (January 20, 1991).

cio-economic differences in our midst. Movies that deal responsibly with class relationships could, in theory, moderate the national evasiveness.

5   But, regrettably, contemporary "class movies" don't deal responsibly with class. The tone of their treatment of rich and poor is new; it is harsher and meaner than that of Frank Capra's "little guy" sagas or George Cukor's social comedies or John Ford's populism that were pleasing to our parents and grandparents in the 30's, 40's and 50's.

6   The harsher tone, however, doesn't bespeak fundamental change. At their best, Hollywood's new-style "class movies" nod at realities of social difference—and then go on to obfuscate them. At their worst these films are driven by near-total dedication to a scam—the maddeningly dangerous deceit that there are no classes in America.

7   One favorite story line stresses discovery: people who think firm class lines exist come to discover, by the end of the tale, that they're mistaken; everybody's really the same.

8   In the 1988 blockbuster "Working Girl," Tess McGill (Melanie Griffith), initially a bottom-dog secretary-gofer, is positive she can make it to the top. But her peers in the word-processing pool regard her aspirations as foolish. They tell her, flat out, that the real world has lines and distinctions and that her daydreams of glory and business power are foolish. "I sing and dance in my underwear," says one pal, "but I'm not Madonna." The implicit message: Get real, Tess. Accept the reality of levels.

9   But Tess, of course, accepts no such thing. She reads *W*, takes classes to improve her accent, seizes her boss's office when the latter breaks her leg skiing—and winds up not only doing deals but ordering the boss (Sigourney Weaver) to get her bony bottom out of sight. What does it take to get to the top? Desire, period. Tess's desire flies her straight up to a managerial perch, allowing her to become, almost effortlessly, all she can be: no problem, few barriers, class dismissed. In the final frame the doubters in the secretarial pool acknowledge their error; they rise to applaud the heroine who proved them wrong.

10   A second familiar story line involves upendings: characters theoretically on the social bottom shake the cages of characters who try to use their position to humiliate those below. The top dogs are so stupid they don't realize that socioeconomic power only lasts for a second and that they can be overcome by any intrepid underling.

11   Consider "Pretty Woman," the 1990 film that became one of the highest-grossing movies ever and is now near the top of video best-seller and rental charts. The would-be humiliators in this movie are snobbish salespeople on chic Rodeo Drive. Vivian (Julia Roberts), a hooker, runs afoul of them when she is sent on a shopping spree by the corporate raider (Richard Gere) who has hired her for a week. The raider wants elegance and the hooker aims to oblige—but on her first pass at the Drive she's suited up in hooker garb, and the salespeople are offended. "I don't

think we have anything for you. *Please leave.*" Quickly the snobs are undone. The corporate raider flashes plastic and tells a shop manager that they'll be spending big and need appropriate cosseting. In minutes—through instruction in fork-tine-counting, for instance—the raider effects the few alterations of manners required to transform Vivian the street hooker into grandeur.

12 Regally togged, her arms filled with sleek clothes boxes, Vivian returns to the salespeople who were mean to her and sticks it to them in economic not moral terms. If they had been nice to her, they would have made a killing. ("You work on commission, don't you?")

13 Power is temporary and snobs are dopes—so goes the message. Ostracize a hooker in midmorning and she'll ruin you before tea. *Class dismissed.*

14 Comparable dismissals occur in movies drawing huge audiences of high school students. They usually have plot lines showing bottom dogs gliding smoothly and painlessly to the top. In "Dirty Dancing" (1987), Patrick Swayze, playing a talented working-class dancer (he has a card in the "housepainters and plasterers union"), competes for esteem with a Yale medical school student—and wins in a breeze.

15 In John Hughes's "Some Kind of Wonderful" (1987) and "Pretty in Pink" (1986), working-class heroes or heroines become romantically interested in classmates who rank above them, in terms of money and status, in the school society. As the attachments develop, the poor students commence to display gifts and talents that prove them equal to or intrinsically superior to the arrogant, insecure characters in whom they've become interested.

16 Once the nonclass, merit-based order or hierarchy has been established, and superficial, class-based gradations have been eliminated, the poor boy or girl chooses whether to continue the relationship with the pseudo-superior as an equal or to end it. Either way, the experience bolsters the belief that, in school and out, social strata are evanescent and meaningless.

17 But what is truly striking is the array of ploys and devices by which movie makers bring off escapes from significant confrontation with class realities. The Vietnam War film "Platoon" (1986), for example, lets on at the beginning that it will show us an upper-middle white soldier learning about differences between himself and the sons of the working class who compose the majority of his comrades in arms.

18 But in place of the experience of learning, we're offered liberal platitudes and star turns. The hero writes his grandmother that his fellow soldiers are the salt of the earth (little corroboration supplied); the soldiers themselves—particularly the blacks among them—are brought on for a succession of amusing monologues, following which they disappear, shipped out dead or alive; at no point is the gritty stuff of class difference even momentarily engaged.

19   In the much-acclaimed "Driving Miss Daisy" (1989), the early intimation is that the focus will be on relations between white employers and black servants. But almost immediately the outlines of that social difference are blurred. The white employer is Jewish and her synagogue is bombed; poor black and rich white become one, joint victims of discriminatory violence. ("You're my best friend, Hoke.") Class dismissed once more.

20   The story is nearly the same even in those unusual movies that focus solely on minority communities. Social difference is glanced at, defined in a few snippets of dialogue—and then trashed, often by means of a joke. In "House Party," Reginald Hudlin's 1990 film about teen-age life, the joke is about sex. Through establishing shots and talk, two girlfriends are placed at a social distance from each other. One lives in "the projects," the other in an expensively middle-class suburban home.

21   The film offers a single moment of reflection on the social difference in question; a young man points out that there is plenty of space for making out in the rich girl's house, none where the projects girl lives. Yet once more, class dismissed.

22   It's hardly surprising that the notion of America as a classless society emerges at its most schematic in movies aimed at relatively youthful, unsophisticated audiences. But the same impulse to paper over social differences surfaces in many more ambitious films purporting to raise subjects considered controversial by Hollywood standards (social injustice, war, the treatment of minorities).

23   And not infrequently that impulse drives film makers—such as Francis Ford Coppola in "The Godfather Part III" and Barry Levinson in "Avalon"—to overplay ethnic influence and underplay class influence on character.

24   The reason all this matters is simple. Treating class differences as totally inconsequential strengthens the national delusion that class power and position are insignificant. It encourages the middle-class—those with the clearest shot at upward mobility—to assume, wrongly, that all citizens enjoy the same freedom of movement that they enjoy. And it makes it easier for political leaders to speak as though class power had nothing to do with the inequities of life in America. ("Class is for European democracies or something else," says George Bush. "It isn't for the United States of America. We are not going to be divided by class.")

25   Movies that deal responsibly with class relationships might help to embolden leaders to begin talking candidly about real as opposed to phony issues of "fairness." But movies obviously can't do this as long as their makers are in terror of allowing class permanently out of the closet.

26   It's true that occasional moments occur when movie audiences can grasp the substantive dimensions of social difference. A person reached

toward from above or below is seen to possess inner, mysterious resources (or limits) about which someone differently placed on the social scale can have no inkling, and can't conceivably lay claim.

27   There is one such moment in "Working Girl." Following orders, Tess, as secretarial underling, books her boss, Katharine Parker (Ms. Weaver), into a chalet for a ski weekend. She is helping Katharine fasten her new ski boots in the office when she is asked where in the chalet the room is located. Tess doesn't know; Katharine dials the resort and at once a flood of flawless German fills the room.

28   The camera angle shows us Tess's awe; we gaze up with her (from the glossy white boots that she, as footman, is buckling) to this animated, magical, Ivy-educated mistress of the world, self-transformed into Europe, performing in another language. Katharine is demonstrating quite casually that bottom dogs have no exact knowledge of what lies between them and their ideal, that top dogs possess secret skills nobody learns overnight, as in charm class, or by changing hairstyles—skills traceable to uncounted indulgent hours of tutoring, study and travel.

29   The bottom dog's eyes widen as frightening truth dawns. If a talent so mesmerizing—this poured-forth foreign self—can be invisible until now, must there not be others equally well-concealed? Maybe this dream to be her *is* foolish. What unimaginable barriers stand between me and my desire?

30   In the movie culture the answer to such questions is, of course: no real barriers, none. "Be all you can be" means, at the bottom as at the top, "Be whatever you wish," fear no obstacle, see no obstacle, there are no obstacles. "Working Girl" is, finally, a story about how ambitious working girls just can't lose—one more movie that obliterates class.

31   "White Palace," for all its initial explicitness about the reality of social differences, is, finally, a story asserting that such differences simply don't matter; pure passion erases them every time.

32   The other week Senator Daniel Patrick Moynihan told a Wall Street Journal reporter that the fundamental issue in this country is "class, not race." It's essential, he said, "to at least start thinking about it, start talking about it. Let's be honest. We're not doing that."

33   One reason we're not is that movies remain firmly resolved against letting us.

Points for Review and Discussion

1. Summarize the chief Hollywood story lines which, in DeMott's view, assert that "there are no classes in America."

2. DeMott believes that even those movies that focus on minorities and ethnic groups tend to preach the message of classlessness. What evidence does he cite?

◆◆ Questions for Writing

1. "Class Struggle in Hollywood" claims that movies encourage "the middle class—those with the clearest shot at upward mobility—to assume, wrongly, that all citizens enjoy the same freedom of movement that they enjoy" (¶ 24). Explain your understanding of why it is "wrong" to induce people to accept this assumption.

2. In movies like "Working Girl" certain scenes bring across the thesis that "bottom dogs have no exact knowledge of what lies between them and their ideal, [no awareness] that top dogs possess secret skills ... traceable to uncounted indulgent hours of tutoring, study and travel" (¶ 28). Look back at Lorene Cary's "Turning Out the Privileged" in Chapter 1. Does lack of knowledge of what separates top dogs from bottom dogs figure in the black students' confidence that they can easily defeat white students? Explain your answer.

3. When Tess, in "Working Girl," takes up a place in her company as an executive rather than secretarial assistant, her former associates in the secretarial pool rise to applaud her. What is the effect of this gesture? What is it meant to tell us about the relation between Tess and those with whom she formerly worked as an equal?

TV AND ALL THE RIGHT COMMODITIES
Mark Crispin Miller

The energy and ingenuity with which messages of equality are developed in popular culture is striking. So, too, is the frequency with which the idea of choice—especially consumer choice—is presented as a foundation of equality. In the following article, Mark Crispin Miller explores the corporate-sponsored interplay of advertising and consumption in "The Cosby Show," and analyzes the ways in which this sitcom sought to dramatize the sameness—and therefore equality—of all Americans. Miller is director of the Film Studies program at Johns Hopkins University and the author of many essays on advertising and television.

> Nobody could watch it all—and that's the point. There *is* a choice. *Your* choice. American television and you.
>
> —JIM DUFFY, *President of Communications, ABC*, in one of a series of ad promoting network television *(1986)*

1   Every evening, TV makes a promise, and seems at once to keep it. TV's nightly promise is something like the grand old promise of America herself. Night after night, TV recalls the promise that was first extended through America's peerless landscape, with its great mountains, cliffs, and canyons, tumbling falls, gigantic woodlands, intricate bayous, lakes the size of seas, heavenly valleys, broiling deserts, and a network of massive rivers hurrying in all directions, through a north thick with trees, through interminable plains, through multicolored tropics, through miles and miles of grass or corn or granite, clay or wheat, until those rushing waters ultimately cascade into the surrounding ocean. And throughout this astonishing land mass lie a multitude of huge and spreading cities, each distinctive and yet each itself diverse, bustling with the restless efforts of a population no less heroically varied than the land itself—white and black and brown and yellow, bespeaking the peculiarities of every creed and culture in the world, and yet all now living here, savoring the many freedoms that distinguish the United States so clearly from those other places where our citizens, or their ancestors, came from.

2   Here all enjoy the promise of that very opportunity, that very differentiation which they, and this great land mass, represent: the promise of unending *choice*. Here they are not ground down by party rule, church

---

From Mark Crispin Miller, "TV and all the Right Commodities," in *Watching Television* (1986), ed. Todd Gitlin.

dictate, authoritarian tyranny, or the daily dangers of fanatical vendetta; and in this atmosphere of peace and plenty, they are free to work and play, have families, and contemplate, if not yet actually enjoy, the bounty of our unprecedented system.

3   Such is the promise of America; and TV, every evening, makes a similar sort of promise. Each night (and every day, all day), TV offers and provides us with an endless range of choices. Indeed, TV can be said to have itself incorporated the American dream of peaceful choice. This development was poignantly invoked by one of the hostages taken, in June of 1985, by the Shiite gunmen who hijacked TWA Flight 847. Back home after his captivity in Lebanon, Clint Suggs observed that "when you go to Beirut, you live war, you hear it, you smell it and it's real. It made me appreciate my freedom, the things we take for granted." In America, such freedom is available to any viewer: "When we sit here in our living room, with the sun setting, the baby sleeping, we can watch television, change channels. We have choices."

4   TV's promise of eternal choice arises from the whole tempting spectacle that is prime time: the full breasts, the gleaming cars, the glistening peaks of ice cream, mounds of candy, long clean highways, colossal frosted drinks, endless laughter, bands of dedicated friends, majestic houses, and cheeseburgers. The inexhaustible multitude of TV's images, sounds, and rhythms, like the dense catalog on every page of *TV Guide*, reassures us again and again that TV points to everything we might ever want or need. Nor is this promise merely implicit. The commercials, perhaps the quintessential components of TV's nonstop display, not only reconfirm our sense of privilege with millions of alluring images, but refer explicitly and often to this extensive "choice" of ours: AT&T offers us "The Right Choice," electricity, we are told, grants us "The Power of Choice," Wendy's reminds us that "There Is No Better Choice," McDonald's is "America's Choice," Coke is "The Real Choice," "In copiers, the choice is Canon," Taster's Choice is "The Choice for Taste"—all such assurances, and the delicious images that bolster them, combining to enhance even further TV's rich, ongoing paean to its own unimaginable abundances.

5   "The Cosby Show" must owe much of its immense success to advertising, for this sitcom is especially well attuned to the commercials, offering a full-scale confirmation of their vision.

6   On the face of it, the Huxtables' milieu is as upbeat and well stocked as a window display at Bloomingdale's, or any of those visions of domestic happiness that graced the billboards during the Great Depression. Everything within this spacious brownstone is luminously clean and new, as if it had all been set up by the state to make a good impression on a group of visiting foreign dignitaries. Here are all the right commodities—lots of bright sportswear, plants and paintings, gorgeous bedding, plenty of copperware, portable tape players, thick carpeting, innumerable knickknacks, and, throughout the house, big, burnished dressers,

tables, couches, chairs, and cabinets (Early American yet looking factory-new). Each week, the happy Huxtables nearly vanish amid the porcelain, stainless steel, mahogany, and fabric of their lives. In every scene, each character appears in some fresh designer outfit that positively glows with newness, never to be seen a second time. And, like all this pricey clutter, the plots and subplots, the dialogue and even many of the individual shots reflect in some way on consumption as a way of life: Cliff's new juicer is the subject of an entire episode; Cliff does a monologue on his son Theo's costly sweatshirt; Cliff kids daughter Rudy for wearing a dozen wooden necklaces. Each Huxtable, in fact, is hardly more than a mobile display case for his/her momentary possessions. In the show's first year, the credit sequence was a series of vivid stills presenting Cliff alongside a shiny Dodge Caravan, out of which the lesser Huxtables then emerged in shining playclothes, as if the van were their true parent, with Cliff serving as the genial midwife to this antiseptic birth. Each is routinely upstaged by what he/she eats or wears or lugs around: in a billowing blouse imprinted with gigantic blossoms, daughter Denise appears, carrying a tape player as big as a suitcase; Theo enters to get himself a can of Coke from the refrigerator, and we notice that he's wearing both a smart beige belt *and* a pair of lavender suspenders; Rudy munches cutely on a piece of pizza roughly twice the size of her own head.

7   As in the advertising vision, life among the Huxtables is not only well supplied, but remarkable for its surface harmony. Relations between these five pretty kids and their cute parents are rarely complicated by the slightest serious discord. Here affluence is magically undisturbed by the pressures that ordinarily enable it. Cliff and Clair, although both employed, somehow enjoy the leisure to devote themselves full-time to the trivial and comfortable concerns that loosely determine each episode: a funeral for Rudy's goldfish, a birthday surprise for Cliff, the kids' preparations for their first day of school. And daily life in this bright house is just as easy on the viewer as it is (apparently) for Cliff's dependents: "The Cosby Show" is devoid of any dramatic tension whatsoever. Nothing happens, nothing changes, there is no suspense or ambiguity or disappointment. In one episode, Cliff accepts a challenge to race once more against a runner who, years before, had beaten him at a major track meet. At the end, the race is run, and—it's a tie!

8   Of course, "The Cosby Show" is by no means the first sitcom to present us with a big, blissful family whose members never collide with one another, or with anything else; "Eight Is Enough," "The Brady Bunch," and "The Partridge Family" are just a few examples of earlier prime-time idylls. There are, however, some crucial differences between those older shows and this one. First of all, "The Cosby Show" is far more popular than any of its predecessors. It is (as of this writing) the top-rated show in the United States and elsewhere, attracting an audience that is not only vast, but often near fanatical in its devotion. Second, and stranger still,

this show and its immense success are universally applauded as an exhilarating sign of progress. Newspaper columnists and telejournalists routinely deem "The Cosby Show" a "breakthrough" into an unprecedented *realism* because it uses none of the broad plot devices or rapid-fire gags that define the standard sitcom. Despite its fantastic ambience of calm and plenty, "The Cosby Show" is widely regarded as a rare glimpse of truth, whereas "The Brady Bunch" et al., though just as cheery, were never extolled in this way. And there is a third difference between this show and its predecessors that may help explain the new show's greater popularity and peculiar reputation for progressivism: Cliff Huxtable and his dependents are not only fabulously comfortable and mild, but also noticeably black.

9   Cliff's blackness serves an affirmative purpose within the ad that is "The Cosby Show." At the center of this ample tableau, Cliff is himself an ad, implicitly proclaiming the fairness of the American system: "Look!" he shows us. "Even *I* can have all this!" Cliff is clearly meant to stand for Cosby himself, whose name appears in the opening credits as "Dr. William E. Cosby, Jr., Ed.D."—a testament both to Cosby's lifelong effort at self-improvement, and to his sense of brotherhood with Cliff. And, indeed, Dr. Huxtable is merely the latest version of the same statement that Dr. Cosby has been making for years as a talk show guest and stand-up comic: "I got mine!" The comic has always been quick to raise the subject of his own success. "What do I care what some ten-thousand-dollar-a-year writer says about me?" he once asked Dick Cavett. And on "The Tonight Show" a few years ago, Cosby told of how his father, years before, had warned him that he'd never make a dime in show business, "and then he walked slowly back to the projects. . . . Well, I just lent him forty thousand dollars!"

10   That anecdote got a big hand, just like "The Cosby Show," but despite the many plaudits for Cosby's continuing tale of self-help, it is not quite convincing. Cliff's brownstone is too crammed, its contents too lustrous, to seem like his—or anyone's—own personal achievement. It suggests instead the corporate showcase which, in fact, it is. "The Cosby Show" attests to the power, not of Dr. Cosby/Huxtable, but of a consumer society that has produced such a tantalizing vision of reality. As Cosby himself admits, it was not his own Algeresque efforts that "caused people to love" him, but those ads put out by Coca-Cola, Ford, and General Foods—those ads in which he looks and acts precisely as he looks and acts in his own show.

11   Cosby's image is divided in a way that both facilitates the corporate project and conceals its true character. On the face of it, the Cosby style is pure impishness. Forever mugging and cavorting, throwing mock tantrums or beaming hugely to himself or doing funny little dances with his stomach pushed out, Cosby carries on a ceaseless parody of some euphoric eight-year-old. His delivery suggests the same childish spontaneity, for in the high, coy gabble of his harangues and monologues there is

a disarming quality of baby talk. And yet all this artful goofiness barely conceals an intimidating hardness—the same uncompromising willfulness that we learn to tolerate in actual children (however cute they may be), but which can seem a little threatening in a grown-up. And Cosby is indeed a most imposing figure, in spite of all his antics: a big man boasting of his wealth, and often handling an immense cigar.

12   It is a disorienting blend of affects, but it works perfectly whenever he confronts us on behalf of Ford or Coca-Cola. With a massive car or Coke machine behind him, or with a calculator at his fingertips, he hunches toward us, wearing a bright sweater and an insinuating grin, and makes his playful pitch, cajoling us to buy whichever thing he's selling, his face and words, his voice and posture all suggesting this implicit and familiar come-on: "Kitchy-koo!" It is not so much that Cosby makes his mammoth bureaucratic masters seem as nice and cuddly as himself (although such a strategy is typical of corporate advertising); rather, he implicitly assures us that *we* are nice and cuddly, like little children. At once solicitous and overbearing, he personifies the corporate force that owns him. Like it, he comes across as an easygoing parent, and yet, also like it, he cannot help but betray the impulse to coerce. We see that he is bigger than we are, better known, better off, and far more powerfully sponsored. Thus, we find ourselves ambiguously courted, just like those tots who eat up lots of Jell-O pudding under his playful supervision.

13   Dr. Huxtable controls his family with the same enlightened deviousness. As widely lauded for its "warmth" as for its "realism," "The Cosby Show" has frequently been dubbed "the "Father Knows Best" of the eighties." Here again (the columnists agree) is a good strong Dad maintaining the old "family values." This equation, however, blurs a crucial difference between Cliff and the early fathers. Like them, Cliff always wins; but this modern Dad subverts his kids not by evincing the sort of calm power that once made Jim Anderson so daunting, but by seeming to subvert himself at the same time. His is the executive style, in other words, not of the small businessman as evoked in the fifties, but of the corporate manager, skilled at keeping his subordinates in line while half concealing his authority through various disarming moves: Cliff rules the roost through teasing put-downs, clever mockery, and amiable shows of helpless bafflement. This Dad is no straightforward tyrant, then, but the playful type who strikes his children as a peach, until they realize, years later, and after lots of psychotherapy, what a subtle thug he really was.

14   An intrusive kidder, Cliff never fails to get his way; and yet there is more to his manipulativeness than simple egomania. Obsessively, Cliff sees to it, through his takes and teasing, that his children always keep things light. As in the corporate culture and on TV generally, so on this show there is no negativity allowed. Cliff's function is therefore to police the corporate playground, always on the lookout for any downbeat tendencies.

15   In one episode, for instance, Denise sets herself up by reading Cliff some somber verses that she's written for the school choir. The mood is despairing; the refrain, "I walk alone . . . I walk alone." It is clear that the girl does not take the effort very seriously, and yet Cliff merrily overreacts against this slight and artificial plaint as if it were a crime. First, while she recites, he wears a clownish look of deadpan bewilderment, then laughs out loud as soon as she has finished, and finally snidely moos the refrain in outright parody. The studio audience roars, and Denise takes the hint. At the end of the episode, she reappears with a new version, which she reads sweetly, blushingly, while Cliff and Clair, sitting side by side in their high-priced pajamas, beam with tenderness and pride on her act of self-correction:

> My mother and my father are my best friends.
> When I'm all alone, I don't have to be.
> It's because of me that I'm all alone, you see.
> Their love is real. . . .
>
> Never have they lied to me, never connived me,
> talked behind my back.
> Never have they cheated me.
> Their love is real, their love is real.

Clair, choked up, gives the girl a big warm hug, and Cliff then takes her little face between his hands and kisses it, as the studio audience bursts into applause.

16   Thus, this episode ends with a paean to the show itself (for "their love" is *not* "real," but a feature of the fiction), a moment that, for all its mawkishness, attests to Cliff's managerial adeptness. Yet Cliff is hardly a mere enforcer. He is himself also an underling, even as he seems to run things. This subservient status is manifest in his blackness. Cosby's blackness is indeed a major reason for the show's popularity, despite his frequent claims, and the journalistic consensus, that "The Cosby Show" is somehow "colorblind," simply appealing in some general "human" way. Although whitened by their status and commodities, the Huxtables are still unmistakably black. However, it would be quite inaccurate to hail their popularity as evidence of a new and rising amity between the races in America. On the contrary, "The Cosby Show" is such a hit with whites in part because whites are just as worried about blacks as they have always been—not blacks like Bill Cosby, or Lena Horne, or Eddie Murphy, but poor blacks, and the poor in general, whose existence is a well-kept secret on prime-time TV.

17   And yet TV betrays the very fears that it denies. In thousands of high-security buildings, and in suburbs reassuringly remote from the cities' "bad neighborhoods," whites may, unconsciously, be further reassured by watching not just Cosby, but a whole set of TV shows that negate the possibility of black violence with lunatic fantasies of containment: "Diff'rent Strokes" and "Webster," starring Gary Coleman and

Emmanuel Lewis, respectively, each an overcute, miniaturized black person, each playing the adopted son of good white parents. Even the oversized and growling Mr. T, complete with Mohawk, bangles, and other primitivizing touches, is a mere comforting joke, the dangerous ex-slave turned comic and therefore innocuous by campy excess; and this behemoth too is kept in line by a casual white father, Hannibal Smith, the commander of the A-Team, who employs Mr. T exclusively for his brawn.

18   As a willing advertisement for the system that pays him well, Cliff Huxtable also represents a threat contained. Although dark-skinned and physically imposing, he ingratiates us with his childlike mien and enviable life-style, a surrender that must offer some deep solace to a white public terrified that one day blacks might come with guns to steal the copperware, the juicer, the microwave, the VCR, even the TV itself. On "The Cosby Show," it appears as if blacks in general can have, or do have, what many whites enjoy, and that such material equality need not entail a single break-in. And there are no hard feelings, none at all, now that the old injustice has been so easily rectified. Cosby's definitive funny face, flashed at the show's opening credits and reproduced on countless magazine covers, is a strained denial of all animosity. With its little smile, the lips pursed tight, eyes opened wide, eyebrows raised high, that dark face shines toward us like the white flag of surrender—a desperate look that no suburban TV Dad of yesteryear would ever have put on, and one that millions of Americans today find indispensable.

19   By and large, American whites need such reassurance because they are now further removed than ever, both spatially and psychologically, from the masses of the black poor. And yet the show's appeal cannot be explained merely as a symptom of class and racial uneasiness, because there are, in our consumer culture, anxieties still more complicated and pervasive. Thus, Cliff is not just an image of the dark Other capitulating to the white establishment, but also the reflection of any constant viewer, who, whatever his/her race, must also feel like an outsider, lucky to be tolerated by the distant powers that be. There is no negativity allowed, not anywhere; and so Cliff serves both as our guide and as our double. His look of tense playfulness is more than just a sign that blacks won't hurt us; it is an expression that we too would each be wise to adopt, lest we betray some devastating sign of anger or dissatisfaction. If we stay cool and cheerful, white like him, and learn to get by with his sort of managerial acumen, we too, perhaps, can be protected from the world by a barrier of new appliances, and learn to put down others as each of us has, somehow, been put down.

20   Such rampant putting-down, the ridicule of all by all, is the very essence of the modern sitcom. Cliff, at once the joker and a joke, infantilizing others and yet infantile himself, is exemplary of everybody's status in the sitcoms, in the ads, and in most other kinds of TV spectacle (as well as in the movies). No one, finally, is immune. That solidarity of un-

derlings enabled by the butt's incursions lasts no longer than whatever takes or gags the others use against him. Once he leaves, disgraced afresh, each performs his function for the others, the status of oaf, jerk, or nerd passing to everyone in turn. Even the one who momentarily plays the put-down artist often seems a bit ridiculous in the very act of putting down the momentary loser. The butt's temporary assailant—the deadpan child, the wry oldster, the sullen maid—may score a hit against the uptight and boorish victim, but then perhaps the attacker him/herself is a bit *too* deadpan, wry, or sullen, and therefore almost as much laughed at as laughed with.

21   On the sitcom, in fact, one is obliged to undercut oneself along with everybody else.

Points for Review and Discussion

1.   Summarize the main points of Miller's attack on corporate America in "TV and All the Right Commodities."
2.   Miller draws a sharp contrast between "The Cosby Show" and earlier sitcoms portraying family life. What differences does he stress?

◆● Questions for Writing

1.   The essay opens by evoking TV's depiction of this country as a world of choice and abundance. How does the vision of America as a world of choice tend to support claims that America is the land of equality?
2.   Throughout "The Cosby Show" the author stresses that an important message driven home by the Huxtable family is that of the basic sameness of Americans. In what ways does the idea that all Americans are the same support the vision of America as the land of equality and mobility?
3.   View an episode or two of "Fresh Prince of Bel Air" and write a page assessing this sitcom from one of the critical perspectives that Miller adopts in discussing "The Cosby Show." Does the "Fresh Prince" develop its own versions of the themes of equality and mobility? Explain your answer.

Connecting the Parts in Chapter 5: Assignments for Extended Essays

1. Write an essay probing your personal opinions about upward mobility as a factor in your own life. Begin the essay by clearly spelling out your opinions in credo form (I believe . . .). Then go on to look into the origins of these opinions. Using examples to clarify your points, assess the influence on your views of each of the following: current economic conditions; your reading of the life experiences of friends, associates, and relatives; your estimate of the intensity of your ambition and the range of your abilities; your belief or disbelief in the continuing validity of the fundamentals of the American Dream (for example, the way to the top lies through hard work).
2. Write an essay on a movie or TV series that either confirms or casts doubt upon the thesis that the entertainment industry is committed to promulgating a vision of America as a classless society. Begin your essay with a statement of the central social themes of the work you have chosen. Then show how that theme is developed in particular scenes, dialogue, and camera work. At the end, compare and contrast the show you have been analyzing with other relevant movies or series.

Leads for Research

1. Look into current thinking about equality and mobility in America by examining recent writing on this subject. Four useful starting points: "Social Mobility in America," a special issue of *The Wilson Quarterly* (Winter 1987); Stephen Rose, *The American Profile Poster* (1986); Kevin Phillips, *The Politics of Rich and Poor* (see Chapter 3 of this book); Katherine S. Newman, *Declining Fortunes, The Withering of the American Dream* (1993). Focus your essay on the nature of the factors militating for and against faith in social mobility as a defining element of American society.
2. Examine historical backgrounds of American faith in mobility. How common was social ascent in the last century? To what extent was the belief in America as the land of opportunity for ordinary men and women grounded in actual fact? Useful starting points for your essay are Herbert Gutman, "The Reality of the Rags-to-Riches Myth," in Stephan Thernstrom and Richard Sennett, eds., *Nineteenth Century Cities: Essays in New Urban History* (1968), and Stephan Thernstrom, *Poverty and Progress: Social Mobility in a Nineteenth Century City* (1964).
3. The history of equality and mobility is different, of course, for blacks than for whites; to this day Americans are poorly acquainted with the full meanings of racial inequality. Begin your research on the kinds of mobility permitted to blacks prior to the 1960s by reading John U. Ogbu, *Minority Education and Caste: The American System in Cross-Cultural Perspective* (1978), and Harvard Sitkoff, *The Struggle for Black Equality* (1981).

6

Lives of the Elites

A wide range of cultural forces continues to revitalize American faith in equality and mobility. And the pattern of thousands of individual lives continues to testify that significant social and economic ascent occurs repeatedly throughout this society.

But many observers believe that politicians, corporate America, and the media nevertheless oversell the values of equality and mobility, and that a balanced account of America needs to say much more about inequality, immobility, and relatively inflexible social structures than officialdom allows itself to say at present. Writers who hold this view often argue that, today as yesterday, working people know far less about structures of power in this society than they need to know if they're to arrive at realistic views of their own situations. These critics explicitly doubt that the men and women at the top got there solely because of superior talent and commitment. And often they imply that the American Dream functions as a fantasy manipulated by authority to keep workers from achieving a level of collective self-consciousness and organizing for the betterment of the group.

Criticism in this vein appears in works of history, journalism, sociological observation, and autobiography; the three essays in "Lives of the Elites" comprise a sampling of it. Implicit in all three essays is that popular belief in America as a classless society is a fundamentally dangerous delusion.

The Power Elite
C. Wright Mills

Lacking clear, neutral labels for the social classes, Americans have adopted an array of terms to define the social divisions in our midst. We speak of "ins" and "outs," of people "above the line" and "below the line," of somebodies and nobodies and has-beens and Joe Sixpacks—on and on. Over the past half-century the search for ways of describing those who combine wealth, social position, and political influence has led to increasing reference to "elites" and to "the Establishment."

C. Wright Mills' *The Power Elite* (1956) ranks among the most famous works anatomizing the people at America's sociopolitical top. Mills, a sociologist at Columbia University, set out to describe interrelationships among the people who "occupy positions in American society from which they can look down upon, so to speak, and by their decision mightily affect, the everyday worlds of ordinary men and women." He offered detailed accounts of Celebrities, The Very Rich, The Metropolitan 400 (the older wealthy families in major Eastern cities and in San Francisco), Chief Executives, The Corporate Rich, Warlords, The Military Ascendancy, and the Political Directorate. The essay below, "The Power Elite," sums up the author's broad argument about the distribution and exercise of power in American society.

1 The power elite, as we conceive it, . . . rests upon the similarity of its personnel, and their personal and official relations with one another, upon their social and psychological affinities. In order to grasp the personal and social basis of the power elite's unity, we have first to remind ourselves of the facts of origin, career, and style of life of each of the types of circle whose members compose the power elite.

2 The power elite is *not* an aristocracy, which is to say that it is not a political ruling group based upon a nobility of hereditary origin. It has no compact basis in a small circle of great families whose members can and do consistently occupy the top positions in the several higher circles which overlap as the power elite. But such nobility is only one possible basis of common origin. That it does not exist for the American elite does not mean that members of this elite derive socially from the full range of strata composing American society. They derive in substantial proportions from the upper classes, both new and old, of local society and the metropolitan 400. The bulk of the very rich, the corporate executives, the political outsiders, the high military, derive from, at most, the upper third of the income and occupational pyramids. Their

From C. Wright Mills, *The Power Elite* (1956).

fathers were at least of the professional and business strata, and very frequently higher than that. They are native-born Americans of native parents, primarily from urban areas, and, with the exceptions of the politicians among them, overwhelmingly from the East. They are mainly Protestants, especially Episcopalian or Presbyterian. In general, the higher the position, the greater the proportion of men within it who have derived from and who maintain connections with the upper classes. The generally similar origins of the members of the power elite are underlined and carried further by the fact of their increasingly common educational routine. Overwhelmingly college graduates, substantial proportions have attended Ivy League colleges, although the education of the higher military, of course, differs from that of other members of the power elite.

3   But what do these apparently simple facts about the social composition of the higher circles really mean? In particular, what do they mean for any attempt to understand the degree of unity, and the direction of policy and interest that may prevail among these several circles? Perhaps it is best to put this question in a deceptively simple way: in terms of origin and career, who or what do these men at the top represent?

4   Of course, if they are elected politicians, they are supposed to represent those who elected them; and, if they are appointed, they are supposed to represent, indirectly, those who elected their appointers. But this is recognized as something of an abstraction, as a rhetorical formula by which all men of power in almost all systems of government nowadays justify their power of decision. At times it may be true, both in the sense of their motives and in the sense of who benefits from their decisions. Yet it would not be wise in any power system merely to assume it.

5   The fact that members of the power elite come from near the top of the nation's class and status levels does not mean that they are necessarily "representative" of the top levels only. And if they were, as social types, representative of a cross-section of the population, that would not mean that a balanced democracy of interest and power would automatically be the going political fact.

6   We cannot infer the direction of policy merely from the social origins and careers of the policy-makers. The social and economic backgrounds of the men of power do not tell us what we need to know in order to understand the distribution of social power. For: (1) Men from high places may be ideological representatives of the poor and humble. (2) Men of humble origin, brightly self-made, may energetically serve the most vested and inherited interests. Moreover (3), not all men who effectively represent the interests of a stratum need in any way belong to it or personally benefit by policies that further its interests. Among the politicians, in short, there are sympathetic *agents* of given groups, conscious and unconscious, paid and unpaid. Finally (4), among the top decision-makers we find men who have been chosen for their positions because of their "expert knowledge." These are some of the obvious

reasons why the social origins and careers of the power elite do not enable us to infer the class interests and policy directions of a modern system of power.

7   Do the high social origin and careers of the top men mean nothing, then, about the distribution of power? By no means. They simply remind us that we must be careful of any simple and direct inference from origin and career to political character and policy, not that we must ignore them in our attempt at political understanding. They simply mean that we must analyze the political psychology and the actual decisions of the political directorate as well as its social composition. And they mean, above all, that we should control, as we have done here, any inference we make from the origin and careers of the political actors by close understanding of the institutional landscape in which they act out their drama. Otherwise we should be guilty of a rather simple-minded biographical theory of society and history.

8   Just as we cannot rest the notion of the power elite solely upon the institutional mechanics that lead to its formation, so we cannot rest the notion solely upon the facts of the origin and career of its personnel. We need both, and we have both—as well as other bases, among them that of the status intermingling.

9   But it is not only the similarities of social origin, religious affiliation, nativity, and education that are important to the psychological and social affinities of the members of the power elite. Even if their recruitment and formal training were more heterogeneous than they are, these men would still be of quite homogeneous social type. For the most important set of facts about a circle of men is the criteria of admission, of praise, of honor, of promotion that prevails among them; if these are similar within a circle, then they will tend as personalities to become similar. The circles that compose the power elite do tend to have such codes and criteria in common. The co-optation of the social types to which these common values lead is often more important than any statistics of common origin and career that we might have at hand.

10   There is a kind of reciprocal attraction among the fraternity of the successful—not between each and every member of the circles of the high and mighty, but between enough of them to insure a certain unity. On the slight side, it is a sort of tacit, mutual admiration; in the strongest tie-ins, it proceeds by intermarriage. And there are all grades and types of connection between these extremes. Some overlaps certainly occur by means of cliques and clubs, churches and schools.

11   If social origin and formal education in common tend to make the members of the power elite more readily understood and trusted by one another, their continued association further cements what they feel they have in common. Members of the several higher circles know one another as personal friends and even as neighbors; they mingle with one another on the golf course, in the gentleman's clubs, at resorts, on

transcontinental airplanes, and on ocean liners. They meet at the estates of mutual friends, face each other in front of the TV camera, or serve on the same philanthropic committee; and many are sure to cross one another's path in the columns of newspapers, if not in the exact cafes from which many of these columns originate. As we have seen, of "The New 400" of cafe society, one chronicler has named forty-one members of the very rich, ninety-three political leaders, and seventy-nine chief executives of corporations.

12 "I did not know, I could not have dreamed," Whittaker Chambers has written, "of the immense scope and power of Hiss' political alliances and his social connections, which cut across all party lines and ran from the Supreme Court to the Religious Society of Friends, from governors of states and instructors in college faculties to the staff members of liberal magazines. In the decade since I had last seen him, he had used his career, and, in particular, his identification with the cause of peace through his part in organizing the United Nations, to put down roots that made him one with the matted forest floor of American upper class, enlightened middle class, liberal and official life. His roots could not be disturbed without disturbing all the roots on all sides of him."

13 The sphere of status has reflected the epochs of the power elite. In the third epoch, for example, who could compete with big money? And in the fourth, with big politicians, or even the bright young men of the New Deal? And in the fifth, who can compete with the generals and the admirals and the corporate officials now so sympathetically portrayed on the stage, in the novel, and on the screen? Can one imagine *Executive Suite* as a successful motion picture in 1935? Or *The Caine Mutiny?*

14 The multiplicity of high-prestige organizations to which the elite usually belong is revealed by even casual examination of the obituaries of the big businessman, the high-prestige lawyer, the top general and admiral, the key senator: usually, high-prestige church, business associations, plus high-prestige clubs, and often plus military rank. In the course of their lifetimes, the university president, the New York Stock Exchange chairman, the head of the bank, the old West Pointer—mingle in the status sphere, within which they easily renew old friendships and draw upon them in an effort to understand through the experience of trusted others those contexts of power and decision in which they have not personally moved.

15 In these diverse contexts, prestige accumulates in each of the higher circles, and the members of each borrow status from one another. Their self-images are fed by these accumulations and these borrowings, and accordingly, however segmental a given man's role may seem, he comes to feel himself a "diffuse" or "generalized" man of the higher circles, a "broad-gauge" man. Perhaps such inside experience is one feature of what is meant by "judgment."

16	The key organizations, perhaps, are the major corporations themselves, for on the boards of directors we find a heavy overlapping among the members of these several elites. On the lighter side, again in the summer and winter resorts, we find that, in an intricate series of overlapping circles; in the course of time, each meets each or knows somebody who knows somebody who knows that one.

17	The higher members of the military, economic, and political orders are able readily to take over one another's point of view, always in a sympathetic way, and often in a knowledgeable way as well. They define one another as among those who count, and who, accordingly, must be taken into account. Each of them as a member of the power elite comes to incorporate into his own integrity, his own honor, his own conscience, the viewpoint, the expectations, the values of the others. If there are no common ideals and standards among them that are based upon an explicitly aristocratic culture, that does not mean that they do not feel responsibility to one another.

18	All the structural coincidence of their interests as well as the intricate, psychological facts of their origins and their education, their careers and their associations make possible the psychological affinities that prevail among them, affinities that make it possible for them to say of one another: He is, of course, one of us. And all this points to the basic, psychological meaning of class consciousness. Nowhere in America is there as great a "class consciousness" as among the elite; nowhere is it organized as effectively as among the power elite. For by class consciousness, as a psychological fact, one means that the individual member of a "class" accepts only those accepted by his circle as among those who are significant to his own image of self.

19	Within the higher circles of the power elite, factions do exist; there are conflicts of policy; individual ambitions do clash. There are still enough divisions of importance within the Republican party, and even between Republicans and Democrats, to make for different methods of operation. But more powerful than these divisions are the internal discipline and the community of interests that bind the power elite together, even across the boundaries of nations at war.

20	Yet we must give due weight to the other side of the case which may not question the facts but only our interpretation of them. There is a set of objections that will inevitably be made to our whole conception of the power elite, but which has essentially to do with only the psychology of its members. It might well be put by liberals or by conservatives in some such way as this:

21	"To talk of a power elite—isn't this to characterize men by their origins and associations? Isn't such characterization both unfair and untrue? Don't men modify themselves, especially Americans such as these, as they rise in stature to meet the demands of their jobs? Don't they arrive at a view and a line of policy that represents, so far as they in their human weaknesses can know, the interests of the nation as a whole? Aren't they merely honorable men who are doing their duty?'

22   What are we to reply to these objections?

23   I. We are sure that they are honorable men. But what is honor? Honor can only mean living up to a code that one believes to be honorable. There is no one code upon which we are all agreed. That is why, if we are civilized men, we do not kill off all of those with whom we disagree. The question is not: are these honorable men? The question is: what are their codes of honor? The answer to that question is that they are the codes of their circles, of those to whose opinions they defer. How could it be otherwise? That is one meaning of the important truism that all men are human and that all men are social creatures. As for sincerity, it can only be disproved, never proved.

24   II. To the question of their adaptability—which means their capacity to transcend the codes of conduct which, in their life's work and experience, they have acquired—we must answer: simply no, they cannot, at least not in the handful of years most of them have left. To expect that is to assume that they are indeed strange and expedient: such flexibility would in fact involve a violation of what we may rightly call their character and their integrity. By the way, may it not be precisely because of the lack of such character and integrity that earlier types of American politicians have not represented as great a threat as do these men of character?

25   It would be an insult to the effective training of the military, and to their indoctrination as well, to suppose that military officials shed their military character and outlook upon changing from uniform to mufti. This background is more important perhaps in the military case than in that of the corporate executives, for the training of the career is deeper and more total.

26   III. To the question of their patriotism, of their desire to serve the nation as a whole, we must answer first that, like codes of honor, feelings of patriotism and views of what is to the whole nation's good, are not ultimate facts but matters upon which there exists a great variety of opinion. Furthermore, patriotic opinions too are rooted in and are sustained by what a man has become by virtue of how and with whom he has lived. This is no simple mechanical determination of individual character by social conditions; it is an intricate process, well established in the major tradition of modern social study. One can only wonder why more social scientists do not use it systematically in speculating about politics.

27   IV. The elite cannot be truly thought of as men who are merely doing their duty. They are the ones who determine their duty, as well as the duties of those beneath them. They are not merely following orders: they give the orders. They are not merely "bureaucrats": they command bureaucracies. They may try to disguise these facts from others and from themselves by appeals to traditions of which they imagine themselves the instruments, but there are many traditions, and they must choose

which ones they will serve. They face decisions for which there simply are no traditions.

28   Now, to what do these several answers add up? To the fact that we cannot reason about public events and historical trends merely from knowledge about the motives and character of the men or the small groups who sit in the seats of the high and mighty. This fact, in turn, does not mean that we should be intimidated by accusations that in taking up our problem in the way we have, we are impugning the honor, the integrity, or the ability of those who are in high office. For it is not, in the first instance, a question of individual character; and if, in further instances, we find that it is, we should not hesitate to say so plainly. In the meantime, we must judge men of power by the standards of power, by what they do as decision-makers, and not by who they are or what they may do in private life. Our interest is not in that: we are interested in their policies and in the *consequences* of their conduct of office. We must remember that these men of the power elite now occupy the strategic places in the structure of American society; that they command the dominant institutions of a dominant nation; that, as a set of men, they are in a position to make decisions with terrible consequences for the underlying populations of the world.

29   Despite their social similarity and psychological affinities, the members of the power elite do not constitute a club having a permanent membership with fixed and formal boundaries. It is of the nature of the power elite that within it there is a good deal of shifting about, and that it thus does not consist of one small set of the same men in the same positions in the same hierarchies. Because men know each other personally does not mean that among them there is a unity of policy; and because they do not know each other personally does not mean that among them there is a disunity. The conception of the power elite does not rest, as I have repeatedly said, primarily upon personal friendship.

30   As the requirements of the top places in each of the major hierarchies become similar, the types of men occupying these roles at the top—by selection and by training in the jobs—become similar. This is no mere deduction from structure to personnel. That it is a fact is revealed by the heavy traffic that has been going on between the three structures, often in very intricate patterns. The chief executives, the warlords, and selected politicians came into contact with one another in an intimate, working way during World War II; after that war ended, they continued their associations, out of common beliefs, social congeniality, and coinciding interests. Noticeable proportions of top men from the military, the economic, and the political worlds have during the last fifteen years occupied positions in one or both of the other worlds: between these higher circles there is an interchangeability of position, based formally upon the supposed transferability of "executive ability," based in sub-

stance upon the co-optation by cliques of insiders. As members of a power elite, many of those busy in this traffic have come to look upon "the government" as an umbrella under whose authority they do their work.

31 As the business between the big three increases in volume and importance, so does the traffic in personnel.... All over the country the corporate leaders are drawn into the circle of the high military and political through personal friendship, trade and professional associations and their various subcommittees, prestige clubs, open political affiliation, and customer relationships. "There is ... an awareness among these power leaders," one first-hand investigator of such executive cliques has asserted, "of many of the current major policy issues before the nation such as keeping taxes down, turning all productive operations over to private enterprises, increasing foreign trade, keeping governmental welfare and other domestic activities to a minimum, and strengthening and maintaining the hold of the current party in power nationally."

32 There are, in fact, cliques of corporate executives who are more important as informal opinion leaders in the top echelons of corporate, military, and political power than as actual participants in military and political organizations. Inside military circles and inside political circles and "on the sidelines" in the economic area, these circles and cliques of corporation executives are in on most all major decisions regardless of topic. And what is important about all this high-level lobbying is that it is done within the confines of that elite.

33 The conception of the power elite and of its unity rests upon the corresponding developments and the coincidence of interests among economic, political, and military organizations. It also rests upon the similarity of origin and outlook, and the social and personal intermingling of the top circles from each of these dominant hierarchies. This conjunction of institutional and psychological forces, in turn, is revealed by the heavy personnel traffic within and between the big three institutional orders, as well as by the rise of go-betweens as in the high-level lobbying. The conception of the power elite, accordingly, does *not* rest upon the assumption that American history since the origins of World War II must be understood as a secret plot, or as a great and co-ordinated conspiracy of the members of this elite. The conception rests upon quite impersonal grounds.

34 There is, however, little doubt that the American power elite—which contains, we are told, some of "the greatest organizers in the world"—has also planned and has plotted. The rise of the elite, as we have already made clear, was not and could not have been caused by a plot; and the tenability of the conception does not rest upon the existence of any secret or any publicly known organization. But, once the conjunction of structural trend and of the personal will to utilize it gave rise to the power

elite, then plans and programs did occur to its members and indeed it is not possible to interpret many events and official policies of the fifth epoch without reference to the power elite. "There is a great difference," Richard Hofstadter has remarked, "between locating conspiracies *in* history and saying that history *is*, in effect, a conspiracy..."

35   The structural trends of institutions become defined as opportunities by those who occupy their command posts. Once such opportunities are recognized, men may avail themselves of them. Certain types of men from each of the dominant institutional areas, more far-sighted than others, have actively promoted the liaison before it took its truly modern shape. They have often done so for reasons not shared by their partners, although not objected to by them either; and often the outcome of their liaison has had consequences which none of them foresaw, much less shaped, and which only later in the course of development came under explicit control. Only after it was well under way did most of its members find themselves part of it and become gladdened, although sometimes also worried, by this fact. But once the co-ordination is a going concern, new men come readily into it and assume its existence without question.

36   So far as explicit organization—conspiratorial or not—is concerned, the power elite, by its very nature, is more likely to use existing organizations, working within and between them, than to set up explicit organizations whose membership is strictly limited to its own members. But if there is no machinery in existence to ensure, for example, that military and political factors will be balanced in decisions made, they will invent such machinery and use it, as with the National Security Council. Moreover, in a formally democratic polity, the aims and the powers of the various elements of this elite are further supported by an aspect of the permanent war economy: the assumption that the security of the nation supposedly rests upon great secrecy of plan and intent. Many higher events that would reveal the working of the power elite can be withheld from public knowledge under the guise of secrecy. With the wide secrecy covering their operations and decisions, the power elite can mask their intentions, operations, and further consolidation. Any secrecy that is imposed upon those in positions to observe high decision-makers clearly works for and not against the operations of the power elite.

37   There is accordingly reason to suspect—but by the nature of the case, no proof—that the power elite is not altogether "surfaced." There is nothing hidden about it, although its activities are not publicized. As an elite, it is not organized, although its members often know one another, seem quite naturally to work together, and share many organizations in common. There is nothing conspiratorial about it, although its decisions are often publicly unknown and its mode of operation manipulative rather than explicit.

38   It is not that the elite "believe in" a compact elite behind the scenes and a mass down below. It is not put in that language. It is just that the

people are of necessity confused and must, like trusting children, place all the new world of foreign policy and strategy and executive action in the hands of experts. It is just that everyone knows somebody has got to run the show, and that somebody usually does. Others do not really care anyway, and besides, they do not know how. So the gap between the two types gets wider.

39 When crises are defined as total, and as seemingly permanent, the consequences of decision become total, and the decisions in each major area of life come to be integrated and total. Up to a point, these consequences for other institutional orders can be assessed; beyond such points, chances have to be taken. It is then that the felt scarcity of trained and imaginative judgment leads to plaintive feelings among executives about the shortage of qualified successors in political, military, and economic life. This feeling, in turn, leads to an increasing concern with the training of successors who could take over as older men of power retire. In each area, there slowly arises a new generation which has grown up in an age of co-ordinated decisions.

40 In each of the elite circles, we have noticed this concern to recruit and to train successors as "broad-gauge" men, that is, as men capable of making decisions that involve institutional areas other than their own. The chief executives have set up formal recruitment and training programs to man the corporate world as virtually a state within a state. Recruitment and training for the military elite has long been rigidly professionalized, but has now come to include educational routines of a sort which the remnants of older generals and admirals consider quite nonsensical.

41 Only the political order, with its absence of a genuine civil service, has lagged behind, creating an administrative vacuum into which military bureaucrats and corporate outsiders have been drawn. But even in this domain, since World War II, there have been repeated attempts, by elite men of such vision as the late James Forrestal's, to inaugurate a career service that would include periods in the corporate world as well as in the governmental.

42 What is lacking is a truly common elite program of recruitment and training; for the prep school, Ivy League College, and law school sequence of the metropolitan 400 is not up to the demands now made upon members of the power elite. Britishers, such as Field Marshall Viscount Montgomery, well aware of this lack, recently urged the adoption of a system "under which a minority of high-caliber young students could be separated from the mediocre and given the best education possible to supply the country with leadership." His proposal is echoed, in various forms, by many who accept his criticism of "the American theory of public education on the ground that it is ill-suited to produce the 'elite' group of leaders ... this country needs to fulfill its obligations of world leadership."

43 In part these demands reflect the unstated need to transcend recruitment on the sole basis of economic success, especially since it is suspect

as often involving the higher immorality; in part it reflects the stated need to have men who, as Viscount Montgomery says, know "the meaning of discipline." But above all these demands reflect the at least vague consciousness on the part of the power elite themselves that the age of co-ordinated decisions, entailing a newly enormous range of consequences, requires a power elite that is of a new caliber. In so far as the sweep of matters which go into the making of decisions is vast and interrelated, the information needed for judgments complex and requiring particularized knowledge, the men in charge will not only call upon one another; they will try to train their successors for the work at hand. These new men will grow up as men of power within the co-ordination of economic and political and military decision.

Points for Review and Discussion

1.   Summarize the chief kinds of relationships Mills discerns among members of the power elite.
2.   The highest levels of class consciousness, Mills says, are found among the elite. How does he account for this? What forces does he believe bind the elite together?
3.   Mills makes four points in rebutting those who claim that the elite consists merely of "honorable men who are doing their duty." What are these four points?

•◆ *Questions for Writing*

1.   "There is a kind of reciprocal attraction among the fraternity of the successful—not between each and every member of the circles of the high and mighty, but between enough of them to insure a certain unity. On the slight side, it is a sort of tacit, mutual admiration; in the strongest tie-ins, it proceeds by intermarriage" (¶ 10). Mills makes his case both through direct argument and through tones that indirectly communicate his attitudes. Reread the sentences above and point to phrases that define Mills' attitude without explicitly spelling it out. Explain your choices.
2.   *The Power Elite* refers throughout to "men," never to "men and women"; someone undertaking to update the book would need to weigh seriously the gains in influence scored by women over the past three to four decades. In your view how much have these gains altered the broad picture of power distribution that Mills sketches?

Money and Class in America
Lewis Lapham

Analysts of the top layers of America's class structure tend to concentrate on the subject of power—how it's exercised and maintained. But some commentators also pay heed to the psychology of the rich—particularly the sense of entitlement among the well-off, and their remoteness from ordinary feelings and ordinary life. The psychology of the rich is closely examined in the essay below, by Lewis Lapham. In his book *Money and Class in America* (1988), Lapham inquires into what he calls "our civil religion"—namely, the pursuit of dollars. His premise is that, even before the American colonists declared their independence, they were of two conflicting minds about the purposes of our national experiment: "One faction thought that money was merely a commodity (as drab as wood, or straw or cloth) and that the American experiment was about the discovery of a moral commonwealth. Another faction, equally idealistic but not so pious, thought that money was a sacrament and that America was about the miracle of self-enrichment." Lapham claims that this argument has continued to rage throughout the whole of American history.

Born into the ranks of the privileged, Lewis Lapham, a journalist who is now the editor of *Harper's* magazine, looks with an insider's eye at various unlovable traits and behaviors of the people on top. Not the least of his contributions is a fresh label for the moneyed: he calls them "the equestrian classes."

The Gilded Cage

> Money is human happiness *in abstracto*; consequently he who is no longer capable of happiness *in concreto* sets his whole heart on money.
>
> —Arthur Schopenhauer
>
> What I want to see above all is that this remains a country where someone can always get rich.
>
> —Ronald Reagan

1   At Yale University in the middle 1950's the man whom I prefer to call George Amory I knew chiefly by virtue of his reputation for wrecking automobiles. He was the heir to what was said to be a large Long Island fortune, and I remembered him as a blond and handsome

---

From Lewis Lapham, *Money and Class in America* (1988).

tennis player embodying the ideal of insouciant elegance seen in a tailor's window. During the whole of our senior year I doubt that I spoke to Amory more than once or twice; we would likely have seen one another in a crowd, probably at a fraternity beer party, and I assume that we exchanged what we thought were witty observations about the differences between the girls from Vassar and those from Smith. At random intervals during the 1960's and 1970's I heard rumors of Amory's exploits in the stock market and the south of France, but I hadn't seen him for almost thirty years when, shortly after President Reagan's second inaugural in the winter of 1985, I ran across him in the bar of the Plaza Hotel. He seemed somehow smaller than I remembered, not as blond or as careless. Ordinarily we would have nodded at one another without a word of recognition, and I remember being alarmed when Amory carried his drink to my table and abruptly began to recite what he apparently regarded as the epic poem of his economic defeat. Presumably he chose me as his confessor because we scarcely knew each other, much less belonged to the same social circles. I wasn't apt to repeat what I heard to anybody whom he thought important enough to matter.

2   "I'm nothing," he said. "You understand that, nothing. I earn $250,000 a year, but it's nothing, and I'm nobody."

3   Amory at Yale had assumed that the world would entertain him as its guest. He had little reason to think otherwise. Together with his grandmother's collection of impressionist paintings and the houses in Southampton and Maine, he looked forward to inheriting a substantial income. Certainly it never had occurred to him that he might be obliged to suffer the indignity of balancing his checkbook or looking at a bill.

4   Things hadn't turned out quite the way he had expected, and in the bar of the Plaza he looked at me with a dazed expression, as if he couldn't believe that he had lost the match. He had three children, but his wife was without substantial means of her own, and somehow he failed to generate enough money to carry him from one week to the next. He explained that most of the paintings had been sold, that he had been forced to rent the house in Southampton for $40,000 during the season, and that the property in Maine had been stolen from him by his sister. He had been busy in the bar making lists of those expenses he deemed inescapable. Handing me a sheet of legal foolscap, he said:

5   "You figure it out. I can't afford to go to a museum, much less to the theater. I'm lucky if I can take Stephanie to dinner once every six months."

6   His list of disbursements appears as he gave it to me, the numbers figured on an annual basis in 1985 dollars and annotated to reflect the narrowness of the margin on which Amory was trying to keep up a decent appearance:

Maintenance of a cooperative apartment on Park Avenue: $20,400[1]
Maintenance of the house in Southampton: $10,000
Private school tuitions (one college, one prep school, one grammar school): $30,000
Groceries: $12,000[2]
Interest on a $200,000 loan adjusted to the prime rate: $30,000
Telephone, household repairs and electricity: $12,000
A full-time maid and a part-time laundress: $25,000
Insurance (on art objects, the apartment and his life): $8,000
Lawyers and accountants: $5,000
Club dues and bills: $5,000[3]
Pharmacy (cosmetics, medicine, notions): $5,000
Doctors (primarily for the children): $4,000
Charitable donations: $6,000[4]
Clothes for his wife: $5,000[5]
Clothes for his children: $7,000
Cash expenditures (taxis, newspapers, coffee shops, balloons, etc.): $8,000
Maintenance of children's expectations (stereo sets, computers, allowances, dancing school, books, winter vacations): $30,000
Maintenance of his own expectations: $3,000
Taxes (city, state, federal): $75,000
Total: $300,400

7   It was no use trying to play the part of a niggling accountant or to suggest that it might be possible to lead a presentable life on less than $250,000 a year. Amory was too desperate to fix his attention on small sums. When I remarked that he might cut back on his children's expectations he said that these were necessary to allow his children to compete with their peers, to give them a sense of their proper place in the world. In answer to a question about the club bills and the charitable do-

---

[1] Given the expense of New York real estate, Amory could count himself lucky to be paying so low a price. He had inherited the apartment, ten rooms at East Seventy-sixth Street, from his mother. By 1985 comparable apartments cost at least $1 million to buy and between $2,000 and $3,000 a month to maintain.

[2] An extremely modest sum, implying the absence of a cook, an inability to give dinner parties and a reliance on canned goods.

[3] Again, a pittance. At his clubs in town Amory could have afforded to do little more than pay his dues and stand his friends to a quarterly round of drinks. At the beach club on Long Island his children would have had to be careful about signing food chits and losing golf balls.

[4] $1,000 to each of his children's schools, the minimum donation acceptable under the rules of what Thorstein Veblen, in *The Theory of the Leisure Class*, defined as "pecuniary decency": $1,000 to Yale University and $2,000 meted out in small denominations to miscellaneous charities dear to Stephanie Amory's friends.

[5] Most of the women in Stephanie Amory's set could draw on an annual clothes allowance of $30,000. Evening dresses designed by Givenchy or Bill Blass cost between $3,000 and $5,000.

nations, Amory pointed out that he allocated nothing for luxury or pleasure, no money for dinner parties, for paintings, for furniture, for a mistress, for psychiatrists, even for a week in Europe.[6]

8 "As it is," he said, "I live like an animal. I eat tuna fish out of cans and hope that when the phone rings it isn't somebody dunning me for a bill."

9 Not knowing what else to do Amory had resolved to leave New York, maybe for Old Westbury or Westport, "someplace unimportant," he said, where he could afford "to stay in the game." He couldn't do for his children what his parents had done for him, and his feeling of failure showed in his eyes. He had the look of a man who was being followed by the police.

10 Seen from a safe distance, Amory's despair seems comic or grotesque, the stuff of dreaming idiocy that Neil Simon could turn into a commercial farce or the *New York Times* editorial page into an occasion for moral outrage. If the average American family of four earns an annual income of $18,000, by what ludicrous arithmetic could a man of Amory's means have the effrontery to feel deprived?

11 It is a question that on a number of occasions in my life I could as easily have asked myself. Like Amory, I was born into the ranks of the equestrian class and educated to the protocols of wealth at prep school and college.[7] Given the circumstances of my childhood in San Francisco, I don't know how I could have avoided an early acquaintance with the pathologies of wealth. The Lapham family enjoyed the advantages of social eminence in a city that cared about little else, and most of its members comforted themselves with the telling and retelling of tales about the mythical riches of my great-grandfather. He died the year I was born, by all accounts a very severe but subtle gentleman who had been one of the partners in the founding of the Texas Oil Company. It was said that he translated poetry from the ancient Greek, played both the organ and the cello, collected shipping companies and oriental jade, and at one point in his life considered the possibility of buying the Monterey Peninsula. That he didn't do so, deciding to acquire instead a less dramatic but more convenient estate in Connecticut, was a source of vast disappointment to his descendants. As a child I occasionally followed my elders around the golf courses at Pebble Beach and Cypress Point, and by listening to their conversation

---

[6] In May 1987 the fashion tabloid *W* fixed the price of keeping a young mistress in New York City at $5,000 per month; the sum included rent, clothes, maid and exercise trainer, but not jewels, furs or weekends in Mexico.

[7] None of the phrases commonly used to describe the holders of American wealth strike me as being sufficiently precise. The United States never has managed to put together an "establishment" in the British sense of the word; "plutocracy" is too vague, and "upper class" implies a veneer of manners that doesn't exist. Borrowed from the Roman usage, equestrian class comprises all those who can afford to ride rather than walk and who can buy any or all of the baubles that constitute the proofs of social status. As with the ancient Romans, the rank is for sale.

gathered that I had been swindled out of a proprietary view of the Pacific Ocean.

12   In 1942, during the first autumn of the Second World War, my grandfather was elected mayor of San Francisco. I often rode in municipal limousines, either to Kezar Stadium for the New Year's Day football game or to the Presidio for military ceremonies among returning generals, and somewhere on the journey through streets that I remember as always crowded, I confused the pretensions of family with the imperatives of the public interest. I came to imagine that I was born to ride in triumph and that others, apparently less fortunate and more numerous, were born to stand smiling in the streets and wave their hats.

13   My self-preoccupation was consistent with the ethos of a city given to believing its own press notices. The citizens of San Francisco dote on a romantic image of themselves, and their provincial narcissism would be difficult to exaggerate. The circumference of the civic interest extends no more than a hundred miles in three directions, as far as Sonoma County on the north, to Monterey on the south and to Yosemite in the east. In a westerly direction the zone of significance doesn't reach beyond the Golden Gate Bridge. We lived in a fashionable quarter of the city, surrounded by spacious houses belonging to people in similar circumstances, and I attended a private school that nurtured social rather than intellectual pretensions. Everybody went to the same dancing classes, and none of us had any sense of other voices in other parts of town.

14   The accident of being born into the American equestrian class has obvious advantages, but it also has disadvantages that are not so obvious. Children encouraged to believe themselves either beautiful or rich assume that nothing further will be required of them, and they revert to the condition of aquatic plants drifting in the shallows. The lack of oxygen in the atmosphere makes them giddy with ruinous fantasy.[8] Together with my classmates and peers, I was given to understand that it was sufficient accomplishment merely to have been born. Not that anybody ever said precisely that in so many words, but the assumption was plain enough, and I could confirm it by observing the mechanics of the local society. A man might become a drunkard, a concert pianist or an owner of companies, but none of these occupations would have an important bearing on his social rank. If he could pay the club dues, if he could present himself at dinner dressed in the correct clothes for whatever the season of the year, if he could retain the minimum good sense necessary to stay out of jail, then he could command the homage of headwaiters. Headwaiters represented the

---

[8] William K. Vanderbilt made the point in a newspaper interview in 1905. "Inherited wealth," he said, "is a big handicap to happiness. It is as certain death to ambition as cocaine is to morality."

world's opinion, and their smiling respect confirmed a man in his definition of himself. That definition would be accepted at par value by everyone whom one knew or would be likely to know. A man's morals or achievements would be admired as if they were lawn decorations, with the same cries of mindless approbation that society women bestow on poets and dogs. The gentleman's inadequacies, whether a tendency toward confused sadism or a habit of cheating the customers on the stock exchange, could be excused as unfortunate lapses of judgment or taste. What was important was the appearance of things, and if these could be decently maintained, a man could look forward to a sequence of pleasant invitations. He would be entitled to a view from the box seats.

15   From the box seats, of course, the world arranges itself into a decorous entertainment conveniently staged for the benefit of the people who can afford the price of admission. The point of view assumes that Australians will play tennis, that Italians will sing or kill one another in Brooklyn, that blacks will dance or riot (always at a seemly distance), and that the holders of a season subscription will live happily ever after, or, if they are very rich, forever.

16   The comfortable assurance of this point of view implies a corollary refusal to see anything that doesn't appear on the program. Nobody could imagine that they might be dislodged by social upheaval, of no matter what force and velocity, and it was taken for granted that the embarrassments of sex and death would be transformed into the lyrics of a Cole Porter song. The Oedipal drama took place only on stage, in road-show companies sent out from the darkness of New York, or possibly in certain poor neighborhoods in the Mission District. All manifestations of intelligence remained suspect, as if they were contraband for which a man could be arrested if they were found in his possession. Later in life, if he discovered that he needed the commodity for the conduct of his business, he could hire a Jew.

17   Similar attitudes of invulnerable privilege were characteristic not only of the students at Hotchkiss and Yale but also of most of the people whom I later came to know in the expensive American professions. Within the labyrinths of the big-time media, in the corridors of Washington law firms and Wall Street brokerage houses, within the honeycombs of most institutions large enough and rich enough to afford their own hermetic models of reality (e.g., the State Department, the Mobil Oil Corporation, Time, Inc.), I found myself in the familiar atmospheres of reverie and dream.

18   Neither at the Hotchkiss School nor at Yale University did I come across many people who placed their trust in anything other than the authority of wealth. The members of the faculty at both institutions often made fine-sounding speeches about the wonders of the liberal arts—as if they (the liberal arts, not the members of the faculty) were a suite of virgins set upon by Philistine dogs—but the systems of value that governed

the workings of the schools were plainly those that prevailed in the better neighborhoods of San Francisco.[9]

19   Hotchkiss received the majority of its students from the affluent middle class resident in New York City, Connecticut and Long Island. Given the plausible expectations of inheritance among these young men, it was hardly surprising that few of them felt obliged to learn much more than the elementary geography of the civilization in which they would happen to be spending the income. They assumed, as did the faculty, that the mere fact of being present ratified their admission to the ranks of "the best people." A prep school education in the autumn of 1948 was something that one couldn't afford to do without (like dancing school or swimming lessons), but it was not something that deserved much thought or attention. It was a necessary ornament, perhaps, but not the equal of a good shotgun or a trust fund yielding $300,000 a year. Ambition, like leather jackets, was best left to the poor. Everybody who mattered already had arrived at all the places that mattered, and anybody who seemed to be in too much of a hurry to get somewhere else (presumably somewhere he or she didn't belong) must be considered a person of doubtful character or criminal intent. Why would anybody want to strive for anything if all the really important prizes had been handed out in the maternity ward at New York Hospital?[10] Scholarship students might be forgiven the wish to become secretary of state or Chief Justice of the United States, but the heirs of affluence didn't need to think beyond the horizon of their amusements. What was necessary would be given to them; for what they desired over and above those necessities they would pay, grudgingly, the going price.[11]

20   The faculty did its best to apply a veneer of cultural polish, to impart a sense that somehow it was important to learn at least a few polite

---

[9] The attitude doesn't appear to have changed much over the last thirty years; if anything, the emphasis on money has become more pronounced. Tuition at an Ivy League college is now $17,000 a year, and the students apparently worry about preserving the assumptions of ease so expensively maintained by their parents.

In *Campus Life*, a study of undergraduate attitudes published in 1987, Helen Lefkowitz Horowitz remarks on the virulent preoccupation with wealth now afflicting students everywhere in the country. She quotes a senior at Duke University, "It seems like all we talk about is money. I try to say that it's not that important. But it's really important to be comfortable, and you can't be comfortable without money."

[10] A variation of this attitude accounted for the more refined Republican opposition to John F. Kennedy's seeking of the presidency in 1960. Politics was an expensive form of social climbing, and the Kennedys conceivably could be forgiven their vulgarity on the ground that they had no other way of being admitted to the Bath and Tennis Club at Palm Beach.

[11] From the point of view of the *jeunesse dorée* matriculating at the Hotchkiss School in the early 1950's the "bare necessities" would have included property equivalent in value to an apartment on Park Avenue, a house in Southampton or Newport, a seat on the New York Stock Exchange, substantial trust funds (both for oneself and one's eventual wife), memberships in the Racquet, Brook and Piping Rock clubs, miscellaneous paintings and art objects falling due on the deaths of various relatives. Luxuries (i.e., those diversions that had to be ordered à la carte) included such items as a divorce, a racing stable, a third house, political office and an art collection.

phrases of Latin or Greek. Nobody stated the operative principles more succinctly than an English master whom I accompanied on a walk through the countryside in the autumn of my sophomore year. The walk was compulsory, the result of an offense against the rules, and the few of us who followed the master across the stubbled fields listened with a degree of attentiveness appropriate to the magnitude of our transgressions. I must have been in fairly bad trouble at the time because I can remember the master's reflections on education with unusual clarity. He was a large and untidy man, notable for his constant puffing on a pipe and the holes in the elbows of his tweed jacket. He spoke slowly and obscurely, the words sometimes garbled by the pipe. His thought revealed itself in cryptic episodes, apparently taking him by surprise. He would interrupt himself just as abruptly, subsiding for no discernible reason into a diffident silence that continued for another two or three miles. As follows:

21   "What we are trying to do here, gentlemen, is to give you an idea of the whole man ... character, you see, character is what we are interested in. The rest is not very important. Politics and business, I suppose, must get done somehow, and I don't mean to say anything against commerce, of course, but none of it has anything to do with character, you see, with the idea of a gentleman...."

22   Or again, some miles down the road at the edge of a stream in which the first skein of ice had formed:

23   "You are the heirs to a great tradition, the magnificent edifice of Western civilization. It's a rich heritage, gentlemen, and we are trying to teach you to find your way around its corridors, its labyrinthine corridors, I might say...."

24   Or lastly, two hours later, while walking up the hill to the gymnasium, with hearty and reassuring laughter:

25   "Never read so much that you wear yourselves out in study. Remember the whole man. No poem can take the place of a tramp through the woods in winter ... know the difference between different orders of things. Most of you have been given a great deal and will be given a great deal more. I think you should learn to respond with informed gratitude."

26   The guarantee of privilege extended to everybody at Hotchkiss, even to the molelike grinds who hoped only to serve the system that temporarily made fun of their accents and their shoes. Nobody seriously questioned the legitimacy of the regime; nor could anybody conceive of an alternative hierarchy of ideas. A small and dissident minority counted among its members several of the most intelligent boys in school, but they were content to make common cause with the social majority in the elaboration of the manner defined as "casual." The motives of the two factions didn't quite coincide—there is a difference between the ennui of people who own things and the ennui of people who fear the owners—but they shared an equivalent egoism. To be casual at prep school was everything—a manner that implied fluidity, grace, ease, absence of commitment, urbanity, lack of sentiment, indifference to the

rules and courage under circumstances always ironic. The style discouraged enthusiasm on the ground that it exposed a person to the risk of failure. Anybody investing time or effort in anything took the appalling risk that the market in his enterprise (i.e., himself) might collapse. Jazz musicians defined the attitude as "cool," and variations of the style later appeared in the 1960's under the rubric of the counterculture. But just as I never met a hippie whom I could have described as a revolutionary, so also I never met a social critic, especially the more eminent among them, whose complaint had more to do with substance than with gesture.

27   At Yale University in the 1950's the expression of "informed gratitude" meant having the good manners to learn the difference between a Beethoven sonata and a logarithm table. Whitney Griswold, then president of the university, welcomed the members of the freshman class to Woolsey Hall and reminded us in his introductory remarks of the many feats performed on our behalf by the venerable sages whose busts could be seen standing on pedestals along the walls. Griswold's discussion of "the well-rounded man" reiterated the word of advice offered by the Hotchkiss English master. Western civilization had apparently been acquired at some cost, and the class of 1956 had an obligation to maintain it in a decent state of repair.

28   As an intellectual proposition Yale proved to be a matter of filling out forms. Over a term of four years the representative celebrities of the human soul (Plato, Montaigne, Goethe et al.) put in guest appearances on the academic talk show, and the audience was expected to welcome them with rounds of appreciative applause. Like producers holding up cue cards, the faculty identified those truths deserving of the adjective "great." The students who received the best marks were those who could think of the most flattering explanations for the greatness of the great figures and the great truths.

29   A few professors made a self-conscious point of taking testimony on all sides of an argument, earnestly considering (pipe thoughtfully in mouth, head inclined diffidently forward and to the left) even the most preposterous hypothesis and keeping an always open mind to the chance of "meaningful dialogue." At the end of the hour or semester, of course, the questions had to be answered in the manner recommended at the beginning. Failure to conform to the presiding truths resulted in second-rate grades and a reputation for being either arrogant or odd.

30   Before the winter of freshman year the students understood that the politics of a Yale education would have little to do with the university's statements of ennobling purpose. A Yale education was a means of acquiring a cash value. Whatever the faculty said or didn't say, what was important was the diploma, the ticket of admission to Wall Street, the professions, the safe havens of the big money. As an undergraduate I thought this discovery profound; it had a cynical glint to it, in keeping with the novels of Albert Camus and the plays of Bertolt Brecht then in vogue among the apprentice intellectuals who frequented the United

Restaurant on Chapel Street. The diner stayed open all night, and one morning at about 3 a.m. I remember telling the cognoscenti about an English professor who had marked one of my papers with an F because I had proposed an unauthorized view of a seventeenth-century divine. In the margin of the paper the professor had written: "I don't care what you think, I'm only interested in knowing that you know what I think." The message pretty much defined the thesis of a Yale education at the time, and the professor was, of course, right. Schools serve the social order and, quite properly, promote the habits of mind necessary to the maintenance of that order.

31   The education offered at Yale (as at Harvard, Princeton or the University of Michigan) bears comparison to the commercial procedure for stunting caterpillars just prior to the moment of their transformation into butterflies. Silkworms can be made useful, but butterflies blow around in the wind and do nothing to add to the profits of the corporation or the power of the state. Brilliance of mind is all well and good if it leads to some visible improvement (preferably technological) or if it can be translated into a redeeming sum of cash. Otherwise, like the Soviet embassy, it is to be placed under surveillance.[12]

32   At Yale I was introduced to the perennial American debate that might well be entitled, "What are the humanities, and why do they mean anything to us here in the last decades of the twentieth century?" The debate has been going on for at least thirty years, becoming more agitated and abstract as it steadily loses its meaning. Nobody wants to say, at least not for publication, that we live in a society that cares as much about the humanities as it cares about the color of the rain in Tashkent. The study of the liberal arts is one of those appearances that must be kept up, like the belief in the rule of law and the devout observances offered to the doctrines of free enterprise and equal opportunity. By advocating the tepid ideals of "the graceful amateur" and "the well-rounded man" the universities make of humanism a pious and wax-faced thing. Works of art and literature become ornaments preserved, like bank notes or trust funds, in the vaults of an intellectual museum. The society doesn't expect its "best people" (i.e., the Hotchkiss students who grow up to become investment bankers and corporation presidents) to have read William Shakespeare or Dante. Nor does anyone imagine that the secretary of state will know much more history than the rudiments of chronology expounded in a sixth-grade synopsis. If it becomes necessary to display the finery of learning, the corporation can hire a speechwriter

[12] Much later in life I became a trustee of schools and universities, and I was sorry to see my earlier impressions so resoundingly confirmed. University presidents devoted their principal time and effort to the labor of raising money. Even if they had entered office with a fondness for literature or scholarship (as did A. Bartlett Giamatti at Yale in the late 1970's) they had no choice but to suppress their enthusiasms when flattering the alumni. Giamatti used to say that he couldn't afford to speak plain English. He was obliged to translate his thought into the empty abstraction of a language that he called "the higher institutional."

or send its chairman to the intellectual haberdashers at the Aspen Institute. Education is a commodity, like Pepsi-Cola or alligator shoes, and freedom is a privilege fully available only to those who can afford it.[13]

The lessons learned at school were confirmed by my experience at different elevations in the choir lofts of the media. After leaving Yale I first found work as a reporter for the *San Francisco Examiner*, a Hearst newspaper known for the artful sensationalism of its headlines. From the *Examiner* I went to the *New York Herald-Tribune* in 1960 and then to various magazines, among them *Life, The Saturday Evening Post* and *Harper's.*

Before I was twenty I thought the pathologies of wealth confined to relatively small numbers of people preserved in the aspic of a specific social class. By the time I was thirty I understood that much of what could be said about the children of the rich also could be said about the nation as a whole and about a society that comforts itself with the dreams of power, innocence and grace.

With the victories over Germany and Japan we learned as Americans to think of ourselves as heirs apparent—not only of the classical and Christian past but also of the earth and all its creation. What was left of Western civilization had passed into the American account, and as the inheritors became increasingly spendthrift (witness over the last forty years the steadily rising curves of inflation, consumption and debt) so also the assumptions of privilege became habitual among larger segments of the population.

In 1905 Edith Wharton published *The House of Mirth*, a novel in which the heroine, a young and beautiful woman named Lily Bart, drifts like a precious ornament on the bright surface of the frivolous, albeit brutal, society summoned into existence by the riches of Twain's Gilded Age. Wharton intended a bitter satire on the self-preoccupation of an ignorant plutocracy. Her heroine declines to sell herself as a commodity, and the novel shows her being inexorably forced out of the soft, well-lighted atmospheres of luxury, "the only climate in which she could breathe," into the deserts of poverty. She cannot live in a world without carriages, engraved invitations, new clothes and the round of frivolous amusements to which she had become accustomed; unable to eat from broken china in a squalid part of town, she prefers to die rather than suffer the "humiliation of dinginess."

The House of Mirth addresses itself to what in 1905 was an irrelevantly small circle of people entranced by their reflections in a trades-

---

[13] The humor implicit in the phrase "the best people" is plain enough even to the editors of journals recommending conservative lines of opinion. Apropos the Reagan administration's practice of the arts of chicane, Thomas Fleming, editor of *Chronicles*, observed, in the winter of 1987, "Except in a few rare and fortunate cases, the powers that be, in this and any land, are a remarkably uniform set of real-estate swindlers, market manipulators and well-oiled office seekers." The observation would not have surprised Tom Paine, Ambrose Bierce or Dorothy Parker.

man's mirror. In the seventy-odd years since Wharton published the novel the small circle has become considerably larger, and the corollary deformations of character show up in all ranks of American society, among all kinds of people caught up in the perpetual buying of their self-esteem.

38   The pathologies of wealth usually afflict the inheritors, not the founders, of fortunes, and by the early 1980's the United States supported a *rentier* class of sizable dimensions. In 1859 the country boasted the presence of only three millionaires—John Jacob Astor, William Vanderbilt and August Belmont; it now entertains at least 500,000 millionaires, not counting the innumerable peers of the same financial realm who fail to pay taxes adjusted to their incomes or who derive their wealth from the criminal trades. The real-estate agents on Manhattan's Upper East Side define a millionaire not as an individual who owns assets worth $1 million but as one who earns $1 million a year.

39   On examining the list of the 400 richest people in America as published last year in *Forbes* magazine, Lester Thurow, the dean of M.I.T.'s Sloan School of Management and a perceptive economist habitually curious about the arithmetic of social class, discovered that all of the 82 wealthiest families, and 241 of the wealthiest individuals, had inherited all or a major part of their fortunes. He also noticed that the $166 billion in business net worth held by the 482 families and individuals named in *Forbes* provided them with effective control over $2.2 billion in business assets—about 40 percent of all fixed, nonresidential private capital in the United States. The richest 10 percent of the American population (i.e., those families earning more than $218,000 a year) now hold roughly 68 percent of the nation's wealth, and in 1982, for the first time in the nation's history, the money that the American people earned from capital (in rents, dividends and interest) equaled the amount earned in wages. The percentages might seem modest, but when counted as absolute numbers, they translate into a large crowd of eager buyers in the markets in luxury.

40   Attitudes of entitlement have become as commonplace among the sons of immigrant peddlers as among the daughters of the *haute bourgeoisie*, among the intellectual as well as the merchant classes. Habits of extravagance once plausible only in the children of the rich can be imitated by people with enough money to obtain lines of illusory credit. As larger numbers of people acquire the emblems of wealth, so also they acquire the habits of mind appropriate to the worship and defense of that wealth.[14]

41   Some weeks after Amory had gone not to Westport but to New Rochelle, I listened to a similar lament from a television producer's wife

---

[14] The habits of entitlement enjoy the fond endorsement of the federal government, which currently donates $400 billion a year (in Social Security, Medicare, military and Civil Service pensions) to the comfort of the middle and upper classes.

who no longer could go confidently into department stores. Her husband granted her an allowance of $75,000 a year for clothes and jewelry, but the money wasn't enough, not nearly enough, to maintain her sense of well-being. Unlike Amory, she had been born poor, in a middle-class suburb of Philadelphia, the daughter of a bank examiner. But she had attended Radcliffe on a scholarship in the early 1960's, and together with almost everybody else in her generation she had come to think herself deserving of everything in the world's gift—success, beauty, happiness, fame. The illusion of unlimited means had done the usual damage.

42   Having been married for some years to the producer, who was successful and often in California, the woman who once had wanted to be a poet had learned to weigh the meaning of her life against the prices paid for clothes, furniture and real estate. She had been unlucky in her assignment of milieu. The producer did business with people who could afford to spend $80,000 for a weekend in Deauville. His wife had learned to value the deference of sales clerks and hotel managers. If somebody else's wife owned a more expensive house in East Hampton, then somebody else's wife obviously had made a better deal with Providence. She no longer could bear to look in department store windows, and if she found herself walking on Fifth Avenue she took care to cross to the opposite side of the street before passing Bergdorf Goodman. Her wariness proceeded from a feeling of humiliation. If she wasn't rich enough to buy whatever she wished to buy, then clearly she was still poor, and what was the point of having any of it? Because she was poor, she was worthless, not fit to be seen in the company of dresses priced at $15,000 or diamond earrings marked down to $33,000 the pair.

43   In the arenas of academic or philanthropic affairs the complaint has a more decorous and muffled sound. I once heard the correct tone expressed at the Russell Sage Foundation in New York by a company of prominent scholars and journalists assembled to address the question of energy policy. The discussants had been invited because of their nominally earnest concern about the global distribution of heat and light. Both commodities at the time seemed to be going in disproportionate amounts to the rich and developed nations of the world. It was hoped that the study group might formulate an ethics of energy consumption whereby the less fortunate members of the international polity could find a place closer to the fire. The gentlemen talked in high-sounding abstractions for the whole of a morning and the better part of an afternoon. They worried about the shadow of famine falling across the map of the Third World; they counted the number of people dying of exposure in deserts that none of them had seen. At the end of the day the study director, an admirably complacent professor from Princeton, asked for specific suggestions. He reminded his guests that the foundation had allocated $250,000 for a five-year assessment of the dilemma, and he wanted to know what was the next step toward implementation. For about an hour various members of the group dutifully examined the question but

failed to come forward with an idea that everybody hadn't already read in *Newsweek*. At last the delegate from Harvard, sharing George Amory's contempt for the meagerness of $250,000, said the sum was so small that it inhibited the surge of imagination.

"Who can do anything with $250,000?" he said. "The thing to do is to leverage it. Anybody with the right connections in the charity business ought to be able to run it up to $1.5 million before the end of the year. If we had $1.5 million, I'm sure we could come up with an idea."

Everybody applauded this initiative, and the seminar adjourned with the resolution to reconvene when the foundation had raised more cash.

The emphasis on what Wharton would have called "the external finish of life," extends across the whole of the social spectrum and accounts for much of the spending in the public as well as the private sectors of superfluous display. Early in 1985, writing in *The New York Times Magazine*, Claude Brown, a student of the Harlem milieu and author of *Manchild in the Promised Land*, recounted a conversation with a teenage boy convicted of murder who explained that he had wanted "to be somebody," to be able to "rock" (i.e., to wear) a different pair of designer jeans at least twice a week. "Man, it's a bring down," the boy said, "to wear the same pants and the same shirt to school three or four times a week when everybody else is 'showin' fly.'" The same spring *The Washingtonian* published a lead article entitled "Going Broke on $100,000 a Year," in which it was explained that a good many young and ambitious couples in Washington had been ruined by their taste for splendor. By way of illustration the magazine reprinted a number of household budgets as hopelessly out of balance as George Amory's.[15]

Two years later, in the spring of 1987, the *New York Times* raised, by 200 percent, the cost of pecuniary decency. On the front page of its Sunday Business Section, under the title "Feeling Poor on $600,000 a Year," a correspondent described the misery of the Wall Street novices "just buying their first $1 million co-ops" and beginning to feel intimations of immortality. The paper relied on the authority of Richard Zorn, an investment banker who retained the vestiges of a social and historical perspective.

"They can ape the styles of the rich and famous," Zorn said. "They earn $600,000 and spend $400,000 out-of-pocket. There's the house in Southampton and the nanny and entertaining and art and the wardrobe. But when the Joneses they are keeping up with are the Basses, it comes to the executive jet and the yachts and the sapphires and the million dollar paintings, and it's all over. What it means is that $10 million in liquid capital is not rich."

---

[15] The nation's consumer debt (i.e., the sum borrowed by individuals) now stands at $2 trillion, roughly equal to the national debt (another $2 trillion); at least in the opinion of a number of respectable economists, this consumer debt presents a far more dangerous threat to the world's financial stability than the $1 trillion owed by the less developed nations of the Third World.

49 Talking to the same point, another banker cited in the same dispatch said, "I never knew how poor I was until I had a little money."

50 The federal government spends a large percentage of its income on the preservation of illusions no less foolish than Lily Bart's. Variations on the theme of dingy humiliation (scored for orchestra and brass band instead of solo flute) echo through the mournful statements of Caspar Weinberger, the former secretary of defense, who wished to enjoy the privilege of conducting simultaneous wars, some nuclear and others merely conventional, on five continents and seven oceans. For this luxury that he perceived as necessity Weinberger asked that the trifling sum of $300 million a day be paid for five years into the Pentagon's account. Let the Congress withhold any part of this allowance, and Weinberger would weep for the loss of Western civilization.[16]

51 Much the same tone of voice appears in the explanations of U.S. senators who say that they cannot possibly keep up what they regard as a decent appearance on a miserable salary of $89,000 a year. Being accustomed to approving sumptuous military budgets and spending $2,453 for circuit breakers that cost $3 in less refined parts of town, the senators ask their sympathetic retainers in the press how they can be expected to maintain at least two residences and attend, suitably dressed, all the civic occasions to which they owe the favor of their presence. Who will deliver them from the humiliation of having to give lectures in dingy halls? Of dodging like beggars for the coins of a campaign contribution?

52 Ask an American what money means, and nine times in ten he will say that it is synonymous with freedom, that it opens the doors of feeling and experience, that citizens with enough money can play at being gods and do anything they wish—drive fast cars, charter four-masted sailing vessels, join a peasant rebellion, produce movies, endow museums, campaign for political office, hire an Indian sage, toy with the conglomeration of companies and drink the wine of orgy. No matter what their income, a depressing number of Americans believe that if only they had twice as much, they would inherit the estate of happiness promised them by the Declaration of Independence.

53 At random intervals over a period of thirty years I have conducted a good many impromptu interviews on this question, asking people of various means to name the combination of numbers that would unlock the vault of paradise. I have put the question to investment bankers and to poets supposedly content with metaphors. The doubling principle holds as firm as the price of emeralds. The man who receives $15,000 a year is sure that he can relieve his sorrow if he had $30,000 a year; the man with

---

[16] Few amenities in the modern world cost as much as a properly equipped military household. To present a decent naval appearance, the United States maintains a fleet of thirteen aircraft carriers, each of which costs $590,000 a day to operate. Each of the 500,000 American soldiers currently stationed abroad costs $88,000 to outfit in an impressively martial livery.

$1 million a year knows that all would be well if he had $2 million a year.

54   All respondents say that if only they could accumulate fortunes of sufficient size and velocity, then they would ascend into the empyrean reflected in the best advertisements; if only they could quit the jobs they loathe, quite pandering to the whim of the company chairman (or the union boss, or the managing editor, or the director of sales); if only they didn't have to keep up appearances, to say what they didn't mean, to lie to themselves and their children; if only they didn't feel so small in the presence of money, then surely they would be free—free of their habitual melancholy, free to act and have, free to rise, like a space vehicle fired straight up from Cape Kennedy, into the thin and intoxicating atmospheres of gratified desire.

55   It is precisely this belief that crowds them into the corners of envy and rage. Imagining that they can be transformed into gods, they find themselves changed into dwarfs. The United States provides life-support systems for the richest and most expensively educated bourgeoisie in the known history of the world, and yet, despite God knows how many opportunities and no matter how elaborate the communication systems or how often everybody goes to Europe, the equestrian classes remain dissatisfied.

56   Nobody ever has enough. It is characteristic of the rich, whether the rich man or the rich nation, to think that they never have enough of anything. Not enough love, time, houses, tennis balls, orgasms, dinner invitations, designer clothes, nuclear weapons or appearances on *The Tonight Show*. This has been the urgent news brought to a sympathetic public for the past twenty years by the chorus of sensitive novelists, Norman Mailer as well as Ann Beattie, who publish the continuous chronicle of disappointment. Given the outward circumstances of their lives, their unhappiness sometimes approaches the margin of parody. There they sit, the wonders of the Western world, surrounded by all the toys available to the customer with a credit card, mourning the loss of innocence, the limits of feminism and the death of bumblebees.

57   Seeking the invisible through the imagery of the visible, the Americans never can get quite all the way to the end of the American dream. Even if we achieve what the world is pleased to acknowledge as success, we discover that the seizing of it fails to satisfy the hunger of our spiritual expectation, which is why we so often feel oppressed by the vague melancholy that echoes like a sad blues through the back rooms of so many American stories. The poor little rich girl and the unhappy movie idol, like J. Gatsby, George Amory and the makers of the nation's foreign policy, compose variations on the same lament. Yes, we have everything that anybody can buy in the department store of the free world: the Ferrari, the third husband, the F-16, the villa at Cap d'Antibes, the indoor tennis court, the Jacuzzi and the Strategic Defense Initiative. But no, it isn't enough. We aren't happy. Somehow we deserve more.

58 As portrayed in Ken Auletta's book, *Greed and Glory on Wall Street: The Fall of the House of Lehman*, the partners in the firm could neither restrain nor appease their appetites for cash. They earned salaries of between $500,000 and $2 million a year, but for reasons that would have been self-evident to George Amory, nothing was ever enough, and everybody always needed more. "Greed was the word that hovered over the troubled partnership.... Traders said the bankers were greedy because they were privately angling to sell the firm. Bankers said the traders were greedy to steal their shares and take such fat bonuses." Joan Ganz Cooney, the founder of Children's Television Workshop and the wife of Pete Peterson, one of the principal Lehman partners, explained to Auletta that her husband wanted to sell the firm so "we'd have no money worries." At the time her husband was receiving the equivalent of $5 million a year after taxes—a sum too small to suppress the feelings of anxiety and panic.[17]

59 Innumerable books by the sons and daughters of the rich remark on a comparable state of deprivation. Gloria Vanderbilt in her autobiography (*Once Upon a Time*, published in 1985) describes her childhood as a vacuum, empty of love or the merest sound of human recognition, as if she were "suspended in a bubble." Sallie Bingham, the reluctant heiress who in 1986 provoked the sale of her family's monopoly interest in the *Louisville Courier Journal*, speaks of being brought up in circumstances similar to those of a political prisoner. She was taught "never to ask the price of anything," but in return for this privilege she was obliged to maintain an attitude of decorous silence—never expressing her thoughts, never presuming to impose "undue stress or criticism" on the men in her family. The historian John A. Garraty noted in his study of *The New Commonwealth* that the unprecedented wealth and comfort of the *alte* nineteenth century in America resulted, paradoxically, in rising levels of exhaustion, anxiety and corruption. He went on to say that "the burgeoning cities of the land expanded the opportunities and fired the imaginations of their inhabitants, yet seemed at the same time to narrow their horizons and reduce them to ciphers."

60 At college I was struck by the way in which heirs to even modest fortunes fitted their lives into small spaces. They had the resources to travel extensively, to underwrite the acts of the imagination (their own or those of others), to make the acquaintance of their own minds. Instead, they fixed their attention on the tiny distinctions between shirts bought at Tripler's and shirts bought at J. Press, between the inflections of voices in Greenwich, Connecticut, and the inflections of voices

---

[17] The arrest in February 1987 of Martin A. Siegel, a Wall Street *Wunderkind*, provoked his peers and confederates to exclamations of surprise. Siegel at the time was earning upwards of $1 million a year as a notable maker of deals for Kidder, Peabody. When it was discovered that he also was selling confidential tips for suitcases filled with cash, a broker said, "How many yachts can you ski behind at the same time?"

twenty miles north in Armonk. Their preoccupations were those of department store clerks or the editors of *New York* magazine.

61   Amory, in his senior year, shared a suite of rooms with a prep-school friend, a boy named Wainwright who barely could muster the energy to go to class. The boy had a talent for painting, but his parents had made a mockery of his ambition to study art, and he had learned at St. Paul's to suppress any sudden or suspicious movement of his imagination. He sometimes thought he would like to travel, maybe to India or Greece. But then he thought of the heat and the flies and what he called "the funny-looking people speaking funny-looking languages," and he decided he was better off seeing the world through the eye of an air-conditioned movie theater on Crown Street. His passivity anticipated the passivity of a subsequent generation brought up to sit in front of television screens, and his xenophobia was not too different from that of the foreign policy establishment that thought it could buy off its fear of Communism by staging a war in what it believed to be the air-conditioned movie theater of Vietnam.

62   Although I have no memory of a specific incident, I know that before I was eight I had begun to suspect that something was wrong with the local presumptions of grace. It was as if a magician at a child's birthday party had made a mistake with the rabbit, thus leaving at least one member of the audience with the awkward suspicion that what was being advertised as paradise might bear a closer resemblance to jail. Possibly it was something about the people waving their hats (not all of whom seemed to be smiling), or perhaps it was a remark overheard in a basement, or a chance encounter with one of Charles Dickens's novels. In San Francisco I had been brought up among people who owned most of what was worth owning in the city; at Yale I had been educated among the heirs to certain affluence; in New York, Los Angeles and Washington I had met many of the people believed to have won all the bets, and yet, despite their ease of manner, hardly anybody seemed to take much pleasure in his or her property. What impressed me was their chronic disappointment and their diminished range of thought and sensibility.

63   Edith Wharton describes the asylum of wealth as a gilded cage, sumptuous in its decor but stupefying in its vacuity.[18] Lily Bart at least had the wit to know that by making money an end in itself she would be required to give up all but the enameled surface of her humanity. She would become a fly embalmed in expensive amber, meant to be stared at, like the celebrities in tomorrow's papers, by the crowd pressing its collective face against the windows of a Fifth Avenue jeweler.

64   Unlike widespread poverty, widespread affluence is something new under the sun, and the criminologists recently have begun to discover what was obvious to both Honoré de Balzac and Talleyrand—that is, that

---

[18] Within a week of being acquitted of the attempted murder of his wife, Claus von Bülow, in an interview with *New York* magazine, observed, "A gilded life may, in many ways, become a gilded cage."

the relation between "subjective dissatisfaction and objective deprivation" is a good deal more complicated than anybody at Harvard previously had thought. Apparently it is not poverty that causes crime, but rather the resentment of poverty. This latter condition is as likely to embitter the "subjectively deprived" in a rich society as the "objectively deprived" in a poor society.[19]

65   In New York the masks of opulence conceal a genuinely terrifying listlessness of spirit. The equestrian classes promenade through the mirrored galleries of the media, their least movements accompanied by a ceaseless murmuring of praise in the fashion magazines as well as in the *New York Times*. Behind the screens of publicity, the mode of feeling is as trivial and cruel as the equivalent modes of feeling prevalent in the ranks of Edith Wharton's plutocracy or F. Scott Fitzgerald's troupe of dancers in the Jazz Age.

Points for Review and Discussion

1. Lapham is quite specific in his account of the effects of encouraging children to believe they are either beautiful or rich. Briefly summarize those effects.

2. Lapham maintains that "as an intellectual proposition Yale proved to be a matter of filling out forms" (¶ 28). What reasons does he give for this low estimate of his higher education?

3. To some extent, Lapham argues, the "pathologies of wealth" surface elsewhere—indeed can be found all through the society. How does he justify this claim?

◆ Questions for Writing

1. Lapham claims that "the attitudes of invulnerable privilege" he encountered at school and college were similar to those of "most of the people I later came to know in the expensive American professions" (¶ 17). On the basis of the examples discussed in the latter part of the essay, explain what you take to be the meaning of the phrase "attitudes of invulnerable privilege."

2. At one point Lapham treats the behavior of government officials seeking large federal appropriations for their departments as essentially the same as that of rich people trying to add to their personal fortunes for self-indulgent reasons. (Reread, for example, the paragraph on the former secretary of defense who "asked that the trifling sum of $300

---

[19] The statistical records show that in the United States in the twentieth century the incidence of crime has risen during periods of prosperity (before 1930 and during the 1960's and 1980's) and declined during the Depression, World War II and the decade of the 1970's.

million a day be paid for five years into the Pentagon's account" [¶ 50].) Does this strike you as a useful perspective on this Cabinet member's behavior? On what does the perspective cast light? What does it obscure?

3. Lewis Lapham seldom explicitly lays out his opinions about those he's discussing; the opinions are built into his choices of language. Reread paragraph 51 about U. S. senators and then, working sentence by sentence, point to phrases that embody the author's attitudes and opinions, and state those opinions in your own language.

Old Money, the Mythology of America's Upper Class
Nelson Aldrich

Moral criticism of the rich usually focuses on self-indulgence, greed, and general uncaringness. But there's one other slightly less familiar but still highly popular target, namely *pretension*. Especially resented are the pretensions of newly rich folk who attempt to suggest that theirs isn't "new money" but is, instead, a legacy from some quasi-aristocratic past.

Nelson Aldrich belongs to the current generation of a relatively old American family that was once as rich as the Rockefellers (and in fact intermarried with Rockefellers). In his book *Old Money* (1988), Aldrich draws sharp contrasts between the manners and values of the newly rich (he sometimes calls the latter "Market Men") and those of the people he grew up with in school and family life. His target in "Class Acts" is the inauthenticity—the artificiality—of the manners and tastes of a famous American entrepreneur.

1   Mark Hampton, a brilliant New York interior decorator whose knowledge of the subtleties of social class is as sophisticated as his knowledge of fine fabrics and furniture, told me once that in the course of his career he has learned to distinguish three kinds of good taste:

> I think good taste sometimes appears like a talent—for singing prettily, say. Perhaps her grandmother sang, and her mother, but you don't have to suppose a genetic inheritance. Background and breeding will do. Then there's a somewhat arid *learned* good taste. One can almost hear the poor creature flipping the pages of *Architectural Digest* and *House and Garden* in her mind. Finally, there's an irregular, intuitive sort of good taste—a personal taste. It's sometimes more difficult to work with such people, but it's always more fun. Their responses are so surprising.

The class contexts are pretty clear. The "background and breeding" sort of good taste I would guess Hampton associates with upper-class antecedence: "learned" good taste he probably sees as a product of middle-class striving; while "personal" taste he doubtless believes to be the result of one of those random descents of the gift, which even the most class-ridden societies are obliged somehow to account for.

2   For expository purposes, the very best connoisseurs of the special beauties of Old Money life usually turn out to be people such as Senator Aldrich, who were born at just the right distance from the manor: close enough to be able to study the basic elements of the design, but not so close as to take it for granted; far enough to see the setting in flattering

---

From Nelson Aldrich, *Old Money* (1988).

perspective, but not so far as to reduce its beauty to a blur. This is the great value of the memoirs of William S. Paley. Born to a provincial manor (Chicago, then Philadelphia), to a suspect race (Jewish), and to substantial wealth (his purchase of the embryonic radio network that became CBS was financed by an advance on his inheritance), Paley's introduction to the aesthetics of the good life began in much the same way as Mark Hampton might expect of one of his more "learned" clients—with magazines. As a young man in Philadelphia, he was an avid reader of *Vogue*, *Harper's Bazaar* and *The New Yorker*. In those slick manuals, the young entrepreneur of a new industry studied the forms and gestures (not to mention the purchases) required of the young entrepreneur of a new self.

3   Aesthetically, however, the self and CBS were two separate spheres of discrimination. In his memoir Paley is frank to admit that the sense of style required to market the network came rather more naturally to him than the style required to advance his person. To program CBS for success, he had only to listen to the promptings of his body. Again and again, he locates the source of his inspiration in his gut, in his nervous system, or in his instincts. The taste that saw "Amos 'n' Andy" as witty, "The Beverly Hillbillies" as amusing, "Cavalcade of America" as touching and informative, or "CBS News" as providing serious and substantial news for the citizens of the republic, this taste, we learn from his memoirs, is the taste Paley was born with.

4   But just as surely as Paley's viscera told him how to present a winning schedule of radio and television programs, they sometimes proved false in telling him how to present a winning self. Visiting Paris in the 1920s with his parents, Paley bought what he evidently believed was a thing of perfect upper-class beauty, a seventeen-thousand-dollar Hispano-Suiza, and engaged a chauffeur to drive him around in it. In Paris, both chauffeur and car seemed to set him off nicely, but back in Philadelphia the chauffeur began to appear inappropriate, somehow, for someone so young. He got rid of him. Then the car proved troublesome. Beautiful and attractive as it was, it was not beautiful in quite the right sort of way, nor was it attracting the attentions of the right sort of people. Ordinary passersby on the street stopped to gawk at it, perhaps to reach out and touch it. Soon, sadly, Paley got rid of the Hispano-Suiza.

5   Paley is proud of the contribution that CBS (and by implication he himself, as a tasteful programmer) has made to American society. When he writes of "CBS News," the tone of his prose takes on the orotund solemnity of Walter Cronkite himself. But he is obviously most pleased by the memory of all those "shows," all the "home entertainment," that he has sent into American households over the years. Yet soon after Paley learned a thing or two about upper-class taste, CBS seldom got brought into *his* home. No sooner had he arrived in New York, a bachelor with a devoted valet and an alluring apartment, than he realized that it would not do to mix his business life and his social life, his associates of the day (many of them necessarily devoted to various aspects of marketing)

with his companions of the evening (many of them so far removed from marketing as never to have known what it is). Later, married and with children, he kept up the *cordon sanitaire* between the two stylistic domains. He recalled that in his youth his father used to discuss the affairs of the Congress Cigar Company, source of the family fortune, around the family dinner table. Paley never did that with CBS. Not, apparently, in front of the children. Much like my great-grandfather before him, Paley seems to have had a sure sense that the world in which he founded an industry was a very different place from the world in which he hoped to found a family.

6   The dinner table, his own and others', was also a good place to further his education in upper-class aesthetics. As an engaging and sociable man, as well as a rich and influential one, Paley quickly entered the round of social entertaining (so different from CBS's home entertainments) that he'd longed for in the pages of *Vogue* and *Harper's Bazaar*. In the process, of course, he soon acquired the sort of friends and acquaintances, many of them Old Money, whose example and instruction would help him in the future to avoid such solecisms as tooling around in a chauffeur-driven Hispano-Suiza. Like so many sensible New World social climbers—like my great-grandfather, for that matter—he was especially impressed with the sort of taste cultivated by the Old Families and Old Money of the Old World. In England during World War II, for example, Paley was delighted to go down to Ditchley, the estate of the Tree family, by then wonderfully restored by massive infusions of Marshall Field's wealth. There he learned the rudiments of the great operating principle of the upper-class aesthetic—*sublimation*. Looking around him at Ditchley, the clichés of Old Money taste seemed to rise spontaneously to his lips, such qualifiers as "understated," "casual," "rich but not ostentatious," combined with such resonant concepts of time as "tradition" and "owned by the same families for generations." What seemed to have impressed him the most, however, was his realization, however dim or informed I don't know, that the furniture and paintings he saw so casually scattered about in this house were "of museum quality."

7   Two generations earlier, Paley would have had little choice in what he could do, back in the New World, with the tastes he was acquiring in the Old. Before World War I, one had to build one's own country house—improvise it, as Henry Adams would say (and as my great-grandfather did). But by the 1920s and 1930s a young entrepreneur such as Paley was able to perceive an actual New World legacy of country houses. In his memoir, he vividly describes a place in Manhasset, Long Island, which he visited one weekend in the 1930s:

> We drove only a few hundred yards down the road and turned into spacious grounds of a lovely old country place. The main house was white clapboard, quite old, very simple, with an elegance and beauty which struck me as being just right. . . . As I wandered about the house and grounds, I could not but think that this house on these grounds represented the kind of home I myself might like to own and live in one day.

8   Paley had always shown a perfect awareness of his place in a line of corporate or technological succession: that his "house" of electronic journalism and entertainment would succeed (or usurp) the "house" of newsprint. His first wife was so enveloped in this dream of historic succession that she appears in the memoirs as, simply, "Dorothy Hearst, wife of Jack Hearst, who was the son of Mr. and Mrs. William Randolph Hearst of the famous newspaper chain." (No satisfaction for the "Who Was She?" class here.) The same sense of historic fittingness could have inflamed Paley's desire for the Manhasset place, for Kiluna Farm, which is what it was called, belonged to Ralph Pulitzer, part heir of another "famous newspaper chain."

9   Paley bought the Pulitzer place and lives there into his late eighties. Sometimes, it is true, the desired effects of his self-setting were lost on visitors. To Lady Diana Cooper, for example, the appointments at Kiluna Farm seemed anything but simple. "A little table in your bedroom was laid as for a nuptial night, with fine lawn, plates, forks, and a pyramid of choice-bloomed peaches, figs and grapes. In the bathroom were all the aids to sleep, masks for open eyes, soothing unguents and potions." Lady Diana noticed everything, not omitting her host's appearance, which was "physically a little Oriental and very attractive." Still, she was depressed by his "luxury taste. . . . [T]he standard is unattainable to us tradition-ridden tired Europeans." But such are the tired reproaches of Old Money everywhere, even American Old Money. Paley should have been flattered; in such people's eyes, success always looks like a succession.

10   In time, Paley's taste became sufficiently self-assured so that he could venture a few forays into modernism. His memoirs show him to be proud of commissioning Eero Saarinen to design a new headquarters for CBS; proud, too, of his collection of modern painting and of his rise to the chairmanship of the board of the Museum of Modern Art. These moves would not have been undertaken if the object in view had not been already certificated as "of museum quality." Even so, I suspect he would never have made them if it hadn't been for his growing acceptance and ease in the company of Old Money. His career in collecting, for example, began in the late 1930s under the tutelage of that "natural patrician" Averell Harriman, who in one summer introduced him to Impressionists in Paris and bird-shooting in the Little Carpathians.

11   It wasn't until 1947, however, that Paley might be said to have secured a firm seat in the class. That was the year he married Barbara Cushing Mortimer, one of the three famous Cushing sisters, daughters of Massachusetts General Hospital's renowned neurosurgeon Harvey Cushing, each of whom was more gloriously lovely than the others, each of whom had a nickname cuter than the next: Minnie, Betsey, and Babe. They had all married well, these girls, all of them to Old Money: Minnie to Vincent Astor, then to James Fosburgh; Betsey to FDR's son James, then to Jock Whitney; Babe to Stanley Mortimer. Paley was

next. His emotions at the joining of this union may be judged by the title he gave to the chapter of his memoirs in which it takes place: "Triumph."

12 In acquiring the hand of Babe Paley, the great programmer finally realized, at least to his own satisfaction, what might be called the program of his own life. Self and setting, mirror image and social image, all had been made new—more accurately, made *old*. In the two long, lovingly detailed paragraphs in which he describes the furnishings of his CBS office, chosen with Babe's help, the word "old" is insisted upon with some frequency, varied only by "antique" and "traditional." The room even manages to look "lived in." But the real triumph of this room is that here Paley came into his own as an instrument of upper-class taste. No more flipping through the pages of magazines to discover what beauties appeal to him. The learned discriminations are natural discriminations now. The old "gut" has been replaced by a new, a finer "gut." How can we tell? We can tell because of the apparent effortlessness with which he, with Babe's help, has created this setting for himself. He tells us, pointedly, that "the first-time visitor might well believe it all came together out of some sort of carelessness." There it is, the key word in the familiar vocabulary of Old Money's most characteristic stance in the world: the casual, easy pose of the ineffably self-assured, the effortlessly *attractive*. With that word, we know that Paley had arrived.

13 When I was at St. Paul's School, the word most of us would have chosen to describe Paley's memoirs is "pathetic." "Pathetic" is the kindest thing we had to say for people who tried too hard to be "attractive," who tried too hard, that is, to be like people who didn't have to try to be anything: people like us, people who already *were*. There was always a touch of vindictiveness in the way we tossed off that word "pathetic," and I daresay there still is. For people like Paley remind us of what we would rather forget. His effortful carelessness, his labored casualness, his heavy-handed understatement, all call attention to what it is that we—authentically enough, because affordably enough—are all so casual and careless about, what it is that we are understating. He reminds us of the object of all this repression: the hideous, vulgar figure of Market Man.

14 In Paley's memoirs, as in Old Money lives, Market Man is conspicuously absent in any number of ways. One that's very significant is the way Paley scants the world of fashion. Fashion is a problem for Old Money, and even more so for any aspirant to Old Money. On the one hand, it is wonderfully alluring, possessing the natural appeal of novelty; and the rich, whether Old or New, are well positioned to respond to novelty wherever it crops up, which is everywhere: in the fine and decorative arts, in resorts, restaurants, and ballet companies, and in the people (celebrities or protocelebrities) who make the art, design the clothes, run the restaurants, choreograph the dances, and so forth. On the other hand, fashion presents Old Money (New Money only if it is trying to become

Old) with the singular difficulty of having to figure out what, in all this welter of novelty, is of "museum quality."

15   The casual, most distinctive, and in some respects most invidious method of dealing with this difficulty is to ignore novelty itself. It is no coincidence that the two American cities most widely known for their hereditary upper classes, Boston and Philadelphia, are the two most notorious for their hostility to fashion. My grandfather's disdain for originality as "a failure of memory" was perfectly characteristic of his circle. Patricians of those old towns never go anywhere unless they've "always" gone there, never know anyone unless they've "always" known them. Fashion never troubles them. Sometimes, indeed, it seems as though anything they do not inherit they do without, buying only the very plain food on their plates. Cleveland Amory tells the story of the Boston lady whose beautiful and otherwise well-furnished Beacon Hill house was bare of rugs, simply because her mother hadn't left her any good ones. The story is a paradigm of one response to the problem of finding "museum quality" in fashion: Have nothing to do with it. I remember once going to Naushon Island in Buzzards Bay, a "country place" not much smaller than Manhattan, which has been "in the family" of Boston Forbeses—that is, in trust for Forbeses—since before the Civil War. The house I stayed in was a somewhat severe H. H. Richardson cottage of twenty-two rooms. The ambience, though "old" and "simple," was as far removed from Kiluna Farm as one could get without becoming actually squalid. Paint peeled from every wall and ceiling; it was a kindness to call the furniture rudimentary; the kitchen seemed well equipped for making sandwiches; everywhere was the odor of mold, carried along by brisk drafts of damp sea air. No automobiles disturbed this idyll; none are permitted on the island. Forbeses walk or go by horse, or sail. Museum quality is assured on Naushon: the buggies, the sailboats, even the Forbeses, whose clothes look as though they, too, had been handed down to them by their mothers and fathers, are all certifiable antiques. On Naushon, only the horses look fashionable.

16   Forbeses, however, are patricians, and the distinctively aristocratic sector of the Old Money class cannot dismiss fashion so easily. To ignore it, they believe, is to deny oneself too much fun, too much beauty, and perhaps power as well. Moreover, the "museum quality" problem can be readily dealt with by cultivating the people who can be counted on to know this quality when they see it, or to make it when they want it. I mean the intelligentsia—the critics, professors, dealers, curators, magazine and book editors, arts journalists, and other such connoisseurs, whose business it is to make such judgments. One may also cultivate the producers of the artifacts, entertainments, and services contending for a place in the museum—artists, writers, architects, decorators, singers and dancers, couturiers, gardeners, restaurateurs, and the like. (The producers can't be trusted to judge their own work, of course, but they can provide critical

insight into everyone else's, some of it occasionally positive.) The presence of these people in (and often of) many Old Money circles in New York and Cambridge, for example, distinguishes the society of those cities from that of much of Boston and Philadelphia, and all of Providence, Rochester, or Hartford.

17 But it is a risky thing they do, these Old Money aristocrats of fashion. The risk goes way beyond the peril of buying something, or reading something, or applauding something that isn't of museum quality. Fashion is appalling to so many Old Money beneficiaries because it carries with it a dreadful reminder of the incredible force and fluidity of the marketplace. Entering any world where fashion is an element, the Old Money participant risks entering a trade or, even more repulsively, becoming a "heavy player" in the trade. One might, for example, become a flack for one's own financial investments in this or that artist or restaurant or dress designer. Babe Paley flirted with that danger every year she appeared on the Ten Best-Dressed Women list; as it was, she embarrassed her children at the Brearley School.

18 Again, the easy solution is to retire completely: to decorate one's setting or person entirely from the attic, as patricians typically do, or from other people's attics, as Paley did. This safe course brings risks of its own, however, both to the overall culture and to Old Money's paternalistic pretensions to lead it. Long ago, in my great-grandfather's day, the brilliant Old Money aristocrat John Jay Chapman scorned the prudent patrician withdrawal from the cultural fray as leading to a culturally disastrous hypocrisy:

> In our ordinary moods we regard the conclusions of the poets as both true and untrue—true to feeling, untrue to fact. . . . Most men have a duplicated philosophy which enables them to love the arts and wit of mankind, at the same time that they conveniently despise them. Life is ugly and necessary; art is beautiful and impossible. . . . The practical problem is to keep them in separate spheres and to enjoy both. . . . Such are the convictions of the average cultivated man. His back is broken, but he lives in the two halves comfortably enough.

But it's not only the man's back that is broken; it is the culture's. Patricians are not much distressed by this. Both my Aldrich grandfathers would have thought the two cultures an inevitable consequence of "emergence": one culture for the emerged, like them, like Bill Paley and his children; and another for everyone else, like the viewers of CBS television programs.

19 Aristocrats of the class take a characteristically bolder course of action. With their allies among the critics and artists, they assume a deliberately exemplary stance toward the marketplace. They "find" and "discover" things; they model things for everyone else, and thereby, or so they hope, influence national taste. In matters of personal appearance, this opportunity to exercise leadership seems to have arisen in the 1920s, the decade of the first mass movement of the middle classes into

colleges and universities. Zelda Fitzgerald pretended to be unhappy about what happened then:

> The flapper is deceased. Her outer accoutrements have been bequeathed to several hundred's girls' schools, and to several million small-town belles, always imitative of the big-town shop girls via the "novelty stores" of their respective small towns. It is a great bereavement to me.

She is joking, surely. If she liked the flapper "line" on herself, she should have been delighted to see it on every other girl. She had only to move on to something else, parading her precious distinction for a while before once again passing it on to the less adventuresome. The result should be gratifying: the maintenance of a certain minimum aesthetic tone in the whole society. Herbert Pell noted the same phenomenon in 1938: "Thirty years ago, it was comparatively easy to recognize a rich man by his clothes, and the distinction among women was patent to the most careless eye. Now it is difficult to distinguish the average New York office worker from the daughter of a millionaire." Pell couldn't have been happier. It was a perfect example of what an Old Money class was supposed to do: elevate the tone of society and thereby justify itself. My father found the same pleasure: not about fashions in clothes (though I would swear he was the first man of his class to wear a pink shirt) but about fashions in art. Through the Institute of Contemporary Art and later the Boston Arts Festival, my father and a number of other Old Money and would-be Old Money Bostonians tried to give their fellow citizens a taste for modernist art. The effort caused a rift between him and his patrician father, which the two of them, for most of their lives, could barely bridge with courtesies. Nevertheless, my father adored trying to move people in this way, to persuade them to love the things he thought lovable. If fashion is a genie that makes markets, including art markets, move, then Old Money and its allies feel obliged to persuade the genie that what *they* want is better than what the masses (think they) want. The risk remains, of course. Fashion leaders come very close to an actual descent *into* the marketplace, where no Old Money beneficiary likes to be. But the risk of not taking that risk may be even worse. As Chapman sensed a hundred years ago, it is the risk of being aesthetically irrelevant.

20   A more conspicuous absence in Paley's memoirs, and so a more conspicuous clue to the repression of Market Man, is the absence of any mention of money. Almost never do he or his wives *buy* anything: They "discover" their treasures in antique stores or "find" them in galleries. The process is one of ingestion, not purchase, the consumer's equivalent of a programmer's "gut reaction." But Old Money taste is always agnostic with respect to money. The whole point of inculcating the peculiar aesthetic of the class is to lift its habitat above the quick and nasty transactions of the cash nexus to the exalted plane of disinterested delight.

21   Another reason to avoid mention of money is that the chink of coin often works unfortunate changes in other people's envy. The task undertaken by the Old Money curriculum is to teach beneficiaries how to *manage* envy, not merely how to arouse it. Children of wealth learn to do this early on. Inviting friends home from school, for example, they find themselves having to explain how it is that the living room looks like the Louis XVI room at the Metropolitan Museum, or what a "conservatory" is. Mark Hampton once told me about an Old Money client who cried out in panic at a proposal he dared make for her dining room.

> "I can't have those *boiseries*," she said. "I mean, they look so expensive. What will Suzie say when she comes home from Radcliffe?"
> Or if it isn't Suzie radicalized at Radcliffe, it's the little boys that Tommy brings home from Collegiate. I've had clients who are afraid that their children might trash the place. Maids are much worse than *boiseries*, of course. No decent little liberal wants to bring his friends home from school when the first thing they're going to see is eight octogenarian Irish ladies padding around the house in uniforms. One of them might be somebody's grandmother, for God's sake!

In time, the children will either leave the house or learn to cope with their friends' envy. But the first rule of envy management is to understate, to the point of repression, the facts of dollar value. Money is democratic. Everybody wants it and it often seems as though everyone were getting it. Money envy can inflame the ugliest proclivities of the hustling world. What beneficiaries must learn to do, therefore, is to redirect envy away from the democratically available powers of money and toward the rather more "exclusive" powers inherent in their own inimitable taste.

22   Finally, money is repressed the better to highlight the ethos of the gift. One notices this aspect of the matter in relation to collecting art. America's Old and would-be Old Rich have usually collected beautiful things for reasons simultaneously self-centered and public-spirited. Their collections beautify their surroundings, ennoble their acquisitiveness, and enhance their reputations for sensitivity and judgment. And for the New Rich seeking to become Old, collecting is a way of making oneself socially attractive to custodians of the extended patrimony. But the rich also collect out of a breeding in, or crude aspiration toward, the gift ethos, with its central impulse to make a gift of what has been given. They might pass on their collections to their own descendants, of course, but this is rarely done in America. Old World collections were accretions; here, even among the Old Rich, they have always been accomplishments, and individual ones at that. Without primogeniture, then, there is no way for a collector to pass on his accomplishment intact, to enter history arm in arm with beauty, except by giving his collection to one of the institutions that care for Old

Money's extended patrimonies. But mention of dollar values spoils all this. It reminds everyone of a hundred different vulgarities they'd rather not think about, vulgarities that the presence of art was meant to dispel. It reminds them of the art world's flagrant commercialization: the noisome rabble of greedy dealers, spoiled painters, corrupt critics, and unctuous museum directors that the art market spawns whenever, as in the last two decades, *art moves*. It reminds them of that most outrageous betrayal of the gift ethos, "deaccessioning." It reminds them of their own anxious aspirations to put together a collection of "museum quality." It reminds them that some people consider their gifts nothing but a tax dodge and their accomplishment nothing but an act of purchase, a jiggle in the movement of a market. Mentioning dollar values around a work of art, in short, amounts to a massive return of the understated. It spoils the careless effect. It will not do.

23 After their settings, the classiest acts by which the Old Rich reveal themselves are matters of an attractive personal presence: postures, demeanor, gestures, speech, manners, and other clues of personality and character that tell those of us who are interested in putting people in the places where, socially speaking, they belong.

24   Of course, to describe the particular significance that Old Money gives the word "attractive" is to risk making comparisons that most people, in a supposedly egalitarian nation, find odious. Perhaps that's why Paley did not attempt it; not in his memoir anyway. But I imagine that Paley on his social and corporate rounds behaves as many Americans do, certainly Old Money Americans. Like a curator on a visit to a strange museum, I'm sure he repeatedly engages in making the discriminatory judgments that mark the passage of a social connoisseur. Like the rest of us, he is probably wrong in some of his attributions. And like us, he may even feel guilty at treating people like this: questioning their authenticity, comparing their aesthetic values, submitting them, in a society where everything is supposed to be possible, to the terrible finality of the pigeonhole.

25   Still, I'm quite certain he does it. And I am certain, too, of what he looks for. It is the equivalent in behavior of Old Money's "understatement" in things. Paley knows what that is. It's in the title of his book. Other tycoons crudely emblazon their memoirs with the name they made for themselves: Boone! Iacocca! Paley's is called, somewhat pathetically, I'm afraid, *As It Happened*. The negligent note is just right, and all social connoisseurs claim to detect it or wish to strike it. Whenever Old Money's characteristic presence is described, the critical vocabulary returns again and again to the same family of words—casual, careless, nonchalant, insouciant, easy, unstudied, natural, effortless.

Points for Review and Discussion

1. Summarize the distinction Nelson Aldrich draws between "Old Money" and "Market Man."
2. "Fashion," Aldrich writes, "is a problem for Old Money" (¶ 14). State the problem and name three ways in which, in his account, Old Money undertakes to solve it.
3. Whether one is Old Money or Market Man, one can become, in Aldrich's opinion, a "social connoisseur" (¶ 24). What (according to Aldrich's definition) is a social connoisseur?

•• Questions for Writing

1. Speaking of the "touch of vindictiveness" in his dismissal of Paley (¶ 13), Aldrich attributes it to the fact that "people like Paley remind us of what we would rather forget"—the "hideous, vulgar . . . Market Man" (¶ 13). Put yourself in Aldrich's place: what other feelings beside revulsion at "Market Man" might enter into your dislike of William Paley?
2. Imagine William Paley reading Nelson Aldrich's account of himself, his traits, his behavior. What might *he* think of Nelson Aldrich? How might he counterattack? Whose side would you yourself take in this scrap? Explain your choice.
3. "What beneficiaries must learn to do . . . is to redirect envy away from the democratically available powers of money and toward the rather more 'exclusive' powers inherent in their own inimitable taste" (¶ 21). How seriously is the reader to regard this assertion? Does Aldrich himself believe that "the beneficiaries" actually possess *exclusive* powers and "inimitable taste"? To what extent does he himself identify with the beneficiaries? To what extent does he wish to be seen as separate from them?

Connecting the Parts in Chapter 6: Assignments for Extended Essays

1. "What impressed me [about the wealthy]," Lewis Lapham writes, was "their diminished range of thought and sensibility." Imagine that you yourself had been brought up in the style of those described in this essay. How might such an upbringing have narrowed your range of thought and feeling? Make notes on what you might not know today that, as things stand, you do know? Use these notes as the basis of an autobiographical essay on the subject of the contributions, to your education, made by your social class. Build the essay on examples drawn from particular life experiences.
2. The attitudes toward the upper class adopted by Lapham and Aldrich differ markedly from those of C. Wright Mills. What exactly is the nature of the difference and what is its significance? Take this question as the starting point for an essay comparing and contrasting—and, finally, evaluating—the attitudes toward class of these three writers. Build your essay on close examination of key, related passages in the three selections.

Leads for Research

1. Three decades ago the two best-known works about "society" and the "upper class" were Cleveland Amory, *Who Killed Society?* (1960) and E. Digby Baltzell, *Protestant Establishment: Aristocracy and Caste in America* (1964). Read these works, comparing their perspectives and tone with either that of Lapham's *Money and Class in America* or Aldrich's *Old Money*. Write an essay describing and accounting for the major changes of attitude that you discern.
2. C. Wright Mills was a sociologist, not a historian; his account of the nature of *The Power Elite* does little to trace the historical development of that phenomenon. Research this development by reading Richard Hofstadter, *Anti-Intellectualism in America* (1963), Chapters 6–8 ("The Decline of the Gentleman," "The Fate of the Reformer," and "The Rise of the Expert"), and Burton J. Bledstein, *The Culture of Professionalism* (1976), Chapters 1–3 ("The Advantage of Being Middle Class," "Space and Words," "The Culture of Professionalism"). Write a paper exploring those aspects of the emergence of class power that seem to you to have been scanted in *The Power Elite*.

7
The Great Equalizer
School

Education lies at the center of many of this country's political and social debates. And some of those debates are conducted on the assumption that issues of class are irrelevant. People argue about (among other subjects) whether academic standards are declining ... about whether America pays its teachers properly ... about whether more attention should be paid to instruction in the basics of math and composition, history and geography. ... These are important matters, obviously—but none of them can be intelligently debated if class realities are left out.

The essays in this section concern the role of schools in fostering (or curbing) democracy, problems of teaching "underprepared" college students, and the absence of a uniform system of school financing. The starting point for each essayist is the belief that understanding the subject addressed demands that we take social differences seriously. Universal equality, whether of students or school systems, is a noble ideal—but miles removed from things as they are.

I Should Never Have Quit School
Benjamin DeMott

As every student and teacher knows, no subject having to do with school is more frequently discussed than grades. And much of the discussion—not only among students—focuses on the *unfairness* of grades: the allegedly willful determination of some teachers to use the grading system as an instrument of punishment, the blindness that prevents some teachers from recognizing an intelligent answer unless the answer is framed in exactly the same words that are in the teacher's head, and other strongly felt provocations to complaint.

The essay below treats the subject of grading in a context larger than that of the defects, real or imagined, of individual teachers. It raises the fundamental question of whether, in a society divided by class, the ideal of fairness in assessing students can ever be reached—and the related question of whether American society is too complacent in its thinking about broad issues of educational equity. The author of the essay is the editor of this book.

1 The will to believe the mythology of classlessness is rooted in personal narrative: the stories of our self-mythologizing lives. *Once upon a time,* says the voice of memory, *I lived through a situation in which rank order was based on ability, work held the key to privilege, all possessed the right to earn privilege, and the allocation of rewards was disinterested and just. I and the others stood equal at the starting line in this situation, dependent solely on personal resources. I was free to race with the pacemakers or hang back and finish last. I knew the contest was consequential for life fortunes. I knew that doing better or worse was up to me. I knew that in this situation—the place and time wherein I individually determined my fate and fashioned my unique self—fairness ruled.*

2 For the American majority the name of the original situation in question is, of course, school. According to an accumulating body of opinion research, the unlucky and badly paid who protest in interviews at their lot often volunteer that they did have a chance—school—and blew it through fault of their own. Successful and well-off interviewees, for their part, accompany expressions of sympathy with the unfortunate with volunteered assertions that the competition in which they gained their own high place was in no way fixed. If, as a millionaire President in the White House put it, Life is unfair, school wasn't. *I earned my edge,*

From Benjamin DeMott, *The Imperial Middle* (1990).

shaped my future, under the rule of fairness; the race that settled things was the same length for all.

3   A number of familiar assumptions about intelligence, the profession of teaching, and public policy concerning the structure and financing of education enter into the sense of school as a fairness zone. One assumption is that intellectual ability—quickness, schoolsmarts, a good mind, college material—is an essence that an individual possesses as the result of biogenetic causes, and develops or fails to develop as a matter of personal volition. Another is that ability can surface anywhere at any time and is quickly recognizable by teachers and testing agencies expert at detecting it. Another is that schools and teachers deal exclusively with ability in its purity, not with extraneous items such as pupils' background, appearance, clothes, economic status. Still another is that school is alert to sudden awakenings and late bloomings. (The authorities see to it that transfer is feasible from vocational to academic tracks and from two-year to four-year institutions of higher learning: private sector, profit-making schools are licensed to serve those whose career decisions—from computer programming to cooking—don't fit orthodox academic calendars or curricula: qualified candidates are allowed to begin professional education in mid-life, etc.)

4   And in addition there's the assumption that policy regarding appropriations for the educational process reflects a more than casual interest, on the part of the public, in preventing domination by unearned privilege. (The interest manifests itself in scholarship and loan funds, state subsidies, efforts to equalize expenditure per pupil among school districts, other economic initiatives.)

5   Understandings of these concepts differ from sector to sector of the population. In upscale quarters pure ability connotes "giftedness" and is admired. Elsewhere it can connote clever facility in a minority member learning to con white folks, and may be patronized as gutless. Among people who don't work with their hands, belief in intellectual ability as a distinct, separable, biopsychic essence is accompanied by certainty that differences in occupation spring from differences in smartness and giftedness (the best minds head for the professions, slow people learn trades). People who work with their hands don't invariably share—sometimes resent—this view.

6   Even the principle that public policy seeks to modify unearned privilege means different things to different people. In 1988 Princeton, New Jersey, spent $7,015 per public school pupil; in the same year Camden, New Jersey, spent $4,500 per pupil; only 7 percent of Princeton pupils failed standard proficiency tests, whereas a percentage eleven times greater failed in Camden. Establishment liberals (including a sitting judge) read the statistics and related material as grounds for overhauling the state's school financing system in order to assure educational equity.

More than a few Princeton parents, on the other hand, opposed to sending their children away, read the same numbers in the context of public school versus private school; fairness, in their view, is what individual communities achieve by taxing themselves heavily enough to create mini-Choates within walking distance. And in many working class communities talk of equalizing pupil expenditures of transforming a local high school into Choate can seem airy. Concern about quality is likely to center, as in Yonkers in 1988, on fear of invasion by a minority perceived as threatening to the safety and values of the majority, or, within the minority, on fear of exclusion and persecution.

7   Pausing over such differences is a useful way of guarding against excessive homogenization of attitudes toward school. Different sectors of society have different agendas, hence define equity in different terms; the price of ignoring the differences is a return to imperial middle universalism.

8   But the fact of differences isn't in this instance the central fact: what matters more is the exceptional breadth of agreement on fairness and evenhandedness as school norms. Certainly that career prospects are related to school performance cuts across social classes from old money to new money through the poverty line; so, too, does trust in the impartially grading teacher, and assurance of the weight of personal choice. The need for vigilance is acknowledged ("Keep politics out of the school"). But the educational process overall is seen as both clean and potent, capable of creating a degree of equality through its own impartiality, capable also of guaranteeing all children—regardless of their parents' success or failure in life—some chance of self-propelled upward movement. The consensus supports the conviction that school is an institution crucial to the survival of an opportunity society. And not uncommonly, as youthful experience is idealized over the years, school becomes memory's democratic home base. Equality on the starting line is recalled as the original reality that later experience—mere illusion, mere pretense—sadly obscures. Hence the popularity of the class reunion (thousands occur yearly). For an hour that institution refreshes memory of the levelness of the first playing field, sanctioning denials of class, affirming the rough justice of life.

9   All democratic societies tend to view education positively, and special circumstances in this society intensify the tendency. In opting for racial and ethnic variety, America chose to add citizens by the tens of millions whose presumed dreams of Americanization could be realized only through schooling. And the succeeding dream of preserving ethnic traditions was also set under school custodianship. It doesn't follow, though, that school's rise to autonomy and consecration was inevitable. Autonomy was hard-gained, with paradox and accident playing roles in its achievement.

10   Two developments were decisive, says hindsight. The first allayed suspicion that school was cowed by the rich, therefore bound to be biased. The second lifted school (in popular estimate) above conflicting interests, beyond coercion by influences other than that of objective truth.

11   Neither development came swiftly. The common schooling system in place in America by the mid-nineteenth century drew together youngsters of widely varying background in a single course of study; the system's founders regarded inclusiveness as a national imperative. But those same founders were far from conceiving of the system as an equalizer. Early readers and grammars took class for granted, preaching resignation, not ambition. McGuffey Readers, in fables entitled "The Rich Boy" and "The Poor Boy," recommended that rich pupils treat poor ones kindly, and that poor pupils accept their condition. "If I were a man," Rich Boy declares, "and had plenty of money, I think no person who lived near me should be very poor." "I have often been told," Poor Boy remarks, "that it is God who makes some poor and others rich—that the rich have many troubles which we know nothing of; and that the poor, if they are but good, may be very happy: indeed, I think that when I am good, nobody can be happier than I am."

12   With the invention of the high school, moreover, "common" in common schooling underwent redefinition. Extended academic education was available to all, but in practice was provided only to pupils who could afford to stay out of the labor market long enough to receive it. (U.S. Office of Education statistics show that in 1890 there were almost seven times as many teenagers at work as at school.) And it was broadly acknowledged that pupils in the immensely larger bottom tier of the two-tier educational system were being prepared for factory work. Authorities responded to corporate complaint about unruly workers by insisting that they themselves understood their obligation to produce disciplined plant hands. One school superintendent and U.S. educational commissioner asserted in 1871 that it was because factory life requires "conformity to the time of the train, to the starting of work in the manufactory," that "the first requisite of the school is *Order*." And he added: "The pupil must have his lessons ready at the appointed time, must rise at the tap of the bell, move to the line, return; in short, go through all the evolutions with equal precision."

13   During the first decades of common schooling, in short, the voice of the system wasn't easily distinguished from voices of moneyed interests. School admitted all comers, taught all comers literacy and numeracy, showed all comers how to live peaceably with each other. (Offensive to our ears, the Rich Boy–Poor Boy fables themselves represented, in their period, evenhanded openness of a sort.) But even as they were included, working people were fixed in their place, offered little that would inspire loyalty, gratitude, or a feeling for the fairness of things.

14   Change came partly because of a developing struggle for control of schools. Periodically, industry leaders sought to displace school administrators, abolish unitary common schooling, and institute job-skills training. Labor reaction was mixed; from the early workingmen's trade associations and parties (the 1820s and 1830s) straight through to the formation of the major, end-of-the-century unions, workers at moments saw advantage in separate, strictly vocational education, and sometimes opposed it only out of an instinct for job protection. (Business-run job-training institutes were on occasion seen as schemes for producing strikebreakers.)

15   Gradually, though, larger issues—those meant to be captured in the phrase educational equity—commenced surfacing. Grasping that business-run schools were inimical to their own interests, educators encouraged labor to stand firm for common schooling—to believe that it offered children of the working class a chance at full democratic citizenship and self-betterment that the alternative denied. As responsiveness to this theme deepened, administrators rejected plant-hand preparation and, in official rhetoric, widened the moral mission of school. Chicago's first woman superintendent of schools, Ella Flagg Young, declared in 1909 that she did not believe "in training the young to belong to a lower industrial class." An unfamiliar idea was ripening: school as an activist in the crusade for social justice.

16   Economic circumstance speeded the growth of trust between working class parents and teachers. Poorly paid, disenfranchised (because female), most teachers in the early decades of this century had reason to identify with working class constituencies. (Unionization prolonged the sympathy, even though subsequent generations of teachers would increasingly label themselves middle class.) The coming of truly bad times—the Depression, mass unemployment—strengthened labor's commitment to the school as one of the few institutions which, if not precisely on workingpeople's side, at least didn't stand to make money by wringing workers and their families.

17   The emerging solidarity of the community of educators and the ranks of labor, each holding school out to the other as a locus of hope, might in time have entangled education in new conflict, rendering idealization impossible. Among the well-off, after all, favorable attitudes toward school stemmed less from appreciation of a democratizing force capable of raising the low and leveling the high than from enthusiasm for the secondary school system as a class preserve. And losing the fight for control had hardly reduced businessmen's suspicion of public education. The most effective weapon educators deployed in the late nineteenth and early twentieth century campaign for autonomy was the concept of school as the adjunct of upward mobility. But that deployment opened up lines of dispute demanding—hindsight speaks again—new weapons.

18 One emerged: science. The public consequences of the triumph of social science in our time lie beyond quick reckoning; one major consequence was the extrication of school from social conflict and the laying of a foundation for the claim that education advanced the cause of justice concretely and objectively. Mass "scientific" intelligence testing during World War I intrigued the nation. Graduate schools of education and school administrators stepped forward as guardians and representatives of a precious methodology capable of functioning as the right arm of equity, freeing evaluation and management of human potential from age-old favoritism and prejudice. In the first half of this century science worship was everywhere, permeating all areas of American life—business, politics, religion, art. But it was in the field of education that the enthusiasm most dramatically connected itself with the ideal of democratic equity. A revolution fought partly in the hope of banishing arbitrary inequality had been followed by a century in which the specter of inequality had returned; the new sciences of psychology and administration promised to ground fairness in impersonal standards; through Stanford-Binet true merit would rise to the top and the original American promise would be realized. And schoolpeople alone—*professionals*—were competent to put the tool to use.

19 The rise or fall in public esteem of any institution touching the lives of an entire population is, needless to say, a complex phenomenon. Definitive word can't be spoken about which force—the original commitment to inclusiveness, the defeat of business and industry school takeover bids, the upsurge of science as the handmaid of equity—most directly furthered the process of idealization. What is clear is that, over a period of a century, different social and intellectual sectors came to have strong reason for doubting that school ever would or could sell them out. From here the step was short to belief in school the equalizer.

20 It is, regrettably, a mistaken belief. During the past three to four decades many educational researchers and historians have worked at the task of explaining why—and at measuring the distance between a meritocratic school system and the system as it is. The pioneering contribution was a mid-century study of the class dimensions of the treatment of poor, middle, and upper middle class pupils by teachers and principals in one midwestern high school. The most influential research—that of the Coleman Commission—was conducted for the U.S. Congress, at the height of the civil rights movement. Inquiry since then has ranged freely over the school and college spectrum, from educational expenditures in relation to pupil performance, to early scholastic ability in relation to ultimate college attendance, to curriculum as abettor of class segmentation.

21 *The Coleman Report* (1966) established that class identity determined student achievement from start to finish—because it shaped attitudes toward teachers, familiarity with the materials of learning,

preparatory experiences of language and reason-giving, and the environment of study. (The most recent confirmation and updating of Coleman appeared, in 1987, in William Julius Wilson's *The Truly Disadvantaged: The Inner City, the Underclass and Public Policy*; Wilson's evidence showed that quality of student performance continues to be unrelated to per-pupil expenditure and other non-class variables.)

22   Other research has shown that well-off students with weak academic records are far more likely to attend college than poor students with strong records; that multi-track, open transfer systems create class enclaves not fluidity; that arrangements in state-supported higher education function similarly (low subsidies for the least advantaged attending two-year colleges, high subsidies for the most advantaged attending flagship universities); and that scholarship funds advertised as democratizing influences in private colleges and universities are frequently awarded to students with family incomes of $100,000 and more per year.

23   A large body of inquiry has suggested, moreover, that public school teachers' conceptions of "ideal" pupils typically fuse responses to class-connected accent, appearance, manner, and deportment with responses to "natural or inborn intelligence:" similar class skewing is noted in testing agencies. The verbal behavior of middle and upper-middle children, identified as "intelligent," becomes a standard of evaluation.

24   Often in the past quarter-century writers and commentators aware of these and related studies have gone so far as to indict public education and standardized testing, charging that both qualify as conscious conspiracies against factory and office workers, tradespeople, "unskilled" laborers. Schools are presented as socioculturally biased institutions whose primary function is to assure that top occupations aren't glutted with credentialed candidates, while preventing the spread of doubt and cynicism about the system as a whole. One thrust of the attacks is directed at curriculum and teaching methods, which are seen as systematically disparaging the knowledge and values of the largest sector of the population—the working class.

25   According to this argument, school everywhere takes middle and upper-middle-class understandings of experience as its standard. It allows post-school status systems—such as that which places mechanics below engineers—to infect the classroom. It refuses to teach scientific principles and theory in shop classes. It gives small motor repair no place in introductory physics. It automatically awards an edge, in arts and humanities education, to those at ease, because of home experience, with the materials that middle and upper-middle-class opinion traditionally holds worthy of "analysis," "appreciation," "discussion." It denies intellectual attention to disciplined excellence in the activities—skills, crafts, practical arts, sports—with which the majority is most conversant and comfortable. And, through the artifices of professionalization, it excludes millions of knowers and workers from the experience of knowledge-sharing, to no social end except that of subordination.

26   Philosophers of education, economists, and socialist revolutionaries are among those who, in the recent past, have levied these or similar charges. Rebuttals stress, among other points, that international studies indicate structural rigidity in education is less marked here than abroad, and that, in America, neither vocational nor non-vocational education has ever been geared solely to occupational demands; school invariably provides competencies beyond those required by employers. A better complaint would be that the left critique, like conventional sociological research, has failed to reach a general audience. In consequence both the extent and nature of class influence on school go unnoticed, as does the role of illusion in sustaining faith in school the equalizer.

27   For a time in the Eighties anxiety about education seemed on the verge of shaking that faith. The decade began with a pessimistic Department of Education study, *A Nation at Risk,* and ended with a declaration by the incoming President that education deserved to be among the highest priorities of the Chief Executive; "I want to become the Education President." But although increased public concern about "poor learning atmospheres" in urban systems has transformed education into a "problem area," it hasn't effectively challenged school's iconographic status.

28   One reason for this is the iron consistency with which educational discourse marginalizes unfairness—focuses chiefly on failure to deliver reading and writing skills to racial and ethnic minorities. The point is made that blacks and Hispanics are "disadvantaged," and that possibly 10 percent of the nation's schools—those dealing with inner city children—are so poorly equipped, staffed, and managed that they're incapable of providing fair opportunity to their student bodies. Political candidates and editorial writers warn that school authorities have failed to arouse, in city and state governments, a proper sense of their public duty to provide special help. But the framing of the issue conceals that the troubles of inner city schools are a special, highly publicized symptom of conditions of inequity that extend far beyond ghettos and barrios. Dropouts and "greasers" who aren't black or Hispanic vastly outnumber the entire American school population of minority students. They're the children of parents whose own experiences of academic English, History, Foreign Language, and Science were frustrating—conducive mainly to doubt that book leaning is connected with the realities of practical life and work.

29   And these parents, to repeat, truly are the majority. It's in the working class at large, not alone in the ghetto (wrongly conceived as separable from the working class), that poetry speaks more often as sport than as Edgar Allan Poe, and that independent study and recreation concentrate on speed shops and soaps instead of upon piano lessons or the elders' favorite novels by Jane Austen.

30   But the notion that only for minorities is school an alien culture neatly excises both the fairness problem and the education problem

from the broader realities of a class society. Four, five, and six decades ago, educational commentary and criticism didn't blink at those realities. A 1927 book on *The Selective Character of American Secondary Education* states flatly that: "The public high school is attended quite largely by the children of the more well-to-do classes. This affords us the spectacle of a privilege being extended at public expense to those very classes that already occupy the privileged positions in modern society. The poor are contributing to provide secondary education for the children of the rich but are either too poor or too ignorant to avail themselves of the opportunities which they help to provide." Twenty years later an academic study based on classroom observation noted that: "Most lower class children do not understand or appreciate the teacher's efforts. In turn, the teacher tends to neglect the lower-class children if she does not actually discriminate against them. They do not reward her with obedience and affection, and she does not reward them with affection, good marks, and special approval. Conversely, when the teacher finds a lower-class child who does respond to her efforts, who does seem to understand middle-class standards, she is the more interested and puts in extra effort where she thinks she can do some good."

31   But more recently protocol demands a near-total excision of class—hedging and equivocation about every mode of inequity that can't be "minoritized." Signs of the excision abound in newspaper stories and popular culture, as well as in academic analyses. Debate about "remediation" isolates minority schools; diagnosis treats internal influences—lazy, permissive, badly educated teachers and principals—as responsible for school failures.

32   *Item:* the principal of a largely black, Paterson, New Jersey, school patrols the corridors with megaphone and baseball bat, locks firedoors (against undesirable intruders), expels indolent students, and succeeds in restoring order to a failed school. Fired by his school board, he's hailed as a pathfinder by the White House and provided with a position in the Department of Education by the sitting Secretary. *Black kids deserve a chance to learn and Joe Clark gave it to them.*

33   *Item:* a fiction film called *Stand and Deliver* (1988), based on the experience of a real-life Los Angeles high school teacher, tells how the man manages to teach the calculus to a class of initially uninterested, unmotivated minority students. (The actual teacher, Jamie Escalante, was named a hero during the 1988 presidential debates.) Tough, streetsmart, knowledgeable not only about math but about the unrealized abilities of his students, the teacher is also resourceful in circumventing obstacles set in his path by school administrators. He coaches, cajoles, browbeats, inspires, works long after school and on weekends, and produces a class of calculus stars. At one point there's a conflict between the teacher and the Educational Testing Service, which suspects him and his class of cheating. But teacher and tester alike share a devotion to fairness, and in the end that value prevails.

34   *Item:* E. D. Hirsch, a respected English professor, argues in a bestseller—*Cultural Illiteracy* (1987)—that the education problem amounts simply to a matter of cultural illiteracy among the minorities. "Disadvantaged children" lack the background knowledge necessary for comprehension of most assigned texts, says Hirsch, but if teachers set them to work learning definitions of key terms (5,000 in number, ranging from *andante* to *sociobiology*), they'll overcome the deficiencies. "If we begin an acculturative program in early grades—that is, if we systematically provide the needed background information from the earliest possible age through third grade—then," says Hirsch, "we can overcome a lot of the knowledge deficit of disadvantaged children.... In my view, the most significant educational reform we could undertake would be to put all children on a level playing-field in literacy skills by the beginning of fourth grade."

35   Fairness once more. And again the conjunction of two leading ideas: inequity as the exception (a minority distress), fairness as the pedagogical obsession. At times the continuing popular and academic trust in school as the equalizer seems actually dependent on the "urban school crisis." The overt function of the crisis is to draw to a head doubt about the health of the democratic ideal of educational equity. The latent function is to lance the doubt by enabling political and educational authority to demonstrate that even tiny infractions of the rule of fairness (there can be no others) rouse fierce democratic concern.

36   But dramas of "concern" at most refurbish belief; they could never father it. In the mythology of school-and-life fairness the concerned educator plays a cameo part; the only true indispensables are the racers, the starting line, and the potent personal will. And it bears emphasizing that the story of the race seems as seductive to the defeated as to the victors. Again excessive homogenization looms as a danger. Scarsdale High School juniors prepping for an English Advanced Placement test are alert to a national context—a horizon of opportunity—different from that, say, of youngsters of the same age completing an apprentice training program in a predominantly Polish high school in northwest Detroit. There are numberless contests; a union apprenticeship in a well-paid trade carries a life-promise different from that implicit in an acceptance letter from the director of admissions at Yale. But in all races there are losers, and at all levels talk of the race is permeated by themes of personal choice and individual responsibility, and by comparisons of "pure" ability and talent.

37   When youngsters aware of their difficulties with schoolwork compare themselves with successful students, they speak not of teachers or of life-circumstances, only of "intelligence." Grownups looking back at a lifetime of unrewarding, poorly paid labor see poor choices of their own as the cause—acts of individual bad judgment. *I should never have quit school* is a refrain in the extended interviews with members of the work-

ing class quoted in Robert Lane's pioneering *Political Ideology* (1962); some responsibility is assigned to parents who didn't insist on school attendance, but in the main the speakers blame themselves.

38. And, predictably, winners praise themselves. Elite liberal arts college student bodies are composed largely of high-achieving children with family incomes in the top tenth percentile. Well brought up, seldom pompous, they adopt tones of sadness and frustration when discussing—in interviews—the gap that widened between themselves and non-achievers. Two separating factors are mentioned. The first is the choice, by the non-achievers, of idleness. Inexplicably, disastrously, the non-achievers simply would not *work*, preferring to hang out at malls. By this act "they threw away their future."

39. The second factor cited is venturesomeness. During years of academic committee service, the present writer has read a fair number of "autobiographical statements" composed by Rhodes, Marshall, Truman, and other fellowship candidates introducing themselves to jurors. Almost by convention the achievers point to entries in their record attesting their readiness to "try everything" in the line of learning experiences. In the highly developed American lesson culture of the Eighties, these experiences include a variety of privately contracted-for instruction—dressage, the bassoon, wilderness survival technique, ballet, dance skating, tennis, chess, Russian, more. "There was only one rule in my family: you had to try everything. You had to give it a fair try and afterward, if you didn't like it, okay: Quit. But you had to make the effort."

40. The sentence-sounds carry the inner concept of self: independent, open to possibility, aware of the endless range of pleasures and satisfactions life offers to those eager to seize the grape, unafraid of embarrassment or failure, delighting in new experiences, proud of the capacity for commitment. Habitually, that capacity is seen as a personal trait; habitually, expensive advantages and options are understood to be, at bottom, self-made.

41. The determination to see them thus underscores the interdependency of the themes of classlessness and unconditionedness in the American psyche. A non-sectarian shrine of the will, as well as of egalitarian moral idealism, school feeds dreams of personal potency, fantasies of self-creation. I am myself alone. What you see is what you get. The need to claim unconditionedness breathes throughout whole lifetimes; school's significance is lessened not a whit by the admission that no single institution or gesture or array of memories can meet the need once for all. As representative citizens, self-mythologizing, individualistic choosers-of-our-separate-paths, we re-invent the school story—the starting line, the momentous decision, the personal turning point—time after time, insistently, lovingly, Frost in one ear, Sinatra in the other. (*Two roads diverged in a wood. I did it my way.*) We use the story as an all-purpose interpretive lens—a means of clarifying experiences remote from school. We do this partly out of hunger for coherence, partly because, for complex reasons, history denies us other choices.

Points for Review and Discussion

1. Summarize DeMott's reasons for denying that the starting line is the same for all students in the educational race.
2. DeMott also denies that intelligence testing ensures fairness based on impersonal standards. What are his reasons for this denial?
3. Summarize DeMott's explication of the nature and effects of "minoritizing" (¶ 28) educational problems.

☙ Questions for Writing

1. Review your own experience as a high school and college student: have you encountered or observed, in the course of your education, what you regard as class bias? Describe the situation as fully as you can.
2. DeMott writes as though "the lesson culture" bestowed unfair advantages on financially well-off students. Does this seem to you a reasonable point? If it does not, explain why not. If it does, explain what advantage you would say that private instruction in dance skating, say, or the bassoon or some other extracurricular subject confers on those who can afford it.
3. In 1909 Ella Flagg Young rejected the idea that schools "should be training the young to belong to a lower industrial class" (¶ 15). In a 500-word essay explain why this rejection can be seen to signal the start of a crusade for social justice in which schools would play an activist role.

THE STRUGGLE AND ACHIEVEMENTS OF AMERICA'S UNDERPREPARED
Mike Rose

One of the most notable and least recognized achievements of the American higher educational system in recent decades has been the development of means of bridging gaps between underprepared students and the college curriculum. A trailblazer in this field is Mike Rose, who teaches "remedial English" at UCLA and is the author of the essay below.

The son of Italian immigrants, Rose grew up a mile from the Watts section of South Los Angeles, had difficulties in school ("two things I couldn't understand and over the years grew to hate: grammar lessons and mathematics"), but at length found his way as an "underprepared student" at Loyola University. After graduate work, he launched himself on a brilliant career as both a teacher and a writer.

Generalizing about the situation of those whose experience matches his own, Mike Rose writes as follows:

> To live your early life on the streets of South L.A.—or Homewood or Spanish Harlem or Chicago's South Side or any one of hundreds of other depressed communities—and to journey up through the top levels of the American educational system will call for support and guidance at many, many points along the way. You'll need people to guide you into conversations that seem foreign and threatening. You'll need models, lots of them, to show you how to get at what you don't know. You'll need people to help you center yourself in your own developing ideas. You'll need people to watch out for you. There is much talk these days about the value of a classical humanistic education, a call for an immersion in the humanities, a return to the great books. These appeals raise lots of suspicions, for such curricula have traditionally served to exclude working-class people from the classroom. It doesn't, of necessity, have to be that way.

1 When I was in the Teacher Corps, I saw daily the effects of background on schooling. Kids came into the schools with hand-me-down skirts and pants, they didn't have lunch money, they were failing. The connections between neighborhood and classroom were striking. This was true, though in different ways, with the veterans. The Tutorial Center also served low-income white and low- and middle-income minority students, but because the kind of students who make it to a place like UCLA enter with a long history of success and, to varying degrees, have removed superficial indicators of their lineage, it's harder, at first glance, to see how profoundly a single assignment or a whole academic

---

From Mike Rose, *Lives on the Boundary* (1989).

career can be affected by background and social circumstance—by interactions of class, race, and gender. But as I settled into Campbell Hall, I saw illustrations continually, ones that complicated easy judgment and expectation.

Sometimes issues of economics and race were brought up by the students themselves. Such issues were also raised by the existence of the Ethnic Studies Centers, the perennial posters in the hallways, or the lobbying of older, politically active students, and they emerged in some of the students' classes. There was wide variation in the students' responses. Some had grown up watching their parents deal with insult, had heard slurs in their schools about skin color and family and language. A young woman writes in her placement exam for Freshman English:

> I could not go into the restroom, the cafeteria, or any place of the high school area alone, without having some girl following me and calling me names or pushing me around. Some of their favorite names for me were "wetback," "beaner," or "illegal alien." I did not pay much attention to the name calling, but when they started pulling my hair, pushing me, or throwing beans at me, I reacted.

Students like her were drawn to issues of race, read the walls of Campbell with understanding, saw connections between the messages on green paper and the hurt in their own past. They had been sensitized to exclusion as they were growing up.

But there were those who came to Campbell Hall with a different past and a different outlook. Some of those who grew up with the protections of middle-class life knew of the wrongs done to their people, but slavery and Nisei internment and agricultural camps seemed distant to them, something heard in their grandmothers' stories—a hazy film playing in an incomprehensible past. Their own coming of age had been shaped by their parents' hard-won assimilation, the irony of that achievement being an erasure of history for the children of the assimilated. These students had passed through a variety of social and religious clubs and organizations in which they saw people of their race exercise power. They felt at the center of things themselves, optimistic, forward-looking, the force of their own personal history leading them to expect an uncomplicated blending into campus life. I think that many of them were ambivalent about Campbell Hall—it was good to have the services, but they felt strange about being marked as different.

"Why are we reading this junk? This is just junk!" Denise was tapping the page and looking at me, then off across the room, then back at me. Underneath the light strikes of her finger was a passage her history professor had excerpted from the Lincoln-Douglas debates:

> ... there is a physical difference between the white and black races which I believe will forever forbid the two races living together on terms of social

and political equality. And inasmuch as they cannot so live, while they do remain together there must be the position of superior and inferior, and I as much as any other man am in favor of having the superior position assigned to the white race.

"Yeah," I said, "Abraham Lincoln. Pretty upsetting, isn't it? Why do you think the professor gave it to the class?" "Well," she said, still angry, "that's not the point. The point is, why do we have to read stuff like this?" The week before, Denise and I had the following exchange. She had to write a paper for her composition class. It was built on an excerpt from Henry Roth's immigrant novel, *Call It Sleep*, and the assignment required her to write about the hardships current immigrants face. Our discussion worked its way around to attitudes, so I suggested to Denise that she write on the things she'd heard said about Hispanic immigrants in Southern California. She looked at me as though I'd whispered something obscene in her ear. "No!" she said emphatically, pulling back her head, "that's rude." "Rude," I said. "Explain to me what's—" She cut in. "You don't want to put that in a paper. That doesn't belong." Some things were better left unsaid. Decent people, Denise had learned, just don't say them. There is a life to lead, and it will be a good life. Put the stuff your grandmother lived and your father saw behind you. It belongs in the past. It need not be dredged up if we're to move on. And, in fact, Denise could not dredge it up—the flow of her writing stopped cold by an ugly historical text that was both confusing and painful for her to see.

5 The counselor's office was always dusky, the sun blocked by thick trees outside the windows. There was an oversize easy chair by his desk. In it sat Marita, thin, head down, hands in her lap, her shiny hair covering her face. The counselor spoke her name, and she looked up, her eyes red in the half-light. The counselor explained that the graduate student who taught her English had accused Marita of plagiarism and had turned her paper over to the director of Freshman English. He asked her to continue, to tell me the story herself.

6 Marita had been at UCLA for about three weeks. This was her first writing assignment. The class had read a discussion of creativity by Jacob Bronowski and were supposed to write papers agreeing or disagreeing with his discussion. What, Marita wondered, would she say? "What is the insight with which the scientist tries to see into nature?" asked Bronowski. Marita wasn't a scientist, and she didn't consider herself to be a particularly creative person, like an artist or an actress. Her father had always been absolute about the expression of opinion, especially with his daughters: "Don't talk unless you know." "All science is the search for unity in hidden likenesses," asserted Bronowski. "The world is full of fools who speak in ignorance," Marita's father would say, and Marita grew up cautious and reticent. Her thoughts on creativity seemed obvious or, worse yet, silly next to this man Bronowski. What did it mean anyway when he said: "We remake nature by the act of discovery,

in the poem or in the theorem"? She wanted to do well on the assignment, so she went to the little library by her house and looked in the encyclopedia. She found an entry on creativity and used some selections from it that had to do with mathematicians and scientists. On the bottom of the last page of her paper, she listed the encyclopedia and her English composition textbook as her references. What had she done wrong? "They're saying I cheated. I didn't cheat." She paused and thought. "You're supposed to use other people, and I did, and I put the name of the book I used on the back of my paper."

7   The counselor handed me the paper. It was clear by the third sentence that the writing was not all hers. She had incorporated stretches of old encyclopedia prose into her paper and had quoted only some of it. I couldn't know if she had lifted directly or paraphrased the rest, but it was formal and dated and sprinkled with high-cultural references, just not what you'd find in freshman writing. I imagined that it had pleased her previous teachers that she cared enough about her work to go find sources, to rely on experts. Marita had come from a tough school in Compton—an area to the southeast of where I'd grown up—and her conscientiousness and diligence, her commitment to the academic way, must have been a great joy to those who taught her. She shifted, hoisting herself back up from the recesses of the counselor's chair. "Are they going to dismiss me? Are they going to kick me out of school?"

8   Marita was adrift in a set of conventions she didn't fully understand; she offended without knowing why. Virtually all the writing academics do is built on the writing of others. Every argument procedes from the texts of others. Marita was only partially initiated to how this works: She was still unsure as to how to weave quotations in with her own prose, how to mark the difference, how to cite whom she used, how to strike the proper balance between her writing and someone else's—how, in short, to position herself in an academic discussion.

9   I told Marita that I would talk with her teacher and that I was sure we could work something out, maybe another chance to write the paper. I excused myself and walked slowly back to my office, half lost in thought, reading here and there in the Bronowski excerpt. It was typical fare for Freshman English anthologies, the sort of essay you'd originally find in places like *The New Yorker*. Bronowski, the eminent scientist, looking back on his career, weaving poetry in with cybernetics, quoting *Faust* in German, allusive, learned, reflective.

10   The people who put together those freshman anthologies are drawn to this sort of thing: It's in the tradition of the English essay and reflects rich learning and polished style. But it's easy to forget how difficult these essays can be and how developed a taste they require. When I was at Loyola, someone recommended I buy Jacques Barzun's *The Energies of Art*, a collection of "fifteen striking essays on art and culture." I remember starting one essay and stopping, adrift, two or three pages later. Then another, but no go. The words arose from a depth of knowledge and

a developed perception and a wealth of received ways to talk about art and a seemingly endless reserve of allusions. I felt like a janitor at a gallery opening, silent, intimidated, little flecks of knowledge—Bagehot, Stendhal, baroque ideology—sticking to the fiber of my broom.

11   Marita's assignment assumed a number of things: an ability to slip into Bronowski's discussion, a reserve of personal experiences that the writer herself would perceive as creative, a knowledge of and facility with—confidence with, really—the kinds of stylistic moves you'd find in those *New Yorker* essays. And it did *not* assume that someone, by family culture, by gender, would be reluctant to engage the reading on its own terms. Marita was being asked to write in a cognitive and social vacuum. I'm sure the other students in her class had a rough time of it as well. Many competent adult writers would too. But the solution Marita used marked her as an outsider and almost tripped the legal switches of the university.

12   At twenty-eight, Lucia was beginning her second quarter at UCLA. There weren't many people here like her. She was older, had a family, had transferred in from a community college. She represented a population that historically hadn't gained much entrance to places like this: the returning student, the single, working mother. She had a network of neighbors and relatives that provided child care. On this day, though, the cousin on tap had an appointment at Immigration, so Lucia brought her baby with her to her psychology tutorial. Her tutor had taken ill that morning, so rather than turn her away, the receptionist brought her in to me, for I had spoken with her before. Lucia held her baby through most of our session, the baby facing her, Lucia's leg moving rhythmically, continually—a soothing movement that rocked him into sleep.

13   Upon entrance to UCLA, Lucia declared a psychology major. She had completed all her preliminary requirements at her community college and now faced that same series of upper-division courses that I took when I abandoned graduate study in English some years before: Physiological Psychology, Learning, Perception . . . all that. She was currently enrolled in Abnormal Psychology, "the study of the dynamics and prevention of abnormal behavior." Her professor had begun the course with an intellectual curve ball. He required the class to read excerpts from Thomas Szasz's controversial *The Myth of Mental Illness*, a book that debunks the very notions underlying the traditional psychological study of abnormal behavior, a book that was proving very difficult for Lucia.

14   My previous encounter with Lucia had convinced me that she was an able student. She was conscientious about her studies—recopied notes, visited professors—and she enjoyed writing: she wrote poems in an old copy book and read popular novels, both in Spanish and English. But Szasz—Szasz was throwing her. She couldn't get through the twelve-and-a-half pages of introduction. I asked her to read some passages out loud and explain them to me as best she could. And as Lucia read and

talked, it became clear to me that while she could, with some doing, pick her way through Szasz's sophisticated prose, certain elements of his argument, particular assumptions and allusions, were foreign to her—or, more precisely, a frame of mind or tradition or set of assumptions that was represented by a single word, phrase, or allusion was either unknown to her or clashed dramatically with frames of mind and traditions of her own.

15   Here are the first few lines of Szasz's introduction:

> Psychiatry is conventionally defined as a medical specialty concerned with the diagnosis and treatment of mental diseases. I submit that this definition, which is still widely accepted, places psychiatry in the company of alchemy and astrology and commits it to the category of pseudoscience. The reason for this is that there is no such thing as "mental illness."

One powerful reason Lucia had decided to major in psychology was that she wanted to help people like her brother, who had a psychotic break in his teens and had been in and out of hospitals since. She had lived with mental illness, had seen that look in her brother's eyes, felt drawn to help people whose mind had betrayed them. The assertion that there was no such thing as mental illness, that it was a myth, seemed incomprehensible to her. She had trouble even entertaining it as a hypothesis, and thus couldn't play out its resonances and implications in the pages that followed. Szasz's bold claim was a bone sticking in her assumptive craw.

16   Here's another passage alongside which she had placed a question mark:

> The conceptual scaffolding of medicine, however, rests on the principles of physics and chemistry, as indeed it should, for it has been, and continues to be, the task of medicine to study and if necessary to alter, the physiochemical structure and function of the human body. Yet the fact remains that human sign-using behavior does not lend itself to exploration and understanding in these terms. We thus remain shackled to the wrong conceptual framework and terminology.

To understand this passage, you need to have some orientation to the "semiotic" tenet that every human action potentially carries some kind of message, that everything we do can be read as a sign of more than itself. This has become an accepted notion in high-powered liberal studies, an inclination to see every action and object as a kind of language that requires interpretation. The notion and its implications—the conversation within which the phrase "sign-using" situates you—was foreign to Lucia. So it was difficult for her to see why Szasz was claiming that medicine was the "wrong conceptual framework" with which to study abnormal behavior.

17   Here's a third passage:

> Man thus creates a heavenly father and an imaginary replica of the protected childhood situation to replace the real or longed-for father and fam-

ily. The differences between traditional religious doctrine, modern political historicism, and psychoanalytic orthodoxy thus lie mainly in the character of the "protectors": they are, respectively, God and the priests, the totalitarian leader and his apologists, and Freud and the psychoanalyst.

While Freud criticized revealed religion for the patent infantilism that it is, he ignored the social characteristics of closed societies and the psychological characteristics of their loyal supporters. He thus failed to see the religious character of the movement he himself was creating.

18   Lucia's working-class Catholicism made it difficult for her to go along with, to intellectually toy with, the comparison of Freud to God, but there was another problem here too, not unlike the problem she had with the "sign-using" passage. It is a standard move in liberal studies to find religious analogues to nonreligious behaviors, structures, and institutions. Lucia could certainly "decode" and rephrase a sentence like: "He thus failed to see the religious character of the movement he himself was creating," but she didn't have the background to appreciate what happens to Freud and psychoanalysis the moment Szasz makes his comparison, wasn't familiar with the wealth of conclusions that would follow from the analogy.

19   And so it went with other key passages. Students like Lucia are often thought to be poor readers or to have impoverished vocabularies (though Lucia speaks two languages); I've even heard students like her referred to as culturally illiterate (though she has absorbed two cultural heritages). It's true there were words Lucia didn't know (*alchemy, orthodoxy*) and sentences that took us two or three passes to untangle. But it seemed more fruitful to see Lucia's difficulties in understanding Szasz as having to do with her belief system and with her lack of familiarity with certain ongoing discussions in humanities and social science—with frames of mind, predispositions, and background knowledge. To help Lucia with her reading, then, I explained five or six central discussions that go on in liberal studies; the semiotic discussion, the sacred-profane discussion, the medical vs. social model discussion. While I did this, I was encouraging her to talk through opinions of her own that ran counter to these discussions. That was how she improved her reading of Szasz. The material the professor assigned that followed the introduction built systematically off it, so once Lucia was situated in that introduction, she had a framework to guide her through the long passages that followed, all of which elaborated those first twelve pages.

20   The baby pulled his face out of his mother's chest, yawned, squirmed, and turned to fix on me, wide-eyed. Lucia started packing up her books with a free hand. I had missed lunch. "Let's go," I said. "I'll walk out with you." Her movement distressed the baby, so Lucia soothed him with soft coos and clicks, stood up, and shifted him to her hip. We left Campbell Hall and headed southeast, me toward a sandwich, Lucia toward the buses that ran up and down Hilgard on UCLA's

east boundary. It was a beautiful California day, and the jacarandas were in full purple bloom. Lucia talked about her baby's little discoveries, about a cousin who worried her, about her growing familiarity with this sprawling campus. "I'm beginning to know where things are," she said, pursing her lips. "You know, the other day some guy stopped me and asked *me* where Murphy Hall was . . . and I could tell him." She looked straight at me: "It felt pretty good!" We walked on like this, her dress hiked up where the baby rode her hip, her books in a bag slung over her shoulder, and I began to think about how many pieces had to fall into place each day in order for her to be a student: The baby couldn't wake up sick, no colic or rashes, the cousin or a neighbor had to be available to watch him, the three buses she took from East L.A. had to be on time—no accidents or breakdowns or strikes—for travel alone took up almost three hours of her school day. Only if all these pieces dropped in smooth alignment could her full attention shift to the complex and allusive prose of Thomas Szasz. "Man thus creates a heavenly father and an imaginary replica of the protected childhood situation to replace the real or longed-for father and family."

21 During the time I was working with Denise and Lucia and the others, all hell was breaking loose in American education. The literacy crisis that has become part of our current cultural vocabulary was taking shape with a vengeance. It was in December 1975 that *Newsweek* informed America that Johnny couldn't write, and in the fall of 1976 the *Los Angeles Times* declared a "Drop in Student Skills Unequalled in History." California, the *Times* article went on to reveal, had "one of the most pronounced drops in achievement of all." Reports on the enrollment and retention of students are a long-standing tradition in the way education conducts its business, but it seemed that every month now a new document was appearing on my desk: reports from a vice-chancellor or the university president's office or from some analyst in the state legislature. What percentage of people from families below a certain income level were entering college? What were their SAT scores? What were the SAT scores of blacks? Chicanos? Asians? More locally, how many UCLA students were being held for remedial English? Remedial math? Were there differences by race or income?

22 This was a new way for me to look at education. My focus had been on particular students and their communities, and it tended to be a teacher's focus, rich in anecdote and observation. Increasingly, my work in the Tutorial Center required that I take a different perspective: I had to think like a policy-maker, considering the balance sheet of economics and accountability. Chip would sit with me in the late afternoon, going over the charts and tables, showing me how to use them to argue for our programs, for in an academic bureaucracy admissions statistics and test scores and retention rates are valued terms of debate. All teaching is embedded in a political context, of course, but the kind of work I had done

before coming to the Tutorial Center tended to isolate me from the immediate presence of institutions: working with a group of kids in the corner of a cafeteria, teaching veterans in a dingy satellite building. I was learning from Chip and from a shrewd vice-chancellor named Chuck Ries how to work within the policy-maker's arena. And though it was, at times, uncomfortable for me and though I would soon come to question the legitimacy of the vision it fostered, it provided an important set of lessons. Probably the central value of being at the Tutorial Center was that it forced me to examine the broad institutional context of writing instruction and underpreparation.

23 The work in the center led to other projects, and during my four years in Campbell Hall, I would be invited to participate in them. One was the Writing Research Project, initiated by Vice-Chancellor Ries, and its purpose was to study the uses of writing and the way it was taught at UCLA. Another was the Freshman Summer Program, six intensive weeks before the freshman year during which students took a writing course linked to an introductory course in political science or psychology or history. There is a lot to tell about these ventures—the politics of evaluating a curriculum at a university, the strains of initiating a curriculum that requires people to cross departmental lines—but the most important thing about both projects was that they led me to do something rarely achieved at a research university. I had to stand on the borders of a number of disciplines and study the way knowledge is structured in the academy and, as well, detail what it means to be unprepared to participate in that disciplinary structure.

24 Students were coming to college with limited exposure to certain kinds of writing and reading and with conceptions and beliefs that were dissonant with those in the lower-division curriculum they encountered. And that curriculum wasn't doing a lot to address their weaknesses or nurture their strengths. They needed practice writing academic essays; they needed opportunities to talk about their writing—and their reading; they needed people who could quickly determine what necessary background knowledge they lacked and supply it in comprehensible ways. What began troubling me about the policy documents and the crisis reports was that they focused too narrowly on test scores and tallies of error and other such measures. They lacked careful analysis of the students' histories and lacked, as well, analysis of the cognitive and social demands of the academic culture the students now faced. The work I was doing in the Tutorial Center, in the Writing Research Project, and in the Summer Program was guiding me toward a richer understanding of what it meant to be underprepared in the American research university. It seemed to me there were five overlapping problem areas—both cognitive and social—that could be used to explain the difficulties experienced by students like Marita . . . and Lucia. These by no means applied equally to all the students whom I came to know, but taken together they represent, better than pie charts and histograms, what it means to

be underprepared at a place like UCLA. Many young people come to the university able to summarize the events in a news story or write a personal response to a play or a movie or give back what a teacher said in a straightforward lecture. But they have considerable trouble with what has come to be called critical literacy: framing an argument or taking someone else's argument apart, systematically inspecting a document, an issue, or an event, synthesizing different points of view, applying a theory to disparate phenomena, and so on. The authors of the crisis reports got tremendously distressed about students' difficulty with such tasks, but it's important to remember that, traditionally, such abilities have only been developed in an elite: in priests, scholars, or a leisure class. Ours in the first society in history to expect so many of its people to be able to perform these very sophisticated literacy activities. And we fail to keep in mind how extraordinary it is to ask *all* our schools to conduct this kind of education—not just those schools with lots of money and exceptional teachers and small classes—but massive, sprawling schools, beleaguered schools, inner-city schools, overcrowded schools. It is a charge most of them simply are not equipped to fulfill, for our educational ideals far outstrip our economic and political priorities.

25   We forget, then, that by most historical—and current—standards, the vast majority of a research university's underprepared students would be considered competently literate. Though they fail to meet the demands made of them in their classes, they fail from a literate base. They are literate people straining at the boundaries of their ability, trying to move into the unfamiliar, to approximate a kind of writing they can't yet command. And as they try, they'll make all the blunders in word choice and sentence structure and discourse strategy that regularly get held up for ridicule, that I made when I was trying to write for my teachers at Loyola. There's a related phenomenon, and we have research evidence of this: As writers move further away from familiar ways of expressing themselves, the strains on their cognitive and linguistic resources increase, and the number of mechanical and grammatical errors they make shoots up. Before we shake our heads at these errors, we should also consider the possibility that many such linguistic bungles are signs of growth, a stretching beyond what college Freshmen can comfortably do with written language. In fact, we should *welcome* certain kinds of errors, make allowance for them in the curricula we develop, analyze rather than simply criticize them. Error marks the place where education begins.

26   Asked to produce something that is beyond them, writers might also fall back on strategies they already know. Asked to take a passage critically apart, they'll summarize it.... I was personally reminded of it when I was writing my dissertation. My chairman was an educational research methodologist and statistician; my background straddled humanities and social science, but what I knew about writing tended to be

shaped by literary models. When it came time to report on the procedures I was using in my study—the methods section of the dissertation—I wrote a detailed chronology of what I did and how I did it. I wanted to relay all the twists and turns of my investigation. About a week later I got it back covered with criticism. My chairman didn't want the vagaries of my investigative life; he wanted a compressed and systematic account. "What do you think this is," he wrote alongside one long, dancing stretch of narrative, "*Travels with Charley?*"

27 Associated with these difficulties with critical literacy are students' diverse orientations toward inquiry. It is a source of exasperation to many freshmen that the university is so predisposed to question past solutions, to seek counterexplanations—to continually turn something nice and clean and clear into a problem. English professor David Bartholomae recalls a teacher of his suggesting that, when stuck, student writers should try the following "machine": "While most readers of_____ have said_____, a close and careful reading shows that_____." The teacher's machine perfectly expresses the ethos of the university, a fundamental orientation toward inquiry. University professors have for so long been socialized into this critical stance, that they don't realize how unsettling it can be to students who don't share their unusual background.

28   There is Scott sitting in an Astronomy tutorial, his jaw set, responding to another student's question about a finite versus an infinite universe: "This is the kind of question," he says, "that you'll argue and argue about. It's stupid. No one wins. So why do it?" And there is Rene who can't get beyond the first few sentences of her essay for Speech. She has to write a critical response to an address of Ronald Reagan's. "You can't criticize the president," she explains. "You've gotta support your president even if you don't agree with him." When students come from other cultures, this discordance can be even more pronounced. Our tutors continually encouraged their students to read actively, to ask why authors say what they say, what their claims are, what assumptions they make, where you, the reader, agree or disagree. Hun's tutor is explaining this to him, then has him try it, has him read aloud so she can guide him. He reads a few lines and stops short. After two more abortive trials, she pulls out of Hun the explanation that what gets written in books is set in tradition, and he is not learned enough to question the authority of the book.

29 It is not usual for students to come to the university with conceptualizations of disciplines that are out of sync with academic reality.... A lot of entering freshmen assume that sociology is something akin to social work, an applied study of social problems rather than an attempt to abstract a theory about social interaction and organization.

Likewise, some think psychology will be a discussion of human motivation and counseling, what it is that makes people do what they do—and some coverage of ways to change what they do. It comes as a surprise that their textbook has only one chapter on personality and psychotherapy—and a half dozen pages on Freud. The rest is animal studies, computer models of thought, lots of neurophysiology. If they like to read novels, and they elect a literature course, they'll expect to talk about characters and motive and plot, but instead they're asked to situate the novel amid the historical forces that shaped it, to examine rhetorical and stylistic devices and search the prose for things that mean more than they seem to mean. Political science should be politics and government and current events—nuclear treaties, trade sanctions, the Iran-Contra scandal—but instead it's Marx and Weber and political economy and organizational and decision-making models. And so goes the litany of misdirection. This dissonance between the academy's and the students' definitions of disciplines makes it hard for students to get their bearings with material: to know what's important, to see how the pieces fit together, to follow an argument, to have a sense of what can be passed over lightly. Thus I would see notebooks that were filled—in frantic script—with everything the professor said or that were scant and fragmented, records of information without coherence.

30 The discourse of academics is marked by terms and expressions that represent an elaborate set of shared concepts and orientations: alienation, authoritarian personality, the social construction of the self, determinism, hegemony, equilibrium, intentionality, recursion, reinforcement, and so on. This language weaves through so many lectures and textbooks, is integral to so many learned discussions, that it's easy to forget what a foreign language it can be. Freshmen are often puzzled by the talk they hear in their classrooms, but what's important to note here is that their problem is not simply one of limited vocabulary. If we see the problem as knowing or not knowing a list or words, as some quick-fix remedies suggest, then we'll force glossaries on students and miss the complexity of the issue. Take, for example, *authoritarian personality*. The average university freshman will know what *personality* means and can figure out *authoritarian*; the difficulty will come from a lack of familiarity with the conceptual resonances that *authoritarian personality* has acquired in the discussions of sociologists and psychologists and political scientists. Discussion . . . you could almost define a university education as an initiation into a variety of powerful ongoing discussions, an initiation that can occur only through the repeated use of a new language in the company of others. More than anything, this was the opportunity people like Father Albertson, my Shakespeare teacher at Loyola, provided to me. The more comfortable and skillful students become with this kind of influential talk, the more they will be included in further conversations and given access to further conceptual tools and re-

sources—the acquisition of which virtually defines them as members of an intellectual community.

31   All students require such an opportunity. But those coming to the university with less-than-privileged educations, especially those from the lower classes, are particularly in need. They are less likely to have participated, in any extended way, in such discussions in the past. They won't have the confidence or the moves to enter it, and can begin to feel excluded, out of place, put off by a language they can't command. Their social marginality, then, is reinforced by discourse and, as happened to me during my first year at Loyola, they might well withdraw, retreat to silence.

32   This sense of linguistic exclusion can be complicated by various cultural differences. When I was growing up, I absorbed an entire belief system—with its own characteristic terms and expressions—from the worried conversations of my parents, from the things I heard and saw on South Vermont, from the priest's fiery tales. I thought that what happened to people was preordained, that ability was a fixed thing, that there was one true religion. I had rigid notions about social roles, about the structure of society, about gender, about politics. There used to be a rickety vending machine at Manchester and Vermont that held a Socialist Workers newspaper. I'd walk by it and feel something alive and injurious: The paper was malevolent and should be destroyed. Imagine, then, the difficulty I had when, at the beginning of my senior year at Mercy High, Jack MacFarland tried to explain Marxism to us. How could I absorb the language of atheistic materialism and class struggle when it seemed so strange and pernicious? It wasn't just that Marxist terms-of-art were unfamiliar; they felt assaultive. What I did was revert to definitions of the social order more familiar to me, and Mr. MacFarland had to draw them out of me and have me talk about them and consider them alongside Marx's vision and terminology, examining points of conflict and points of possible convergence. It was only then that I could appropriate Marx's strange idiom.

33   Once you start to think about underprepared students in terms of these overlapping problem areas, all sorts of solutions present themselves. Students need more opportunities to write about what they're learning and guidance in the techniques and conventions of that writing—what I got from my mentors at Loyola. They need more opportunities to develop the writing strategies that are an intimate part of academic inquiry and what has come to be called critical literacy—comparing, synthesizing, analyzing—the sort of thing [I tried to give my students]. They need opportunities to talk about what they're learning: to test their ideas, reveal their assumptions, talk through the places where new knowledge clashes with ingrained belief. They need a chance, too, to talk about the ways they may have felt excluded from all this in the past and may feel threatened by it in the present. They need the occasion to rise above the

fragmented learning the lower-division curriculum encourages, a place within a course or outside it to hear about and reflect on the way a particular discipline conducts its inquiry: Why, for example, *do* so many psychologists who study thinking rely on computer modeling? Why is mathematics so much a part of economics? And they need to be let in on the secret talk, on the shared concepts and catchphrases of Western liberal learning.

34   There is nothing magical about this list of solutions. In fact, in many ways, it reflects the kind of education a privileged small number of American students have received for some time. The basic question our society must ask, then, is: How many or how few do we want to have this education? If students didn't get it before coming to college—and most have not—then what are we willing to do to give it to them now? Chip and I used to talk about our special programs as attempts to create an Honors College for the underprepared. People would smile as we spoke, but, as our students would have said, we were serious as a heart attack. The remedial programs we knew about did a disservice to their students by thinking of them as *remedial*. We wanted to try out another perspective and see what kind of program it would yield. What would happen if we thought of our students' needs and goals in light of the comprehensive and ambitious program structures more often reserved for the elite?

Points for Review and Discussion

1.   Summarize "the effects of background on schooling" (¶ 1) that Rose details in this essay.
2.   Rose believes that some failing students "thought to be poor readers or to have impoverished vocabularies" (¶ 19) actually fail for quite different reasons. In the case of the student he calls Lucia, what does he see as the causes of her academic problems?

◆ *Questions for Writing*

1.   "The remedial programs we knew about did a disservice to their students by thinking of them as *remedial*. We wanted to try out another perspective..." (¶ 34). On the basis of the examples Rose gives in this essay, describe in your own words the perspective he tried out in working with underprepared students. What do you see as its essentials?
2.   Denise "could not dredge [the past] up" (¶ 4), and Rose believes the reason for this is fear that dredging it up would stop her forward progress. Put yourself in Denise's place: what other reasons might a person have for not wanting to write about his or her Hispanic family's immigrant past? (For assistance with this question see the selection by Richard Rodriguez in Chapter 8, page 318.)

3. "Asked to produce something that is beyond them, writers ... fall back on strategies they already know" (¶ 26). Describe as fully as you can an experience in your career as a student in which you yourself fared badly on an assignment by falling back, defensively, on an old strategy.

4. Implicit throughout Rose's essay is the assumption that greater alertness to class differences among students on the part of institutions and teachers would speed the learning process. In a short paper give reasons for and against accepting this assumption.

Savage Inequalities of Public Education
Jonathan Kozol

Firsthand reporting, by nonacademic writers, on what actually happens in American public schools took a great leap forward in the 1960s. Several young, Ivy League-educated idealists just starting careers as elementary or high school teachers found themselves stunned by what they encountered and put their discoveries on paper, in books that reached large audiences. Among the best known of these works was a National Book Award winner entitled *Death at an Early Age* (1967), a work about poor kids in Boston's public schools by a Harvard-educated grammar school teacher in his twenties—Jonathan Kozol.

Over the past quarter-century Kozol has written six more books about education, the poor, and the homeless. The most recent, *Savage Inequalities* (1991), focuses on the impact, on individual student lives, of this country's class-skewed system of school financing. The essay below describes the theory and background of that system, as well as an ongoing effort in Texas to change it.

The Dream Deferred, Again, in San Antonio

1   When low-income districts go to court to challenge the existing system of school funding, writes John Coons, the natural fear of the conservative is "that the levelers are at work here sapping the foundations of free enterprise."

2   In reality, he says, "there is . . . no graver threat to the capitalist system than the present cyclical replacement of the 'fittest' of one generation by their artificially advantaged off-spring. Worse, when that advantage is proffered to the children of the successful *by the state,* we can be sure that free enterprise has sold its birthright. . . . To defend the present public school finance system on a platform of economic or political freedom is no less absurd than to describe it as egalitarian. In the name of all the values of free enterprise, the existing system . . . is a . . . scandal."

3   There is something incongruous, he goes on, about "a differential of any magnitude" between the education of two children, "the sole justification for which is an imaginary school district line" between those children. The reliance of our public schools on property taxes and the localization of the uses of those taxes "have combined to make the public school into an educator for the educated rich and a keeper for the uneducated poor. There exists no more powerful force for rigidity of social class and the frustration of natural potential. . . ."

From Jonathan Kozol, *Savage Inequalities* (1991).

4   The freedom claimed by a rich man, he says, "to give his child a preferential education, and thereby achieve the transmission of advantage by inheritance, denies the children of others the freedom inherent in the notion of free enterprise." Democracy "can stand certain kinds and amounts" of inherited advantage. "What democracy cannot tolerate is an aristocracy padded and protected by the state itself from competition from below. . . ." In a free-enterprise society, he writes, "differential provision by the public school marks the intrusion of . . . heresy, for it means that certain participants in the economic race are hobbled at the gate—and hobbled by the public handicapper."

5   According to our textbook rhetoric, Americans abhor the notion of a social order in which economic privilege and political power are determined by hereditary class. Officially, we have a more enlightened goal in sight: namely, a society in which a family's wealth has no relation to the probability of future educational attainment and the wealth and station it affords. By this standard, education offered to poor children should be at least as good as that which is provided to the children of the upper-middle class.

6   If Americans had to discriminate directly against other people's children, I believe most citizens would find this morally abhorrent. Denial, in an active sense, of other people's children is, however, rarely necessary in this nation. Inequality is mediated for us by a taxing system that most people do not fully understand and seldom scrutinize. How this system really works, and how it came into existence, may enable us to better understand the difficulties that will be confronted in attempting to revise it.

7   The basic formula in place today for education finance is described as a "foundation program." First introduced during the early 1920s, the formula attempts to reconcile the right of local districts to support and govern their own schools with the obligation of the state to lessen the extremes of educational provision between districts. The former concern derives from the respect for liberty—which is defined, in this case, as the freedom of the district to provide for its own youth—and from the belief that more efficiency is possible when the control of local schools is held by those who have the greatest stake in their success. The latter concern derives from the respect for equal opportunity for all school-children, regardless of their parents' poverty or wealth.

8   The foundation program, in its pure form, operates somewhat like this: (1) A local tax upon the value of the homes and businesses within a given district raises the initial funds required for the operations of the public schools. (2) In the wealthiest districts, this is frequently enough to operate an adequate school system. Less affluent districts levy a tax at the same rate as the richest district—which assures that the tax burden on all citizens is equally apportioned—but, because the property is

worth less in a poor community, the revenues derived will be inadequate to operate a system on the level of the richest district. (3) The state will then provide sufficient funds to lift the poorer districts to a level ("the foundation") roughly equal to that of the richest district.

9   If this formula were strictly followed, something close to revenue equality would be achieved. It would still not satisfy the greater needs of certain districts, which for instance may have greater numbers of retarded, handicapped, or Spanish-speaking children. It would succeed in treating districts, but not children, equally. But even this degree of equal funding has not often been achieved.

10 The sticking point has been the third and final point listed above: what is described as the "foundation." Instead of setting the foundation at the level of the richest district, the states more frequently adopt what has been called "a low foundation." The low foundation is a level of subsistence that will raise a district to a point at which its schools are able to provide a "minimum" or "basic" education, but not an education on the level found in the rich districts. The notion of a "minimum" (rather than a "full") foundation represents a very special definition of the idea of equality. It guarantees that every child has "an equal minimum" but not that every child has the same. Stated in a slightly different way, it guarantees that every child has a building called "a school" but not that what is found within one school will bear much similarity, if any, to that which is found within another.

11 The decision as to what may represent a reasonable "minimum" (the term "sufficient" often is employed) is, of course, determined by the state officials. Because of the dynamics of state politics, this determination is in large part shaped by what the richer districts judge to be "sufficient" for the poorer; and this, in turn, leads to the all-important question: "sufficient" for what purpose? If the necessary outcome of the education of a child of low income is believed to be the capability to enter into equal competition with the children of the rich, then the foundation level has to be extremely high. If the necessary outcome is, however, only the capacity to hold some sort of job—perhaps a job as an employee of the person who was born in a rich district—then the foundation could be very "minimal" indeed. The latter, in effect, has been the resolution of this question.

12 This is not the only factor that has fostered inequality, however. In order to win backing from the wealthy districts for an equalizing plan of any kind, no matter how inadequate, legislatures offer the rich districts an incentive. The incentive is to grant some portion of state aid to *all* school districts, regardless of their poverty or wealth. While less state aid is naturally expected to be given to the wealthy than the poor, the notion of giving something to all districts is believed to be a "sweetener" that will assure a broad enough electoral appeal to raise the necessary funds through statewide taxes. [In] several states, however, these

"sweeteners" have been so sweet that they have sometimes ended up by deepening the preexisting inequalities.

13   All this leads us to the point, acknowledged often by school-finance specialists but largely unknown to the public, that the various "formulas" conceived—and reconceived each time there is a legal challenge—to achieve some equity in public education have been almost total failures. In speaking of the equalizing formula in Massachusetts, for example, the historian Joel Weinberg makes this candid observation: "The state could actually have done as well if it had made no attempt to relate its support system to local ability [i.e., local wealth] and distributed its 'largesse' in a completely random fashion"—as, for example, "by the State Treasurer throwing checks from an airplane and allowing the vagaries of the elements to distribute them among the different communities." But even this description of a "random" distribution may be generous. If the wind had been distributing state money in New Jersey, for example, it might have left most disparities unchanged, but it would not likely have increased disparities consistently for 20 years, which *is* what the state formula has done without exception.

14   The contest between liberty and equity in education has, in the past 30 years, translated into the competing claims of local control, on the one hand, and state (or federal) intervention on the other. Liberty, school conservatives have argued, is diminished when the local powers of school districts have been sacrificed to centralized control. The opposition to desegregation in the South, for instance, was portrayed as local (states') rights as a sacred principle infringed upon by federal court decisions. The opposition to the drive for equal funding in a given state is now portrayed as local (district) rights in opposition to the powers of the state. While local control may be defended and supported on a number of important grounds, it is unmistakable that it has been historically advanced to counter equity demands; this is no less the case today.

15   [The] recent drive for "schools of excellence" (or "schools of choice") within a given district carries this historic conflict one step further. The evolution of a dual or tripartite system in a single district, as we have observed in New York City and Chicago, has counterposed the "freedom" of some parents to create some enclaves of selective excellence for their own children against the claims of equity made on behalf of all the children who have been excluded from these favored schools. At every level of debate, whether it is states' rights versus federal intervention, local district versus state control, or local school versus the district school board, the argument is made that more efficiency accrues from local governance and that equity concerns enforced by centralized authority inevitably lead to waste and often to corruption. Thus, "efficiency" joins "liberty" as a rhetorical rebuttal to the claims of equal opportunity and equal funding. "Local control" is the sacred principle in all these arguments.

16   Ironically, however, as in the New Jersey situation, "local control" is readily ignored when state officials are dissatisfied with local leadership. A standard reaction of state governors, when faced with what they judge to be ineptitude at local levels, is to call for less—and not more—local governance by asking for a state takeover of the failing district. The liberty of local districts, thus, is willingly infringed on grounds of inefficiency. It is only when equal funding is the issue that the sanctity of district borders becomes absolute.

17   But this is not the only way in which the states subvert local control. They do it also by prescription of state guidelines that establish uniform curricula for all school districts, by certifying teachers on a statewide basis, and—in certain states like Texas, for example—by adopting textbooks on a statewide basis. During the past decade, there have also been conservative demands for national controls—a national teachers' examination, for example, and a national examination for all students—and we have been told that the commanding reason for these national controls is an alleged decline in national competitiveness against Japan and other foreign nations: a matter that transcends the needs or wishes of a local state or district. The national report that launched the recent "excellence" agenda bore the title "A Nation at Risk." It did not speak of East St. Louis, New York City or Winnetka. Testing of pupils is, in a sense, already national. Their reading scores are measured "at," "above," or else "below" a national norm. Children, whether in Little Rock, Great Neck, or the Bronx, compete with all American children when they take the college-entrance tests. Teacher preparation is already standardized across the nation. Textbooks, even before the states began adoptions, were homogenized for national consumption. With the advent of TV instruction via satellite, national education will be even more consistent and, in large part, uncontested.

18   Then too, of course, the flag in every classroom is the same. Children do not pledge allegiance to the flag of Nashua, New Hampshire, or to that of Fargo, North Dakota. The words of the pledge are very clear: They pledge allegiance to "one nation indivisible" and, in view of what we've seen of the implacable divisions that exist and are so skillfully maintained, there is some irony in this. The nation is hardly "indivisible" where education is concerned. It is at least two nations, quite methodically divided, with a fair amount of liberty for some, no liberty that justifies the word for many others, and justice—in the sense of playing on a nearly even field—only for the kids whose parents can afford to purchase it.

19   We may ask again, therefore, what "local governance" in fact implies in public education. The local board does not control the manufacture of the textbooks that its students use. It does not govern teacher preparation or certification. It does not govern political allegiance. It does not govern the exams that measure math and reading. It does not govern the exams that will determine or prohibit university admissions.

It does not even really govern architecture. With few exceptions, elementary schools constructed prior to ten years ago are uniform boxes parted by a corridor with six rooms to the left, six to the right, and maybe twelve or twenty-four more classrooms in the same configuration on the floor or floors above.

20 What the local school board *does* determine is how clean those floors will be; how well the principal and teachers will be paid; whether the classrooms will be adequately heated; whether a class of 18 children will have 18 textbooks or whether, as in some cities, a class of 30 children will be asked to share the use of 15 books; whether the library is stocked with up-to-date encyclopedias, computers, novels, poetry, and dictionaries or whether it's used instead for makeshift classrooms, as in New York City; whether the auditorium is well equipped for real theatrical productions or whether, as in Irvington, NJ, it must be used instead to house 11 classes; whether the gymnasium is suitable for indoor games or whether it is used for reading classes; whether the playground is equipped with jungle gyms and has green lawns for soccer games and baseball or whether it is a bleak expanse of asphalt studded with cracked glass.

21 If the school board has sufficient money, it can exercise some real control over these matters. If it has very little money, it has almost no control; or rather it has only negative control. Its freedom is to choose which of the children's needs should be denied. This negative authority is all that local governance in fact implies in places such as Camden and Detroit. It may be masked by the apparent power to advance one kind of "teaching style," one "approach," or one "philosophy" over another. But, where the long-standing problems are more basic (adequate space, sufficient teachers for all classrooms, heating fuel, repair of missing window-panes and leaking roofs and toilet doors), none of the pretended power over tone and style has much meaning. Style, in the long run, is determined by the caliber and character of teachers, and this is an area in which the poorest schools have no real choice at all.

22 Stephen Lefelt, a judge who tried a legal challenge to New Jersey's system of school financing, concluded from the months of testimony he had heard, that "local control," as it is presently interpreted to justify financial inequality, denies poor districts *all* control over the things that matter most in education. So, in this respect, the age-old conflict between liberty and equity is largely nonexistent in this setting. The wealthy districts have the first and seldom think about the second, while the very poor have neither.

23 In surveying the continuing tensions that exist between the claims of local liberty and those of equity in public education, historians have noted three distinguishable trends within this century. From the turn of the century until the 1950s, equity concerns were muted and the courts did not intrude much upon local governance. From 1954 (the year in which

Brown v. *Board of Education* was decided) up to the early 1970s, equity concerns were more pronounced, although the emphasis was less on economic than on racial factors. From the early 1970s to the present, local control and the efficiency agenda have once again prevailed. The decisive date that scholars generally pinpoint as the start of the most recent era is March 21 of 1973: the day on which the high court overruled the judgment of a district court in Texas that had found the local funding scheme unconstitutional—and in this way halted in its tracks the drive to equalize the public education system through the federal courts.

24 We have referred often to the Texas case. It is time now to examine it in detail.

25 A class-action suit had been filed in 1968 by a resident of San Antonio named Demetrio Rodriguez and by other parents on behalf of their own children, who were students in the city's Edgewood district, which was very poor and 96 percent nonwhite. Although Edgewood residents paid one of the highest tax rates in the area, the district could raise only $37 for each pupil. Even with the "minimum" provided by the state, Edgewood ended up with only $231 for each child. Alamo Heights, meanwhile, the richest section of the city but incorporated as a separate schooling district, was able to raise $412 for each student from a lower tax rate and, because it also got state aid (and federal aid), was able to spend $543 on each pupil. Alamo Heights, then as now, was a predominantly white district.

26 The difference between spending levels in these districts was, moreover, not the widest differential to be found in Texas. A sample of 110 Texas districts at the time showed that the ten wealthiest districts spent an average of three times as much per pupil as the four poorest districts, even with the funds provided under the state's "equalizing" formula.

27 Late in 1971, a three-judge federal district court in San Antonio held that Texas was in violation of the equal protection clause of the U.S. Constitution. "Any mild equalizing effects" from state aid, said the court, "do not benefit the poorest districts."

28 It is this decision that was then appealed to the Supreme Court. The majority opinion of the high court, which reversed the lower court's decision, noted that, in order to bring to bear "strict scrutiny" upon the case, it must first establish that there had been "absolute deprivation" of a "fundamental interest" of the Edgewood children. Justice Lewis Powell wrote that education is not "a fundamental interest" inasmuch as education "is not among the rights afforded explicit protection under our Federal Constitution." Nor, he wrote, did he believe that "absolute deprivation" was at stake. "The argument here," he said, "is not that the children in districts having relatively low assessable property values are receiving no public education; rather, it is that they are receiving a poorer quality education than that available to children in districts having more assessable wealth." In cases where wealth is involved, he said, "the Equal Protection Clause does not require absolute equality. . . ."

29   Attorneys for Rodriguez and the other plaintiffs, Powell wrote, argue "that education is itself a fundamental personal right because it is essential to the exercise of First Amendment freedoms and to intelligent use of the right to vote. [They argue also] that the right to speak is meaningless unless the speaker is capable of articulating his thoughts intelligently and persuasively.... [A] similar line of reasoning is pursued with respect to the right to vote."

30   "Yet we have never presumed to possess either the ability or the authority to guarantee ... the most *effective* speech or the most *informed* electoral choice." Even if it were conceded, he wrote, that "some identifiable quantum of education" is a prerequisite to exercise of speech and voting rights, "we have no indication ... that the [Texas funding] system fails to provide each child with an opportunity to acquire the basic minimal skills necessary" to enjoy a "full participation in the political process."

31   This passage raised, of course, some elemental questions. The crucial question centered on the two words "minimal" and "necessary." In the words of O. Z. White of Trinity University in San Antonio: "We would always want to know by what criteria these terms had been defined. For example, any poor Hispanic child who could spell three-letter words, add and subtract, and memorize the names and dates of several presidents would have been viewed as having been endowed with 'minimal' skills in much of Texas 50 years ago. How do we update those standards? This cannot be done without the introduction of subjective notions as to what is needed in the present age. Again, when Powell speaks of what is 'necessary' to enjoy what he calls 'full participation' in the nation's politics, we would want to know exactly what he has in mind by 'full' participation. A lot of wealthy folks in Texas think the schools are doing a sufficiently good job if the kids of poor folks learn enough to cast a vote—just not enough to cast it in their own self-interest. They might think it fine if kids could write and speak—just not enough to speak in ways that make a dent in public policy. In economic terms, a lot of folks in Alamo Heights would think that Edgewood kids were educated fine if they had all the necessary skills to do their kitchen work and tend their lawns. How does Justice Powell settle on the level of effectiveness he has in mind by 'full participation'? The definition of this term is at the essence of democracy. If pegged too low, it guarantees perpetuation of disparities of power while still presenting an illusion of fair play. Justice Powell is a human being and his decision here is bound to be subjective. When he tells us that the Edgewood kids are getting all that's 'full' or 'necessary,' he is looking at the world from Alamo Heights. This, I guess, is only natural. If he had a home here, that is where he'd likely live.

32   "To a real degree, what is considered 'adequate' or 'necessary' or 'sufficient' for the poor in Texas is determined by the rich or relatively rich; it is decided in accord with their opinion of what children of the poor are fitted to become, and what their social role should be. This role has al-

ways been equated with their usefulness to us; and this consideration seems to be at stake in almost all reflections on the matter of the 'minimal' foundation offered to schoolchildren, which, in a sense, is only a metaphor for 'minimal' existence. When Justice Powell speaks of 'minimal' skills, such as the capacity to speak, but argues that we have no obligation to assure that it will be the 'most effective' speech, he is saying something that may seem quite reasonable and even commonplace, but its something which would make more sense to wealthy folks in Alamo than to the folks in Edgewood."

33   Powell, however, placed great emphasis on his distinction between "basic minimal" skills, permitting some participation, and no skills at all, which might deny a person all participation; and he seemed to acquiesce in the idea that some inequity would always be inevitable. "No scheme of taxation ...," he wrote, "has yet been devised which is free of all discriminatory impact."

34   In any case, said Justice Powell in a passage that anticipates much of the debate now taking place, "experts are divided" on the question of the role of money in determining the quality of education. Indeed, he said, "one of the hottest sources of controversy concerns the extent to which there is a demonstrable correlation between educational expenditures and the quality of education."

35   In an additional comment that would stir considerable reaction among Texas residents, Powell said the district court had been in error in deciding that the Texas funding system had created what is called "a suspect class"—that is to say, an identifiable class of unjustly treated people. There had been no proof, he said, that a poor district such as Edgewood was necessarily inhabited mainly or entirely by poor people and, for this reason, it could not be said that poverty was the real cause of deprivation, even if there *was* real deprivation. There is, said Powell, "no basis ... for assuming that the poorest people ... are concentrated in the poorest districts." Nor, he added, is there "more than a random chance that racial minorities are concentrated" in such districts.

36   Justice Thurgood Marshall, in his long dissent, challenged the notion that an interest, to be seen as "fundamental," had to be "explicitly or implicitly guaranteed" within the Constitution. Thus, he said, although the right to procreate, the right to vote, the right to criminal appeal are not guaranteed, "these interests have nonetheless been afforded special judicial consideration ... because they are, to some extent, interrelated with constitutional guarantees." Education, Marshall said, was also such a "related interest" because it "directly affects the ability of a child to exercise his First Amendment interests both as a source and as a receiver of information and ideas. ... [Of] particular importance is the relationship between education and the political process."

37   Marshall also addressed the argument of Justice Powell that there was no demonstrated "correlation between poor people and poor districts." In support of this conclusion, Marshall wrote, the majority "of-

fers absolutely no data—which it cannot on this record...." Even, however, if it were true, he added, that *all* individuals within poor districts are not poor, the injury to those who *are* poor would not be diminished. Nor, he went on, can we ignore the extent to which state policies contribute to wealth differences. Government zoning regulations, for example, "have undoubtedly encouraged and rigidified national trends" that raise the property values in some districts while debasing them in others.

38   Marshall also challenged the distinction, made by Justice Powell, between "absolute" and "relative" degrees of deprivation, as well as Powell's judgment that the Texas funding scheme, because it had increased the funds available to local districts, now provided children of low income with the "minimum" required. "The Equal Protection Clause is not addressed to ... minimal sufficiency," said Marshall, but to equity; and he cited the words of *Brown* to the effect that education, "where the State has undertaken to provide it, is a right which must be made available to all on equal terms."

39   On Justice Powell's observation that some experts questioned the connection between spending and the quality of education, Marshall answered almost with derision: "Even an unadorned restatement of this contention is sufficient to reveal its absurdity." It is, he said, "an inescapable fact that if one district has more funds available per pupil than another district," it "will have greater choice" in what it offers to its children. If, he added, "financing variations are so insignificant" to quality, "it is difficult to understand why a number of our country's wealthiest school districts," which, he noted, had no obligation to support the Texas funding scheme, had "nevertheless zealously pursued its cause before this Court"—a reference to the *amicus* briefs that Bloomfield Hills, Grosse Pointe and Beverly Hills had introduced in their support of the defendants.

40   On the matter of local control, Marshall said this: "I need not now decide how I might ultimately strike the balance were we confronted with a situation where the State's sincere concern for local control inevitably produced educational inequality. For, on this record, it is apparent that the State's purported concern with local control is offered primarily as an excuse rather than as a justification for interdistrict inequality.... [If] Texas had a system truly dedicated to local fiscal control one would expect the quality of the educational opportunity provided in each district to vary with the decision of the voters in that district as to the level of sacrifice they wish to make for public education. In fact, the Texas scheme produces precisely the opposite result." Local districts, he observed, *cannot* "choose to have the best education in the State" because the education offered by a district is determined by its wealth—"a factor over which local voters [have] no control."

41   If, for the sake of local control, he concluded, "this court is to sustain interdistrict discrimination in the educational opportunity afforded

Texas school children, it should require that the State present something more than the mere sham now before us...."

42   Nonetheless, the court's majority turned down the suit and in a single word—"reversed"—Justice Powell ended any expectations that the children of the Edgewood schools would now be given the same opportunities as children in the richer districts. In tandem with the *Milliken* decision two years later, which exempted white suburban districts from participating in desegregation programs with the cities, the five-to-four decision in *Rodriguez* ushered in the ending of an era of progressive change and set the tone for the subsequent two decades which have left us with the present-day reality of separate and unequal public schools.

43   Unlike the U.S. Constitution, almost all state constitutions are specific in their references to public education. Since the decision in the Texas case, therefore, the parents of poor children have been centering their legal efforts on the various state courts, and there have been several local victories of sorts. In the absence of a sense of national imperative, however, and lacking the unusual authority of the Supreme Court, or the Congress, or the president, local victories have tended to deliver little satisfaction to poor districts. Even favorable decisions have led frequently to lengthly exercises of obstruction in the legislative process, eventuating often in a rearrangement of the old state "formula" that merely reconstructs the old inequities.

44   There is another way, however, in which legal victories have been devalued by the states, and this is seen most vividly in California. Even before the Texas case had been reversed, parents from Southern California had brought suit in the state courts, alleging that the funding system was unconstitutional because of the wide differential between funding for the children of the rich and poor. At the time of the trial, for example, Baldwin Park, a low-income city near Los Angeles, was spending $595 for each student while Beverly Hills was able to spend $1,244, even though the latter district had a tax rate less than half that of the former. Similar inequities were noted elsewhere in the state.

45   The court's decision found the California scheme a violation of both state *and* federal constitutions. For this reason, it was not affected by the later finding in the Texas case. In 1974 a second court decision ordered the state legislature to come up with a different system of school funding. A new system was at last enacted in the spring of 1977. As soon as Californians understood the implications of the plan—namely, that funding for most of their public schools would henceforth be approximately equal—a conservative revolt surged through the state. The outcome of this surge, the first of many tax revolts across the nation in the next ten years, was a referendum that applied a "cap" on taxing and effectively restricted funding for *all* districts. Proposition 13, as the tax cap would be known, may be interpreted in several ways. One interpretation was described succinctly by a California legislator: "This is the revenge

of wealth against the poor. 'If the schools must actually be equal,' they are saying, 'then we'll undercut them all.'"

46   It is more complex than that, but there is an element of truth in this assessment and there is historic precedent as well. Two decades earlier, as U.S. Commissioner of Education Francis Keppel had observed, voters responded to desegregation orders in the South by much the same approach. "Throughout much of the rural South," he wrote, "desegregation was accompanied by lowering the tax base for [the] public schools [while] granting local and state tax exemptions for [a parallel system of private white] academies...."

47   Today, in all but 5 percent of California districts, funding levels are within $300 of each other. Although, in this respect, the plaintiffs won the equity they sought, it is to some extent a victory of losers. Though the state ranks eighth in per capita income in the nation, the share of its income that now goes to public education is a meager 3.8 percent—placing it at forty-sixth among the 50 states. Its average class size is the largest in the nation.

48   These developments in California, which may soon be replicated in some other states as local courts begin to call for equitable funding of the schools, tell us much about the value we assign to "excellence." If excellence must be distributed in equitable ways, it seems, Americans may be disposed to vote for mediocrity.

49   Meanwhile, for the children of the rich and very rich in California, there is still an open door to privileged advancement. In the affluent school districts, tax-exempt foundations have been formed to channel extra money into local schools. Afternoon "Super Schools" have been created also in these districts to provide the local children with tutorials and private lessons. And 5 percent of California's public schools remain outside the "spread" ($300) that exists between the other districts in official funding. The consequence is easily discerned by visitors. Beverly Hills still operates a high school that, in academic excellence, can rival those of Princeton and Winnetka. Baldwin Park still operates a poorly funded and inferior system. In Northern California, Oakland remains a mainly nonwhite, poor and troubled system while the schools that serve the Piedmont district, separately incorporated though it is surrounded on four sides by Oakland, remains richly funded, white, and excellent. The range of district funding in the state is still extremely large. The poorest districts spend less than $3,000 while the wealthiest spend more than $7,000.

50   For those of the affluent who so desire, there are also private schools; and because the tax cap leaves them with more money, wealthy parents have these extra funds available to pay for private school tuition—a parallel, in certain ways, to the developments that Keppel outlined in the South after the *Brown* decision.

51   The lesson of California is that equity in education represents a formidable threat to other values held by many affluent Americans. It will

be resisted just as bitterly as school desegregation. Nor is it clear that even an affirmative decision of the high court, if another case should someday reach that level, would be any more effective than the California ruling in addressing something so profoundly rooted in American ideas about the right and moral worth of individual advancement at whatever cost to others who may be less favored by the accident of birth.

52 Despite the evidence, suburbanites sometimes persist in asking what appears at first a reasonable question: "So long as every child has a guarantee of education, what harm can it really be to let us spend a little more? Isn't this a very basic kind of freedom? And is it fair to tell us that we *cannot* spend some extra money if we have it?"

53 This sentiment is so deeply held that even advocates for equity tend to capitulate at this point. Often they will reassure the suburbs: "We don't want to take away the good things that you have. We just want to lift the poorer schools a little higher." Political accommodation, rather than conviction, dictates this approach because, of course, it begs the question: Since every district is competing for the same restricted pool of gifted teachers, the "minimum" assured to every district is immediately devalued by the district that can add $10,000 more to teacher salaries. Then, too, once the richest districts go above the minimum, school suppliers, textbook publishers, computer manufacturers adjust their price horizons—just as teachers raise their salary horizons—and the poorest districts are left where they were before the minimum existed.

54 Attorneys in school-equalization suits have done their best to understate the notion of "redistribution" of resources. They try instead, wherever possible, to speak in terms that seem to offer something good for everyone involved. But this is a public relations approach that blurs the real dynamics of a transfer of resources. No matter what devices are contrived to bring about equality, it is clear that they require money-transfer, and the largest source of money is the portion of the population that possesses the *most* money. When wealthy districts indicate they see the hand of Robin Hood in this, they are clear-sighted and correct. This is surely why resistance to these suits, and even to court orders, has been so intense and so ingeniously prolonged. For, while, on a lofty level, wealthy districts may be fighting in defense of a superb abstraction— "liberty," "local control," or such—on a mundane level they are fighting for the right to guarantee their children the inheritance of an ascendant role in our society.

55 There is a deep-seated reverence for fair play in the United States, and in many areas of life we see the consequences in a genuine distaste for loaded dice; but this is not the case in education, health care, or inheritance of wealth. In these elemental areas we want the game to be unfair and we have made it so; and it will likely so remain.

56	Let us return, then, for a final time to San Antonio—not to the city of 1968, when the *Rodriguez* case was filed, but to the city of today. It is 23 years now since Demetrio Rodriguez filed suit against the state of Texas. Things have not changed very much in the poor neighborhoods of Texas. After 23 years of court disputes and numerous state formula revisions, per-pupil spending ranges from $2,000 in the poorest districts to some $19,000 in the richest. The minimum foundation that the state allows the children in the poorest districts—that is to say, the funds that guarantee the minimal basic education—is $1,477. Texas, moreover, is one of the ten states that gives no financial aid for school construction to the local districts.

57	In San Antonio, where Demetrio Rodriguez brought his suit against the state in 1968, the children of the poor still go to separate and unequal schools.

58	"The poor live by the water ditches here," said O. Z. White as we were driving through the crowded streets on a hot day in 1989. "The water is stagnant in the ditches now but, when the rains come, it will rise quite fast—it flows south into the San Antonio River. . . .

59	"The rich live on the high ground to the north. The higher ground in San Antonio is Monte Vista. But the very rich—the families with old money—live in the section known as Alamo Heights."

60	Alamo Heights, he told me, is a part of San Antonio. "It's enclosed by San Antonio but operated as a separate system. Dallas has a similar white enclave known as Highland Park, enclosed on four sides by the Dallas schools but operated as a separate district. We call these places 'parasite districts' since they give no tax support to the low-income sections.

61	"Alamo Heights is like a different world. The air is fresher. The grass is greener. The homes are larger. And the schools are richer."

62	Seven minutes from Alamo Heights, at the corner of Hamilton and Guadalupe, is Cassiano—a low-income housing project. Across the street from Cassiano, tiny buildings resembling shacks, some of them painted pastel shades, house many of the children who attend the Cooper Middle School, where 96 percent of children qualify by poverty for subsidized hot lunches and where 99.3 percent are of Hispanic origin. At Cooper, $2,800 is devoted to each child's education and 72 percent of children read below grade level. Class size ranges from 28 to 30. Average teacher salary is $27,000.

63	In Alamo Heights, where teachers average $31,000, virtually all students graduate and 88 percent of graduates go on to college. Classes are small and $4,600 is expended yearly on each child.

64	Fully 10 percent of children at the Cooper Middle School drop out in seventh and eighth grades. Of the survivors, 51 percent drop out of high school.

65	In 1988, Alamo Heights spent an average of $46 per pupil for its "gifted" program. The San Antonio Independent District, which includes the Cooper Middle School, spent only $2 for each child for its "gifted" program. In the Edgewood District only $1 was spent per child for the "gifted" program.

66   Although the property tax in Alamo Heights yielded $3,600 for each pupil, compared to $924 per pupil in the San Antonio district and only $128 in Edgewood, Alamo Heights also received a share of state and federal funds—almost $8,000 yearly for a class of 20 children. Most of this extra money, quite remarkably, came to Alamo Heights under the "equalizing" formula.

67   Some hope of change was briefly awakened in the fall of 1989 when front-page headlines in the *New York Times* and other leading papers heralded the news that public schools in Texas had been found unconstitutional under state law. In a nine-to-zero decision, the state supreme court, citing what it termed "glaring disparities" in spending between wealthy and poor districts, said that the funding system was in violation of the passage in the Texas constitution that required Texas to maintain an education system for "the general diffusion of knowledge" in the state. The court's decision summarized some of the most extreme inequities: District spending ranged from $2,112 to $19,333. The richest district drew on property wealth of $14 million for each student while the poorest district drew on property worth only $20,000 for each student. The 100 wealthiest districts taxed their local property, on the average, at 47 cents for each $100 of assessed worth but spent over $7,000 for each student. The 100 poorest districts had an average tax rate more than 50 percent higher but spent less than $3,000 for each student. Speaking of the "evident intention" of "the framers of our [Texas] Constitution to provide equal educational advantages for all," the court said, "Let there be no misunderstanding. A remedy is long overdue." There was no reference this time to the U.S. Constitution.

68   Stories related to the finding dominated the front page and the inside pages of the *San Antonio Express-News*. "Students cheered and superintendents hugged lawyers in an emotional display of joy," the paper said. In the library of John F. Kennedy High School in the Edgewood district, Demetrio Rodriguez put his hand on his chest to fight back tears as students, teachers and community leaders cheered his vindication and their victory. As the crowd rose to applaud the 64-year-old man, Rodriguez spoke in halting words: "I cried this morning because this is something that has been in my heart.... My children will not benefit from it.... Twenty-one years is a long time to wait." Rodriguez, a sheet-metal worker at a nearby U.S. Air Force base, had lived in San Antonio for 30 years. "My children got caught in this web. It wasn't fair . . . but there is nothing I can do about it now." The problem, he said to a reporter, should have been corrected 20 years before.

69   In an editorial that day, the paper said that what the court had found "should have been obvious to anyone" from the beginning.

70   The Edgewood superintendent, who had been the leader in the latest round of litigation, spoke of the attacks that he had weathered in the

course of years. He had been a high school principal in 1974 when the original *Rodriguez* finding had been overruled by the U.S. Supreme Court. "It was like somebody had died...," he said. In the years since, he had gone repeatedly to the state capital in Austin, where he was met by promises from legislators that they would "take care of it," he said. "More and more task forces studied education," he recalled, while another generation of poor children entered and passed through the Edgewood schools. At length, in 1984, Edgewood joined with seven other poor school districts and brought suit against the state and 48 rich districts. The suit was seen by some as a class war, he said. He was accused of wanting to take away the "swimming pools," the "tennis courts" and "carpeted football fields" from wealthy districts. "They'd say I was being Robin Hood...," he said. The district, he assured reporters, was not looking to be given swimming pools. All the district wanted, he said, was "to get us up to the average...." Children in Edgewood, he said, had suffered most from being forced to lower their horizons. "Some of the students don't ... know how to dream.... They have accepted [this]," he said, as if it were "the way [that] things should be."

71   The governor of Texas, who had opposed the suit and often stated he was confident the court would find against the claims of the poor districts, told the press of his relief that the Supreme Court hadn't mandated an immediate solution. "I am extremely pleased," he said, "that this is back in the hands of the legislature...."

72   The chairman of the Texas Railroad Commission, who was running for governor as a Republican, voiced his concern that people might use this court decision to impose an income tax on Texas.

73   The U.S. Secretary of Education, Lauro Cavazos, came to Texas and provided fuel for those who sought to slow down implementation of the court's decision. "First," he said, "money is clearly not the answer...." Furthermore, he said, "there is a wide body of research" to support that view and, he added, in apparent disregard of the conclusions of the court, "the evidence here in Texas corroborates those findings." He then went on to castigate Hispanic parents for not caring about education.

74   Meanwhile, the press observed that what it termed "the demagoguery" of "anti-tax vigilantes" posed another threat. "Legions of tax protestors" had been mobilized, a local columnist said. It was believed that they would do their best to slow down or obstruct the needed legislative action. Others focused on the likelihood that wealthy people would begin to look outside the public schools. There were already several famous private schools in Texas. Might there soon be several more?

75   Predictions were heard that, after legislative red tape and political delays, a revised state formula would be developed. The court would look it over, voice some doubts, but finally accept it as a reasonable effort. A few years later, O. Z. White surmised, "we'll discover that they didn't do the formula 'exactly' right. Edgewood probably will be okay. It's been in the news so it will have to be a showpiece to improvement. What of the children in those other districts where the poor Hispanic

families have no leaders, where there isn't a Rodriguez? Those are the ones where children will continue to be cheated and ignored.

76 "There's lots of celebration now because of the decision. Wait a year. Watch and see the clever things that people will contrive. You can bet that lots of folks are thinking hard about this 'Robin Hood' idea. Up in Alamo Heights I would expect that folks have plenty on their minds tonight. I don't blame them. If I lived in Alamo Heights, I guess I'd be doing some hard thinking too. . . .

77 "We're not talking about some abstraction here. These things are serious. If all of these poor kids in Cassiano get to go to real good schools—I mean, so they're educated *well* and so they're smart enough to go to colleges and universities—you have got to ask who there will be to trim the lawns and scrub the kitchen floors in Alamo Heights. Look at the lights up there. The air is nice and clean when you're up high like that in Texas. It's a different world from Guadalupe. Let me tell you something. Folks can hope, and folks can try, and folks can dream. But those two worlds are never going to meet. Not in my life. Not in yours. Not while any of those little kids in Cassiano are alive. Maybe it will happen someday. I'm not going to be counting."

78 Around us in the streets, the voices of children filled the heavy air. Teen-age girls stood in the doorways of the pastel houses along Guadalupe while the younger children played out in the street. Mexican music drifted from the houses and, as evening came to San Antonio, the heat subsided and there was a sense of order and serenity as people went about their evening tasks, the task of children being to play and of their older sisters to go in and help their mothers to make dinner.

79 "Everything is acceptance," said O. Z. "People get used to what they have. They figure it's the way it's supposed to be and they don't think it's going to change. All those court decisions are so far away. And Alamo Heights seems far away, so people don't compare. And that's important. If you don't know what you're missing, you're not going to get angry. How can you desire what you cannot dream of?" But this may not really be the case; for many of the women in this neighborhood do get to see the richer neighborhoods because they work in wealthy people's homes.

80 According to the principal of Cooper Middle School, crack addiction isn't a real problem yet for younger children. "Here it's mainly chemical inhalants. It can blind you, I've been told. They get it mainly out of spray-paint cans and liquid paper," he says wearily.

81 But a social worker tells me there's a crack house right on Guadalupe. "There is a lot of prostitution here as well," she says. "Many of these teen-age girls helping their mothers to make supper will be pregnant soon. They will have children and leave school. Many will then begin the daily trip to Alamo Heights. They'll do domestic work and bring up other people's kids. By the time they know what they were missing, it's too late."

82   It is now the spring of 1991. A year and a half has passed since these events took place. The Texas legislature has at last, and with much rhetoric about what many legislators call "a Robin Hood approach," enacted a new equalizing formula but left a number of loopholes that perpetuate the fiscal edge enjoyed by very wealthy districts. Plaintiffs' attorneys are guarded in their expectations. If the experience of other states holds true in Texas, there will be a series of delays and challenges and, doubtless, further litigation. The implementation of the newest plan, in any case, will not be immediate. Twenty-three years after Demetrio Rodriguez went to court, the children of the poorest people in the state of Texas still are waiting for an equal chance at education.

Points for Review and Discussion

1.   Summarize the essentials of the school financing formula known as the "foundation program."
2.   Kozol sees three trends in the twentieth-century history of tensions between liberty and equity in public education. Name and explain the trends.
3.   Summarize the essentials of the Supreme Court majority opinion, by Justice Lewis Powell, and the dissent, by Justice Thurgood Marshall, in the Edgewood School District case.

•◆ Questions for Writing

1.   As Kozol demonstrates, "local governance" has limited meaning in many school districts. Yet local control of schools remains a powerful political rallying cry. In communities in which local control is virtually nonexistent, people continue to speak and act as though it's still fully intact. Write an essay exploring the various dimensions of this paradox.
2.   "The lesson of California," Kozol writes, "is that equity in education represents a formidable threat to other values held by many affluent Americans" (¶ 51). Define these "other values" as you understand them, and assess their strengths and weaknesses.
3.   The metaphor of "the race" turns up repeatedly in debate about class inequities in the schools. Kozol's essay quotes a writer who attempts to "correct" the claim that "the starting line is the same for all." The writer argues that "certain participants in the economic race are hobbled at the gate—and hobbled by the public handicapper" (¶ 4). Write a page discussing the pros and cons of the race metaphor as a means of clarifying educational realities.

Connecting the Parts in Chapter 7: Assignments for Extended Essays

1. Questions about "the role of money in determining the quality of education" can be clarified at least in part by considering them in the light of personal experience. Review your own experience as a student, going back as far as you trust your memory, and write an essay describing and analyzing instances in which levels of school funding—whether high or low—made a difference to you as a learner. How did money enter into the "style" of teaching favored in your schools? Might a different style have improved your rate of learning? Support your answer with clear reasons.
2. The authors of most of the selections in this work would be likely to hold firm convictions for or against equal funding for all public schools. Write an essay couched in the form of a debate between two of them—Anna Quindlen versus Paul Fussell, for example, or Donna Gaines versus Mortimer Levitt—on this subject. Make certain to adjust the content and the tone of the arguments you put in the mouths of your debaters to the style of thought and expression evident in the selections from their work included in this book.

Leads for Research

1. Research the current state of controversy regarding the funding of public schools by reading the whole of Jonathan Kozol's *Savage Inequalities* (1991) and looking up the public response to the book. (Read the full text of the reviews excerpted in *Book Review Digest* and check out journals not covered by *BRD*; a particularly interesting review of the Kozol book, not mentioned in *BRD*, appeared in *Boston Review*.) Write a paper summarizing and assessing the main lines of response to Kozol; in your conclusion explain how that response has strengthened or weakened your belief in the plausibility of Kozol's arguments.
2. Explore the history of American debates on educational opportunity by consulting some standard works in this field: David Tyack, *The One Best System: A History of American Urban Education* (1974); Diane Ravitch, *The Great School Wars: New York City, 1805–1973* (1974); Ira Katznelson and Margaret Weir, *Schooling for All* (1985). Choose a topic of special interest to you—vocational education, ethnic clashes, or another topic—and write a paper tracing the origins, development and current resolution of conflict in this area.
3. In recent years scholarship has focused productively on the interplay of social class with educational opportunity and career planning. A research paper reporting on recent findings in this area could profitably consult three books written or edited by Lois Weis, *Between Two Worlds: Black Students in an Urban Community College* (1985); *Schooling and the Silenced Others* (1992); *Beyond Silenced Voices* (1993).

8

Superiors and Inferiors (II)
The Problem of Guilt

As noted at the start of *Created Equal*, awareness of social differences stirs complex responses. The essays in this section explore feelings traceable to that awareness—feelings of embarrassment, guilt, or obligation.

A famous entertainer and writer fashions mildly self-critical comedy out of memories of the strain imposed on him, as an adolescent, by his impoverished family's provinciality. A labor lawyer reflects on the gap between his own social circumstances and those of the union members whose cause he makes his own. A young teacher returns to her working-class origins in Queens, New York, and "shakes hands with [her] discreetly rebellious past." A successful writer and broadcaster remembers with shame his effort, as a promising, upward-bound, scholarship boy, to distance himself from his working-class Chicano roots. A black activist whose personal successes threaten to separate her from her family and friends argues passionately to her peers that blacks who make it professionally must seek to improve the situation of the people they've left behind.

The statements and narratives each testify, in distinctly separate and complicated ways, to the pressure on individual human beings of class consciousness in the United States.

Protestant
Garison Keillor

Differences in beliefs and manners as well as in incomes and property determine social class, and differences in manners often provide the material of popular entertainment. The thrust can be harshly satirical, focused on affectation and snobbery, or it can be gentle and affectionate—as when someone who's risen from humble beginnings looks back fondly at an earlier, unsophisticated self. Among the most successful comedy of the latter, tender kind is that produced by Garrison Keillor—writer, performer, and inventor of a musical variety show ("A Prairie Home Companion") that has charmed large audiences, on public radio, for nearly two decades.

One well-loved feature of this show is Keillor's weekly monologue recounting current events in a mythical rural Minnesota community called Lake Wobegon. Materials from the monologues figure in the performer's bestselling autobiographical memoir, *Lake Wobegon Days* (1985). The following pages are an excerpt from that book.

1   Our family was dirt poor, which I figured out as a child from the fact we had such a bad vacuum. When you vacuumed the living room, it would groan and stop and you had to sit and wait for it to groan and start up, then vacuum like mad before it quit again, but it didn't have good suction either. You had to stuff the hairballs into it. I also knew it because Donald Hoglund told me. He asked me how much my dad earned, and I said a thousand dollars, the most money I could imagine, and he shrieked, "You're poor! You're poor!" So we were. And, in a town where everyone was either Lutheran or Catholic, we were neither one. We were Sanctified Brethren, a sect so tiny that nobody but us and God knew about it, so when kids asked what I was, I just said Protestant. It was too much to explain, like having six toes. You would rather keep your shoes on. . . .

2   The Cox Brethren of St. Cloud held to the same doctrines as we did but they were not so exclusive, more trusting of the world—for example, several families owned television sets. They kept them in their living rooms, out in the open, and on Sunday, after meeting and before dinner, the dad might say, "Well, I wonder what's on," knowing perfectly well what was on, and turn it on—a Green Bay Packers game—and watch it. On Sunday.

3   I ate a few Sunday dinners at their houses, and the first time I saw a television set in a Brethren house, I was dumbfounded. None of the

---

From Garrison Keillor, *Lake Wobegon Days* (1985).

Wobegonian Brethren had one; we were told that watching television was the same as going to the movies—*no*, in other words. I wondered why the St. Cloud people were unaware of the danger. You start getting entangled in the things of the world, and one thing leads to another. First it's television, then it's worldly books, and the next thing you know, God's people are sitting around drinking whiskey sours in dim smoky bars with waitresses in skimpy black outfits and their bosoms displayed like grapefruit.

4   That was not my view but my parents'. "Beer is the drunkard's kindergarten," said Dad. Small things led to bigger ones. One road leads up, the other down. A man cannot serve two masters. Dancing was out, even the Virginia reel: it led to carnal desires. Card-playing was out, which led to gambling, though we did have Rook and Flinch—why those and not pinochle? "Because. They're different." No novels, which tended to glamorize iniquity. "How do you know if you don't read them?" I asked, but they *knew*. "You only have to touch a stove once to know it's hot," Mother said. (Which novel had she read? She wasn't saying.) Rock 'n' roll, jazz, swing, dance music, nightclub singing: all worldly. "How about Beethoven?" I asked, having heard something of his in school. "That depends," she said. "Was he a Christian?" I wasn't sure. I doubted he was.

5   On the long Sunday-night drive home, leaning forward from the back seat, I pressed them on inconsistencies like a little prosecutor: if dancing leads to carnal desire, how about holding hands? Is it wrong to put your arm around a girl? People gamble on football: is football wrong? Can you say "darn"? What if your teacher told you to read a novel? Or a short story? What if you were hitch-hiking in a blizzard and were picked up by a guy who was listening to rock 'n' roll on the radio, should you get out of the car even though you would freeze to death? "I guess the smart thing would be to dress warmly in the first place," offered Dad. "And wait until a Ford comes along." All Brethren drove Fords.

6 In Lake Wobegon, car ownership is a matter of faith. Lutherans drive Fords, bought from Bunsen Motors, the Lutheran car dealer, and Catholics drive Chevies from Main Garage, owned by the Kruegers, except for Hjalmar Ingqvist, who has a Lincoln. Years ago, John Tollerud was tempted by Chevyship until (then) Pastor Tommerdahl took John aside after church and told him it was his (Pastor Tommerdahl's) responsibility to point out that Fords get better gas mileage and have a better trade-in value. And he knew for a fact that the Kruegers spent a share of the Chevy profits to purchase Asian babies and make them Catholics. So John got a new Ford Falcon. It turned out to be a dud. The transmission went out after ten thousand miles and the car tended to pull to the left. In a town where car ownership is by faith, however, a person doesn't complain about these things, and John figured there must be a good rea-

son for his car trouble, which perhaps he would understand more fully someday.

7   The Brethren, being Protestant, also drove Fords, of course, but we distinguished ourselves from Lutherans by carrying small steel Scripture plates bolted to the top of our license plates. The verses were written in tiny glass beads so they showed up well at night. We ordered these from the Grace & Truth Scripture Depot in Erie, Pennsylvania, and the favorites were "The wages of sin is death. Rom. 6:23" and "I am the way, the truth and the life. Jn. 10:6." The verse from John was made of white beads, the Romans of lurid red, and if your car came up behind a Brethren car on the road at night, that rear verse jumped right out at you. It certainly jumped out at me the night I drove Karen Mueller back from Avon, where we had had two whiskey sours apiece on her fake ID. I was going seventy on the old post road when we flew over a hill and there was a pair of taillights and what looked like a red stripe between them. I hit the brakes, we skidded at an angle so that for one split second, looking out the side window, I saw "The wages of sin is death" like a flashbulb exploding in my face, and then we were halfway in the ditch. I hit the gas, and we passed Brother Louie on the low side, and I got Karen home before eleven, and nobody was the wiser except me. "You're a wonderful driver. You saved our lives," Karen said, but I knew the truth. Drinking whiskey sours with a Catholic girl and thinking lustful thoughts, I had earned death three times over, and God was reminding me of this at the same time as He took the wheel for those few seconds, probably because He had a purpose for Brother Louie's life.

8   Perhaps God had a purpose for mine, too, but He must have wondered why I showed so little curiosity about what it might be. My own purpose was escape, first in my dad's car (a Ford Fairlane station wagon) and then in the car he gave me (a 1956 Tudor sedan). Both of these cars had verses bolted to the plates, so I carried pliers with me and pulled over just outside town and removed the evidence of our faith and put it in the trunk. Then I raced off and did what I could to debauch myself, and, on the way back, sometimes reeling from the effects of a couple Grain Belts and half a pack of Pall Malls, I bolted the verses back on.

9   The Grace & Truth catalog offered many items with Scripture emblazoned on them, including birthday cards ("Ye must be born again"), a Gospel mailbox with handsome nameplate and "My Word shall not pass away. Matt. 24:35" painted on the lid, a telephone-book cover ("Let no corrupt communication pass out of your mouth, but that which is good to the use of edifying. Eph. 4:29"), a doormat ("Now ye are no more strangers and foreigners, but fellow-citizens with the saints, and of the household of God. Eph. 2:19"), a wastebasket ("Touch not the unclean thing. 2 Cor. 6:17"), and even an umbrella ("Giving thanks always for all things. Eph. 5:20"). There were paper napkins and placemats in the Bible Families, Familiar Parables, Our Lord's Miracles, and Bible Prophecies

series—once, my friend Lance came to supper and found Armageddon and the Seven-Headed Beast under his plate. Grace & Truth even offered matchbooks. If a smoker asked for a light, you could give him the book ("Your body is the temple of the Holy Ghost, therefore glorify God in your body, which is God's").

10   Testimony was the aim of this merchandise. The Grace & Truth people believed that unregenerate man has hardened his heart against God and that the Spirit works to exercise and open the heart but that these openings of grace may be very brief, perhaps only a few seconds, during which the wicked may repent—especially if God's Word is before them. Thus, the need to place Scripture in plain view. A fellow motorist's heart might be opened on the road; our license-plate verse would be right there at the right moment to show the way.

11   I felt that so much Scripture floating around might tend to harden some hearts, that Scripture should be treated with reverence and not pasted to any flat surface you could find—at least, that was what I said when Brethren asked why I didn't carry a "The Peace of God Passeth All Understanding" bookbag to school. In fact, I was afraid I would be laughed off the face of the earth.

12   My dad's car sported a compass on the dashboard, with "I am the Way" inscribed in luminescent letters across its face, clearly visible in the dark to a girl who might be sitting beside me. "Why do you have that?" she might say. "It's not mine, it's my dad's," I'd say. "I don't know why, I guess he likes it there." I wanted her and me to be friends and our conversation to head in the direction of personal feelings, The Importance of Being Free and Sharing Love, and not toward the thorny subject of obedience, which tended to put a damper on things. The compass wasn't easily removed; you'd have to get behind the instrument panel to remove the nuts. I thought of covering it with masking tape, but that might only draw attention to it. So I hung my cap on it.

13   Brother Louie wasn't so timid. His car (a Fairlane four-door) was a rolling display of Scripture truth, equipped not only with verses on the license plates but also across the dashboard, both sunvisors, the back of the front seat, all four armrests, the rubber floormats, the ashtray and glove compartment, and just in case you weren't paying attention, he had painted a verse across the bottom of the passenger side of the windshield—"The earth is full of the goodness of the Lord"—for your edification as you gazed at the scenery. Brother Louie kept a plastic bucket by his left leg, where he kept Gospel tracts, rolled up and wrapped in bright cellophane, which he tossed out at mailboxes as he drove along. The cellophane was to protect the Word from rain and also to attract the eye. And finally, one year, he found a company in Indiana that advertised custom-made musical horns. Louie's horn played the first eight notes of the Doxology. It sounded like a trumpet. He blew it at pedestrians, oncoming traffic, while passing, and sometimes just for his own pleasure. On occasion, vexed by a fellow driver, he gave in to wrath and leaned on the

horn, only to hear "Praise God from Whom all blessings flow." It calmed him down right away. The horn cost Louie more than a hundred dollars, and when he traded in the Fairlane on a Galaxie, he took the horn along.

14   Brother Louie was assistant cashier at the First Ingqvist State Bank, which entitled him to a cubicle, three feet of oak paneling topped with two feet of frosted glass. He sat in there and received loan applicants, the small-time ones, and also some depositors. Many older people who remembered their elders' memories of the failure of the New Albion Bank in the Panic of 1873 did not quite trust a bank per se and were uneasy about shoving their money under the grill to Mary Dahl, who was nineteen years old and chewed gum. They wanted Louie to accept it personally.

15   It was touching to see Mrs. Fjelde and Mrs. Ruud and Mrs. Diener, old farm ladies in farm-lady dresses and their best black hats with the veils, their cotton stockings and old cloth coats, shuffling into Louie's cubicle. Sitting by his desk, enjoying the little ritual conversation. "Good morning. You certainly look well." "Thank you, Louie. Actually, my back has been bothering me." "I'm sorry to hear that." "Oh, it's nothing. I'll feel better when it warms up." Some weather talk. "How's Lena doing? And Harold? What do you hear from Elsie?" Louie knew everybody by name. Some news, and then the grand moment: reaching in her purse for the coin purse, emptying the egg money out on the desk. A few crumpled ones, a lot of quarters and dimes. Louie, impressed: "Well, look at that! Doing pretty well, I'd say." The careful count of the treasure. Filling out the deposit slip. The customer inquiring about Louie's wife, Gladys, and his four daughters. Some customers could make a fifteen-minute transaction out of less than five bucks. At the end, Louie stood up and held out his hand. "Thanks," he said. "Appreciate your coming in." And out they went.

16   Brother Louie, a heavy-set young man with a full head of black hair and elegant mustache who had a weakness for two-toned summer shoes and red bow ties, grew old and fat and bald at the bank, where he stayed assistant cashier for thirty years until he retired in 1961, after forty-five years of employment there. It never occurred to me until he retired that once Louie had wanted to make something of himself in the banking business.

17   In the flush of pride that accompanied retirement—his picture appeared on the front page of the *Herald Star* along with an extensive article, "Town Lauds Louie For Years of Service," and a photo of a Certificate of Distinguished Citizenship that Hjalmar, using his considerable influence, had wangled for Louie from Governor Elmer L. Andersen himself, signed by him *and* by Minnesota's Secretary of State Joseph L. Donovan, and presented to Louie at a banquet at the Sons of Knute temple, attended by everyone, even Fr. Emil—Louie went so far as to show me his scrapbook and talk about his salad days, which was utterly unlike him: on Louie's Grace & Truth shaving mirror was, "Not me, but

Christ in me, be magnified," and he lived by that precept. I never knew a man who tried so hard to avoid the personal pronoun.

18   In the scrapbook, along with photos of his parents (who glared at the photographer as if this moment was a terrible insult, even though they had paid for it) and of him and Gladys in the front seat of a Buick roadster (his only non-Ford car) and souvenirs of a honeymoon in the Black Hills, was a certificate from the St. Paul College of Commerce proclaiming in fancy script bedecked with patriotic bunting that Louie had successfully completed a course in finance and banking and earned the degree of Associate of Commerce. It was dated 1931.

19   He earned the degree studying at night, and when it came in the mail, he said, "I told Gladys we were moving to the Cities. It was our chance.

20   "We packed everything we owned in the back of the Buick and took off a week later. Sandy and Marylee stayed with their grandma. They cried to see us go, they thought Minneapolis was on the other side of the world, where there were missionaries. We had a flat this side of St. Cloud and another near Anoka and then one in Osseo. Gladys thought I could've checked those tires before we left, which I had, but I was too mad to talk about it, so we hauled in around midnight at the Cran Hotel on Hennepin Avenue, which looked to have reasonable rates in the tourist guide, and got a room. The lobby was dirty, and there were old men sitting around the lobby in their undershirts, and the desk clerk was rude. He said, 'Whaddaya want?' Gladys wouldn't let me pick up the change. She said, 'You don't know where that money has been.' The room was small and it smelled of disinfectant. I opened the closet and almost fell to my death—no floor, it was a shaft of some sort, it went down to the basement; I dropped my shirt in it. We got undressed for bed, and now we were wide awake. Gladys said, 'Someone died in here, that's why the Pine-Sol. I'm not about to get into a deathbed.' She said she would prefer to sleep on a park bench. So we got dressed and snuck down the backstairs to avoid notice. We drove to the Hotel Nicollet. It was a swank place with walnut paneling and potted palms and a carpet like walking in mud. Well, we must've looked like orphans in the storm because the clerk asked if we had reservations and then he got snooty with us, he said, 'Ordinarily we're full weeks in advance. You really should have written on ahead a long time ago. But you're lucky, I do have a room for $15.' Gladys thought it was the weekly rate. She said, 'No, we're only staying the one night.' But I knew. I looked him straight in the eye and I said, 'You wouldn't happen to have something better, would you?' I didn't want him to think we were green. No, he said, so I said we'd take it and I peeled off a twenty, my only one. Gladys was in shock, and so was I. We got to the room which was like a royal suite, and we couldn't sleep for thinking about all that money. Fifteen dollars! Gladys said, 'What made you say that?' Well, it was pride talking, worldly pride. I was so ashamed. I thought of the girls, the things I

could've done for them with that money. I sat up all night thinking. I decided that if Minneapolis had that effect on me, that I'd rather spend what I didn't have than admit to not having it, then I'd better go back where I belonged, and the next day we did. And then I told a lie: I said I'd looked for a job and didn't find one good enough. It took me a long time to get Minneapolis off my conscience."

21   The Brethren did not hold with ambition of worldly success, and their hopes for their children were modest ones: to earn an honest living, take pleasure in the Lord, and suffer trouble cheerfully. College was not necessary, nor was a well-paying job. Mr. Milburn of the St. Cloud Brethren earned a good dollar as a wholesale hardware salesman for Benson Brothers, but salesmanship forced a man to put his faith on the shelf—if a client cursed and told dirty jokes, he'd have to bite his tongue. Farming was the most godly livelihood, and show business was the least. When Bernie Carlson ("Mister Midwest"), host of the popular "Happy Day" and "Farm Hour" shows, got fired for a drunken remark to the Sweetheart of Song, it was noted as "what happens to people who get too big," the logical consequence of success. Bernie was "big" in nobody's eyes but ours. WFPT in Freeport was a Quonset hut in a cornfield by the tower. Nevertheless, he drove a white Olds and was on the radio, so he was pointed out to me as a sign of "what happens." I was ten and I liked to read from the newspaper into a cardboard tube, cupping a hand behind my ear to hear if I had Bernie's deep bass tones.

Points for Review and Discussion

1.   Summarize the Keillor family position regarding recreation. What entertainments are approved and disapproved, and for what reasons?
2.   Keillor remembers that, people in his hometown believed the Spirit intervenes in the course of human events for specific purposes. Explain, on the basis of an example in "Protestant," how this intervention is thought to take place.

❧ *Questions for Writing*

1.   When a girl asks young Garrison why his car compass has a religious message on it, he answers vaguely, "I don't know why, I guess [my Dad] likes it there" (¶ 12). And he explains to the reader that his reason for saying this was to keep the conversation with the girl headed toward making out rather than the "thorny subject of obedience." What other reasons might he have for answering as he does? Why does he carry pliers to remove the religious messages—"the evidence of our faith"—from the license plates on the family car?
2.   Reread the account of the old farm ladies banking their egg money (¶ 15). Keillor writes that it was "touching" to see them with Brother

Louie. To whom would it be "touching?" Where on the social ladder must this person be located in order to be touched by such a moment?

3. Brother Louie asks the desk clerk at the "swank" Minneapolis hotel whether he "wouldn't happen to have something better" than a $15 room (¶ 20). Why does Louie ask this question? How does his social class affect his feelings at this moment?

4. After reflecting on your answers to questions 1–3, write a page describing as precisely as you can Garrison Keillor's attitude toward his Minnesota past.

Free Trade
Thomas Geoghegan

Daily encounters with class differences are the norm for doctors, lawyers, and teachers, especially if they're employed in the nonprofit sector. And often these encounters become shaping influences on the moral education of the professionals in question. They learn not merely about the size and impact of the gaps separating the classes, but, in addition, about the reasons why their own assumptions of superiority warrant questioning.

When Thomas Geoghegan (pronounced Guh-HEE-gun) was in law school, his roommate persuaded him to serve as a poll watcher in a union election in which a group of coal miners was attempting to vote corrupt leaders out of office. Later Geoghegan became a Chicago-based labor lawyer, representing teamsters, steelworkers, nurses, and carpenters. In "Free Trade," below, Geoghegan reflects on several factors that separate him from his clients; he also confronts the possibility that the relatively humble and poorly paid people he represents may possess a higher order of moral intelligence than that found in the topmost reaches of American society. Geoghegan's first book, *Which Side Are You on? Trying to Be for Labor When It's Flat on Its Back*, was published in 1991.

1 It may sound odd to say, but I am one of the rich. Compared with many of my friends, I make very little money. Yet in personal income I am still in the upper one-fifth of the country: I make, on average, $60,000 a year, which is a laughably low salary to my friends, who take me out to dinner, pick up the bill, and regard me as a kind of monk. It frightens me to realize I'm upper one-fifth, for several reasons:

1. It is frightening because I can do it by defending the poor. That seems wrong to me right there.
2. It is frightening because I really am poor. I can barely get by on $60,000 a year.

2 For now, I can keep up appearances, go out to the same restaurants as my friends, even walk into Convito Italiano on the night after the Great Crash and spend eight dollars for a glass of wine. But I know if I ever get married, the jig is up. I would be exposed, my world would collapse, because then I would have to buy some $400,000 house. Sure, I may be upper one-fifth, but I am not really a serious person. A friend of mine put his hand on my shoulder and said, "Tom, what if you want to get married and have children?"

From Thomas Geoghegan, *Which Side Are You On? Trying to Be for Labor When It's Flat on Its Back* (1991).

3   I crawl at the very bottom of the upper class. This makes me a natural political radical or malcontent: $60,000 a year is probably what Lenin made just before the Revolution. Or what George Orwell made when he was down and out in Paris and London. This is the income bracket that starts all the trouble and keeps a person on edge. Somewhere in a Raymond Chandler novel, I read that Marlowe did not make a lot of money either and it helped him as a detective to stay in touch with real life. I flatter myself that on $60,000 a year I can be like Marlowe himself and look deep into the heart of darkness.

4   In fact, I have no idea how anyone else lives, how the bottom four-fifths of the country gets along. When I hear that the median family income in America is $29,000 a year (in 1986), I take out my passport and wonder what country I have wandered into. Did you know that? $29,000 a year? That means the income of roughly half the families in America is below that. Why isn't this fact on the front page of the *New York Times* every single day? Imagine what it would be like on $29,000 a year, or less, just you and your family of four—with both you *and* your spouse working. What would you do? Eat out at Pizza Hut once a week, that would be it, or so I used to think. A Teamsters member told me once, "Pizza Hut? You can't even do *that*." When I think of that number, $29,000 a year, I feel as cut off from the U.S. as someone living in Malaysia. I cannot even begin to guess what the real, unwritten life of my own country is like. And I am a labor lawyer, too. I represent them. My friends rely on *me*, as if I were Marco Polo, a traveler in Malay, and other places, to come back to tell them what the pizza at Pizza Hut is like.

5   And if that's so, we're all in trouble.

6   I was at the ball game the other night with a friend of mine who said, "Come on, it's not that bad, $29,000 a year..."

7   "For a family of four?" I said.

8   "You're thinking of Chicago, where the cost of living's really high."

9   "I don't think it is high here."

10 "I bet $29,000 goes a lot further in Des Moines..."

11 "Not that much, I bet..."

12 We ran out of things to say. As we did, I looked out in the bleachers, which were totally empty.

13 It is not the low median income that is so shocking to me but the fact that we (i.e., me and my friends) do not even know about it. In *The Ancien Régime and the French Revolution,* Tocqueville says that the great evil in France on the eve of the Revolution was not the existence of class but the fact that the classes never saw each other. The French upper class, isolated, lost any feeling of responsibility for the common people, or, indeed, for the nation.

14 Maybe that is happening here. I notice it in the way we talk about the "economy." In fact, it is impossible to talk about the American econ-

omy now as if it were a single, seamless thing. If I try to talk about the "economy" with anyone in my "class," it turns into a wild lunging conversation, and I talk about A, and he or she talks about B, and both of us end up utterly frustrated and angry. In the old days, it was pretty clear when the American economy was "good" and when it was "bad." Now, with the growing class division, this is a much trickier exercise. "Good" or "bad" for whom?

15   Of course, this has been true before. In his book *The Age of Empire*, E. J. Hobsbawm writes that in the 1870s, when wages rose but profits fell, the period was called the Great Depression. Then, around 1900, when profits rose but wages fell, the period was called the Belle Epoque. Now it seems true again. In the 1980s, profits rose but wages were flat or falling in real terms, and this period is called the Reagan boom. It is eerie how even in South Chicago, even as people were being laid off, they still assumed that, well, yes, this is a "boom." And in the Reagan years, it is true, for most people, not steelworkers but most people, it was a much slower, subtler, not unnerving kind of decline, like cutting your wrists and bleeding into warm bath water.

16   For labor, the "boom" was the "crash." Our "boom" was their "crash." But even in my "class," not everyone thinks it was the Belle Epoque. Robert Reich and James Fallows are two of the best writers who worry over the new class division in the country. Both men are not so much economists as *moralistes*, who both write in the *Atlantic* for a large educated audience. Even when the two argue with each other, they seem to share a sense that we are being driven now, not by the old Newtonian economic laws, but by new forces, to some new, unknown, probably terrible place, past the last moon of Neptune, into a cold and lawless beyond.

17   Reich, quite grimly, says that the new global economy has turned the U.S. into a class society, and there is nothing we can do but watch. There will be three kinds of American workers: (1) symbolic analysts, i.e., those who process information, like lawyers, bankers, scientists, and consultants; (2) routine production workers, like steelworkers and miners; and (3) routine personal service workers, like secretaries and shoeshine boys. Reich claims that those in the first category, symbolic analysts, i.e., the lawyers, bankers, yuppies—have cut loose from the American economy and are no longer dependent on it. They are now part of a global economy, which will always need their services and always enrich them, even if the American economy falls apart.

18   So, Reich says, America's industrial base can disappear and people at the top will still get richer and richer. For them, i.e., for "us," the American economy is as meaningless a concept as the economy of Delaware.

19   Now this, to Reich, is a new development. Formerly, the rich depended in some way on the well-being of the whole nation. Henry Ford paid his autoworkers good wages, Reich says, so they could go out and buy his Model T, and he knew his prosperity was tied to theirs. But now

we can let the workers shine our shoes, and it will not hurt "our" prosperity one bit. Other countries will pay the bills we run up at Convito Italiano, because other countries will always need the fancy postgrad services we provide, with our fancy postgrad educations. There is no such thing as a national economy.

20 Fallows, writing from Japan, has a different view. He says that once, like Reich, he, too, thought a national economy was a meaningless concept, like the economy of Delaware. Then he went to Japan and saw that in Japan a national economy is not meaningless at all. The Japanese elite, their upper one-fifth, sure as hell have a national economy. Indeed, to Fallows, the Japanese economy is a kind of super-Delaware devouring the world.

21 So who is right, Fallows or Reich? Maybe both of them. Maybe there are two paths open to an "upper one-fifth," namely: (1) love your country and build up its economy, or (2) throw in with the world economy and send your own people into Third World hell. This is the choice facing us. And in a way, so little was asked of us, historically, as an elite: simply that we not make America any worse than it was, any more of a class society. And we blew it, we could not even do that.

22 It may not be a question of free will. I know I should save money, and I even have saved some, but I could spend it any minute on a condominium. I often think that tonight, at Convito Italiano, I will pass up dessert and maybe, if I push myself away from the table, just once, for one night, and put what I save in a bank, there could be money for a steel mill in South Chicago. I feel guiltier than most, I suppose, because I made my money off steelworkers. It is horrible to be sitting at a wine bar, looking in my date's eyes, then suddenly to see the apparition of a steelworker before me.

23 In Tom Wolfe's *Bonfire of the Vanities,* supposed novel of our time, the hero, an investment banker, discovers the "other class" when he takes a wrong turn and runs over a black kid in a ghetto. Imagine if Wolfe had written a novel in which an investment banker runs over a middle-aged steelworker. It would not even have occurred to Wolfe. Nor would it sell. Yet it happens every day.

24 I would be in favor of Free Trade if we had an upper class like Japan's. I would be in favor of Free Trade if we, my generation, the Reaganites, could be more patriotic, if we could go out and make something, if we could save a little and not keep forcing ourselves to throw up, like the ancient Romans, so we could go out and consume more.

25 I would be in favor of Free Trade if we were not so corrupt.

26 Recently I spoke to my friend Ann, the economist, and asked her the following:

27 "Look, Ann, I know all about the economic reasons for deindustrialization. I mean, the high dollar, the high interest rates, the debt crisis,

the loss of markets in the Third World. But isn't the real reason just that we're corrupt? I mean the upper class, people in the upper one-fifth?"

28   She looked at me. "Are *you* in the upper one-fifth?"
29   "Yes."
30   "Isn't that amazing? So am I."
31   "As an economist, do you think it's silly for me to say, 'It's corruption'?"
32   She said, relieved, almost in a whisper, "I think it *is* corruption. When I talk to groups, and talk about the steel industry and its decline, I think some of them feel ashamed. They feel embarrassed."
33   I know this is true. More people are feeling embarrassed. I feel embarrassed, now that I let adult men kneel before me and shine my shoes. I just started having my shoes shined. Sometimes the man who shines them looks up at me and gives me a horrible grin, and I feel sick, but I keep going. I tell myself, "It's good discipline," and he is a personal service worker, and I should not cringe, this is the way it's going to be from now on. But still, I feel like I have one foot in Babylon.
34   My friend Len said to me recently, "In the 1950s and 1960s, things always seemed to be getting better. Every year, it seemed, wages were higher, there were more civil rights, more social justice. You had this sense of progress . . . Now it's gone, this whole sense. Now, each year, there's more racism, more poverty, unions get busted. Everywhere you look. We're headed *down.*"
35   A friend told me that his sister, a medical researcher, was being courted by a big drug company. She turned them down, but they persisted: "How much do you want? $150,000? No? $200,000? How about $300,000?" O.K., she said, she would try the job for a week. Every day, at her door, there was a limousine waiting for her, driven by a Teamster. As she came to know him, and they started talking, she found out he and the other drivers had not had a raise at this company in three years. The company had tons of money, it was doing great, it was just stiffing these guys because . . . well, why not? Labor is weak now.
36   The role of these people, in the global economy, is just to drive around the upper "one-fifth."
37   Reich says there is no way we can stop this from happening. Real wages will keep falling. All we can do, he says, is to change the tax code to increase transfer payments from the rich to the poor.
38   When I reached this point, I thought, "What a wimp this guy is." Americans do not like to use the tax code this way. No Democrat is even talking about making the income tax more progressive, and it was luck we had as much tax reform as we did in 1984. If people on the left want to redistribute income, they can only hope the economy, and not the tax code, is going to do it.
39   But Reich says there is no hope. So maybe we can have voluntary transfer payments from rich to poor. There are several ways we could do it:

40   We could take more cabs.
41   We could leave bigger tips at restaurants.
42   We could give presents to them. For example, a friend of mine at Skadden, Arps just gave his secretary a car. He really wanted to give her more money, but he couldn't: it would have upset the firm's salary structure. So, in lieu of that, he gave her a car and set an example for us, in the century or so to come: just pick out the workers we like down there in the lower four-fifths and give them new cars.

43   In this new global economy, I worry about the Third World. Not the Third World "over there," but the Third World down the street. This is the real threat to organized labor: not Brazil, not Korea. Indeed, why is there such a problem competing with *that* Third World when we have such a large one of our own here at home?
44   I speak now of the "underclass," a growth sector of the economy, the people who are under the personal service workers. The whole class did not exist as such twenty or twenty-five years ago. If I call them Third World, it must seem for rhetorical effect. This is still America, not Brazil, etc. But the Third World recognizes its own, and in little gestures, almost invisible, it is welcoming us to the club.
45   Mother Teresa has even sent her nuns over from India to work on the West Side of Chicago, to feed people. When she came here, she said Chicago was *worse* than anything she had seen in India. A priest I know said to me, "And she wasn't kidding."
46   "I don't believe it," I said. "That woman is shameless."
47   "Go see for yourself," he said.
48   So I did. I went to a kitchen run by the little nuns brought by Mother Teresa. The hardest part is just getting there, to the West Side. While it makes up a quarter or even a third of the city, it is not quite clear to me where it is. It seems to me like Brigadoon, shrouded in mist, occupying no real "place." Although it is only four miles or so away from me, it does not seem possible to get in a car and drive there, any more than it would to get in a car and drive to France.
49   One point I have to clear up: The kitchen to which I went, at St. Malachy's, is not like a homeless shelter one might see in a white, liberal church. This is India, not Lincoln Park. The nuns serve food here every day, at ten in the morning, and the most ordinary people come in to eat, not bag ladies, not weirdos wearing winter coats in August. Neighborhood people, you know? Of course, there is a cop in a squad car around the corner, not quite in sight of the kitchen, and he sits there all morning as food is being served.
50   To get in the kitchen, when I arrive on Sunday, I have to push through a crowd of fifty or so men who have been waiting for the nuns to open the door. This is the part I hate, the two or three minutes waiting for the nuns to open the door, when it is just me and fifty young, desperate black men: and I have my back to them. They say, "Knock louder," then they laugh.

51 Then a little nun from Calcutta opens the door, just wide enough for me to get through, so I can go in and they can't.

52 On Sunday, which is the big day here, about 200 or more people will go through the line. There is a Gospel reading at the start. The first Sunday I came, it was the passage in which Jesus is telling the disciples to give up everything, to take nothing with them, when they go out to preach the good news. The men in the room looked blank. I thought, "This is not the Gospel I would have picked..."

53 There are very few women or children. Most are young men, twenty to thirty-five years old. While the men are thinner than steelworkers I know, slighter, even gaunt, many of them seem very strong in their upper arms, as if they work out in a gym or on a Nautilus. They looked darker, more Ethiopian, and yet I had a feeling that I *knew* these men ... I had seen them before. This was the shock for me: I could have seen these people in my own office, I could imagine them in a mill.

54 Now, maybe, if organized labor had not collapsed, they would not be steelworkers. They would be busboys or dishwashers, and the men who are busboys or dishwashers now would be working in the mills instead. Everyone would advance in the queue: the part-time dishwashers would be full-time, the full-time ones would be in mills. And the little nuns could go back to India.

55 We could not have created this soup kitchen without busting the unions.

56 Going through the line, most of the men say nothing. If they don't want green vegetables, for example, they shake their heads. Or they make grunting sounds. Once in a while, someone says, "Thank you." It is always the two words, "Thank you," not "Thanks." Mostly they say nothing, but then I don't say anything either.

57 The nuns did not exactly swoon over me when I volunteered. But they did put me to work. Sister Arjay, the boss, told me where to stand and what to do. She and Sister Colleta are both about four feet eleven and probably they are peasant girls from villages. They talk in that furiously fast way that Indians can, and the men talk back as slow as molasses, and it is impossible to understand anybody here.

58 My first time, it was a brutally hot morning, in the mid-90s. The smell in the room was overpowering. The T-shirts seemed pasted on the men with fourteen days of sweat. I would stink of cabbage and ammonia and sweat for days after I left. Waiting for the nuns to open the door, I had almost gagged, and I wondered how the men could even bear to eat. As I watched them sitting and eating, in dead quiet, I thought, "This could be a prison cafeteria." Except a prison cafeteria would not smell this bad.

59 I was at the end of the serving line. My job was to pour the iced tea into cups, which were mostly old Dannon yogurt cups. I was told to fill up the cup by two-thirds, *no more*, because it was hot, and we might run out. Sister Colleta watched me carefully, to make sure I was not too gen-

erous. A man would ask me, please, to fill it to the top. I would say, "No." I felt like a guard in a concentration camp.

60   A child came up and asked for more. Sister saw me hesitate, so she came over and said, "No."

61   "Gee, I thought she'd let the kids have seconds," one of the volunteers whispered.

62   I almost gave Sister twenty dollars and said, "Let's give the kids some iced tea," but it was a bit late to wave my money around, like a big shot.

63   Anyway, Sister was right. It was a big crowd.

64   I would later ask George, an unemployed man who acts as a volunteer, "George, why is the crowd so much bigger on Sunday?"

65   "Because the men who work during the week are here."

66   "You mean, some of these men have *jobs*?" I said.

67   George looked thoughtful. "A few."

68   Just as the last man came through the line, I ran out of iced tea. The nuns were impressed. Sister Colleta came over and gave me a big smile. "You're very good," she said.

69   But now I knew I would have nightmares all night: Did I give one little child too much? And maybe his sister not enough? I felt like Sophie in *Sophie's Choice*, standing behind the iced tea.

70   I had expected, at the end of it all, to love the poor, to be filled with a warm glow. But I didn't feel any love for the men here. Around the room, on the wall, I could read the sayings of Mother Teresa, like New England samplers. But there was something hollow about the whole experience. I complained about it to my friend the priest.

71   He said, "You're not down there for self-actualization."

72   I said, "I didn't feel any love for them."

73   "So what?"

74   "Isn't that the point?"

75   "No. The Church says nothing about that."

76   "I thought Jesus did."

77   Look, he said, these nuns aren't liberals. They are conservative, semi-cloistered, probably in Opus Dei. They don't care about "love" in our modern, interpersonal way. We, the liberals, want love: we go to soup kitchens to *be* loved. The nuns go there to feed people. That's it. Give them something to eat. Period.

78   I wish I had talked to this woman, Mother Teresa, before I had gone into labor law.

79   One saying of Mother Teresa I did not see on the wall was: Chicago is worse than anything I have seen in India. Now, I admit that things are bad in Chicago, but I just can't believe they are worse than anything she has ever seen in India. I know, of course, what she means. India has been struggling with a caste system for centuries, whereas here, in the United States, we have created ours, the "underclass," etc., in just one decade, the 1980s. But what is this woman's problem? Is she against Free Trade?

Does she want to take food from the tables of starving Third World workers?

80 Sometimes it is depressing to be there, on the West Side. But now when I am depressed, I think of Free Trade. That beautiful idea, that noble thing, which does such credit to the human race which binds the nations and the peoples together. And when I think of Free Trade, I do not mind filling the Dannon yogurt cups two-thirds of the way. I always feel, in my own little way, I am doing something for Free Trade.

81 Last summer I met an undergraduate at Columbia University, and she told me, "I worked in a soup kitchen, and what's the point in it? It just seems hopeless."

82 I wanted to say, "Then join us, organized labor. If we had had strong unions, they wouldn't have let this happen."

83 Then I realized it was 1989 and she was only twenty-two. She had probably never heard of organized labor.

84 Anyway, in the 1970s, there had been strong unions, and everything I deplored had happened in any event. This is the problem that torments me.

85 Planning could have saved the basic industry of the United States. I have no doubt of it. Just as Germany, Japan, and many other countries saved their manufacturing sector through planning, we could have done the same.

86 Now, the U.S. has a tradition of *not* planning, or of not using industrial-type planning, the way other countries do. But when I was in school, in the 1960s, I was convinced we would have to change. I read books like Andrew Schonfield's *Modern Capitalism*, Charles Lindbloom's *Markets and Politics*, and Samuel Beer's *British Politics in the Collectivist Age*. From all these books, I learned how Western Europe and Japan engaged in industrial planning and how the U.S. would have to do the same to survive. By "planning," one meant not centralized Soviet-style planning but something like the Ministry of International Trade and Industry in Japan or the Commissariat du Plan in France. These "plans" were really proposals for capital investment, for letting some industries grow and others die.

87 I believed in this kind of planning fervidly. It was one reason I became a labor lawyer. It seemed to me that the U.S., with its excess of individualism, with its shortsighted brand of liberal capitalism, had no constituency with any interest in the long term, or in long-term economic planning, except organized labor. Indeed, in the 1930s, John L. Lewis had been one of the few who supported the kind of industry planning that Western Europe and Japan now routinely do. When led by Lewis, labor saw its future tied up with planning. It was one of the unknown tragedies of American history that Lewis lost out in this battle in the early stages of the New Deal. Lewis, Rexford Tugwell, and the other American planners were routed, in an early power struggle, by Felix

Frankfurter, Louis Brandeis, and others on the left who abhorred the idea of planning and were urging a strong program of antitrust and laissez-faire.

88   So the great opportunity for planning had been lost. But I was convinced, from reading all my books, that the opportunity would come again. It had to, or we would deindustrialize and lose much or all of our industrial base. When the opportunity came again, organized labor would again be the champion. America would find itself in its own desperate "Battle of Britain," and it would at last realize it would have to go to war and *plan*, just like our enemies, Germany and Japan. And a Winston Churchill would come out of exile to lead us. And he would have as his strongest support the leaders of organized labor, who would naturally support long-term planning and responsible actions to save our manufacturing sector. This is how we would steer ourselves through the storms of the rising global economy.

89   Now I wonder if planning in this country could have ever worked. The whole culture is against it. In the U.S., even organized labor would be walking into Convito Italiano on the night of the Great Crash. It is not just the yuppies, I found out, to my horror. Everybody in this country has the same disease.

90   I am thinking of 1979, that damned, horrible year, the last year organized labor could have saved itself, although not many in labor may realize it now. This was the year, 1979, when Iran imposed the oil embargo; when OPEC then tripled the price of oil to $30 a barrel; when the U.S. economy then crashed in flames, with double-digit inflation *and* unemployment; when mobs started forming to throw Jimmy Carter out of the White House; and when Paul Volcker became chairman of the Federal Reserve Board and could more or less run the country under martial law. After 1979, everything was lost. If it were not for that year, the Democrats might still be in the White House; some people might still call themselves liberals; we might still have an organized labor. Everything began in that one horrible year.

91   It did not have to happen either. None of it was inevitable. For, oddly enough, just at that moment, 1979, we had, for the first time, an Administration willing to *plan:* and plan European-style, too. Not every industry, just one industry, which was energy. But energy would have been enough. The Administration had a plan that would have saved just enough oil to stop a catastrophe: to keep OPEC at bay, to head off Reagan's election, to hold off the darkness of the 1980s to come.

92   I know, I was there. In my one brief departure from being a labor lawyer, I had joined the Department of Energy in 1977. My two DOE years make no sense in terms of my career, if that is the word, but there was this much logic to it: I had tried the mystical, populist approach to changing the world by being in the Mineworkers and then in the Sadlowski campaign, and neither had worked. I thought, "Look, if I want to change the world, why not try the direct approach?" Like any normal

Harvard graduate, I would do it from the top, work for someone in the White House, be a special assistant to some special assistant. But I would not work just anywhere. In the Carter Administration, "energy" was the one and only thing I would have considered. It was the only thing that was new and exciting. I would even work for that ... mandarin, James Schlesinger, who was a hawk, too, Nixon's own Secretary of Defense, although I admit, for a liberal like me, this had a slightly adulterous thrill.

93   Anyway, I had always wanted to be a planner. And Carter was proposing in his plan just the right answer to the problem. We were consuming too much oil, because oil was too cheap. Our domestic oil had been price-controlled since 1973, to keep oil companies from reaping a windfall at the higher OPEC price. The National Energy Plan, or NEP, would have solved the problem in a neat manner. NEP would tax the price of our domestic oil up to the higher OPEC price and thereby discourage consumption. Then NEP would rebate the proceeds of the tax back to consumers, American citizens, on an equal per capita basis, so that consumers, the middle- and lower-income ones especially, would not be any worse off.

94   In other words, NEP was a redistribution of income. A fairly major one, too. So NEP would have saved us from destruction, made our society more equal, and kept the Democrats in power. Also, NEP had a special benefit for organized labor. It would have raised energy costs in Texas and the South, to which anti-union employers were moving from the North and Midwest.

95   NEP was the first time since the thirties that the federal government had tried to "plan" for a whole industry. If successful, NEP could have led into a new era of European-style industrial planning. It could have realized Lewis's dream in the 1930s. Organized labor, at last, could have a greater role in planning the economy. It could have been the start of a wider, bolder program to save our manufacturing base and plan our way through the perils of Free Trade and the Global Economy.

96   So you might think that in that fateful year, 1979, organized labor supported NEP. Spent millions in pushing it. Took its last stand in supporting it. Said, "This is it, on this one we live or die."

97   Actually, labor opposed it. Yes. Opposed it. Teamed up with the oil companies and the Republicans to kill NEP in the Senate. The AFL-CIO, in its wisdom, set out to kill the very type of thing for which John L. Lewis had fought. Seemingly, labor does not want any kind of economic planning.

98   I couldn't believe it. I gasped. I was dumbfounded. I went to meetings with labor people, to explain NEP. They wouldn't even listen to us. I remember one of them, a lobbyist, was especially contemptuous.

99   He said, "Now, this NEP ... you're going to tax people, and then give the money back to them?"

100   "Yes," we said.

101   He sneered. Crazy Harvard liberals, he must have thought.

102   "You people," he said. "Do you think you can just play with people's lives like that?"

103   Yes, actually, we did think that. We, the Kennedy School graduates, the Rhodes scholars, etc., the second lieutenants in Schlesinger's army, we had thought up NEP, and it had sprung full-blown out of our heads. Yes, this was elitist. But what was our alternative? Work with these chuckleheads?

104   NEP was giving these people *free money.* And they still were against it. They just wanted to gas-guzzle, keep driving their cars, keep driving and driving and driving until they went over the cliff.

105   I had known labor was dumb. But until now, I had had no idea how dumb it was. Now I was not fighting for the rank and file but fighting them, and it was quite chilling to see them from the other side.

106   Boy, they were dumb. And to think I had believed, once, in *democratic* planning?

107   Lewis would have laughed at me for being such a fool. Labor, plan? Lewis thought all the leaders of organized labor, except for himself, were a bunch of rubes, bunglers, and self-serving idiots. He called them, regularly, the worst purple-prose names. And as to my idea, democratic planning? By the rank and file? Poor, ignorant people in coal mines and steel mills? Lewis never even remotely thought of democratic planning in that sense. To him, the whole notion would have been cruel, to turn such matters over to the rank and file. I may have believed in these people, but he didn't.

108   So after the defeat of NEP, we had nothing, no "plan" at all. The clock ticked away, Iran exploded, and the rest is history.

109   I knew I had to get out of D.C. Anyone could see the Democrats were through. I remember the summer I left, 1979, going to a party, and someone asked me, "Don't you work at the Department of Energy?" When I said yes, I could hear my answer ricochet around the room, and I could hear people whisper angrily, "He works at DOE." Who could blame them? It was not our fault, but . . . At this point, it seemed everything I touched in my life had been a disaster: the UMW blew up, too democratic; Sadlowski lost, too honest, maybe; and my dream of democratic planning was in shambles, because organized labor was so damned dumb.

110   So I went far, far away on a long journey. I went to Chicago and became a labor lawyer again. But now I would live simply. No changing the world. I would stay away from the East for at least ten years, all through the 1980s, and I would do little cases now, with little local unions. Because here, I thought, is where it starts, with the little people, in the local-union halls. Here is where I can get back my faith again. Maybe one day I can come back to the East again, after years in the mysterious Midwest, with faith, with knowledge, like Carlos Castaneda.

111　　And now that the 1980s are over, now that I've been out here in the local-union halls, and been out here with real people . . . did I get back my old faith?

112　　Well . . . I've only been here ten years.

113　　In fact, I did try to change the world in the 1980s. It was the suit to recover the pensions for the men and women of Wisconsin Steel. The suit in itself was no big deal. But I now believe that anything that consumes a person, any one of us, whatever it is, has a greenhouse effect: it changes the earth's atmosphere. Anyway, here is what I wanted to say about planning:

114　　Once a year, the "women of Wisconsin Steel" invited me to speak to them. Until now, I have referred only to the men of Wisconsin Steel, but there was also a large group of women, who were union as well, most of them "office and clerical." Every spring, about fifty or sixty of the women took over a restaurant in Lansing, rented a private banquet room, and had a reunion. You would expect that these women would eat a lot of salad, but in fact, the food here was "chicken, beef, and sausage," or "CBS." It was just as carnivorous here as in a union hall. The women never went to the rallies with the men, even when the settlement was voted on. They stayed apart, in their own private banquet room.

115　　There were no men, except Frank Lumpkin and me, as the honorary male guests, to report on the status of our case. Then one year Camille, who organized the banquet, said that I should bring a date. "I don't know. . . " I said. (It was always a problem getting a date to the South Side.) Oh, she said, bring your girlfriend, and she made a point of pressing the idea. So I asked J. if she would come to the banquet. J., who had never been to Lansing or anywhere near it, was very troubled by it all. "What is this thing?" she said, and I tried to explain it. "I don't think this is appropriate," she said, and she seemed rather upset.

116　　"Oh, it is appropriate," I said, so she finally went.

117　　I wish I could describe what it is like to have dinner with "the women of Wisconsin Steel." You see women like these in the Loop on State Street, at 5:05, pouring into the buses, headed for the South Side, or taking the South Shore train, and I almost envy them some nights, especially in winter, when it is cold and already dark, and they are off to the bungalows and to a long, drowsy evening in front of the TV. I think, as I go back to work, how much I would like to be on that bus or train.

118　　Most of the women of Wisconsin Steel have jobs, and they seem to be doing much better than the men. For them, the 1980s could have been worse. Sometimes I think the rank and file have switched sexes, and now the women, not the men, should be wearing the union windbreakers, because they are the real "proles" in the new global economy.

119　　Yet the women of Wisconsin Steel miss the mill, almost bitterly. They seem to miss the idea of working with their husbands, who were in the mill, not in sight perhaps but nearby. Often, the women would work for a few years, then leave to raise the kids, then come back to their old jobs. The men, their husbands, would keep working steadily. And all through the sixties and seventies, the wages of the men, their husbands, kept going up and up.

120 At every banquet, the program is the same. At the end of the meal, going around the room, one by one, each woman stands up to speak a little about herself. I explained all this to J.

121 The first woman stood up and said, "Hi, I'm Millie N."

122 Someone laughed. "We know, we know."

123 Millie got the giggles. "And I'm a receptionist at Leo Burnett . . . and, uh . . . uh . . . "

124 "Tell us about your grandchildren, Millie."

125 "I have two lovely grandchildren, two girls. . . " One of them was in a fashion show recently, and she's only four.

126 "And two years ago . . . my husband, Bill, passed away . . . Millie stopped.

127 Some "oohs" and "aahs" from the crowd here.

128 "And I love my job, I really do . . . but oh, I miss the mill, and I miss you all, and I miss all the great times we used to have there. . . " Millie just burst out with this, very rapidly. Many women speeded up at the end.

129 Then Millie sat down, and the next woman stood up. Her name, I think, was Irene, and she was a big, fat woman who had a wonderful laugh. She was very funny talking about the jobs she had after the mill closed.

130 "I had a job at McDonald's," she said, "at $3.25 an hour . . . and I was the *boss*." She roared with laughter, and so did everyone else.

131 I should add, everyone had been drinking.

132 Then another woman stood up, and she froze. Stage fright. Could not speak a word.

133 Other women yelled, "Come on, Grace, speak, *speak*. . . "

134 Grace tried to speak, but nothing came out.

135 Some of the women laughed. "Next, next. . . "

136 Grace sat down, but as she did, she gave us a look that was full of . . . well, love.

137 It startled me to see it. I don't know who else did.

138 Then the next woman stood up and said she had a job with Waste Management, Inc., which owns several dumps in the area.

139 Some women booed.

140 She said, "Well, you know our slogan . . . 'Better us than in your backyard.'"

141 "It *is* in our backyard," a lady snapped.

142 More women stood up. More grandchildren were described. More alcohol was consumed. Some of these women, with their bouffant hairdos, looked like the old babysitters I had as a child.

143 As the women spoke, I looked over at J. to see how she was doing. She seemed to be very moved. Later, much later on, she said to me, "I

didn't know anything about people like these ... who are in unions, I mean."

144   I must have seemed blank, so she went on.

145   "I grew up as a Republican, remember. Oh yes, I'm a liberal now. . . "

146   "Like everyone," I said.

147   "Yes, but I still thought people in unions were grubby, materialistic, just concerned about their wages. . . "

148   "Well . . . they are," I said.

149   "No," she said, "they're *not*. That's not what I saw. These women, they have. . . " She was looking for a word. "They have. . . "

150   She gave up. She didn't want to be corny and say ". . . nobility of character."

151   I know this, because the same corny thought has come to me.

152   But that night I had a quite different, perhaps cornier thought: What if these women who stood up and told the stories, what if they had been in charge of the economy in the 1980s? What would they have done with all the money we drop every night at Convito Italiano?

153   I feel that somehow they would have spent it on their grandchildren. They would have spent it on education. They would have looked to the future, the long term, etc., not in the priggish, self-conscious way of a planner, but more like a family member, a grandmother, one whose husband was dead, and who herself might soon face death. I am convinced they would have spent it not on themselves but on the kids. These women ask for little and lead very simple lives.

Points for Review and Discussion

1. Geoghegan says that America may have to choose between two paths. Name those paths and explain why he believes "this is the choice facing us" (¶ 21).

2. Geoghegan finds "something hollow about the whole experience" of working in a soup kitchen. How does he himself account for this feeling?

Questions for Writing

1. At one point in this essay Geoghegan sees workers as "dumb" (¶ 115); at another he sees them as possessing "nobility of character" (¶ 150). Summarize his reasons for each view. Which seems closest, finally, to his true feelings?

2. Geoghegan and his friend Ann agree that "the real reason" for the disaster of deindustrialization is that privileged people like themselves are "corrupt" (¶ 27). On what ground do they arrive at this conclusion? Does it strike you as rational or irrational? Explain your answer.

3. Following his discussion of Robert Reich and "voluntary transfer payments from rich to poor," Geoghegan tells the story of a lawyer friend who gave his secretary a "car and set an example for us, in the century or so to come: just pick out the workers we like down there in the lower four-fifths and give them new cars" (¶ 42). How do you read the phrase "set an example for us"? Is Geoghegan serious or not? How can you tell?

THE HIDDEN INJURIES OF CLASS
Richard Sennett and Jonathan Cobb

Upward movement from one class to another is, in theory, the stuff of basic American success stories. But the real-life human beings who live these stories don't always speak positively about them. They may not be convinced, for one thing, that the work they have risen to has as much dignity as that which they left behind. They may feel, in addition, that they are still at a disadvantage—because the people on the rung to which they have climbed belong, by birth, to a higher social class, and hence retain the power to judge them. They may even feel, at bottom, illegitimate and inauthentic—undeserving of the position to which they have risen.

In their book *The Hidden Injuries of Class* (1972) the sociologists Richard Sennett and Jonathan Cobb interviewed a number of "successes" who were ambivalent about their own achievements. One of the most poignant interviews, with a bank loan officer the interviewers call Frank Rissarro, appears below.

1 Frank Rissarro,* a third-generation Italian-American, forty-four years old when we talked with him, had worked his way up from being a shoeshine boy at the age of nine to classifying loan applications in a bank. He makes $10,000 a year, owns a suburban home, and every August rents a small cottage in the country. He is a man who at first glance appears satisfied—"I know I did a good job in my life"—and yet he is also a man who feels defensive about his honor, fearing that people secretly do not respect him; he feels threatened by his children, who are "turning out just the way I want them to be," and he runs his home in a dictatorial manner.

2 Rissarro was born in 1925, the second-eldest child and only son of parents who lived in a predominantly Italian section of Boston. His father, an uneducated day laborer, worked hard, drank hard, and beat his wife and children often. As a young boy, Rissarro was not interested in school—his life was passed in constant fear of his father's violence. He was regarded by his family as a spoiled brat, with no brains and no common sense. His sisters and cousins did better than he scholastically, all finishing high school. Yet even as a child, Rissarro worked nights and weekends helping to support his family. At sixteen he quit school, feel-

---

From Richard Sennett and Jonathan Cobb, *The Hidden Injuries of Class* (1972).

* This is not his real name, nor are the details that follow about his job, age, and income precisely accurate.

ing incapable of doing the work and out of place. After two years in the military, he worked as a meat-cutter for nearly twenty years.

3 Rissarro was and is a man of ambition. The affluence spreading across America in the decades following the Second World War made him restless—he wanted to either get a butcher shop of his own or get out. The capital for a small business being beyond his reach, he had a friend introduce him to the branch manager of a bank setting up a new office in his neighborhood. He won a job processing loans for people who come in off the street; he helps them fill out the forms, though he is still too low-level to have the power to approve or disapprove the loans themselves.

4 A success story: from chaos in the Depression, from twenty years of hacking away at sides of beef, Rissarro now wears a suit to work and has a stable home in respectable surroundings. Yes, it is a success story—except that *he* does not read it that way.

5 As we explored with Rissarro the reasons why these good things have come to him, we found the declarations of self-satisfaction almost instantly giving way to a view of himself as a passive agent in his own life, a man who has been on the receiving end of events rather than their cause: "I was just at the right place at the right time," he says again and again. "I was lucky," he claims, in describing how he emotionally withstood the terrors of his father's home.

6 Is this modesty? Not for him. He feels passive in the midst of his success because he feels illegitimate, a pushy intruder, in his entrance to the middle-class world of neat suburban lawns, peaceable families, happy friendships. Despite the fact that he has gained entrée, he doesn't believe he deserves to be respected. In discussing, for instance, his marriage—to a woman somewhat more educated than he, from an Italian background equivalent to "lace-curtain Irish"—Rissarro told us something impossible to believe, considering his ungrammatical speech, his obsession with his childhood, his mannerisms and gestures: "My wife didn't know that I had no background to speak of, or else she would never have married me." The possibility that she accepted him for himself, and never made an issue of where he came from, he simply cannot accept.

7 Sociologists have a neat formula to explain the discontent caused by upward mobility; they call Frank's malaise a product of "status incongruity": Because Frank does not yet know the rules of his new position, because he is caught between two worlds, he feels something is wrong with him. This formula falls back on an image of the antithesis between working-class struggle and educated, "higher" culture.

8 The trouble here, however, is that Frank *doesn't* feel caught between two worlds. He knows what the rules of middle-class life are, he has played at them now for some years; furthermore, he is not in any way ashamed of his working-class past. Indeed, he is proud of it, he thinks it makes him a more honest person at work:

9   "I'm working, like I said, with fellows that are educated, college boys, in that office. I'm about the only one in there in any straits to say I'm educated. I'm enjoying this job, I'm going in with the big shots. I go in at nine, I come out at five. *The other fellows, because they got an education, sneaks out early and comes in late.* The boss knows I'm there, a reliable worker. 'Cause I've had the factory life, I know what it is. I mean, a man deserves—the least you can do is put your hours in and do your job. I'm a good employee. I know I am because I see others who are educated."

10 In fact, toward educated white-collar work itself, beyond all its symbolic connotations of success, Frank Rissarro harbors an innate disrespect: "These jobs aren't real work where you make something—it's just pushing papers."

11 Then why has he striven so hard to be upwardly mobile? One ready answer is that he wanted the house, the suit, the cottage in the country. And Rissarro himself gives that answer at first. After a few hours of talk, however, he conveys a more complicated and difficult set of feelings.

12 The poverty of his childhood he speaks about as something shameful, not because there was a lack of things, but rather because the people who had nothing acted like animals. He remembers this particularly in terms of his father—his father's poverty and his drunken brutality toward Frank and Frank's mother are interwoven in Frank's memory. Other images in his conversation concerning the poor, both white and black, similarly fuse material deprivation with chaotic, arbitrary, and unpredictable behavior; he sees poverty, in other words, as depriving men of the capacity to act rationally, to exercise self-control. A poor man, therefore, *has* to want upward mobility in order to establish dignity in his own life, and dignity means, specifically, moving toward a position in which he deals with the world in some controlled, emotionally restrained way. People who have been educated, on the other hand, are supposed to already possess this capacity. They are supposed to have developed skills for taming the world without force or passion.

13 Frank feels that it is such people on whom he ought to model the changes he wants in his own life. And yet, paradoxically, he doesn't respect the content of their powers: just as intellect gives a man respect in the world, the educated do nothing worth respecting; their status means they can cheat. In a further twist, Rissarro then proceeds to turn the paradox into a terrible accusation against himself: "As far as I'm concerned, I got through life by always trying to depend on the other guy to do my work. But when it came to my hands, I could do all the work myself."

14 Capturing respect in the larger America, then, means to Frank getting into an educated position; but capturing that respect means that he no longer respects himself. This contradiction ran through every discussion we held, as an image either of what people felt compelled to do with their own lives or of what they sought for their sons. If the boys could

get educated, anybody in America would respect them; and yet, as we shall see, the fathers felt education would lead the young into work not as "real" as their own.

15   A workingman looks at the privileges high culture bestows in much the same light as does Ortega y Gasset or William Pfaff—that high culture permits a life in which material need can be transcended by a higher form of self-control; he looks at the claims of intellectual privilege, however, with the same jaundiced eyes as does Sartre. On this ground, the workingman's feelings about his leaving the isolated, poor ethnic community have the same ambivalence that the radical intellectual experiences when he seeks to define his place in relation to the workingman.

16   Yet, why should Frank Rissarro be worrying about his legitimacy? And why has he chosen as a "prestige model" a kind of work activity he despises?

17   This paradox might, of course, be read simply as a conflict in the individual personalities of men like Frank Rissarro. It is more accurate, however, to see it as an issue introduced into their lives by the America outside the urban village. The story these workingmen have to tell is not just who they are but what are the contradictory codes of respect in the America of their generation.

18   How Frank Rissarro talked to his interviewer provides some beginning clues in this regard. Frank Rissarro did not so much grant an interview as give a confession. The interviewer began by asking a neutral question, something about what Rissarro remembered of Boston while he was growing up. He replied by talking with little interruption for more than three hours about intimate feelings and experiences to this stranger whom he had never met before. Rissarro talked to the interviewer in a peculiar way: he treated him as an emissary from a different way of life, as a representative of a higher, more educated class, before whom he spread a justification of his entire life. At various points where he spoke of situations where he felt powerless and the interviewer sympathized, Rissarro would suddenly respond to him as simply a human being, not as an emissary sent in judgment; but then, as he returned to the story of his life, which he seemed to live through again as he described it, the interviewer once again became a representative of a class of people who could do what they wanted and who made him feel inadequate. It was Rissarro's chief concern throughout to show why circumstances had not permitted him to take charge of his life in the same way.

19   Yet this man is someone who feels he has done a good job in establishing a stable family and margin of security in contrast to the life of poverty and turmoil he knew as a child during the Depression. Why then is he so defensive?

20   The word "educated" as used by Rissarro, and by other men and women we talked to, is what psychologists call a "cover term"; that is, it stands for a whole range of experiences and feelings that may in fact have little to do with formal schooling. Education covers, at the most ab-

stract level, the development of capacities within a human being. At the most concrete level, education meant to the people we interviewed getting certificates for social mobility and job choice, and they felt that American society parcels out the certificates very unequally and unfairly, so that middle-class people have more of a chance to become educated than themselves. But if the abstract is connected to the concrete, this means middle-class people have more of a chance than workers to escape from becoming creatures of circumstance, more chance to develop the defenses, the tools of personal, rational control that "education" gives. Why should one class of human beings get a chance to develop the weapons of self more than another? And yet, if that class difference is a *fait accompli,* what has a man without education got inside himself to defend against this superior power?

21   Rissarro believes people of a higher class have a power to judge him because they seem internally more developed human beings; and he is afraid, because they are better armed, that they will not respect him. He feels compelled to justify his own position, and in his life he has felt compelled to put himself up on their level in order to earn respect. All of this, in turn—when he thinks just of himself and *is not comparing himself* to his image of people in a higher class—all of this is set against a revulsion against the work of educated people in the bank, and a feeling that manual labor has more dignity.

22   What does he make of this contradiction in his life? That he is an impostor—but more, that the sheer fact that he is troubled must prove he really is inadequate. After all, he has played by the rules, he has gained the outward signs of material respectability; if, then, he still feels defenseless, something must be wrong with *him:* his unhappiness seems to him a sign that he simply cannot become the kind of person other people can respect.

23   This tangle of feelings appeared again and again as we talked to people who started life as poor, ethnically isolated laboring families, and have been successful in making the sort of material gains that are supposed to "melt" people into the American middle class.

24   The children who get formal education are no more exempt than parents like Rissarro from a feeling of inadequate defenses in the very midst of success. Nationally, about half the children from white, blue-collar homes get started in the kind of schooling their parents want—that is, about half go beyond high school. There is a large difference between girls and boys in this; depending on whose figures you use, between ten and twenty-five percent of boys from blue-collar homes receive some further schooling, while between forty and fifty percent of the girls do. A much smaller percentage of boys gets through four years of college or technical school (three to five percent); a slightly higher, though still small, percentage of girls do.

25   As with blue-collar workers who have moved into offices, we are dealing with a minority—a minority, however, on whom much hope is

pinned. Observers of the college scene like John McDermott have suggested that this may be a more desperately unhappy group of students than the disaffected young from suburban homes. McDermott and, in another context, David Riesman believe these working-class boys and girls are made to feel inadequate by a "laying-on of culture" practiced in college by their teachers and the more privileged students—a process that causes people to feel inadequate in the same way "status incongruity" does, by subjecting them to an unfamiliar set of rules in a game where respect is the prize.

26 Yet here is James, in his third year at a local college accessible to sons and daughters from blue-collar homes. James's father works as a clerk for the city by day and mends rugs at night and on the weekend. James knows the rules for making it in college, and he has survived the weeding-out process of the first years with good grades. But James disrespects school in the same way Frank disrespects pushing papers around at the bank; the status of "educated man" is greater than that of a craftsman, but the intrinsic satisfaction seems less. James feels, however, that he must stay in school, above all for his father's sake:

27 "The American Dream for my father is to see his kids get a college education, something he never had. If it had to kill them, they were gonna get a college education. He never really forced it on us, but we knew that this was really gonna make him happy—that we could get a college degree."

28 James also knows what leaving school would mean materially: a loss of security, status jobs, money. He is going to stay in school, because he feels compelled by these material considerations even as he disrespects them on their own.

29 How does he deal with the conflict success in school has set up in his life? Like Frank Rissarro, he blames himself for feeling so ambivalent. On the one hand he says, "I still don't have the balls to go out into the world," i.e., to quit school; on the other hand, "If I really had what it takes, I could make this school thing worthwhile." He takes personal responsibility for his social position, and the result is that he makes himself feel inadequate no matter which way he turns in attempting to deal with success.

30 James has gone through a profound dislocation in his life, and his discontent is pronounced. His problem, however, is shared in more muted form by others who have made more modest gains. These are kids who have had a little schooling beyond high school and then gone into such jobs as saleswork or management traineeships. They feel they have had more opportunity open to them than their manual-laboring parents. At the same time, they see the parents' work as intrinsically more interesting and worthwhile, and they suffer, therefore, from a feeling of not having made use of their opportunities. When all the discipline of sticking it out in school yields an occupation they feel little engagement in, they hold themselves to blame, for not feeling more self-confidence, for having failed to develop. "If only I had what it

takes," says a young shoe salesman, son of a factory laborer, "things would have been different."

31   One way to make sense of these confusing metaphors of self-worth is to recast them as issues of *freedom* and *dignity*. Class is a system for limiting freedom: it limits the freedom of the powerful in dealing with other people, because the strong are constricted within the circle of action that maintains their power; class constricts the weak more obviously in that they must obey commands. What happens to the dignity men see in themselves and in each other, when their freedom is checked by class?

32   In England or France today, one would have to give a different reply to this general question than one would in the United States. In cultures with still-strong working-class traditions, or a sense of working-class solidarity, the respect as equals that workingmen may not get from those who command them they can get from each other. Richard Hoggart's *The Uses of Literacy* is a beautiful evocation of the feeling among laborers that we are unfree, but dignified in our oppression because we have each other. In the *faubourgs rouges* around Paris, workers similarly take real pride in their class position.

33   But if it is possible, then, to feel dignified even as one recognizes that he has less material freedom, fewer work options, less chance of education than others, why is it that in America men like Frank Rissarro feel their dignity is on the line? Why do they take their class position so personally? And especially someone like James, who is actively engaged in self-development, in acquiring the education Rissarro feels he lacks—why does he have a similar feeling of vulnerability?

34   ... The circumstances of urban workers in America ... provide some partial answers: the ethnic refuge is fragmenting as the ethnic turf in the city is being destroyed; both these men have changed classes in a society that, unlike Britain, celebrates the myth of permeation of social classes, and social mobility creates status anxiety. But these circumstantial answers are too simple. That an increase in material power and freedom of choice should be accompanied by a crisis in self-respect deserves more probing study.

35   It is worth remarking here on the obtuseness of the position advanced by B. F. Skinner in *Beyond Freedom and Dignity*, when his clichés of behavioral psychology are applied to actual human lives. Skinner says that freedom of the individual and his dignity as an autonomous man are unscientific myths; yet here are two human beings, Rissarro and James, reared in a class where men have severe limits imposed on their individual freedom to choose, men struggling to establish more freedom in order to gain dignity—dignity they find hard to define—men whose struggle, while successful on the surface, is eroding their confidence in themselves. What insight do we gain into their actions by calling the search for freedom and dignity a myth, what do we learn about the culture, and why it is so structured that the more it gives them the more it makes them feel vulnerable? Why talk about getting "beyond"

the idea of freedom and dignity in individual lives when the society is so arranged that these men have as yet had little taste of either? . . .

36   The one bit of information appearing so far that will be crucial, in fact, for understanding how the struggle for freedom and dignity has become destructive in America is the value men like Frank Rissarro and James put on knowledge. Knowledge through formal education they see as giving a man the tools for achieving freedom—by permitting him to control situations, and by furnishing him with access to a greater set of roles in life. As things actually stand, however, Certified Knowledge does not mean dignity for either of these men; indeed, it is the reverse, it is a sham. What needs to be understood is how the class structure in America is organized so that *the tools of freedom become sources of indignity.*

37   Since the life histories presented thus far touch on the issue of social mobility, one moral might be that people are happier if they don't try to push themselves. Perhaps class change in America is such a viciously destructive process that, no matter how it works psychologically, "melting" into the middle classes is not what people from the disintegrating urban villages should do with their lives. The problem with this idea is that the same issues of dignity and self-respect appear in the lives of people who remain manual laborers. These issues concern the everyday experiences of working-class survival as well as the exceptional issues of success.

Points for Review and Discussion

1. Summarize the view of education that Sennett and Cobb attribute to Frank Rissarro.
2. What is the meaning of the phrase "status incongruity" (¶ 7)? Support your definition with details from the interview.

•⊷ Questions for Writing

1. Review your account of the view of education that Sennett and Cobb attribute to Frank Rissarro. Do Rissarro's thoughts and feelings on this subject strike you as unique to him or as shared by others in similar situations? Give reasons for your answer.
2. The interviewers assert that class is a system for limiting freedom. "It limits the freedom of the powerful in dealing with other people, because the strong are constricted within the circle of action that maintains their power; class constricts the weak more obviously in that they must obey commands" (¶ 31). Write a page in which, on the basis of your personal experience, you challenge or endorse this claim.
3. Sennett and Cobb raise the possibility that "class change in America is . . . a viciously destructive process" (¶ 37). Again on the basis of your personal experience, write a page challenging or endorsing this proposition.

On Being White, Female, and Born in Bensonhurst
Marianna De Marco Torgovnick

The influence of class often seems indistinguishable from that of ethnic background, race, and gender; the forces interact in ways that make it difficult to treat any one of them as independent of others. The interdependence is suggested in the title of the essay below—"On Being White, Female, and Born in Bensonhurst." More than once, as Marianna Torgovnick tells her life story, she pauses to point out complexities in her motives and feelings that no single strand of her background can fully explain.

A professor at Duke University, Torgovnick is the author of three books on literature, society, and the arts. She's now at work on a volume of autobiographical essays to be called *Crossing Ocean Parkway*.

1 The mafia protects the neighborhood, our fathers say, with that peculiar satisfied pride with which law-abiding Italian Americans refer to the Mafia: the Mafia protects the neighborhood from "the coloreds." In the fifties and sixties, I heard that information repeated, in whispers, in neighborhood parks and in the yard at school in Bensonhurst. The same information probably passes today in the parks (the word now "blacks," not "coloreds") but perhaps no longer in the schoolyards. From buses each morning, from neighborhoods outside Bensonhurst, spill children of all colors and backgrounds—American black, West Indian black, Hispanic, and Asian. But the blacks are the only ones especially marked for notice. Bensonhurst is no longer entirely protected from "the coloreds." But in a deeper sense, at least for Italian Americans, Bensonhurst never changes.

2 Italian-American life continues pretty much as I remember it. Families with young children live side by side with older couples whose children are long gone to the suburbs. Many of those families live "down the block" from the last generation or, sometimes still, live together with parents or grandparents. When a young family leaves, as sometimes happens, for Long Island or New Jersey or (very common now) for Staten Island, another arrives, without any special effort being required, from Italy or a poorer neighborhood in New York. They fill the neat but anonymous houses that make up the mostly tree-lined streets: two-, three-, or four-family houses for the most part (this is a working, lower to middle-middle class area, and people need rents to pay mortgages), with a few single family or small apartment houses tossed in at random.

From Marianna De Marco Torgovnick, "On Being White, Female, and Born in Bensonhurst," in *Best American Essays* (1991), ed. Joyce Carol Oates.

Tomato plants, fig trees, and plaster madonnas often decorate small but well-tended yards which face out onto the street; the grassy front lawn, like the grassy back yard, is relatively uncommon.

3   Crisscrossing the neighborhood and marking out ethnic zones—Italian, Irish, and Jewish, for the most part, though there are some Asian Americans and some people (usually Protestants) called simply Americans—are the great shopping streets: Eighty-sixth Street, Kings Highway, Bay Parkway, Eighteenth Avenue, each with its own distinctive character. On Eighty-sixth Street, crowds bustle along sidewalks lined with ample, packed fruit stands. Women wheeling shopping carts or baby strollers check the fruit carefully, piece by piece, and often bargain with the dealer, cajoling for a better price or letting him know that the vegetables, this time, aren't up to snuff. A few blocks down, the fruit stands are gone and the streets are lined with clothing and record shops, mobbed by teenagers. Occasionally, the el rumbles overhead, a few stops out of Coney Island on its way to the city, a trip of around one hour.

4   On summer nights, neighbors congregate on stoops which during the day serve as play yards for children. Air conditioning exists everywhere in Bensonhurst, but people still sit outside in the summer—to supervise children, to gossip, to stare at strangers. "*Buona sera,*" I say, or "*Buona notte,*" as I am ritually presented to Sal and Lily and Louie, the neighbors sitting on the stoop. "*Grazie,*" I say when they praise my children or my appearance. It's the only time I use Italian, which I learned at high school, although my parents (both second-generation Italian Americans, my father Sicilian, my mother Calabrian) speak it at home to each other but never to me or my brother. My accent is the Tuscan accent taught at school, not the southern Italian accents of my parents and the neighbors.

5   It's important to greet and please the neighbors; any break in this decorum would seriously offend and aggrieve my parents. For the neighbors are the stern arbiters of conduct in Bensonhurst. Does Mary keep a clean house? Did Gina wear black long enough after her mother's death? Was the food good at Tony's wedding? The neighbors know and pass judgment. Any news of family scandal (my brother's divorce, for example) provokes from my mother the agonized words: "But what will I *tell* people?" I sometimes collaborate in devising a plausible script.

6   A large sign on the church I attended as a child sums up for me the ethos of Bensonhurst. The sign urges contributions to the church building fund with the message, in huge letters: "EACH YEAR ST. SIMON AND JUDE SAVES THIS NEIGHBORHOOD ONE MILLION DOLLARS IN TAXES." Passing the church on the way from largely Jewish and middle-class Sheepshead Bay (where my in-laws live) to Bensonhurst, year after year, my husband and I look for the sign and laugh at the crass level of its pitch, its utter lack of attention to things spiritual. But we also understand exactly the values it represents.

7   In the summer of 1989, my parents were visiting me at my house in Durham, North Carolina, from the apartment in Bensonhurst where they have lived since 1942: three small rooms, rent-controlled, floor clean enough to eat off, every corner and crevice known and organized. My parents' longevity in a single apartment is unusual even for Bensonhurst, but not that unusual; many people live for decades in the same place or move within a ten-block radius. When I lived in this apartment, there were four rooms; one has since been ceded to a demanding landlord, one of the various landlords who have haunted my parents' life and must always be appeased lest the ultimate threat—removal from the rent-controlled apartment—be brought into play. That summer, during their visit, on August 23 (my younger daughter's birthday) a shocking, disturbing, news report issued from the neighborhood: it had become another Howard Beach.

8   Three black men, walking casually through the streets at night, were attacked by a group of whites. One was shot dead, mistaken, as it turned out, for another black youth who was dating a white, although part-Hispanic, girl in the neighborhood. It all made sense: the crudely protective men, expecting to see a black arriving at the girl's house and overreacting; the rebellious girl dating the outsider boy; the black dead as a sacrifice to the feelings of the neighborhood.

9   I might have felt outrage, I might have felt guilt or shame, I might have despised the people among whom I grew up. In a way I felt all four emotions when I heard the news. I expect that there were many people in Bensonhurst who felt the same rush of emotions. But mostly I felt that, given the set-up, this was the only way things could have happened. I detested the racial killing, but I also understood it. Those streets, which should be public property available to all, belong to the neighborhood. All the people sitting on the stoops on August 23 knew that as well as they knew their own names. The black men walking through probably knew it too—though their casual walk sought to deny the fact that, for the neighbors, even the simple act of blacks walking through the neighborhood would be seen as invasion.

10 Italian Americans in Bensonhurst are notable for their cohesiveness and provinciality; the slightest pressure turns those qualities into prejudice and racism. Their cohesiveness is based on the stable economic and ethical level that links generation to generation, keeping Italian Americans in Bensonhurst and the Italian-American community alive as the Jewish-American community of my youth is no longer alive. (Its young people routinely moved to the suburbs or beyond and were never replaced, so that Jews in Bensonhurst today are almost all very old people.) Their provinciality results from the Italian Americans' devotion to jealous distinctions and discriminations. Jews are suspect, but (the old Italian women admit) "they make good husbands." The Irish are okay, fellow Catholics, but not really "like us"; they make bad husbands because they drink and gamble. Even Italians come in varieties, by region (Sicil-

ian, Calabrian, Neapolitan, very rarely any region further north) and by history in this country (the newly arrived and ridiculed "gaffoon" versus the second or third generation).

11   Bensonhurst is a neighborhood dedicated to believing that its values are the only values; it tends toward certain forms of inertia. When my parents visit me in Durham, they routinely take chairs from the kitchen and sit out on the lawn in front of the house, not on the chairs on the back deck; then they complain that the streets are too quiet. When they walk around my neighborhood (these De Marcos who have friends named Travaglianti and Occhipinti), they look at the mailboxes and report that my neighbors have strange names. Prices at my local supermarket are compared, in unbelievable detail, with prices on Eighty-sixth Street. Any rearrangement of my kitchen since their last visit is registered and criticized. Difference is not only unwelcome, it is unacceptable. One of the most characteristic things my mother ever said was in response to my plans for renovating my house in Durham. When she heard my plans, she looked around, crossed her arms, and said, "If it was me, I wouldn't change nothing." My father once asked me to level with him about a Jewish boyfriend who lived in a different part of the neighborhood, reacting to his Jewishness, but even more to the fact that he often wore Bermuda shorts: "Tell me something, Marianna. Is he a Communist?" Such are the standards of normality and political thinking in Bensonhurst.

12   I often think that one important difference between Italian Americans in New York neighborhoods like Bensonhurst and Italian Americans elsewhere is that the others moved on—to upstate New York, to Pennsylvania, to the Midwest. Though they frequently settled in communities of fellow Italians, they did move on. Bensonhurst Italian Americans seem to have felt that one large move, over the ocean, was enough. Future moves could be only local: from the Lower East Side, for example, to Brooklyn, or from one part of Brooklyn to another. Bensonhurst was for many of these people the summa of expectations. If their America were to be drawn as a *New Yorker* cover, Manhattan itself would be tiny in proportion to Bensonhurst and to its satellites, Staten Island, New Jersey, and Long Island.

13   "Oh, no," my father says when he hears the news about the shooting. Though he still refers to blacks as "coloreds," he's not really a racist and is upset that this innocent youth was shot in his neighborhood. He has no trouble acknowledging the wrongness of the death. But then, like all the news accounts, he turns to the fact, repeated over and over, that the blacks had been on their way to look at a used car when they encountered the hostile mob of whites. The explanation is right before him but, "Yeah," he says, still shaking his head, "yeah, but what were they *doing* there? They didn't belong."

14   Over the next few days, the television news is even more disturbing. Rows of screaming Italians lining the streets, most of them looking like

my relatives. I focus especially on one woman who resembles almost completely my mother: stocky but not fat, mid-seventies but well preserved, full face showing only minimal wrinkles, ample steel-gray hair neatly if rigidly coiffed in a modified beehive hairdo left over from the sixties. She shakes her fist at the camera, protesting the arrest of the Italian-American youths in the neighborhood and the incursion of more blacks into the neighborhood, protesting the shooting. I look a little nervously at my mother (the parent I resemble), but she has not even noticed the woman and stares impassively at the television.

15   What has Bensonhurst to do with what I teach today and write? Why did I need to write about this killing in Bensonhurst, but not in the manner of a news account or a statistical sociological analysis? Within days of hearing the news, I began to plan this essay, to tell the world what I knew, even though I was aware that I could publish the piece only someplace my parents or their neighbors would never see or hear about it. I sometimes think that I looked around from my baby carriage and decided that someday, the sooner the better, I would get out of Bensonhurst. Now, much to my surprise, Bensonhurst—the antipodes of the intellectual life I sought, the least interesting of places—had become a respectable intellectual topic. People would be willing to hear about Bensonhurst—and all by the dubious virtue of a racial killing in the streets.

16   The story as I would have to tell it would be to some extent a class narrative: about the difference between working class and upper middle class, dependence and a profession, Bensonhurst and a posh suburb. But I need to make it clear that I do not imagine myself as writing from a position of enormous self-satisfaction, or even enormous distance. You can take the girl out of Bensonhurst (that much is clear), but you may not be able to take Bensonhurst out of the girl. And upward mobility is not the essence of the story, though it is an important marker and symbol.

17   In Durham today, I live in a twelve-room house surrounded by an acre of trees. When I sit on my back deck on summer evenings, no houses are visible through the trees. I have a guaranteed income, teaching English at an excellent university, removed by my years of education from the fundamental economic and social conditions of Bensonhurst. The one time my mother ever expressed pleasure at my work was when I got tenure, what my father still calls, with no irony intended, "ten years." "What does that mean?" my mother asked when she heard the news. Then she reached back into her experience as a garment worker, subject to periodic layoffs. "Does it mean they can't fire you just for nothing and can't lay you off?" When I said that was exactly what it means, she said, "Very good. Congratulations. That's *wonderful*." I was free from the *padrones*, from the network of petty anxieties that had formed, in large part, her very existence. Of course, I wasn't really free of petty anxieties: would my salary increase keep pace with my colleagues', how would my office compare, would this essay be accepted for

publication, am I happy? The line between these worries and my mother's is the line between the working class and the upper middle class.

18   But getting out of Bensonhurst never meant to me a big house, or nice clothes, or a large income. And it never meant feeling good about looking down on what I left behind or hiding my background. Getting out of Bensonhurst meant freedom—to experiment, to grow, to change. It also meant knowledge in some grand, abstract way. All the material possessions I have acquired, I acquired simply along the way—and for the first twelve years after I left Bensonhurst, I chose to acquire almost nothing at all. Now, as I write about the neighborhood, I recognize that although I've come far in physical and material distance, the emotional distance is harder to gauge. Bensonhurst has everything to do with who I am and even with what I write. Occasionally I get reminded of my roots, of their simultaneously choking and nutritive power.

19   Scene one: It's after a lecture at Duke, given by a visiting professor from Princeton. The lecture was long and a little dull and—bad luck—I had agreed to be one of the people having dinner with the lecturer afterward. We settle into our table at the restaurant: this man, me, the head of the comparative literature program (also a professor of German), and a couple I like who teach French, the husband at my university, the wife at one nearby. The conversation is sluggish, as it often is when a stranger, like the visiting professor, has to be assimilated into a group, so I ask the visitor from Princeton a question to personalize things a bit. "How did you get interested in what you do? What made you become a professor of German?" The man gets going and begins talking about how it was really unlikely that he, a nice Jewish boy from Bensonhurst, would have chosen, in the mid-fifties, to study German. Unlikely indeed.

20   I remember seeing *Judgment at Nuremberg* in a local movie theater and having a woman in the row in back of me get hysterical when some clips of a concentration camp were shown. "My God," she screamed in a European accent, "look at what they did. Murderers, MURDERERS!"—and she had to be supported out by her family. I couldn't see, in the dark, whether her arm bore the neatly tattooed numbers that the arms of some of my classmates' parents did—and that always affected me with a thrill of horror. Ten years older than me, this man had lived more directly through those feelings, lived with and *among* those feelings. The first chance he got, he raced to study in Germany. I myself have twice chosen not to visit Germany, but I understand his impulse to identify with the Other as a way of getting out of the neighborhood.

21   At the dinner, the memory about the movie pops into my mind but I pick up instead on the Bensonhurst—I'm also from there, but Italian American. Like a flash, he asks something I haven't been asked in years: Where did I go to high school and (a more common question) what was my maiden name? I went to Lafayette High School, I say, and my name was De Marco. Everything changes: his facial expression, his posture, his accent, his voice. "Soo, Dee Maw-ko," he says, "dun anything wrong at

school today—got enny pink slips? Wanna meet me later at the park or maybe bye the Baye?" When I laugh, recognizing the stereotype that Italians get pink slips for misconduct at school and the notorious chemistry between Italian women and Jewish men, he says, back in his Princetonian voice: "My God, for a minute I felt like I was turning into a werewolf."

22   It's odd that although I can remember almost nothing else about this man—his face, his body type, even his name—I remember this lapse into his "real self" with enormous vividness. I am especially struck by how easily he was able to slip into the old, generic Brooklyn accent. I myself have no memory of ever speaking in that accent, though I also have no memory of trying not to speak it, except for teaching myself, carefully, to say "oil" rather than "earl."

23   But the surprises aren't over. The female French professor, whom I have known for at least five years, reveals for the first time that she is also from the neighborhood, though she lived across the other side of Kings Highway, went to a different, more elite high school, and was Irish American. Three of six professors, sitting at an eclectic vegetarian restaurant in Durham, all from Bensonhurst—a neighborhood where (I swear) you couldn't get the *New York Times* at any of the local stores.

24   Scene two: I still live in Bensonhurst. I'm waiting for my parents to return from a conference at my school, where they've been summoned to discuss my transition from elementary to junior high school. I am already a full year younger than any of my classmates, having skipped a grade, a not uncommon occurrence for "gifted" youngsters. Now the school is worried about putting me in an accelerated track through junior high, since that would make me two years younger. A compromise was reached: I would be put in a special program for gifted children, but one that took three, not two, years. It sounds okay.

25   Three years later, another wait. My parents have gone to school this time to make another decision. Lafayette High School has three tracks: academic, for potentially college-bound kids; secretarial, mostly for Italian-American girls or girls with low aptitude-test scores (the high school is de facto segregated, so none of the tracks is as yet racially coded, though they are coded by ethnic group and gender); and vocational, mostly for boys with the same attributes, ethnic or intellectual. Although my scores are superb, the guidance counselor has recommended the secretarial track; when I protested, the conference with my parents was arranged. My mother's preference is clear: the secretarial track—college is for boys; I will need to make a "good living" until I marry and have children. My father also prefers the secretarial track, but he wavers, half proud of my aberrantly high scores, half worried. I press the attack, saying that if I were Jewish I would have been placed, without question, in the academic track. I tell him I have sneaked a peek at my files and know that my IQ is at genius level. I am allowed to insist on the change into the academic track.

26   What I did, and I was ashamed of it even then, was to play upon my father's competitive feelings with Jews: his daughter could and should be as good as theirs. In the bank where he was a messenger, and at the insurance company where he worked in the mailroom, my father worked with Jews, who were almost always his immediate supervisors. Several times, my father was offered the supervisory job but turned it down after long conversations with my mother about the dangers of making a change, the difficulty of giving orders to friends. After her work in a local garment shop, after cooking dinner and washing the floor each night, my mother often did piecework making bows; sometimes I would help her for fun, but it *wasn't* fun, and I was free to stop while she continued for long, tedious hours to increase the family income. Once a week, her part-time boss, Dave, would come by to pick up the boxes of bows. Short, round, with his shirttails sloppily tucked into his pants and a cigar almost always dangling from his lips, Dave was a stereotyped Jew but also, my parents always said, a nice guy, a decent man.

27   Years later, similar choices come up, and I show the same assertiveness I showed with my father, the same ability to deal for survival, but tinged with Bensonhurst caution. Where will I go to college? Not to Brooklyn College, the flagship of the city system—I know that, but don't press the invitations I have received to apply to prestigious schools outside of New York. The choice comes down to two: Barnard, which gives me a full scholarship, minus five hundred dollars a year that all scholarship students are expected to contribute from summer earnings, or New York University, which offers me one thousand dollars above tuition as a bribe. I waver. My parents stand firm: they are already losing money by letting me go to college; I owe it to the family to contribute the extra thousand dollars plus my summer earnings. Besides, my mother adds, harping on a favorite theme, there are no boys at Barnard; at NYU I'm more likely to meet someone to marry. I go to NYU and do marry in my senior year, but he is someone I didn't meet at college. I was secretly relieved, I now think (though at the time I thought I was just placating my parents' conventionality), to be out of the marriage sweepstakes.

28   The first boy who ever asked me for a date was Robert Lubitz, in eighth grade: tall and skinny to my average height and teenage chubbiness. I turned him down, thinking we would make a ridiculous couple. Day after day, I cast my eyes at stylish Juliano, the class cutup; day after day, I captivated Robert Lubitz. Occasionally, one of my brother's Italian-American friends would ask me out, and I would go, often to ROTC dances. My specialty was making political remarks so shocking that the guys rarely asked me again. After a while I recognized destiny: the Jewish man was a passport out of Bensonhurst. I of course did marry a Jewish man, who gave me my freedom and, very important, helped remove me from the expectations of Bensonhurst. Though raised in a largely Jewish section of Brooklyn, he had gone to college in Ohio and knew how important it was, as he put it, "to get past the Brooklyn Bridge." We

met on neutral ground, in Central Park, at a performance of Shakespeare. The Jewish-Italian marriage is a common enough catastrophe in Bensonhurst for my parents to have accepted, even welcomed, mine—though my parents continued to treat my husband like an outsider for the first twenty years ("Now Marianna. Here's what's going on with your brother. But don't tell-a you husband").

29   Along the way I make other choices, more fully marked by Bensonhurst cautiousness. I am attracted to journalism or the arts as careers, but the prospects for income seem iffy. I choose instead to imagine myself as a teacher. Only the availability of NDEA fellowships when I graduate, with their generous terms, propels me from high school teaching (a thought I never much relished) to college teaching (which seems like a brave new world). Within the college teaching profession, I choose offbeat specializations: the novel, interdisciplinary approaches (not something clear and clubby like Milton or the eighteenth century). Eventually I write the book I like best about primitive others as they figure within Western obsessions: my identification with "the Other," my sense of being "Other," surfaces at last. I avoid all mentoring structures for a long time but accept aid when it comes to me on the basis of what I perceive to be merit. I'm still, deep down, Italian-American Bensonhurst, though by this time I'm a lot of other things as well.

30   Scene three: In the summer of 1988, a little more than a year before the shooting in Bensonhurst, my father woke up trembling and in what appeared to be a fit. Hospitalization revealed that he had a pocket of blood on his brain, a frequent consequence of falls for older people. About a year earlier, I had stayed home, using my children as an excuse, when my aunt, my father's much loved sister died, missing her funeral; only now does my mother tell me how much my father resented my taking his suggestion that I stay home. Now, confronted with what is described as brain surgery but turns out to be less dramatic than it sounds, I fly home immediately.

31   My brother drives three hours back and forth from New Jersey every day to chauffeur me and my mother to the hospital: he is being a fine Italian-American son. For the first time in years, we have long conversations alone. He is two years older than I am, a chemical engineer who has also left the neighborhood but has remained closer to its values, with a suburban, Republican inflection. He talks a lot about New York, saying that (except for neighborhoods like Bensonhurst) it's a "third-world city now." It's the summer of the Tawana Brawley incident, when Brawley accused white men of abducting her and smearing racial slurs on her body with her own excrement. My brother is filled with dislike for Al Sharpton and Brawley's other vocal supporters in the black community—not because they're black, he says, but because they're troublemakers, stirring things up. The city is drenched in racial hatred that makes itself felt in the halls of the hospital: Italians and Jews in the beds and as doctors; blacks as nurses and orderlies.

32   This is the first time since I left New York in 1975 that I have visited Brooklyn without once getting into Manhattan. It's the first time I have spent several days alone with my mother, living in her apartment in Bensonhurst. My every move is scrutinized and commented on. I feel like I am going to go crazy.

33   Finally, it's clear that my father is going to be fine, and I can go home. She insists on accompanying me to the travel agent to get my ticket for home, even though I really want to be alone. The agency (a Mafia front?) has no one who knows how to ticket me for the exotic destination of North Carolina and no computer for doing so. The one person who can perform this feat by hand is out. I have to kill time for an hour and suggest to my mother that she go home, to be there for my brother when he arrives from Jersey. We stop in a Pork Store, where I buy a stash of cheeses, sausages, and other delicacies unavailable in Durham. My mother walks home with the shopping bags, and I'm on my own.

34   More than anything I want a kind of *sorbetto* or ice I remember from my childhood, a *cremolata*, almond-vanilla-flavored with large chunks of nuts. I pop into the local bakery (at the unlikely hour of 11 A.M.) and ask for a *cremolata*, usually eaten after dinner. The woman—a younger version of my mother—refuses: they haven't made a fresh ice yet, and what's left from the day before is too icy, no good. I explain that I'm about to get on a plane for North Carolina and want that ice, good or not. But she has her standards and holds her ground, even though North Carolina has about the same status in her mind as Timbuktoo and she knows I will be banished, perhaps forever, from the land of *cremolata*.

35   Then, while I'm taking a walk, enjoying my solitude, I have another idea. On the block behind my parents' house, there's a club for men, for men from a particular town or region in Italy: six or seven tables, some on the sidewalk beneath a garish red, green, and white sign; no women allowed or welcome unless they're with men, and no women at all during the day when the real business of the club—a game of cards for old men—is in progress. Still, I know that inside the club would be coffee and a *cremolata* ice. I'm thirty-eight, well dressed, very respectable looking; I know what I want. I also know I'm not supposed to enter that club. I enter anyway, asking the teenage boy behind the counter firmly, in my most professional tones, for a *cremolata* ice. Dazzled, he complies immediately. The old men at the card table have been staring at this scene, unable to place me exactly, though my facial type is familiar. Finally, a few old men's hisses pierce the air. "*Strega*," I hear as I leave, "*mala strega*"—"witch," or "brazen whore." I have been in Bensonhurst less than a week, but I have managed to reproduce, on my final day there for this visit, the conditions of my youth. Knowing the rules, I have broken them. I shake hands with my discreetly rebellious past, still an outsider walking through the neighborhood, marked and insulted—though unlikely to be shot.

Points for Review and Discussion

1.   Italian Americans in Bensonhurst, says the author, see blacks walking in their neighborhood as an "invasion." What in her opinion causes this perception?
2.   Torgovnick describes her past as "discreetly rebellious" (¶ 35). Describe her rebellions and explain why they qualify as discreet.

◆◇ Questions for Writing

1.   Torgovnick asserts that "upward mobility is not the essence of [her] story, though it is an important marker and symbol" (¶ 16). Choose a passage in which the author's upward mobility seems to you a centrally important influence on her behavior and feelings, and explain your choice.
2.   Choose a second passage in this essay in which matters of class seem to you less important influences on behavior and feelings than gender or ethnicity. Again: explain your choice.
3.   After describing the Bensonhurst sign advertising that the local Roman Catholic church saves the community a million dollars in taxes, Torgovnick notes that she and her husband laugh at its "crass level," but nevertheless "also understand exactly the values it represents" (¶ 6). What are those values? To what degree are they class values? On what grounds do they warrant respect?
4.   "I detested the racial killing, but I also understood it. Those streets, which should be public property available to all, belong to the neighborhood" (¶ 9). These sentences express conflicting loyalties. Spell out as clearly as you can, in a short paper, the nature and substance of the conflicts.

The Achievement of Desire
Richard Rodriguez

In telling their life stories, people who succeed often create an impression of themselves as Super-Beings. Never were they in doubt about where they were going, what they wanted, why they wanted it. Never did they ask themselves whether the cost might be too high. So much confidence, so much clarity: how could they be so self-assured?

The story of ascent that's told in Richard Rodriguez's *Hunger of Memory*, an autobiographical memoir, is of a different kind. It shows us a Chicano youth who's ambitious—but also sensitive, and often puzzled and uncertain. Not until the start of his fourth decade does he begin to understand what his ascent means and how to avoid falsely exaggerating or falsely minimizing its true human significance.

Rodriguez earned a doctorate in English at Stanford, went on to teach at Yale. As a writer he has entered many recent controversies involving minority groups, including the one about affirmative action. (He opposes affirmative action.) The PBS MacNeil-Lehrer news show includes Rodriguez on its roster of regular "essayists."

In the selection below Rodriguez comes to grips with a pivotally important discovery about the relation between himself and his parents.

1   The boy who first entered a classroom barely able to speak English, twenty years later concluded his studies in the stately quiet of the reading room in the British Museum. Thus with one sentence I can summarize my academic career. It will be harder to summarize what sort of life connects the boy to the man.

2   With every award, each graduation from one level of education to the next, people I'd meet would congratulate me. Their refrain always the same: "Your parents must be very proud." Sometimes then they'd ask me how I managed it—my "success." (How?) After a while, I had several quick answers to give in reply. I'd admit, for one thing, that I went to an excellent grammar school. (My earliest teachers, the nuns, made my success their ambition.) And my brother and both my sisters were very good students. (They often brought home the shiny school trophies I came to want.) And my mother and father always encouraged me. (At every graduation they were behind the stunning flash of the camera when I turned to look at the crowd.)

3   As important as these factors were, however, they account inadequately for my academic advance. Nor do they suggest what an odd success I managed. For although I was a very good student, I was also a very

---

From Richard Rodriguez, *Hunger of Memory* (1983).

bad student. I was a "scholarship boy," a certain kind of scholarship boy. Always successful, I was always unconfident. Exhilarated by my progress. Sad. I became the prized student—anxious and eager to learn. Too eager, too anxious—an imitative and unoriginal pupil. My brother and two sisters enjoyed the advantages I did, and they grew to be as successful as I, but none of them ever seemed so anxious about their schooling. A second-grade student, I was the one who came home and corrected the "simple" grammatical mistakes of our parents. ("Two negatives make a positive.") Proudly I announced—to my family's startled silence—that a teacher had said I was losing all trace of a Spanish accent. I was oddly annoyed when I was unable to get parental help with a homework assignment. The night my father tried to help me with an arithmetic exercise, he kept reading the instructions, each time more deliberately, until I pried the textbook out of his hands, saying, "I'll try to figure it out some more by myself."

4   When I reached the third grade, I outgrew such behavior. I became more tactful, careful to keep separate the two very different worlds of my day. But then, with ever-increasing intensity, I devoted myself to my studies. I became bookish, puzzling to all my family. Ambition set me apart. When my brother saw me struggling home with stacks of library books, he would laugh, shouting: "Hey, Four Eyes!" My father opened a closet one day and was startled to find me inside, reading a novel. My mother would find me reading when I was supposed to be asleep or helping around the house or playing outside. In a voice angry or worried or just curious, she'd ask: "What do you see in your books?" It became the family's joke. When I was called and wouldn't reply, someone would say I must be hiding under my bed with a book.

5   (How did I manage my success?)

6   What I am about to say to you has taken me more than twenty years to admit: *A primary reason for my success in the classroom was that I couldn't forget that schooling was changing me and separating me from the life I enjoyed before becoming a student.* That simple realization! For years I never spoke to anyone about it. Never mentioned a thing to my family or my teachers or classmates. From a very early age, I understood enough, just enough about my classroom experiences to keep what I knew repressed, hidden beneath layers of embarrassment. Not until my last months as a graduate student, nearly thirty years old, was it possible for me to think much about the reasons for my academic success. Only then. At the end of my schooling, I needed to determine how far I had moved from my past. The adult finally confronted, and now must publicly say, what the child shuddered from knowing and could never admit to himself or to those many faces that smiled at his every success. ("Your parents must be very proud. . . .")

7   At the end, in the British Museum (too distracted to finish my dissertation) for weeks I read, speed-read, books by modern educational theorists, only to find infrequent and slight mention of students like me.

(Much more is written about the more typical case, the lower-class student who barely is helped by his schooling.) Then one day, leafing through Richard Hoggart's *The Uses of Literacy*, I found, in his description of the scholarship boy, myself. For the first time I realized that there were other students like me, and so I was able to frame the meaning of my academic success, its consequent price—the loss.

8   Hoggart's description is distinguished, at least initially, by deep understanding. What he grasps very well is that the scholarship boy must move between environments, his home and the classroom, which are at cultural extremes, opposed. With his family, the boy has the intense pleasure of intimacy, the family's consolation in feeling public alienation. Lavish emotions texture home life. *Then*, at school, the instruction bids him to trust lonely reason primarily. Immediate needs set the pace of his parents' lives. From his mother and father the boy learns to trust spontaneity and nonrational ways of knowing. *Then*, at school, there is mental calm. Teachers emphasize the value of a reflectiveness that opens a space between thinking and immediate action.

9   Years of schooling must pass before the boy will be able to sketch the cultural differences in his day as abstractly as this. But he senses those differences early. Perhaps as early as the night he brings home an assignment from school and finds the house too noisy for study.

10   He has to be more and more alone, if he is going to "get on." He will have, probably unconsciously, to oppose the ethos of the hearth, the intense gregariousness of the working-class family group. Since everything centres upon the living-room, there is unlikely to be a room of his own; the bedrooms are cold and inhospitable, and to warm them or the front room, if there is one, would not only be expensive, but would require an imaginative leap—out of the tradition—which most families are not capable of making. There is a corner of the living-room table. On the other side Mother is ironing, the wireless is on, someone is singing a snatch of song or Father says intermittently whatever comes into his head. The boy has to cut himself off mentally, so as to do his homework, as well as he can.*

11   The next day, the lesson is as apparent at school. There are even rows of desks. Discussion is ordered. The boy must rehearse his thoughts and raise his hand before speaking out in a loud voice to an audience of classmates. And there is time enough, and silence, to think about ideas (big ideas) never considered at home by his parents.

12   Not for the working-class child alone is adjustment to the classroom difficult. Good schooling requires that any student alter early childhood habits. But the working-class child is usually least prepared for the

---

* All quotations in this chapter are from Richard Hoggart, *The Uses of Literacy* (London: Chatto and Windus, 1957), ch. 10.

change. And, unlike many middle-class children, he goes home and sees in his parents a way of life not only different but starkly opposed to that of the classroom. (He enters the house and hears his parents talking in ways his teachers discourage.)

13   Without extraordinary determination and the great assistance of others—at home and at school—there is little chance for success. Typically most working-class children are barely changed by the classroom. The exception succeeds. The relative few become scholarship students. Of these, Richard Hoggart estimates, most manage a fairly graceful transition. Somehow they learn to live in the two very different worlds of their day. There are some others, however, those Hoggart pejoratively terms "scholarship boys," for whom success comes with special anxiety. Scholarship boy: good student, troubled son. The child is "moderately endowed," intellectually mediocre, Hoggart supposes—though it may be more pertinent to note the special qualities of temperament in the child. High-strung child. Brooding. Sensitive. Haunted by the knowledge that one *chooses* to become a student. (Education is not an inevitable or natural step in growing up.) Here is a child who cannot forget that his academic success distances him from a life he loved, even from his own memory of himself.

14   Initially, he wavers, balances allegiance. ("The boy is himself [until he reaches, say, the upper forms] very much of *both* the worlds of home and school. He is enormously obedient to the dictates of the world of school, but emotionally still strongly wants to continue as part of the family circle.") Gradually, necessarily, the balance is lost. The boy needs to spend more and more time studying, each night enclosing himself in the silence permitted and required by intense concentration. He takes his first step toward academic success, away from his family.

15   From the very first days, through the years following, it will be with his parents—the figures of lost authority, the persons toward whom he feels deepest love—that the change will be most powerfully measured. A separation will unravel between them. Advancing in his studies, the boy notices that his mother and father have not changed as much as he. Rather, when he sees them, they often remind him of the person he once was and the life he earlier shared with them. He realizes what some Romantics also know when they praise the working class for the capacity for human closeness, qualities of passion and spontaneity, that the rest of us experience in like measure only in the earliest part of our youth. For the Romantic, this doesn't make working-class life childish. Working-class life challenges precisely because it is an *adult* way of life.

16   The scholarship boy reaches a different conclusion. He cannot afford to admire his parents. (How could he and still pursue such a contrary life?) He permits himself embarrassment at their lack of education. And to evade nostalgia for the life he has lost, he concentrates on the benefits education will bestow upon him. He becomes especially ambitious. Without the support of old certainties and consolations, almost mechan-

ically, he assumes the procedures and doctrines of the classroom. The kind of allegiance the young student might have given his mother and father only days earlier, he transfers to the teacher, the new figure of authority. "[The scholarship boy] tends to make a father-figure of his formmaster," Hoggart observes.

17   But Hoggart's calm prose only makes me recall the urgency with which I came to idolize my grammar school teachers. I began by imitating their accents, using their diction, trusting their every direction. The very first facts they dispensed, I grasped with awe. Any book they told me to read, I read—then waited for them to tell me which books I enjoyed. Their every casual opinion I came to adopt and to trumpet when I returned home. I stayed after school "to help"—to get my teacher's undivided attention. It was the nun's encouragement that mattered most to me. (She understood exactly what—my parents never seemed to appraise so well—all my achievements entailed.) Memory gently caressed each word of praise bestowed in the classroom so that compliments teachers paid me years ago come quickly to mind even today.

18   The enthusiasm I felt in second-grade classes I flaunted before both my parents. The docile, obedient student came home a shrill and precocious son who insisted on correcting and teaching his parents with the remark: "My teacher told us. . . ."

19   I intended to hurt my mother and father. I was still angry at them for having encouraged me toward classroom English. But gradually this anger was exhausted, replaced by guilt as school grew more and more attractive to me. I grew increasingly successful, a talkative student. My hand was raised in the classroom; I yearned to answer any question. At home, life was less noisy than it had been. (I spoke to classmates and teachers more often each day than to family members.) Quiet at home, I sat with my papers for hours each night. I never forgot that schooling had irretrievably changed my family's life. That knowledge, however, did not weaken ambition. Instead, it strengthened resolve. Those times I remembered the loss of my past with regret, I quickly reminded myself of all the things my teachers could give me. (They could make me an educated man.) I tightened my grip on pencil and books. I evaded nostalgia. Tried hard to forget. But one does not forget by trying to forget. One only remembers. I remembered too well that education had changed my family's life. I would not have become a scholarship boy had I not so often remembered.

20   Once she was sure that her children knew English, my mother would tell us, "You should keep up your Spanish." Voices playfully groaned in response. '¡Pochos!' my mother would tease. I listened silently.

21   After a while, I grew more calm at home. I developed tact. A fourth-grade student, I was no longer the show-off in front of my parents. I became a conventionally dutiful son, politely affectionate, cheerful enough, even—for reasons beyond choosing—my father's favorite. And

much about my family life was easy then, comfortable, happy in the rhythm of our living together: hearing my father getting ready for work; eating the breakfast my mother had made me; looking up from a novel to hear my brother or one of my sisters playing with friends in the backyard; in winter, coming upon the house all lighted up after dark.

22   But withheld from my mother and father was any mention of what most mattered to me: the extraordinary experience of first-learning. Late afternoon: In the midst of preparing dinner, my mother would come up behind me while I was trying to read. Her head just over mine, her breath warmly scented with food. "What are you reading?" Or, "Tell me all about your new courses." I would barely respond, "Just the usual things, nothing special." (A half smile, then silence. Her head moving back in the silence. Silence! Instead of the flood of intimate sounds that had once flowed smoothly between us, there was this silence.) After dinner, I would rush to a bedroom with papers and books. As often as possible, I resisted parental pleas to "save lights" by coming to the kitchen to work. I kept so much, so often, to myself. Sad. Enthusiastic. Troubled by the excitement of coming upon new ideas. Eager. Fascinated by the promising texture of a brand-new book. I hoarded the pleasures of learning. Alone for hours. Enthralled. Nervous. I rarely looked away from my books—or back on my memories. Nights when relatives visited and the front rooms were warmed by Spanish sounds, I slipped quietly out of the house.

23   It mattered that education was changing me. It never ceased to matter. My brother and sisters would giggle at our mother's mispronounced words. They'd correct her gently. My mother laughed girlishly one night, trying not to pronounce *sheep* as *ship*. From a distance I listened sullenly. From that distance, pretending not to notice on another occasion, I saw my father looking at the title pages of my library books. That was the scene on my mind when I walked home with a fourth-grade companion and heard him say that his parents read to him every night. (A strange-sounding book—*Winnie the Pooh*.) Immediately, I wanted to know, "What is it like?" My companion, however, thought I wanted to know about the plot of the book. Another day, my mother surprised me by asking for a "nice" book to read. "Something not too hard you think I might like." Carefully I chose one, Willa Cather's *My Ántonia*. But when, several weeks later, I happened to see it next to her bed unread except for the first few pages, I was furious and suddenly wanted to cry. I grabbed up the book and took it back to my room and placed it in its place, alphabetically on my shelf.

24   "Your parents must be very proud of you." People began to say that to me about the time I was in sixth grade. To answer affirmatively, I'd smile. Shyly I'd smile, never betraying my sense of the irony: I was not proud of my mother and father. I was embarrassed by their lack of education. It was not that I ever thought they were stupid, though stupidly I

took for granted their enormous native intelligence. Simply, what mattered to me was that they were not like my teachers.

25   But, "Why didn't you tell us about the award?" my mother demanded, her frown weakened by pride. At the grammar school ceremony several weeks after, her eyes were brighter than the trophy I'd won. Pushing back the hair from my forehead, she whispered that I had "shown" the *gringos*. A few minutes later, I heard my father speak to my teacher and felt ashamed of his labored, accented words. Then guilty for the shame. I felt such contrary feelings. (There is no simple road-map through the heart of the scholarship boy.) My teacher was so soft-spoken and her words were edged sharp and clean. I admired her until it seemed to me that she spoke too carefully. Sensing that she was condescending to them, I became nervous. Resentful. Protective. I tried to move my parents away. "You both must be very proud of Richard," the nun said. They responded quickly. (They were proud.) "We are proud of all our children." Then this afterthought: "They sure didn't get their brains from us." They all laughed. I smiled.

26   The scholarship boy pleases most when he is young—the working-class child struggling for academic success. To his teachers, he offers great satisfaction; his success is their proudest achievement. Many other persons offer to help him. A businessman learns the boy's story and promises to underwrite part of the cost of his college education. A woman leaves him her entire library of several hundred books when she moves. His progress is featured in a newspaper article. Many people seem happy for him. They marvel. "How did you manage so fast?" From all sides, there is lavish praise and encouragement.

27   In his grammar school classroom, however, the boy already makes students around him uneasy. They scorn his desire to succeed. They scorn him for constantly wanting the teacher's attention and praise. "Kiss Ass," they call him when his hand swings up in response to every question he hears. Later, when he makes it to college, no one will mock him aloud. But he detects annoyance on the faces of some students and even some teachers who watch him. It puzzles him often. In college, then in graduate school, he behaves much as he always has. If anything is different about him it is that he dares to anticipate the successful conclusion of his studies. At last he feels that he belongs in the classroom, and this is exactly the source of the dissatisfaction he causes. To many persons around him, he appears too much the academic. There may be some things about him that recall his beginnings—his shabby clothes; his persistent poverty; or his dark skin (in those cases when it symbolizes his parents' disadvantaged condition)—but they only make clear how far he has moved from his past. He has used education to remake himself.

28   It bothers his fellow academics to face this. They will not say why exactly. (They sneer.) But their expectations become obvious when they are disappointed. They expect—they want—a student less changed by

his schooling. If the scholarship boy, from a past so distant from the classroom, could remain in some basic way unchanged, he would be able to prove that it is possible for anyone to become educated without basically changing from the person one was.

29   Here is no fabulous hero, no idealized scholar-worker. The scholarship boy does not straddle, cannot reconcile, the two great opposing cultures of his life. His success is unromantic and plain. He sits in the classroom and offers those sitting beside him no calming reassurance about their own lives. He sits in the seminar room—a man with brown skin, the son of working-class Mexican immigrant parents. (Addressing the professor at the head of the table, his voice catches with nervousness.) There is no trace of his parents' accent in his speech. Instead he approximates the accents of teachers and classmates. Coming from *him* those sounds seem suddenly odd. Odd too is the effect produced when *he* uses academic jargon—bubbles at the tip of his tongue: "*Topos* . . . negative capability . . . vegetation imagery in Shakespearean comedy." He lifts an opinion from Coleridge, takes something else from Frye or Empson or Leavis. He even repeats exactly his professor's earlier comment. All his ideas are clearly borrowed. He seems to have no thought of his own. He chatters while his listeners smile—their look one of disdain.

30   When he is older and thus when so little of the person he was survives, the scholarship boy makes only too apparent his profound lack of *self*-confidence. This is the conventional assessment that even Richard Hoggart repeats:

> [The scholarship boy] tends to over-stress the importance of examinations, of the piling-up of knowledge and of received opinions. He discovers a technique of apparent learning, of the acquiring of facts rather than of the handling and use of facts. He learns how to receive a purely literate education, one using only a small part of the personality and challenging only a limited area of his being. He begins to see life as a ladder, as a permanent examination with some praise and some further exhortation at each stage. He becomes an expert imbiber and doler-out; his competence will vary, but will rarely be accompanied by genuine enthusiasms. He rarely feels the reality of knowledge, of other men's thoughts and imaginings, on his own pulses . . . He has something of the blinkered pony about him. . . .

But this is criticism more accurate than fair. The scholarship boy is a very bad student. He is the great mimic; a collector of thoughts, not a thinker; the very last person in class who ever feels obliged to have an opinion of his own. In large part, however, the reason he is such a bad student is because he realizes more often and more acutely than most other students—than Hoggart himself—that education requires radical self-reformation. As a very young boy, regarding his parents, as he struggles with an early homework assignment, he knows this too well. That is why he lacks self-assurance. He does not forget that the classroom is responsible for remaking him. He relies on his teacher, depends on all that he hears in the classroom and reads in his books. He becomes in every obvious way the worst student, a dummy mouthing the opinions of others. But he would not be so bad—nor would he become so successful, a *scholarship* boy—if he did not accurately perceive that the best synonym for primary "education" is "imitation."

31 Those who would take seriously the boy's success—and his failure—would be forced to realize how great is the change any academic undergoes, how far one must move from one's past. It is easiest to ignore such considerations. So little is said about the scholarship boy in pages and pages of educational literature. Nothing is said of the silence that comes to separate the boy from his parents. Instead, one hears proposals for increasing the self-esteem of students and encouraging early intellectual independence. Paragraphs glitter with a constellation of terms like *creativity* and *originality*. (Ignored altogether is the function of imitation in a student's life.) Radical educationists meanwhile complain that ghetto schools "oppress" students by trying to mold them, stifling native characteristics. The truer critique would be just the reverse: not that schools change ghetto students too much, but that while they might promote the occasional scholarship student, they change most students barely at all.

32 From the story of the scholarship boy there is no specific pedagogy to glean. There is, however, a much larger lesson. His story makes clear that education is a long, unglamorous, even demeaning process—*a nurturing never natural to the person one was before one entered a classroom*. At once different from most other students, the scholarship boy is also the archetypal "good student." He exaggerates the difficulty of being a student, but his exaggeration reveals a general predicament. Others are changed by their schooling as much as he. They too must re-form themselves. They must develop the skill of memory long before they become truly critical thinkers. And when they read Plato for the first several times, it will be with awe more than deep comprehension.

33 The impact of schooling on the scholarship boy is only more apparent to the boy himself and to others. Finally, although he may be laughable—a blinkered pony—the boy will not let his critics forget their own change. He ends up too much like them. When he speaks, they hear themselves echoed. In his pedantry, they trace their own. His ambitions are theirs. If his failure were singular, they might readily pity him. But he is more troubling than that. They would not scorn him if this were not so.

34 Like me, Hoggart's imagined scholarship boy spends most of his years in the classroom afraid to long for his past. Only at the very end of his schooling does the boy-man become nostalgic. In this sudden change of heart, Richard Hoggart notes:

> He longs for the membership he lost, "he pines for some Nameless Eden where he never was." The nostalgia is the stronger and the more ambiguous because he is really "in quest of his own absconded self yet scared to

find it." He both wants to go back and yet thinks he has gone beyond his class, feels himself weighted with knowledge of his own and their situation, which hereafter forbids him the simpler pleasures of his father and mother.

According to Hoggart, the scholarship boy grows nostalgic because he remains the uncertain scholar, bright enough to have moved from his past, yet unable to feel easy, a part of a community of academics.

35   This analysis, however, only partially suggests what happened to me in my last year as a graduate student. When I traveled to London to write a dissertation on English Renaissance literature, I was finally confident of membership in a "community of scholars." But the pleasure that confidence gave me faded rapidly. After only two or three months in the reading room of the British Museum, it became clear that I had joined a lonely community. Around me each day were dour faces eclipsed by large piles of books. There were the regulars, like the old couple who arrived every morning, each holding a loop of the shopping bag which contained all their notes. And there was the historian who chattered madly to herself. ("Oh dear! Oh! Now, what's this? What? Oh, my!") There were also the faces of young men and women worn by long study. And everywhere eyes turned away the moment our glance accidentally met. Some persons I sat beside day after day, yet we passed silently at the end of the day, strangers. Still, we were united by a common respect for the written word and for scholarship. We did form a union, though one in which we remained distant from one another.

36   More profound and unsettling was the bond I recognized with those writers whose books I consulted. Whenever I opened a text that hadn't been used for years, I realized that my special interests and skills united me to a mere handful of academics. We formed an exclusive—eccentric!—society, separated from others who would never care or be able to share our concerns. (The pages I turned were stiff like layers of dead skin.) I began to wonder: Who, beside my dissertation director and a few faculty members, would ever read what I wrote? And: Was my dissertation much more than an act of social withdrawal? These questions went unanswered in the silence of the Museum reading room. They remained to trouble me after I'd leave the library each afternoon and feel myself shy—unsteady, speaking simple sentences at the grocer's or the butcher's on my way back to my bed-sitter.

37   Meanwhile my file cards accumulated. A professional, I knew exactly how to search a book for pertinent information. I could quickly assess and summarize the usability of the many books I consulted. But whenever I started to write, I knew too much (and not enough) to be able to write anything but sentences that were overly cautious, timid, strained brittle under the heavy weight of footnotes and qualifications. I seemed unable to dare a passionate statement. I felt drawn by professionalism to the edge of sterility, capable of no more than pedantic, lifeless, unassailable prose.

38   *Then* nostalgia began.

39   After years spent unwilling to admit its attractions, I gestured nostalgically toward the past. I yearned for that time when I had not been so alone. I became impatient with books. I wanted experience more immediate. I feared the library's silence. I silently scorned the gray, timid faces around me. I grew to hate the growing pages of my dissertation on genre and Renaissance literature. (In my mind I heard relatives laughing as they tried to make sense of its title.) I wanted something—I couldn't say exactly what. I told myself that I wanted a more passionate life. And a life less thoughtful. And above all, I wanted to be less alone. One day I heard some Spanish academics whispering back and forth to each other, and their sounds seemed ghostly voices recalling my life. Yearning became preoccupation then. Boyhood memories beckoned, flooded my mind. (Laughing intimate voices. Bounding up the front steps of the porch. A sudden embrace inside the door.)

40   For weeks after, I turned to books by educational experts. I needed to learn how far I had moved from my past—to determine how fast I would be able to recover something of it once again. But I found little. Only a chapter in a book by Richard Hoggart . . . I left the reading room and the circle of faces.

41   I came home. After the year in England, I spent three summer months living with my mother and father, relieved by how easy it was to be home. It no longer seemed very important to me that we had little to say. I felt easy sitting and eating and walking with them. I watched them, nevertheless, looking for evidence of those elastic, sturdy strands that bind generations in a web of inheritance. I thought as I watched my mother one night: Of course a friend had been right when she told me that I gestured and laughed just like my mother. Another time I saw for myself: My father's eyes were much like my own, constantly watchful.

42   But after the early relief, this return, came suspicion, nagging until I realized that I had not neatly sidestepped the impact of schooling. My desire to do so was precisely the measure of how much I remained an academic. *Negatively* (for that is how this idea first occurred to me): My need to think so much and so abstractly about my parents and our relationship was in itself an indication of my long education. My father and mother did not pass their time thinking about the cultural meanings of their experience. It was I who described their daily lives with airy ideas. And yet, *positively:* The ability to consider experience so abstractly allowed me to shape into desire what would otherwise have remained indefinite, meaningless longing in the British Museum. If, because of my schooling, I had grown culturally separated from my parents, my education finally had given me ways of speaking and caring about that fact.

43   My best teachers in college and graduate school, years before, had tried to prepare me for this conclusion, I think, when they discussed texts of aristocratic pastoral literature. Faithfully, I wrote down all that

they said. I memorized it: "The praise of the unlettered by the highly educated is one of the primary themes of 'elitist' literature." But, "the importance of the praise given the unsolitary, richly passionate and spontaneous life is that it simultaneously reflects the value of a reflective life." I heard it all. But there was no way for any of it to mean very much to me. I was a scholarship boy at the time, busily laddering my way up the rungs of education. To pass an examination, I copied down exactly what my teachers told me. It would require many more years of schooling (an inevitable miseducation) in which I came to trust the silence of reading and the habit of abstracting from immediate experience—moving away from a life of closeness and immediacy I remembered with my parents, growing older—before I turned unafraid to desire the past, and thereby achieved what had eluded me for so long—the end of education.

Points for Review and Discussion

1. In educational literature, Rodriguez writes, nothing is said about "the silence that comes to separate the scholarship boy from his parents" (¶ 31). Summarize Rodriguez's reasons for believing that this silence is crucially important.
2. Richard Hoggart's *The Uses of Literacy* was an important moment of awakening in Rodriguez's life. To what did this book awaken him?

•◦ Questions for Writing

1. Rodriguez speaks repeatedly of the guilt he felt toward his parents (¶ 19, 25, etc.). What causes this guilt? Does it strike you as a genuine or as an invented feeling? Explain your answer.
2. "Working-class life challenges precisely because it is an *adult* way of life" (¶ 15). Explain this assertion as clearly as you can. Whom does working-class life challenge? When and why? What does meeting this challenge do for a human being?
3. At the end of "The Achievement of Desire" Rodriguez describes the negative and positive impact of his schooling. State that impact in your own words, and write an essay comparing and contrasting the effects of your schooling on yourself with the effects Rodriguez describes.

Forum on the Responsibility of Intellectuals
Anthony Appiah, Henry Louis Gates Jr., bell hooks, Glenn Loury, Eugene Rivers, and Cornel West

When people who have moved up from one class to another are told they should extend a hand to those they've left behind, they've been known to turn resentful or angry. *Why me? Everybody has the same chance in life. Why am I responsible for other people's failures?* Behind this response lies the belief that, in a society that prizes individualism, successful people are under no obligation to help anybody except, perhaps, members of their own immediate families.

In 1993 a series of forums at Harvard's John F. Kennedy School of Government posed a challenge to this way of thinking. Eugene Rivers, pastor of an African American community church near Boston, convened a group of the country's most successful and best-placed black intellectuals, and asked them to face the following question: "What is the Responsibility of Black Intellectuals in the Age of Crack?"

In addition to Rivers himself, the panelists included Henry Louis Gates, director of the W. E. B. Du Bois Institute at Harvard, Glenn Loury, professor of economics at Boston University, bell hooks, professor of women's studies at City College of New York, and Anthony Appiah, professor of African-American studies at Harvard. The following are excerpts from that discussion.

1   EUGENE RIVERS: I would like first to thank God for this opportunity to engage in a public discussion of some issues which are very *pressing* for a growing number of African-American people who are suffering in our inner-cities. And I would like to thank Professor Gates, the DuBois Institute, and the African-American Studies department, and Anthony Appiah and Josh Cohen of the *Boston Review*, for the courage, sensitivity, and humanity implicit in sponsoring this forum.

2   The issues we will discuss this evening are very challenging. They speak to questions of class, race, identity, moral obligation, and the responsibility of intellectuals. We need to have a serious discussion that moves beyond ideological posturing, dysfunctional rhetoric, ugga-bugga nationalism, and Afrocentrism to talk about ways that those of us who have extraordinary class privilege can coordinate and use our resources to alleviate some of the irrational and unnecessary suffering of, in particular, people of African descent.

3   ANTHONY APPIAH: Cornel, do you want to start us off?

From "The Responsibility of Intellectuals in the Age of Crack" (*Boston Review*, Vol. 18, 1993).

CORNEL WEST: This is an ongoing conversation, and the issues he raises here are arresting and complex. To start with, I think we have to acknowledge the degree to which we live in a market civilization, which affects all of our values and sensibilities. That makes it so very difficult to talk about ways of life that can serve as countervailing forces against the market moralities and market mentalities that go into what I call the "gangsterization" of America—especially the gangsterization of black America with territorial imperatives, with guns, with very little value on life and property. Black America is still a mirror of a larger American civilization. There are some real continuities between what happens on Wall Street, what we see in the White House, and what Ice Cube is talking about in "The Predator," in his recent album which is already number one pop and rhythm and blues.

We need to start with that broader context in order to get at the specificity of the condition of the black working poor and very poor. We must not get caught with just external explanations in terms of what's outside the black community. Nor should we get caught in internal explanations in terms of black behavior and black people trying to reach for themselves as if that can be done without addressing the larger circumstances. We need a dialectic here to keep in mind just the balance. I am convinced that it's so difficult to live a human and humane life in a market-driven civilization in general that the only way I can begin to talk about it is to begin with a very simple notion of nonmarket values—love, care, service to others, kindness, those things that we have forgotten about. How do you give those notions *life* in a market civilization? That's the challenge. To meet it, we need what I call a politics of conversion—because we are going to have to turn these brothers and sisters around. Some turning of the soul.

Now of course, I come from the church. We have ways of turning people around, but we have our faults and our foibles too—patriarchalism, homophobia—so not enough turnaround is actually taking place in those churches. But there has to be some discourse about convincing persons to live a different kind of life. And it's a *moral* discourse, it's a *spiritual* discourse. But this discourse is very difficult and dangerous in American society. The right wing tends to have monopoly on it—or, if not a monopoly, certainly a twist. A very powerful twist. But responsible, progressive intellectuals have to talk a moral and spiritual language—a language of love, joy, communion, support, effective bonds—those notions which are requisite of any human being coming to terms with the terrors and traumas of being human.

BELL HOOKS: I think that we have to do more than talk. People look at us and say: they are up there talking about love and communion, but we don't really see that love and communion taking place among *them*. We don't really see them living the anti-bourgeois life that would actually be against market forces. Cornel and I talked at the Schomburg on Tuesday night, and I said to him there that I felt very alienated from other black intellectuals precisely because I wonder how we can we talk about transforming the lives of black under-class people and ourselves if we are not talking about being anti-capitalist—that black self-determination is not the same as black capitalism.

8 GLENN LOURY: As I look on the panel, it looks like I am probably the appointed defender of capitalism. But I venture out on that shaky ground not so much out of ideological conviction as pragmatism. We don't have an alternative model to capitalism in the world today. That's just a fact. The cultural degradation abetted by the for-profit dynamic that makes everything a commodity and that infringes upon what should be sacred is an issue. The question is how one insulates and nurtures that sacred space against the infringement of this market pressure. And it seems to me that that is not just, or even mainly, a political question. It's a question that engages spiritual issues.

9 In the context of Gene Rivers's provocative indictment—his concern about the responsibility of the intellectual and especially the black intellectual in the age of crack—we need to consider the issue of being in relationship with the persons of concern. This is not just a process of thinking or of organizing or of being engaged in activity. It's a question of being *present*, of *knowing* some of the people who are the object of the inquiry, of where you place yourself. In a Christian context, we are, after all, all sinners; we are, after all, *all* subject to these degrading forces of moral decay. We are all in some way vulnerable, and we are all, therefore, responsible to each other. I am especially moved to ask about the peculiar responsibility of blacks. Gene asks about the responsibility of the *black* intellectual in the age of crack. What's special about blackness in that context? I have the intuition that there *is* something special about blackness, but I am very uneasy with that intuition because it cuts against the universalistic principle that, as human beings, we all ought to be concerned about these things. But there is history, there are traditions here.

10 Finally, the other side of the black intellectual is the intellectual side; as intellectuals, we have been virtually contemptuous of the spiritual, of the transcendent. We think that we can reduce all of these questions to dialectical analyses of certain social processes.

11 HOOKS: I don't feel that I have been that kind of intellectual, Glenn, and I don't want to be represented in that way. There are varying kinds of black intellectuals. I ask you to make that acknowledgement because I feel that it does a *dis*service to those of us who have not been disassociated to erase what we have done and lump us in this category of black intellectuals who have felt this disconnection. We keep reproducing this binary opposition that's not true for all of us.

12 HENRY LOUIS GATES JR.: I want to respond to something Glenn said, and put a twist on it. One of the sad things for me is that such a large part of our community has become virtually contemptuous of the intellectual. I remember a survey in the *Washington Post* last summer that listed things inner-city black kids considered "white"—getting straight A's, doing well at school, going to the Smithsonian. That was a horrible moment for me and for those of us who were raised to *be* here, to be in this room. Our community produced us. We are not an aberration of the tradition, we are what the tradition wanted us to be.

13   Let me come now to the responsibility of the African-American intellectual and of our generation—particularly those of us who were undergraduates in the late 60s when institutions such as Harvard decided to "open up and train a new black elite" (all of that of course in quotation marks). Our responsibility is, in part, to produce new organizational structures where the kinds of analysis necessary for long-term change in the society can take place. If you look at the history of African-American intellectuals and examine the discourse even as early as Absolom Jones, there is always a sense of urgency that undergirds our rhetoric. Why? Because we had the most horrendous sociopolitical economic system on our backs and we needed to get it off *yesterday*. That sense of urgency has led to wonderful moments, heroic moments in our history, but it has at times also led to action based on a lack of adequate reflection. It's incumbent upon us, as urgent as these problems are, to do the analysis, to stop feeling guilty about being an intellectual and do the hard work that will lead to social transformation. Everything we do does not have to have a hand grenade effect to slay the dragon tomorrow. And I think that's a very, very difficult message to get through to our community and often to our students, and students in rooms like this.

14 APPIAH: Is there a way of taking that and asking the question this way—what responsibility do black intellectuals have apart from as intellectuals?

15 HOOKS: I tried to start with how we live our lives because I think that when you are in a classroom with a progressive affluent black intellectual who is humiliating you, and who is using discourse in such a way that does not affirm you, you don't feel that this person is really about something. I believe deeply, from both my spiritual and political practice, that we are first and foremost an example by our lives. I thought really deeply about coming here precisely because when I think about the responsibility of intellectuals in the age of crack, I don't see myself as dealing with a community "out there." I am thinking about my brother who is a crack addict. I talked to him *last week* about his electricity bill. What is my responsibility on the concrete level as an individual? How do I use my resources and how do I work with the larger community to deal with the question of crack and all the other genocidal forces in our lives? I think that we have got to believe, as intellectuals of varying political persuasions, that the example of our lives matters *as much* as our testimony in words and in public settings.

16 RIVERS: I would like to ask: to what extent has our old class segregation reproduced and exacerbated the anti-intellectualism that we decry? To what extent have we, by virtue of *removing* ourselves from the community, actually fed *into* the very thing we lament? Take the periodically sexy topic of anti-Semitism. One of the things that's interesting to me about that concept as a force in our community is that it raises the question: to what extent have we anti-anti-Semitic intellectuals *contributed* to the negative social forces in our community by segregating *ourselves*, leaving a weak social group *defenseless*, left to their own devices they do all these negative anti-Semitic things that we *then* turn around and lecture them against as we *ensure* that

they never get close to us. So, one part of this discussion has to do with our class identity, and how we *distance* ourselves. We talk in theoretical terms about emancipating the poor, for the sake of humanity; just don't let the unwashed and the illiterate rub shoulders with me. I wouldn't want to be caught dead having to interface with them to *reduce* the negativism and the nihilism that produces these dysfunctional social patterns.

17 WEST: I think you have raised a number of issues that can be easily confused and conflated. The assumption at times, Gene, is that if the middle class—of which the black intellectuals are one species—were to *stay*, that middle class could, in a messianic way, uplift and fundamentally transform the black poor condition. I don't believe that.

18 RIVERS: Not necessarily. But they could just have a conversation periodically.

19 WEST: They have conversations all the time. I think you have to raise the question: why did the middle class leave? They left because they had opportunities heretofore not available to them. And let's keep in mind that the majority of black folk are very much like the Harvard Union of Clerical and Technical Workers: they are working-class people. They are not middle class, they are not so-called under class or working poor. They are like "roc." They are hard working brothers and sisters on the edge of poverty, if the check doesn't show up on the 30th—but that's not middle class. And they are trying to get out. Why? Because of the *levels* of crime, the *fear* of crime, the combat zones and the existential wastelands. That's why they leave, they are human beings. They want their children to have *some* sense of walking the streets safely. Given that reality, though, brother, the question is: what can the middle class do? Especially a parvenu bourgeoisie, a newly arrived middle class.

20 Every middle class we know in human history becomes intoxicated with bourgeois-ness. Every one we know. The black middle class has, too. You see, part of what we are talking about is the difficulty of being an intellectual in a business civilization. An intellectual has a *profound* dedication to the life of the mind, believes in a playfulness of the life of the mind, understands it requires discipline like a jazz musician. That's serious discipline. You can do that anywhere—inner-city, vanilla suburbs, wherever you go. But to be an intellectual, to cut against the grain of a business civilization, means that intellectuals actually surface precisely when they are *experts*—like here at the Kennedy School. But experts aren't intellectuals. Some are. But most aren't. Experts are something else. That's something else, it's *very important*. And Eugene might be asking us to be *experts*. But that's something else, Gene. I am not against it. But that's something else than being intellectual.

21 But the other side of this thing is *celebrity*, which is part of the commodification of academic star . . .

22 HOOKS: One of my concerns in coming here tonight was precisely that my voice, as a black female voice would be overshadowed by homosocial bonding among the men here. One of the things that Eugene evoked was women and children. Part of why I wish to see a greater voice from radical black women intellectuals is that many of us experience our intellectuality, our

stardom very differently. As I listen I feel more and more divorced from this discussion precisely because I feel that my sense of being an intellectual first comes out of being nurtured by black women in black institutions—the church, the school—and so I am trying to suggest that we have something to learn from many voiceless black women who have tried to keep alive the pursuit of intellectuality in diverse black communities, among all classes. We need mechanisms to hear from those people, and to learn how they devote their resources to keeping that pursuit alive.

23   On this issue of resources: I recognize, Glenn, that I participate in capitalism. But I *never* hear black intellectuals—progressive, affluent, black intellectuals, or conservatives—talk about what we do with our money. A redistribution of resources begins fundamentally with: what am I willing to give up? If I am unwilling to give up some of my resources, then I don't believe that I am going to convince masses of other people that they should give up some of their resources, because we know capitalism is not going to end tomorrow, and that a lot of us black folks are going to be more affluent. The question for me, then, is how do we share our resources within diverse black communities? And I see that as a concrete question.

24   For me, dealing with addicts in the family raises a concrete question of co-dependency: to what extent do you share resources to enable or to allow people to *redeem* their lives? To me these are practical concrete questions, and I venture to say that many black women are dealing with them. I tell my students all the time that black folks who are crack addicted are not bleeding white people to death. It is the families that get bled. So if we want to look for a model of responsibility we need to look at productive models in those domestic contexts where people are trying to talk about how do you share resources effectively without further disenabling.

25 LOURY: I don't have an answer to bell's question, but I have accumulated several points that I want to make . . . : I think this discussion is too abstract. I don't mean that to put anybody *down*, but I mean, I think there is an answer to the question that somebody raised about things the middle-class can do. There are tens upon tens of thousands of children, for example, who are in foster care, who don't have homes. Now, you can talk about a tenuous middle class. But those people who are one pay-check away nevertheless have the capacity to nurture, support, and love these children. We ask ourselves as black people, what are our responsibilities? *Surely* those responsibilities include seeing after those children. Where is the movement amongst our leaders—political and intellectual—to create the institutional capacity for us to see that those children are looked after better than they are now? That's not unfeasible. That's not pie in the sky. That's something that can actually happen, and again, it has to happen in particular places. It has to happen in Boston, in Mattapan, it has to happen because 20 people, and then 200, and then 2,000 determine that it's going to happen someplace. It's not going to happen because Bill Clinton runs for president saying he would like to see it happen.

26 GATES: But Glenn—. . . there are attempts like Marion Wright Edelman's Children's Defense Fund, which is a very, very

important movement for us all, and which Cornel and I both belong to. That, it seems to me, is an attempt of the so-called new middle class to reach back, and to make bridges to the community that was left behind....

27 I have four statistics that I would like to share. In 1960, 24% of black households were headed by women: in 1990 that number is 56%, and 55% of these women live in poverty. The percentage of births out of wedlock in the black community in 1960 was 21.6%; in 1988 it is 63.7%. In 1960 19.9% of our children lived only with their mothers, in 1990 that number was 51.2%. In 1960, finally, two percent of our children had mothers who had never been married; in 1990 that number was 35%. If raising our children is the most important work of a society, its burdens now fall disproportionately on the much-demonized single mother.

28 What's happened is that our community has been divided into two. We now have two black communities, not one. We probably have more than that. Yet each of us tends to speak of the black community as if blackness were a class. We have to decide if blackness really does constitute a class. We have to start with this issue, and recognize that the community we were children in no longer exists. There is a new black community—or new black communities—out there, and if we are trying to put it back together then we have to recognize that reality and then talk about new solutions to new problems. That is, I think, the signal failure of our generation of black intellectuals. More often than not we resort to romantic black nationalism or to some other way to assuage the guilt that we feel, and everybody in here knows what I am talking about, about leaving that other community behind.

29 HOOKS: I don't know what Skip [Gates] is talking about. I am going to testify from the location that I inhabit. I don't feel like I have left that community behind. That community has been in my life every single day. I know lots of middle-class and upper-class black people who are one pay check away from poverty because of accumulated debt in their lives. One of my sisters who was leading a very bourgeois life found herself homeless after she lost her job. I saw her spiral from her Mercedes, her BMW, her whole $400,000 life into homelessness in a matter of months. If we want to talk about why a black middle class or upper middle class has to have different values, then we need to deal with our own materialism. We cannot talk about sharing resources that we don't have to share because of our own levels of greed. I mean I am interested in talking about what kind of values do we replace market values with and how do we do that?

30 WEST: I don't think the black middle class is any more greedy than any other middle class that existed, in fact, in some ways it is less so because we do have certain survivor's guilt that we talked about before. I mean this is one of the reasons why I don't want to lose the dialectic we started off with in terms of what's internal to the black community and what's external. We are living in a society that has certain obligations to its citizens. I don't care *who* they are. We have got a lumpen bourgeoisie, we have got a middle class that's never truly been a middle class even though it does have certain obligations—though all wealth in

the black middle class is equivalent to the wealth of white workers. We have *income* that's higher, not wealth, because we could not get houses because of *discrimination* and keeping suburbs vanilla. It was federal policy that did that and we can tell the story about that. So I do not want to lose sight of the external. We cannot sit here and allow American society in its broad reaches to get off the hook here. The black middle class is not a messianic middle class and it never will be. It is going to behave middle class. We are talking about a critical minority of black middle-class folk who are willing to sacrifice themselves.

31 RIVERS: What does that mean for us in this room, Cornel? To move the conversation along we need to bring it home personally, to what one does with one's own notions of greed—not to call for the state to redistribute wealth when I am not personally willing to do it myself.

32 WEST: That analogy doesn't work. It doesn't work at all—individual black middle-class person and the state and corporate America?

33 RIVERS: I am not talking about equivalence in magnitude. I am saying that you can't tell somebody else that they should distribute their wealth, however they got it, while you are sitting on all kinds of disposable income and flying all around the world cooling out and letting black people suffer. We can't make that argument anymore. What we have to do is talk about how we are, in this existential nightmare, morally obligated with our class privilege and our access and opportunity to alleviate the suffering of black people. I can't talk—we can't talk—about white America and *their* thing when we are sitting up here with Yellowstone Forest in our own eyes. That's the issue that Glenn and bell are pushing us on. How do we talk about personal commitment?

34 WEST: We have been talking about both at the same time.

35 RIVERS: I agree with that. But talking about white people is easy.

36 WEST: Not white people, but well-to-do white people, powerful white people, not working-class folk.

37 RIVERS: Talking about rich white folk is easy.

38 WEST: We are not talking about them personally, we are talking about the wealth they have.

39 RIVERS: I agree with that, Cornel. I am with you. All I am saying is: let's do something uncharacteristic and bring it home and talk about what we are going to do. We have got celebrities up here. How do we mobilize your celebrity status so that we can produce an infrastructure so that those who live on the ground, in the bush, working with Leroy and Rahim, have the kinds of resources they need. You do your thing. That's cool. We have to have everybody everywhere. But we need an infrastructure that says that Rahim and Catrina and Rashida have resources coming to them. That's where our celebrity intelligentsia can help. They have the access.

40 APPIAH: Let me ask this question: why should black intellectuals use their celebrity anymore than other black celebrities, who on the whole have a great deal more celebrity than most intellectuals? What is the obligation over and above the obligation to act as an intellectual, to do the thinking that is necessary? Obviously we *all* have obligations as citizens, we *all* have obligations as members of churches or resistors of church membership in my case.

But the idea of talking about the responsibilities of black intellectuals is to talk about responsibilities *specific* to people as intellectuals.

41 HOOKS: One of the resources that I feel I have, specific to intellectual experience, is critical thinking and critical consciousness. I think particularly because I came out of the working black poor, I feel strongly the need to share that resource because I feel that what enabled me was that capacity to think critically and analytically and to act in relationship to my thoughts. So I think a lot about how that can be effectively shared beyond the academy with diverse black communities, and it seems to me that one of the big issues as I think about us here is a question of literacy and the fact that so much of black intellectual thought is shared in written discourse. In forms that are apart from a diversity of black presence and experience, and it seems to me I would like us to have a space where we share what we concretely do. I think that one, I feel deeply that black intellectuals have to move outside the academy to share how we think and what we think about, and there are many ways to do that. I know that people like Cornel and Eugene do that through the church. I myself try to go to cities and ask people, where do black people hang out.

42 APPIAH: Say some more about what you do.

43 HOOKS: I will break it down to my individual circumstances. White people will invite me someplace to come and talk and pay me $5,000 and there may not be any black people there. So what is my obligation? One of the things I feel I can do is contact black community leaders and say: where do black people hang out? Regular folks doing what they do. A lot of times it's restaurants and I can call the people who own a particular restaurant and I can go there for a couple of hours to talk to people who want to share questions like: how do you deal with an addict? How do our elders deal with the fact that many of our elders live in prisons—that they have to lock every room in their house because the addicts living with them prey upon them. How do you deal with that concretely? And how do I link that to some education for critical consciousness? That may seem trivial, but it's one concrete thing that I feel we don't do enough of. Where are our literacy programs? Literacy without education for critical consciousness is not enough, we need a *critical* literacy.

44 RIVERS: Can I cite two quick examples in Boston? There's a young doctoral candidate at M.I.T. named Alan Shaw—a graduate of Harvard in Applied Math, and here in the audience tonight. Alan set up a software company in black Dorchester called Amani Information Systems. He has been using his considerable intellectual talent as an expert and an intellectual to develop alternative approaches to learning computer literacy. He's in the hood teaching brothers and sisters computer literacy and using computer literacy as a mechanism for resocializing them in terms of values situating it in a black historical context and promoting the point that bell was making about critical consciousness. An extraordinary program that deserves a lot more attention and concrete support.

45 Then there's the Algebra Project of Robert Moses of SNCC fame. He's got a second tier of younger intellectual activists—

for example, Cynthia Parker and Jaqueline Rivers—who are very skilled young people working on an alternative approach to math literacy. Concrete, no nonsense, no ugga-bugga, on the ground.

46 LOURY: I think what Eugene is saying warrants emphasis. I think there are a ring of programs that we can think about, but one thing that's in common is that the people in question are looking at the talents that they have and they are finding specific ways in which those talents can be made available. I think that there will be more answers to your question when there are more relationships between the people with the talents and the people with the need. That's why I would stress that this not be programmatic so much as it be directed at people to ask how are they living their lives. In response to something Skip said earlier, Marion Wright Edelman is very fine but that's not an answer to the question I raised about who's going to care for kids. That's an answer to how are we going to put progressive pressure on the state in order to implement a certain kind of child care program. The distinction is vital.

Points for Review and Discussion

1. Reverend Rivers and Professor West differ about the responsibilities of successful black intellectuals with regard to the redistribution of wealth. Summarize carefully the point at issue between them.
2. Professors Loury and Gates differ about the responsibility of black people with regard to black foster children. Summarize carefully the point at issue in the exchanges between them.

•◦ Questions for Writing

1. Professor Gates refers to the "guilt that we feel ... about leaving that other community behind" (¶ 28). Describe the causes of this guilt as you understand them.
2. Professor hooks describes one way in which, in the course of her public lecture dates, she attempts to meet her obligations to the class—the "working black poor" (¶ 41)—from which she has risen. She acknowledges that what she does "may seem trivial," but she argues that "it's one concrete thing ... we don't do enough of" (¶ 43). In your view is the activity she mentions "trivial"? Explain your reasoning.
3. The repeated theme in this forum is that of *group* responsibility—the obligation of one class (upper-middle-class black intellectuals) to exert itself, person by person, to help another class (the urban black poor). Do you believe the concept of group responsibility can flourish in an individualistic and highly competitive society? Should it flourish? Again: explain your reasoning.

Connecting the Parts in Chapter 8: Assignments for Extended Essays

1.   Several of the writers of the selections in Chapter 8—several people written about as well—experience complex feelings in their dealings with those who belong to a class different from their own. These feelings include (among others) pride, intransigence, discomfort, embarrassment, and shame. From among your own encounters with people whose social situation differs from yours, choose one encounter that seems to you especially instructive about relations between superiors and inferiors. Write an essay fully describing the encounter and analyzing currents of your own mental and emotional response to it that strike you as particularly revelatory.

2.   Rodriguez quotes the following two passages from notes he made on college lectures about "aristocratic pastoral literature."

> The praise of the unlettered by the highly educated is one of the primary themes of "elitist" literature.

> The importance of the praise given the unsolitary, richly passionate, and spontaneous life is that it simultaneously reflects the value of a reflective life.

Write an essay in which you probe likenesses and differences between this "praise" and that which you find in the essays by Thomas Geoghegan and Marianna De Marco Torgovnick. Conclude your essay with a statement setting forth your own evaluation of unsolitary, passionate, and spontaneous life.

Leads for Research

1.   Look into the question of international differences in class consciousness by reading Richard Hoggart's *The Uses of Literacy* (1955) and comparing it with Rodriguez's *Hunger of Memory*. Write a paper focused on the degrees of explicitness and particularity with which these two writers treat the subject of class. What does Hoggart's account of membership in his class include that Rodriguez's account of *his* class membership doesn't include? (And vice versa.) What does the difference between these two writers' approach to class identity tell us about differences between England and America?

2.   Research the "other community [left] behind" by the black intellectuals who debate each other in the forum on responsibility. Write a paper answering these questions: What degree of social mobility exists in this community? How much movement out of the ghetto has taken place in recent years? Useful starting points for your inquiry are David Swinton,

"The Economic Status of African-Americans: 'Permanent' Poverty and Inequality," in *The State of Black America* (1991, a National Urban League report), and Andrew Hacker, *Two Nations, Black and White, Separate, Hostile, Unequal* (1992).

3. Over the last quarter of a century moral and political philosophers have developed a fascinating and complicated discourse on the problem of the responsibilities of society to its least well-off members. (The issues in question figure throughout the exchanges in the black intellectuals' forum.) The key contribution to the discourse was John B. Rawls's *A Theory of Justice* (1971); other important contributions are Robert Nozick's *Anarchy, State, and Utopia* (1974) and Alisdair MacIntyre's *After Virtue* (1981). A central phrase in this discourse is "distributive justice." Read one or more of the books in question and write an essay on how major issues in the debate on responsibility are conceived and framed in political philosophy.

9

Class Consequences
Five Public Issues

Every public issue of our time, from tax rates to illiteracy rates, has clear class dimensions. But more often than not, media and legislative debate neglects those dimensions. The neglect stems at least partly from protectiveness about the nation's self-image. A classless society shouldn't have to worry about differences, from class to class, in the impact of changes in policy. And America's self-image is that of a classless society.

The essays in Chapter 9 focus on particular policies (legislative, judicial, and administrative decisions made in the past or facing the society in the future). With one exception, the essays seek to establish the relevance of class concerns, and they argue, implicitly or explicitly, that policymakers who neglect the class consequences of public policies are likely to make bad decisions. The essayists share no common political perspective. The idea that class counts in America isn't essentially conservative, liberal, or moderate. As the essays below illustrate in different ways, the idea is a tool enabling citizens of a democracy to see deeper into the meanings of the choices that they call on their leaders to make.

THE AFFLUENT DRAFT RESISTER
William G. Smith

The most dramatic recent instance of class injustice traceable to state-administered public policy occurred during the Vietnam War. Between America's formal entry into the war, in 1964, and the taking of Saigon by Viet Cong troops in 1973, 27 million men came of draft age; 60 percent of them escaped military service. Only about 3 percent of these 16 million men were draft offenders who took flight to Canada or Europe or elsewhere. Nine out of ten escapees missed the war because they were officially deferred on grounds of mental or physical handicap. Most of the escapees belonged to the American middle class.

The inequities of the draft were no secret. A Chicago-based wartime study showed that "youths from neighborhoods with low education levels [were] four times as likely to die in Vietnam as youths from better-educated neighborhoods." A Wisconsin congressman polled a randomly selected one hundred inductees from his district—unlucky young men who had missed out on deferments—and found that all belonged to families with incomes at or below the poverty level. The editor of the Harvard University undergraduate newspaper learned, also by polling, that of the 1200 members of the class of 1970, only two went to Vietnam.

Social commentators with middle class bases were remarking, as early as 1972, that they "had never known a single family that had lost a son in Vietnam, or indeed, one with a son wounded, missing in action, or held prisoner of war. And by the mid-1970s, some journalists were describing Vietnam explicitly as a "class war."

The report below, "The Affluent Draft Resister," details some of the strategies that proved useful to young, male, middle-class citizens determined to avoid military service. The author, William G. Smith, is a lawyer who was an active draft counselor throughout the entire period of U. S. involvement in Vietnam. He continues to specialize in litigating military cases.

1   I was in a law firm that had been very active in the National Lawyers Guild; I'd done a lot of work in Mississippi in Freedom Summer (1964). By the end of 1966, we had a fairly active antidraft movement going in this country. I was one of the first "left" lawyers to be involved in it. (There were lawyers associated with various pacifist groups—Quakers, Mennonites, Jehovah's Witnesses—involved earlier than I had been, but those lawyers weren't particularly "political" lawyers.)

2   Because of the reputation our law firm had, we began getting calls from parents and from young people who were affected by the draft. I had

---

From William G. Smith, "The Affluent Draft Resister," in *Hell No, We Won't Go* (1991), ed. Sherry G. Gottlieb.

to educate myself, because no one knew anything about the draft law at that time; it was a very obscure set of regulations that nobody had ever paid any attention to—there had not been any significant political opposition to the draft until that time. I quickly decided that the work load was going to be far more than one lawyer could accomplish. We formed the Selective Service Law Panel in Los Angeles, which grew to over a hundred lawyers; we began holding regular meetings every three weeks. We used those as educational forums, and as devices to sign out cases to lawyers. Our primary activity, however, was in counseling.

3   We tried to make counseling available to everybody. My standard rate was four hundred dollars. We each had a commitment to do so much free counseling, particularly among minority groups. We set up [free] draft counseling sessions in Compton and East Los Angeles. The effort to get draft counseling into the working-class neighborhoods and minority communities was not successful. We tried, but it was not successful for a variety of reasons. People stayed out of the draft primarily by medical deferments or conscientious objection. (Medical deferments outweighed conscientious objection by fifty to one.)

4   For a medical deferment, the person would get his family doctor's medical records, and if they were not sufficient, we had a panel of several hundred doctors who were willing to examine people and come up with medical reports which would suggest that the person was not physically qualified for military service. There's a vast difference between a kid growing up in Watts and a kid growing up in Beverly Hills in terms of medical treatment that he has received. For example, if the kid's ever had any allergies, or asthma, if he grew up in Watts, chances are he never got any treatment for it. If he grew up in Beverly Hills, he got lots of treatment; we could easily get those people out of the draft. People in Watts, unless they were "lucky" enough to have an asthma attack during their induction physical, were found acceptable and drafted.

5   Same for psychiatric problems: kids in Beverly Hills who couldn't adjust to their affluent life-style went to therapists at an early age, often developing significant psychological histories, which could be used to try to get them out of the draft. General medical care in affluent communities permitted you to build on that, and send them to another doctor who could find enough in the medical problem that the person would be medically disqualified. In those days, I could give anyone who came to me for counseling at least a 70 percent chance of flunking the physical exam—legitimately, not because we were faking it. ([Though] it's true the doctors would sometimes "stretch" their reports more than they would in a personal-injury case, for example.)

6   We could also choose where the physical exam would occur. There were about one hundred places in the U.S. where you could take your physical examination, depending on where you lived. But you could transfer your physical to anyplace in the country, as long as you happened to be there when your physical was scheduled. We soon developed

a network which would tell us exactly where we could expect someone to fail a physical examination for any given physical condition. For example, we discovered that in Albuquerque, New Mexico, there was a psychiatrist who virtually would flunk anybody who came in with a report from another psychiatrist: so we sent clients with psychiatric reports to Albuquerque. There was no conspiracy—we were simply taking advantage of the law. Examining centers in rural areas were not accustomed to seeing young men with long hair, and you looked very strange if you came in looking like the typical California hippie; so we would send kids to those places with psychiatric reports, and they were convinced that those people were out of their marbles and [would] find them disqualified, whereas they would have been found qualified in Los Angeles.

7   Essentially, the affluent draft resister had a far better chance of winning because of all the advantages he had: he could afford to transfer his physical exam because his parents could send him to Albuquerque; he had plenty of medical care when he was a kid—and if he didn't have enough, we could send him to a doctor, and he could pay for that doctor. If we couldn't get him out on medical grounds, chances are he had the advantage of a much better education and could therefore write a much more cogent conscientious objector claim. An average kid growing up in a black or Latino community had real difficulty expressing himself in English, a prerequisite for filing a successful conscientious objector claim. Also, the general idea of draft resistance was prevalent primarily in the student community (primarily white, of course) and received support from peers, whereas in a minority or working-class community, they stuck out like a sore thumb. The people who went to Vietnam were primarily minority people, poor people, or working-class people, because they didn't have the support mechanism to get out of the draft. I'm not so sure there's anything we could have done at the time to prevent it—we tried, because that was very much on our minds—[and] I don't think anything can be done in the future to prevent it, even with our experience and hindsight.

8   Before 1965, it was extremely difficult to be classified as a conscientious objector unless you had been raised in a traditional pacifist religion such as the Quakers, Mennonites, Jehovah's Witnesses. Even after '65, it took a long time to overcome the perceptions of draft board members about conscientious objection; some boards absolutely refused to abide by the new Supreme Court decision.

9   In 1965, they changed the rules so that if you were married, you could still be drafted. Then student deferments were gradually phased out. Then, finally, they phased out deferments for people who had children.

10   In 1965, five-year sentences [for refusing induction] were very common; then they began tapering off. Two years was probably the average sentence during that ten-year period—mostly [in] minimum-security

federal penitentiaries, which tend to be better than state prisons, because they don't get the same kind of criminal; they don't get many crimes of violence in federal courts.

11   Two federal District Court judges within the Ninth Circuit, who had been sentencing young men who were prosecuted for draft evasion in their own courtrooms to jail, sent their own sons to see me for counseling.

12   I took an extensive tour of Canada very early in the game, and spoke at all the major universities in Canada, because they all had draft-resister assistance groups. From that, I had contacts in every major Canadian city, and some of the smaller ones, so that if a kid wanted to go to Canada, it could be arranged before he got there. I tended to try to discourage people from going to Canada, because I felt that with adequate counseling, nobody had to go.

13   The problems that developed were that some people were very angry when they got there, to the point that they would go into the American consulate offices to tell the people there they were renouncing their citizenship. Others simply gradually became Canadian citizens. Then, when we were trying to get these people back into the United States, we ran into some severe problems, because they lost their U.S. citizenship in this process. Under the immigration law, if you become a citizen of another country, you automatically lose your citizenship in the United States. A lot of kids who could have easily stayed out of the draft if they'd simply stayed in the United States got themselves into the worst possible mess in Canada because they were no longer eligible to return to the United States, even after their draft status was resolved. We have a number of people whose status in the United States is still not clarified. We still have some people in Canada; we have a large number of people in the United States who are here illegally, technically, because they don't qualify for residence here. Those are residual problems from the Vietnam war that will continue for a long time.

14   I counseled about three thousand people during the Vietnam war. I can only think of one who actually went into the service. Not one of my counselees ever went to jail, unless they were already under indictment when they first came for counseling—there wasn't a lot we could do for those guys. My name got to be fairly well known around the country; people came to see me from all over, because I was on "60 Minutes" on the draft, and a lot of other nationwide programs.

15   If I get with a group of Vietnam vets, and we start talking about draft resistance, and how easy it was to stay out of the draft, there are a lot of variable attitudes. Some people's attitude is basically "More power to the people who got out; I wish I had." [But there's] also a lot of resentment, particularly when [they're] told it was primarily an affluent, upper-middle-class phenomenon, and would be in the future if it ever occurred again.

16   I guess my attitude now is different because, although I was caught up in it, and all my clients at the time seemed to share my attitudes about the antiwar movement in general, almost all of them have sold out. Today's yuppies—some of them are even rabid Reagan supporters. I don't have a whole lot of empathy for them today. A very small percentage remained active after their draft status was resolved. In fact, we saw a dramatic change in the antidraft activities in this country, when they changed from an "oldest first" system to a lottery system [1970]. A great deal of opposition to the draft dissipated among people after they became [twenty-one], [or] too old under the lottery system to be drafted, or who received lottery numbers that could prevent them from being drafted. Draft resistance was a function of the danger a person faced, to a large extent.

17   We saw it again when the draft registration program resumed in 1980: although we had an initial burst of activity, and it looked as though it would be very similar to the Vietnam war, that activity soon diminished to almost nothing. People quickly became aware that they were in no particular danger. The Selective Service System has been very astute in changing their regulations so that in any future draft, the exposure time will be very limited. It will be primarily young people who are exposed to liability, who have less opportunity to formulate political opposition to the war or to the draft, and who will be in the military before they realize what's happened.

18   I don't anticipate seeing an antidraft movement in the future, even if we get involved in a conflict like Nicaragua where we're actually using draftees—nothing like what we had in the past. We'll have an active opposition, and it'll be easy to keep kids out of the draft again; but don't expect to see a movement, because of the way the regulations have been manipulated to prevent that. Under the [current] lottery system, your exposure is going to be sometime between January 1 and December 31 of the year you reach your twentieth birthday; so after you've passed [that date], you have absolutely no real liability. For people twenty-one and over, it's not likely we're going to see a whole lot of activity. It's going to be confined to a very narrow age band.

19   It remains to be seen whether they're going to need ever again the numbers that they needed even in the Vietnam war, which weren't very large in comparison with what they had been in World War II, for example. Even with the largest draft call in the Vietnam era, in 1965, you would not have exhausted more than one year under the lottery system. What this is going to cause is some assertion on the part of the government that the young people are supporting the war more than they did, say, in the Vietnam conflict. It'd only be because of the nature of the draft system, not necessarily because people support what's going on.

Points for Review and Discussion

1. Summarize the basic activities of "draft counselors." Exactly what services did they perform for their clients?
2. Smith says his "attitude now [to draft evaders] is different" (¶ 16). What is the difference and how does he himself account for it?

●◆ Questions for Writing

1. William Smith speaks of "the effort to get draft counseling into the working-class neighborhoods and minority communities" (¶ 3) as a failure. Summarize the reasons for that failure in your own words.
2. In discussing "examining centers," Smith explains how clients with psychiatric reports were sent to the Albuquerque, New Mexico center because it had a psychiatrist who automatically flunked anybody who came in with a report from another psychiatrist. Smith asserts that "there was no conspiracy—we were simply taking advantage of the law" (¶ 6). Write a page in which you judge the morality of the strategy Smith describes.
3. A common reply to those who attack as unfair government policies such as those concerning the draft, is that life itself is unfair. On what assumptions does this justification rest? In your view what is the strongest criticism that can be mounted against such assumptions?

THE FUTILE WAR ON DRUGS
Elliott Currie

One method of simplifying social problems is to see them as resulting from countless individual failures of personal character. According to this view, people are jobless because they're lazy; they're homeless because they lack forehandedness; they're addicted because they have no moral discipline. When public disasters are seen this way, the complex question of how to balance public and private responsibility can be neatly bypassed.

Coming to terms with this question doesn't mean dismissing character and conduct as irrelevant. It does mean looking hard at the social and economic backgrounds of behavior, and also into the influence that public policy may be exerting. In "The Futile War on Drugs" Elliott Currie looks hard at the drug crisis of our time. He probes the effects of specific public policies on specific sectors of the urban population, relating state and federal law to the daily life of a social class.

Elliott Currie has taught criminology and sociology at Yale and the University of California (Berkeley), and is a consultant to the National Council on Crime and Delinquency. His most recent book is *Reckoning: Drugs, the Cities, and the American Future* (1993).

1 To some observers it is as if the drug plague of the 1980s had come out of the blue. As one noted commentator puts it,

> The explosion of drug use—particularly use of crack—in the mid-1980s seemed to have nothing to do with any decline in opportunities, or indeed any change that should have increased the sense of despair and hopelessness that some claim is the reason for the resort to drugs.

2 The belief that the drug crisis was detached from any precipitating social context—a reflection of some mysterious failure of individual moral character, unrelated to systemic changes in the society as a whole—lends itself to the argument that the drug problem will be solved, if at all, by some combination of moral exhortation, force, and fear. But it does not square with the evidence. In fact, the drug crisis of the 1980s flourished in the context of an unparalleled social and economic disaster that swept low-income communities in America in ways that virtually ensured that the drug problem would worsen. To be sure, the sheer increase in the availability of drugs—especially crack, which is not only powerfully appealing but also remarkably inexpensive and easy

---

From Elliott Currie, *Reckoning: Drugs, the Cities, and the American Future* (1993).

to distribute—was a crucial factor. But crack was like a match thrown on dry tinder.

3   The most fundamental and far-reaching change, from which much else has followed, has been the continuing decline of what the researchers of the fifties and sixties called the "opportunity structure." We've seen that mass drug abuse is closely associated both with long-term joblessness and with long-term employment in jobs that offer no challenge and no future—jobs that cannot support families or sustain communities. It should not be surprising, therefore, that the drug crisis has worsened simultaneously with one of the most radical shifts in economic opportunities in American history. That shift was predicted more than once in the 1950s and 1960s; but it has gone much farther than anyone then imagined.

4   A crucial part of that change has been the accelerating disappearance of the traditional blue-collar jobs that once provided decent pay and a path into stable community and family life for less-educated workers. As John Kasarda has shown, the deindustrialization of the past fifteen to twenty years has struck hardest at the central cities, where the loss of blue-collar jobs was so great that it usually offset any gains in other sectors of the urban economy—even in the years when some areas of the country were enjoying considerable economic growth. Between 1970 and 1980, New York City gained almost 275,000 managerial, professional, technical, and administrative jobs, but lost over 360,000 in blue-collar manufacturing, clerical work, and sales—a net loss of over 95,000 jobs in the central city. Those losses were particularly devastating for people without much formal schooling—not, however, only those who had dropped out of school, but the entire "noncollege" half of younger Americans. Thus Detroit lost well over 100,000 jobs held by people without a high-school diploma and over 55,000 held by high-school graduates, and simultaneously gained 22,000 jobs for college graduates and 35,000 for people with some college.

5   By the 1980s, as a result, young people growing up in the cities could see less and less connection between completing high school and landing a decent job, unless they expected to go on to college; and that profound change has been especially crippling for minorities. As Kasarda points out, blacks in the cities are still "highly concentrated in the education category where city employment has rapidly declined ... and greatly underrepresented in the educational-attainment categories where city employment is quickly expanding." This helps explain what seems at first to be a paradox; even the "boom" years of the eighties and the rapid growth of jobs in some urban areas generally failed to reverse the decline in opportunities for less educated minority workers. To some observers, the coexistence of economic growth with lingering joblessness in the inner cities points to a cultural or "behavioral" explanation of the plight of the urban unemployed. But there is a more parsimonious explanation: by the 1970s, the fruits of economic growth were being dis-

tributed differently than in the past—increasingly divided by education, race, and residence.

6   Up through the late 1960s, economic growth pulled in the less educated and the better educated more equally. Between 1950 and 1970, Kasarda notes, "there was considerable growth in all cities in the number of blacks employed who had not completed twelve years of education." But "after 1970, the bottom fell out in urban industrial demand for poorly educated blacks." In Philadelphia, for example, the number of jobs lost in the seventies for blacks without a high-school diploma almost equaled the number added in the previous *two* decades.

7   What is critical about these declines is that they have not only affected the individuals who have lost jobs, but have essentially placed entire communities on the margins of the productive economy. In the Chicago ghetto neighborhoods of Oakland and Grand Boulevard, according to William J. Wilson and his colleagues, fewer than one adult in four was gainfully employed by 1980, where well over half had been employed thirty years before.

8   The sharp decline in prospects for less-educated urban workers was partly—but only partly—matched by increased opportunities in the suburbs. Thus while New York City lost 95,000 jobs during the seventies, its suburbs gained almost 500,000; Chicago lost 88,000 jobs while its suburbs gained a whopping 630,000. But several formidable barriers kept most of those suburban jobs out of the hands of minorities from the inner cities. The economic boom in fast-growing Atlanta, for example, as Gary Orfield has shown, "did not produce strong outreach for black workers but drew many young, highly skilled, well-educated non-Southerners into the area, most of whom moved to the suburbs." Nor was this result entirely accidental. The maldistribution of job opportunities between suburbs and inner city was exacerbated by the deliberate restriction of housing opportunities for low-income people in the job-rich suburbs—and even deliberate resistance to extending public transportation from the inner city to suburban worksites, which meant that the new jobs were often as unreachable for poorer inner-city residents as if they had been on another planet. (Relatively few poor inner-city workers have access to a car: over three-quarters of the households in Chicago's West Side ghetto, for example, had no car in 1980.) Recent research by Mark Schneider and Thomas Phelan, moreover, shows that even when blacks moved to the suburbs, they were usually "found in highly segregated communities with comparatively slow job growth." Many newer, "clean" industries moved to some suburbs in the 1970s and early 1980s, but much more slowly, if at all, to those suburbs with "expanding black population concentrations."

9   Nor were inner-city blacks the only losers from these changes in the labor market. The sociologist Marta Tienda has shown how these shifts away from manufacturing and toward the suburbanization of new jobs have had an enormous impact on Puerto Rican Americans—among

whom, as we've seen, hard-drug abuse has raged at crisis levels since the seventies. Because they are heavily concentrated in areas where good jobs for less educated workers have vanished, and are confined to the bottom of the "ethnic hiring queue," both unemployment and what Tienda calls "detachment from the labor force" have risen sharply among Puerto Ricans—more rapidly than among other Hispanic groups. In the early 1970s, about 13 percent of adult Puerto Rican men were "unstably active" in the labor force—that is, still connected to the job market but periodically unemployed. That was already exceptionally high, but ten years later, the proportion had risen to 19 percent, and to those had been added another 6 percent who were "stably inactive"— that is, they were out of the labor force and had not looked for work over a five-year period.

10   The rapid decline of industrial jobs, then—along with a mismatch between urban and suburban job growth—left many less educated workers stranded even in areas where the total number of jobs grew dramatically in the seventies and eighties. But equally crucial has been the downward trend in the quality of the *new* jobs available to most Americans—rural and small-town as well as urban. It is not just that the less prepared are being left behind in an economy increasingly dominated by high-tech postindustrial jobs requiring ever-higher skills and formal education. Though many new jobs do require more education than most poor people—black or white, urban or rural—possess, we have not created nearly enough of them to provide most Americans with good, stable work even if they *did* have the requisite education. The most conspicuous trend in the American labor market since the seventies, in fact, has been the growth of poorly paying, unstable jobs with little future.

11   In a 1988 study, for example, researchers from the Budget Committee of the U.S. Senate divided the jobs created in the American economy between 1979 and 1987 into three categories—those that paid poverty-level wages or below, those that paid more than four times the poverty level, and "middle-wage" jobs in between. The "dominant trend in American job creation in the 1980s," the committee reported, "has been for low-paying jobs to replace those which provided a middle-class standard of living." The growth of low-wage jobs was not, of course, the whole story: many high-wage jobs were created in those years. But the share of new jobs paying below-poverty wages grew twice as fast. More than four out of five net new jobs for men in the American economy in those years paid poverty-level wages or below. Though this shift varied regionally (at least until the recession of the early 1990s), with some Northeastern and Midwestern states creating higher proportions of good jobs, the overall trend nationwide was toward "downward wage polarization."

12   What is especially relevant in understanding the social context of the drug crisis is that this decline in job quality struck hardest—indeed almost wholly—at *younger* workers. Between 1979 and 1987, the Senate committee calculates, there was a net loss of about 1.6 million middle-

wage jobs for workers under thirty-five and a vast increase in low-wage ones, while for workers *over* thirty-five things actually improved slightly on the national level.

13   Increasingly, too, the jobs available to the young were more likely to be less than full-time. Overall, the proportion of American jobs that are part-time has grown by half since the late 1950s. Not all part-time jobs, of course, are poor ones. But as Chris Tilly has shown, most of the growth since the seventies has been in what he calls "secondary" part-time work, in jobs "characterized by low skill requirements, low pay and fringe benefits, low productivity, and high turnover" as well as little chance for advancement. Over a fourth of part-time workers, versus one in twenty full-time workers, earned no more than minimum wages in 1984. And the largest share of the growth in secondary part-time work was among youth aged sixteen to twenty-one and "prime age" men aged twenty-two to sixty-four—not among women, who were steadily shifting toward full-time work in those years. In short, not only were youth (and young adult men) facing the loss of traditional entry-level jobs, but their options were increasingly limited to jobs that were both poorly paid and part-time.

14   Once again, as Tilly makes clear, this shift was not accidental. It was one aspect of a quite deliberate strategy on the part of many employers to reduce their costs and become economically competitive by adopting a "low-wage, low-skill, high-turnover" policy rather than by increasing the skills and productivity of their work force. That choice, rather than the inevitable effects of neutral technological changes, is most responsible for the rapid downward shift in America's "opportunity structure." Besides the move toward part-time work, that strategy has involved the transfer of millions of jobs to low-wage havens both in poorer parts of the United States and overseas; aggressive resistance to unionization; the deliberate refusal to invest in serious training and retraining of workers (about which we shall hear more later); and fierce opposition to raises in the federal minimum wage, which consequently remained stagnant in the face of sharply rising costs of living throughout the 1980s. In 1974, full-time, year-round work at the minimum wage (then $2.00 an hour) brought an income fractionally more than that required to support a family of three at the poverty level, and about 80 percent of the poverty level for a family of four. By 1987, the same level of work at the minimum wage of $3.35 brought only 74 percent of what it took to support a family of three at the poverty level and merely 58 percent of the poverty level for a family of four.

15   When we add the trends in low-wage and part-time work to those in unemployment, we begin to see just how deeply the "opportunity structure" has been slashed for people in the bottom third of the income scale—especially the young. Robert Sheak and David Dabelko have compiled figures on the numbers of people who fall into one of four categories of what they call the "underemployed": the officially unemployed; those who are out of the labor force but would like a job now;

those working part-time involuntarily, for economic reasons; and those working year-round, full-time, but earning less than the federal poverty level for a family of four. Together, they were about 23 percent of the total number of Americans employed in 1972, and 29 percent by 1987—in all, nearly 32 million people, up from only 19 million fifteen years before. Thirteen million people, in short, had joined the ranks of the poorly employed in the course of a decade and a half—a period that included several years of the Reagan economic "recovery."

16 The pervasive decline in job quality has reduced opportunities not only for minorities, but for younger and less educated whites as well—so much so that by the mid-1980s, young white men without much education were facing job prospects as bleak as those that blacks or Hispanics faced twenty years before. They were, in effect, falling into the same kinds of economic conditions that confronted urban blacks at the time of the ghetto riots of the sixties.

17 In one of the most revealing studies of this troubling pattern, the sociologist Daniel Lichter of Pennsylvania State University traced the growth of four types of "economic underemployment" between 1970 and 1982—the years immediately preceding the drug epidemic of the 1980s. In addition to looking at unemployment as officially defined—that is, being out of a job but actively looking for one within the past thirty days—Lichter also included what he called "subunemployment"—being without a job but not looking in the belief that none were available; underemployment resulting from low hours of work (working less than full-time and unable to find a full-time job); and underemployment resulting from low wages—which he defined as working full-time but earning less than 125 percent of the federal poverty level.

18 Measured in this way, Lichter shows, the 1970s and early 1980s were an economic catastrophe for younger and less educated American men of all races. Between 1970 and 1982, the overall level of underemployment roughly doubled among men in central cities; by 1982 more than one in three black men—but also nearly one in five white men—fell into one of those four categories of the "underemployed." 1982 was a recession year and 1970 was not, but that accounted for only part of the decline. By 1980, before the recession, underemployment had already risen by about 50 percent from its level in 1970. As many white men were underemployed in 1982 as black men had been in 1970—so that although black men remained twice as likely to be unemployed or in poor jobs as whites did, the situation was significantly and rapidly deteriorating for white men as well. (Black men were increasingly likely to be out of work altogether, but whites were closing the gap when it came to working in poor jobs with low pay and insufficient hours.)

19 Not surprisingly, Lichter found the problem of urban underemployment to be considerably worse for younger men, of both races. Already in 1970, 24 percent of young black men and 14 percent of young white men living in central cities were underemployed. By 1980 the figures had risen to 37 and 20 percent respectively, and in the recession of 1982

shot to 54 and 26 percent. In that year, in other words, over *half* of young black men and a quarter of young white men were either out of work or working at jobs with too few hours or too meager wages to provide a minimally decent living.

20   When we look at the connection between underemployment and education the portrait sharpens. Between 1970 and 1980 underemployment among *white* men with less than twelve years of schooling doubled; by 1982 it had tripled. In that recession year almost a third of white men with less than a high-school education were either jobless or working in poverty-level or near-poverty-level jobs—as were nearly half of blacks. Again, there was some racial convergence in the rates of underemployment in low-income work, but as Lichter tellingly comments, "this was largely because of increases in the white 'working poor' rather than declines in the fraction of less-educated blacks who were working at poverty wages." The narrowing of the difference between the races, in other words, was due to the declining economic conditions of young white men, rather than improving conditions for blacks.

21   Lichter concludes that in the seventies and early eighties there was a growing split by class and age in the "adequacy of employment among urban men." Men with low levels of education, in particular, were in *much* worse shape in the early eighties than their counterparts had been a decade earlier; the economic consequences of poor schooling had sharply increased. It was not that the skills or competence of younger urban men had fallen; rather, the kind of work available to them had changed markedly for the worse. More recent research shows that this trend has continued. Between 1973 and 1987, according to Sheldon Danziger and Gregory Acs, levels of schooling increased for working men of all races: the proportion of employed black men who had a high-school education or better, for example, more than doubled. But that increasing education did little for their chances of landing a good job. Indeed, men with a high-school education were more than twice as likely to be working in a low-wage job in 1987 as their counterparts in 1973. White men with a high-school diploma were as likely to be working in low-wage jobs in 1987 as blacks had been fifteen years before. What that has meant in human terms is that much greater numbers of younger people of all races, even if they successfully complete high school, now realistically have very little to look forward to in the world of work.

22   These adverse shifts in the "opportunity structure" were exacerbated by the simultaneous reduction in the public benefits that could have cushioned the economic impact of declining earnings from poorer jobs. To understand just how fateful the slashing of public income support has been since the early 1980s, we need to emphasize that even *before* the Reagan administration began a deliberate assault on the welfare state, the United States already ranked lowest among advanced industrial societies in the generosity of its safety net for the disadvantaged and in the degree to which income benefits kept people from sinking into poverty.

The dimensions of this gap have been illuminated by the recent Luxemburg Income Study, which compares rates of poverty and the effectiveness of government benefits in the United States, Canada, Australia, West Germany, Sweden, and the United Kingdom at the start of the 1980s. With the exception of Australia, the American rate of what economists call "pretransfer" poverty—that is, the level of poverty before income benefits and taxes are counted—was already sharply higher than that of the other countries: more than half again as high as Sweden and nearly twice that of West Germany. But the gaps were even wider once the much more generous government benefits for the poor in other countries were added in. Families with children in the United States were three times as likely to be poor after transfers as families in Sweden, twice as likely as families in West Germany. Overall, according to the economist Timothy Smeeding, at the end of the 1970s it was already true that "government programs reduce poverty twice as much on average in the other countries as in the United States." One reason for these differences was that the benefit levels in our income support programs were far lower than those in the other countries. Another was that many American families, unlike those in other Western industrial democracies, did not participate in the meager programs available: they fell through the safety net altogether. In the United States, according to Smeeding, 27 percent of poor families with children "receive no public income support from the programs studied," while in every other country in this study, "at least 99 percent" of poor families with children received some form of income support.

23   And that was *before* the deliberate reductions in income support in the United States in the 1980s propelled hundreds of thousands more American families into poverty. (The effect of these cuts, too, was magnified because they came after several years of inflation that had already reduced the real value of income benefits for the poor.) Between 1979 and 1986, the average benefit under Aid to Families with Dependent Children (AFDC) fell by about 20 percent in real terms, while the proportion of poor children actually receiving benefits fell from 72 to 60 percent. By the late 1980s, thirty-five states and the District of Columbia paid average welfare benefits that were less than *half* the federal poverty level. And what was true for AFDC was also true for other kinds of income support, notably unemployment insurance. The proportion of jobless workers receiving benefits under the unemployment compensation system fell from a little more than half in the late 1970s (already extremely low by European standards) to less than a third by the late 1980s. All of this meant that, as the 1980s wore on, public benefits lifted fewer and fewer people out of poverty. In 1979, according to the Center on Budget and Policy Priorities, only about one poor family in five was pulled above the poverty line by some combination of AFDC, social security, and unemployment insurance: but by 1986, just one in *nine*. In absolute numbers, this meant that about half a million families re-

mained in poverty who would have ceased to be poor had benefits been maintained at even their already minimal late-seventies levels.

24 The savage combination of a deteriorating job structure and reductions in income support benefits was responsible for sharply declining economic conditions for lower-income Americans in the seventies and eighties, both within the races and between them, and a deepening and hardening of poverty which, again, crossed racial and ethnic boundaries.

25 These adverse income shifts have struck hardest at the groups that are already most vulnerable to drug abuse—particularly disadvantaged young men and younger women raising children. By 1983, just before the crack epidemic leveled the inner cities, the median income of black families with a child under the age of six had fallen 23 percent since 1974, and for Hispanic families by 17 percent. Families headed by a single *woman* of *any* race with a child under six had seen their income drop by 25 percent since the mid-1970s.

26 The worst effects were at the bottom. More Americans became poor or nearly poor in the years just before the drug crisis, and the living conditions of those below the poverty line worsened by virtually every measure from the late 1970s onward—reversing what had been an erratic but generally upward twenty-year trend. Between 1979 and 1984, just when the drug epidemic of the eighties began to explode, 7 million white and 1.3 million black people joined the ranks of those living below 125 percent of the federal poverty level. The growth in poverty was especially dramatic in some cities, particularly those suffering sharp losses in relatively well-paying jobs—and it was already underway, in many cases, well before the eighties. The proportion of Hispanic families living in poverty, for example, more than doubled between 1969 and 1979 in several cities, including Cleveland and Bridgeport, and nearly doubled in Boston, Detroit, and Milwaukee.

27 Not only were there *more* of the poor, however; they were also poorer. The depth of poverty is sometimes measured by the "income deficit"—the amount of money it would take a poor family or individual to *reach* the poverty level. During the 1980s the average income deficit of poor families increased for all races and ethnic groups—but, again, it was worst of all for minorities. By the close of the decade the average poor black or Hispanic family was subsisting at more than $5,000 *below* the federal poverty level.

28 A recent Census Bureau study shows that this trend toward deepening deprivation among the poor occurred for both poor women and poor men, for both poor families and "unrelated individuals"—and that, in fact, it was *understated* by the conventional statistics. The average income deficit for all poor families rose by about 12 percent from 1973 to 1986; but since the average poor family was smaller over those years, the income deficit *per family member* rose more dramatically, by nearly 30 percent. Measured in terms of the real resources available to their fami-

lies, indeed, the American poor were considerably poorer in 1986 than they had been in 1959, when the federal government first began collecting poverty data—and well before the "war on poverty" of the sixties.

29   It is sometimes argued that the decline in income among the poor simply reflects a rising proportion of poor people in families headed by women, who are more likely to be severely poor. But the deepening of the poverty gap was more general: the income deficit increased for families headed by men as well as by women, and for unrelated individuals of both sexes. Those hardest hit were poor men living outside of families, whose *average* income was less than half the poverty level in the eighties (less than $3,000) and who were considerably *worse* off than their counterparts had been in the early 1970s. Moreover, as the study points out, the growing ranks of the homeless are mostly not even included in these figures: the government's poverty statistics are based on a survey of *households,* which by definition—as we've seen in the case of surveys of drug use—excludes most people who live outside them. Were we to factor in the economic condition of men and women without stable homes who eluded the official surveys, the number of poor men and women who have sunk below half of the official poverty line would loom even larger. Ominously, too, the rising income deficit among the poor continued more or less steadily throughout the much-vaunted economic "recovery" of the 1980s; the state of the poorest, that is, was little affected by a growing economy, even when we had one.

30   Poverty, moreover, not only deepened but also became more concentrated geographically. More of the poor were trapped in communities mainly inhabited by other poor people. That was particularly true for blacks and Hispanics: persistent residential segregation and rising poverty rates worked together to cram growing numbers of people into neighborhoods that, as a result, were unusually lacking in collective economic and social resources. According to William J. Wilson and his colleagues, the proportion of blacks living in "extreme poverty areas"—where over 40 percent of the residents were poor—more than doubled between 1970 and 1980. Similarly, as Anne Santiago and Margaret Wilder have shown, by 1979 roughly 50 percent of the Hispanic poor in Boston, Cincinnati, Newark, and Philadelphia were living in areas of concentrated poverty, reflecting a "growing spatial isolation of impoverished Latinos from the larger population."

31   It is sometimes argued that the rises in poverty have been only among people who have chosen not to work, or whose inappropriate behavior has forced them out of the labor market—and that things have steadily improved for people who behave responsibly and work regularly. But that isn't true. Indeed, one of the most telling economic shifts during the 1970s and 1980s has been that the rewards of working regularly have fallen, not risen, for those at the lower end of the job scale. Marta Tienda, for example, shows that Mexican-American and Puerto Rican men who were "stably active" in the work force were more likely to be

poor in 1985 than their counterparts fifteen years earlier. Hispanics, in particular, greatly increased their participation in the labor force in the 1970s and early 1980s, but their poverty rates rose faster than any other groups, mainly because of their increasing concentration in low-wage jobs. Among all races, the numbers of people who worked full-time and year-round but earned less than a poverty-level wage rose significantly from the early 1970s onward: they were about 8 percent of the total employed in 1972 and 12 percent by 1987. Moreover, their numbers steadily increased after the middle of the 1970s, growing—like the income deficit of the poor—even during the economic "recovery" after the early 1980s. Nor was the increase in the working poor confined to the inner cities; it was a national phenomenon that cut across the rural-urban divide as well as the racial one. In 1979, 32 percent of rural workers and 23 percent of urban workers earned less than enough from full-time, year-round work to support four people at the poverty level. By 1987 their numbers had risen sharply in *both* country and city, to 42 percent and 29 percent respectively. In many Southern and some Mid-western and Mountain states, nearly *half* of rural full-time workers, by the late 1980s, could not earn enough to bring a family of four above the poverty line.

32   What these bare statistics mean in real life is not only that growing numbers of working Americans face extremes of economic deprivation—but also that, more and more, working hard and hewing to middle-class norms of behavior may get you nothing more than long hours and continued poverty. That is obviously a recipe for frustration and alienation, and it has been psychologically aggravated by the simultaneous growth in conspicuous affluence at the other end of the income scale.

33   As poverty deepened and spread, many other American families of all races and ethnic groups were doing better and better, contributing to the stark splitting of life chances and material well-being that distinguishes the past fifteen years from any comparable period in our history. The proportion of white families making over $50,000 a year nearly doubled from the late sixties to the end of the eighties—and grew even more rapidly among blacks, by 168 percent from 1967 to 1989. Overall, measured by gains and losses at each fifth of the American income distribution, as reported by the House Ways and Means Committee, the bottom fifth of Americans lost about 12 percent in income between 1977 and 1990 while the top fifth gained over 30 percent—and the top 5 percent gained nearly 50 percent.

34   A recent Census Bureau study illustrates the growth of inequality from another vantage point. The study measures trends in "relative income"—defined as the proportion of the population with incomes either less than half or more than twice the national average. During the 1970s and 1980s, more and more Americans—white, black, and Latino—fell into one or the other of those extremes, with the numbers in the middle correspondingly shrinking. Given what we've seen about the impact of

the changing job structure on younger and less educated people, it is not surprising that they suffered most from this growing economic bifurcation. In 1969 only 19 percent of people under eighteen had incomes below half the national average; by 1989, the figure was about 30 percent. Among people without a high-school diploma, the proportion with low relative incomes jumped from 23 percent in 1964 to 38 percent in 1989, and the rise was actually slightly *faster* for those who had finished high school but had not completed college. In short, a substantial part of the younger population, especially, saw its comparative fortunes plummeting—not only relative to the most affluent, but also to the middle; and they were therefore progressively less able to participate fully in the good life as it was lived by more fortunate Americans.

35 But the decline in living standards among poorer Americans has involved more than income alone. Shrinking opportunities and falling incomes have been exacerbated by the crisis in low-income housing and the effects of government retreat from the provision of public services. These have combined to increase the "surplus of vulnerability" that has laid many communities open to the ravages of hard drugs.

36 The housing crisis has contributed particularly heavily to that vulnerability. Without a stable place to live, people lose the community supports that could provide a buffer against the impact of economic decline. As Gary Orfield puts it,

> Without being able to afford housing where the family can stay securely, there is no basic stability in a family's life and no consistent lasting relationship with institutions, friends, and community. Housing determines access to schooling, safety, friends for the children, and the ability to get to work in a reasonable time.

37 But stable housing became far more elusive for lower-income people in the eighties, as the result of skyrocketing housing costs, declining incomes, and the retreat of the federal government from housing support for the poor and near-poor. During the years when the drug crisis struck with greatest force, the federal government had virtually abandoned its already weak commitment to the ideal of "a decent home and a suitable living environment for every American family" embodied in the Federal Housing Act passed just after World War II. Indeed, low-income housing programs were "slashed more deeply than any other federal activity" during the 1980s—by roughly 75 percent from 1981 through 1989. Meanwhile, costs in the private housing market were spinning out of control; between 1974 and 1983, the number of rental units going for less than $300 a month (in 1986 dollars) fell by almost a million. Thus, just as the incomes of the poor fell steadily and the value of housing benefits for poor families plummeted, housing costs rose, in a perverse triple whammy. As a result, for families with children in the bottom fifth of the income scale, the "median rent burden"—rent as a proportion of to-

tal family income—went up by fifty percent from 1974 to 1987. In Atlanta, families below the poverty level were "forced to spend more than two-thirds of their cash incomes for housing costs by the early 1980s," according to Orfield, which meant that many could not both meet those costs and "provide other basic essentials for their children." The significance of this is illuminated if we look back at what the Kerner Commission on the ghetto riots of the 1960s had to say about the state of housing for the poor a quarter-century ago. "Grievances related to housing," the commission found, "were important factors in the structure of Negro discontent" that led to the disorders. The commission singled out the rising rent burden as especially troubling, and found it ominous that increasing numbers of black families had to spend more than *25 percent* of their income for rent, thereby "sacrificing other essential needs." They called, accordingly, for the provision of six million new units of low-and moderate-income housing to be built over the next five years. Instead, low-income housing construction dropped precipitously from roughly 50,000 units a year in the mid-sixties—which the commission regarded as desperately inadequate—to less than 25,000 in the 1980s. The results were entirely predictable. According to a survey by the U.S. Conference of Mayors, the wait for federal housing assistance had reached two years, on average, by 1989; so many people had signed up for federal help that two-thirds of the cities surveyed had closed their waiting lists to new applicants.

[38] The whipsaw effect of rising housing costs, falling incomes, and the withdrawal of federal housing funds has aggravated the vulnerability to drugs in several ways. It not only drove some of the poor into homelessness but forced many more to move repeatedly in search of an affordable place to live—undermining the social cohesion of local communities and eroding traditional sources of social support for families hard-pressed by other social and economic adversities. Those trends have been much aggravated by the simultaneous collapse of other parts of the public sector in poor neighborhoods under the impact of budget cuts at the federal, state, and local levels. Especially significant was the withdrawal of many public services—from hospitals to recreation facilities to fire protection—in the 1970s and 1980s. In a startling analysis, Rodrick and Deborah Wallace have shown how cutbacks in fire protection in the South Bronx helped to create what they describe as a "general collapse of public health," including rises in tuberculosis, homicide, infant mortality—and drug abuse. From 1972 to 1976, they write, "some fifty New York firefighting units were either disbanded or removed, mainly from ... overcrowded areas such as the South Bronx.... Fire department staffing fell from 14,700 to 10,200 between 1970 and 1976." The result was a massive "burnout" of local housing, which in turn "forced a vast transfer of population within the city, stressing not only disintegrating communities, but those overburdened by refugees." The consequent disintegration of social supports, they argue, was especially devastating for the minority poor.

39   The policies of the seventies and eighties, then, did more than merely strip individuals of jobs and income. They created communities that lacked not only viable economic opportunities, but also hospitals, fire stations, movie theaters, stores, and neighborhood organizations—communities without strong ties of friendship or kinship, disproportionately populated by increasingly deprived and often disorganized people locked into the bottom of a rapidly deteriorating job market. In many cities these disruptive trends were accelerated by the physical destruction left by the ghetto riots of the 1960s or by urban-renewal projects and freeways that split or demolished older, more stable neighborhoods and dispersed their residents.

40   Some of the consequences of this community fragmentation are suggested in Carl Taylor's investigation of the youth drug-gang culture in Detroit. Taylor describes how certain neighborhoods were transformed, after the late 1960s, from "a close-knit, cooperative network of extended families and friends to a declining, less stable community with no vital organization and transient residents." The process was compounded by the virtual collapse of even the most basic institutions of the private and public economy. Recreational centers were closed down: "Institutions such as drugstores and movie houses were demolished. Neighborhood children were left idle." Neighborhoods were simultaneously depleted of both economic opportunities and anything resembling a sense of community or of mutual obligations. In the course of his research, Taylor asked gang members several questions about their relationship to their neighborhoods. When asked "Do you know your neighbors on your street?" only fourteen of eighty gang members said yes. Only twelve answered yes when asked if there were any businesses such as drugstores, grocery stores, or clothing stores in their neighborhood. Only five said they "cared about their neighborhood," or that it would matter to them if there was a dope house on their street. And only two of the eighty said that they helped their neighbors "with problems in the community."

41   The destruction of community institutions has also contributed to a more subtle and less easily measured demoralization of many low-income communities—a transformation of values and norms, especially among the young, that contributes to the spread of drug abuse. I do not intend to romanticize the way of life of the urban or rural slums in the past. But there is important, if scattered, evidence that the culture of many poor communities has altered hand in hand with the economic decline of the past twenty years. The weakening of their institutions by impoverishment, forced migration, and the retreat of public services has left a vacuum that has been filled by the norms and values of the increasingly strident consumer culture of post-1980s America.

42   We do not have hard, quantitative evidence to show the extent of the downward spread of that culture. But opinion surveys do tell us that through that decade more and more Americans, especially the young, came to define their life purpose in terms of acquiring large amounts of

money and consumer goods. Research on the attitudes of high-school seniors, for example, shows a clear and sometimes startling national shift toward "consumption aspirations" between 1976 and 1986—including a sharp rise in the number of teenagers who considered "having lots of money" one of the most important goals in life, and who felt that it is very important to own "at least two cars," "clothes in the latest style," and other luxury goods. It is difficult not to see the connection between the broadcasting of those values at all levels of the economy and society and the growth of the mentality of predatory acquisition illuminated in street-level studies of the youth drug culture as in these comments by female gang members Taylor interviewed in Detroit:

> If a guy ain't got no crew [gang], he probably ain't got no cash. Guys with no paper don't interest us. If you ain't got no paper, what do I need you for?

> This boy at my school wants to get with me. He's cute, plays on the basketball team at school.... This fool told me he had a job at the gas station. I said, "Look here, fella, how you going to get with me and you ain't got no paper?"... Fuck them. Got no cash, got no time.

> I want nice things. I like BMWs, Volvos, and Benzos. Some niggah tried rapping to me, talking about going out on a date, taking the *bus*..... I said, "Niggah, please!"

43   It would be a mistake to imagine that these attitudes are confined to an urban underclass or that they reflect a distinct culture of the disadvantaged that stands apart from that of "mainstream" America. They are better understood as an only somewhat distorted version of the values that came to dominate all too much of mainstream economic life in the United States during the 1980s. The celebration of the consumer culture and its rewards—and the denigration of "ordinary" work and nonpecuniary values—hammered home through the media, has grown by default in the absence of countervailing values and norms rooted in viable communities and transmitted and enforced by effective families.

44   The transformation of poor communities has, in short, been cultural as well as structural—involving subtler changes in values and attitudes as well as massive shifts in economic opportunities and standards of living. Much discussion of the pathologies of the inner city—whether poverty, crime, or drugs—tends to fasten on one level of explanation or the other. But they are not mutually exclusive; they are intimately related, and indeed it is the simultaneous withering of economic opportunities and intensification of consumer values that has made the urban drug culture both so alluring and so difficult to dislodge through conventional policies. Rapidly constricting economic opportunities have severely weakened the indigenous institutions and traditions of poor communities, and the weakening of those institutions, in turn, has helped make possible the rise of a violent and materialistic street culture.

45   On closer examination, then, there is little mystery to why the 1980s drug crisis emerged when and where it did. Quite simply, life for many Americans had become bleaker, more stressful, less hopeful, and more atomized. These changes have been not only material, but cultural and familial. Black or white, men or women, urban or rural, the quality and character of life among less advantaged Americans, especially the young, have changed sharply for the worse, in ways that predictably increase their vulnerability to drug abuse.

46   It is not simply that many people have become poorer, but that they have become poorer in the context of declining opportunities for ever attaining a better life. It is not just that more young people, especially young men, are out of work, but that more and more are increasingly locked in to a future without anything much better. It is not just that material prospects have dimmed for the relatively young and poor, but that they have dimmed just when there has been an explosion of affluence and a growing celebration of material consumption at the other end. It is not just that families must contend with less, but that their sources of resilience and support have been sharply undermined. Never before in our recent history have so many been excluded from the realistic prospect of living the good life as their society defines it; never have so many been subjected to such severe and pervasive social and economic stress and such persistent insecurity; never have the public and private sources of help been so uncertain.

47   These changes were not the reflection of neutral forces over which we had no control. To be sure, there were profound technological and demographic changes rocking the foundations of American society just as they affected every other industrial country. But their specific impact on American life was decisively shaped by deliberate public policies. Indeed, had we set out consciously to prepare the ground for a fast-moving drug epidemic, we could hardly have done a better job. Over the course of the past twenty years, we have been busily "warring" on drugs with one hand while steadily exacerbating the social conditions that breed drug abuse with the other.

48   We know that social and economic deprivation and a sense of exclusion from the "good life" breed drug abuse; but we have consciously chosen policies that have spread and deepened poverty and widened the gap between the deprived and the affluent. We know that shrinking opportunities for stable and challenging work are central to the growth of drug abuse and the drug culture; but we have adopted policies toward economic development and the distribution of work and wages that have dramatically narrowed the chances for dignified and steady work, especially for the young and poorly educated. We know that the resulting stresses and deprivations place enormous pressures on the capacity of families and communities to resist the encroachment of drugs, but we have simultaneously gutted the public services and benefits that could help families and communities cope.

We know that a culture of consumption married to a systematic denial of legitimate opportunities feeds the distorted values that animate the street drug culture; but we have steadily bombarded the young with the message that the most important sources of personal worth and identity are acquisition and display rather than contribution and creativity.

49   These are not separate trends, they are all strands of an ongoing attempt to reshape American society and culture which, following the British writer Alan Walker, we may call a "strategy of inequality." That strategy has been justified in the name of stimulating economic growth, of shrinking wasteful and costly government, and of spurring the poor to work harder and enter the mainstream of society. What it has given us is deepening poverty, widening inequality, fragmented communities, collapsing families—and a drug problem of unprecedented proportions. That is the situation we face as we try to come up with a workable strategy to reduce the dimensions of drug abuse in the United States.

Points for Review and Discussion

1.   Summarize the major recent changes in the "opportunity structure," in neighborhoods and in cultural values, described in this essay.
2.   Currie argues that the U. S. safety net for the disadvantaged in 1980, *before* the Reagan assault on welfare, was the least effective among those of the world's advanced industrial nations. On what does he base this view?

•◦ Questions for Writing

1.   The author denies that poverty has worsened "only among people who have chosen not to work" (¶ 31) or who have behaved inappropriately. What evidence does he offer in support of this denial? Are you persuaded? Explain your answer.
2.   One reviewer of Currie's work wrote that he shows that "the war on drugs is futile, because it does nothing to reverse the epidemic of hopelessness that nourishes the drug culture." Is this a fair account of the argument in this essay? Does Currie's primary emphasis fall on personal feelings such as hopelessness or pessimism? Again, explain your answer.
3.   Write a one-page newspaper editorial on the functions of drug use among the nonworking poor and among the comparatively well-off middle class. End with a brief conclusion on what's wrong with conventional thinking about drug use.

The Ethics of Limits and the Abortion Debate
Christopher Lasch

Some public issues appear to arise solely from differences in moral and religious beliefs and to have no footing in class interests. The most passionately debated of these issues in our time is probably that of abortion. Both pro-life and pro-choice forces struggle to keep discussion centered on the moral ramifications they see as central, and their efforts in this direction have been largely successful.

It doesn't follow from this, however, that the abortion issue is without class dimensions. As Christopher Lasch demonstrates in "The Ethics of Limits and the Abortion Debate," hostility between social groups is clearly responsible for no small measure of the intensity of the debate. Lasch's probe of the class issues involved starts with an examination of current meanings of familiar social categories: working class, lower middle class, professional classes, the poor; it then moves on to argue that changes in the composition of these groups have a direct bearing on both pro-life and pro-choice attitudes.

Christopher Lasch, who taught history at Rochester University, until his untimely death in 1994, came to national prominence in 1979, when President Jimmy Carter singled out his book, *The Culture of Narcissism*, as a valuable diagnosis of America's late twentieth century maladies. Lasch's other books include *The New Radicalism in America* (1965) and *Haven in a Heartless World: The Family Besieged* (1977).

1   The decline of its standard of living makes it harder than ever to figure out just what Americans mean when they speak of a middle class. In Europe, where the bourgeoisie stood between the remnants of the feudal nobility and a class-conscious proletariat, the term had a sociological precision it never achieved in the United States. American workers never came to see themselves unambiguously as a proletariat. The American dream of equal opportunity encouraged them to hope that their children would move up the social scale. Very few of those children climbed into the salaried class, as it turned out, but they achieved a precarious level of security, in the years of the great postwar expansion, that made it seem reasonable enough for them to think of themselves as a middle class, if only because they were doing better than their parents and better, certainly, than blacks and Hispanics who lived in the "culture of poverty."

From Christopher Lasch, *The True and Only Heaven* (1991).

2   The boundary between the middle class and the working class was further blurred by a long-term decline in the position of the old proprietary class of shopkeepers, small businessmen, and independent professionals. In 1900, the middle class could not possibly have been confused with the working class. It was self-employed and not a little self-satisfied. It employed wage labor and domestic servants. Wives did not work—a point of considerable pride. Middle-class professional men were engaged for the most part in private practice, and even when they worked for salaries it was usually in organizations—colleges, hospitals, small firms of various kinds—over which they retained a good deal of responsibility. By the sixties and seventies, however, it was impossible to find a large category of people who shared all these characteristics. Small businessmen had lost out to the big corporations, tradesmen to the retail chains. Salaried professionals now worked mostly in gigantic bureaucracies, in which some of them earned princely incomes and wielded considerable influence while others earned very little money and wielded no influence at all.

3   The enormous range of wealth and power among professionals makes it difficult to use the concept of a professional-managerial class with precision, but that designation describes the upper levels of the salaried class much better than the usual designation of them as a middle class. Except as a rough description of relative income levels, the middle class, for all practical purposes, has ceased to exist. At the upper levels, it has dissolved into a "new class" with interests and an outlook on life that cannot be called "middle-class" in any conventional sense of the term. At the lower levels, the middle class has become increasingly indistinguishable from a working class whose climb out of poverty stopped well short of affluence.

4   *Time*'s report on the declining middle class, published at the height of the presidential campaign of 1988, includes a revealing vignette that illustrates the difficulty of distinguishing between the lower reaches of the middle class and the working class, especially in a period when both are faced with straitened circumstances. Bob Forrester, now sixty years old, settled on the west coast in 1953, having grown up in a blue-collar family in East St. Louis. His wife, Carol, was the daughter of a longshoreman on Staten Island. Neither went to college. In 1957, Forrester took a unionized job as a tankerman in Los Angeles harbor, at an annual wage of $5,512, while his wife stayed home to raise their three children. Today he makes $40,000 a year and owns three houses worth a total of $600,000. *Time* refers to him as a member of the middle class, and most Americans—including Forrester himself, perhaps—would probably agree with this classification, even though he clearly owes his material security to the labor movement and continues to serve it as a union official. But *Time* itself acknowledges the ambiguity of middle-class status when it describes Forrester's story as part of a "fundamental shift in the social and economic structure of old working-class neighborhoods."

5   "I'm definitely better off than my father was," Forrester says. None of his children, however, can make the same claim. The eldest, Billy, went to work on the boats when he graduated from high school. He was making $27,000 a year by the mid-eighties, when the company he worked for began to lay off unionized workers and to replace them with scabs. Having lost his job, Billy moved up the coast to Washington and went into business for himself as a gardener. His income fluctuated between $10,000 and $20,000. In 1987 he bought a house for $43,000, thanks to his father's ability to make the down payment of $11,000. His income barely supports his four children, but he has been unable to find a harbor job in Washington. "You've got to stand in line three days just to get your name on a list," he says. "It's a rat race."

6   Forrester's youngest child, Bob, is also looking for work in the harbor, but the Longshoremen's Union in Los Angeles has kept his application for three years without offering him a position. "They pass out 50,000 or 60,000 applications," he says, "... for about three hundred jobs." Meanwhile he drives a delivery truck at $8.25 an hour. Until 1987, he lived with his parents, as did his sister, Peggy. Now he and his wife live in a one-bedroom apartment. "What I'm afraid of," his wife says, "is to be living like this forever." As for Peggy herself, she earns $25,000 as the manager of a retail clothing store but pays out two-thirds of her income in rent, household expenses, and car payments. Saving is out of the question, and she has no hope of owning a house—the last vestige of proprietary status.[1] Her car, a Ford Tempo purchased for $8,500, cost her almost as much as the house her father bought in 1957. The down payment came to 6 percent of her salary, whereas her father paid only 14 percent of his annual income as a down payment on his first house, which he sold in 1973 for nearly five times what he paid for it. Peggy's car, on the other hand, is now worth less than half its original price.[2]

7   The convergence of the working class and the lower middle class, in an era of downward mobility, reveals itself not only in their standard of living but in a common outlook. If the middle class is a state of mind, as so many observers insist, it is a petty-bourgeois state of mind that holds it together. The petty bourgeoisie has no socioeconomic importance now that artisans, farmers, and other small proprietors no longer make up a large part of the population; but its time-honored habits and its characteristic code of ethics linger on, nowhere more vigorously than in

---

[1] Home ownership is a poor substitute for the kind of property that formerly supported a family and relieved people of the need to work for wages. It is not a source of material sustenance, let alone a source of the "virtue" formerly associated with property ownership. It remains an important symbol of independence and responsibility, however, and the decline of home ownership, more vividly than any other development, dramatizes for many people the collapse of the American dream.

[2] While Bob Forrester and his wife, still loyal to the party that had done so much for the labor movement, planned to vote for Dukakis in 1988, all of his children planned to vote for Bush—a choice that obviously cannot be attributed to upward mobility or "embourgeoisement."

the heart of the American worker. The worker's culture and political outlook bear little resemblance to those of his European counterparts. In many ways, however, they bear a close resemblance to the outlook of the old European peasantry and petty bourgeoisie—from which the American working class was recruited in the first place.

8   It is not just that American workers, unlike European workers, fail to support socialist or communist parties ... or that they have never shown much interest in remodeling the Democratic party along the lines of the British Labour party. The differences go deeper. American workers are more religious than workers in Europe: they declare an affiliation with some church, profess a belief in God, and even attend services occasionally. They have a stronger sense of ethnic and racial identity. They have a heavier investment in the ethic of personal accountability and neighborly self-help, which tempers their enthusiasm for the welfare state. They carry the code of manly independence to extremes—as in the assertion of their sacred right to bear arms—that would be considered ridiculous in Europe. Above all, they define themselves as a "middle class." They also define themselves as "workers," of course, but the meaning of that term, in America, is still closer to "producers" than to "proletarians." In his study of Canarsie, a beleaguered ethnic community in Brooklyn, Jonathan Rieder notes that the residents "showed their hostility to people on welfare"—and also to corporate wealth—"by contrasting parasites and producers." A spokesman for one civic group wrote in its newspaper, "For years, we have witnessed the appeasement of nonproductive and counter-productive 'leeches' at the expense of New York's middle-class work force." This populist language, together with the reference to a "middle-class work force," captures the ambiguity of working-class identity in America.

9   Lower-middle-class culture, now as in the past, is organized around the family, church, and neighborhood. It values the community's continuity more highly than individual advancement, solidarity more highly than social mobility. Conventional ideals of success play a less important part in lower-middle-class life than the maintenance of existing ways. Parents want their children to get ahead, but they also want them to respect their elders, resist the temptation to lie and cheat, willingly shoulder the responsibilities that fall to them, and bear adversity with fortitude. More concerned with honor than with worldly ambition, they have less interest in the future than do upper-middle-class parents, who try to equip their children with the qualities required for competitive achievement. They do not subscribe to the notion that parents ought to provide children with every possible advantage. The desire "to preserve their way of life," as E. E. LeMasters writes in a study of construction workers, takes precedence over the desire to climb the social ladder. "If my boy wants to wear a goddamn necktie all his life and bow and scrape to some boss, that's his right, but by God he should also have the right to earn an honest living with his hands if that is what he likes."

10 In his historical studies of nineteenth-century Massachusetts, Stephan Thernstrom found that neither the Irish nor the Italians thought of schooling primarily as a means for their children to climb into a higher social class and to leave their old neighborhoods behind. In Newburyport, Irish parents sometimes sacrificed their children to their passion for home ownership, forcing them into the workplace instead of sending them to school. Irrational by upper-middle-class standards, this choice made sense to people bent on holding their communities together and on assuring the continuation of their own way of life in the next generation. Social workers and educators, however, condemned child labor and sought to create a system of universal education, which would make it possible for children to surpass their parents, break the old ties, and make their own way in the larger world beyond the ethnic ghetto. In the same way, civil service reformers tried to replace the tribal politics of the Irish-American machine with a system more consistent with the principles of meritocracy and administrative efficiency.

11 Sociologists observed, usually with a suggestion of disapproval, that working people seemed to have no ambition. According to Lloyd Warner, who studied Newburyport in the 1930s, working-class housewives set the dominant tone of cultural conservatism. They adhered to a "rigid" and "conventional" code of morality and seldom dared to "attempt anything new." They took no interest in long-range goals. "Their hopes are basically centered around carrying on [and] take the form of not wanting their present routine disturbed—they want to continue as they are, but, while doing so, better their circumstances and gain more freedom." Anthony Lukas, a journalist, made the same point in his account of the Boston school conflicts of the mid-seventies. Lukas contrasted the "Charlestown ethic of getting by" with the "American imperative to get ahead." The people of Charlestown, deserted by the migration of more ambitious neighbors to the suburbs, had renounced "opportunity, advancement, adventure" for the "reassurance of community, solidarity, and camaraderie."[3]

12 Conflicting attitudes about the future, much more than abstract speculation about the immortality of the embryonic soul, underlay the controversy about abortion touched off by the Supreme Court's 1973 decision in *Roe* v. *Wade.* No other issue more clearly revealed the chasm between "middle-class" values and those of the educated elite. "I think people are foolish to worry about things in the future," an anti-abortion activist declared. "The future takes care of itself." Another woman active in the pro-life movement said, "You can't plan everything in life."

---

[3] They regarded Boston's "urban renaissance" across the river without enthusiasm, just as the working-class residents of Oakland, as Lillian Rubin portrayed them in her 1976 study of family patterns, resented the highly publicized development of new "life styles" in Berkeley and San Francisco. As far as Oakland workers were concerned, Berkeley and San Francisco "might just as well be on another planet," according to Rubin.

For the pro-choice forces, however, the "quality of life" depended on planned parenthood and other forms of rational planning for the future. From their point of view, it was irresponsible to bring children into the world when they could not be provided with the full range of material and cultural assets essential to successful competition. It was unfair to saddle children with handicaps in the race for success: congenital defects, poverty, or a deficiency of parental love. A pro-choice activist argued that "raising a child is a contract of twenty years at least, . . . so if you're not in a life situation where you can [make] the commitment to raising a child, you should have the option of not doing so at that time." Teenage pregnancy was objectionable to advocates of legalized abortion not because they objected to premarital sex but because adolescents, in their view, had no means of giving their offspring the advantages they deserved.

13   For opponents of abortion, however, this solicitude for the "quality of life" looked like a decision to subordinate ethical and emotional interests to economic interests. They believed that children needed ethical guidance more than they needed economic advantages. Motherhood was a "huge job," in their eyes, not because it implied long-range financial planning but because "you're responsible, as far as you possibly can be, for educating and teaching them . . . what you believe is right—moral values and responsibilities and rights." Women opposed to abortion believed that their adversaries regarded financial security as an indispensable pre-condition of motherhood. One such woman dismissed "these figures that it takes $65,000 from birth" to raise a child as "ridiculous." "That's a new bike every year. That's private colleges. That's a complete new outfit when school opens. . . . Those figures are inflated to give those children everything, and I think that's not good for them."

14   The debate about abortion illustrates the difference between the enlightened ethic of competitive achievement and the petty-bourgeois or working-class ethic of limits. "The values and beliefs of pro-choice [people] diametrically oppose those of pro-life people," Kristin Luker writes in her study of the politics of abortion in California. Pro-life activists resented feminist disparagement of housework and motherhood. They agreed that women ought to get equal pay for equal work in the marketplace, but they did not agree that unpaid work in the home was degrading and oppressive. What they found "disturbing [in] the whole abortion mentality," as one of them put it, "is the idea that family duties—rearing children, managing a home, loving and caring for a husband—are somehow degrading to women." They found the pretense that "there are no important differences between men and women" unconvincing. They believed that men and women "were created differently and . . . meant to complement each other." Upper-middle-class feminists, on the other hand, saw the belief in biologically determined gender differences as the ideological basis of women's oppression.

15   Their opposition to a biological view of human nature went beyond the contention that it served to deprive women of their rights. Their insistence that women ought to assume "control over their bodies" evinced an impatience with biological constraints of any kind, together with a belief that modern technology had liberated humanity from those constraints and made it possible for the first time to engineer a better life for the human race as a whole. Pro-choice people welcomed the medical technologies that made it possible to detect birth defects in the womb, and they could not understand why anyone would knowingly wish to bring a "damaged" child, or for that matter an "unwanted" child, into the world. In their eyes, an unwillingness to grant such children's "right not to be born" might itself be considered evidence of unfitness for parenthood. "I think if I had my druthers," one of them told Luker, "I'd probably advocate the need for licensing pregnancies."

16   For people in the right-to-life movement, this kind of thinking led logically to full-scale genetic engineering, to an arrogant assumption of the power to make summary judgments about the "quality of life," and to a willingness to consign not only a "defective" fetus but whole categories of defective or superfluous individuals to the status of nonpersons.[4] A pro-life activist whose infant daughter died of a lung disease objected to the idea that her "baby's life, in a lot of people's eyes, wouldn't have been very meaningful. . . . She only lived twenty-seven days, and that's not a very long time, but whether we live ninety-nine years or two hours or twenty-seven days, being human is being human, and what it involves, we really don't understand."

17   Perhaps it was the suggestion that "we really don't understand" what it means to be human that most deeply divided the two parties to the abortion debate. For liberals, such an admission amounted to a betrayal not only of the rights of women but of the whole modern project: the conquest of necessity and the substitution of human choice for the blind workings of nature. An unquestioning faith in the capacity of the rational intelligence to solve the mysteries of human existence, ultimately the secret of creation itself, linked the seemingly contradictory

---

[4] These fears are by no means fanciful or exaggerated. A 1970 article in the journal of the California Medical Association welcomed the growing acceptance of abortion as a "prototype of what is to occur," the harbinger of a "new ethic" that would substitute the quality of life, in effect, for the sanctity of life. The article predicted that "problems of birth control and birth selection [would be] extended inevitably to death selection and death control" and would lead to an acceptance of the need for "public and professional determination of when and when not to use scarce resources." The courts have tended to transform the right to prevent birth defects by means of abortion into a duty to prevent birth defects and then to apply this kind of thinking to all those whose lives have "no meaning," in the words of a recent decision authorizing a "life-shortening course of action" in the case of an elderly patient—to all those unfortunate human beings, in other words, who can be said "for all practical purposes" to be "merely existing."

positions held by liberals—that abortion is an "ethical private decision" and sex a transaction between "consenting adults" but that the state might well reserve the right to license pregnancy or even to embark on far-reaching programs of eugenic engineering. The uneasy coexistence of ethical individualism and medical collectivism grew out of the separation of sex from procreation, which made sex a matter of private choice while leaving open the possibility that procreation and child rearing might be subjected to stringent public controls. The objection that sex and procreation cannot be severed without losing sight of the mystery surrounding both struck liberals as the worst kind of theological obscurantism. For opponents of abortion, on the other hand, "God is the creator of life, and . . . sexual activity should be open to that. . . . The contraceptive mentality denies his will, 'It's my will, not your will.'"

18   If the abortion debate confined itself to the question of just when an embryo becomes a person, it would be hard to understand why it elicits such passionate emotions or why it has become the object of political attention seemingly disproportionate to its intrinsic importance. But abortion is not just a medical issue or even a woman's issue that has become the focus of a larger controversy about feminism. It is first and foremost a class issue. Kristin Luker's study of activists on both sides of the question leaves no doubt about that. The pro-choice women in her survey were better educated and made more money than their counterparts in the anti-abortion movement. They worked in the professional, managerial, and entrepreneurial sector of the economy. Many were unmarried, many were divorced, and the married women among them had small families. More than 60 percent of Luker's sample of pro-choice women said they had no religion, while most of the rest described themselves as vaguely Protestant. Anti-abortion activists, on the other hand, were housewives with large families. Eighty percent of them were Catholics. These differences defined the difference between two social classes, each with its own view of the world—the one eager to press its recent gains and to complete the modern revolution of rising expectations, the other devoted to a last-ditch defense of the "forgotten American."

Points for Review and Discussion

1.   Summarize Lasch's reasons for believing that the convergence of the working class and the lower middle class is pertinent to the abortion debate.

2.   Lasch and others contrast the "ethic of getting by" with the "American imperative of getting ahead." State the difference between the two in your own words.

⇢ Questions for Writing

1. Attitudes toward the future are a key factor in shaping convictions about abortion, according to the author (¶ 12). Write a paragraph explaining why this is so. How in your opinion does social class influence attitudes toward the future?
2. This essay quotes a journalist's distinction between the values of "community, solidarity and camaraderie" that he finds in a working-class Boston neighborhood, and the values of "opportunity, advancement, adventure" that characterize the suburbs (¶ 11). Does your own experience confirm or deny the existence of such a distinction? Give reasons for your answer.
3. Lasch states flatly that "abortion is not just a medical issue or even a woman's issue. . . . It is first and foremost a class issue" (¶ 18). If abortion came to be recognized, throughout the society, as a class issue, would it be—in your view—easier or harder to resolve the conflict? Why so?

CENSORING STUDS
Ellen Goodman

Increasingly in recent years public school systems and school boards have become embroiled in censorship controversies. A parent finds that a story, novel, or other work assigned as required reading for class contains offensive language, or an objectionable point of view, or both. The parent brings the matter to the attention of the teacher and/or the school board. The board responds by telling the teacher who made the original assignment to drop the work from the reading list. And sometimes at this point other parents—or the publisher or author, or the American Civil Liberties Union—speaks up in defense of the book, and a battle begins.

In the article below Ellen Goodman describes one such episode that occurred in Girard, Pennsylvania. The work found objectionable was Studs Terkel's *Working* (excerpted on pages 13–20 of this book), and Terkel himself traveled to Pennsylvania to make the case for his book. Goodman's Boston *Globe* newspaper column is syndicated to 400 newspapers throughout the country, and it has been awarded a Pulitzer Prize.

1   In early February 1982, Studs Terkel went down to Girard, Pennsylvania, to defend his book against the banners. His performance in the school and at the open meeting was, I am told, vintage Terkel: intimate, winning, honest.

2   Those who know this man from Chicago could imagine the itch he felt to turn on his own tape recorder and capture the voices and the feelings of the people who had accused him of writing a dirty book.

3   Terkel is, after all, a professional listener. He has listened to Americans who survived the Depression and listened to Americans who make it through life one working day at a time in a factory or a restaurant. He has a passion for words as they are really spoken—expletives not deleted. The folk of Girard, even those who challenged the school's right to assign *Working* to the students, are much like the people between the pages of his book. As Terkel put it, "The exquisite irony is that they are the heroes and heroines of this book."

4   What was unusual about this scene was that Terkel came and even conquered.

5   But without Terkel's star performance, it would have been another version of a stock play that has run in hundreds of other places with names as unfamiliar as Girard. Warsaw, Indiana, St. Anthony, Idaho, Gardner, Kansas, Drake, North Dakota, are only a few entries on the huge roll call of towns that have staged a censorship show.

From Ellen Goodman, *Keeping in Touch* (1986).

6   The list of books that have been challenged or banned from school curricula and libraries in the last few years reads like a Who's Who of American authors. The words of challengers read sometimes like a parody. It is tempting to repeat the lines of the parent from Richford, Vermont, who criticized the school use of *Grapes of Wrath*, saying, "You would never find a book like that in the *Reader's Digest*."

7   But the censorship incidents are real and growing. The American Library Association's Office for Intellectual Freedom, which keeps track of these things, tells us that in 1981, reported challenges tripled nationally from 300 to 900. These come sometimes from the left and mostly from the right. But they almost always come from people who want limits: limits on what the libraries can hold, limits on what the schools can assign, limits on what the students can read.

8   If Robert Doyle, the ALA's assistant to the president, had to pick the hottest issues for censoring they would be "language," sexual references, agnostic and atheistic viewpoints, and secular humanism. Not far behind would be protests against books without a strong moral viewpoint, in which good is not always rewarded and evil not always punished.

9   When you listen, censorship controversy is not really between liberal and conservative, left and right. It's between those who think that the business of books is to expand our vision and those who only want to read what they believe. It's between those who think the business of schools is to describe the world as it is, warts and all, and those who worry that the warts will spread unless they are removed from the pages, the shelves, the schools.

10   Maybe the library, even the school library, seems like an odd place for such a noisy conflict. Doyle says that, in fact, libraries try to maintain some political neutrality by "promoting the widest viewpoint." But in an era when the major intellectual struggle is against those who want to ensure a narrow viewpoint, this belief isn't neutral anymore.

11   The schools in particular are increasingly a focus for conflicting ideas, our investment in the future. All the regular procedures to approve textbooks, to define appropriate reading, have become more complex and more controversial. But there is a difference between an orderly review process and the lynch-mob censorship by which schools are hung one by one.

12   Most of the time, as Doyle says, a book doesn't even get a day in court. Only 15 percent of the censorship challenges even make news. Most of the rest are handled quietly. In about half the cases, the ALA tells us, some form of censorship is imposed almost immediately. Sometimes this censorship is as informal as a Magic Marker in the hand of a teacher in Idaho who blacks out every damn and hell in the book.

13   Terkel did get his "day in court," a public court. He defended his work against people who hunt for words instead of meanings. He defended the real world, the wide lands. He left Girard with a farewell that should, with any luck, stave off the censors of one more book for one more day: "I hope you have a long, decent life, work hard, and READ."

Points for Review and Discussion

1. Ellen Goodman holds that believers in censorship favor a variety of publicly imposed limits. Summarize the specific limits she mentions in your own words.
2. Make a list of the words and phrases used in this column to characterize protesters against "'language,' sexual references, agnostic and atheistic arguments and secular humanism" (¶ 8). Where do these terms place the protesters in the social class system?

•◦ Questions for Writing

1. Goodman asserts that the "censorship controversy is not really between liberal and conservative, left and right" but between "those who think the business of books is to expand our vision and those who only want to read what they believe" (¶ 9). On what ground could it be claimed that this is an oversimplification?
2. Write a coherently argued, one-page "Answer to Ellen Goodman on Censorship." Begin by defining the place of critics of censorship in the social class system; then go on to explain why it's unfair to describe those who advocate restrictions on reading lists as members of a "lynch mob." (Note: for help with this critique, reread the previous selection, by Christopher Lasch, on the issue of abortion.)
3. Now write a newspaper column of your own in which, after taking account of the class dimensions of censorship controversies, you go on to stake out a position of your own about how these controversies should be handled.

Death of a Princess
Charles Krauthammer

Among the more widely debated cultural issues of the 1990s was that of doctor-assisted suicide. State law and court cases centered on the activities of Dr. Jack Kevorkian, a Michigan-based physician who continued to answer requests for aid from terminally ill patients even after state authorities forbade him to do so. It soon became evident that resolution of the debate would come only through a decision of the Supreme Court.

"Death of a Princess" focuses on a suicide which, in the 1980s, became the subject of a one-hour documentary shown on public television—a program called "Choosing Suicide." Krauthammer's point of view is critical, and in the course of setting it forth, he pauses more than once to reflect on divergent class attitudes toward the behavior he's criticizing.

Charles Krauthammer studied political theory at McGill and Oxford universities before deciding to become a medical doctor. He graduated from Harvard Medical School, became Chief Resident in Psychiatry at Massachusetts General Hospital—and then switched careers, signing on as a political columnist for *The New Republic* and commenting frequently on politics for various television talk shows.

1   On July 10, 1979, alone and off-camera, Jo Roman, a New York artist, killed herself with an overdose of sleeping pills. It was not an impulsive act. As early as 1975, she had made up her mind that she would end her life on her own terms, purposefully and "rationally." Several years later, when she learned that she had breast cancer, she moved up the date. She would do it within a year, she decided, and proceeded to tell friends, family, and a TV film crew. Thus began a drama that culminated in a sensational front-page story in the *New York Times* and a harrowing one-hour documentary entitled "Choosing Suicide" that aired June 16, 1980 on PBS.

2   The documentary is a faithful record of the gatherings Jo held during that year to prepare for her great deed. It records the deliberations of a Greek chorus of chosen literati and hapless family relations drawn into her web as co-conspirators, spectators and participants. At these meetings, all sit in the obligatory circle. Jo, the queen bee, presides. She is quiet, controlled, in command. She is experiencing no pain or disability, but her mind is made up. No one can change her resolve, but all "acknowledge" and "respect" her feelings. There is much touching, hugging, crying and stroking. No one seems distracted by the bobbing microphones and clanking camera stands.

From Charles Krauthammer, *Cutting Edges* (1985).

3   All the while, I am trying to figure out why they are there. The film crew, I suppose, thinks that if she delivers they've got a hot property, and, if it is done with taste, maybe an Emmy. Friends and family must feel the weight of the contemporary obligation to "be there" and share the experience. And how do you turn down an invitation to a suicide?

4   But what's in it for Jo? Perhaps, like Tom Sawyer, she simply wants to live the fantasy of attending, indeed directing, her own wake. Jo herself invokes loftier motives with more decidedly romantic pretensions: she considers this act a work of art, "the final brush stroke on the canvas of my life." It is a claim taken with utmost seriousness by her friends, who seem to believe that art is anything that artists do (and then proceed to frame). "This is the greatest creative act of your life" gushes one friend. And because it is art, Jo Roman's son can assure her that rational suicide is not something he would recommend for the masses. He has told his friends and co-workers of Jo's plans, he says, but they are all into apple pie, baseball and religion, and they don't understand.

5   The masses, I infer, could begin to understand the angry crash into the highway abutment, the impulsive leap from the apartment window. They could begin to understand the everyday anguished acts of self-destruction full of killing and pain and suffering. What they would find difficult to understand is the bloodless, careless, motiveless, meaningless art of Jo Roman's rational suicide. Jo's friends, however, are awed by her innovation. After all, one friend comments, we need something more dignified than sidewalk splatter (as passé as action painting, I suppose). And Jo, in a burst of creativity, has given them the ultimate soufflé, the stylish alternative to such crude gaucheries, the artistic way to end it all. She has produced the last word in sophistication: the meticulously orchestrated, thoroughly psychoanalyzed, faithfully filmed, year-long death watch.

6   Jo has other reasons for suicide besides art. She and her flock coo responsively about how all this has brought them closer together, put them in touch with their own feelings, given them a profound "learning experience." In an interview taped twelve days after Jo's death, husband Mel, looking grave and lost, reflects on how the whole year leading up to Jo's death caused him great pain and suffering. But it has been worthwhile, he says, because he has learned a lot about himself. I found this a particularly sad sight: a grown man in his bereavement seeking solace in the shallowest cliché of adolescent solipsism—the world as an instrument of one's own education. It marked the moment in the show when the banality finally transcended the pathos.

7   Jo herself occasionally gropes for some deeper philosophic justification for her act. She proclaims suicide as the enricher and clarifier of life. Her friends stroke her hand and nod sagely in the classic group-therapy mode; but I have no idea what she meant. Another group favorite was

the idea that Jo is "taking control of her own life," taking responsibility for herself, finishing a job she started. They congratulate Jo for preempting God or cancer and taking her own life. In their preoccupation with the agency of her act, however, they avoid the question of its consequences. And the documentary shows us just what these consequences are: feelings of acute loss for her friends, suffering for her loved ones, bewilderment and self-doubt for her husband. When one of the pernicious seeds of her act begins to flower before her eyes—when her daughter, who also has had cancer, begins to contemplate her own suicide—Jo sees not horror but raised consciousness.

8   Our usual response to a victim of suicide is, as Pasternak says, to "bow compassionately before [his] suffering" because "what finally makes him kill himself is not the firmness of his resolve, but the unbearable quality of his anguish." Jo Roman, however, denies us our compassion because she denies herself her anguish. She opens the film looking into the camera and calmly proclaiming that her suicide, unlike others, does not involve killing and hurting, but is a reasoned response to her life. But her very coldness persuades us that we are watching not a suicide but a murder. This is why we experience not sorrow but emptiness, why we feel not pity but anger.

9   The anger is directed both at the murderer and at her mesmerized accomplices. A protesting voice is difficult to find. One friend says to her "I can't understand you. If someone say at age seventy-five said to me 'I have arthritis and I can't type'—O.K. I can understand that, but you ..." Can't type! What next? Suicide over a lost backhand? A clogged Cuisinart? The anger turns to bewilderment. What happens when these people are threatened by something worse than pain or age or travail? What happens when their children or their values are threatened? Is their reward for sophistication a capacity for self-delusion so prodigious as to turn cowardice into courage, death into creativity and suicide into art?

10 Not that voluntary death is either new or necessarily eccentric. History contains many acts of voluntary death from Socrates and Christ to the mother who gives up her seat on the lifeboat for her child. But they died for truth or salvation or love. They died for more than a dose of good feelings or artistic conceit. What is most pathetic about Jo Roman's death is that, in her enervated and alienated circle, she died for the illusion that her death would express some transcendent reality. Like the Dadaists, she believed that her life and death were art. But at least the Dadaists, were under no illusion. They considered both equally worthless.

11 "Choosing Suicide" is disturbing because it leaves us with the feeling that the Dadaists were right after all. For all its voguish psychobabble and pseudophilosophic paradoxes, this documentary leaves us with one conviction: that on the altar of her savage household gods—art, growth, feeling, control, creativity—Jo Roman died for nothing.

Points for Review and Discussion

1. Summarize the reasons for Jo Roman's suicide that are cited in this column.
2. Spell out in your own words Krauthammer's objections to Roman's action.

•◆ Questions for Writing

1. People of "sophistication" (¶ 5, 6) appear ready to accept the suicide as a "profound 'learning experience.'" How do you explain this readiness?
2. The "masses" (¶ 5) on the other hand, seem incapable of or unwilling to see the behavior as a learning experience. How do you yourself account for this unwillingness?
3. In your opinion should class differences in attitudes toward "rational suicide" be ignored in the ultimate decision, by authority, to approve or outlaw such acts? Explain your answer.

Connecting the Parts in Chapter 9: Assignments for Extended Essays

1. In one or more passages in each of their essays the authors in Chapter 9 reveal a class sympathy or hostility of their own. (The existence of this sympathy or hostility doesn't tell us anything definitive about the writers' individual class situations; people are sometimes hostile to their own class and sympathetic with another.)

   The presence of fellow feeling or animus shows itself in tones of voice, choices of phrase, "loaded" expressions. Reread the selections, this time making notes on passages in which class sympathy or hostility seems to you evident. Then write an essay in which you compare and contrast these passages for the purpose of bringing to light ways in which personal class feeling, muted or otherwise, can affect the treatment of large public issues.

2. Taxes, interest rates, unemployment, housing, health care, crime—each of these and practically every other public concern of our time directly touches the lives of students whether young or mature, full-time or part-time. And the aspects of these issues that matter most to each individual vary in accordance with the individual's social class.

   Choose the two or three issues that are most urgent to you. Then write an essay explaining the connection between that urgency and the realities of your class identity.

Leads for Research

1. Many issues less well-publicized than those alluded to previously in Chapter 9 are equally rich in class dimensions. One example worth exploring is the debate over the goals and priorities of feminist political activism. Consensus-building in the women's movement has required, almost from the beginning, uncommon alertness to differences in class meanings of "equal justice." A useful starting point for a research paper on current class issues in feminism is Judith Stacey's *Brave New Families* (1990).

2. No less rich in class dimensions is the ongoing debate about cultural assimilation—the question of whether ethnic groups should or should not resist the process of "Americanization" that loosens ties to the cultural past. The following works are useful starting points for a research paper exploring class issues in the assimilation debate: Andrew Greeley, *Why Can't They Be Like Us? America's White Ethnic Groups* (1971); Stephen Steinberg, *The Ethnic Myth: Race, Ethnicity, and Class in America* (1981).

3. The past decade witnessed the emergence of an issue of "fairness" centered on alleged special privileges awarded to African-Americans; the issue has moved gradually to the center of this country's race politics. Useful starting points for a paper exploring the political and cultural backgrounds of the so-called fairness issue are Thomas Byrne Edsall and Mary D. Edsall, *Chain Reaction: The Impact of Race, Rights, and Taxes on American Politics* (1991); Derrick Bell, *Faces at the Bottom of the Well: The Permanence of Racism* (1992).

10

Tomorrow's Class Politics

Much of the writing in this book addresses events and issues closely connected to contemporary experience. But writers interested in the shape of the future are also strongly drawn to the subjects of social difference and inequality. Some are utopians, bent on imagining model societies remote in time from the present—ideal communities capable of illuminating today's wrongs and correcting them. Other writers offer practical suggestions for change—particular directions that could be followed now. Still others offer analysis designed to show why the immediate future cannot bring major change.

The essays in this section sample the latter two kinds of writing. Mickey Kaus and James MacGregor Burns and Stewart Burns, authors of the section's opening and closing essays, present positive agendas for change and take up essentially optimistic positions. Derrick Bell's outlook is pessimistic. Tracing the complex relation between white racism and class conflicts that persist unresolved for generations, he argues against the notion that the prospect is good for early, positive change in the direction of equality.

THE CASE FOR CLASS-MIXING
Mickey Kaus

A decade of conservative leadership in the White House followed by extreme anxiety about the national debt created a climate unfavorable to discussion of class inequality in America. Yet the subject has by no means disappeared. One of the most widely commented-upon works of political analysis to appear in the early 1990s was Mickey Kaus's *The End of Equality* (1992). And although, as the title suggests, the book foresaw no early lessening of class differences, it devoted much space to the exposition of ways of moderating social problems arising from those differences. The book's major theme—the need to create a new American melting pot capable of easing class relations—is developed in the essay below.

Mickey Kaus has contributed significantly to the school of thought dubbed "neoliberalism" or "New Democratic" and embraced by President Bill Clinton in the period when he was governor of Arkansas and head of the Democratic Leadership Council. Kaus is a senior editor of *The New Republic* magazine.

1   What really bothers liberals about American society? Is it that William Gates, the 35-year-old founder of a computer software company, is worth $4 billion, and that some people drive Mercedeses and Acuras while others drive Hyundais and used K-cars? Is it that the wealthiest 40 percent of families receive 67.3 percent of the national income?

2   Or is it that the experience of confronting degraded beggars is now a daily occurrence for Americans who live or work in our major cities? Is it that a whole class of Americans—mainly poor, black Americans—has become largely isolated from the rest of society and is acquiring the status of a despised foreign presence? Is it that the wealthiest 20 or 30 percent of Americans are "seceding," as Harvard's Robert Reich puts it, into separate, often self-sufficient suburbs, where they rarely even meet members of non-wealthy classes, except in the latter's role as receptionists or repairmen? And is it the gnawing sense that, in their isolation, these richer Americans not only pass on their advantages to their children, but are coming to think that those advantages are deserved, that they and their children are essentially not just better off, but better?

3   If I'm right, distaste for this second sort of inequality—social inequality—is at the core of liberal discontent. Yet the primacy of this

---

From Mickey Kaus, "The Case for Class-Mixing," *The Washington Monthly* (July–August 1992).

value is only occasionally made explicit in our ordinary political conversations. It is "subliminal" in the sense that it forms the unacknowledged motive of liberal policies that are justified on more familiar rhetorical grounds. Specifically, liberals tell themselves they are for "more equality" of income and wealth, when if they asked themselves, I think, they would probably discover they're actually after social equality—equality of dignity, of the way we treat each other in everyday life.

4   The point is that money equality isn't the only factor that determines social equality, and it may not be the crucial one. More important, perhaps, are the social attitudes and institutions that determine how much weight the money variable has. But if that's true, why spend all our energies trying to twiddle the dial that produces greater or lesser money inequality? An equally promising approach would focus on changing those attitudes and institutions that translate money differences, however large or small, into invidious social differences.

5   This is the Civic Liberal alternative. Confronted with vast disparities of wealth, it attempts, not to redistribute wealth "progressively," but to circumscribe wealth's power—to prevent money inequality from translating into social inequality. The primary way it does this is through social institutions that create a second, noneconomic sphere of life—a public, community sphere—where money doesn't "talk," where the principles of the marketplace (i.e., rich beats poor) are replaced by the principle of equality of citizenship. As the pre-1989 Eastern European champions of "civil society" tried to carve out a social space free of communist domination, so Civic Liberals would carve out a space free of capitalist domination, of domination by wealth.

6   The foundation of this community sphere in the United States is, of course, the political institution of democracy. There the marketplace stops, and the rule is not "one dollar, one vote" but "one citizen, one vote." The same principle applies to other important components of our community life, such as public schools, libraries, highways, parks, and the military draft. Each of these institutions attempts to treat all citizens, rich and poor, with equal dignity. They are especially valuable parts of the public sphere because, in contrast with the rather formal and abstract equality of voting, they require rich and poor to actually rub shoulders with each other as equals. So do many other, less obvious but important institutions such as museums and post offices, even parades and softball leagues.

7   Now, you can argue that money "talks" in our democracy, too, and that it talks even louder these days as politicians depend more and more upon rich donors to fund their increasingly expensive campaigns. Meanwhile, the affluent and the poor no longer rub shoulders in the public schools of even small cities, as the middle class flees to its suburban enclaves or else abandons public education entirely. In bigger cities, the everyday experience of public life in streets, parks, subways, and li-

braries has been ruined by crime, incivility, and neglect. The draft has been replaced by a volunteer army that the rich can simply avoid.

8   But these are precisely the sort of things with which Civic Liberalism concerns itself. Instead of worrying about distributing and redistributing income, it worries about rebuilding, preserving, and strengthening community institutions in which income is irrelevant, about preventing their corruption by the forces of the market. It tries to reduce the influence of money in politics, to revive the public schools as a common experience, to restore the draft. And it searches for new institutions that could enlarge the sphere of egalitarian community life.

9   Not all components of the public sphere have deteriorated in the late twentieth century. The jury system, for example, still brings disparate members of the community together, if only occasionally, in a way that often convinces those who serve that common sense isn't a function of income or race. More generally, the courts still treat a Michael Milken or Leona Helmsley with an inspiring lack of deference. But other institutions have not been so hardy. Let's start with the institution that has deteriorated most dramatically: the military.

10 There are perfectly good military reasons for replacing the current all-volunteer force (AVF). Some of these reasons are related to social equality. The Gulf war proved that the egalitarian objections to an AVF become loudest at the worst time, just as the prospect of combat and death looms. At the very moment we were trying to intimidate Saddam Hussein in the winter of 1990–91, our country was split by a debate over whether the rich would bear their fair share of the fighting. The only reason the controversy wasn't crippling may have been that the battle turned out to be short, with few casualties on our side.

11 There are other, more technical problems with the AVF that have less to do with egalitarianism, such as the fact that the pool of young men from which we must buy our volunteers is shrinking (from 8.6 million men aged 18 to 21 in 1981 to an estimated 6.6 million in 1995). But the main justification for a draft remains moral. Volunteer-army advocates rely on the logic of the private sphere, in which everything, even soldiers' lives, is convertible into cash. If some young Americans are freely willing to go into battle for $25,000 a year—well, it's a deal. ("You took the money, now shut up and die," as former Navy Secretary James Webb caricatured the argument during the Iraq crisis.) But it is one thing for society to pay people to pick up its garbage and drive buses. It's another to pay them to risk their necks in battle. If dying in combat isn't outside the economic sphere, what is? The draft is the most natural and—again, because it involves the risk of death—most potent, arena of democratic experience. It doesn't only break down class barriers for a couple of years; it breaks them down for life, in part by giving all who serve a network of military acquaintances that crosses class lines. Even Henry Kissinger used to hang out with his old Army buddies.

12   A democratic draft is hardly a bold, idealistic step into the future. It's something America has done before. To reinstate it, we don't need new taxes or new leaders—simply a new law.

13   True, thanks to communism's collapse, the military will only need about 11 percent of America's draft-age men by 1995. But, however modest the manpower needs of the military, a draft is the most socially egalitarian way of meeting them. Even if only 11 percent of men in the upper, middle, and lower classes served—and all the others had to think about serving—it would do more to promote social equality than all the "transfer payments" liberals might conceivably legislate.

Genuine Draft

14   Yet it would be even more effective to involve more than 11 percent, and more than just men—to make the military part of a broader scheme of national service, including civilian service. Here is an idea that separates Civic Liberals from those with other priorities.

15   "At the age of 18, you should be focusing on your dreams and ambitions, not picking up cans in Yellowstone," sniffs Republican Jack Kemp. For social egalitarians, however, national service is valuable precisely because it would force Americans to pause in their disparate career trajectories and immerse themselves in a common, public enterprise. It is the draft in a weaker dose, more widely dispensed.

16   The notion of national service was revived in the eighties—to no apparent effect. Universal service was endorsed by Gary Hart, who predicted it "might be the biggest issue" of the decade. Senator Sam Nunn and Rep. Dave McCurdy introduced legislation that would have made federal student aid contingent on one or two years of service. (The Nunn-McCurdy bill went nowhere when the education establishment realized it would supplant existing loan programs.) William F. Buckley distinguished himself from most on the right by calling for a service scheme that would enroll 80 percent of America's youth by means of various "inducements" and "sanctions." Buckley's proposal, too, went nowhere.

17   For Civic Liberals the overriding goal, of course, is class-mixing. This helps clarify the sort of national service program we're talking about. For example, it excludes Job Corps-type programs designed to help salvage underclass kids through elaborate vocational training. The more national service "targets" the poor, the less it will be seen as a duty for all classes. Nor is the Civic Liberal test of success whether national service participants become less selfish. It's simply whether a large cross section of the population winds up serving together under conditions of equality.

18   Purely voluntary programs fail to meet this test; the ambitious sons and daughters of upper-class families simply don't sign up. Some na-

tional service advocates (like Buckley) nevertheless hope that "incentives" of various sorts might subtly induce participation by the rich. But such financial inducements can still be easily ignored by the wealthy. The only way to guarantee class-mixing is to make national service mandatory. That requires the threat of a penalty harsh enough to be coercive. It could be jail. It could also be a heavy monetary penalty that judges could tailor to fit the financial circumstances of any refuseniks—though it would have to be a potential fine of hundreds of thousands, perhaps even millions, of dollars if it were going to guarantee the participation of the truly wealthy.

19   A mandatory service scheme would enlist a lot of people—3 to 4 million a year, assuming the plan targeted young men and women of draft age. What would they be doing? Here again, it matters that social equality is the main goal. If we see national service mainly as an antidote to the "culture of selfishness," then the grungier the work, the better. Cleaning up mud slides is just the thing to teach incipient yuppies a thing or two. But the Civic Liberal imperative is to mix the classes, not to beat the selfishness out of them. National service jobs could be enjoyable, even career-enhancing. What's important is that they have a heterogeneous, communal aspect.

20   There are plenty of worthy tasks that fit this bill. Care for the infirm elderly is probably the most pressing need. Buckley notes that between 125,000 and 300,000 older Americans now living in nursing homes could move back into the "normal community" if there were enough workers to assist them with their daily chores. Those who are incapable of leaving nursing homes often lead lives of brutal loneliness—but the cost of professional attendants is simply too great for the vast majority of American families to bear by themselves.

21   In strict economic terms, national service is almost surely an inefficient way to help these lonely, old and ill Americans. It would be cheaper (once you count the "opportunity costs" of forgoing all the other things the servers could be doing with their time) to raise taxes to pay for a lot of nurses and handholders. But national service lets us do something in addition to providing services. It allows us to carve out a part of life where the market is negated, where common, nonmarket values that even conservatives like Buckley invoke—fellowship, solidarity, and social equality—can flourish.

22   There are other needs almost as critical: tutoring the illiterate and semiliterate, helping maintain or patrol public spaces, sorting library books, perhaps assisting in the care of preschool children in day care. As long as the tasks are class-mixing and valuable, a national service would be free to do whatever work the market, for one reason or another, cannot do—whether that work is grungy or exhilarating, and whether or not the government could do it more cheaply some other way.

23   Unfortunately, an emphasis on the most useful work puts national service on a collision course with public employee unions, which see young draftees as threats to their jobs (the same reason they also fear a WPA-style guaranteed jobs program). The more useful the work, the greater the chance some union member is already doing it.

24   One solution is to restrict national service to a few concrete tasks of proven utility and practicality. "There are four or five jobs we clearly know how to train kids to do," says Kathleen Kennedy Townsend, who runs a student service organization for the state of Maryland. Her list: teachers' aides, police aides, nurses' aides, a rural "conservation corps" to clean up the environment, plus a similar corps to repair and maintain urban public spaces. Put those together and you probably have enough jobs to keep several million young people usefully employed at a time.

25   The final question facing any mandatory national service scheme is how to integrate it with the military. That's trickier than you might think. The armed forces, as noted, need only a small fraction of those eligible to serve. What's more, they require stints of service lasting at least two years (otherwise training costs become too high). Requiring two years of civilian service seems a bit much. But one year of civilian service could hardly be treated as the equivalent of two years in the army.

26   Clearly, military service should count as the fulfillment of any service requirement. Beyond that, young Americans could be given a choice of military or civilian service—but the military's wages would have to be set much higher to compensate for the greater risks and longer tour of duty. Because the rich would be less tempted by such financial incentives than the nonrich, the result would probably be class division, with the military disproportionately poor and the affluent opting to avoid the perils of potential combat.

27   A better approach, for social egalitarians, would combine universal service with conscription. Teenagers would first be subject to a military draft, with no civilian alternative. If they escaped in the draft lottery, they'd have to do a year of civilian service. This hybrid draft/service setup might well be perceived as fairer than any attempt to allow more freedom of choice at the expense of universal exposure to military risks. Rich and poor teenagers would take their chances in the draft together. If chosen, they would serve together for two years. If they weren't chosen, they would still serve together as civilians for one year.

28   This sort of service scheme is the most intrusive Civic Liberal strategy; it would interrupt the lives of all Americans. But precisely because it is intrusive, it holds out the possibility of doing for everyone what Joseph Epstein, editor of *The American Scholar*, remembers the peacetime draft did for him: "[I]t jerked me free, if only for a few years, from the social class in which I have otherwise spent nearly all my days. It jerked everyone free. . . ."

Doctored Results

29   Given the continuing threats to social equality, Civic Liberals can hardly be satisfied with restoring the public sphere where it has deteriorated. They need to seize on new possibilities to expand it. Of all the potential new egalitarian institutions on the horizon, the biggest involves the provision of health care.

30   Health isn't a good like other goods. If somebody can't afford a car, we're willing to say, well, he doesn't have a car. But if a man who can't afford medical care is bleeding on the sidewalk, we are going to provide him with it one way or another, at public expense if necessary. As with the draft, the issue is life or death.

31   Of course, saying health care should be available to everyone doesn't necessarily mean it must be available in equal measure, or that the experience of getting it will necessarily be one that mixes classes. But the goal of universal coverage offers a solid base for building a potent democratic institution. We know it cements social equality to have Americans attend the same schools and serve in the same army. What effect would it have if they used the same doctors? The experience might not be as intense as school or service, but it would be repeated throughout a person's life.

32   Certainly universal health insurance seems to play a major socially equalizing role in Western Europe, where every country has some sort of universal national health plan. In most of them, the plan's egalitarianism is a source of fierce national pride. When everyone uses the same system, it not only reinforces "solidarity," it also ensures the quality of care. Upper-middle-class Americans will not tolerate bad treatment for very long (just as they wouldn't have tolerated the Vietnam war if their sons had been drafted).

33   In the United States, we have a patchwork system that, rather than putting everyone in the same boat, puts different groups in different boats and lets some fall in between. At the bottom, Medicaid covers only about 42 percent of the poor, mainly those on welfare or other mothers with young children. At the top, the revenue code heavily subsidizes generous employer-paid health plans by not counting them as income (a $40 billion tax break). Falling between boats are those who are unemployed, self-employed, or whose employers don't have a company plan. They are left to fend for themselves, to buy private insurance (with after-tax dollars). Between 31 and 37 million people in this group aren't insured at all, and that number has been growing. But if Americans reach the magic age of 65, they can relax. They qualify for Medicare, which will cover most of their bills.

34   It's not necessarily true that the more "socialized" a system is, the better it satisfies the demands of social equality. The British, German, and Canadian systems all currently meet the goal. The "socialized" British system allows those with money to purchase private insurance, but that

doesn't undermine class-mixing because most of the private insurance merely supplements the national health system, where the most advanced, high-tech medicine is still practiced. Only about 10 percent of the population uses the private system (though that percentage is growing).

35 Germany also manages to include about 90 percent of its population in a single system. The Germans do this by the simple expedient of requiring 75 percent of the population to join one of several "statutory sickness funds." Those with incomes above a certain threshold can opt out, but once they've done so, they can never opt back in. Not surprisingly, most remain with their assigned funds. The system's motto might be, "We have ways of making you stay." An even simpler, more effective strategy can be found in Canada, where it is flat-out illegal to buy basic private health insurance. Canadian waiting rooms mix virtually 100 percent of the population.

36 But less sweeping plans are less likely to achieve this objective. Senator Edward Kennedy's patchwork employer-based insurance scheme, in particular, looks like a loser for social equality. Medicaid and Medicare would still exist, probably with differential standards of care. Some employers would still provide lavish, fee-for-service insurance; some would consign their employees to spartan HMOs. Taxpayers (most of whom would already be covered, one way or another) probably wouldn't want to pay for much in the way of gap-filling last-resort insurance. We'd still have a system in which different classes report to different waiting rooms.

37 Even under the most promising plans, the crunch for Civic Liberalism will come when attempts to control the overall cost of health care force some method of rationing ever-more expensive medical procedures. What happens when affluent Americans—*increasingly* affluent Americans—are faced with this rationing? They will not calmly take their place in the queue for CAT scanners or proton-beam accelerators or artificial hearts. They will go outside the "universal" system and pay more money to get the expensive technology they want.

38 The temptation will be to let them, with the result of producing a two-tier health system of elaborate care for the affluent and basic care for everyone else. A Civic Liberal strategy would require regulations, such as those in Germany, making it unappealing to opt out of the "universal" system. At the very least a heavy tax disincentive will be necessary. The goal would only be to make enough (say, 90 percent) of the populace use the public sphere's waiting rooms. It's one thing, Civic Liberals could argue, for the rich to be able to buy the nicest cars, or the houses with the nicest views. It's another thing to make it easy for money to buy life itself.

Kids or Cash?

39 Health care isn't the only new public sphere possibility. Day care is another service with impressive potential for growth. The debate over day care has been between those (mainly Democrats) who want to encourage

communal day care centers and those (like President Bush) who would simply give cash to parents with preschool kids and let the parents decide whether to use the money to buy day care. Civic Liberals would tend to favor communal centers. Indeed, day care is a public sphere institution offering a unique escape from the tyranny of suburban class-segregation. Unlike schools, day care centers can be conveniently located near places of work rather than near homes. And poor preschool children aren't nearly as threatening to upper-middle-class parents as, say, poor adolescents. Locate the day care centers near work, and let the toddlers of secretaries mix with the toddlers of bank presidents. Let their parents worry together and visit together.

40   A range of other government institutions—museums, post offices, libraries—at least potentially reinforce social equality by providing services to all citizens. There is an important distinction to be made here—one typically ignored by American admirers of European social democracies—between provision of such common services and the provision of cash. With "in-kind, universal" services, Robert Kuttner notes, people of all classes actually meet and interact with each other and with those doing the servicing. They wait together, flirt, swap sob stories and advice, save each other's place in line, keep an eye on each other's kids. The "middle class is . . . reminded that poor people are human," Kuttner writes. This is the stuff of social equality.

41   But none of these virtues is evident when all the government does is send out checks—even if, as liberals typically recommend, benefits go to the middle class and rich as well as the poor. Recipients receive their benefit checks in isolation. The cash is spent, and is intended to be spent, in the private, money sphere. No communal experience is involved. On the contrary, the recipient's attention is focused more intensely on the importance of money and what it can buy. How much solidarity is there in cashing a check? Rich and poor don't even cash them in the same places.

Out at Third

42 Civic Liberalism would also recognize and protect the social-egalitarian power of class-mixing institutions that are technically in the "private sector." Particularly important are casual gathering places like taverns, coffee houses, and drug stores. Ray Oldenburg calls these "third places" because they offer an alternative to the other two main sites of our lives—home and work. One essential characteristic of a good third place is that it is accessible to people of all income levels; as Oldenburg puts it, "Worldly status claims must be checked at the door in order that all within remain equals." In the mid-seventeenth century, he points out, coffee houses were actually called "levelers" because they mixed the various classes in a way unheard of in the old feudal order.

43 It's easy to underestimate the significance of such unpretentious institutions. But they embody much of what Americans feel they've lost since the move from small towns—the general store, the pharmacy soda fountain of *It's a Wonderful Life*, the neighborhood bar romanticized on "Cheers."

44 The decline of those "private" democratic places is bound up in the process of suburbanization. Zoning changes that allow coffee shops, stores, and taverns to locate near residences, instead of in single-purpose commercial strips, would help. Still, it would be hard for even a nearby neighborhood tavern to mix classes in a neighborhood that is itself segregated by class. Fully restoring third places as class-mixing institutions will have to await the success of longer-term strategies to integrate the suburbs by income, as well as by race.

45 But some privately operated enterprises that are part of our public life don't rely on class-mixing at the neighborhood level. Organized professional sports are an obvious example. Going to a major league baseball game remains one of the few enjoyable experiences shared at the same time, in the same place, by people of various classes—one reason it's considered so precious. But even the democratic aspects of spectator sports are threatened by a number of recent developments. Attending a ball game has become a distinctly less egalitarian experience, for example, with the unfortunate invention of the tax-deductible corporate "skybox." Team owners now routinely demand stadium renovations that enable them to maximize the square-footage devoted to the rich. Another inegalitarian development is cable television, which allows broadcasters to restrict spectatorship to those who can afford to subscribe. In 1987, most New York Yankee home games were available only on cable. The result was a tremendous protest and a threat of congressional action, in part because large sections of New York—the poorer sections—weren't even wired for cable.

46 In general, the decline of network broadcasting (and the advent of demographically targeted "narrowcasting" on cable) should disturb social egalitarians. Network TV is often awful, but it once had the virtue of giving all Americans a common, classless set of cultural experiences. As the network audience share declines (it's fallen from 92 percent to 64 percent), that is increasingly no longer true. Instead of everybody watching Milton Berle, young professionals watch the Arts & Entertainment Network while the less cultured tune in to "Married with Children."

47 But once the egalitarian importance of these private institutions is acknowledged, Civic Liberals will be able to take steps to halt their deterioration. The tax deduction for stadium skyboxes and season tickets could be completely eliminated, for example—not on economic grounds, but on social-egalitarian grounds. Television coverage of sporting events could be regulated to keep it universal, preventing cable companies from buying the rights and then broadcasting only to the cable-ready affluent.

If necessary, the sports franchises themselves could be regulated, purchased by municipalities, or even seized by eminent domain. If the TV networks collapse completely, the government could establish a BBC-style network, less snooty than the current Public Broadcasting System, with a preferred spot on the broadcast spectrum nationwide. These may seem like relatively small things, compared with the draft or national health care. But they matter.

48   The point isn't that the Civic Liberal reforms suggested above would ensure social equality. That will require something more. The point is that once we set out to rebuild the public sphere, we can make fairly large improvements fairly expeditiously. It requires nothing we haven't done ourselves in the past—or that we can't copy, with appropriate modifications, from other democratic capitalist nations. We can frame our obligations so that rich and poor Americans serve the nation together. We did that in World War II. We did it in the fifties. We can have a society in which the various classes use the same subways and drop off their kids at the same day care centers and run into each other at the post office. We don't have to equalize incomes or make incomes "more equal" or even stop incomes from getting more unequal to do these things. We just have to do them.

Points for Review and Discussion

1.   Mickey Kaus believes that "class mixing" is the surest strategy now available to those intent on fostering the cause of equality. Summarize his reasons for believing this.
2.   Explain the specifics of Kaus's proposal to "combine universal service with conscription"(¶ 27).

•◆ *Questions for Writing*

1.   List the specific proposals to advance "Civic Liberalism" that Kaus sets forth in his article. Which of them seems to you most significant and useful? Which seems least significant and useful? Explain your answers.
2.   Kaus writes as follows about one kind of class-mixing situation as follows: "[People] wait together, flirt, swap sob stories and advice, save each other's place in line, keep an eye on each other's kids. The 'middle class is . . . reminded that poor people are human' . . . This is the stuff of social equality" (¶ 40). On what grounds might one challenge the claim that "this is the stuff of social equality?"
3.   Write a page assessing one of your own recent experiences of class-mixing. Was the effect of the experience "equalizing?" Why or why not?

Racism's Secret Bonding
Derrick Bell

According to conventional wisdom, ignorance is a major stumbling block to the achievement of justice and equality for all U.S. citizens. On this view the reason people fall into racist, classist attitudes is that they're badly educated; as levels of schooling rise, racism and classism will diminish; the nation's commitment to the improvement of public education ensures ultimate defeat for the forces of bigotry.

Not every contemporary thinker buys this version of the future. Among its strongest doubters is Derrick Bell, author of *Faces at the Bottom of the Well* (1992), the work from which the following essay is excerpted. Bell is visiting professor of law at New York University. In 1990 he was fired from his job as Weld Professor of Law at Harvard for refusing to end his two-year leave protesting the absence of minority women on the law faculty.

"Racism's Secret Bonding" is cast in the form of a dialogue between Bell and an imaginary character, Geneva Crenshaw—a civil rights lawyer and prophet who made her debut in Bell's first book (*And We Are Not Saved: The Elusive Quest for Racial Justice* [1987]).

1 "Well," Geneva asked, "do you think sweeping reforms are possible?"

2 "I am far less certain than I was twenty, even ten, years ago," I replied, "that our long-held belief in education is the key to the race problem. You know," and I explained the old formula, "education leads to enlightenment. Enlightenment opens the way to empathy. Empathy foreshadows reform. In other words, that whites—once given a true understanding of the evils of racial discrimination, once able to *feel* how it harms blacks—would find it easy, or easier, to give up racism."

3 "Yes, that is certainly what we have hoped for," Geneva agreed, "but now you have doubts? Doubts based on—"

4 "Experience, Geneva, experience. Even older and wiser, it's hard for me to admit, but we fool ourselves when we argue that whites do not know what racial subordination does to its victims. Oh, they may not know the details of the harm, or its scope, but they *know*. Knowing is the key to racism's greatest value to individual whites and to their interest in maintaining the racial status quo."

5 "Watch it, friend!" Geneva cautioned. "Your civil rights colleagues who consider your giving up on integration to be an abject surrender to

---

From Derrick Bell, *Faces at the Bottom of the Well* (1992).

racism, will deem blasphemy your loss of faith in the value of educating whites to racism's evils."

6 "Don't I know it?" I replied sadly, thinking of some of the motivations for racist behavior that we understand, and trying to connect them with other factors, possibly hidden ones we haven't yet considered. We've long known, as I told Geneva, that poor whites prefer to identify with what Professor Kimberlè Crenshaw calls the "dominant circle" of well-to-do whites, particularly those who attribute social problems to blacks rather than to the policies that they, the upper-class policymakers, have designed and implemented. No less accurate, if more earthy, than Crenshaw's is the novelist Toni Morrison's assessment of how the presence of blacks enables a bonding by whites across a vast socioeconomic divide. When asked why blacks and whites can't bridge the abyss in race relations, Morrison replied:

> [B]ecause black people have always been used as a buffer in this country between powers to prevent class war, to prevent other kinds of real conflagrations.
> If there were no black people here in this country, it would have been Balkanized. The immigrants would have torn each other's throats out, as they have done everywhere else. But in becoming an American, from Europe, what one has in common with that other immigrant is contempt for *me*—it's nothing else but color. Wherever they were from, they would stand together. They could all say, "I am not *that*." So in that sense, becoming an American is based on an attitude: an exclusion of me.
> It wasn't negative to them—it was unifying. When they got off the boat, the second word they learned was "nigger." Ask them—I grew up with them. I remember in the fifth grade a smart little boy who had just arrived and didn't speak any English. He sat next to me. I read well, and I taught him to read just by doing it. I remember the moment he found out that I was black—a nigger. It took him six months; he was told. And that's the moment when he belonged, that was his entrance. Every immigrant knew he would not come at the very bottom. He had to come above at least one group—and that was us.

7 "You know, Geneva," I mused, "Morrison's observation gains in validity as the Eastern Europeans—freed of the authoritarian domination of Communist control—engage in fierce and bloody ethnic conflicts. Those conflicts, and their violent counterparts in other parts of the world, reveal the role of blacks that enables Americans to boast that this nation is a melting pot of people from many origins."

8 "I understand," Geneva interrupted. "Americans achieve a measure of social stability through their unspoken pact to keep blacks on the bottom—an aspect of social functioning that more than any other has retained its viability and its value to general stability from the very beginning of the American experience down to the present day. Indeed, as Professor Jennifer Hochschild has recognized, racism is in a state of symbiosis with liberal democracy in this country. And, if all this is true, does that not mean that we need a truly extraordinary educational campaign, something like a data deluge?"

9 "So, I would think, but I have the sense that it's an open secret everyone has agreed on, however much individuals may deplore it from time to time. Indeed, I wonder whether the plight of black people in this country isn't caused by factors more fundamental even than white racism, more essential than good government to a civilized society? While some racial reform can be pressured by financial considerations, disaster, threat, guilt, love, and, yes, even education, there may be a primary barrier to the racial reformation which nullifies all these. I wonder, that is, whether—in the melding of millions of individuals into a nation—some within it *must* be sacrificed, killed, or kept in misery so that the rest who share the guilt for this monstrous wrong, can bring out of their guilt those qualities of forbearance and tolerance essential to group survival and growth? And, if so, then who in the legal system plays the more important role—the prosecutors who are the instruments of the sacrifices mandated by a social physics we do not understand, or the defendants whose efforts are destined to fail but who, by those efforts, serve to camouflage the bitter reality of those sacrifices from the society and—alas—from themselves as well?"

10 As I wound up, Geneva just looked at me blankly, her face reflecting my own stark frame of mind.

11 "A grim outlook, I know," I said, "and one that has taken on confirming, metaphorical muscle for me in Ursula Le Guin's haunting short story 'The Ones Who Walk Away from Omelas.'"

12 I went on to give a brief account of the idyllic community in the story, of a prosperous and sophisticated people, much given to carnivals, parades, and festivals of all kinds; their leaders, wise and free of corruption.

13 "There is in Omelas neither crime nor want. In a word, its people are extremely happy.

14 "But there is a problem, an open secret. It's a secret that forces some who learn of it—and some who have known it for a long time—to conclude that they cannot remain, and they leave Omelas. They leave and never look back, never return."

15 Reaching over to my bookshelf, I took down the book of Le Guin's short stories and opened it to the passage that had haunted me since I'd read it some days earlier.

> In a basement under one of the beautiful public buildings of Omelas, or perhaps in the cellar of one of its spacious private homes, there is a room. It has one locked door, and no window. A little light seeps in dustily between cracks in the boards, secondhand from a cobwebbed window somewhere across the cellar.... The floor is dirt, a little damp to the touch, as cellar dirt usually is. The room is about three paces long and two wide: a mere broom closet or disused tool room. In the room a child is sitting. It might be a boy or a girl. It looks about six, but actually is nearly ten. It is feebleminded. Perhaps it was born defective, or perhaps it has become imbecile

through fear, malnutrition, and neglect.... The door is always locked, and nobody ever comes, except that sometimes—the child has no understanding of time or interval—sometimes the door rattles terribly and opens, and a person, or several people, are there. One of them may come in and kick the child to make it stand up. The others never come close, but peer in at it with frightened, disgusted eyes. The food bowl and water jug are hastily filled, the door is locked, the eyes disappear. The people at the door never say anything, but the child, who has not always lived in the tool room, and can remember sunlight and its mother's voice, sometimes speaks. "I will be good," it says. "Please let me out. I will be good!" They never answer.

They all know it is there, all the people of Omelas. Some of them have come to see it, others are content merely to know it is there. They all know that it has to be there. Some of them understand why, and some do not, but they all understand that their happiness, the beauty of their city, the tenderness of their friendships, the health of their children, the wisdom of their scholars, the skill of their makers, even the abundance of their harvest and the kindly weathers of their skies, depend wholly on this child's abominable misery.

16 Geneva sat quietly for a time, absorbed in thought. "A fine story," she said finally, "and an apt metaphor for the knowing but unspoken alliance whereby all whites are bonded—as bell hooks says—by racism. And," she added, "as paradoxical as it seems, viewing racism as an amalgam of guilt, responsibility, and power—all of which are generally known but never acknowledged—may explain why educational programs are destined to fail. More important, the onus of this open but unmentionable secret about racism marks the critical difference between blacks and whites in this country, the unbreachable barrier, the essence of why blacks can never be deemed the orthodox, the standard, the conventional. Indeed, the fact that, as victims, we suffer racism's harm but, as a people, cannot share the responsibility for that harm, may be the crucial component in a definition of what it is to be black in America."

17 "So," I said,... "For all the reasons we have been discussing, being black in America means we are ever the outsiders. As such, we are expendable and must live always at risk of some ultimate betrayal by those who will treat such treachery as a right."

18 Geneva frowned. "I guess what you say is right, but now that we have expanded—exploded, really—the education-as-cure-for-racism notion, there is something more. Toni Morrison, you know, is not the only witness to the fact that learning the term *nigger* made new immigrants from Europe 'feel instantly American.' Why, 'every white immigrant who got off the boat was allowed,' as Andrew Hacker writes, 'to talk about "the niggers" within 10 minutes of landing in America.' Ralph Ellison, too, saw that 'whites could look at the social position of blacks and feel that color formed an easy and reliable gauge for determining to what extent one was or was not an American.' But he saw this as 'tricky magic,' because despite the racial difference and social status, 'something indisputably American about Negroes not only raised doubts

about the white man's value system but aroused the troubling suspicion that whatever else the true American is, he is also somehow black.'"

19   In the essay of Ellison's from which Geneva was quoting, he reviews the long history—fantasy, he calls it—of an America free of blacks. He calls it an absurd fantasy, one that fascinates blacks no less than whites and that becomes operative whenever the nation grows weary of the struggle toward the ideal of American democratic equality. In arguing that blacks are a unique and essential part of American culture, Ellison contends that without blacks, the nation's economic, political, and cultural history would have been far different. And, because they are an essential component of this country's make-up, he warns that those who would use the removal of blacks as a radical therapy to achieve a national catharsis, would destroy rather than cure the patient.

20   "Do you think," I asked, "that recognition of our essential cultural role may protect us from the ultimate betrayal we both fear?"

21   "On the contrary," she said firmly, "I believe that the notion that we blacks, the immutable outsiders, might nevertheless be the bearers of the culture, increases our risk dramatically."

22   "Then, you differ with Ralph Ellison," and I took his book from the shelf. "He concludes his essay by acknowledging that blacks, of the many groups that compose this country, suffered the harsh realities of the human condition. Because of our past fate, 'for blacks, there are no hiding places down here, not in suburbia or in penthouse, neither in country nor in city. They are an American people who are geared to what *is* and who yet are driven by a sense of what is possible for human life to be in this society.' He predicts that the nation could not survive being deprived of blacks' presence because, 'by the irony implicit in the dynamics of American democracy, they symbolize both its most stringent testing and the possibility of its greatest human freedom.'

23   "Ellison's optimism cannot conceal the additional dimension he provides to the scapegoat theme in Le Guin's story. He is telling—or, rather, reminding—us that black people are not innocent children chosen at random to perform the psychologically necessary role of social cohesion. Rather, they are the nation's conscience, but he says it better than I."

24   Taking the book from me, Geneva read the passage I pointed to:

> Listen: it is the black American who puts pressure upon the nation to live up to its ideals. It is he who gives creative tension to our struggle for justice and for the elimination of those factors, social and psychological, which make for slums and shaky suburban communities.... Without the black American, something irrepressibly hopeful and creative would go out of the American spirit, and the nation might well succumb to the moral slobbism that has ever threatened its existence from within.

25   "In other words," I suggested when she looked up, "we're a race of Jeremiahs, prophets calling for the nation to repent."

26   "Exactly!" Geneva said. "And you know what nations do to their prophets?"

27   "I do. About the least dire fate for a prophet is that one preaches, and no one listens; that one risks all to speak the truth, and nobody cares."

Points for Review and Discussion

1. In a passage quoted in this essay the novelist Toni Morrison asserts that "if there were no black people in this country . . . immigrants would have torn each other's throats out" (¶ 6). On what stated grounds does she believe this?
2. According to Bell, "for all the reasons we have been discussing, being black in America means we are ever the outsiders" (¶ 17). What *are* the reasons?

↔ Questions for Writing

1. Explain in your own words Ralph Ellison's thesis that blacks are the true bearers of American culture. What does this statement mean? How do you yourself assess its accuracy?
2. Bell argues that the bloody conflicts tormenting Eastern European nations confirm that it's the presence of black people that "enables Americans to boast that this nation is a melting pot of people from many origins" (¶ 7). How do you interpret this statement? And again, what is your assessment of its accuracy?
3. Bell ends this essay on a depressed note. What are the reasons for the depression and how valid are they? Explain your answer.

The Nurturing of Rights
James MacGregor Burns and Stewart Burns

Hopefulness about class relations in the future sometimes rests on anticipation of policy changes, sometimes on belief in the possibility of changes in the national outlook—new conceptions of enlightened self-interest that will recharge democratic energies. Optimism of this sort resounds in "The Nurturing of Rights" by James MacGregor Burns and Stewart Burns. The authors' vision of "empowering rights" and "nurturing rights" owes much to ideas developed in "women's activism" over the past quarter-century; the same holds for their vision of a new kind of leadership capable of creating a "Great Majority" that can "put through a massive rights program."

James MacGregor Burns is a biographer, historian, and teacher who was awarded both a Pulitzer Prize and a National Book Award for his *Roosevelt: The Soldier of Freedom* (1970). Stewart Burns (James's son) is a social historian and editor of the Martin Luther King papers at Stanford University.

1 To think about rights in a wholly new way calls for rights claimants to make a leap of the imagination into a kind of intellectual shadowland. It means breaking out of the world of contractual rights in which Americans are so deeply immersed that they take it for granted, and plunging into a nascent world of nurturing rights. Currently some may live in that environment for a few years after birth and then largely abandon it for the familiar territory of impersonal contracts and fleeting personal contacts.

2 To make that leap into the world of nurturing rights, the best starting point is at the side of the newborn child, where—as was noted at the outset—rights begin. The birth of that infant establishes a claim to the right to survive and to grow, a right that must be assured first of all by the mother and other family members, who make up a "rights microcosm" of nurturing persons.

3 For centuries the family has been presented as a benign microcosmic model for the larger society. "The most ancient of all societies, and the only one that is natural, is the family," Rousseau wrote in 1762, and thus the family "may be called the first model of political societies," and "all, being born free and equal, alienate their liberty only for their own advantage." The family, wrote John Stuart Mill a century later, must be more than a school of obedience. "Justly constituted," it would be "the real school of the virtues of freedom," a "school of sympathy in equality, of living together in love, without power on one side or obedience on the other."

4 An ancient dream—and a dream often shattered on the rocks of social reality. The vast majority of American children, growing, going to

---

From James MacGregor Burns and Stewart Burns, *The People's Charter* (1991).

school, taking jobs, enter a society far more patriarchal than nurturing or communitarian—a competitive, hierarchical society in which they will be treated generally as means to others' ends rather than as ends in themselves. The rights secured by justice, John Rawls argues, echoing Kant's central concern with human beings as ends in themselves, "are not subject to political bargaining or to the calculus of social interests." But it is precisely the bargaining among interests that dominates American political and social—and even intellectual—life.

5   Some feminists, notes Virginia Held, have urged that the right of women to enter freely and fairly into contractual relations in the broader society should be extended to their lives at home, with their mates and families. But other feminists have advocated the reverse process. "Instead of importing into the household principles derived from the marketplace," Held herself contends, "perhaps we should export to the wider society the relations suitable for mothering persons and children," so that relations in that wider society would be "characterized by more care and concern and openness and trust and human feeling than are the contractual bargains" in current political and economic life. Thus the household would replace the marketplace as a model for society.

6   Society as a caring, trusting "extended household"—would it also realize people's needs for personal and economic and social rights? Would it meet the test, in short, of real opportunity? This might be its supreme achievement. For the essence of the ideal nurturing family is not only caring and sharing but its willingness and capacity to open up opportunities for children to develop and pursue self-fulfillment, and to thwart the great enemies of the child's real opportunity, such as ill health, low motivation, emotional disability, damaged self-esteem. Could the potential of the nurturing family for fostering real opportunity be extended to the whole society?

7 To propagate the ideal of nurturing parents, supportive families, caring households, and spread it to society at large—this has been the dream of visionaries for centuries. Utopian societies in the nineteenth century hoped to demonstrate that men and women might live in a spirit of communal equality, of loving solidarity, of mutual aid and protection. Religious communities sent out missionaries to preach Christian love and charity as well as hellfire and damnation. Populist farmers and others established economic cooperatives that incorporated family values of sharing and reciprocity on a larger scale.

8   Perhaps it would seem even more utopian today to expect that the ideal and the practices of the nurturing family could be extended to the broader society with more success than in the past. To achieve such an objective, rights activists and strategists would need first to identify and mobilize a huge coalition of Americans who would be devoted to the pursuit of nurturing rights for themselves and others. Next such a coalition must be ready either to form its own party or to convert an estab-

lished party into a stronger rights force, and in either case to win elective offices. Yet the new coalition must be more than electoral if it expects to galvanize the commitment and moral passion needed to effect basic change; it must at the same time become a coalition of grass-roots activists and social movement groups involved in community organizing, direct action, and public education—a rich federation of diverse social forces. This broad rights coalition and its winning party must then be prepared to refashion governmental institutions, if necessary, in order to carry through rights legislation and implement it. And all these requisites would require something more—transforming leadership.

9   Does a "Great Majority" for the pursuit of rights lie out there for the mobilizing? One weakness of reform movements historically has been their certainty that their cause was so self-evidently just and noble that there must be a tremendous majority simply waiting to make it its own. Such a majority has rarely shown up at the polls on election day. Rights strategists would need to be realistic about potential support and the heavy task of mobilizing and extending it. They would have to understand too that most Americans think of rights not in terms of human, nurturing rights embedded in relationships and in an ethic of caring, but in terms of abstract Bill of Rights protections or individualistic and property-oriented economic rights.

10   Still, a Great Majority is there to be mobilized, in the homes and neighborhoods, schools and sanctuaries, streets and workplaces of the nation. It would include low-income workers, the inner-city and rural poor, activists in such human service professions as teaching and social work, peace activists, environmentalists. It would gather energy and staying power from millions of committed young people. Women of all ages—especially women of color—would be the common denominator and the unifying force in such a coalition and central to its leadership; women form the majority in most of these categories and constitute the great majority of those who are economically deprived or destitute. And women outnumber men in census tallies and voting rolls.

11   The numbers and the needs are there. Can they be mobilized? Success will turn largely on unity within and among the constituent groups, and unity in turn would depend on the capacity of such groups to rise above internal divisions and external rivalries to form the foundation of a rights majority. One of the striking aspects of these groups is how far they are fragmented into smaller, single-issue subgroups in many separate localities. Skillful negotiation would be needed to bring them together behind a program that transcended their differences, along with arguments—most notably that their particular and separate goals have a far better chance of realization if they united in a Great Majority coalition to win political power.

12   To forge a majority that can win nationwide electoral power—this is the toughest endeavor of all. Indeed, the American system of checks and balances raises a series of hurdles that require activists to wage cam-

paigns for president, senators, representatives, governors, and state legislators in staggered elections over an extended period. Forging a new majority would call for most of the traditional techniques of informing and registering would-be voters and getting them to the polls, but committed and savvy activists could do this with much more efficiency and spirit than is typically found in American elections today, especially if Congress finally passes an automatic and universal registration law, as proposed by Human SERVE and other organizations. The steadily falling numbers of voters indicate that the major parties do a poor job even by the criteria of conventional electioneering.

13 That decline in voting, so deplorable in itself, offers a special opportunity to a rights majority, for it can deploy its large array of troops on a smaller battlefield. Conventional politicians are particularly vulnerable in nominating contests, since primaries, even presidential primaries, attract exceptionally low turnouts. If a rights majority carefully marshaled supporters in crucial primary contests, it could secure a dominant role in the selection of nominees. Such an effort would call for big turnouts not only at the polls but at candidates' speeches and debates and at party conclaves, and for high-visibility rallies at key points in congressional, state, and presidential primary campaigns—in short, for directly confronting candidates with both the numbers and the determination of rights activists.

14 Standing above these tactical and organizational matters, for both the shorter and longer term, must be the moral and mobilizing power of the rights majority itself. Only an enduring and articulate commitment to overriding goals could carry a popular majority to continuing election victories. Only an abiding concern for the needs and aspirations and for the real opportunity of fellow Americans could sustain that commitment. Equally important would be the capacity to stand up against strong opposition, an opposition that should be regarded not as unfair or diabolical but rather as an opportunity to strengthen one's own ranks, to sharpen one's own commitment, and to pose for the American people policies and programs strikingly different from the consensus positions of the two major parties. Conflict has historically been the great engine of progressive politics in the United States; it could be a major weapon in the success of a Great Majority.

15 That success will turn ultimately on the capacity of a new majority to convert its principles into workable policies and programs. And that step will encounter perhaps the hardest obstacle—the intellectual and institutional resistance of the gridlocked political system to new initiatives and radical programs and to structural change. Systemic reform of the government would indeed require a great majority both quantitatively and qualitatively. Quantitatively, because sheer numbers in Congress and elsewhere would be essential to put through reforms when two-thirds majorities, for example, were required. Qualitatively because reformers would be so committed to rights purposes that they would

adapt institutions to clear goals; they would restructure institutions to fit those objectives, in the process creating new centers of democratic power. In fashioning and implementing the necessary means to realize their ends, they would understand that just as ends should not be subordinated to means, neither should they unduly subordinate means to ends. Ends and means must be carefully matched since, as Gandhi stressed, means are ends-in-the-making.

16 For a Great Majority to win power and put through a massive rights program will call for leadership of an extraordinary nature. Few contemporary American politicians could even begin to meet the tests of that kind of leadership. Today's standard practices of transactional leadership—the favor-swapping, the deal-making, the special-interest representation, all based on an ethic of calculated self-interest—are woefully inadequate, as two centuries of delay and deadlock have shown, to rise above brokerage and address the enduring wants, needs, and demands of millions of the less privileged.

17 Such large purposes call for a new generation of transforming leaders with the vision of a Thomas Jefferson on a Franklin Roosevelt, a Walter Reuther or a Martin Luther King, Jr.; and even more of an Elizabeth Cady Stanton, an Eleanor Roosevelt, an Ella Baker or Marian Wright Edelman. Far more important will be the leadership engendered at the grass roots. No fundamental advance in rights programs will be possible without the leadership of tens of thousands of activists, acting in the tradition of the agrarian rebels, the union militants, the black marchers and jailgoers who were the heart of the great radical and reform movements.

18 A Great Majority will depend heavily on the leadership of women, particularly women of color, who will face old hurdles and new. One of the oldest and highest is the assumption, "embedded in culture" and perpetuated by male scholars, in Sue Tolleson Rinehart's words, "that leadership would be exercised by physical males, and that the qualities of leadership are the qualities of masculinity." A related assumption is that if women do wish to lead, they must adopt traits of competitiveness, aggressiveness, person-to-person domination, on the model of former British Prime Minister Margaret Thatcher. Over the centuries femininity has been stereotyped as "dependent, submissive and conforming," in contrast to the masculine conception of leadership as command and control.

19 Ironically, it will be precisely these "feminine" qualities—better described as caring and sharing—that will be crucial to the leadership of a Great Majority. Feminist or nurturing leadership will draw its strength from the closeness of leaders to the evolving wants and needs of followers. The world of nurturing leadership and followership will not be hierarchical but mutually interactive, as leaders recognize the human wants of followers, legitimate them as needs, and begin to satisfy those needs. Followers, both fulfilled and emboldened as needs are met, will escalate their hopes and expectations; they will intensify their claims to entitle-

ments and convert them into still higher demands on the leaders. Eventually, as leaders respond to followers' rising activism, they will in a sense become followers of their followers. Indeed the mutuality has been so deep in this spiral from wants to demands that the process is increasingly a reciprocal relation between leaders and followers in a dynamic interplay of forces, until leadership and followership are interwoven. Hierarchy and command yield to equality and mutuality.

20   Ultimately leadership means the exercise of power—the question is what kind of power, for the benefit of whom? A last intellectual barrier to feminist leadership is the contention that men know how to handle power—it is their daily currency—and women do not. Men's kind of power is defined in terms of certain resources—money, guns, status, connections. This definition of power, traditional in political science, is so inadequate as to be dangerously misleading. It is not these resources alone but whether and how activists and potential followers are motivated to make the best use of such resources as are available to them that is pivotal. This was one of the lessons of Vietnam—soldiers relatively poor in military resources but high in motivation and group support defeated soldiers armed with vast quantities of modern weapons but poorly motivated. Whether or not the traditional model of power will remain paramount in American politics and society will depend in part on the capacity of a Great Majority and its rights party to convert a collective desire for real opportunity into the motivational force behind dynamic social activism and the emergence of transformational leadership at all levels.

21   The prospects for success of a rights party are not high. The grip of tradition, intellectual rigidity, institutional gridlock, and transactional leadership is very strong. Even vitalizing our leadership, even mobilizing a new majority, even restructuring our institutions may not be enough. We must ultimately make the most daring leap of all—to change ourselves, in our families and neighborhoods and communities.

22   From Rousseau's *Social Contract* to "second wave" feminist thinking of recent times, democratic theorists have faced the fact that people have to change themselves in order to make democracy work. Although the transformation of individuals and of institutions must reinforce each other, a critical mass of citizens with changed values, aspirations, and self-concepts would seem to be a precondition for building and sustaining an effective coalition for rights. Moreover, even if an electoral majority won sweeping legislative and constitutional reforms, little real social change would result if citizens were not motivated to actualize the new rights in their everyday lives.

23   American history abounds with precedent for rights creation from the bottom up. Over two centuries, millions of oppressed Americans defined and asserted basic entitlements long before these were officially recognized, and they transformed themselves in the process. The past generation has seen remarkable advances in the right to personal auton-

omy, particularly in areas of sexuality and "body rights." This right has been realized far more by individuals asserting it directly than by laws and court decisions that were, in fact, the consequence of people's changing conduct and expectations. For nurturing rights to achieve similar legitimacy in order to become the object of new national policies and programs, the informal practice of such rights would need to well up from the grass roots, prefiguring a nurturing society. A wide array of educational forums, organizing projects, community development efforts, and cooperative institutions would be needed to generate a base of common consciousness and commitment as catalyst for the large-scale implementation of nurturing rights by a restructured government. With transformation under way at the personal and community levels, the mobilization of a new majority would be less difficult to accomplish and more likely to translate new policies into real opportunity.

24 Thus the place to begin is with citizen education that would instill the nurturing rights ethic into the folkways and culture of the citizenry, a process of learning by doing in the spirit of John Dewey and Myles Horton.

25 Underlying nurturing rights is the assumption that rights are interwoven with responsibility. Unlike the liberal individualist paradigm that sees the individual as independent, unencumbered, and linked to others primarily by contract, nurturing rights are predicated upon people's interdependence and are constituted by social relationships. Feminists have taken the lead in showing that rights and an ethic of care are not contradictory. Carol Gilligan has illustrated how women have been socialized to perceive their claims to personhood as expressions of selfishness. But an underpinning of women's activism has been the opposite principle that asserting rights is a moral and social responsibility. Rather than dissolve "natural" bonds of family and community in order to promote individual claims, nurturing rights would involve a "morality of responsibility that knits such claims into a fabric of relationship, blurring the distinction between self and other through the representation of their interdependence." Self and other, individual and community, Gilligan suggests, would be experienced as "different but connected" not "separate and opposed." In some respects, as feminist practice has exemplified, individuality and community are less at odds than mutually reinforcing; the question becomes how to cultivate their cross-fertilization to bring out the best in each.

26 If nurturing rights are rooted in responsibility for oneself *and* for other people, not just in one's own circle but in the wider community, they are necessarily communal. While some communal rights, as Staughton Lynd stresses, involve means of political expression—the right to act in concert, for instance—the most vital are entitlements to social resources, such as universal child-care services, that aim to foster personal growth—physical, emotional, intellectual, cultural, spiritual. Thus nurturing rights would satisfy not only basic needs for nutrition,

physical health, shelter, and a healthy environment, but such higher needs as education, cultural development, and emotional well-being, all of these in turn prerequisites to the fulfillment of everyone's right to individuality.

27   Moving beyond the liberal conception of rights as protections of due process and procedural fairness, nurturing rights are substantive, embodying explicit values and purposes. They would not jettison the liberal concern with process, however, but refashion it to serve directly these values and purposes. Substantive rights devoid of democratic process can be as deficient as procedural rights without concrete content. Animated by citizen responsibility and commitment, nurturing rights would combine substantive ends with modes of political participation and self-governance tailored to those ends. Socioeconomic entitlements would have democratic forms and mandates institutionally built in: for example, community-controlled health services, patient participation in federal AIDS policy-making, local planning councils for economic conversion of war industry, democratized welfare agencies. Such structures of grassroots democracy would not be mere window dressing but empowered by law. The Johnson administration's war on poverty might have been more effective if its rhetoric of "maximum feasible participation" had been translated into real empowerment of poor people. Even if the implementation of nurturing rights required that revenue allocation and overall policy-making be somewhat centralized, the nature and delivery of services would have to be democratically determined in localities—and not, as with "revenue sharing," by unaccountable state and local bureaucracies. Democratic empowerment, through the integration of political and socioeconomic rights, would lie at the heart of nurturing rights.

28   To empower themselves, people would need to alter both their identity as citizens and their conception of democracy. Citizenship, rather than merely an "outer frame" of duties such as voting, paying taxes, and obeying laws, would be experienced as "the core of our life," in Michael Walzer's formulation, which "assumes a closely knit body of citizens, its members committed to one another." Such an activist citizenship would express itself through the development of participatory democracy, an ideal crystallized in the 1962 "Port Huron Statement" of Students for a Democratic Society: "We would replace power rooted in possession, privilege, or circumstance by power and uniqueness rooted in love, reflectiveness, reason, and creativity. As a *social system* we seek the establishment of a democracy of individual participation, governed by two central aims: that the individual share in those social decisions determining the quality and direction of his life"; and that society be restructured to encourage both autonomy and common participation. Implicit in the SDS manifesto was the importance of combining movement-based grass-roots democracy with electoral politics, without compromising the former's principles, purposes, and passion.

29   Progress toward this ideal of democratic citizenship would not, however, replace a conformity of apathy with a conformity of activism, or substitute political duties for political rights. Participatory democracy would violate its own values if citizens did not have a right *not* to participate, or to participate differently or unconventionally. But perhaps as the experience of democracy came to mean more than hollow forms and smoke and mirrors, as it came to be a rewarding experience of fellowship and community and a means of enhancing self-esteem, self-confidence, and self-fulfillment, more and more people would rise to the challenge.

30   The new spirit of democratic citizenship would embrace an ongoing citizen responsibility not only to assert rights and strive to translate them into law but to engage actively in the further stages of implementation and enforcement. Reformers have proven more successful at legalizing rights than at actualizing them. Mobilizing diverse constituencies to push a comprehensive agenda of nurturing rights through a divided and sometimes deadlocked political system will not be easy. But no less formidable will be the continuing democratic process of deciding how the new entitlements, once enacted, should be put into effect.

31   Daunting dilemmas and differences will arise right away, threatening the endurance of the majority coalition. If, for whatever reasons, some rights had to be implemented before others, or for some groups ahead of others, how would these priorities be determined? How would various entitlements, especially economic ones, be fairly apportioned, given a national context of material and fiscal scarcity? If certain types of entitlement required a disproportionate share of resources, for an interim period at least, how would the groups having to make do with less be persuaded to cooperate, deferring what is due them? What if different rights seemed to clash, such as those to a decent livelihood and to a sustainable environment, or to free speech versus freedom from the discriminatory harassment of "hate speech"? Rights conflicts in the future will likely be less than in the past clear-cut clashes between "just" and "unjust" claims—as between the rights of slaves and of slaveholders—but will more tend to be conflicts between valid and even fundamental rights, each expressing cherished values and legitimate moral claims, which can be reconciled only through prudent and principled compromise.

32   Resolving such conflicts of rights will be a major purpose of the new, or renewed, institutions of participatory democracy that should foster the fullest possible debate and deliberation and ensure that all views are heard. Yet even the most appropriate structures to link ends and means would not succeed in reconciling serious differences without the commitment and perseverance of many citizens learning how to engage in constructive conflict. Transforming leadership will need to be cultivated at every level.

33   Is it too late? Has the United States become so fragmented along crosscutting lines of class, race, ethnicity, gender, age, sexual orientation, cul-

ture, and education that it would be impossible to build a broad and powerful rights movement uniting diverse constituencies? Growing divisions, even within groups (such as African-Americans) previously more homogeneous, present the most fundamental obstacle to the creation of a new majority coalition. Is it pie-in-the-sky to imagine that social conflict can be waged constructively, without divisiveness, resentment, hostility, or violence, and within a larger context of solidarity? Here is the ultimate test of how far citizens can change their own values and attitudes.

34   As Audre Lorde, Charlotte Bunch, and other feminist thinkers have urged, citizens must learn to redefine and reclaim difference in order to bridge divisions. Throughout history, human differences have been distorted or misnamed in order to serve as tools of domination—racial distinction being the most odious example. Yet differences that to a large extent have been "socially constructed" can be reconstructed and turned into tools of empowerment. Speaking to women in particular, Lorde writes that "we must recognize differences among women who are our equals, neither inferior nor superior, and devise ways to use each others' difference to enrich our visions and our joint struggles. The future of our earth may depend upon the ability of all women to identify and develop new definitions of power and new patterns of relating across difference."

35   How can activist citizens, both women and men, recast differences as building blocks of authentic and lasting solidarity? Facing them honestly would help to overcome fears and prejudices and the perception of differences as more than they are. Moreover, seeing them clearly would enable diverse groups to understand not only their particular perspective in relation to others but the multiplicity of perspectives and the complex ways that these interact to constitute the social whole. If in the past, active citizenship and "civic virtue" were practiced mainly in homogeneous communities, the comprehension of multiple oppressions, needs, and aspirations might open the door to true citizenship in a heterogeneous, multicultural society. The more that differences are recognized and valued, the less difficulty citizens will have discovering and embracing what they have in common, and the more prepared they will be for trusting cooperation over the long haul.

36   In a sense activists "must strive to become 'one-woman coalitions,'" Bunch suggests, "capable of understanding and raising all issues of oppression and seeing our relationship to them—whites speaking about racism, heterosexuals about homophobia, the able-bodied about disabilities." The more that activists are able to gain a broadened, holistic view of social relationships—internalizing the ethic that "an injury to one is an injury to all"—the more personal wholeness they may come to feel as individuals. The surer their grasp of the multiplicity of social experience, the better equipped they will be to carry out a common program of nurturing rights that values equally the needs, expectations, and priorities of all groups.

37	A coalition for nurturing rights would thus diverge sharply from the traditional model that reflects the liberal individualist paradigm: coalitions motivated by narrow self-interest, entailing least common denominators, short-run goals, expedient compromise, and division—not difference—as the organizing principle. According to the old model, movements or pressure groups are "assumed to be competitive," Joshua Cohen and Joel Rogers explain. Their coordination is "limited to select points of convergent interest" with no basis for "continuing coordination among fragmented groups." The guiding assumption is that no broader agreement is feasible and, ironically, that to pursue such agreement is itself divisive, threatening the fragile, superficial, and temporary "unity."

38	The concept of a coalition has to be redefined as an alliance or federation motivated by cooperation not competition, by common needs more than self-interest, and by respect for difference. "A true alliance is based upon some self-interest of each component group and a common interest into which they merge," Martin Luther King, Jr., wrote shortly before his death. "For an alliance to have permanence and loyal commitment from its various elements, each of them must have a goal from which it benefits and none must have an outlook in basic conflict with the others." As King associate Reverend James Lawson, Jr., has put it, each group's self-interest has to be "an enlightened self-interest within the context of the entire community." Tocqueville called this "self-interest rightly understood."

39	Perhaps women have begun to offer the answer. As the feminist movement has put diversity at the center, and as women of color have assumed more leadership, especially intellectual leadership, the formation of alliances—among women and with other rights forces—has become a growing priority. Theorists such as Lisa Albrecht, Rose Brewer, and Davida Alperin argue that alliances are essential to understand and confront the interconnectedness of political issues, particularly the simultaneous and interactive nature of various oppressions, by gender, race, class, and so forth. Unlike traditional coalitions, these alliances are intended to be "ongoing, long-term arrangements" for fundamental reform. Creating such alliances will mean learning how to make principled compromises, with people of diverse backgrounds, styles, and perspectives, that are in the long-run interest of all participants. This type of coalition activity "is not work done in your home," cautions singer-historian Bernice Johnson Reagon. "You shouldn't look for comfort." With feminists blazing the trail, alliance-building could be taken up as an intermediate objective by all progressive social movements, leading to a national federation of alliances that could exercise power both inside and outside political parties and the electoral system.

40	Forging movement alliances and fostering an activist citizenry would aim at the "structural renewal" of society, in Martin Buber's words, creating a more cooperative and nurturing society that would strive to fulfill pluralist ideals that have remained out of reach. The establishment of real pluralism is both more pressing and more possible (as well as more threatening to many whites) now that peoples of color, including many new immigrants from Latin America and Asia, are increasing their proportions at an unprecedented rate, and consequently their influence and power. Such pluralism would be more than the fruitful interaction of racial, ethnic, and other autonomous groups. The true measure of a pluralist society is the extent to which each group exercises equal political, economic, and cultural power. For power to be equalized, however, it would have to be democratized; for power to be democratized it would have to be transformed, replacing "power-over," power as control and manipulation, by "power-with," power widely shared, power as self-empowerment—above all, power as an enabling and energizing force, the capacity to nurture growth in human beings.

41   As power is transformed, democracy would take on new dimensions. It would mean not only the right of individuals to define their identities and determine their futures; and not only the right of groups and communities to preserve their autonomy and control their common life. Most important, it would mean the right of individuals and groups to participate fully in shaping the values, culture, priorities, and aims of the whole society.

42   At the dawn of the twentieth century, W. E. B. Du Bois cast light on the travail of African-Americans to hold on to their cultural roots while aspiring to make the nation better and happier for all. The black citizen did not seek to "Africanize America," Du Bois wrote in *The Souls of Black Folk*, "for America has too much to teach the world and Africa." Neither would this citizen "bleach his Negro soul in a flood of white Americanism, for he knows that Negro blood has a message for the world. He simply wishes to make it possible for a man to be both a Negro and an American, without being cursed and spit upon by his fellows, without having the doors of Opportunity closed roughly in his face."

43   The realization of equal participation in, and equal contribution to, the remaking of American society during its third century not only might create a nation of singular cultural and intellectual richness but might offer the best possibility for fulfilling the original American creed. Moreover, the growth of democracy might bolster the prospects for economic justice in an age of economic decline, while, to venture a utopian thought, gains in cultural wealth and in emotional and spiritual well-being might offset losses in material affluence—that is, for those who have enjoyed it. Still, it is likely to be an arduous journey forward, one that will call for new generations of Americans who have grown up in nurturing family, school, and community environments and will have learned since early childhood the value of personal empowerment.

44   Poet Langston Hughes, grandnephew of nineteenth-century black leader John Mercer Langston, voiced a bittersweet hope for the nation's rebirth, and for the rebirth of the human rights whose promise lay at the nation's core:

> O, let America be America again—
> The land that never has been yet. . . .
> O, yes,
> I say it plain,
> America never was America to me,
> And yet I swear this oath—
> America will be!

Points for Review and Discussion

1. Summarize three reasons that the authors give for being hopeful about the possibility of this nation taking an imaginative leap "into the world of nurturing rights" (¶ 2).
2. This essay draws a contrast between "hierarchical" and "mutually interactive" worlds. Explain the meaning of the contrast, and tell why the authors find it significant.

❧ Questions for Writing

1. The Burnses lay heavy stress on the relation between nurturing rights and substantive rights (¶ 27). What in your opinion is the essence of this relation and how significant do you yourself believe it to be? Give reasons for your answer.
2. The essay also lays heavy stress on the distinction between transactional and transformative leadership (¶ 16, 17). What in your opinion is the essence of this distinction and how significant do you believe it to be? Again: give reasons for your answer.
3. The authors write that "the growth of democracy" might produce "gains in cultural welath and in emotional and spiritual well-being" that could "offset losses in material affluence—that is, for those who have enjoyed it" (¶ 43). The authors don't themselves describe the gains they have in mind. Speculate as concretely as you can on the nature of the "gains" that might compensate the formerly affluent for their material losses. Do you believe such gains are possible? Desirable? Explain your thinking.

Connecting the Parts in Chapter 10: Assignments for Extended Essays

1. The writers represented in this book would undoubtedly have distinctly individual responses to the argument for class-mixing advanced by Mickey Kaus. Write an essay in which you imagine, articulate, compare, and evaluate the probable responses to Kaus of Paul Fussell, Jonathan Kozol, and bell hooks.
2. From among the writers in this book choose two who, in your opinion, would be likely to respond positively to Derrick Bell's analysis of the prospects for early achievement, in the United States, of higher levels of justice and equality. Write an essay giving reasons for your choice, citing relevant passages from individual works.

Leads for Research

1. The writers in Chapter 10 share the belief that tomorrow's class relationships are necessarily a critical consideration for anyone attempting to think seriously about the future. But theirs are hardly the only ways of articulating that belief. Lester Thurow's *Head to Head* (1992) and James Fallows' *More Like Us* (1989) put the matter of class relationships and the future in wholly different contexts. Read these books and write a paper comparing and contrasting their perspectives with that of either the Burnses or of Mickey Kaus.
2. Write a research report on the nonfiction sources of the basic themes of Derrick Bell's "Racism's Secret Bonding." Your starting points are the key works cited in Bell's own text, namely Jennifer Hochschild, *The New American Dilemma* (1984) and Ralph Ellison's *Going to the Territory* (1986).
3. The distinction between transactional and transformational leadership mentioned in the Burnses' "The Nurturing of Rights" originated and receives its fullest expression in James Burns' *Leadership* (1978). Read this work; consult reviews of it cited in *Book Review Digest* and combine their insights and your own reactions in a critical analysis of the book.

11

Class Textures (I)
Adventure, Superstition, Enigma

Much can be learned from autobiographical accounts and interviews in which individuals reflect on the content of their own experience of social difference, and on the meanings that they draw from these experiences. Read in combination with political, cultural, and sociological studies, such accounts help to clarify the American class system—its degree of fairness, its structures of opportunity, its passionate commitment to myths of classlessness.

But there are limits to all these materials. They tell us too little about the ways in which actualities of class are interwoven, in daily life, with the other major forces that shape and color inner character and external events. These interweaving processes differ vastly from person to person, and differ, too, at every stage of any individual life; they are at once complicated and fascinating. Priceless insight into the processes comes through literary art: stories and novels in which writers reach beyond the constraints of personal experience and specialized academic languages toward comprehensive imaginative understanding.

Chapter 11 consists of four works of narrative fiction notable for that understanding. In the first story we see what social difference means to a young wife driven by her need for "adventure." In the second story we watch the interplay of class stereotypes and superstition. The third story shows us a child attempting to pray her way past a class-driven family crisis. The fourth story probes the difficulty of locating any meaning in the constant remaking of human pecking orders. What comes across in each of the tales is the variety of ways in which class colors responses to the texture of daily life.

Sorghum
Bobbie Ann Mason

The phrase "social mobility" conjures up a person climbing the ladder in business or the professions—an ambitious person intent on gaining money, power, and/or public esteem. But the pull of the idea of social ascent isn't as simple as this version of it implies. Part of the interest of Bobbie Ann Mason's short story "Sorghum" lies in the heroine's semi-awakenings to that truth. Liz learns about rewards of mobility that aren't usually mentioned in success stories.

Bobbie Ann Mason published her first collection of stories in 1973, when she was 33; the book won the prestigious PEN/Hemingway Award. Mason was born in Mayfield, Kentucky, did her undergraduate work at the University of Kentucky, and holds a doctorate in English Literature from the University of Connecticut. Her best-known work of fiction is the novel *In Country*, the film version of which starred Bruce Willis.

1   Liz woke up at 3 A.M., when she recognized Danny's car rumbling into the driveway. It had a hole in the muffler. Then she heard the car turn around and speed down the street. In the distance, the tires kept squealing as Danny tore up and down the streets of the subdivision. She waited for the crash, but the car returned. Again, Danny backed out of the driveway and went zooming down the street, the tires screeching. Someone will call the police, she thought, terrified.

2   "What's Daddy doing?" said Melissa, a little silhouette in the dim light of the bedroom doorway. She was dragging her Cabbage Patch-style doll by an arm.

3   "It's all right, sugar." Liz got out of bed and bent down to hug her child.

4   "Kiss Maretta Louise, too," Melissa said.

5   Liz held on to Melissa, her free hand untangling the little girl's hair. To be fair, Liz patted Maretta Louise's hair, too.

6   "He's just having a little joy ride, sweetie," Liz said. "There's isn't any traffic, so he has the street all to himself."

7   "Daddy doesn't love Maretta Louise," Melissa said, whining. "He told her she was ugly."

8   "She's not ugly! She's precious." Liz herded Melissa back to her own bed. "I'll stay in here with you," she said. "Let's be real quiet so we won't wake Michael up."

9   The car roared into the driveway again, and the door slammed. Danny worked the four-to-midnight shift at the tire plant, and for the

---

From Bobbie Ann Mason, *Love Life* (1989).

past several Friday nights he had been coming in late, usually drunk. Liz worked all day at a discount store, and the only times she was with Danny during the week, they were asleep. Weekends were shocking, when they saw each other awake and older. They had something like a commuter marriage, she thought, with none of the advantages. Liz didn't love Danny in the same way anymore. When he was drunk, he made love as though he were plowing corn, and she did not enjoy it.

10   "I'm home!" yelled Danny, bursting into the house.

11   On Thursday after supper, when Michael and Melissa were playing at friends' houses down the street, Liz tuned in to Sue Ann Grooms, a psychic on the radio.

12   "Hello. You're on the air."

13   A man said, "Could you tell me if I'm going to get laid off?"

14   "No, you're not," said Sue Ann Grooms.

15   "O.K.," the man said.

16   "Hello, you're on the air."

17   A woman with a thin, halting voice said, "I lost my wedding ring. Where can I go find it?"

18   "I see a tall building," said Sue Ann. "With a basement."

19   "You must mean when I worked at the courthouse."

20   "I'm getting a strong picture of a large building with a basement."

21   "Well, I'll look there, then."

22   Sue Ann Grooms was local. Liz's brother had been in her class at school. Her show had been on for nearly a year, and people called up with money problems, family troubles, a lot of cancer operations. Sue Ann always had an answer on the tip of her tongue. It was amazing. She was right, too. Liz knew people who had called in.

23   Nervously, Liz dialed the radio station. She had to dial several times before she got through. She was put on hold, and she sat in a kitchen chair while music played in her ear. When Sue Ann Grooms said, "You're on the air," Liz jumped. Flustered, she said, "Uh—is my husband cheating on me?"

24   Sue Ann paused. The psychic didn't normally pause for thought. "I'm afraid the answer is yes," she said.

25   "Oh."

26   Sue Ann Grooms went into fast-forward, it seemed, on other calls. Sick babies, cancer, husbands out of work. The answers blurred together. Chills rushed over Liz. Her friend Faye, at the store, had urged Liz to go out and have adventures. Faye, who was divorced, dumped her children at her mother's on weekends and went out on dates to fancy restaurants up in Paducah. It wasn't just men Faye was after. She had an interest in the peculiar. It could be a strange old woman who raised peacocks and made her own apple butter, or a belly dancer. Faye had met a belly dancer at the Western Inn, a woman who learned the art just to please her husband, because her navel turned him on, but then she took her

show on the road. She had belly-danced her way across America, Faye said.

27   It was still daylight, and Liz went for a drive, wishing she had a little sports car instead of a Chevette. She passed the Holiday Inn, the marquee said "WELCOME TEXACO BIGWIGS." She stopped for a fill-up at a Texaco, wondering what bigwigs would come to this little town. The conventions centered in Paducah, where they could buy liquor. A surly teenager gassed her up.

28   "Where are the bigwigs?" she asked.

29   "Huh?"

30   She explained about the Holiday Inn sign.

31   "I don't know." He shrugged and fumbled with the change. He didn't look retarded, just devoid of life. Liz shot out of the station. She felt a burning desire, for no one in particular, nothing she knew, but she expected it would make sense sooner or later. She slowed down at a triangle intersection on the highway where some teenagers were washing windshields for leukemia victims.

32   "Why don't we go out to eat at someplace fancy sometime?" she asked Danny that weekend. Faye had been to a restaurant at the Lake where the bread was baked in flowerpots. The restaurant was decorated with antiques and stuffed wild animals.

33   "You're always wanting something we can't afford," Danny said, as he twisted open a bottle of beer. "You wanted a microwave, and now you've got it. The more you get, the more you want."

34   Liz started to remind him about the Oldsmobile he was longing for (his father swore by Oldsmobiles), but it took too much energy. He hauled her toward him in a rough embrace. "What have I done to you?" he asked when she pushed him away.

35   "Nothing."

36   "You're acting funny."

37   "I'm just frustrated. I want to go back to college and finish. I didn't finish, and I think I ought to finish."

38   "But the two years you went didn't do you any good. There's not any jobs around here that call for college."

39   "I just wish I could finish what I started," she said.

40   He grinned, cocking his beer bottle at her, "This fellow at work says his wife went to college, and she changed one hundred percent. She changed her hair and the way she cooked and everything. He keeps looking at her picture, thinking maybe he's been tricked and she's not the same person. There's a lot of that going around," he said thoughtfully.

41   "Well, there's more to life than just getting by," Liz snapped. Danny looked at her strangely.

42   Faye had told Liz about a man who made sorghum molasses. "He's a darling old man I met at a flea market, and he makes it with all the old

equipment and stuff." Liz had a craving for sorghum. She hadn't had any since she was a child. On Friday after work, she drove out to the place.

43   The Summer farm was five miles out in the country, near a run-down old settlement with an old-fashioned general store (peeling paint, Dr Pepper sign). Cletus Summer lived in a new brick ranch house, with a shiny white dish antenna squatting possessively in the backyard. The outbuildings were gray and sagged with age. Near a shed, several visitors were watching the old man boiling down cane syrup in a vat. The heat from the fire beneath the vat burned Liz's face, and she stepped back. This old man had been making sorghum for generations, she thought. Yet she couldn't even get Danny to grill chickens.

44   The vat was sectioned like a rat maze, and Cletus Summer was swooshing the fluid through the maze with a spade. Now and then he scooped foam from the surface. It was green, like pond slime.

45   "This is the second batch," he said to the visitors. "Yesterday I throwed away a whole batch that took all day to make. It didn't taste right. It tasted green."

46   "It sure looks green," Liz said.

47   A younger man, in a red T-shirt and a cowboy hat, said, "You're supposed to have mules walking in a circle to mash the cane. But Daddy built a machine to squeeze the juice out." He laughed. "The real old-timers don't like that, do they, Daddy?" The man wore a large brass belt buckle that said "ED" in large letters superimposed on crossed Confederate rifles. "Remember the time that old farmer made some hooch out of his sorghum and the pigs got into it and got drunk?"

48   The men howled together. The older man said, "It was 'soo-ee' all over the place! The farmer got plowed, too, and he passed out in the pigpen." Viciously, he kicked at a log on the fire. "Damn! Them logs ain't burning. They're plumb green."

49   "Everything's green here," Liz said, gazing at the slippery scum. The cane leaves strewn around on the ground were bright green.

50   "An old-timey sorghum-making had a picnic, and the whole neighborhood helped," Ed said, gazing straight at Liz. She decided he was good-looking.

51   "Nowadays people ain't work brittle," the old man mumbled.

52   "What do you mean?" Liz asked.

53   "If you ain't work brittle, it means you're lazy."

54   Later, after she had taken the gallon of sorghum she bought to the car and had stopped to pet some cats, Liz saw the man named Ed under a tree, reading a paperback. He had a good build and a strong, craggy face. He smiled at her, a crooked smile like the label pasted on the sorghum can.

55   "Do you live here?" she asked. "I never saw a farmer laze around under a tree with a book before."

56   "No, I just came up from Memphis to help Daddy out. I've got a business there—I sell sound systems?" He closed the book on his thumb. The book was about Hitler.

57   "I always liked sorghum on pancakes," Liz said. "But I never knew what all went into it."

58   "It's an education being around Daddy. He could do everything the old way. But he doesn't have to anymore." Ed glanced over at his father, who was hunched over the vat and tasting the syrup from a wooden spoon. He still seemed dissatisfied with the taste. "Daddy's getting real bad—forgetful and stuff. It's not stopping him, though. He's got a girlfriend and he still drives to town. By the way, my name's Ed."

59   "That's what I figured. I'm Liz."

60   "What's your favorite food, Liz?" he asked.

61   "Ice cream. Why?"

62   "Just asking. Who's your favorite star?"

63   "Sometimes Clint Eastwood. Sometimes Paul Newman."

64   "You want to go out with me for ice cream and then a Paul Newman movie?"

65   She laughed. "My husband might not like it if he found out."

66   Ed said, "If ifs and buts was candy and nuts, we'd have Christmas every day."

67   She laughed, and he tilted his cowboy hat down over his eyes and peered out from under it flirtatiously. He said, "What's your husband got that I ain't got?" he asked.

68   "I don't know. I never see him," she said, wishing she hadn't mentioned she had a husband. "We don't get along."

69   "Well, there you go. Come on."

70   In Ed's red Camaro, they headed for Paducah, on back roads, past ripening tobacco fields and corn scorching in the late-summer haze. Ed was a careful driver. Liz couldn't imagine him terrorizing the neighborhood at 3 A.M. As the road twisted through abandoned towns, past run-down farms and shabby gas stations, Liz felt excited. It was all so easy. This was what Faye did every weekend.

71   "When I die, I don't want to be cremated," Ed said when they passed a small family cemetery.

72   "A lot of people are getting cremated now. I guess it's all right."

73   "My sister burnt her dog. The vet had to put it to sleep, and she had it cremated. She keeps it in a milk jug on the mantel. It's antique."

74   Liz felt goose bumps rush over her arms. She saw herself as a character in a movie, in one of those romantic boy-meets-girl scenes. She said, "There's this new movie I want to see that has Chevy Chase in it."

75   "I thought he was dead."

76   "No, he's not."

77   "I can't remember what stars have died," he said.

78   At the mall, they priced some stereo components in a Radio Shack ("a little check on the competition," Ed said), and then they had their pictures made in Wild West costumes at a booth in the center of the mall. From a rack of old clothing, Liz selected a low-cut gown and a feather boa. She giggled at herself in the mirror as she changed behind a

curtain. Ed chose a severe black hat, a string tie, a worn green jacket, and wool pants with suspenders. The woman who ran the booth said, "Y'all look good. Everybody gets such a kick out of this. I guess it takes them back to a simpler time."

79   "If there ever *was* such a time," Ed said, nodding. As they posed for the camera, he said, "This is the seduction of Miss Jones by the itinerant preacher." Liz spotted a woman she knew across the corridor in front of a shoe store. Liz turned her head, hoping she wouldn't be recognized, while Ed filled out a form for the picture to be mailed to him in Memphis.

80   "Order anything you want," Ed said at a restaurant in the mall. Liz ordered Cajun chicken and a margarita. She had never had Cajun chicken. It was expensive, but she suspected Ed must have a lot of money. She began to relax and enjoy herself. She liked margaritas. She said, "My friend Faye at work went out to eat last week at a place where you choose your meat from a big platter they bring and then you grill it at your table. I told her I didn't see the point in going out to eat if you had to cook it yourself." She licked salt from the edge of her glass.

81   "Does your husband take you out to eat?"

82   "No. He works the four-to-midnight shift. And his idea of going out to eat is McDonald's."

83   "Does he make you happy?" Ed sipped his drink and stared at her.

84   "No," Liz said, embarrassed. "He gets drunk, and he's fooling around with somebody, so what I do is none of his business." She explained about the psychic.

85   "I had my palm read once," he said. "There's this whole town of psychics in Florida."

86   "Really?"

87   "Yeah. I was there once and had my palm read by six different palm readers."

88   "What did you find out?"

89   "My life line is squiggly. I'm supposed to have a dangerous and unfulfilled life." He held his palm out and traced his life line. Liz could see the squiggle, like those back roads to Paducah.

90   "Do you have any kids?" she asked.

91   "Not exactly. I never stayed married long enough."

92   Liz laughed. "It doesn't take long to make kids."

93   "Have you got any?"

94   "Yeah—two, Michael and Melissa. They're eight and six. They drive me crazy, but I wouldn't take anything for them."

95   After ordering more drinks, Ed said, "Once I saw this great little kid who played Little League. He was a perfect little guy—blond hair and blue eyes and smart as a whip. He had a good grip on that bat, and he could run. You know what I did? I found his mother and married her and had an instant great kid. Somebody I could take fishing and play catch with."

96 "What happened to him—and her?"

97 "Oh, he grew up and got in trouble. I left a long time before that."

98 "Tell me about yourself," she said eagerly. "I want to know everything."

99 Feeling reckless and liberated, Liz began meeting Ed on occasional Friday nights throughout the late summer and fall. It was easy to get Michael and Melissa to spend Friday evenings with her parents, who had cable. Supposedly, Liz was playing cards with Faye and the girls.

100 Ed called her at the store on those weekends when he came up from Memphis to help his father out. Mr. Summer had a girlfriend who looked after him during the week, but she spent weekends traveling to visit her family (her husband was in jail and her son was in a mental institution). Ed had been married twice, both times to women who worked in dress stores and always looked like fashion plates. But he insisted neither of them was as good-looking as Liz. He told her she was sexy and that he liked the way she said whatever came to mind. She met him at the mall, and they usually ate something, and then Liz left her car there and went with Ed out to the Summer farm, to a small apartment Ed had fixed up in the shed where the sorghum-making equipment was stored. The place had been his clubhouse when he was a boy. The room was nice. Ed had even installed a sound system, and sonorous music Liz couldn't identify flooded the room like a church organ as they made passionate love on a single bed by the window. Liz felt happy, but the moon shining made her shiver with the knowledge of what she was doing, as if the moon were spying on her. But she couldn't believe it mattered. She wondered what Danny would do if he found out, whether he could take the kids from her. She didn't think so. She didn't know any woman who had lost custody of her kids, especially when the father was drunk and unfaithful. Some people thought an unfaithful woman was worse, though. They expected it of men, but women were supposed to be better. Liz didn't understand this. And she didn't know how she could possibly leave Danny and support the kids on her own. She wished she could take her kids to Memphis and live with Ed. He had told her his apartment building had a swimming pool, and he belonged to a country club. Liz didn't know whether to believe him. His reported life-style seemed farfetched, incongruous with the old farm and the sorghum shed. But in that shed on those Friday nights, she felt her whole life take off, like a car going into fifth gear. Liz never saw Ed's father, who was alone in his small brick ranch house, watching something that soared in from outer space to his satellite dish.

101 One Friday in the fall, Ed told Liz he wanted to take her down to Reelfoot Lake the next weekend. He straightened the quilt out and brushed dirt and debris from it. He began dressing. He said, "I want to take you to the annual game dinner me and my hunting buddies have."

102 "But it's too far to get back by midnight."

103   "You could stay there. A friend of mine has a house on the lake."

104   "Danny would find out." She couldn't see Ed's face in the dark. He was by the window, pulling on his boots, with one foot propped on a sorghum can.

105   He said, "I wouldn't care if he did, except he might come after me and blow my head off."

106   "He's not very big," said Liz, buttoning her blouse. "He's not as big as you are. But I'm afraid. I don't know what I'm getting into with you."

107   "Well, I don't know what I'm getting into with you either," Ed said, buckling his "ED" belt. "But we'll have a good time down at Reelfoot. This game dinner's something. We'll have duck and all kinds of game—possum, coon, bunny-rabbit, armadillo. . . ."

108   "Oh, you're teasing!" she cried. "You're such a kidder."

109   "But you come down with me. It's a tradition, one of those things that's supposed to mean something."

110   On Thursday night, Liz stayed up late to speak to Danny when he got in. She had ignored his Friday-night sprees, not wanting to pick a fight with him. As he shed his work clothes, tossing them into the laundry basket, she said, "I might not be here when you come in tomorrow night."

111   "Why not?"

112   "I'm going with Faye to this place down in Tennessee where you can go to a mall that's nothing but factory outlets." It was true that there was such a mall, and Faye had been there. "It's so far we thought we'd go down Friday night and stay with this friend of Faye's." Liz had worked out this story with Faye.

113   "Fine," Danny said. "If you can get a good price on some 501 jeans, I need a pair."

114   "O.K.," said Liz. "I'll look." She suddenly realized Danny had gained weight—maybe ten pounds.

115   After work, Liz left her car at the train depot in Fulton, and Ed met her there. He looked handsome in a green blazer and a tie printed with geese in flight. She was nervous about meeting his friends. "Wow, look at Miss America," he said after they had stopped at a gas station for her to change clothes. She had brought her clothes in tote bags instead of a suitcase, to avoid suspicion.

116   "I never get to dress up," Liz said, pleased. "But I love this dress, and I got it on sale."

117   By the time Reelfoot Lake came into view, the sun was setting and Liz was hungry. Ed slowed down and said, "Look at that lake. Can you imagine the earthquake that made that lake—way back yonder? They say we're due for another one."

118   "I hope it's not this weekend," Liz said. "That's what I always thought about going to California—it would be just my luck for it to hit

when I was there. If there was an earthquake here this weekend, it would be to punish me. Maybe I should have called up Sue Ann Grooms."
119   Ed reached for her hand. "Don't be nervous," he said.
120   "Don't you get nervous when you're on the verge of something?"
121   "Verge of what?"
122   "I don't know. I just feel like something's going to happen."
123   "I always feel like I'm on the verge of something," said Ed.
124   "Well, you've done a lot, and you've got a lot to show for it."
125   "I can't complain. I made it off the farm, and that's something."
126   "Happy?"
127   "Have you got what you want?"
128   "Nobody ever gets all they want," he said. "Everybody's always dissatisfied. The sad thing is, money ain't everything."
129   Liz said, "It's not everything, but it helps."
130   Ed turned into a narrow dirt road. "We're just about there," he said. "Joe's country house is real nice. Speaking of money, he made his off of women's hats, in Memphis." He laughed. "His store is called Le Chateau Chapeau."
131   "Is he rich?" cried Liz. "I've never been around people with money. I won't know how to act."
132   "Oh, he's not really rich," Ed assured her.
133   "Will they have finger bowls? They're rich if they've got finger bowls. And a lot of forks." She giggled.
134   Ed laughed. "You've been watching too much 'Dynasty.'"
135   "Yes, they *are* rich," Liz said when she saw the house. "I know what lakefront property goes for! I bet that house cost a hundred and fifty thousand dollars."
136   "Hey, it's O.K.," Ed said. "For one thing, you're younger and better-looking than anybody here. Just remember that. They'll all be jealous."
137   It was a two-story chalet-style house with large windows. Ed led Liz inside, on the basement level, where there was a wet bar. Several people in subdued, tasteful clothing were standing around, drinking and laughing. Liz had worn her loud red dress—Faye's idea. As she was introduced, Liz felt out of place and all the names instantly escaped her. When Ed had kissed her in the car, his shaving lotion was strong, like something from Christmas, and he seemed warm and familiar. But in this classy house, plunging into hunting talk with his buddies, he was a stranger. For all she knew, Ed could be a drug dealer.
138   "Margarita?" Ed asked, and Liz nodded.
139   With her drink, Liz explored the house. A woman named Nancy showed her around. Liz figured out that she was the owner's wife. "We haven't had this much company in months," Nancy said, laughing. "I'm so proud!" "That's a pretty love seat," Liz murmured. She wondered what it cost. It was Wedgwood-blue velvet, with white wood trim. In her house, the kids would spill something on it within ten minutes.

140 "We bought that love seat to celebrate our tenth anniversary," Nancy said. "Ten years and still in love! We thought it was romantic." She laughed giddily and sipped something pale from a long-stemmed glass. "But we're romantic fools," she said. "When our son was born, in 1979, I wrote a whole book of poems! They just came pouring out, while I was in the hospital. We got a friend of ours who's a printer to print them up. It turned out real nice."

141 Liz combed her hair in a luxurious gold-and-beige bathroom large enough to dance in. She set her drink on a long marble counter. Next to a greenhouse window—with huge hanging fuchsias and airplane plants—was a Jacuzzi, sunken into the floor. Liz had never seen a hot tub before. The water was bubbling, steaming up the windows of the greenhouse. It was dark outside now, but she could dimly make out the tall cypress trees standing in the lake like gigantic wading birds. She hurried out of the bathroom, wobbling on her high heels. She suddenly had the scary thought that the guests were going to strip naked and get in that hot tub together. Otherwise, why would it be heated up? She had heard about orgies among trendy sets of people.

142 Liz found Ed in the den, talking to a short fat man wearing a dinner jacket made of camouflage material. The den had shelves and shelves of wooden duck decoys, lined up, all facing the same way. Liz expected them to move, the way they did at the carnival. She felt like pitching baseballs at them.

143 "I've been collecting these little babies for twenty years," said the man in the camouflage jacket to the guests gathered around him. For several minutes, he narrated the history of the duck decoys, pointing out which ones were antiques.

144 "Hey, Ed. That's a good-looking gal you've got there with you," he said suddenly. His voice sounded off-key, like an artificial voice from a mechanical box.

145 "I think I'll keep her," Ed said, grinning. "Joe, meet Liz. This is Joe Callaway. This is his house. Joe and me go way back."

146 "Nice to meet you," Liz said. "I've been talking to your wife. She showed me around."

147 In front of a gun rack, Ed said to Liz, "What's wrong? You look funny."

148 "Nothing. I'm just nervous."

149 "You're fine," he said, patting her on the behind.

150 "I guess I expected a lot of mannequins in hats—not ducks. That jacket's a scream. My kid has some jeans made out of that material."

151 At the dinner table—two forks, no finger bowls—Liz sat between Ed and Joe and across from a man in a black curly wig that sat on his head askew. A small pink plastic goose marked each place setting, and the centerpiece of the table was an enormous duck decoy resting on a bed of cabbage leaves, the curly kind. The duck had artificial flowers sprouting out of holes in its back and a smug expression. Liz noticed a woman us-

ing her fingers to pick out the cherries in her fruit cocktail, and she realized that if you had enough money it didn't matter how you behaved. The thought was comforting, and it made her feel a little reckless. Maybe if Liz used bad manners, they would just think she was being original. The woman eating with her fingers wore a derby hat and reminded Liz of Susan St. James on "Kate & Allie." There were five men and five women at the table, and Liz couldn't keep their names straight because most of them reminded her of someone else. Then she almost shrieked as she turned to face a platter of little birds, posed exactly like tiny roast turkeys. They were quail.

152 "Welcome to our critter dinner," Nancy said to Liz. "It's a tradition. We've been doing this every duck season for ten years."

153 Liz had forgotten what Ed had said about the game dinner. Several dishes circulated, and Ed served Liz, plopping something from each one on her plate.

154 "We've got everything but rattlesnake here," Ed said, smiling.

155 "I think I've got some of that on my plate," joked a man who had said he owned his own bush-hog rental company.

156 "Most of it's out of season, but we freeze it and then the women fix it up and we have everything at once," Ed explained to Liz.

157 "I was cooking all day on this rabbit," the woman in the hat said. "It was so tough I must have used a quart of tenderizer."

158 "It tastes just divine, Cindy," said Nancy. Earlier, Nancy had passed around souvenir tie tacks for the men—little silver ducks in flight. She gave the women oven mitts in the shape of fish. Liz had seen them in craft stores, and they were worth ten dollars. She stuffed hers in her purse. An irresistible bargain from a housewares outlet—fifty cents, she would tell Danny.

159 "What's this?" Liz asked, when a dish of something that looked like cat paws reached her.

160 "Possum," Joe said. "I claim credit for that."

161 "They say you have to trap a possum and feed it milk for ten days before you butcher it," the woman in the hat, Cindy, said.

162 "Did you do that, Joe?"

163 "Hell, no. I just blasted it out of my sycamore tree out front." He whooped, a clown guffaw.

164 "Possum's gamy, but you acquire a taste for it," said the woman who was with the man in the wig. Her hair looked real.

165 The goose had a cream sauce on it; the duck was cooked with cherries and felt leathery; the quail was stuffed with liver; the rabbit seemed to be pickled. Liz stared at her plate. Ed was discussing duck calls with the bush-hog man. The women chattered about someone's custom-made drapes.

166 The bush-hog man's wife, who looked older than he did, said to Liz, "Don't you just hate it when somebody says they'll come out to work on something and you stay home and then they don't show up?"

167 "Excuse me," Liz said, rising. "I'll be right back."

168 Her face burned red. Everyone at the table looked at her. In the large bathroom she tried to throw up, but she had been too excited all day to eat. Her face in the mirror was younger. The wrinkles under her eyes had plumped out, as her new eye cream had promised. She looked young, innocent. If she dropped dead of a heart attack—or lead poisoning from eating buckshot—and Danny found out where she was, what would he make of it?

169 She clutched a gold towel rack, trying to steady herself. She stared hard in the mirror at the person she had become for the evening, in the red dress Faye had recommended. It was like a whore dress, she thought. Danny was right about the way she always wanted something she didn't have. What did she really want? She didn't know. She didn't want to lose her kids. She didn't want to stay with Danny. She *would* like a hot tub—but she didn't need any duck decoys. She would not have paid even fifty cents for that fish mitt.

170 The assorted dishes at the dinner reminded her of a picture she saw once of a vase of flowers, impossible combinations: pansies, irises, daisies, zinnias, roses, a fantasy mixture of flowers throughout the seasons, from the early-spring hyacinths to the fall asters. The arrangement was beautiful, but it was something you could never see in real life. That was the way she thought of life with Ed, in a house like this—something grand that could never come true.

171 The greenhouse windows were steamy, and the hanging plants dripped moisture. The whirling water in the tub sounded like the ocean. Liz wished she could go to the ocean, just once in her life. That was one thing she truly wanted. She checked the lock on the door and slipped out of her shoes. She laid her purse on the counter next to the sink and carefully removed her stockings and dress. She touched her toe in the hot water. It seemed too hot to bear, but she decided she would bear it—like a punishment, or an acquired taste that would turn delicious when she was used to it.

Points for Review and Discussion

1. Liz's husband tells her that "The more you get, the more you want." Is this a fair or unfair analysis of her character and behavior?

2. List the defects and virtues of Ed and Dan as an outsider might see them. Which character do you regard as more likable? Why?

◆◆ Questions for Writing

1. Mason defines social differences in "Sorghum" through a variety of facts—about everything from clothes and occupations to manners and

styles of driving cars. Make a list of the factual details that you regard as most important in clarifying social levels in this story.

2. Mason also defines social differences through styles of speech. Compare and contrast Nancy's way of talking with Liz's. How do you describe the differences? Do you see these differences as reflecting character differences? Explain your answer.

3. Liz tells Ed at the dinner party that she's "nervous" (¶ 148). What are the main causes of this nervousness as you see them?

4. When she sees a guest eating with her fingers, Liz "realized that if you had enough money it didn't matter how you behaved. The thought was comforting" (¶ 151). What kinds of comfort might Liz have gained from this "thought?"

5. The final sentence of the story says that Liz intends to bear the steamy hot tub water either as "a punishment" or as "an acquired taste that would turn delicious when she was used to it" (¶ 171). Both the wording and the punctuation of the sentence stress the either-or aspect of the immersion in Liz's thinking. This far-out reckless act of hers will turn out to be positive or negative, but not, she thinks, as a mixture. Does this idea strike you as realistic? Look back at the whole series of events and decisions in which Liz has involved herself. Is it likely that these events will lead to pure punishment or pure delight? Again, explain your answer.

The Jinx
Charles Dickinson

Charles Dickinson's "The Jinx" is a story about men and women—students, manual workers, a foreman, a husband and wife—adjusting and readjusting day by day to self-created, ceaselessly changing rank orders. One character in the story sees some advantage for himself in descending to the level of black magician. Other characters near the bottom invent their own rank orders within which they qualify as superior—"above" at least some of the coworkers or neighbors who are on their level. And people who live at close adjacency to all this class-shuttling try not to become confused—or superstitious.

The author of two novels and a volume of short stories, Charles Dickinson has published fiction in *The New Yorker*, *The Atlantic*, and *Esquire*. He was born in Detroit in 1951, attended the University of Kentucky, and now lives in Palatine, Illinois, with his wife and children.

1 The time is four-thirty on a cold Monday morning and the men of the Ultra Scavenger Service await the week's assignments of trucks and crews. Monday is the day Dooster, the foreman, must select a partner for Sweet, the Ultra jinx. Each truck has a driver, and two men called "tail gunners" who ride on small footholds at the rear of the truck and load the garbage into the compactor. These men engage in exhausting and dangerous work, and being paired with a jinx makes them understandably nervous.

2 Dooster begins to call out names. Everyone listens, smokes, coughs into his gloves. No one leaves, even after his name is called. Sweet himself leans patiently against the plate-glass window at the front of the room. He is not unaware of his station at Ultra, but he needs the money too much to quit and release everyone from the danger of working with him.

3 "You have your assignments," Dooster says to the men who still pack the room. But they have not heard the jinx's name called. "What . . . are you scared of the cold?" the foreman says.

4 One man pops out the door to the yard and his departure is like a cork being forced: drivers and tail gunners follow almost in a gush.

5 Dooster takes a moment, then announces the last crews. "Lupkin and Hayes with Reed on 24. Singh and Sweet with Cribones on 11."

6 And with that, the foreman's cup of coffee spills almost of its own volition.

From Charles Dickinson, *With or Without* (1987).

7   Word passes in an instant among the men of Ultra that the jinx and Singh have been put together. Most agree this is a stroke of genius by Dooster. Nobody likes Singh because he is so obviously a foreigner. He wears a turban and a scraggly black beard, and has a high-pitched, unfamiliar voice. But he has endeared himself to his fellow workers by being easy for them to look down on. He and the jinx make a perfect couple. An upbeat mood infects the men of Ultra as they begin their day's work.

8   When Sweet awoke for work that morning at three-thirty, Rachel was still studying. He cleared a space at the kitchen table amid her books and papers, in order that he could eat his breakfast alongside her. She was tapping numbers into a calculator and humming. She kissed him and told him he possessed an unpleasant odor. Then she yawned.

9   Rachel was Sweet's age, and hard on the trail of a master's degree in Actuarial Sciences. Sweet had a bachelor's in History and was the Ultra Scavenger Service jinx. They had been married less than a year.

10   Sweet had gone to work at Ultra strictly for the money, rising well before dawn to apply for the job, and being turned down the first three times he tried because no one was absent those mornings. But on his fourth attempt, a Monday, two men did not appear, and Sweet became a tail gunner. The season was summer, tropically hot and damp.

11   On Sweet's first day, his partner, Stuckman, was lifting a bundle of newspapers when the dirty tin binding strap sliced surgically through his glove, then nearly through his thumb. He wanted to finish the route but his glove fingers kept filling with blood. Like test tubes, Sweet told Rachel.

12   Sweet was regarded suspiciously by the men of Ultra when they heard the story. Fourteen stitches were required to close Stuckman's wound, but he reported that thirteen had been taken. Something already in motion was given impetus by that misstatement.

13   A certain wariness attended the following morning's announcement of Stuckman's replacement. Becker, also new on the job, with a month's seniority over Sweet, was given the assignment. The others approved of this pairing. They sensed something important taking place around them, a threat to the prevailing order, and they appreciated having a new man to test their suspicions and theories on.

14   The trucks and crews went out on another hot day. Sweet and Becker did not say much to each other but harbored their energy for the work, which went uneventfully until the next-to-last stop of the day. There, a customer was discarding an old lawn-mower. Becker, looking for a bargain, yanked the starter cord to see if the mower was worth salvaging. The engine did not start but the blade made one revolution and neatly sheared off the little toe on Becker's left foot. A call was put in to the dispatcher for an ambulance, and the men of Ultra heard the truck number and the nature of the emergency and looked very uneasily at one another.

15 Sweet, Singh, and Cribones are working through a neighborhood on the north side of town. Lunchtime is approaching, and Cribones has maintained a pace that will deliver them at the appointed hour to a convenience store where a girl he has dated works. She gives him free ham-salad sandwiches and coffee. Cribones's tail gunners don't disrupt his plans, which is all he asks of them. He knows Sweet's reputation, but he feels safe in the cab, behind the wheel, thinking about lunch.

16 The ambulance took Becker away, his toe riding along in a baggie of shaved ice, and Sweet and the driver made the route's last stop, emptied the truck at the landfill, then returned to the yard. Sweet was eager to provide his version of the incident but no one wanted to hear it. The men of Ultra had not heard even Becker's side of the story, but they had heard enough: a man had lost a toe while working with Sweet, one day after a man nearly lost a thumb working with Sweet.

17 Sweet was kept in the garage the next day. Dooster explained that they had an odd number of tail gunners, and on such an occasion somebody was held back to work around the yard. Sweet got the idea when he saw a truck go out with three men on the back. He spent the day hosing down the repair bays, washing the windshields on the idle trucks, filling the pop machine, and pulling weeds along the fence that surrounded the yard.

18 Later, he cornered the foreman. "Why aren't I on a truck today?"

19 "I told you. Odd number of gunners. Low man has to stay behind and do the menials."

20 "One truck had three guys on it, I noticed."

21 "A special route," Dooster said. He would not meet Sweet's eye. "Something new we're trying."

22 "Not very cost-efficient."

23 "We'll see, won't we?"

24 "Tell me the truth. Nobody wanted to work with me, right?"

25 "Did I say that?"

26 "I didn't cut off Becker's toe. I didn't slice Stuckman's thumb."

27 "You were there, though." Dooster said. "Two bad accidents your first two days on the job. That makes these men very nervous. They know they're never going to make a living with their brains, sitting in a nice safe office, so they become much more conscious of their body's condition. They're like athletes, Sweet. They see Becker go down for two, three months at least, and Stuckman out a couple weeks. It scares them. They look for someone to blame."

28 "That's absurd," Sweet said.

29 "Sure it is. Maybe," the foreman said. "Tomorrow I'll put you on a truck with someone. But these men don't like to change their minds. I want you to know that."

30 Sweet went home and his wife was in the shower washing her hair. She finished, held out a hand, and hooked the towel Sweet tossed.

31   "Open the window," Rachel said. She was rosy and a little out of breath. "God, you stink! You smell like something crawled inside your shirt and died."

32   "They think I'm a jinx. Nobody will work with me."

33   "What a silly thing to say," she said, laughing. "From what you told me, you had nothing to do with those men getting hurt."

34   "I *didn't*. But I was there, I'm new, so I must be guilty," Sweet said. "The foreman told me the others are like athletes—they make a living with their bodies."

35   "*Athletes?*" Rachel scoffed. "Athletes choose to be what they are. Would these guys be garbagemen if they had the smarts to be anything else?"

36   "No," Sweet said. "But they understand that. They know they'll never be anything else—so it's vital to them that they stay in one piece. A jinx scares them witless."

37   "Witless is the word exactly," she said. "Don't take it so seriously. You aren't one of them. You know you'll move on before too long."

38   "But I want them to be able to count on me," Sweet said.

39   "Can I count on you to burn those clothes."

40   He watched his wife wrap herself in the towel and step from the tub. He was conducting a test of his own there in the damp, slippery bathroom, to see if he had also become a jinx in his own home. But Rachel moved deftly across the slick tile and into their bedroom, although when she sat down to study while combing the knots from her hair she cut her finger on the sharp edge of a page. Sweet did not hear her cry out because he was already in the shower, and Rachel did not make the connection.

41   Sweet and Singh are eating lunch in the convenience store, leaning against a frozen-food cooler at the rear. They must eat there because Cribones is using the truck's warm cab to entertain his girlfriend, who did indeed have three free ham-salad sandwiches and a large black coffee waiting for him. The driver dropped Sweet and Singh at the store, and picked up the girl and the food. Cribones told his tail gunners he would retrieve them in a half-hour.

42   Sweet buys a newspaper and reads while he eats his sandwich. He is angry, because he has been on his feet all morning, and must now remain standing through lunch. Singh touches Sweet's arm and asks, "May I read the financial section, please?"

43   An hour passes before Cribones returns. The girl jumps down out of the cab wearing Cribones's hat, and he has to yell after her to bring it back. She teases him, twirling the hat on a finger, daring him to come for it. Sweet snatches the hat from her on his way to the truck and angrily wings it in at the smirking driver.

44   Sweet and Singh take their places on the tail but the truck does not move for nearly five minutes, and when it finally does, Cribones ignores

the remainder of the route and returns with undue speed and gnashing of gears to the garage. The driver immediately goes into a conference with Dooster, and when the meeting is finished Cribones goes to Sweet and loudly declares, "You are bad luck *in person*."

45 Dooster kept his promise and put Sweet back on a truck. By rotating the jinx through the roster of gunners and drivers, he kept complaints to a minimum. Working with Sweet became a trial to be weathered, like a bout with the flu. Rachel's summer session ended, but her new semester began just after Labor Day, and with their schedules Sweet sometimes would not speak to her for two or three days at a time. She would be only a muttering in the next room while he slept, or a dark shape in bed when he left for work at a quarter after four in the morning.

46 The foreman takes Sweet aside after the trucks are put away and the men either have gone home or are horsing around in the yard.
47 "What happened today? At lunch?" Dooster asks.
48 "I don't know. What happened?"
49 "I couldn't reach Cribones on the radio for nearly an hour. He's kinda vague as to why."
50 "That's between you and him, then."
51 "Was he with a girl?"
52 "Take it up with him," Sweet says.
53 "I did. He won't admit to anything. He's been caught before with his radio off. We've found evidence he's had girls in his cab, which is automatic dismissal. I'm putting him back on the tail for a month," Dooster says.
54 "He no doubt blames me."
55 "You can count on that."
56 Cribones is waiting for Sweet when he comes into the yard. A few men are still around, talking, smoking, laughing.
57 "What'd you tell him?" Cribones asks sullenly.
58 "Nothing."
59 "I don't believe you."
60 Sweet shrugs. He is exhausted and cold.
61 "I've gotta ride the tail for thirty days because of you." Cribones says.
62 "I didn't turn off the radio. I didn't turn it off the other time you got caught, either."
63 "You *did* talk about me!"
64 "He asked questions that were none of my business," Sweet says. "I didn't answer them."
65 "When are you going to quit here?"
66 "I need the money," Sweet says. "I have to put my wife through school."

67 "Are you bad luck for her, too?" Cribones asks.
68 "You'd have to ask her."
69 A block away he is crossing the street when Singh pedals by on a bicycle. He waves and gives the handlebar bell a jingle. Sweet wonders where he came from. He watches him until he is out of sight, and all the time he watches he expects Singh to fall off the bike, to snag a chain, to snag his unraveling turban in the spokes and break his neck.
70 Rachel is studying when he gets home. The book she reads from is *Theories of Life Expectancy.* He sniffs himself surreptitiously for that dead smell she sometimes accuses him of possessing.
71 She asks, looking up at him, "Why no kiss?"
72 "You'll say I stink."
73 "Do you?"
74 "I don't know."
75 "Kiss me," she says, with an impatient tapping of her pencil against her palm. He kisses her lips. She presses a hand to his chest, he feels the faint prick of the pencil point through his shirt. He steps back and she tests the air with a series of delicate sniffs; she samples his taste by running her tongue lightly over her mouth.
76 "Not bad," she says. "Not *fragrant,* but I know you work hard. Did I ever tell you I once followed you for a block when you were working near school? You were so fixated on that garbage. Lift the cans, empty them, ride to the next stop. Lift, empty, ride. Lift, empty, ride. I don't know if I'd do the same to put you through school. I loved you for doing it for me."
77 "They asked me at work if I brought you bad luck, too," Sweet says.
78 Rachel grimaces. "Still the jinx, huh?"
79 "Do I?"
80 "I *am* a little blue. I don't feel so hot," she says. "Did you cause that?"
81 "Don't feel so hot how?"
82 "Random pains. I'm smoking off and on again."
83 "I know. I smelled it," Sweet says. "If you smoke—and spend time with the jinx—you're sure to get cancer."
84 "Well, I don't spend time with you—so I'm safe, aren't I?" she says.
85 He hangs his work clothes on a nail driven into the wall outside the back door, and arranges his boots there on the floor. Rachel follows him into the kitchen, carrying the pencil, keeping a beat against her palm.
86 "Can you handle some bad news?" she asks. And before he can answer yes or no, she says, "Tuition's going up."
87 "How much?"
88 "Twelve percent."
89 "When did you hear this?" Sweet asks. He does not bother to compute the new figure; the school will do that for him. He asks questions of Rachel as a way to bleed off the anger and frustration that fill him.

90 "A while ago," she says. "I didn't want to tell you because we were having a tough time."
91 "Is there a *good* time to hear about a tuition increase?" Sweet asks.
92 "Well, now I've told you," she says. She nibbles the end of the pencil. "I've been feeling pretty alone lately. I imagine you have, too."
93 "It's just the hours we keep," Sweet says.
94 "And in forty years we'll laugh about this?"

95 The following morning, Sweet is paired with Cribones. They go out into the cold, and the day is exhausting for Sweet, because Cribones sulks about being a tail gunner at all and doesn't do his share. Sweet, having heard Rachel's assessment of his job, also thinks too much about what he is doing, and the hazed rhythm of the work eludes him.
96 At lunch, Cribones says, "I asked to be paired with you. Nobody could believe it."
97 "I'm honored."
98 "But I'm smarter than they think. I want you to do to me what you did to Becker."
99 "I didn't do anything to Becker," Sweet says.
100 "You did something," Cribones says. "He's getting paid what we make to sit home and watch TV. Now, I'm not willing to give up a toe—but I'll take a bad sprained ankle if it means I can sit out this suspension. This here is too much like work."
101 "I can't help you." Sweet says.
102 "Sure you can. You're a jinx."
103 "I am not a jinx."
104 "You *are,* though. Just work your old black magic on me. I'll gladly limp home."
105 "No," Sweet says.
106 "I'll pay you."
107 Sweet does not reply. He merely listens.
108 "How about twenty-five dollars for each week of disability?"
109 "Fifty," Sweet says. "For fifty dollars a week, I'll see what I can do."

Points for Review and Discussion

1. Sweet's truck is dogged by events that rouse superstitious fears. List those events and the related superstitions.
2. Sweet's decision to work as a garbageman could be described as self-sacrificing. And Rachel's decision to allow him to continue in the job could be described as exploitative. Explain why each of these terms—*self-sacrificing* and *exploitative*—does or does not seem to you to fit the case.

◆◦ Questions for Writing

1. Where do Sweet and Rachel place themselves socially in relation to the drivers and tailgunners employed by Ultra Scavenger Service? Cite passages supporting your answer.
2. Where does Dooster, the foreman, place Sweet in relation to the other employees? Again: cite supporting passages.
3. Where do the nonsupervisory Scavenger Service employees place Sweet in relation to themselves? Why? What is their justification for this placement? Does it change in the course of the story? How so?
4. Sweet's wife Rachel knows for certain that Sweet does not fit the stereotype of "garbageman." Name the grounds of her certainty. Is there ever a moment at which she wavers in this certainty? Explain your answer.
5. At the close of the story Sweet consents to become a black magician. Why does he do this? What comment on class identity seems implicit in his decision? What comment on class identity does this story make as a whole?

The Water-Faucet Vision
Gish Jen

In Gish Jen's "The Water-Faucet Vision" a grown woman remembers herself as a pious fifth-grader—a child who imagined herself to be a miracle-worker capable of conquering, by prayer, the terrifying parental strife that racked her home. The strife in question had its roots in class frustrations: social facts of life that are sometimes farther removed from children's understanding than the sexual facts of life, and that have immense power to wound. One theme of the story is the persistence, among grown-ups as well as children, of the fantasy that prayer can "solve" socioeconomic frustration.

Gish Jen was born in 1956, the daughter of Chinese parents, and describes herself as a "writing Mom." Her first novel, *Typical American* (1991), was nominated for a National Book Critics Circle Award and in 1992 she received a Guggenheim Fellowship in fiction.

1   To protect my sister Mona and me from the pains—or, as they pronounced it, the "pins"—of life, my parents did their fighting in Shanghai dialect, which we didn't understand; and when my father one day pitched a brass vase through the kitchen window, my mother told us he had done it by accident.

2   "By accident?" said Mona.

3   My mother chopped the foot off a mushroom.

4   "By accident?" said Mona. "By *accident?*"

5   Later I tried to explain to her that she shouldn't have persisted like that, but it was hopeless.

6   "What's the matter with throwing things," she shrugged. "He was mad."

7   That was the difference between Mona and me: Fighting was just fighting to her. If she worried about anything, it was only that she might turn out too short to become a ballerina, in which case she was going to be a piano player.

8   I, on the other hand, was going to be a martyr. I was in fifth grade then, and the hyperimaginative sort—the kind of girl who grows morbid in Catholic school, who longs to be chopped or frozen to death but then has nightmares about it from which she wakes up screaming and clutching a stuffed bear. It was not a bear that I clutched, though, but a string of three malachite beads that I had found in the marsh by the old aqueduct one day. Apparently once part of a necklace, they were each won-

---

From Gish Jen, "The Water-Faucet Vision," in *Charlie Chan Is Dead: An Anthology of Contemporary Asian-American Fiction* (1993), ed. Jessica Hagedorn.

derfully striated and swirled, and slightly humped toward the center, like a jellyfish; so that if I squeezed one, it would slip smoothly away, with a grace that altogether enthralled and—on those dream-harrowed nights—soothed me, soothed me as nothing had before or has since. Not that I've lacked occasion for soothing: Though it's been four months since my mother died, there are still nights when sleep stands away from me, stiff as a well-paid sentry. But that is another story. Back then I had my malachite beads, and if I worried them long and patiently enough, I was sure to start feeling better, more awake, even a little special—imagining, as I liked to, that my nightmares were communications from the Almighty Himself, preparation for my painful destiny. Discussing them with Patty Creamer, who had also promised her life to God, I called them "almost visions"; and Patty, her mouth wadded with the three or four sticks of doublemint she always seemed to have going at once, said, "I bet you'll be doin' miracleth by seventh grade."

9   Miracles. Today Patty laughs to think she ever spent good time stewing on such matters, her attention having long turned to rugs, and artwork, and antique Japanese bureaus—things she believes in.

10   "A good bureau's more than just a bureau," she explained last time we had lunch. "It's a hedge against life. I tell you, if there's one thing I believe, it's that cheap stuff's just money out the window. Nice stuff, on the other hand—now that you can always cash out, if life gets rough. *That* you can count on."

11   In fifth grade, though, she counted on different things.

12   "You'll be doing miracles too," I told her, but she shook her shaggy head and looked doleful.

13   "Na' me," she chomped. "Buzzit's okay. The kin' things I like, prayers work okay on."

14   "Like?"

15   "Like you 'member that dreth I liked?"

16   She meant the yellow one, with the criss-cross straps.

17   "Well gueth what."

18   "Your mom got it for you."

19   She smiled. "And I only jutht prayed for it for a week," she said.

20   As for myself, though, I definitely wanted to be able to perform a wonder or two. Miracle-working! It was the carrot of carrots: It kept me doing my homework, taking the sacraments; it kept me mournfully on key in music hour, while my classmates hiccuped and squealed their carefree hearts away. Yet I couldn't have said what I wanted such powers *for*, exactly. That is, I thought of them the way one might think of, say, an ornamental sword—as a kind of collectible, which also happened to be a means of defense.

21   But then Patty's father walked out on her mother, and for the first time, there was a miracle I wanted to do. I wanted it so much I could see it: Mr. Creamer made into a spitball; Mr. Creamer shot through a straw into the sky; Mr. Creamer unrolled and re-plumped, plop back on Patty's

doorstep. I would've cleaned out his mind and given him a shave en route. I would've given him a box of peanut fudge, tied up with a ribbon, to present to Patty with a kiss.

22   But instead all I could do was try to tell her he'd come back.

23   "He will not, he will not!" she sobbed. "He went on a boat to Rio Deniro. To Rio Deniro!"

24   I tried to offer her a stick of gum, but she wouldn't take it.

25   "He said he would rather look at water than at my mom's fat face. He said he would rather look at water than at me." Now she was really wailing, and holding her ribs so tightly that she almost seemed to be hurting herself—so tightly that just looking at her arms wound around her like snakes made my heart feel squeezed.

26   I patted her on the arm. A one-winged pigeon waddled by.

27   "He said I wasn't even his kid, he said I came from Uncle Johnny. He said I was garbage, just like my mom and Uncle Johnny. He said I wasn't even his kid, he said I wasn't his Patty, he said I came from Uncle Johnny!"

28   "From your Uncle Johnny?" I said stupidly.

29   "From Uncle Johnny," she cried. "From Uncle Johnny!"

30   "He said that?" I said. Then, wanting to go on, to say *something*. I said, "Oh Patty, don't cry."

31   She kept crying.

32   I tried again. "Oh Patty, don't cry," I said. Then I said, "Your dad was a jerk anyway."

33   The pigeon produced a large runny dropping.

34   It was a good twenty minutes before Patty was calm enough for me just to run to the girls' room to get her some toilet paper; and by the time I came back she was sobbing again, saying "To Rio Deniro, to Rio Deniro" over and over again, as though the words had stuck in her and couldn't be gotten out. As we had missed the regular bus home and the late bus too, I had to leave her a second time to go call my mother, who was only mad until she heard what had happened. Then she came and picked us up, and bought us each a fudgsicle.

35   Some days later, Patty and I started a program to work on getting her father home. It was a serious business. We said extra prayers, and lit votive candles; I tied my malachite beads to my uniform belt, fondling them as though they were a rosary, I a nun. We even took to walking about the school halls with our hands folded—a sight so ludicrous that our wheeze of a principal personally took us aside one day.

36   "I must tell you," she said, using her nose as a speaking tube, "that there is really no need for such peee-ity."

37   But we persisted, promising to marry God and praying to every saint we could think of. We gave up gum, then gum and slim jims both, then gum and slim jims and ice cream—and when even that didn't work, we started on more innovative things. The first was looking at flowers. We held our hands beside our eyes like blinders as we hurried by the violets

by the flagpole, the window box full of tulips outside the nurse's office. Next it was looking at boys: Patty gave up angel-eyed Jamie Halloran and I, gymnastic Anthony Rossi. It was hard, but in the end our efforts paid off. Mr. Creamer came back a month later, and though he brought with him nothing but dysentery, he was at least too sick to have all that much to say.

38   Then, in the course of a fight with my father, my mother somehow fell out of their bedroom window.

39   Recently—thinking a mountain vacation might cheer me—I sublet my apartment to a handsome but somber newlywed couple, who turned out to be every bit as responsible as I'd hoped. They cleaned out even the eggshell chips I'd sprinkled around the base of my plants as fertilizer, leaving behind only a shiny silverplate cake server and a list of their hopes and goals for the summer. The list, tacked precariously to the back of the kitchen door, began with a fervent appeal to God to help them get their wedding thank-yous written in three weeks or less. (You could see they had originally written "two weeks" but scratched it out—no miracles being demanded here.) It went on:

> Please help us, Almighty Father in Heaven Above, to get Ann a teaching job within a half-hour drive of here in a nice neighborhood.
> Please help us, Almighty Father in Heaven Above, to get John a job doing anything where he won't strain his back and that is within a half-hour drive of here.
> Please help us, Almighty Father in Heaven Above, to get us a car.
> Please help us, A.F. in H.A., to learn French.
> Please help us, A.F. in H.A., to find seven dinner recipes that cost less than 60 cents a serving and can be made in a half-hour. And that don't have tomatoes, since You in Your Heavenly Wisdom made John allergic.
> Please help us, A.F. in H.A., to avoid books in this apartment such as You in Your Heavenly Wisdom allowed John, for Your Heavenly Reasons, to find three nights ago (June 2nd).

40   Et cetera. In the left hand margin they kept score of how they had fared with their requests, and it was heartening to see that nearly all of them were marked "Yes! Praise the Lord" (sometimes shortened to PTL), with the sole exception of learning French, which was mysteriously marked "No! PTL to the Highest."

41   That note touched me. Strange and familiar both, it seemed like it had been written by some cousin of mine—some cousin who had stayed home to grow up, say, while I went abroad and learned what I had to, though the learning was painful. This, of course, is just a manner of speaking; in fact I did my growing up at home, like anybody else.

42   But the learning *was* painful: I never knew exactly how it happened that my mother went hurdling through the air that night years ago, only that the wind had been chopping at the house, and that the argument had started about the state of the roof. Someone had been up to fix it the

year before, but it wasn't a roofer, it was some man my father had insisted could do just as good a job for a quarter of the price. And maybe he could have, had he not somehow managed to step through a knot in the wood under the shingles and break his uninsured ankle. Now the shingles were coming loose again, and the attic insulation was mildewing besides, and my father was wanting to sell the house altogether, which he said my mother had wanted to buy so she could send pictures of it home to her family in China.

43 "The Americans have a saying," he said. "They saying, 'You have to keep up with Jones family.' I'm saying if Jones family in Shanghai, you can send any picture you want, *an-y* picture. Go take picture of those rich guys' house. You want to act like rich guys, right? Go take picture of those rich guys' house."

44 At that point my mother sent Mona and me to wash up, and started speaking Shanghaiese. They argued for some time in the kitchen, while we listened from the top of the stairs, our faces wedged between the bumpy Spanish scrolls of the wrought iron railing. First my mother ranted, then my father, then they both ranted at once until finally there was a thump, followed by a long quiet.

45 "Do you think they're kissing now?" said Mona. "I bet they're kissing, like this." She pursed her lips like a fish and was about to put them to the railing when we heard my mother locking the back door. We hightailed it into bed; my parents creaked up the stairs. Everything at that point seemed fine. Once in their bedroom, though, they started up again, first softly, then louder and louder, until my mother turned on a radio to try to disguise the noise. A door slammed; they began shouting at one another; another door slammed; a shoe or something banged the wall behind Mona's bed.

46 "How're we supposed to *sleep?*" said Mona, sitting up.

47 There was another thud, more yelling in Shanghaiesé, and then my mother's voice pierced the wall, in English. "So what you want I should do? Go to work like Theresa Lee?"

48 My father rumbled something back.

49 "You think you're big shot because you have job, right? You're big shot, but you never get promotion, you never get raise. All I do is spend money, right? So what do you do, you tell me. So what do you do!"

50 Something hit the floor so hard that our room shook.

51 "So kill me," screamed my mother. "You know what you are? You are failure. Failure! You are failure!"

52 Then there was a sudden, terrific, bursting crash—and after it, as if on a bungled cue, the serene blare of an a cappella soprano, picking her way down a scale.

53 By the time Mona and I knew to look out the window, a neighbor's pet beagle was already on the scene, sniffing and barking at my mother's body, his tail crazy with excitement; then he was barking at my stunned and trembling father, at the shrieking ambulance, the police, at crying

Mona in her bunny-footed pajamas, and at me, barefoot in the cold grass, squeezing her shoulder with one hand and clutching my malachite beads with the other.

54   My mother wasn't dead, only unconscious, the paramedics figured that out right away, but there was blood everywhere, and though they were reassuring about her head wounds as they strapped her to the stretcher, commenting also on how small she was, how delicate, how light, my father kept saying, "I killed her, I killed her" as the ambulance screeched and screeched headlong, forever, to the hospital. I was afraid to touch her, and glad of the metal rail between us, even though its sturdiness made her seem even frailer than she was; I wished she was bigger, somehow, and noticed, with a pang, that the new red slippers we had given her for Mother's Day had been lost somewhere along the way. How much she seemed to be leaving behind, as we careened along—still not there, still not there—Mona and Dad and the medic and I taking up the whole ambulance, all the room, so there was no room for anything else; no room even for my mother's real self, the one who should have been pinching the color back to my father's grey face, the one who should have been calming Mona's cowlick—the one who should have been bending over us, to help us to be strong, to help us get through, even as we bent over her.

55   Then suddenly we were there, the glowing square of the emergency room entrance opening like the gates of heaven; and immediately the talk of miracles began. Alive, a miracle. No bones broken, a miracle. A miracle that the hemlocks cushioned her fall, a miracle that they hadn't been trimmed in a year and a half. It was a miracle that all that blood, the blood that had seemed that night to be everywhere, was from one shard of glass, a single shard, can you imagine, and as for the gash in her head, the scar would be covered by hair. The next day my mother cheerfully described just how she would part it so that nothing would show at all.

56   "You're a lucky duck-duck," agreed Mona, helping herself, with a little *pirouette*, to the cherry atop my mother's chocolate pudding.

57   That wasn't enough for me, though. I was relieved, yes, but what I wanted by then was a real miracle, not for her simply to have survived but for the whole thing never to have happened—for my mother's head never to had to have been shaved and bandaged like that, for her high, proud forehead to never have been swollen down over her eyes, for her face and neck and hands never to have been painted so many shades of blueblack, and violet, and chartreuse. I still want those things—for my parents not to have had to live with this affair like a prickle-bush between them, for my father to have been able to look my mother in her swollen eyes and curse the madman, the monster that could have dared done this to the woman he loved. I wanted to be able to touch my mother without shuddering, to be able to console my father, to be able to get that crash out of my head, the sound of that soprano—so many things that I didn't know how to pray for them, that I wouldn't have known where to start even if I had the power to work miracles, right there, right then.

58 A week later, when my mother was home, and her head beginning to bristle with new hairs, I lost my malachite beads. I had been carrying them in a white cloth pouch that Patty had given me, and was swinging the pouch on my pinky on my way home from school, when I swung just a bit too hard, and it went sailing in a long arc through the air, whooshing like a perfectly thrown basketball through one of the holes of a nearby sewer. There was no chance of fishing it out: I looked and looked, crouching on the sticky pavement until the asphalt had crazed the skin of my hands and knees, but all I could discern was an evil-smelling musk, glassy and smug and impenetrable.

59 My loss didn't quite hit me until I was home, but then it produced an agony all out of proportion to my string of pretty beads. I hadn't cried at all during my mother's accident, and now I was crying all afternoon, all through dinner, and then after dinner too, crying past the point where I knew what I was crying for, wishing dimly that I had my beads to hold, wishing dimly that I could pray but refusing, refusing, I didn't know why, until I finally fell into an exhausted sleep on the couch, where my parents left me for the night—glad, no doubt, that one of the more tedious of my childhood crises seemed to be finally winding off the reel of life, onto the reel of memory. They covered me, and somehow grew a pillow under my head, and, with uncharacteristic disregard for the living-room rug, left some milk and pecan sandies on the coffee table, in case I woke up hungry. Their thoughtfulness was prescient: I did wake up in the early part of the night; and it was then, amid the unfamiliar sounds and shadows of the living room, that I had what I was sure was a true vision.

60 Even now what I saw retains an odd clarity: the requisite strange light flooding the room, first orange, and then a bright yellow-green, then a crackling bright burst like a Roman candle going off near the piano. There was a distinct smell of coffee, and a long silence. The room seemed to be getting colder. Nothing. A creak; the light starting to wane, then waxing again, brilliant pink now. Still nothing. Then, as the pink started to go a little purple, a perfectly normal middle-aged man's voice, speaking something very like pig latin, told me quietly not to despair, not to despair, my beads would be returned to me.

61 That was all. I sat a moment in the dark, then turned on the light, gobbled down the cookies—and in a happy flash understood I was so good, really, so near to being a saint that my malachite beads would come back through the town water system. All I had to do was turn on all the faucets in the house, which I did, one by one, stealing quietly into the bathroom and kitchen and basement. The old spigot by the washing machine was too gunked up to be coaxed very far open, but that didn't matter. The water didn't have to be full blast, I understood that. Then I gathered together my pillow and blanket and trundled up to my bed to sleep.

62 By the time I woke up in the morning I knew that my beads hadn't shown up, but when I knew it for certain, I was still disappointed; and as if that weren't enough, I had to face my parents and sister, who were all

abuzz with the mystery of the faucets. Not knowing what else to do, I, like a puddlebrain, told them the truth. The results were predictably painful.

63   "Callie had a *vision*," Mona told everyone at the bus stop. "A vision with lights, and sinks in it!"

64   Sinks, visions. I got it all day, from my parents, from my classmates, even some sixth and seventh graders. Someone drew a cartoon of me with a halo over my head in one of the girls' room stalls; Anthony Rossi made gurgling noises as he walked on his hands at recess. Only Patty tried not to laugh, though even she was something less than unalloyed understanding.

65   "I don't think miracles are thupposed to happen in *thewers*," she said.

66   Such was the end of my saintly ambitions. It wasn't the end of all holiness; the ideas of purity and goodness still tippled my brain, and over the years I came slowly to grasp of what grit true faith was made. Last night, though, when my father called to say that he couldn't go on living in our old house, that he was going to move to a smaller place, another place, maybe a condo—he didn't know how, or where—I found myself still wistful for the time religion seemed all I wanted it to be. Back then the world was a place that could be set right: One had only to direct the hand of the Almighty and say, just here, Lord, we hurt here—and here, and here, and here.

Points for Review and Discussion

1.   Praying seems to be a central activity in "The Water-Faucet Vision." List those who engage in it and explain their states of mind as clearly as you can.
2.   Children of immigrants can adopt any of several attitudes—pride, resentment, irritation, shame, others—toward their parents' "foreignness." How do you describe the attitudes taken by the children in this story toward their parents' Shanghai background?

•❖ *Questions for Writing*

1.   The argument between the grownups in this story "started about the state of the roof" (¶ 42). Summarize in your own words the matters that the husband and wife dealt with before the argument ended.
2.   Describe as fully as you can, citing relevant passages, the state of mind in which Callie turns to prayer. Why does she have no alternative except to set all her hopes on divine intervention?
3.   Where is "The Water-Faucet Vision" most explicit on the subject of the entanglement of religion and the dream of success? What do you take to be the narrator's attitude toward that entanglement? Again: comment on specific passages in your answer.

THE SUPERINTENDENT
John Cheever

Complaints about the unfairness or injustice of a society's rank order carry within them doubts about the logic of the system—its underlying rationale. For what *reason* does A stand above B? What measure or yardstick determines that this person behaves as a Superior and that one behaves as an Inferior? Why do people defer to Ted and Mary and disrespect Sally and Bill?

The usual answers to such questions invoke money or job status or celebrity—but they're not wholly satisfying. Implicit in every rank order or class system is the notion that the higher-ups are in some genuine way *better* than those below them. And when "better" means only that they have more money or a professional degree or publicly recognizable name, the nagging question returns: Why does A stand above B?

In John Cheever's "The Superintendent" a modestly educated New York City apartment house super, Chester Coolidge, repeatedly seems on the verge of asking that question. He's somewhat disturbed by the relations between his richer and poorer tenants. His own status is challenged—by his employers and others. He notices a tenant behaving haughtily toward a stranger. When at length Chester Coolidge does ask a question—Why does his workday lack meaning?—the question becomes a challenge for the reader. It's up to us to explain why the endless topsy-turvy of class and status in this narrative finally "add[s] up to nothing."

John Cheever (1912–1982) was born in Quincy, Massachusetts, attended Thayer Academy in that state, and did not go to college. His short stories began appearing in *The New Yorker* magazine shortly after the end of World War II. They evoke, as he once wrote, "a long-lost world when the city of New York was still filled with a river light, when you heard the Benny Goodman quartets from a radio in the corner stationery store, and when almost everybody wore a hat." Cheever's best known novels are *Falconer* (1977) and *The Wapshot Chronicle* (1957).

1 The alarm began ringing at six in the morning. It sounded faintly in the first-floor apartment that Chester Coolidge was given as part wages of an apartment-house superintendent, but it woke him at once, for he slept with the percussive noises of the building machinery on his consciousness, as if they were linked to his own well-being. In the dark, he dressed quickly and ran through the lobby to the back stairs, where his path was obstructed by a peach basket full of dead roses and carnations. He kicked this aside and ran lightly down

---

From John Cheever, *The Stories of John Cheever* (1978).

the iron stairs to the basement and along a hall whose brick walls, encrusted with paint, looked like a passage in some catacomb. The ringing of the bell grew louder as he approached the room where the pump machinery was. The alarm signified that the water tank on the roof was nearly empty and that the mechanism that regulated the water supply wasn't working. In the pump room, Chester turned on the auxiliary pump.

2   The basement was still. Far up the back elevator shaft he could hear the car moving down, floor by floor, attended by the rattle of milk bottles. It would take an hour for the auxiliary to fill the roof tank, and Chester decided to keep an eye on the gauge himself, and let the handyman sleep. He went upstairs again, and shaved and washed while his wife cooked breakfast. It was a moving day, and before he sat down to breakfast, he saw that the barometer had fallen and, looking out of the window and up eighteen stories, he found the sky as good as black. Chester liked a moving day to be dry and fair, and in the past, when everyone moved on the first of October, the chances for good weather had been favorable; but now all this had been changed for the worse, and they moved in the snow and the rain. The Bestwicks (9-E) were moving out and the Neguses (1-A) were moving up. That was all. While Chester drank his first cup of coffee, his wife talked about the Bestwicks, whose departure excited in her some memories and misgivings. Chester did not answer her questions, nor did she expect him to that early in the day. She talked loosely and, as she put it herself, to hear the sound of her own voice.

3   Mrs. Coolidge had come with her husband twenty years earlier from Massachusetts. The move had been her idea. Ailing and childless, she had decided that she would be happier in a big city than in New Bedford. Entrenched in a superintendent's apartment in the East Fifties, she was perfectly content. She spent her days in the movies and the stores, and she had seen the Shah of Persia with her own eyes. The only part of city life that troubled her was the inhibitions that it put on her native generosity.

4   "That poor Mrs. Bestwick," she said. "Oh, that poor woman! You told me they sent the children out to stay with their grandmother, didn't you, until they get settled? I wish there was something I could do to help her. Now, if this was in New Bedford, we could ask her to dinner or give her a basket with a nice dinner in it. You know, I'm reminded by her of those people in New Bedford—the Fenners. The two sisters, they were. They had diamonds as big as filberts, just like Mrs. Bestwick, and no electricity in the house. They used to have to go over to Georgiana Butler's to take a bath."

5   Chester did not look at his wife, but her mere presence was heartening and wonderful, for he was convinced that she was an extraordinary woman. He felt that there was a touch of genius in her cooking, that her housework was marked with genius, that she had a geniuslike memory,

and that her ability to accept the world as she found it was stamped with genius. She had made johnnycake for breakfast, and he ate it with an appreciation that verged on awe. He knew for a fact that no one else in the world could make johnnycake like his wife and that no one else in Manhattan that morning would have tried.

6   When he had finished breakfast, he lighted a cigar and sat thinking about the Bestwicks. Chester had seen the apartment building through many lives, and it seemed that another was commencing. He had, since 1943, divided the tenants into two groups, the "permanents" and the "ceilings." A rent increase had been granted the management, and he knew that that would weed out a number of the "ceilings." The Bestwicks were the first to go under these conditions, and, like his wife, he was sorry to see them leave. Mr. Bestwick worked downtown. Mrs. Bestwick was a conscientious citizen and she had been building captain for the Red Cross, the March of Dimes, and the Girl Scouts. Whatever Mr. Bestwick made, it was not enough—not for that neighborhood. The liquor store knew. The butcher knew. The doorman and the window washer knew, and it had been known for a year to Retail Credit and the Corn Exchange Bank. The Bestwicks had been the last people in the neighborhood to face the facts. Mr. Bestwick wore a high-crowned felt hat, suit coats that were cut full around the waist, tight pants, and a white raincoat. He duck-footed off to work at eight every morning in a pair of English shoes that seemed to pinch him. The Bestwicks had been used to more money than they now had, and while Mrs. Bestwick's tweed suits were worn, her diamonds, as Mrs. Coolidge had noticed, were as big as filberts. The Bestwicks had two daughters and never gave Chester any trouble.

7   Mrs. Bestwick had called Chester late one afternoon about a month before and asked him if he would come upstairs. It was not urgent, she explained in her pleasant voice, but if it was not inconvenient, she would like to see him. She let him in graciously, as she did everything. She was a slender woman—a too slender woman with a magnificent bust and a graceful way of moving. He followed her that afternoon into the living room, where an older woman was sitting on a sofa. "This is my mother, Mrs. Doubleday, Chester," Mrs. Bestwick said. "Mother, this is Chester Coolidge, our superintendent." Mrs. Doubleday said she was pleased to meet him, and Chester accepted her invitation to sit down. From one of the bedrooms, Chester heard the older Bestwick girl singing a song. "Up with Chapin, / Down with Spence," she sang. "Hang Miss Hewitt / To a back-yard fence."

8   Chester knew every living room in the building, and by his standards the Bestwicks' was as pleasant as any of them. It was his feeling that all the apartments in his building were intrinsically ugly and inconvenient. Watching his self-important tenants walk through the lobby, he sometimes thought that they were a species of the poor. They were poor in space, poor in light, poor in quiet, poor in repose, and poor in the atmosphere of privacy—poor in everything that makes a man's home his cas-

tle. He knew the pains they took to overcome these deficiencies: the fans, for instance, to take away the smells of cooking. A six-room apartment is not a house, and if you cook onions in one end of it, you'll likely smell them in the other, but they all installed kitchen exhausts and kept them running, as if ventilating machinery would make an apartment smell like a house in the woods. All the living rooms were, to his mind, too high-ceilinged and too narrow, too noisy and too dark, and he knew how tirelessly the women spent their time and money in the furniture stores, thinking that another kind of carpeting, another set of end tables, another pair of lamps would make the place conform at last to their visions of a secure home. Mrs. Bestwick had done better than most, he thought, or perhaps it was because he liked her that he liked her room.

9 "Do you know about the new rents, Chester?" Mrs. Bestwick said.

10 "I never know about rents or leases," Chester said untruthfully. "They handle all of that at the office."

11 "Our rent's been raised," Mrs. Bestwick said, "and we don't want to pay that much. I thought you might know if there was a less expensive apartment vacant in the building."

12 "I'm sorry, Mrs. Bestwick," Chester said. "There isn't a thing."

13 "I see," Mrs. Bestwick said.

14 He saw that she had something in mind; probably she hoped that he would offer to speak to the management and persuade them that the Bestwicks, as old and very desirable tenants, should be allowed to stay on at their present rental. But apparently she wasn't going to put herself in the embarrassing position of asking for his help, and he refrained, out of tact, from telling her that there was no way of his bringing pressure to bear on the situation.

15 "Isn't this building managed by the Marshall Cavises?" Mrs. Doubleday asked.

16 "Yes," Chester said.

17 "I went to Farmington with Mrs. Cavis," Mrs. Doubleday said to her daughter. "Do you think it would help if I spoke with her?"

18 "Mrs. Cavis isn't around here very much," Chester said. "During the fifteen years I worked here, I never laid eyes on either of them."

19 "But they do manage the building?" Mrs. Doubleday said to him.

20 "The Marshall Cavis Corporation manages it," Chester said.

21 "Maude Cavis was engaged to Benton Towler," Mrs. Doubleday said.

22 "I don't expect they have much to do with it personally," Chester said. "I don't know, but it seems to me I heard they don't even live in New York."

23 "Thank you very much, Chester." Mrs. Bestwick said. "I just thought there might be a vacancy."

24 When the alarm began ringing again, this time to signify that the tank on the roof was full, Chester lit out through the lobby and down the iron stairs and turned off the pump. Stanley, the handyman, was awake and

moving around in his room by then, and Chester told him he thought the float switch on the roof that controlled the pump was broken and to keep an eye on the gauge. The day in the basement had begun. The milk and the newspapers had been delivered; Delaney, the porter, had emptied the waste cans in the back halls; and now the sleep-out cooks and maids were coming to work. Chester could hear them greeting Ferarri, the back-elevator man, and their clear "Good mornings" confirmed his feeling that the level of courtesy was a grade higher in the basement than in the lobby upstairs.

25   At a little before nine, Chester telephoned the office management. A secretary whose voice he did not recognize took the message. "The float switch on the water tank is busted," he told her, "and we're working the auxiliary manually now. You tell the maintenance crew to get over here this morning."

26   "The maintenance crew is at one of the other buildings," the unfamiliar voice said, "and we don't expect them back until four o'clock."

27   "This is an emergency, God damn it!" Chester shouted. "I got over two hundred bathrooms here. This building's just as important as those buildings over on Park Avenue. If my bathrooms run dry, you can come over here and take the complaints yourself. It's a moving day, and the handyman and me have got too much to do to be sitting beside the auxiliary all the time." His face got red. His voice echoed through the basement. When he hung up, he felt uncomfortable and his cigar burned his mouth. Then Ferarri came in with a piece of bad news. The Bestwicks' move would be delayed. They had arranged for a small moving company to move them to Pelham, and the truck had broken down in the night, bringing a load south from Boston.

28   Ferarri took Chester up to 9-E in the service car. One of the cheap, part-time maids that Mrs. Bestwick had been hiring recently had thumbtacked a sign onto the back door. "To Whom It May Concern," she had printed. "I never play the numbers and I never will play the numbers and I never played the numbers." Chester put the sign in the waste can and rang the back bell. Mrs. Bestwick opened the door. She was holding a cracked cup full of coffee in one hand, and Chester noticed that her hand was trembling. "I'm terribly sorry about the moving truck, Chester," she said. "I don't quite know what to do. Everything's ready," she said, gesturing toward the china barrels that nearly filled the kitchen. She led Chester across the hall into the living room, where the walls, windows, and floors were bare. "Everything's ready," she repeated. "Mr. Bestwick has gone up to Pelham to wait for me. Mother took the children."

29   "I wish you'd asked my advice about moving companies," Chester said. "It isn't that I get a cut from them or anything, but I could have put you onto a reliable moving firm that wouldn't cost you any more than the one you got. People try to save money by getting cheap moving companies and in the end they don't save anything. Mrs. Negus—she's in 1-A—she wants to get her things in here this morning."

30 Mrs. Bestwick didn't answer. "Oh, I'll miss you, Mrs. Bestwick," Chester said, feeling that he might have spoken unkindly. "There's no question about that. I'll miss you and Mr. Bestwick and the girls. You've been good tenants. During the eight years you've been here, I don't believe there's been a complaint from any of you. But things are changing, Mrs. Bestwick. Something's happening. The high cost of living. Oh, I can remember times when most of the tenants in this building wasn't rich nor poor. Now there's none but the rich. And, oh, the things they complain about, Mrs. Bestwick. You wouldn't believe me. The day before yesterday, that grass widow in 7-F called up, and you know what she was complaining about? She said the toilet seats in the apartment wasn't big enough."

31 Mrs. Bestwick didn't laugh at his joke. She smiled, but her mind seemed to be on something else.

32 "Well, I'll go down and tell Mrs. Negus that they'll be a delay," Chester said.

33 Mrs. Negus, who was replacing Mrs. Bestwick, took piano lessons. Her apartment had an entrance off the lobby, and in the afternoon she could be heard practicing her scales. The piano was a difficult instrument for her and she had mastered only a few jingles. Piano lessons were a new undertaking for Mrs. Negus. When she first moved into the building, during the war, her name had been Mary Toms, and she had lived with Mrs. Lasser and Mrs. Dobree. Chester suspected that Mrs. Lasser and Mrs. Dobree were loose women, and when Mary Toms joined them, Chester had worried about her, because she was so young and so pretty. His anxiety was misplaced—the loose life didn't depress or coarsen her at all. Coming in there as a poor girl in a cloth coat, she had at the end of the year more furs than anybody else and she seemed to be as happy as a lark. It was in the second winter that Mr. Negus began to call. He went there by chance, Chester guessed, and the visit changed his whole life. He was a tough-looking middle-aged man and Chester remembered him because when he came through the lobby on his way to I-A, he used to bury his nose in the collar of his coat and pull his hat brim down over his eyes.

34 As soon as Mr. Negus began to visit Mary Toms regularly, she eliminated all her other friends. One of them, a French naval officer, made some trouble, and it took a doorman and a cop to get him out. After this, Mr. Negus pointed out the door to Mrs. Lasser and Mrs. Dobree. It was nothing against Mary Toms, and she tried hard to get her friends another apartment in the building. Mr. Negus was stubborn, and the two older women packed their trunks and moved to an apartment on West Fifty-eighth Street. After they had gone, a decorator came in and overhauled the place. He was followed by the grand piano, the poodles, the Book-of-the-Month Club membership, and the crusty Irish maid. That winter, Mary Toms and Mr. Negus went down to Miami and got married there, but even after his marriage Mr. Negus still skulked through the lobby as

if he was acting against his better judgment. Now the Neguses were going to move the whole caboodle up to 9-E. Chester didn't care one way or the other, but he didn't think the move was going to be permanent. Mrs. Negus was on the move. After a year or two in 9-E, he figured she'd ascend to one of the penthouses. From there, she'd probably take off for one of the fancier buildings on upper Fifth.

35   When Chester rang the bell that morning, Mrs. Negus let him in. She was still as pretty as a picture. "Hi, Chet," she said. "Come on in. I thought you didn't want me to start moving until eleven."

36   "Well, there may be a delay," Chester said. "The other lady's moving truck hasn't come."

37   "I got to get this stuff upstairs, Chet."

38   "Well, if her men don't come by eleven," Chester said, "I'll have Max and Delaney move the stuff down."

39   "Hi, Chet," Mr. Negus said.

40   "What's that on the seat of your pants, honey?" Mrs. Negus said.

41   "There's nothing on my pants," Mr. Negus said.

42   "Yes, there is, too," Mrs. Negus said. "There's a spot on your pants."

43   "Look," Mr. Negus said, "these pants just come back from the dry cleaner's."

44   "Well, if you had marmalade for breakfast," Mrs. Negus said, "you could have sat in that. I mean, you could have got marmalade on them."

45   "I didn't have marmalade," he said.

46   "Well, butter, then," she said. "It's awfully conspicuous."

47   "I'll telephone you," Chester said.

48   "You get her stuff out of there, Chet," Mrs. Negus said, "and I'll give you ten dollars. That's been my apartment since midnight. I want to get my things in there." Then she turned to her husband and began to rub his pants with a napkin. Chester let himself out.

49   In Chester's basement office, the telephone was ringing. He picked up the receiver and a maid spoke to him and said that a bathroom in 5-A was overflowing. The telephone rang repeatedly during the time that he was in the office, and he took down several complaints of mechanical failures reported by maids or tenants—a stuck window, a jammed door, a leaky faucet, and a clogged drain. Chester got the toolbox and made the repairs himself. Most of the tenants were respectful and pleasant, but the grass widow in 7-F called him into the dining room and spoke to him curtly.

50   "You are the janitor?" she asked.

51   "I'm the superintendent," Chester said. "The handyman's busy."

52   "Well, I want to talk with you about the back halls," she said. "I don't think this building is as clean as it should be. The maid thinks that she's seen roaches in the kitchen. We've never had roaches."

53   "It's a clean building," Chester said. "It's one of the cleanest buildings in New York. Delaney washes the back stairs every second day and

we have them painted whenever we get the chance. Sometime when you don't have anything better to do, you might come down cellar and see my basement. I take just as much pains with my basement as I do with my lobby."

"I'm not talking about the basement," the woman said. "I'm talking about the back halls."

Chester left for his office before he lost his temper. Ferarri told him that the maintenance crew had come and were up on the roof with Stanley. Chester wished that they had reported to him, for since he was the superintendent and carried the full burden of the place on his shoulders, he felt he should have been consulted before they went to work on his domain. He went up to Penthouse F and climbed the stairs from the back hall to the roof. A north wind was howling in the television antennas, and there was a little snow left on the roofs and terraces. Tarpaulins covered the porch furniture, and hanging on the wall of one of the terraces was a large straw hat, covered with ice. Chester went to the water tank and saw two men in overalls way up the iron ladder, working on the switch. Stanley stood a few rungs below them, passing up tools. Chester climbed the iron ladder and gave them his advice. They took it respectfully, but as he was going down the ladder, he heard one of the maintenance men ask Stanley, "Who's that—the janitor?"

Hurt for the second time that day, Chester went to the edge of the roof and looked out over the city. On his right was the river. He saw a ship coming down it, a freighter pressing forward on the tide, her deck and porthole lights burning in the overcast. She was off to sea, but her lights and her quietness made her look to Chester as warmed and contained as a farmhouse in a meadow. Down the tide she came like a voyaging farmhouse. Compared to his own domain, Chester thought, a ship was nothing. At his feet, there were thousands of arteries hammering with steam; there were hundreds of toilets, miles of drainpipe, and a passenger list of over a hundred people, any one of whom might at that minute be contemplating suicide, theft, arson, or mayhem. It was a huge responsibility, and Chester thought with commiseration of the relatively paltry responsibilities of a ship's captain taking his freighter out to sea.

When he got back to the basement, Mrs. Negus was on the telephone to ask him if Mrs. Bestwick had gone. He said he would call her back, and hung up. Mrs. Negus's ten dollars seemed to commit Chester to building a fire under Mrs. Bestwick, but he didn't want to add to her troubles, and he thought with regret of what a good tenant she had been. The overcast day, the thought of Mrs. Bestwick and the people who had called him janitor convinced Chester that he needed to be cheered up, and he decided to get his shoes shined.

But the shoeshine parlor that morning was still and empty, and Bronco, the shoeshine man, bent mournfully over Chester's shoes. "I'm sixty-two years old, Chester," Bronco said, "and I got a dirty mind. You think it's because I'm around shoes all the time? You think it has something to do with the way the polish smells?" He lathered Chester's shoes and rubbed in the polish with a coarse brush. "That's what my old lady thinks," Bronco said. "She thinks it's got something to do with being around shoes all the time. All I think about," Bronco said sadly, "is love, love, love. It's disgusting. I see in the paper a picture of a young couple eating supper. For all I know, they're nice young clean-minded people, but I've got different thoughts. A lady comes in to have a pair of heels put on her shoes. 'Yes, madam. No, madam. They'll be ready for you tomorrow, madam,' I'm saying to her, but what's going through my mind I'd be ashamed to tell you. But if it's from being around shoes all the time, how can I help myself? It's the only way I got to make a living. For a job like yours, you got to be a carpenter, a painter, a politician, a regular nursemaid. Oh, that must be some job you got, Chester! A window gets stuck. A fuse burns out. They tell you to come up and fix it. The lady of the house, she opens the door. She's all alone. She's got on her nightgown. She—" Bronco broke off and applied the shoe rag vigorously.

59   When Chester returned to the building, Mrs. Bestwick's moving truck still hadn't come, and he went directly to 9-E and rang the back bell. There was no answer. There was no sound. He rang and rang, and then he opened the door with the pass key, just as Mrs. Bestwick came into the kitchen. "I didn't hear the bell," she said. "I'm so upset by this delay that I didn't hear the bell. I was in the other room." She sat down at the kitchen table. She looked pale and troubled.

60   "Cheer up, Mrs. Bestwick," Chester said. "You'll like it in Pelham. Isn't Pelham where you're moving to? Trees, birds. The children'll put on weight. You'll have a nice house."

61   "It's a small house, Chester," Mrs. Bestwick said.

62   "Well, I'm going to tell the porters to take your stuff—your things—out now and put them in the alley," Chester said. "They'll be just as safe there as they will be in here, and if it rains, I'll see that everything's covered and kept dry. Why don't you go up to Pelham now, Mrs. Bestwick?" he asked. "I'll take care of everything. Why don't you just get onto a train and go up to Pelham?"

63   "I think I'll wait, thank you, Chester," Mrs. Bestwick said.

64   Somewhere a factory whistle blew twelve o'clock. Chester went downstairs and inspected the lobby. The rugs and the floor were clean, and the glass on the hunting prints was shining. He stood under the canopy long enough to see that the brass stanchions were polished, that the rubber doormat was scrubbed, and that his canopy was a good canopy and, unlike some others, had withstood the winter storms. "Good morning," someone said to him elegantly while he was standing there, and he said, "Good morning, Mrs. Wardsworth," before he realized that it was Katie Shay, Mrs. Wardsworth's elderly maid. It was an understandable mistake, for Katie was wearing a hat and a coat that had been discarded by Mrs. Wardsworth and she wore the dregs of a bottle of

Mrs. Wardsworth's perfume. In the eclipsed light the old woman looked like the specter of her employer.

65   Then a moving van, Mrs. Bestwick's moving van, backed up to the curb. This improved Chester's spirits, and he went in to lunch with a good appetite.

66   Mrs. Coolidge did not sit down at the table with Chester, and because she was wearing her purple dress, Chester guessed that she was going to the movies.

67   "That woman up in 7-F asked me if I was the janitor today," Chester said.

68   "Well, don't you let it worry you, Chester," Mrs. Coolidge said. "When I think of all the things you have on your mind, Chester—of all the things you have to do—it seems to me that you have more to do than almost anybody I ever knew. Why, this place might catch fire in the middle of the night, and there's nobody here knows where the hoses are but you and Stanley. There's the elevator machines and the electricity and the gas and the furnace. How much oil did you say that furnace burned last winter, Chester?"

69   "Over a hundred thousand gallons, Chester said.

70   "Just think of that," Mrs. Coolidge said.

71   The moving was proceeding in an orderly way when Chester got downstairs again. The moving men told him that Mrs. Bestwick was still in the apartment. He lighted a cigar, sat down at his desk, and heard someone singing, "Did you ever see a dream walking?" The song, attended with laughing and clapping, came from the far end of the basement, and Chester followed the voice down the dark hall, to the laundry. The laundry was a brightly lighted room that smelled of the gas dryer. Banana peels and sandwich papers were spread over the ironing boards, and none of the six laundresses were working. In the center of the room, one of them, dressed in a negligee that someone had sent down to have washed, was waltzing with a second, dressed in a tablecloth. The others were clapping and laughing. Chester was wondering whether or not to interfere with the dance when the telephone in his office rang again. It was Mrs. Negus. "Get that bitch out of there, Chester," she said. "That's been my apartment since midnight. I'm going up there now."

72   Chester asked Mrs. Negus to wait for him in the lobby. He found her there wearing a short fur coat and dark glasses. They went up to 9-E together and he rang Mrs. Bestwick's front bell. He introduced the two women, but Mrs. Negus overlooked the introduction in her interest in a piece of furniture that the moving men were carrying across the hall.

73   "That's a lovely piece," she said.

74   "Thank you," Mrs. Bestwick said.

75   "You wouldn't want to sell it?" Mrs. Negus said.

76 "I'm afraid I can't," Mrs. Bestwick said. "I'm sorry that I'm leaving the place in such a mess," she went on. "There wasn't time to have someone come in and clean it up."

77 "Oh, that doesn't matter," Mrs. Negus said. "I'm going to have the whole thing painted and redecorated anyhow. I just wanted to get my things in here."

78 "Why don't you go up to Pelham now, Mrs. Bestwick?" Chester said. "Your truck's here, and I'll see that all the stuff is loaded."

79 "I will in a minute, Chester," Mrs. Bestwick said.

80 "You've got some lovely stones there," Mrs. Negus said, looking at Mrs. Bestwick's rings.

81 "Thank you," Mrs. Bestwick said.

82 "Now, you come down with me, Mrs. Bestwick," Chester said, "and I'll get you a taxi and I'll see that everything gets into the moving van all right."

83 Mrs. Bestwick put on her hat and coat. "I suppose there are some things I ought to tell you about the apartment," she said to Mrs. Negus, "but I can't seem to remember any of them. It was very nice to meet you. I hope you'll enjoy the apartment as much as we have." Chester opened the door and she went into the hall ahead of him. "Wait just a minute, Chester," she said. "Wait just a minute, please." Chester was afraid then that she was going to cry, but she opened her purse and went through its contents carefully.

84 Her unhappiness at that moment, Chester knew, was more than the unhappiness of leaving a place that seemed familiar for one that seemed strange; it was the pain of leaving the place where her accent and her looks, her worn suit and her diamond rings could still command a trace of respect; it was the pain of parting from one class and going into another, and it was doubly painful because it was a parting that would never be completed. Somewhere in Pelham she would find a neighbor who had been to Farmingdale or wherever it was; she would find a friend with diamonds as big as filberts and holes in her gloves.

85 In the foyer, she said goodbye to the elevator man and the doorman. Chester went outside with her, expecting that she would say goodbye to him under the canopy, and he was prepared again to extol her as a tenant, but she turned her back on him without speaking and walked quickly to the corner. Her neglect surprised and wounded him, and he was looking after her with indignation when she turned suddenly and came back. "But I forgot to say goodbye to you, Chester, didn't I?" she said. "Goodbye, and thank you, and say goodbye to Mrs. Coolidge for me. Give Mrs. Coolidge my best regards." Then she was gone.

86 "Well, it looks as though it was trying to clear up, doesn't it?" Katie Shay said as she came out the door a few minutes later. She was carrying a paper bag full of grain. As soon as Katie crossed the street, the pi-

geons that roost on the Queensboro Bridge recognized her, but she did not raise her head to see them, a hundred of them, leave their roost and fly loosely in a circle, as if they were windborne. She heard the roar of their wings pass overhead and saw their shadows darken the puddles of water in the street, but she seemed unconscious of the birds. Her approach was firm and gentle, like that of a nursemaid with importunate children, and when the pigeons landed on the sidewalk and crowded up to her feet, she kept them waiting. Then she began to scatter the yellow grain, first to the old and the sick, at the edges of the flock, and then to the others.

87 A workman getting off a bus at the corner noticed the flock of birds and the old woman. He opened his lunch pail and dumped onto the sidewalk the crusts from his meal. Katie was at his side in a minute. "I'd rather you didn't feed them," she said sharply. "I'd just as soon you didn't feed them. You see, I live in that house over there, and I can keep an eye on them, and I see that they have everything they need. I give them fresh grain twice a day. Corn in the winter. It costs me nine dollars a month. I see that they have everything they need and I don't like to have strangers feed them." As she spoke, she kicked the stranger's crusts into the gutter. "I change their water twice a day, and in the winter I always see that the ice is broken on it. But I'd just as soon that strangers didn't feed them. I know you'll understand." She turned her back on the workman and dumped the last of the feed out of her bag. She was queer, Chester thought, she was as queer as the Chinese language. But who was queerer—she, for feeding the birds, or he, for watching her?

88 What Katie had said about the sky was true. The clouds were passing, and Chester noticed the light in the sky. The days were getting longer. The light seemed delayed. Chester went out from under the canopy to see it. He clasped his hands behind his back and stared outward and upward. He had been taught, as a child, to think of the clouds as disguising the City of God, and the low clouds still excited in him the curiosity of a child who thought that he was looking off to where the saints and the prophets lived. But it was more than the liturgical habits of thought that he retained from his pious childhood. The day had failed to have any meaning, and the sky seemed to promise a literal explanation.

89 Why had it failed? Why was it unrewarding? Why did Bronco and the Bestwicks and the Neguses and the grass widow in 7-F and Katie Shay and the stranger add up to nothing? Was it because the Bestwicks and the Neguses and Chester and Bronco had been unable to help one another; because the old maid had not let the stranger help her feed the birds? Was that it? Chester asked, looking at the blue air as if he expected an answer to be written in vapor. But the sky told him only that it was a long day at the end of winter, that it was late and time to go in.

Points for Review and Discussion

1. Imagine yourself in Chester Coolidge's job as superintendent of a large urban apartment house. What would be the chief satisfactions—and the chief frustrations—of your work life?
2. Mrs. Negus is perhaps this story's least attractive character. Why so? Point to examples of offensive behavior on her part and explain why they give offense.

•• Questions for Writing

1. On several occasions characters in this story render judgments on the relative human worth of the Bestwicks and Neguses. Make a list of the occasions and briefly explain the rankings.
2. Chester Coolidge himself is often ranked by others. Make a list of these rankings and briefly explain the reasoning on which they rest.
3. Katie's behavior (¶ 87) indicates that she ranks herself considerably higher than the other pigeon feeder. Briefly explain the basis of this ranking.
4. As your answers to 1–3 indicate, evaluations and rankings in the world of Chester Coolidge are made in accordance with a variety of standards. Do any of these standards seem to you to provide an adequate basis for judging the worth of individual human beings? Why so?
5. "The day had failed to have any meaning.... Why did Bronco and the Bestwicks and the Neguses and the grass widow in 7-F and Katie Shay and the stranger add up to nothing?" (¶ 88, 89). Write a page in which you answer this question by explaining what's lacking in the pecking orders that rule the world of "The Superintendent."
6. From among the nonfiction readings in *Created Equal*, choose one that seems to you to cast interesting light on "The Superintendent" and go on to explain your choice.

12

Class Textures (II)
Varieties of Human Love

In fairy tales and myths the power of love is absolute; it can bridge any social gap. Spying beauty in a scullery maid, the prince instantly loses his heart; his feeling for Cinderella, and hers for him, burns off all merely factual, merely social circumstance. In fantasies love is inviolable; coarse material stuff cannot touch it.

But matters are otherwise in ordinary lived experience: love is entangled and embedded in an array of gritty influences that make it hard to imagine it as an independent, unconditioned force. Sexual love, the love of parent for child or of student for mentor—all take some of their form from the immediate environment. The stories in Chapter 12 explore, in various ways, the environment and social construction of love.

Tillie Olsen shows us a single mother remembering the fierce discipline of feeling she imposed, of necessity, on her youngest child. Stuart Dybek writes about the impact of ethnicity, race, class, and aesthetic taste on the development of love. Sandra Cisneros's heroine learns a vision of "pure" love from TV—and is obliged to unlearn it in marriage. And Russell Banks's hero comes finally to the beginnings of an understanding of the class origins of the ideas of beauty and "lovableness" that mold his emotional life.

I Stand Here Ironing
Tillie Olsen

The truth about any family embraces both subjective and objective reality. Parental income and employment history matters, as does the number of children, the size of abode, frequency of changes of address, and so on. But no less important are the attitudes and feelings of parents toward children and vice versa. And these subjective and objective factors are tightly connected; separating feelings from socioeconomics is often next to impossible.

In Tillie Olsen's story "I Stand Here Ironing" we listen to a mother probing her memories of rearing her first child, now a nineteen-year-old college student. The behavior and feelings she describes have clear roots in personal character—traits and eccentricities that define the uniqueness of this particular parent and this particular child. But the mother is wholly aware that character is inseparable from social situation; she knows, that is, that both she and her daughter *are* what they have jointly suffered, and that the quality of their love is directly related to the life circumstances they shared.

Tillie Olsen was born in Nebraska in 1912, and raised a family of four daughters in San Francisco. Although simple survival was a struggle, Olsen managed to keep alive her own literary ambitions, and, relatively late in life, she finally won a foundation grant in literature that eased her domestic burdens. Not long afterward she produced *Tell Me a Riddle* (1961), a prizewinning collection of short stories.

1 I stand here ironing, and what you asked me moves tormented back and forth with the iron.

2 "I wish you would manage the time to come in and talk with me about your daughter. I'm sure you can help me understand her. She's a youngster who needs help and whom I'm deeply interested in helping."

3 "Who needs help?" Even if I came what good would it do? You think because I am her mother I have a key, or that in some way you could use me as a key? She has lived for nineteen years. There is all that life that has happened outside of me, beyond me.

4 And when is there time to remember, to sift, to weigh, to estimate, to total? I will start and there will be an interruption and I will have to gather it all together again. Or I will become engulfed with all I did or did not do, with what should have been and what cannot be helped.

5 She was a beautiful baby. The first and only one of our five that was beautiful at birth. You do not guess how new and uneasy her tenancy in

---

From Tillie Olsen, *Tell Me a Riddle* (1961).

her now-loveliness. You did not know her all those years she was thought homely, or see her poring over her baby pictures, making me tell her over and over how beautiful she had been—and would be, I would tell her—and was now, to the seeing eye. But the seeing eyes were few or nonexistent. Including mine.

6   I nursed her. They feel that's important nowadays. I nursed all the children, but with her, with all the fierce rigidity of first motherhood, I did like the books said. Though her cries battered me to trembling and my breast ached with swollenness, I waited till the clock decreed.

7   Why do I put that first? I do not even know if it matters, or if it explains anything.

8   She was a beautiful baby. She blew shining bubbles of sound. She loved motion, loved light, loved color and music and textures. She would lie on the floor in her blue overalls patting the surface so hard in ecstasy her hands and feet would blur. She was a miracle to me, but when she was eight months old I had to leave her daytimes with the woman downstairs to whom she was no miracle at all, for I worked or looked for work and for Emily's father, who "could no longer endure" (he wrote in his good-by note) "sharing want with us."

9   I was nineteen. It was the pre-relief, pre-WPA world of the depression. I would start running as soon as I got off the streetcar, running up the stairs, the place smelling sour, and awake or asleep to startle awake, when she saw me she would break into a clogged weeping that could not be comforted, a weeping I can yet hear.

10   After a while I found a job hashing at night so I could be with her days, and it was better. But it came to where I had to bring her to his family and leave her.

11   It took a long time to raise the money for her fare back. Then she got chicken pox and I had to wait longer. When she finally came, I hardly knew her, walking quick and nervous like her father, looking like her father, thin, and dressed in a shoddy red that yellowed her skin and glared at the pock marks. All the baby loveliness gone.

12   She was two. Old enough for nursery school they said, and I did not know then what I know now—the fatigue of the long day, and the lacerations of group life in nurseries that are only parking places for children.

13   Except that it would have made no difference if I had known. It was the only place there was. It was the only way we could be together, the only way I could hold a job.

14   And even without knowing, I knew. I knew the teacher that was evil because all these years it has curdled into my memory, the little boy hunched in the corner, her rasp, "why aren't you outside, because Alvin hits you? That's no reason, go out coward." I knew Emily hated it even if she did not clutch and implore "don't go Mommy" like the other children, mornings.

15   She always had a reason why we should stay home. Momma, you look sick, Momma. I feel sick. Momma, the teachers aren't there today,

they're sick. Momma there was a fire there last night. Momma it's a holiday today, no school, they told me.

16   But never a direct protest, never rebellion. I think of our others in their three-, four-year-oldness—the explosions, the tempers, the denunciations, the demands—and I feel suddenly ill. I stop the ironing. What in me demanded that goodness in her? And what was the cost, the cost to her of such goodness?

17   The old man living in the back once said in his gentle way: "You should smile at Emily more when you look at her." What *was* in my face when I looked at her? I loved her. There were all the acts of love.

18   It was only with the others I remembered what he said, so that it was the face of joy, and not of care or tightness or worry I turned to them—but never to Emily. She does not smile easily, let alone almost always as her brothers and sisters do. Her face is closed and somber, but when she wants, how fluid. You must have seen it in her pantomimes, you spoke of her rare gift for comedy on the stage that rouses a laughter out of the audience so dear they applaud and applaud and do not want to let her go.

19   Where does it come from, that comedy? There was none of it in her when she came back to me that second time, after I had had to send her away again. She had a new daddy now to learn to love, and I think perhaps it was a better time. Except when we left her alone nights, telling ourselves she was old enough.

20   "Can't you go some other time Mommy, like tomorrow?" she would ask. "Will it be just a little while you'll be gone?"

21   The time we came back, the front door open, the clock on the floor in the hall. She rigid awake. "It wasn't just a little while. I didn't cry. I called you a little, just three times, and then I went downstairs to open the door so you could come faster. The clock talked loud, I threw it away, it scared me what it talked."

22   She said the clock talked loud that night I went to the hospital to have Susan. She was delirious with the fever that comes before red measles, but she was fully conscious all the week I was gone and the week after we were home when she could not come near the baby or me.

23   She did not get well. She stayed skeleton thin, not wanting to eat, and night after night she had nightmares. She would call for me, and I would sleepily call back, "you're all right, darling, go to sleep, it's just a dream," and if she still called, in a sterner voice, "now go to sleep Emily, there's nothing to hurt you." Twice, only twice, when I had to get up for Susan anyhow, I went in to sit with her.

24   Now when it is too late (as if she would let me hold and comfort her like I do the others) I get up and go to her at her moan or restless stirring. "Are you awake? Can I get you something?" And the answer is always the same: "No, I'm all right, go back to sleep Mother."

25   They persuaded me at the clinic to send her away to a convalescent home in the country where "she can have the kind of food and care you can't manage for her, and you'll be free to concentrate on the new baby."

They still send children to that place. I see pictures on the society page of sleek young women planning affairs to raise money for it, or dancing at the affairs, or decorating Easter eggs or filling Christmas stockings for the children.

26. They never have a picture of the children so I do not know if they still wear those gigantic red bows and the ravaged looks on the every other Sunday when parents can come to visit "unless otherwise notified"—as we were notified the first six weeks.

27. Oh it is a handsome place, green lawns and tall trees and fluted flower beds. High up on the balconies of each cottage the children stand, the girls in their red bows and white dresses, the boys in white suits and giant red ties. The parents stand below shrieking up to be heard and the children shriek down to be heard, and between them the invisible wall "Not To Be Contaminated by Parental Germs or Physical Affection."

28. There was a tiny girl who always stood hand in hand with Emily. Her parents never came. One visit she was gone. "They moved her to Rose Cottage," Emily shouted in explanation. "They don't like you to love anybody here."

29. She wrote once a week, the labored writing of a seven-year-old. "I am fine. How is the baby. If I write my letter nicely I will have a star. Love." There never was a star. We wrote every other day, letters she could never hold or keep but only hear read—once. "We simply do not have room for children to keep any personal possessions," they patiently explained when we pieced one Sunday's shrieking together to plead how much it would mean to Emily to keep her letters and cards.

30. Each visit she looked frailer. "She isn't eating," they told us. (They had runny eggs for breakfast or mush with lumps, Emily said later, I'd hold it in my mouth and not swallow. Nothing ever tasted good, just when they had chicken.)

31. It took us eight months to get her released home, and only the fact that she gained back so little of her seven lost pounds convinced the social worker.

32. I used to try to hold and love her after she came back, but her body would stay stiff, and after a while she'd push away. She ate little. Food sickened her, and I think much of life too. Oh she had physical lightness and brightness twinkling by on skates, bouncing like a ball up and down up and down over the jump rope, skimming over the hill; but these were momentary.

33. She fretted about her appearance, thin and dark and foreign-looking at a time when every little girl was supposed to look or thought she should look a chubby blond replica of Shirley Temple. The doorbell sometimes rang for her, but no one seemed to come and play in the house or be a best friend. Maybe because we moved so much.

34. There was a boy she loved painfully through two school semesters. Months later she told me how she had taken pennies from my purse to buy him candy. "Licorice was his favorite and I brought him some every

day, but he still liked Jennifer better'n me. Why Mommy why?" A question I could never answer.

35   School was a worry to her. She was not glib or quick in a world where glibness and quickness were easily confused with ability to learn. To her overworked and exasperated teachers she was an overconscientious "slow learner" who kept trying to catch up and was absent entirely too often.

36   I let her be absent, though sometimes the illness was imaginary. How different from my now-strictness about attendance with the others. I wasn't working. We had a new baby, I was home anyhow. Sometimes, after Susan grew old enough, I would keep her home from school, too, to have them all together.

37   Mostly Emily had asthma, and her breathing, harsh and labored, would fill the house with a curiously tranquil sound. I would bring the two old dresser mirrors and her boxes of collections to her bed. She would select beads and single earrings, bottle tops and shells, dried flowers and pebbles, old postcards and scraps, all sorts of oddments; then she and Susan would play Kingdom, setting up landscapes and furniture, peopling them with action.

38   Those were the only times of peaceful companionship between her and Susan. I have edged away from it, that poisonous feeling between them, that terrible balancing of hurts and needs I had to do between the two, and did so badly, those earlier years.

39   Oh there are conflicts between the others too, each one human, needing, demanding, hurting, taking—but only between Emily and Susan, no, Emily toward Susan that corroding resentment. It seems so obvious on the surface, yet it is not obvious. Susan, the second child, Susan, golden and curly haired and chubby, quick and articulate and assured, everything in appearance and manner Emily was not; Susan, not able to resist Emily's precious things, losing or sometimes clumsily breaking them; Susan telling jokes and riddles to company for applause while Emily sat silent (to say to me later: that was *my* riddle, Mother, I told it to Susan); Susan, who for all the five years' difference in age was just a year behind Emily in developing physically.

40   I am glad for that slow physical development that widened the difference between her and her contemporaries, though she suffered over it. She was too vulnerable for that terrible world of youthful competition, of preening and parading, of constant measuring of yourself against every other, of envy, "If I had that copper hair," or "If I had that skin . . . " She tormented herself enough about not looking like the others, there was enough of the unsureness, the having to be conscious of words before you speak, the constant caring—what are they thinking of me? what kind of an impression am I making—there was enough without having it all magnified unendurably by the merciless physical drives.

41   Ronnie is calling. He is wet and I change him. It is rare there is such a cry now. That time of motherhood is almost behind me when the ear is

not one's own but must always be racked and listening for the child cry, the child call. We sit for a while and I hold him, looking out over the city spread in charcoal with its soft aisles of light. "Shuggily" he breathes. A funny word, a family word, inherited from Emily, invented by her to say comfort.

42   In this and other ways she leaves her seal, I say aloud. And startle at my saying it. What do I mean? What did I start to gather together, to try and make coherent? I was at the terrible, growing years. War years. I do not remember them well. I was working, there were four smaller ones now, there was not time for her. She had to help be a mother, and housekeeper, and shopper. She had to set her seal. Mornings of crisis and near hysteria trying to get lunches packed, hair combed, coats and shoes found, everyone to school or Child Care on time, the baby ready for transportation. And always the paper scribbled on by a smaller one, the book looked at by Susan then mislaid, the homework not done. Running out to that huge school where she was one, she was lost, she was a drop; suffering over the unpreparedness, stammering and unsure in her classes.

43   There was so little time left at night after the kids were bedded down. She would struggle over books, always eating (it was in those years she developed her enormous appetite that is legendary in our family) and I would be ironing, or preparing food for the next day, or writing V-mail to Bill, or tending the baby. Sometimes, to make me laugh, or out of her despair, she would imitate happenings or types at school.

44   I think I said once: "Why don't you do something like this in the school amateur show?" One morning she phoned me at work, hardly understandable through the weeping. "Mother, I did it. I won, I won; they gave me first prize; they clapped and clapped and wouldn't let me go."

45   Now suddenly she was Somebody, and as imprisoned in her difference as in anonymity.

46   She began to be asked to perform at other high schools, even in colleges, then at city and state-wide affairs. The first one we went to, I only recognized her that first moment when thin, shy, she almost drowned herself into the curtains. Then: Was this Emily? the control, the command, the convulsing and deadly clowning, the spell, then the roaring, stamping audience, unwilling to let this rare and precious laughter out of their lives.

47   Afterwards: You ought to do something about her with a gift like that—but without money or knowing how, what does one do? We have left it all to her, and the gift has as often eddied inside, clogged and clotted, as been used and growing.

48   She is coming. She runs up the stairs two at a time with her light graceful step, and I know she is happy tonight. Whatever it was that occasioned your call did not happen today.

49   "Aren't you ever going to finish the ironing, Mother? Whistler painted his mother in a rocker. I'd have to paint mine standing over an ironing board." This is one of her communicative nights and she tells

me everything and nothing as she fixes herself a plate of food out of the icebox.

50   She is so lovely. Why did you want me to come in at all? Why were you concerned? She will find her way.

51   She starts up the stairs to bed. "Don't get me up with the rest in the morning." "But I thought you were having midterms." "Oh, those," she comes back in and says quite lightly, "in a couple of years when we'll all be atom-dead they won't matter a bit."

52   She has said it before. She believes it. But because I have been dredging the past, and all that compounds a human being is so heavy and meaningful in me, I cannot endure it tonight.

53   I will never total it all now. I will never come in to say: She was a child seldom smiled at. Her father left me before she was a year old. I worked her first six years when there was work, or I sent her home and to his relatives. There were years she had care she hated. She was dark and thin and foreign-looking in a world where the prestige went to blondness and curly hair and dimples, slow where glibness was prized. She was a child of anxious, not proud, love. We were poor and could not afford for her the soil of easy growth. I was a young mother, I was a distracted mother. There were the other children pushing up, demanding. Her younger sister was all that she was not. She did not like me to touch her. She kept too much in herself, her life was such she had to keep too much in herself. My wisdom came too late. She has much in her and probably nothing will come of it. She is a child of her age, of depression, of war, of fear.

54   Let her be. So all that is in her will not bloom—but in how many does it? There is still enough left to live by. Only help her to believe—help make it so there is cause for her to believe that she is more than this dress on the ironing board, helpless before the iron.

Points for Review and Discussion

1. What differences does the narrator see in her treatment of her children and why do these differences trouble her?

2. "I Stand Here Ironing" evokes dimensions of parenthood that are omitted from most family sitcoms as well as from most political discussion of "family values." Name one of these dimensions and explain why you see it as significant.

Questions for Writing

1. The mother who speaks in "I Stand Here Ironing" has suffered many humiliations in her lifetime. Make a list of these humiliations, name the one that seems to you most harrowing, and explain in a paragraph why it strikes you as the worst.

2. The narrator is afraid that she "will become engulfed with all I did or did not do, with what should have been and what cannot be helped" (¶ 4). What lies behind this fear? Is it guilt or something else? Explain your answer.

3. Thinking of Emily's behavior in relation to that of her other children, the mother "feels suddenly ill" (¶ 16). What causes this response in her? Why did she never turn "the face of joy" to her oldest child?

4. "I Stand Here Ironing" has been praised for rendering truths of poverty and deprivation with power seldom matched in short fiction. Name the truth that impresses you most, and spell out its ramifications as fully as you can.

5. From among the nonfiction texts in *Created Equal*, choose one that seems to cast interesting light on "I Stand Here Ironing" and go on to explain your choice.

Chopin in Winter
Stuart Dybek

Money and occupation separate the classes, and the same holds for cultural tastes. (See Paul Fussell, at the beginning of this book, pages 39–45.) People divide the worlds of art into the respectable and the improper; there are "right" and "wrong" books, paintings and music; social ascent requires that a person abhor "junk."

But tastes are complicated matters. They reflect—among other things—career aspirations, ethnic loyalties and resentments, political and moral feeling, features of personal character, the accidents, turning points, and patterns of development of individual lives. Stuart Dybek's "Chopin in Winter" focuses on three characters—a boy, his grandfather, and a gifted and pregnant young pianist who lives in the apartment above them. Reading it carefully you see how tastes and class are connected not just to each other but to every other element that gives shape to our humanness—including our capacity for love.

Born in Chicago in 1942, Dybek published his first work in 1979. His stories have appeared often in prize anthologies and were collected in *The Coast of Chicago* (1990). Dybek lives in Kalamazoo, Michigan, and teaches at Western Michigan University.

1 The winter Dzia-Dzia came to live with us in Mrs. Kubiac's building on Eighteenth Street was the winter that Mrs. Kubiac's daughter, Marcy, came home pregnant from college in New York. Marcy had gone there on a music scholarship, the first person in Mrs. Kubiac's family to go to high school, let alone college.

2 Since she had come home I had seen her only once. I was playing on the landing before our door, and as she came up the stairs we both nodded hi. She didn't look pregnant. She was thin, dressed in a black coat, its silvery fur collar pulled up around her face, her long blonde hair tucked into the collar. I could see the snowflakes on the fur turning to beads of water under the hall light bulb. Her face was pale and her eyes the same startled blue as Mrs. Kubiac's.

3 She passed me almost without noticing and continued up the next flight of stairs, then paused and, leaning over the banister, asked, "Are you the same little boy I used to hear crying at night?"

4 Her voice was gentle, yet kidding.

5 "I don't know," I said.

6 "If your name is Michael and if your bedroom window is on the fourth floor right below mine, then you are," she said. "When you were

---

From Stuart Dybek, *The Coast of Chicago* (1990).

little sometimes I'd hear you crying your heart out at night. I guess I heard what your mother couldn't. The sound traveled up."

7   "I really woke you up?"

8   "Don't worry about that. I'm a very light sleeper. Snow falling wakes me up. I used to wish I could help you as long as we were both up together in the middle of the night with everyone else snoring."

9   "I don't remember crying," I said.

10   "Most people don't once they're happy again. It looks like you're happy enough now. Stay that way, kiddo." She smiled. It was a lovely smile. Her eyes seemed surprised by it. "Too-da-loo." She waved her fingers.

11   "Too-da-loo." I waved after her. A minute after she was gone I began to miss her.

12   Our landlady, Mrs. Kubiac, would come downstairs for tea in the afternoons and cry while telling my mother about Marcy. Marcy, Mrs. Kubiac said, wouldn't tell her who the child's father was. She wouldn't tell the priest. She wouldn't go to church. She wouldn't go anywhere. Even the doctor had to come to the house, and the only doctor that Marcy would allow was Dr. Shtulek, her childhood doctor.

13   "I tell her, 'Marcy, darling, you have to do something,'" Mrs. Kubiac said. "'What about all the sacrifices, the practice, the lessons, teachers, awards? Look at rich people—they don't let anything interfere with what they want.'"

14   Mrs. Kubiac told my mother these things in strictest confidence, her voice at first a secretive whisper, but growing louder as she recited her litany of troubles. The louder she talked the more broken her English became, as if her worry and suffering were straining the language past its limits. Finally, her feelings overpowered her; she began to weep and lapsed into Bohemian, which I couldn't understand.

15   I would sit out of sight beneath the dining-room table, my plastic cowboys galloping through a forest of chair legs, while I listened to Mrs. Kubiac talk about Marcy. I wanted to hear everything about her, and the more I heard the more precious the smile she had given me on the stairs became. It was like a secret bond between us. Once I became convinced of that, listening to Mrs. Kubiac seemed like spying. I was Marcy's friend and conspirator. She had spoken to me as if I was someone apart from the world she was shunning. Whatever her reasons for the way she was acting, whatever her secrets, I was on her side. In daydreams I proved my loyalty over and over.

16   At night we could hear her playing the piano—a muffled rumbling of scales that sounded vaguely familiar. Perhaps I actually remembered hearing Marcy practicing years earlier, before she had gone on to New York. The notes resonated through the kitchen ceiling while I wiped the supper dishes and Dzia-Dzia sat soaking his feet. Dzia-Dzia soaked his feet every night in a bucket of steaming water into which he dropped a

tablet that fizzed, immediately turning the water bright pink. Between the steaming water and pink dye, his feet and legs, up to the knees where his trousers were rolled, looked permanently scalded.

17 Dzia-Dzia's feet seemed to be turning into hooves. His heels and soles were swollen nearly shapeless and cased in scaly calluses. Nails, yellow as a horse's teeth, grew gnarled from knobbed toes. Dzia-Dzia's feet had been frozen when as a young man he walked most of the way from Krakow to Gdansk in the dead of winter escaping service in the Prussian army. And later he had frozen them again mining for gold in Alaska. Most of what I knew of Dzia-Dzia's past had mainly to do with the history of his feet.

18 Sometimes my uncles would say something about him. It sounded as if he had spent his whole life on the move—selling dogs to the Igorot in the Philippines after the Spanish-American War; mining coal in Johnstown, Pennsylvania; working barges on the Great Lakes; riding the rails out West. No one in the family wanted much to do with him. He had deserted them so often, my uncle Roman said, that it was worse than growing up without a father.

19 My grandma had referred to him as *Pan Djabel*, "Mr. Devil," though the way she said it sounded as if he amused her. He called her a *gorel*, a hillbilly, and claimed that he came from a wealthy, educated family that had been stripped of their land by the Prussians.

20 "Landowners, all right!" Uncle Roman once said to my mother. "Besides acting like a bastard, according to Ma, he actually *was* one in the literal sense."

21 "Romey, shhh, what good's bitter?" my mother said.

22 "Who's bitter, Ev? It's just that he couldn't even show up to bury her. I'll never forgive that."

23 Dzia-Dzia hadn't been at Grandma's funeral. He had disappeared again, and no one had known where to find him. For years Dzia-Dzia would simply vanish without telling anyone, then suddenly show up out of nowhere to hang around for a while, ragged and smelling of liquor, wearing his two suits one over the other, only to disappear yet again.

24 "Want to find him? Go ask the bums on skid row," Uncle Roman would say.

25 My uncles said he lived in boxcars, basements, and abandoned buildings. And when, from the window of a bus, I'd see old men standing around trash fires behind billboards, I'd wonder if he was among them.

26 Now that he was very old and failing he sat in our kitchen, his feet aching and numb as if he had been out walking down Eighteenth Street barefoot in the snow.

27 It was my aunts and uncles who talked about Dzia-Dzia "failing." The word always made me nervous. I was failing, too—failing spelling, English, history, geography, almost everything except arithmetic, and that only because it used numbers instead of letters. Mainly, I was failing

penmanship. The nuns complained that my writing was totally illegible, that I spelled like a DP, and threatened that if I didn't improve they might have to hold me back.

28   Mother kept my failures confidential. It was Dzia-Dzia's they discussed during Sunday visits in voices pitched just below the level of an old man's hearing. Dzia-Dzia stared fiercely but didn't deny what they were saying about him. He hadn't spoken since he had reappeared, and no one knew whether his muteness was caused by senility or stubbornness, or if he'd gone deaf. His ears had been frozen as well as his feet. Wiry white tufts of hair that matched his horned eyebrows sprouted from his ears. I wondered if he would hear better if they were trimmed.

29   Though Dzia-Dzia and I spent the evenings alone together in the kitchen, he didn't talk any more than he did on Sundays. Mother stayed in the parlor, immersed in her correspondence courses in bookkeeping. The piano rumbled above us through the ceiling. I could feel it more than hear it, especially the bass notes. Sometimes a chord would be struck that made the silverware clash in the drawer and the glasses hum.

30   Marcy had looked very thin climbing the stairs, delicate, incapable of such force. But her piano was massive and powerful-looking. I remembered going upstairs once with my mother to visit Mrs. Kubiac. Marcy was away at school then. The piano stood unused—top lowered, lid down over the keys—dominating the apartment. In the afternoon light it gleamed deeply, as if its dark wood were a kind of glass. Its pedals were polished bronze and looked to me more like pedals I imagined motormen stamping to operate streetcars.

31   "Isn't it beautiful, Michael?" my mother asked.

32   I nodded hard, hoping that Mrs. Kubiac would offer to let me play it, but she didn't.

33   "How did it get up here?" I asked. It seemed impossible that it could fit through a doorway.

34   "Wasn't easy," Mrs. Kubiac said, surprised. "Gave Mr. Kubiac a rupture. It come all the way on the boat from Europe. Some old German, a great musician, brang it over to give concerts, then got sick and left it. Went back to Germany. God knows what happened to him—I think he was a Jew. They auctioned it off to pay his hotel bill. That's life, huh? Otherwise who could afford it? We're not rich people."

35   "It must have been very expensive anyway," my mother said.

36   "Only cost me a marriage," Mrs. Kubiac said, then laughed, but it was forced. "That's life too, huh?" she asked. "Maybe a woman's better off without a husband?" And then, for just an instant, I saw her glance at my mother, then look away. It was a glance I had come to recognize from people when they caught themselves saying something that might remind my mother or me that my father had been killed in the war.

37   The silverware would clash and the glasses hum. I could feel it in my teeth and bones as the deep notes rumbled through the ceiling and

walls like distant thunder. It wasn't like listening to music, yet more and more often I would notice Dzia-Dzia close his eyes, a look of concentration pinching his face as his body swayed slightly. I wondered what he was hearing. Mother had said once that he'd played the fiddle when she was a little girl, but the only music I'd even seen him show any interest in before was the "Frankie Yankovitch Polka Hour," which he turned up loud and listened to with his ear almost pressed to the radio. Whatever Marcy was playing, it didn't sound like Frankie Yankovitch.

38   Then one evening, after weeks of silence between us, punctuated only by grunts, Dzia-Dzia said, "That's boogie-woogie music."

39   "What, Dzia-Dzia?" I asked, startled.

40   "Music the boogies play."

41   "You mean from upstairs? That's Marcy."

42   "She's in love with a colored man."

43   "What are you telling him, Pa?" Mother demanded. She had just happened to enter the kitchen while Dzia-Dzia was speaking.

44   "About boogie-woogie." Dzia-Dzia's legs jiggled in the bucket so that the pink water sloshed over onto the linoleum.

45   "We don't need that kind of talk in the house."

46   "What talk, Evusha?"

47   "He doesn't have to hear that prejudice in the house," Mom said. "He'll pick up enough on the street."

48   "I just told him boogie-woogie."

49   "I think you better soak your feet in the parlor by the heater," Mom said. "We can spread newspaper."

50   Dzia-Dzia sat, squinting as if he didn't hear.

51   "You heard me, Pa. I said soak your feet in the parlor," Mom repeated on the verge of shouting.

52   "What, Evusha?"

53   "I'll yell as loud as I have to, Pa."

54   "Boogie-woogie, boogie-woogie, boogie-woogie," the old man muttered as he left the kitchen, slopping barefoot across the linoleum.

55   "Go soak your head while you're at it," Mom muttered behind him, too quietly for him to hear.

56   Mom had always insisted on polite language in the house. Someone who failed to say "please" or "thank you" was as offensive to her ears as someone who cursed.

57   "The word is 'yes,' not 'yeah,'" she would correct. Or "If you want 'hey,' go to a stable." She considered "ain't" a form of laziness, like not picking up your dirty socks.

58   Even when they got a little drunk at the family parties that took place at our flat on Sundays, my uncles tried not to swear—and they had all been in the army and the marines. Nor were they allowed to refer to the Germans as Krauts, or the Japanese as Nips. As far as Mom was con-

cerned, of all the misuses of language, racial slurs were the most ignorant, and so the most foul.

59 My uncles didn't discuss the war much anyway, though whenever they got together there was a certain feeling in the room as if beneath the loud talk and joking they shared a deeper, sadder mood. Mom had replaced the photo of my father in his uniform with an earlier photo of him sitting on the running board of the car they'd owned before the war. He was grinning and petting the neighbor's Scottie. That one and their wedding picture were the only photos that Mom kept out. She knew I didn't remember my father, and she seldom talked about him. But there were a few times when she would read aloud parts of his letters. There was one passage in particular that she read at least once a year. It had been written while he was under bombardment, shortly before he was killed.

> When it continues like this without letup you learn what it is to really hate. You begin to hate them as a people and want to punish them all—civilians, women, children, old people—it makes no difference, they're all the same, none of them innocent, and for a while your hate and anger keep you from going crazy with fear. But if you let yourself hate and believe in hate, then no matter what else happens, you've lost. Eve, I love our life together and want to come home to you and Michael, as much as I can, the same man who left.

60 I wanted to hear more but didn't ask. Perhaps because everyone seemed to be trying to forget. Perhaps because I was afraid. When the tears would start in Mom's eyes I caught myself wanting to glance away as Mrs. Kubiac had.

61 There was something more besides Mom's usual standards for the kind of language allowed in the house that caused her to lose her temper and kick Dzia-Dzia out of his spot in the kitchen. She had become even more sensitive, especially where Dzia-Dzia was concerned, because of what had happened with Shirley Popel's mother.

62 Shirley's mother had died recently. Mom and Shirley had been best friends since grade school, and after the funeral, Shirley came back to our house and poured out the story.

63 Her mother had broken a hip falling off a curb while sweeping the sidewalk in front of her house. She was a constantly smiling woman without any teeth who, everyone said, looked like a peasant. After forty years in America she could barely speak English, and even in the hospital refused to remove her babushka.

64 Everyone called her Babushka, Babush for short, which meant "granny," even the nuns at the hospital. On top of her broken hip, Babush caught pneumonia, and one night Shirley got a call from the doctor saying Babush had taken a sudden turn for the worse. Shirley rushed right over, taking her thirteen-year-old son, Rudy. Rudy was Babushka's favorite, and Shirley hoped that seeing him would instill the will to live

in her mother. It was Saturday night and Rudy was dressed to play at his first dance. He wanted to be a musician and was wearing clothes he had bought with money saved from his paper route. He'd bought them at Smoky Joe's on Maxwell Street—blue suede loafers, electric-blue socks, a lemon-yellow one-button roll-lapel suit with padded shoulders and pegged trousers, and a parrot-green satin shirt. Shirley thought he looked cute.

65   When they got to the hospital they found Babush connected to tubes and breathing oxygen.

66   "Ma," Shirley said, "Rudy's here."

67   Babush raised her head, took one look at Rudy, and smacked her gray tongue.

68   "Rudish," Babush said, "you dress like nigger." Then suddenly her eyes rolled; she fell back, gasped, and died.

69   "And those were her last words to any of us, Ev," Shirley wept, "words we'll carry the rest of our lives, but especially poor little Rudy—*you dress like nigger.*"

70   For weeks after Shirley's visit, no matter who called, Mom would tell them Shirley's story over the phone.

71   "Those aren't the kind of famous last words we're going to hear in this family if I can help it," she promised more than once, as if it were a real possibility. "Of course," she'd sometimes add, "Shirley always has let Rudy get away with too much. I don't see anything cute about a boy going to visit his grandmother at the hospital dressed like a hood."

72   Any last words Dzia-Dzia had he kept to himself. His silence, however, had already been broken. Perhaps in his own mind that was a defeat that carried him from failing to totally failed. He returned to the kitchen like a ghost haunting his old chair, one that appeared when I sat alone working on penmanship.

73   No one else seemed to notice a change, but it was clear from the way he no longer soaked his feet. He still kept up the pretense of sitting there with them in the bucket. The bucket went with him the way ghosts drag chains. But he no longer went through the ritual of boiling water: boiling it until the kettle screeched for mercy, pouring so the linoleum puddled and steam clouded around him, and finally dropping in the tablet that fizzed furiously pink, releasing a faintly metallic smell like a broken thermometer.

74   Without his bucket steaming, the fogged windows cleared. Mrs. Kubiac's building towered a story higher than any other on the block. From our fourth-story window I could look out at an even level with the roofs and see the snow gathering on them before it reached the street.

75   I sat at one end of the kitchen table copying down the words that would be on the spelling test the next day. Dzia-Dzia sat at the other, mumbling incessantly, as if finally free to talk about the jumble of the past he'd never mentioned—wars, revolutions, strikes, journeys to

strange places, all run together, and music, especially Chopin. "Chopin," he'd whisper hoarsely, pointing to the ceiling with the reverence of nuns pointing to heaven. Then he'd close his eyes and his nostrils would widen as if he were inhaling the fragrance of sound.

76 It sounded no different to me, the same muffled thumping and rumbling we'd been hearing ever since Marcy had returned home. I could hear the intensity in the crescendos that made the silverware clash, but it never occurred to me to care what she was playing. What mattered was that I could hear her play each night, could feel her playing just a floor above, almost as if she were in our apartment. She seemed that close.

77 "Each night Chopin—it's all she thinks about, isn't it?"
78 I shrugged.
79 "You don't know?" Dzia-Dzia whispered, as if I were lying and he was humoring me.
80 "How should I know?"
81 "And I suppose how should you know the 'Grande Valse brillante' when you hear it either? How should you know Chopin was twenty-one when he composed it?—about the same age as the girl upstairs. He composed it in Vienna, before he went to Paris. Don't they teach you that in school? What are you studying?"
82 "Spelling."
83 "Can you spell *dummkopf?*"
84 The waves of the keyboard would pulse through the warm kitchen and I would become immersed in my spelling words, and after that in penmanship. I was in remedial penmanship. Nightly penmanship was like undergoing physical therapy. While I concentrated on the proper slant of my letters my left hand smeared graphite across the loose-leaf paper.
85 Dzia-Dzia, now that he was talking, no longer seemed content to sit and listen in silence. He would continually interrupt.
86 "Hey, Lefty, stop writing with your nose. Listen how she plays."
87 "Don't shake the table, Dzia-Dzia."
88 "You know this one? No? 'Valse brillante.'"
89 "I thought that was the other one."
90 "What other one? The E-flat? That's 'Grande Valse brillante.' This one's A-flat. Then there's another A-flat—Opus 42—called 'Grande Valse.' Understand?"
91 He rambled on like that about A- and E-flat and sharps and opuses and I went back to compressing my capital *M*'s. My homework was to write five hundred of them. I was failing penmanship yet again, my left hand, as usual, taking the blame it didn't deserve. The problem with *M* wasn't my hand. It was that I had never been convinced that the letters could all be the same widths. When I wrote, *M* automatically came out twice as broad as *N*, *H*, double the width of *I*.
92 "This was Paderewski's favorite waltz. She plays it like an angel."

93 I nodded, staring in despair at my homework. I had made the mistake of interconnecting the *M*'s into long strands. They hummed in my head, drowning out the music, and I wondered if I had been humming aloud. "Who's Paderewski?" I asked, thinking it might be one of Dzia-Dzia's old friends, maybe from Alaska.

94 "Do you know who's George Washington, who's Joe DiMaggio, who's Walt Disney?"

95 "Sure."

96 "I thought so. Paderewski was like them, except he played Chopin. Understand? See, deep down inside, Lefty, you know more than you think."

97 Instead of going into the parlor to read comics or play with my cowboys while Mom pored over her correspondence courses, I began spending more time at the kitchen table, lingering over my homework as an excuse. My spelling began to improve, then took a turn toward perfection; the slant of my handwriting reversed toward the right; I began to hear melodies in what had sounded like muffled scales.

98 Each night Dzia-Dzia would tell me more about Chopin, describing the preludes or ballades or mazurkas, so that even if I hadn't heard them I could imagine them, especially Dzia-Dzia's favorites, the nocturnes, shimmering like black pools.

99 "She's playing her way through the waltzes," Dzia-Dzia told me, speaking as usual in his low, raspy voice as if we were having a confidential discussion. "She's young but already knows Chopin's secret—a waltz can tell more about the soul than a hymn."

100 By my bedtime the kitchen table would be shaking so much that it was impossible to practice penmanship any longer. Across from me, Dzia-Dzia, his hair, eyebrows, and ear tufts wild and white, swayed in his chair, with his eyes squeezed closed and a look of rapture on his face as his fingers pummeled the tabletop. He played the entire width of the table, his body leaning and twisting as his fingers swept the keyboard, left hand pounding at those chords that jangled silverware, while his right raced through runs across tacky oilcloth. His feet pumped the empty bucket. If I watched him, then closed my eyes, it sounded as if two pianos were playing.

101 One night Dzia-Dzia and Marcy played so that I expected at any moment the table would break and the ceiling collapse. The bulbs began to flicker in the overhead fixture, then went out. The entire flat went dark.

102 "Are the lights out in there, too?" Mom yelled from the parlor. "Don't worry, it must be a fuse."

103 The kitchen windows glowed with the light of snow. I looked out. All the buildings down Eighteenth Street were dark and the streetlights were out. Spraying wings of snow, a snow-removal machine, its yellow lights revolving, disappeared down Eighteenth like the last blinks of electricity. There wasn't any traffic. The block looked deserted, as if the

entire city was deserted. Snow was filling the emptiness, big flakes floating steadily and softly between the darkened buildings, coating the fire escapes, while on the roofs a blizzard swirled up into the clouds.

104   Marcy and Dzia-Dzia never stopped playing.

105   "Michael, come in here by the heater, or if you're going to stay in there put the burners on," Mom called.

106   I lit the burners on the stove. They hovered in the dark like blue crowns of flame, flickering Dzia-Dzia's shadow across the walls. His head pitched, his arms flew up as he struck the notes. The walls and windowpanes shook with gusts of wind and music. I imagined plaster dust wafting down, coating the kitchen, a fine network of cracks spreading through the dishes.

107   "Michael?" Mother called.

108   "I'm sharpening my pencil." I stood by the sharpener grinding it as hard as I could, then sat back down and went on writing. The table rocked under my point, but the letters formed perfectly. I spelled new words, words I'd never heard before, yet as soon as I wrote them their meanings were clear, as if they were in another language, one in which words were understood by their sounds, like music. After the lights came back on I couldn't remember what they meant and threw them away.

109   Dzia-Dzia slumped back in his chair. He was flushed and mopped his forehead with a paper napkin.

110   "So, you liked that one," he said. "Which one was it?" he asked. He always asked me that, and little by little I had begun recognizing their melodies.

111   "The polonaise," I guessed. "In A-flat major."

112   "Ahhh," he shook his head in disappointment. "You think everything with a little spirit is the polonaise."

113   "The 'Revolutionary' étude!"

114   "It was a waltz," Dzia-Dzia said.

115   "How could that be a waltz?"

116   "A posthumous waltz. You know what 'posthumous' means?"

117   "What?"

118   "It means music from after a person's dead. The kind of waltz that has to carry back from the other side. Chopin wrote it to a young woman he loved. He kept his feelings for her secret but never forgot her. Sooner or later feelings come bursting out. The dead are as sentimental as anyone else. You know what happened when Chopin died?"

119   "No."

120   "They rang the bells all over Europe. It was winter. The Prussians heard them. They jumped on their horses. They had cavalry then, no tanks, just horses. They rode until they came to the house where Chopin lay on a bed next to a grand piano. His arms were crossed over his chest, and there was plaster drying on his hands and face. The Prussians rode right up the stairs and barged into the room, slashing with

their sabers, their horses stamping and kicking up their front hooves. They hacked the piano and stabbed the music, then wadded up the music into the piano, spilled on kerosene from the lamps, and set it on fire. Then they rolled Chopin's piano to the window—it was those French windows, the kind that open out and there's a tiny balcony. The piano wouldn't fit, so they rammed it through, taking out part of the wall. It crashed three stories into the street, and when it hit it made a sound that shook the city. The piano lay there smoking, and the Prussians galloped over it and left. Later, some of Chopin's friends snuck back and removed his heart and sent it in a little jeweled box to be buried in Warsaw."

121   Dzia-Dzia stopped and listened. Marcy had begun to play again very faintly. If he had asked me to guess what she was playing I would have said a prelude, the one called "The Raindrop."

122 I heard the preludes on Saturday nights, sunk up to my ears in bathwater. The music traveled from upstairs through the plumbing, and resonated as clearly underwater as if I had been wearing earphones.

123   There were other places I discovered where Marcy's playing carried. Polonaises sometimes reverberated down an old trash chute that had been papered over in the dining room. Even in the parlor, provided no one else was listening to the radio or flipping pages of a newspaper, it was possible to hear the faintest hint of mazurkas around the sealed wall where the stovepipe from the space heater disappeared into what had once been a fireplace. And when I went out to play on the landing, bundled up as if I was going out to climb on the drifts piled along Eighteenth Street, I could hear the piano echoing down the hallways. I began to creep higher up the stairs to the top floor, until finally I was listening at Mrs. Kubiac's door, ready to jump away if it should suddenly open, hoping I would be able to think of some excuse for being there, and at the same time almost wishing they would catch me.

124   I didn't mention climbing the stairs in the hallway, nor any of the other places I'd discovered, to Dzia-Dzia. He never seemed interested in anyplace other than the kitchen table. It was as if he were attached to the chair, rooted in his bucket.

125   "Going so early? Where you rushing off to?" he'd ask at the end of each evening, no matter how late, when I'd put my pencil down and begun buckling my books into my satchel.

126   I'd leave him sitting there, with his feet in his empty bucket, and his fingers, tufted with the same white hair as his ears, still tracing arpeggios across the tabletop, though Marcy had already stopped playing. I didn't tell him how from my room, a few times lately after everyone was asleep, I could hear her playing as clearly as if I were sitting at her feet.

127 Marcy played less and less, especially in the evenings after supper, which had been her regular time.

128   Dzia-Dzia continued to shake the table nightly, eyes closed, hair flying, fingers thumping, but the thump of his fingers against the oilcloth was the only sound other than his breathing—rhythmic and labored as if he were having a dream or climbing a flight of stairs.

129   I didn't notice at first, but Dzia-Dzia's solos were the start of his return to silence.

130   "What's she playing, Lefty?" he demanded more insistently than ever, as if still testing whether I knew.

131   Usually now, I did. But after a while I realized he was no longer testing me. He was asking because the sounds were becoming increasingly muddled to him. He seemed able to feel the pulse of the music but could no longer distinguish the melodies. By asking me, he hoped perhaps that if he knew what Marcy was playing he would hear it clearly himself.

132   Then he began to ask what she was playing when she wasn't playing at all.

133   I would make up answers. "The polonaise . . . in A-flat major."

134   "The polonaise! You always say that. Listen harder. Are you sure it's not a waltz?"

135   "You're right, Dzia-Dzia. It's the 'Grande Valse'."

136   "The 'Grande Valse' . . . which one is that?"

137   "A-flat, Opus 42. Paderewski's favorite, remember? Chopin wrote it when he was twenty-one, in Vienna."

138   "In Vienna?" Dzia-Dzia asked, then pounded the table with his fist. "Don't tell me numbers and letters! A-flat, Z-sharp, Opus 0, Opus 1,000! Who cares? You make it sound like a bingo game instead of Chopin."

139   I was never sure if he couldn't hear because he couldn't remember, or couldn't remember because he couldn't hear. His hearing itself still seemed sharp enough.

140   "Stop scratching with that pencil all the time, Lefty, and I wouldn't have to ask you what she's playing," he'd complain.

141   "You'd hear better, Dzia-Dzia, if you'd take the kettle off the stove."

142   He was slipping back into his ritual of boiling water. The kettle screeched like a siren. The windows fogged. Roofs and weather vanished behind a slick of steam. Vapor ringed the overhead light bulbs. The vaguely metallic smell of the fizzing pink tablets hung at the end of every breath.

143   Marcy played hardly at all by then. What little she played was muffled, far off as if filtering through the same fog. Sometimes, staring at the steamed windows, I imagined Eighteenth Street looked that way, with rings of vapor around the streetlights and headlights, clouds billowing from exhaust pipes and manhole covers, breaths hanging, snow swirling like white smoke.

144   Each night water hissed from the kettle's spout as from a blown valve, rumbling as it filled the bucket, brimming until it slopped over onto the warped linoleum. Dzia-Dzia sat, bony calves half submerged, trousers rolled to his knees. He was wearing two suits again, one over

the other, always a sure sign he was getting ready to travel, to disappear without saying good-bye. The fingers of his left hand still drummed unconsciously along the tabletop as his feet soaked. Steam curled up the arteries of his scalded legs, hovered over his lap, smoldered up the buttons of his two vests, traced his mustache and white tufts of hair until it enveloped him. He sat in a cloud, eyes glazed, fading.

145 I began to go to bed early. I would leave my homework unfinished, kiss Mother good night, and go to my room.

146 My room was small, hardly space for more than the bed and bureau. Not so small, though, that Dzia-Dzia couldn't have fit. Perhaps, had I told him that Marcy played almost every night now after everyone was sleeping, he wouldn't have gone back to filling the kitchen with steam. I felt guilty, but it was too late, and I shut the door quickly before steam could enter and fog my window.

147 It was a single window. I could touch it from the foot of the bed. It opened onto a recessed, three-sided air shaft and faced the roof of the building next door. Years ago a kid my age named Freddy had lived next door and we still called it Freddy's roof.

148 Marcy's window was above mine. The music traveled down as clearly as Marcy said my crying had traveled up. When I closed my eyes I could imagine sitting on the Oriental carpet beside her huge piano. The air shaft actually amplified the music just as it had once amplified the arguments between Mr. and Mrs. Kubiac, especially the shouting on those nights after Mr. Kubiac had moved out, when he would return drunk and try to move back in. They'd argued mostly in Bohemian, but when Mr. Kubiac started beating her, Mrs. Kubiac would yell out in English, "Help me, police, somebody, he's killing me!" After a while the police would usually come and haul Mr. Kubiac away. I think sometimes Mom called them. One night Mr. Kubiac tried to fight off the police, and they gave him a terrible beating. "You're killing him in front of my eyes!" Mrs. Kubiac began to scream. Mr. Kubiac broke away and, with the police chasing him, ran down the hallways pounding on doors, pleading for people to open up. He pounded on our door. Nobody in the building let him in. That was their last argument.

149 The room was always cold. I'd slip, still wearing my clothes, under the goose-feather—stuffed *piersyna* to change into my pajamas. It would have been warmer with the door open even a crack, but I kept it closed because of the steam. A steamed bedroom window reminded me too much of the winter I'd had pneumonia. It was one of the earliest things I could remember: the gurgling hiss of the vaporizer and smell of benzoin while I lay sunk in my pillows watching steam condense to frost on the pane until daylight blurred. I could remember trying to scratch through the frost with the key to a windup mouse so that I could see how much snow had fallen, and Mother catching me. She was furious that I had climbed out from under the warmth of my covers and

asked me if I wanted to get well or to get sicker and die. Later, when I asked Dr. Shtulek if I was dying, he put his stethoscope to my nose and listened. "Not yet." He smiled. Dr. Shtulek visited often to check my breathing. His stethoscope was cold like all the instruments in his bag, but I liked him, especially for unplugging the vaporizer. "We don't need this anymore," he confided. Night seemed very still without its steady exhaling. The jingle of snow chains and the scraping of shovels carried from Eighteenth Street. Maybe that was when I first heard Marcy practicing scales. By then I had grown used to napping during the day and lying awake at night. I began to tunnel under my *piersyna* to the window and scrape at the layered frost. I scraped for nights, always afraid I would get sick again for disobeying. Finally, I was able to see the snow on Freddy's roof. Something had changed while I'd been sick—they had put a wind hood on the tall chimney that sometimes blew smoke into our flat. In the dark it looked as if someone was standing on the roof in an old-fashioned helmet. I imagined it was a German soldier. I'd heard Freddy's landlord was German. The soldier stood at attention, but his head slowly turned back and forth and hooted with each gust of wind. Snow drove sideways across the roof, and he stood banked by drifts, smoking a cigar. Sparks flew from its tip. When he turned completely around to stare in my direction with his faceless face, I'd duck and tunnel back under my *piersyna* to my pillows and pretend to sleep. I believed a person asleep would be shown more mercy than a person awake. I'd lie still, afraid he was marching across the roof to peer in at me through the holes I'd scraped. It was a night like that when I heard Mother crying. She was walking from room to room crying like I'd never heard anyone cry before. I must have called out because she came into my room and tucked the covers around me. "Everything will be all right," she whispered; "go back to sleep." She sat on my bed, toward the foot where she could look out the window, crying softly until her shoulders began to shake. I lay pretending to sleep. She cried like that for nights after my father was killed. It was my mother, not I, whom Marcy had heard.

150 It was only after Marcy began playing late at night that I remembered my mother crying. In my room, with the door shut against the steam, it seemed she was playing for me alone. I would wake already listening and gradually realize that the music had been going on while I slept, and that I had been shaping my dreams to it. She played only nocturnes those last weeks of winter. Sometimes they seemed to carry over the roofs, but mostly she played so softly that only the air shaft made it possible to hear. I would sit huddled in my covers beside the window listening, looking out at the white dunes on Freddy's roof. The soldier was long gone, his helmet rusted off. Smoke blew unhooded; black flakes with sparking edges wafted out like burning snow. Soot and music and white gusts off the crests buffeted the pane. Even when the icicles began to

leak and the streets to turn to brown rivers of slush, the blizzard in the air shaft continued.

Marcy disappeared during the first break in the weather. She left a note that read: "Ma, don't worry."

"That's all," Mrs. Kubiac said, unfolding it for my mother to see. "Not even 'love,' not even her name signed. The whole time I kept telling her 'do something,' she sits playing the piano, and now she does something, when it's too late, unless she goes to some butcher. Ev, what should I do?"

My mother helped Mrs. Kubiac call the hospitals. Each day they called the morgue. After a week, Mrs. Kubiac called the police, and when they couldn't find Marcy, any more than they had been able to find Dzia-Dzia, Mrs. Kubiac began to call people in New York—teachers, old roommates, landlords. She used our phone. "Take it off the rent," she said. Finally, Mrs. Kubiac went to New York herself to search.

When she came back from New York she seemed changed, as if she'd grown too tired to be frantic. Her hair was a different shade of gray so that now you'd never know it had once been blonde. There was a stoop to her shoulders as she descended the stairs on the way to novenas. She no longer came downstairs for tea and long talks. She spent much of her time in church, indistinguishable among the other women from the old country, regulars at the morning requiem mass, wearing babushkas and dressed in black like a sodality of widows, droning endless mournful litanies before the side altar of the Black Virgin of Czestochowa.

By the time a letter from Marcy finally came, explaining that the entire time she had been living on the South Side in a Negro neighborhood near the university, and that she had a son whom she'd named Tatum Kubiac—"Tatum" after a famous jazz pianist—it seemed to make little difference. Mrs. Kubiac visited once but didn't go back. People had already learned to glance away from her when certain subjects were mentioned—daughters, grandchildren, music. She had learned to glance away from herself. After she visited Marcy she tried to sell the piano, but the movers couldn't figure how to get it downstairs, nor how anyone had ever managed to move it in.

It took time for the music to fade. I kept catching wisps of it in the air shaft, behind walls and ceilings, under bathwater. Echoes traveled the pipes and wallpapered chutes, the bricked-up flues and dark hallways. Mrs. Kubiac's building seemed riddled with its secret passageways. And, when the music finally disappeared, its channels remained, conveying silence. Not an ordinary silence of absence and emptiness, but a pure silence beyond daydream and memory, as intense as the music it replaced, which, like music, had the power to change whoever listened. It hushed the close-quartered racket of the old building. It had always been there behind the creaks and drafts and slamming doors, behind the staticky radios, and the flushings and footsteps and crackling fat, behind the wails of vacuums and kettles and babies, and the voices with their scraps of conversation and arguments and laughter floating out of flats where people locked themselves in with all that was private. Even after I no longer missed her, I could still hear the silence left behind.

Points for Review and Discussion

1. "Chopin in Winter" is heavily populated with elders who are anxious about their children. Which anxiety dramatized in the story seems to you the most reasonable? Which seems least reasonable? Explain your answers.
2. Dzia-Dzia is clearly a racist. What do you see as the causes of his racism?

Question for Writing

1. Reread "Chopin In Winter" making notes on the responses to music of Michael, Dzia-Dzia, and Marcy. Then write a page about one of these characters in which you define connections between his or her social identity and musical likes and dislikes.
2. Marcy's life "in a Negro neighborhood" with a child named Tatum stirs Marcy's mother to mournful prayer (¶ 155). Explain how class and ethnic factors figure in her response.
3. Reread the quarrel between Michael's mother and grandfather about boogie-woogie (¶ 43–55). What other subjects besides music are at stake in this quarrel? Explain your answer.
4. On the basis of your reading of "Chopin in Winter," reconsider the familiar phrase "climbing the social ladder." Who are the climbers in this story? To what do they aspire? Choose one of these aspirations and write a page explaining why you do or do not believe it to be a worthwhile human goal.
5. From among the nonfiction texts in *Created Equal*, choose one that seems to you to cast interesting light on "Chopin in Winter" and go on to explain your choice.

Woman Hollering Creek
Sandra Cisneros

Face to face with harsh and seemingly inescapable social facts, human beings find hope and refuge in two places: religious faith and secular or romantic love. The heroine of Sandra Cisneros' "Woman Hollering Creek" awakens during the story from romantic dreams to a fearfully brutish reality—but, before the end, catches a glimpse of a resource she never knew existed.

The author of two short story collections and a book of poetry called *My Wicked Wicked Ways*, Cisneros was born in 1954 in Chicago. Her father is Mexican, her mother Mexican-American; she has six brothers but is, she writes, "nobody's mother and nobody's wife." During the past decade Cisneros has worked as a teacher of high school dropouts, as an arts administrator, and as a visiting writer at various universities; she currently lives in San Antonio, Texas.

1   The day Don Serafín gave Juan Pedro Martínez Sánchez permission to take Cleófilas Enriqueta DeLeón Hernández as his bride, across her father's threshold, over several miles of dirt road and several miles of paved, over one border and beyond to a town *en el otro lado*—on the other side—already did he divine the morning his daughter would raise her hand over her eyes, look south, and dream of returning to the chores that never ended, six good-for-nothing brothers, and one old man's complaints.

2   He had said, after all, in the hubbub of parting: I am your father, I will never abandon you. He *had* said that, hadn't he, when he hugged and then let her go. But at the moment Cleófilas was busy looking for Chela, her maid of honor, to fulfill their bouquet conspiracy. She would not remember her father's parting words until later. *I am your father, I will never abandon you.*

3   Only now as a mother did she remember. Now, when she and Juan Pedrito sat by the creek's edge. How when a man and a woman love each other, sometimes that love sours. But a parent's love for a child, a child's for its parents, is another thing entirely.

4   This is what Cleófilas thought evenings when Juan Pedro did not come home, and she lay on her side of the bed listening to the hollow roar of the interstate, a distant dog barking, the pecan trees rustling like ladies in stiff petticoats—*shh-shh-shh, shh-shh-shh*—soothing her to sleep.

From Sandra Cisneros, *Woman Hollering Creek and Other Stories* (1991).

5   In the town where she grew up, there isn't very much to do except accompany the aunts and godmothers to the house of one or the other to play cards. Or walk to the cinema to see this week's film again, speckled and with one hair quivering annoyingly on the screen. Or to the center of town to order a milk shake that will appear in a day and a half as a pimple on her backside. Or to the girlfriend's house to watch the latest *telenovela* episode and try to copy the way the women comb their hair, wear their makeup.

6   But what Cleófilas has been waiting for, has been whispering and sighing and giggling for, has been anticipating since she was old enough to lean against the window displays of gauze and butterflies and lace, is passion. Not the kind on the cover of the *¡Alarma!* magazines, mind you, where the lover is photographed with the bloody fork she used to salvage her good name. But passion in its purest crystalline essence. The kind the books and songs and *telenovelas* describe when one finds, finally, the great love of one's life, and does whatever one can, must do, at whatever the cost.

7   *Tú o Nadie.* "You or No One." The title of the current favorite *telenovela*. The beautiful Lucía Méndez having to put up with all kinds of hardships of the heart, separation and betrayal, and loving, always loving no matter what, because *that* is the most important thing, and did you see Lucía Méndez on the Bayer aspirin commercials—wasn't she lovely? Does she dye her hair do you think? Cleófilas is going to go to the *farmacía* and buy a hair rinse; her girlfriend Chela will apply it—it's not that difficult at all.

8   Because you didn't watch last night's episode when Lucía confessed she loved him more than anyone in her life. In her life! And she sings the song "You or No One" in the beginning and end of the show. *Tú o Nadie.* Somehow one ought to live one's life like that, don't you think? You or no one. Because to suffer for love is good. The pain all sweet somehow. In the end.

9   *Seguín.* She had liked the sound of it. Far away and lovely. Not like *Monclova. Coahuia.* Ugly.

10 *Seguín, Tejas.* A nice sterling ring to it. The tinkle of money. She would get to wear outfits like the women on the *tele*, like Lucía Méndez. And have a lovely house, and wouldn't Chela be jealous.

11 And yes, they will drive all the way to Laredo to get her wedding dress. That's what they say. Because Juan Pedro wants to get married right away, without a long engagement since he can't take off too much time from work. He has a very important position in Seguin with, with . . . a beer company, I think. Or was it tires? Yes, he has to be back. So they will get married in the spring when he can take off work, and then they will drive off in his new pickup—did you see it?—to their new home in Seguin. Well, not exactly new, but they're going to repaint the house. You know newlyweds. New paint and new furniture. Why not?

He can afford it. And later on add maybe a room or two for the children. May they be blessed with many.

12   Well, you'll see. Cleófilas has always been so good with her sewing machine. A little *rrrr, rrrr, rrrr* of the machine and *¡zas!* Miracles. She's always been so clever, that girl. Poor thing. And without even a mama to advise her on things like her wedding night. Well, may God help her. What with a father with a head like a burro, and those six clumsy brothers. Well, what do you think! Yes, I'm going to the wedding. Of course! The dress I want to wear just needs to be altered a teensy bit to bring it up to date. See, I saw a new style last night that I thought would suit me. Did you watch last night's episode of *The Rich Also Cry?* Well, did you notice the dress the mother was wearing?

13   La Gritona. Such a funny name for such a lovely *arroyo*. But that's what they called the creek that ran behind the house. Though no one could say whether the woman had hollered from anger or pain. The natives only knew the *arroyo* one crossed on the way to San Antonio, and then once again on the way back, was called Woman Hollering, a name no one from these parts questioned, little less understood. *Pues, allá de los indios, quién sabe*—who knows, the townspeople shrugged, because it was of no concern to their lives how this trickle of water received its curious name.

14   "What do you want to know for?" Trini the laundromat attendant asked in the same gruff Spanish she always used whenever she gave Cleófilas change or yelled at her for something. First for putting too much soap in the machines. Later, for sitting on a washer. And still later, after Juan Pedrito was born, for not understanding that in this country you cannot let your baby walk around with no diaper and his pee-pee hanging out, it wasn't nice, *¿entiendes? Pues*.

15   How could Cleófilas explain to a woman like this why the name Woman Hollering fascinated her. Well, there was no sense talking to Trini.

16   On the other hand there were the neighbor ladies, one on either side of the house they rented near the *arroyo*. The woman Soledad on the left, the woman Dolores on the right.

17   The neighbor lady Soledad liked to call herself a widow, though how she came to be one was a mystery. Her husband had either died, or run away with an ice-house floozie, or simply gone out for cigarettes one afternoon and never came back. It was hard to say which since Soledad, as a rule, didn't mention him.

18   In the other house lived *la señora* Dolores, kind and very sweet, but her house smelled too much of incense and candles from the altars that burned continuously in memory of two sons who had died in the last war and one husband who had died shortly after from grief. The neighbor lady Dolores divided her time between the memory of these men and her garden, famous for its sunflowers—so tall they had to be supported with

broom handles and old boards; red red cockscombs, fringed and bleeding a thick menstrual color; and, especially, roses whose sad scent reminded Cleófilas of the dead. Each Sunday *la señora* Dolores clipped the most beautiful of these flowers and arranged them on three modest headstones at the Seguin cemetery.

19 The neighbor ladies, Soledad, Dolores, they might've known once the name of the *arroyo* before it turned English but they did not know now. They were too busy remembering the men who had left through either choice or circumstance and would never come back.

20 Pain or rage, Cleófilas wondered when she drove over the bridge the first time as a newlywed and Juan Pedro had pointed it out. *La Gritona*, he had said, and she had laughed. Such a funny name for a creek so pretty and full of happily ever after.

21 The first time she had been so surprised she didn't cry out or try to defend herself. She had always said she would strike back if a man, any man, were to strike her.

22 But when the moment came, and he slapped her once, and then again, and again; until the lip split and bled an orchid of blood, she didn't fight back, she didn't break into tears, she didn't run away as she imagined she might when she saw such things in the *telenovelas*.

23 In her own home her parents had never raised a hand to each other or to their children. Although she admitted she may have been brought up a little leniently as an only daughter—*la consentida*, the princess—there were some things she would never tolerate. Ever.

24 Instead, when it happened the first time, when they were barely man and wife, she had been so stunned, it left her speechless, motionless, numb. She had done nothing but reach up to the heat on her mouth and stare at the blood on her hand as if even then she didn't understand.

25 She could think of nothing to say, said nothing. Just stroked the dark curls of the man who wept and would weep like a child, his tears of repentance and shame, this time and each.

26 The men at the ice house. From what she can tell, from the times during her first year when still a newlywed she is invited and accompanies her husband, sits mute beside their conversation, waits and sips a beer until it grows warm, twists a paper napkin into a knot, then another into a fan, one into a rose, nods her head, smiles, yawns, politely grins, laughs at the appropriate moments, leans against her husband's sleeve, tugs at his elbow, and finally becomes good at predicting where the talk will lead, from this Cleófilas concludes each is nightly trying to find the truth lying at the bottom of the bottle like a gold doubloon on the sea floor.

27 They want to tell each other what they want to tell themselves. But what is bumping like a helium balloon at the ceiling of the brain never

finds its way out. It bubbles and rises, it gurgles in the throat, it rolls across the surface of the tongue, and erupts from the lips—a belch.

28   If they are lucky, there are tears at the end of the long night. At any given moment, the fists try to speak. They are dogs chasing their own tails before lying down to sleep, trying to find a way, a route, an out, and—finally—get some peace.

29   In the morning sometimes before he opens his eyes. Or after they have finished loving. Or at times when he is simply across from her at the table putting pieces of food into his mouth and chewing. Cleófilas thinks, This is the man I have waited my whole life for.

30   Not that he isn't a good man. She has to remind herself why she loves him when she changes the baby's Pampers, or when she mops the bathroom floor, or tries to make the curtains for the doorways without doors, or whiten the linen. Or wonder a little when he kicks the refrigerator and says he hates this shitty house and is going out where he won't be bothered with the baby's howling and her suspicious questions, and her requests to fix this and this and this because if she had any brains in her head she'd realize he's been up before the rooster earning his living to pay for the food in her belly and the roof over her head and would have to wake up again early the next day so why can't you just leave me in peace, woman.

31   He is not very tall, no, and he doesn't look like the men on the *telenovelas*. His face still scarred from acne. And he has a bit of a belly from all the beer he drinks. Well, he's always been husky.

32   This man who farts and belches and snores as well as laughs and kisses and holds her. Somehow this husband whose whiskers she finds each morning in the sink, whose shoes she must air each evening on the porch, this husband who cuts his fingernails in public, laughs loudly, curses like a man, and demands each course of dinner be served on a separate plate like at his mother's, as soon as he gets home, on time or late, and who doesn't care at all for music or *telenovelas* or romance or roses or the moon floating pearly over the *arroyo*, or through the bedroom window for that matter, shut the blinds and go back to sleep, this man, this father, this rival, this keeper, this lord, this master, this husband till kingdom come.

33   A doubt. Slender as a hair. A washed cup set back on the shelf wrong-side-up. Her lipstick, and body talc, and hairbrush all arranged in the bathroom a different way.

34   No. Her imagination. The house the same as always. Nothing.

35   Coming home from the hospital with her new son, her husband. Something comforting in discovering her house slippers beneath the bed, the faded housecoat where she left it on the bathroom hook. Her pillow. Their bed.

36   Sweet sweet homecoming. Sweet as the scent of face powder in the air, jasmine, sticky liquor.

37   Smudged fingerprint on the door. Crushed cigarette in a glass. Wrinkle in the brain crumpling to a crease.

38 Sometimes she thinks of her father's house. But how could she go back there? What a disgrace. What would the neighbors say? Coming home like that with one baby on her hip and one in the oven. Where's your husband?

39   The town of gossips. The town of dust and despair. Which she has traded for this town of gossips. This town of dust, despair. Houses farther apart perhaps, though no more privacy because of it. No leafy *zócalo* in the center of the town, though the murmur of talk is clear enough all the same. No huddled whispering on the church steps each Sunday. Because here the whispering begins at sunset at the ice house instead.

40   This town with its silly pride for a bronze pecan the size of a baby carriage in front of the city hall. TV repair shop, drugstore, hardware, dry cleaner's, chiropractor's, liquor store, bail bonds, empty storefront, and nothing, nothing, nothing of interest. Nothing one could walk to, at any rate. Because the towns here are built so that you have to depend on husbands. Or you stay home. Or you drive. If you're rich enough to own, allowed to drive, your own car.

41   There is no place to go. Unless one counts the neighbor ladies. Soledad on one side, Dolores on the other. Or the creek.

42   Don't go out there after dark, *mi'jita*. Stay near the house. *No es bueno para la salud. Mala suerte.* Bad luck. *Mal aire.* You'll get sick and the baby too. You'll catch a fright wandering about in the dark, and then you'll see how right we were.

43   The stream sometimes only a muddy puddle in the summer, though now in the springtime, because of the rains, a good-size alive thing, a thing with a voice all its own, all day and all night calling in its high, silver voice. Is it La Llorona, the weeping woman? La Llorona, who drowned her own children. Perhaps La Llorona is the one they named the creek after, she thinks, remembering all the stories she learned as a child.

44   La Llorona calling to her. She is sure of it. Cleófilas sets the baby's Donald Duck blanket on the grass. Listens. The day sky turning to night. The baby pulling up fistfuls of grass and laughing. La Llorona. Wonders if something as quiet as this drives a woman to the darkness under the trees.

45 What she needs is ... and made a gesture as if to yank a woman's buttocks to his groin. Maximiliano, the foul-smelling fool from across the road, said this and set the men laughing, but Cleófilas just muttered. *Grosera*, and went on washing dishes.

46 She knew he said it not because it was true, but more because it was he who needed to sleep with a woman, instead of drinking each night at the ice house and stumbling home alone.

47 Maximiliano who was said to have killed his wife in an ice-house brawl when she came at him with a mop. I had to shoot, he had said—she was armed.

48 Their laughter outside the kitchen window. Her husband's, his friends'. Manolo, Beto, Efrain, el Perico. Maximiliano.

49 Was Cleófilas just exaggerating as her husband always said? It seemed the newspapers were full of such stories. This woman found on the side of the interstate. This one pushed from a moving car. This one's cadaver, this one unconscious, this one beaten blue. Her ex-husband, her husband, her lover, her father, her brother, her uncle, her friend, her co-worker. Always. The same grisly news in the pages of the dailies. She dunked a glass under the soapy water for a moment—shivered.

50 He had thrown a book. Hers. From across the room. A hot welt across the cheek. She could forgive that. But what stung more was the fact it was *her* book, a love story by Corín Tellado, what she loved most now that she lived in the U.S., without a television set, without the *telenovelas*.

51 Except now and again when her husband was away and she could manage it, the few episodes glimpsed at the neighbor lady Soledad's house because Dolores didn't care for that sort of thing, though Soledad was often kind enough to retell what had happened on what episode of *María de Nadie*, the poor Argentine country girl who had the ill fortune of falling in love with the beautiful son of the Arrocha family, the very family she worked for, whose roof she slept under and whose floors she vacuumed, while in that same house, with the dust brooms and floor cleaners as witnesses, the square-jawed Juan Carlos Arrocha had uttered words of love, I love you, Maria, listen to me, *mi querida*, but it was she who had to say No, no, we are not of the same class, and remind him it was not his place nor hers to fall in love, while all the while her heart was breaking, can you imagine.

52 Cleófilas thought her life would have to be like that, like a *telenovela*, only now the episodes got sadder and sadder. And there were no commercials in between for comic relief. And no happy ending in sight. She thought this when she sat with the baby out by the creek behind the house. Celófilas de . . . ? But somehow she would have to change her name to Topazio, or Yesenia, Cristal, Adriana, Stefania, Andrea, something more poetic than Cleófilas. Everything happened to women with names like jewels. But what happened to a Cleófilas? Nothing. But a crack in the face.

53 Because the doctor has said so. She has to go. To make sure the new baby is all right, so there won't be any problems when he's born, and the

appointment card says next Tuesday. Could he please take her. And that's all.

54   No, she won't mention it. She promises. If the doctor asks she can say she fell down the front steps or slipped when she was out in the backyard, slipped out back, she could tell him that. She has to go back next Tuesday, Juan Pedro, please, for the new baby. For their child.

55   She could write to her father and ask maybe for money, just a loan, for the new baby's medical expenses. Well then if he'd rather she didn't. All right, she won't. Please don't anymore. Please don't. She knows it's difficult saving money with all the bills they have, but how else are they going to get out of debt with the truck payments? And after the rent and the food and the electricity and the gas and the water and the who-knows-what, well, there's hardly anything left. But please, at least for the doctor visit. She won't ask for anything else. She has to. Why is she so anxious? Because.

56   Because she is going to make sure the baby is not turned around backward this time to split her down the center. Yes. Next Tuesday at five-thirty. I'll have Juan Pedrito dressed and ready. But those are the only shoes he has. I'll polish them, and we'll be ready. As soon as you come from work. We won't make you ashamed.

57   Felice? It's me, Graciela.
58   No, I can't talk louder. I'm at work.
59   Look, I need kind of a favor. There's a patient, a lady here who's got a problem.
60   Well, wait a minute. Are you listening to me or what?
61   I can't talk real loud 'cause her husband's in the next room.
62   Well, would you just listen?
63   I was going to do this sonogram on her—she's pregnant, right?—and she just starts crying on me. *Hijole,* Felice! This poor lady's got black-and-blue marks all over. I'm not kidding.
64   From her husband. Who else. Another one of those brides from across the border. And her family's all in Mexico.
65   Shit. You think they're going to help her? Give me a break. This lady doesn't even speak English. She hasn't been allowed to call home or write or nothing. That's why I'm calling you.
66   She needs a ride.
67   Not to Mexico, you goof. Just to the Greyhound. In San Anto.
68   No, just a ride. She's got her own money. All you'd have to do is drop her off in San Antonio on your way home. Come on, Felice. Please? If we don't help her, who will? I'd drive her myself, but she needs to be on that bus before her husband gets home from work. What do you say?
69   I don't know. Wait.
70   Right away, tomorrow even.
71   Well, if tomorrow's no good for you . . .
72   It's a date, Felice. Thursday. At the Cash N Carry off I-10. Noon. She'll be ready.

73   Oh, and her name's Cleófilas.
74   I don't know. One of those Mexican saints, I guess. A martyr or something.
75   Cleófilas. C-L-E-O-F-I-L-A-S. Cle. O. Fi. Las. Write it down.
76   Thanks, Felice. When her kid's born she'll have to name her after us, right?
77   Yeah, you got it. A regular soap opera sometimes. *Qué vida, comadre. Bueno* bye.

78   All morning that flutter of half-fear, half-doubt. At any moment Juan Pedro might appear in the doorway. On the street. At the Cash N Carry. Like in the dreams she dreamed.
79   There was that to think about, yes, until the woman in the pickup drove up. Then there wasn't time to think about anything but the pickup pointed toward San Antonio. Put your bags in the back and get in.
80   But when they drove across the *arroyo*, the driver opened her mouth and let out a yell as loud as any mariachi. Which startled not only Cleófilas, but Juan Pedrito as well.
81   *Pues*, look how cute. I scared you two, right? Sorry. Should've warned you. Every time I cross that bridge I do that. Because of the name, you know. Woman Hollering. *Pues*, I holler. She said this in a Spanish pocked with English and laughed. Did you ever notice, Felice continued, how nothing around here is named after a woman? Really. Unless she's the Virgin. I guess you're only famous if you're a virgin. She was laughing again.
82   That's why I like the name of that *arroyo*. Makes you want to holler like Tarzan, right?
83   Everything about this woman, this Felice, amazed Cleófilas. The fact that she drove a pickup. A pickup, mind you, but when Cleófilas asked if it was her husband's, she said she didn't have a husband. The pickup was hers. She herself had chosen it. She herself was paying for it.
84   I used to have a Pontiac Sunbird. But those cars are for *viejas*. Pussy cars. Now this here is a *real* car.
85   What kind of talk was that coming from a woman? Cleófilas thought. But then again, Felice was like no woman she'd ever met. Can you imagine, when we crossed the *arroyo* she just started yelling like a crazy, she would say later to her father and brothers. Just like that. Who would've thought?
86   Who would've? Pain or rage, perhaps, but not a hoot like the one Felice had just let go. Makes you want to holler like Tarzan, Felice had said.
87   Then Felice began laughing again, but it wasn't Felice laughing. It was gurgling out of her own throat, a long ribbon of laughter, like water.

Points for Review and Discussion

1. "Woman Hollering Creek" tells of a bitterly painful learning experience. What kinds of knowledge would the heroine have needed in order to spare herself this experience?
2. Juan Pedro is an abusive husband. What do you see as the causes of his abusiveness?

❦ Questions for Writing

1. Summarize in your own words the basic social facts that define the lives and marriage of Cleófilas and Juan Pedro.
2. Summarize—again in your own words—the fantasy of love that colors Cleófilas's initial perceptions of those social facts. Where did the fantasy originate? What keeps it alive? How does it ease the class realities of this young woman's life?
3. Felice's hollering and laughter at the story's end might be said to suggest a safer refuge and stronger hope than any hitherto known to Cleófilas. How would you describe this refuge and hope?
4. From among the nonfiction texts in *Created Equal,* choose one that seems to you to cast interesting light on "Woman Hollering Creek" and go on to explain your choice.

SARAH COLE: A TYPE OF LOVE STORY
Russell Banks

Schooling, tastes, "values," income, occupation, property—all these potent factors in determining class identity have received attention in *Created Equal*. But one highly important factor has been neglected—physical appearance: beauty or homeliness. Russell Bank's "Sarah Cole: A Type of Love Story" corrects the omission. On nearly every page this story shows us beauty and homeliness interacting powerfully with the whole range of other forces shaping social differences. The story's hero and heroine, Ron and Sarah, are unlike in many ways besides that of appearance, and well before the end their mutual preoccupation with physical beauty and its opposite comes to seem life-killing. But the power of that preoccupation is overwhelming from start to finish.

A native New Englander, Russell Banks was born in 1940, and has lived and worked in a variety of jobs in Florida, Jamaica, and other parts of the Caribbean. He now teaches at Princeton and New York universities and makes his home in Brooklyn. His best known book is *Continental Drift* (1985), described by the *New York Times* as "a shattering dissection of American life," and by *The Atlantic* magazine as "a great American novel."

1

1   To begin, then, here is a scene in which I am the man and my friend Sarah Cole is the woman. I don't mind describing it now, because I'm a decade older and don't look the same now as I did then, and Sarah Cole is dead. That is to say, on hearing this story you might think me vain if I looked the same now as I did then, because I must tell you that I was extremely handsome then. And if Sarah were not dead, you'd think I was cruel, for I must tell you that Sarah was very homely. In fact, she was the homeliest woman I have ever known. Personally, I mean. I've *seen* a few women who were more unattractive than Sarah, but they were clearly freaks of nature or had been badly injured or had been victimized by some grotesque, disfiguring disease. Sarah, however, was quite normal, and I knew her well, because for three and a half months we were lovers.

2   Here is the scene. You can put it in the present, even though it took place ten years ago, because nothing that matters to the story depends on when it took place, and you can put it in Concord, New Hampshire,

---

From Russell Banks, *Success Stories* (1986).

even though that is indeed where it took place, because it doesn't matter where it took place, so it might as well be Concord, New Hampshire, a place I happen to know well and can therefore describe with sufficient detail to make the story believable. Around six o'clock on a Wednesday evening in late May, a man enters a bar. The bar, a cocktail lounge at street level, with a restaurant upstairs, is decorated with hanging plants and unfinished wood paneling, butcher-block tables and captain's chairs, with a half-dozen darkened, thickly upholstered booths along one wall. Three or four men between the ages of twenty-five and thirty-five are drinking at the bar and, like the man who has just entered, wear three-piece suits and loosened neckties. They are probably lawyers, young, unmarried lawyers gossiping with their brethren over martinis so as to postpone arriving home alone at their whitewashed town-house apartments, where they will fix their evening meals in radar ranges and afterwards, while their TVs chuckle quietly in front of them, sit on their couches and do a little extra work for tomorrow. They are, for the most part, honorable, educated, hard-working, shallow and moderately unhappy young men.

3   Our man, call him Ronald, Ron, in most ways is like these men, except that he is unusually good-looking, and that makes him a little less unhappy than they. Ron is effortlessly attractive, a genetic wonder, tall, slender, symmetrical and clean. His flaws—a small mole on the left corner of his square, not-too-prominent chin, a slight excess of blond hair on the tops of his tanned hands, and somewhat underdeveloped buttocks—insofar as they keep him from resembling too closely a men's store mannequin, only contribute to his beauty, for he is beautiful, the way we usually think of a woman as being beautiful. And he is nice too, the consequence, perhaps, of his seeming not to know how beautiful he is, to men as well as women, to young people (even children) as well as old, to attractive people (who realize immediately that he is so much more attractive than they as not to be competitive with them) as well as unattractive people.

4   Ron takes a seat at the bar, unfolds the evening paper in front of him, and before he can start reading, the bartender asks to help him, calling him "Sir," even though Ron has come into this bar numerous times at this time of day, especially since his divorce last fall. Ron got divorced because, after three years of marriage, his wife chose to pursue the career that his had interrupted, that of a fashion designer, which meant that she had to live in New York City while he had to continue to live in New Hampshire, where his career got its start. They agreed to live apart until he could continue his career near New York City, but after a few months, between conjugal visits, he started sleeping with other women and she started sleeping with other men, and that was that. "No big deal," he explained to friends, who liked both Ron and his wife, even though he was slightly more beautiful than she. "We really were too young when we got married, college sweethearts. But we're still best

friends," he assured them. They understood. Most of Ron's friends were divorced by then too.

5   Ron orders a Scotch and soda with a twist and goes back to reading his paper. When his drink comes, before he takes a sip of it, he first carefully finishes reading an article about the recent reappearance of coyotes in northern New Hampshire and Vermont. He lights a cigarette. He goes on reading. He takes a second sip of his drink. Everyone in the room—the three or four men scattered along the bar, the tall, thin bartender and several people in the booths at the back—watches him do these ordinary things.

6   He has got to the classified section, is perhaps searching for someone willing to come in once a week and clean his apartment, when the woman who will turn out to be Sarah Cole leaves a booth in the back and approaches him. She comes up from the side and sits next to him. She's wearing heavy tan cowboy boots and a dark brown suede cowboy hat, lumpy jeans and a yellow T-shirt that clings to her arms, breasts and round belly like the skin of a sausage. Though he will later learn that she is thirty-eight years old, she looks older by about ten years, which makes her look about twenty years older than he actually is. (It's difficult to guess accurately how old Ron is; he looks anywhere from a mature twenty-five to a youthful forty, so his actual age doesn't seem to matter.)

7   "It's not bad here at the bar," she says, looking around. "More light, anyhow. Whatcha readin'?" she asks brightly, planting both elbows on the bar.

8   Ron looks up from his paper with a slight smile on his lips, sees the face of a woman homelier than any he has ever seen or imagined before, and goes on smiling lightly. He feels himself falling into her tiny, slightly crossed, dark brown eyes, pulls himself back, and studies for a few seconds her mottled, pocked complexion, bulbous nose, loose mouth, twisted and gapped teeth and heavy but receding chin. He casts a glance over her thatch of dun-colored hair and along her neck and throat, where acne burns against gray skin, and returns to her eyes and again feels himself falling into her.

9   "What did you say?" he asks.

10   She knocks a mentholated cigarette from her pack, and Ron swiftly lights it. Blowing smoke from her large, wing-shaped nostrils, she speaks again. Her voice is thick and nasal, a chocolate-colored voice. "I asked you whatcha readin', but I can see now." She belts out a single, loud laugh. "The paper!"

11   Ron laughs too. "The paper! The *Concord Monitor!*" He is not hallucinating, he clearly sees what is before him and admits—no, he asserts—to himself that he is speaking to the most unattractive woman he has ever seen, a fact that fascinates him, as if instead he were speaking to the most beautiful woman he has ever seen or perhaps ever will see, so he treasures the moment, attempts to hold it as if it were a golden ball, a disproportionately heavy object which—if he does not hold it lightly,

with precision and firmness—will slip from his hand and roll across the lawn to the lip of the well and down, down to the bottom of the well, lost to him forever. It will be a memory, that's all, something to speak of wistfully and with wonder as over the years the image fades and comes in the end to exist only in the telling. His mind and body waken from their sleepy self-absorption, and all his attention focuses on the woman, Sarah Cole, her ugly face, like a warthog's, her thick, rapid speech, her dumpy, off-center wreck of a body. To keep this moment here before him, he begins to ask questions of her, he buys her a drink, he smiles, until soon it seems, even to him, that he is taking her and her life, its vicissitudes and woe, quite seriously.

12   He learns her name, of course, and she volunteers the information that she spoke to him on a dare from one of the two women still sitting in the booth behind her. She turns on her stool and smiles brazenly, triumphantly, at her friends, two women, also homely (though nowhere as homely as she), and dressed, like her, in cowboy boots, hats and jeans. One of the women, a blond with an underslung jaw and wearing heavy eye makeup, flips a little wave at her, and as if embarrassed, she and the other woman at the booth turn back to their drinks and sip fiercely at straws.

13   Sarah returns to Ron and goes on telling him what he wants to know, about her job at Rumford Press, about her divorced husband, who was a bastard and stupid and "sick," she says, as if filling suddenly with sympathy for the man. She tells Ron about her three children, the youngest, a girl, in junior high school and boy-crazy, the other two, boys, in high school and almost never at home anymore. She speaks of her children with genuine tenderness and concern and Ron is touched. He can see with what pleasure and pain she speaks of her children; he watches her tiny eyes light up and water over when he asks their names.

14   "You're a nice woman," he informs her.

15   She smiles, looks at her empty glass. "No. No, I'm not. But you're a nice man, to tell me that."

16   Ron, with a gesture, asks the bartender to refill Sarah's glass. She is drinking white Russians. Perhaps she has been drinking them for an hour or two, for she seems very relaxed, more relaxed than women usually do when they come up and without introduction or invitation speak to Ron.

17   She asks him about himself, his job, his divorce, how long he has lived in Concord, but he finds that he is not at all interested in telling her about himself. He wants to know about her, even though what she has to tell him about herself is predictable and ordinary and the way she tells it unadorned and clichéd. He wonders about her husband. What kind of man would fall in love with Sarah Cole?

2

18   That scene, at Osgood's Lounge in Concord, ended with Ron's departure, alone, after having bought Sarah a second drink, and Sarah's return

to her friends in the booth. I don't know what she told them, but it's not hard to imagine. The three women were not close friends, merely fellow workers at Rumford Press, where they stood at the end of a long conveyor belt day after day packing *TV Guides* into cartons. They all hated their jobs, and frequently after work, when they worked the day shift, they would put on their cowboy hats and boots, which they kept all day in their lockers, and stop for a drink or two on their way home. This had been their first visit to Osgood's, however, a place that, prior to this, they had avoided out of a sneering belief that no one went there but lawyers and insurance men. It had been Sarah who had asked the others why that should keep them away, and when they had no answer for her, the three had decided to stop at Osgood's. Ron was right, they had been there over an hour when he came in, and Sarah was a little drunk. "We'll hafta come in here again," she said to her friends, her voice rising slightly.

19   Which they did, that Friday, and once again Ron appeared with his evening newspaper. He put his briefcase down next to his stool and ordered a drink and proceeded to read the front page, slowly, deliberately, clearly a weary, unhurried, solitary man. He did not notice the three women in cowboy hats and boots in the booth in back, but they saw him, and after a few minutes Sarah was once again at his side.

20   "Hi."

21   He turned, saw her, and instantly regained the moment he had lost when, two nights ago, once outside the bar and on his way home, he had forgotten about the ugliest woman he had ever seen. She seemed even more grotesque to him now than before, which made the moment all the more precious to him, and so once again he held the moment as if in his hands and began to speak with her, to ask questions, to offer his opinions and solicit hers.

22   I said earlier that I am the man in this story and my friend Sarah Cole, now dead, is the woman. I think back to that night, the second time I had seen Sarah, and I tremble, not with fear but in shame. My concern then, when I was first becoming involved with Sarah, was merely with the moment, holding on to it, grasping it wholly, as if its beginning did not grow out of some other prior moment in her life and my life separately and at the same time did not lead into future moments in our separate lives. She talked more easily than she had the night before, and I listened as eagerly and carefully as I had before, again with the same motives, to keep her in front of me, to draw her forward from the context of her life and place her, as if she were an object, into the context of mine. I did not know how cruel this was. When you have never done a thing before and that thing is not simply and clearly right or wrong, you frequently do not know if it is a cruel thing, you just go ahead and do it and maybe later you'll be able to determine whether you acted cruelly. That way you'll know if it was right or wrong of you

to have done it in the first place; too late, of course, but at least you'll know.

23   While we drank, Sarah told me that she hated her ex-husband because of the way he treated the children. "It's not so much the money," she said, nervously wagging her booted feet from her perch on the high barstool. "I mean, I get by, barely, but I get them fed and clothed on my own okay. It's because he won't even write them a letter or anything. He won't call them on the phone, all he calls for is to bitch at me because I'm trying to get the state to take him to court so I can get some of the money he's s'posed to be paying for child support. And he won't even think to talk to the kids when he calls. Won't even ask about them."

24   "He sounds like a sonofabitch."

25   "He is, he is!" she said. "I don't know why I married him. Or stayed married. Fourteen years, for Christ's sake. He put a spell over me or something. I don't know," she said, with a note of wistfulness in her voice. "He wasn't what you'd call good-looking."

26   After her second drink, she decided she had to leave. Her children were at home, it was Friday night and she liked to make sure she ate supper with them and knew where they were going and who they were with when they went out on their dates. "No dates on school nights," she said to me. "I mean, you gotta have rules, you know."

27   I agreed, and we left together, everyone in the place following us with his or her gaze. I was aware of that, I knew what they were thinking, and I didn't care, because I was simply walking her to her car.

28   It was a cool evening, dusk settling onto the lot like a gray blanket. Her car, a huge, dark green Buick sedan at least ten years old, was battered almost beyond use. She reached for the door handle on the driver's side and yanked. Nothing. The door wouldn't open. She tried again. Then I tried. Still nothing.

29   Then I saw it, a V-shaped dent in the left front fender, binding the metal of the door against the metal of the fender in a large crimp that held the door fast. "Someone must've backed into you while you were inside," I said to her.

30   She came forward and studied the crimp for a few seconds, and when she looked back at me, she was weeping. "Jesus, Jesus, Jesus!" she wailed, her large, froglike mouth wide open and wet with spit, her red tongue flopping loosely over gapped teeth. "I can't pay for this! I *can't!*" Her face was red, and even in the dusky light I could see it puff out with weeping, her tiny eyes seeming almost to disappear behind wet cheeks. Her shoulders slumped, and her hands fell limply to her sides.

31   Placing my briefcase on the ground, I reached out to her and put my arms around her body and held her close to me, while she cried wetly into my shoulder. After a few seconds, she started pulling herself back together and her weeping got reduced to snuffling. Her cowboy hat had been pushed back and now clung to her head at a precarious, absurdly

jaunty angle. She took a step away from me and said, "I'll get in the other side."

32   "Okay," I said, almost in a whisper. "That's fine."

33   Slowly, she walked around the front of the huge, ugly vehicle and opened the door on the passenger's side and slid awkwardly across the seat until she had positioned herself behind the steering wheel. Then she started the motor, which came to life with a roar. The muffler was shot. Without saying another word to me or even waving, she dropped the car into reverse gear and backed it loudly out of the parking space and headed out of the lot to the street.

34   I turned and started for my car, when I happened to glance toward the door of the bar, and there, staring after me, were the bartender, the two women who had come in with Sarah, and two of the men who had been sitting at the bar. They were lawyers, and I knew them slightly. They were grinning at me. I grinned back and got into my car, and then, without looking at them again, I left the place and drove straight to my apartment.

3

35   One night several weeks later, Ron meets Sarah at Osgood's, and after buying her three white Russians and drinking three Scotches himself, he takes her back to his apartment in his car—a Datsun fastback coupe that she says she admires—for the sole purpose of making love to her.

36   I'm still the man in this story, and Sarah is still the woman, but I'm telling it this way because what I have to tell you now confuses me, embarrasses me and makes me sad, and consequently I'm likely to tell it falsely. I'm likely to cover the truth by making Sarah a better woman than she actually was, while making me appear worse than I actually was or am; or else I'll do the opposite, make Sarah worse than she was and me better. The truth is, I was pretty, extremely so, and she was not, extremely so, and I knew it and she knew it. She walked out the door of Osgood's determined to make love to a man much prettier than any she had seen up close before, and I walked out determined to make love to a woman much homelier than any I had made love to before. We were, in a sense, equals.

37   No, that's not exactly true. (You see? This is why I have to tell the story the way I'm telling it.) I'm not at all sure she feels as Ron does. That is to say, perhaps she genuinely likes the man, in spite of his being the most physically attractive man she has ever known. Perhaps she is more aware of her homeliness than of his beauty, for Ron, despite what I may have implied, does not think of himself as especially beautiful. He merely knows that other people think of him that way. As I said before, he is a nice man.

38   Ron unlocks the door to his apartment, walks in ahead of her and flicks on the lamp beside the couch. It's a small, single-bedroom, modern apartment, one of thirty identical apartments in a large brick building on the Heights just east of downtown Concord. Sarah stands nervously at the door, peering in.

39   "Come in, come in," Ron says.

40   She steps timidly in and closes the door behind her. She removes her cowboy hat, then quickly puts it back on, crosses the living room and plops down in a blond easy chair, seeming to shrink in its hug out of sight to safety. Behind her, Ron, at the entry to the kitchen, places one hand on her shoulder, and she stiffens. He removes his hand.

41   "Would you like a drink?"

42   "No ... I guess not," she says, staring straight ahead at the wall opposite, where a large framed photograph of a bicyclist advertises in French the Tour de France. Around a corner, in an alcove off the living room, a silver-gray ten-speed bicycle leans casually against the wall, glistening and poised, slender as a thoroughbred racehorse.

43   "I don't know," she says. Ron is in the kitchen now, making himself a drink. "I don't know ... I don't know."

44   "What? Change your mind? I can make a white Russian for you. Vodka, cream, Kahlua and ice, right?"

45   Sarah tries to cross her legs, but she is sitting too low in the chair and her legs are too thick at the thigh, so she ends, after a struggle, with one leg in the air and the other twisted on its side. She looks as if she has fallen from a great height.

46   Ron steps out from the kitchen, peers over the back of the chair, and watches her untangle herself, then ducks back into the kitchen. After a few seconds, he returns. "Seriously. Want me to fix you a white Russian?"

47   "No."

48   Ron, again from behind and above her, places one hand on Sarah's shoulder, and this time she does not stiffen, though she does not exactly relax, either. She sits there, a block of wood, staring straight ahead.

49   "Are you scared?" he asks gently. Then he adds, "*I* am."

50   "Well, no. I'm not scared." She remains silent for a moment. "You're scared? Of what?" She turns to face him but avoids his blue eyes.

51   "Well ... I don't do this all the time, you know. Bring home a woman I ...," he trails off.

52   "Picked up in a bar."

53   "No. I mean, I like you, Sarah. I really do. And I didn't just pick you up in a bar, you know that. We've gotten to be friends, you and me."

54   "You want to sleep with me?" she asks, still not meeting his steady gaze.

55   "Yes." He seems to mean it. He does not take a gulp or even a sip from his drink. He just says, "Yes," straight out, and cleanly, not too quickly, either, and not after a hesitant delay. A simple statement of a simple fact. The man wants to make love to the woman. She asked him, and he told her. What could be simpler?

56   "Do you want to sleep with *me?*" he asks.

57   She turns around in the chair, faces the wall again, and says in a low voice, "Sure I do, but ... it's hard to explain."

58   "What? But what?" Placing his glass down on the table between the chair and the sofa, he puts both hands on her shoulders and lightly kneads them. He knows he can be discouraged from pursuing this, but he is not sure how easily. Having got this far without bumping against obstacles (except the ones he has placed in his way himself), he is not sure what it will take to turn him back. He does not know, therefore, how assertive or how seductive he should be with her. He suspects that he can be stopped very easily, so he is reluctant to give her a chance to try. He goes on kneading her doughy shoulders.

59   "You and me . . . we're real different." She glances at the bicycle in the corner.

60   "A man . . . and a woman," he says.

61   "No, not that. I mean, different. That's all. Real different. More than you . . . You're nice, but you don't know what I mean, and that's one of the things that makes you so nice. But we're different. Listen," she says, "I gotta go. I gotta leave now."

62   The man removes his hands and retrieves his glass, takes a sip and watches her over the rim of the glass, as, not without difficulty, the woman rises from the chair and moves swiftly toward the door. She stops at the door, squares her hat on her head, and glances back at him.

63   "We can be friends, okay?"

64   "Okay. Friends."

65   "I'll see you again down at Osgood's, right?"

66   "Oh, yeah, sure."

67   "Good. See you," she says, opening the door.

68   The door closes. The man walks around the sofa, snaps on the television set, and sits down in front of it. He picks up a *TV Guide* from the coffee table and flips through it, stops, runs a finger down the listings, stops, puts down the magazine and changes the channel. He does not once connect the magazine in his hand to the woman who has just left his apartment, even though he knows she spends her days packing *TV Guides* into cartons that get shipped to warehouses in distant parts of New England. He'll think of the connection some other night, but by then the connection will be merely sentimental. It'll be too late for him to understand what she meant by "different."

4

69 But that's not the point of my story. Certainly, it's an aspect of the story, the political aspect, if you want, but it's not the reason I'm trying to tell the story in the first place. I'm trying to tell the story so that I can understand what happened between me and Sarah Cole that summer and early autumn ten years ago. To say we were lovers says very little about what happened; to say we were friends says even less. No, if I'm to understand the whole thing, I'll have to say the whole thing, for, in the end, what I need to know is whether what happened between me and Sarah Cole was right or wrong. Character is fate,

which suggests that if a man can know and then to some degree control his character, he can know and to that same degree control his fate.

70   But let me go on with my story. The next time Sarah and I were together we were at her apartment in the south end of Concord, a second-floor flat in a tenement building on Perley Street. I had stayed away from Osgood's for several weeks, deliberately trying to avoid running into Sarah there, though I never quite put it that way to myself. I found excuses and generated interest in and reasons for going elsewhere after work. Yet I was obsessed with Sarah by then, obsessed with the idea of making love to her, which, because it was not an actual *desire* to make love to her, was an unusually complex obsession. Passion without desire, if it gets expressed, may in fact be a kind of rape, and perhaps I sensed the danger that lay behind my obsession and for that reason went out of my way to avoid meeting Sarah again.

71   Yet I did meet her, inadvertently, of course. After picking up shirts at the cleaner's on South Main and Perley streets, I'd gone down Perley on my way to South State and the post office. It was a Saturday morning, and this trip on my bicycle was part of my regular Saturday routine. I did not remember that Sarah lived on Perley Street, although she had told me several times in a complaining way—it's a rough neighborhood, packed-dirt yards, shabby apartment buildings, the carcasses of old, half-stripped cars on cinder blocks in the driveways, broken red and yellow plastic tricycles on the cracked sidewalks—but as soon as I saw her, I remembered. It was too late to avoid meeting her. I was riding my bike, wearing shorts and T-shirt, the package containing my folded and starched shirts hooked to the carrier behind me, and she was walking toward me along the sidewalk, lugging two large bags of groceries. She saw me, and I stopped. We talked, and I offered to carry her groceries for her. I took the bags while she led the bike, handling it carefully, as if she were afraid she might break it.

72   At the stoop we came to a halt. The wooden steps were cluttered with half-opened garbage bags spilling eggshells, coffee grounds and old food wrappers to the walkway. "I can't get the people downstairs to take care of their garbage," she explained. She leaned the bike against the banister and reached for her groceries.

73   "I'll carry them up for you," I said. I directed her to loop the chain lock from the bike to the banister rail and snap it shut and told her to bring my shirts up with her.

74   "Maybe you'd like a beer?" she said as she opened the door to the darkened hallway. Narrow stairs disappeared in front of me into heavy, damp darkness, and the air smelled like old newspapers.

75   "Sure," I said, and followed her up.

76   "Sorry there's no light. I can't get them to fix it."

77   "No matter. I can see you and follow along," I said, and even in the dim light of the hall I could see the large, dark blue veins that cascaded

thickly down the backs of her legs. She wore tight, white-duck Bermuda shorts, rubber shower sandals and a pink sleeveless sweater. I pictured her in the cashier's line at the supermarket. I would have been behind her, a stranger, and on seeing her, I would have turned away and studied the covers of the magazines, *TV Guide, People,* the *National Enquirer,* for there was nothing of interest in her appearance that in the hard light of day would not have slightly embarrassed me. Yet here I was inviting myself into her home, eagerly staring at the backs of her ravaged legs, her sad, tasteless clothing, her poverty. I was not detached, however, was not staring at her with scientific curiosity, and because of my passion, did not feel or believe that what I was doing was perverse. I felt warmed by her presence and was flirtatious and bold, a little pushy, even.

78   Picture this. The man, tanned, limber, wearing red jogging shorts, Italian leather sandals, a clinging net T-shirt of Scandinavian design and manufacture, enters the apartment behind the woman, whose dough-colored skin, thick, short body and homely, uncomfortable face all try, but fail, to hide themselves. She waves him toward the table in the kitchen, where he sets down the bags and looks good-naturedly around the room. "What about the beer you bribed me with?" he asks.

79   The apartment is dark and cluttered with old, oversized furniture, yard sale and secondhand stuff bought originally for a large house in the country or a spacious apartment on a boulevard forty or fifty years ago, passed down from antique dealer to used-furniture store to yard sale to thrift shop, where it finally gets purchased by Sarah Cole and gets hauled over to Perley Street and shoved up the narrow stairs, she and her children grunting and sweating in the darkness of the hallway—overstuffed armchairs and couch, huge, ungainly dressers, upholstered rocking chairs, and in the kitchen, an old flat-topped maple desk for a table, a half-dozen heavy oak dining room chairs, a high, glass-fronted cabinet, all peeling, stained, chipped and squatting heavily on a dark green linoleum floor.

80   The place is neat and arranged in a more or less orderly way, however, and the man seems comfortable there. He strolls from the kitchen to the living room and peeks into the three small bedrooms that branch off a hallway behind the living room. "Nice place!" he calls to the woman. He is studying the framed pictures of her three children arranged as if on an altar atop the buffet. "Nice-looking kids!" he calls out. They are. Blond, round-faced, clean and utterly ordinary-looking, their pleasant faces glance, as instructed, slightly off camera and down to the right, as if they are trying to remember the name of the capital of Montana.

81   When he returns to the kitchen, the woman is putting away her groceries, her back to him. "Where's that beer you bribed me with?" he asks again. He takes a position against the doorframe, his weight on one hip, like a dancer resting. "You sure are quiet today, Sarah," he says in a low voice. "Everything okay?"

82 Silently, she turns away from the grocery bags, crosses the room to the man, reaches up to him, and holding him by the head, kisses his mouth, rolls her torso against his, drops her hands to his hips and yanks him tightly to her and goes on kissing him, eyes closed, working her face furiously against his. The man places his hands on her shoulders and pulls away, and they face each other, wide-eyed, as if amazed and frightened. The man drops his hands, and the woman lets go of his hips. Then, after a few seconds, the man silently turns, goes to the door, and leaves. The last thing he sees as he closes the door behind him is the woman standing in the kitchen doorframe, her face looking down and slightly to one side, wearing the same pleasant expression on her face as her children in their photographs, trying to remember the capital of Montana.

5

83 Sarah appeared at my apartment door the following morning, a Sunday, cool and rainy. She had brought me the package of freshly laundered shirts I'd left in her kitchen, and when I opened the door to her, she simply held the package out to me, as if it were a penitent's gift. She wore a yellow rain slicker and cap and looked more like a disconsolate schoolgirl facing an angry teacher than a grown woman dropping a package off at a friend's apartment. After all, she had nothing to be ashamed of.

84 I invited her inside, and she accepted my invitation. I had been reading the Sunday *New York Times* on the couch and drinking coffee, lounging through the gray morning in bathrobe and pajamas. I told her to take off her wet raincoat and hat and hang them in the closet by the door and started for the kitchen to get her a cup of coffee, when I stopped, turned and looked at her. She closed the closet door on her yellow raincoat and hat, turned around and faced me.

85 What else can I do? I must describe it. I remember that moment of ten years ago as if it occurred ten minutes ago, the package of shirts on the table behind her, the newspapers scattered over the couch and floor, the sound of wind-blown rain washing the side of the building outside and the silence of the room, as we stood across from one another and watched, while we each simultaneously removed our own clothing, my robe, her blouse and skirt, my pajama top, her slip and bra, my pajama bottom, her underpants, until we were both standing naked in the harsh gray light, two naked members of the same species, a male and female, the male somewhat younger and less scarred than the female, the female somewhat less delicately constructed than the male, both individuals pale-skinned, with dark thatches of hair in the area of their genitals, both individuals standing slackly, as if a great, protracted tension between them had at last been released.

6

86 We made love that morning in my bed for long hours that drifted easily into afternoon. And we talked, as people usually do when they spend

half a day or half a night in bed together. I told her of my past, named and described the people whom I had loved and had loved me, my ex-wife in New York, my brother in the Air Force, my mother in San Diego, and I told her of my ambitions and dreams and even confessed some of my fears. She listened patiently and intelligently throughout and talked much less than I. She had already told me many of these things about herself, and perhaps whatever she had to say to me now lay on the next inner circle of intimacy or else could not be spoken of at all.

87   During the next few weeks, we met and made love often, and always at my apartment. On arriving home from work, I would phone her, or if not, she would phone me, and after a few feints and dodges, one would suggest to the other that we get together tonight, and a half hour later she'd be at my door. Our lovemaking was passionate, skillful, kindly and deeply satisfying. We didn't often speak of it to one another or brag about it, the way some couples do when they are surprised by the ease with which they have become contented lovers. We did occasionally joke and tease each other, however, playfully acknowledging that the only thing we did together was make love but that we did it so frequently there was no time for anything else.

88   Then one hot night, a Saturday in August, we were lying in bed atop the tangled sheets, smoking cigarettes and chatting idly, and Sarah suggested that we go out for a drink.

89   "Out? Now?"

90   "Sure. It's early. What time is it?"

91   I scanned the digital clock next to the bed. "Nine forty-nine."

92   "There. See?"

93   "That's not so early. You usually go home by eleven, you know. It's almost ten."

94   "No, it's only a little after nine. Depends on how you look at things. Besides, Ron, it's Saturday night. Don't you want to go out and dance or something? Or is this the only thing you know how to do?" she said, and poked me in the ribs. "You know how to dance? You like to dance?"

95   "Yeah, sure . . . sure, but not tonight. It's too hot. And I'm tired."

96   But she persisted, happily pointing out that an air-conditioned bar would be as cool as my apartment, and we didn't have to go to a dance bar, we could go to Osgood's. "As a compromise," she said.

97   I suggested a place called the El Rancho, a restaurant with a large, dark cocktail lounge and dance bar located several miles from town on the old Portsmouth highway. Around nine the restaurant closed and the bar became something of a roadhouse, with a small country-and-western band and a clientele drawn from the four or five villages that adjoined Concord on the north and east. I had eaten at the restaurant once but had never gone to the bar, and I didn't know anyone who had.

98   Sarah was silent for a moment. Then she lighted a cigarette and drew the sheet over her naked body. "You don't want anybody to know about us, do you? Do you?"

99 "That's not it.... I just don't like gossip, and I work with a lot of people who show up sometimes at Osgood's. On a Saturday night especially."

100 "No," she said firmly. "You're ashamed of being seen with me. You'll sleep with me, all right, but you won't go out in public with me."

101 "That's not true, Sarah."

102 She was silent again. Relieved, I reached across her to the bed table and got my cigarettes and lighter.

103 "You owe me, Ron," she said suddenly, as I passed over her. "You owe me."

104 "What?" I lay back, lighted a cigarette, and covered my body with the sheet.

105 "I said, 'You owe me.'"

106 "I don't know what you're talking about, Sarah. I just don't like a lot of gossip going around, that's all. I like keeping my private life private, that's all. I don't *owe* you anything."

107 "Friendship you owe me. And respect. Friendship and respect. A person can't do what you've done with me without owing them friendship and respect."

108 "Sarah, I really don't know what you're talking about," I said. "I am your friend, you know that. And I respect you. I do."

109 "You really think so, don't you?"

110 "Yes. Of course."

111 She said nothing for several long moments. Then she sighed and in a low, almost inaudible voice said, "Then you'll have to go out in public with me. I don't care about Osgood's or the people you work with, we don't have to go there or see any of them," she said. "But you're gonna have to go to places like the El Rancho with me, and a few other places I know, too, where there's people *I* know, people *I* work with, and maybe we'll even go to a couple of parties, because *I* get invited to parties sometimes, you know. I have friends, and I have some family, too, and you're gonna have to meet my family. My kids think I'm just going around barhopping when I'm over here with you, and I don't like that, so you're gonna have to meet them so I can tell them where I am when I'm not at home nights. And sometimes you're gonna come over and spend the evening at my place!" Her voice had risen as she heard her demands and felt their rightness, until now she was almost shouting at me. "You *owe* that to me. Or else you're a bad man. It's that simple, Ron."

112 It was.

7

113 The handsome man is overdressed. He is wearing a navy blue blazer, taupe shirt open at the throat, white slacks, white loafers. Everyone else, including the homely woman with the handsome man, is dressed appropriately—that is, like everyone else—jeans and cowboy boots,

blouses or cowboy shirts or T-shirts with catchy sayings or the names of country-and-western singers printed across the front, and many of the women are wearing cowboy hats pushed back and tied under their chins.

114 The man doesn't know anyone at the bar or, if they're at a party, in the room, but the woman knows most of the people there, and she gladly introduces him. The men grin and shake his hand, slap him on his jacketed shoulder, ask him where he works, what's his line, after which they lapse into silence. The women flirt briefly with their faces, but they lapse into silence even before the men do. The woman with the man in the blazer does most of the talking for everyone. She talks for the man in the blazer, for the men standing around the refrigerator, or if they're at a bar, for the other men at the table, and for the other women too. She chats and rambles aimlessly through loud monologues, laughs uproariously at trivial jokes and drinks too much, until soon she is drunk, thick-tongued, clumsy, and the man has to say her goodbyes and ease her out the door to his car and drive her home to her apartment on Perley Street.

115 This happens twice in one week and then three times the next—at the El Rancho, at the Ox Bow in Northwood, at Rita and Jimmy's apartment on Thorndike Street, out in Warner at Betsy Beeler's new house and, the last time, at a cottage on Lake Sunapee rented by some kids in shipping at Rumford Press. Ron no longer calls Sarah when he gets home from work; he waits for her call, and sometimes, when he knows it's she, he doesn't answer the phone. Usually, he lets it ring five or six times, and then he reaches down and picks up the receiver. He has taken his jacket and vest off and loosened his tie and is about to put his supper, frozen manicotti, into the radar range.

116 "Hello?"
117 "Hi."
118 "How're you doing?"
119 "Okay, I guess. A little tired."
120 "Still hung over?"
121 "Naw. Not really. Just tired. I hate Mondays."
122 "You have fun last night?"
123 "Well, yeah, sorta. It's nice out there, at the lake. Listen," she says, brightening. "Whyn't you come over here tonight? The kids're all going out later, but if you come over before eight, you can meet them. They really want to meet you."
124 "You told them about me?"
125 "Sure. Long time ago. I'm not supposed to tell my own kids?"
126 Ron is silent.
127 She says, "You don't want to come over here tonight. You don't want to meet my kids. No, you don't want my kids to meet *you*, that's it."
128 "No, no, it's just . . . I've got a lot of work to do. . . ."
129 "We should talk," she announces in a flat voice.
130 "Yes," he says. "We should talk."

131. They agree that she will meet him at his apartment, and they'll talk, and they say goodbye and hang up.
132. While Ron is heating his supper and then eating it alone at his kitchen table and Sarah is feeding her children, perhaps I should admit, since we are nearing the end of my story, that I don't actually know that Sarah Cole is dead. A few years ago I happened to run into one of her friends from the press, a blond woman with an underslung jaw. Her name, she reminded me, was Glenda; she had seen me at Osgood's a couple of times and we had met at the El Rancho once when I had gone there with Sarah. I was amazed that she could remember me and a little embarrassed that I did not recognize her at all, and she laughed at that and said, "You haven't changed much, mister!" I pretended to recognize her then, but I think she knew she was a stranger to me. We were standing outside the Sears store on South Main Street, where I had gone to buy paint. I had recently remarried, and my wife and I were redecorating my apartment.
133. "Whatever happened to Sarah?" I asked Glenda. "Is she still down at the press?"
134. "Jeez, no! She left a long time ago. Way back. I heard she went back with her ex-husband. I can't remember his name, something Cole. Eddie Cole, maybe."
135. I asked her if she was sure of that, and she said no, she had only heard it around the bars and down at the press, but she had assumed it was true. People said Sarah had moved back with her ex-husband and was living for a while with him and the kids in a trailer in a park near Hooksett, and then when the kids, or at least the boys, got out of school, the rest of them moved down to Florida or someplace because he was out of work. He was a carpenter, she thought.
136. "He was mean to her," I said. "I thought he used to beat her up and everything. I thought she hated him."
137. "Oh, well, yeah, he was a bastard, all right. I met him a couple times, and I didn't like him. Short, ugly and mean when he got drunk. But you know what they say."
138. "What do they say?"
139. "Oh, you know, about water seeking its own level and all."
140. "Sarah wasn't mean when she was drunk."
141. The woman laughed. "Naw, but she sure was short and ugly!"
142. I said nothing.
143. "Hey, don't get me wrong," Glenda said. "I liked Sarah. But you and her . . . well, you sure made a funny-looking couple. She probably didn't feel so self-conscious and all with her husband," she said somberly. "I mean, with you, all tall and blond, and poor old Sarah . . . I mean, the way them kids in the press room used to kid her about her looks, it was embarrassing just to have to hear it."
144. "Well . . . I loved her," I said.

145   The woman raised her plucked eyebrow in disbelief. She smiled. "Sure, you did, honey," she said, and she patted me on the arm. "Sure, you did." Then she let the smile drift off her face, turned and walked away from me.

146   When someone you have loved dies, you accept the fact of his or her death, but then the person goes on living in your memory, dreams and reveries. You have imaginary conversations with him or her, you see something striking and remind yourself to tell your loved one about it and then get brought up short by the knowledge of the fact of his or her death, and at night, in your sleep, the dead person visits you. With Sarah, none of that happened. When she was gone from my life, she was gone absolutely, as if she had never existed in the first place. It was only later, when I could think of her as dead and could come out and say it, my friend Sarah Cole is dead, that I was able to tell this story, for that is when she began to enter my memories, my dreams and my reveries. In that way, I learned that I truly did love her, and now I have begun to grieve over her death, to wish her alive again, so that I can say to her the things I could not know or say when she was alive, when I did not know that I loved her.

8

147 The woman arrives at Ron's apartment around eight. He hears her car, because of the broken muffler, blat and rumble into the parking lot below, and he crosses quickly from the kitchen and peers out the living room window and, as if through a telescope, watches her shove herself across the seat to the passenger's side to get out of the car, then walk slowly in the dusky light toward the apartment building. It's a warm evening, and she's wearing her white Bermuda shorts, pink sleeveless sweater and shower sandals. Ron hates those clothes. He hates the way the shorts cut into her flesh at the crotch and thigh, hates the large, dark caves below her arms that get exposed by the sweater, hates the sucking noise made by the sandals.

148   Shortly, there is a soft knock at his door. He opens it, turns away and crosses to the kitchen, where he turns back, lights a cigarette and watches her. She closes the door. He offers her a drink, which she declines, and somewhat formally, he invites her to sit down. She sits carefully on the sofa, in the middle, with her feet close together on the floor, as if she were being interviewed for a job. Then he comes around and sits in the easy chair, relaxed, one leg slung over the other at the knee, as if he were interviewing her for the job.

149   "Well," he says, "you wanted to talk."

150   "Yes. But now you're mad at me. I can see that. I didn't do anything, Ron."

151   "I'm not mad at you."

152   They are silent for a moment. Ron goes on smoking his cigarette.

153 Finally, she sighs and says, "You don't want to see me anymore, do you?"

154 He waits a few seconds and answers, "Yes. That's right." Getting up from the chair, he walks to the silver-gray bicycle and stands before it, running a fingertip along the slender crossbar from the saddle to the chrome-plated handlebars.

155 "You're a sonofabitch," she says in a low voice. "You're worse than my ex-husband." Then she smiles meanly, almost sneers, and soon he realizes that she is telling him that she won't leave. He's stuck with her, she informs him with cold precision. "You think I'm just so much meat, and all you got to do is call up the butcher shop and cancel your order. Well, now you're going to find out different. You *can't* cancel your order. I'm not meat, I'm not one of your pretty little girlfriends who come running when you want them and go away when you get tired of them. I'm *different!* I got nothing to lose, Ron. Nothing. So you're stuck with me, Ron."

156 He continues stroking his bicycle. "No, I'm not."

157 She sits back in the couch and crosses her legs at the ankles. "I think I *will* have that drink you offered."

158 "Look, Sarah, it would be better if you go now."

159 "No," she says flatly. "You offered me a drink when I came in. Nothing's changed since I've been here. Not for me and not for you. I'd like that drink you offered," she says haughtily.

160 Ron turns away from the bicycle and takes a step toward her. His face has stiffened into a mask. "Enough is enough," he says through clenched teeth. "I've given you enough."

161 "Fix me a drink, will you, honey?" she says with a phony smile.

162 Ron orders her to leave.

163 She refuses.

164 He grabs her by the arm and yanks her to her feet.

165 She starts crying lightly. She stands there and looks up into his face and weeps, but she does not move toward the door, so he pushes her. She regains her balance and goes on weeping.

166 He stands back and places his fists on his hips and looks at her. "Go on, go on and leave, you ugly bitch," he says to her, and as he says the words, as one by one they leave his mouth, she's transformed into the most beautiful woman he has ever seen. He says the words again, almost tenderly. "Leave, you ugly bitch." Her hair is golden, her brown eyes deep and sad, her mouth full and affectionate, her tears the tears of love and loss, and her pleading, outstretched arms, her entire body, the arms and body of a devoted woman's cruelly rejected love. A third time he says the words. "Leave me now, you disgusting, ugly bitch." She is wrapped in an envelope of golden light, a warm, dense haze that she seems to have stepped into, as into a carriage. And then she is gone, and he is alone again.

167 He looks around the room, as if searching for her. Sitting down in the easy chair, he places his face in his hands. It's not as if she has died; it's as if he has killed her.

Points for Review and Discussion

1. "You and me," says Sarah, "we're real different" (¶ 59). Make a list of the differences (other than in beauty) between Ron and Sarah that you find in the story. Which of these differences seem to you to be class differences? Explain your answer.
2. In the course of this story the narrator sometimes speaks in the first person singular, as "I," and sometimes he's spoken of in the third person, as "Ron." Look back over a few places where these changes of person occur (¶ 22 or ¶ 147, for example). State in your own words what purpose these changes of person serve.

•◆ Questions for Writing

1. After the couple's second meeting, Sarah leaves Osgood's in her car with the shot muffler, and Ron exchanges grins with two lawyers who are watching (¶ 34). Explain as clearly as you can what the grinning is about. What are the lawyers wordlessly saying to Ron? What is he wordlessly answering?
2. Ron dresses inappropriately for his date with Sarah at El Rancho (¶ 113). What makes him do this? Working slowly and patiently, explain his motives in your own words.
3. "I listened as eagerly and carefully as I had before, again with the same motives, to keep her in front of me, to draw her forward from the context of her life and place her, as if she were an object, into the context of mine. I did not know how cruel this was" (¶ 22). Define the nature of the cruelty of which Ron is guilty. Is he too self-critical, in your opinion—or not critical enough? Explain your answer.
4. At one point in the story Ron says: "We were, in a sense, equals" (¶ 36). The comment can be seen as expressing all Ron's strengths and weaknesses as a human being (and those of many other human beings as well). Explain as clearly as you can why this is so.

Acknowledgments

Nelson Aldrich, "Class Acts" from *Old Money, The Mythology of America's Upper Class* by Nelson Aldrich. Copyright © 1988 by Nelson Aldrich. Used by permission.

Anthony Appiah, Henry Louis Gates Jr., bell hooks, Glenn Loury, Eugene Rivers, and Cornel West, "Forum on the Responsibility of Intellectuals" by Anthony Appiah, Henry Louis Gates Jr., bell hooks, Glenn Loury, Eugene Rivers, and Cornel West. Reprinted by permission of the authors.

Howard M. Bahr, "Ups and Downs: Three Middletown Families," from *Social Mobility in America* by Howard M. Bahr. Reprinted by permission.

Russell Banks, "Sarah Cole: A Type of Love Story," pages 162–176 from *Success Stories* by Russell Banks. Copyright © 1986 by Russell Banks. Reprinted by permission of HarperCollins Publishers, Inc.

Derrick Bell, "Racism's Secret Bonding" from *Faces at the Bottom of the Well* by Derrick Bell. Copyright © 1992 by BasicBooks, Inc. Reprinted by permission of BasicBooks, a division of HarperCollins Publishers, Inc.

James MacGregor Burns and Stewart Burns, "Nurturing Rights" from *A People's Charter*. Copyright © 1993 by James MacGregor Burns and Stewart Burns. Reprinted by permission of Alfred A. Knopf, Inc.

Lorene Cary, excerpts from *Black Ice* by Lorene Cary. Copyright © 1991 by Lorene Cary. Reprinted by permission of Alfred A. Knopf, Inc.

Sandra Cisneros, "Woman Hollering Creek" by Sandra Cisneros from *There Was a Man There Was a Woman*. Reprinted by permission of The Susan Bergholz Agency.

John Cheever, "The Superintendent" by John Cheever. Copyright © 1957 by John Cheever. Used by permission.

Robert Coles and Jane Hallowell, "The Maid and the Missus" by Robert Coles and Jane Hallowell, first appeared in *Radcliffe Quarterly*, March 1979. Reprinted by permission.

Elliott Currie, "The Futile War on Drugs" from *Reckoning: Drugs, the Cities, and the American Future* by Elliott Currie. Copyright © 1993 by Elliott Currie. Reprinted by permission of Hill & Wang.

Benjamin DeMott, "I Should Never Have Quit School" and "Class Struggle in Hollywood" from *Why Americans Can't Think Straight About Class* by Benjamin DeMott. Copyright © 1990 by Benjamin DeMott. Reprinted by permission.

Alexis de Tocqueville, "More Equal Than In Any Other Country" from *Democracy in America* by Alexis de Tocqueville. Copyright © 1954 by Random House, Inc. Reprinted by permission of Random House, Inc.

Stuart Dybek, "Chopin in Winter," from *The Coast of Chicago* by Stuart Dybek. Copyright © 1990 by Stuart Dybek. Reprinted by permission.

Barbara Ehrenreich, excerpt from *Fear of Falling* by Barbara Ehrenreich. Copyright © 1989 by Barbara Ehrenreich. Reprinted by permission of Random House, Inc.

Paul Fussell, "A Touchy Subject," from *Class* by Paul Fussell. Copyright © 1983 by Paul Fussell. Reprinted by permission of Simon & Schuster, Inc.

Donna Gaines, excerpt from *Teenage Wasteland* by Donna Gaines. Copyright © 1991 by Donna Gaines. Reprinted by permission of Pantheon Books, a division of Random House, Inc.

Thomas Geoghegan, "Free Trade," from *Which Side Are You On?* by Thomas Geoghegan. Copyright © 1991 by Thomas Geoghegan. Reprinted by permission of Farrar, Straus & Giroux, Inc.

Ellen Goodman, "Censoring Studs" by Ellen Goodman. Copyright © 1994 by The Boston Globe Company. Reprinted by permission.

Sherry Gershon Gottlieb, "William G. Smith Interview," from *Hell No, We Won't Go!* by Sherry Gershon Gottlieb. Copyright © 1991 by Sherry Gershon Gottlieb. Used by permission of Viking Penguin, a division of Penguin Books USA Inc.
John Langston Gwaltney, "Cleaning Up After the Masters," by John Langston Gwaltney, interview with Al Davidoff. Reprinted by permission.
Richard Huber, "The Heritage" from *The American Idea of Success* by Richard Huber. Copyright © 1971 by Richard Huber. Reprinted by permission.
Gish Jen, "The Water-Faucet Vision," by Gish Jen from *Charlie Chan is Dead*. Copyright © 1987 by Gish Jen. First published in Nimrod. Reprinted by permission of the author.
Michael B. Katz, excerpt from *The Undeserving Poor* by Michael B. Katz. Copyright © 1989 by Michael B. Katz. Reprinted by permission of Pantheon Books, a division of Random House, Inc.
Mickey Kaus, "The Case for Class-Mixing," by Mickey Kaus from *The Washington Monthly*, July/August 1992. Reprinted by permission.
Garrison Keillor, "Protestant," from *Lake Wobegon Days* by Garrison Keillor. Copyright © 1985 by Garrison Keillor. Used by permission of Viking Penguin, a division of Penguin Books USA Inc.
Jonathan Kozol, "The Dream Deferred, Again, in San Antonio," from *Savage Inequalities* by Jonathan Kozol. Copyright © 1991 by Jonathan Kozol. Reprinted by permission of Crown Publishers, Inc.
Charles Krauthammer, "Death of a Princess," by Charles Krauthammer from *The New Republic*, July 1980. Reprinted by permission.
Lewis Lapham, "The Gilded Cage," from *Money and Class in America* by Lewis Lapham. Copyright © 1988 by Lewis Lapham. Reprinted by permission.
Christopher Lasch, excerpt from pages 483–491 from "The Ethics of Limits and the Abortion Debate," by Christopher Lasch from *The True and Only Heaven*. Copyright © 1991 by Christopher Lasch. Reprinted with the permission of W.W. Norton & Company, Inc.
Mortimer Levitt, excerpts from *Class: What It Is and How To Acquire It* by Mortimer Levitt. Copyright © 1984 by Mortimer Levitt. Reprinted with the permission of Atheneum Publishers, an imprint of Macmillan Publishing Company.
Bobbie Ann Mason, "Sorghum," from *Love Life* by Bobbie Ann Mason. Copyright © 1989 by Bobbie Ann Mason. Reprinted by permission of HarperCollins Publishers.
Mark Crispin Miller, "Deride and Conquer," by Mark Crispin Miller. Copyright © 1991 by Mark Crispin Miller. Used by permission.
C. Wright Mills, "The Power Elite," by C. Wright Mills. Used by permission of Oxford University Press.
Tillie Olsen, "I Stand Here Ironing," from *Tell Me a Riddle* by Tillie Olsen. Copyright © 1956, 1957, 1960, 1961 by Tillie Olsen. Used by permission of Delacorte Press/Seymour Lawrence, a division of Bantam Doubleday Dell Publishing Group, Inc.
Tony Parker, "Harold Albert, The Richest Man in the World, and Louie, His Wife," from *Bird, Kansas* by Tony Parker. Copyright © 1989 by Alfred A. Knopf, Inc. Reprinted by permission of Alfred A. Knopf, Inc.
Kevin Phillips, excerpt from *The Politics of Rich and Poor* by Kevin Phillips. Copyright © 1990 by Kevin Phillips. Reprinted by permission of Random House, Inc.
Anna Quindlen, "The Skirt Standard," by Anna Quindlen. Copyright © 1992 by The New York Times Company. Reprinted by permission.
Richard Rodriguez, "The Achievement of Desire" from *Hunger of Memory* by Richard Rodriguez. Used by permission of David R. Godine Publishers, Inc.
Mike Rose, excerpts from *Lives on the Boundary: The Struggles and Achievements of America's Underprepared* by Mike Rose. Copyright © 1989 by Mike Rose. Reprinted with the permission of The Free Press, an imprint of Simon & Schuster.
Richard Sennett and Jonathan Cobb, "Hidden Injuries," from *The Hidden Injuries of Class* by Richard Sennett and Jonathan Cobb. Reprinted by permission of Alfred A. Knopf, Inc.
Brent Staples, "A Brother's Murder," by Brent Staples. First appeared in the *New York Times*. Reprinted by permission of the author.
Studs Terkel, "Airline Stewardess," pages 41–49 from *Working* by Studs Terkel. Copyright © 1972, 1974 by Studs Terkel. Reprinted by permission of Pantheon Books, a division of Random House, Inc.
Marianna Torgovnick, "On Being White, Female and Born in Bensonhurst," from *Crossing Ocean Parkway* by Marianna Torgovnick. Reprinted by permission of The University of Chicago Press.
"A Sociologist Looks at an American Community" from *Life*, 1953. Reprinted by permission.

Index

Achievement of Desire, The (Rodriguez), 318–329
Affluent Draft Resister, The (Smith), 345–349
Aldrich, Nelson, 212–221
American Idea of Success, The (Huber), 115–123
Appiah, Anthony, 330–339

Bahr, Howard M., 156–162
Banks, Russell, 501–518
Bell, Derrick, 400–405
Bird's Eye View of American Plutographics, A (Phillips), 93–110
Brother's Murder, A (Staples), 28–30
Burns, James MacGregor, 406–418
Burns, Stewart, 406–418

Cary, Lorene, 32–34
Case for Class-Mixing, The (Kaus), 389–399

Censoring Studs (Goodman), 377–378
Cheever, John, 452–463
Chopin in Winter (Dybek), 475–490
Cisneros, Sandra, 491–499
Class Struggle in Hollywood (DeMott), 164–168
Cleaning Up After the Masters (Gwaltney), 3–6
Cobb, Jonathan, 299–306
Coles, Jane Hallowell, 7–12
Coles, Robert, 7–12
Conwell, Russell, 125–132
Currie, Elliott, 351–367

Death of a Princess (Krauthammer), 380–382
DeMott, Benjamin, 164–168, 227–237
Dickinson, Charles, 436–442
Dirtbags, Burnouts, Metalheads, and Thrashers (Gaines), 54–64

522

Discovery of the Working Class, The (Ehrenreich), 69–81
Dybek, Stuart, 475–490

Ehrenreich, Barbara, 69–81
Emergence of the Underclass as a Public Issue, The (Katz), 82–91
Ethics of Limits and the Abortion Debate, The (Lasch), 368–375

Forum on the Responsibility of Intellectuals (Appiah et al), 330–339
Free Trade (Geoghegan), 283–297
Fussell, Paul, 39–44
Futile War on Drugs, The (Currie), 351–367

Gaines, Donna, 54–64
Gates, Henry Louis Jr., 330–339
Geoghegan, Thomas, 283–297
Goodman, Ellen, 377–378
Gwaltney, John Langston, 3–6

Harold Albert, the Richest Man in the World, and Louie, His Wife (Parker), 133–141
Hidden Injuries of Class, The (Sennett and Cobb), 299–306
hooks, bell, 330–339
Huber, Richard, 115–123

I Should Never Have Quit School (DeMott), 227–237

I Stand Here Ironing (Olsen), 467–473

Jen, Gish, 444–451
Jinx, The (Dickinson), 436–442

Katz, Michael, 82–91
Kaus, Mickey, 389–399
Keillor, Garrison, 275–281
Kozol, Jonathan, 254–271
Krauthammer, Charles, 380–382

Lapham, Lewis, 192–210
Lasch, Christopher, 368–375
Levitt, Mortimer, 46–53
Life, Editors of, 150–154
Loury, Glenn, 330–339

Maid and the Missus, The (Coles and Coles), 7–12
Mamet, David, 25–26
Mason, Bobbie Ann, 423–434
Miller, Mark Crispin, 170–177
Mills, C. Wright, 181–191
Money and Class in America (Lapham), 192–210
More Equal Than in Any Other Country (de Tocqueville), 147–149
My House (Mamet), 25–26

Nurture of Rights, The (Burns and Burns), 406–418

Old Money, the Mythology of America's Upper Class (Aldrich), 212–221

Olsen, Tillie, 467–473
On Being White, Female, and Born in Bensonhurst (Torgovnick), 307–316

Parker, Tony, 133–141
Pecking Order, A (Terkel), 13–20
Phillips, Kevin, 93–110
Power Elite, The (Mills), 181–191
Protestant (Keillor), 275–281

Quindlen, Anna, 22–23

Racism's Secret Bonding (Bell), 400–405
Rivers, Eugene, 330–339
Rodriguez, Richard, 318–329
Rose, Mike, 239–252

Sarah Cole: A Type of Love Story (Banks), 501–518
Savage Inequalities of Public Education (Kozol), 254–271
Sennett, Richard, 299–306
Skirt Standard, The (Quindlen), 22–23
Smith, William G., 345–349
Sociologist Looks at an American Community, A (Editors of Life), 150–154
Sorghum (Mason), 423–434

Staples, Brent, 28–30
Struggle and Achievements of America's Underprepared, The (Rose), 239–252
Superintendent, The (Cheever), 452–463

Terkel, Studs, 13–20
Tocqueville, Alexis de, 147–149
Torgovnick, Marianna De Marco, 307–316
Touchy Subject, A (Fussell), 39–44
Toward a Definition of Class (Levitt), 46–53
Turning Out the Privileged (Cary), 32–34
TV and All the Right Commodities (Miller), 170–177

Ups and Downs: Three Middletown Families (Bahr), 156–162

Water-Faucet Vision, The (Gish Jen), 444–451
West, Cornel, 330–339
Where to Get Rich (Conwell), 125–132
Woman Hollering Creek (Cisneros), 491–499